D1245685

The Definitive Guide to DAX: Business intelligence with Microsoft Excel, SQL Server Analysis Services, and Power BI

Marco Russo and Alberto Ferrari

PUBLISHED BY
Microsoft Press
A division of Microsoft Corporation
One Microsoft Way
Redmond, Washington 98052-6399

Library of Congress Control Number: 2014955069
ISBN: 978-0-7356-9835-2

Printed and bound in the United States of America.

4   17

Microsoft Press books are available through booksellers and distributors worldwide. If you need support related to this book, email Microsoft Press Support at mspinput@microsoft.com. Please tell us what you think of this book at http://aka.ms/tellpress.

Acquisitions Editor: Devon Musgrave
Developmental Editor: Carol Dillingham
Project Editor: Carol Dillingham
Editorial Production: Christian Holdener, S4Carlisle Publishing Services
Technical Reviewer: Gerhard Brueckl and Andrea Benedetti; Technical Review services provided by Content Master, a member of CM Group, Ltd.
Copyeditor: Leslie Phillips
Indexer: Maureen Johnson, MoJo's Indexing and Editorial Services
Cover: Twist Creative • Seattle

We dedicate this book to the Picasso team.

Contents at a glance

	Foreword	*xvii*
	Introduction	*xix*
CHAPTER 1	**What is DAX?**	1
CHAPTER 2	**Introducing DAX**	17
CHAPTER 3	**Using basic table functions**	45
CHAPTER 4	**Understanding evaluation contexts**	61
CHAPTER 5	**Understanding *CALCULATE* and *CALCULATETABLE***	93
CHAPTER 6	**DAX examples**	129
CHAPTER 7	**Time intelligence calculations**	155
CHAPTER 8	**Statistical functions**	213
CHAPTER 9	**Advanced table functions**	233
CHAPTER 10	**Advanced evaluation context**	285
CHAPTER 11	**Handling hierarchies**	339
CHAPTER 12	**Advanced relationships**	367
CHAPTER 13	**The VertiPaq engine**	399
CHAPTER 14	**Optimizing data models**	425
CHAPTER 15	**Analyzing DAX query plans**	457
CHAPTER 16	**Optimizing DAX**	495
	Index	*537*

Table of contents

Foreword . . . . *xvii*

Introduction . . . . *xix*

Chapter 1   What is DAX?   1

Understanding the data model 1

    Understanding the direction of a relationship 3

DAX for Excel users. 5

    Cells versus tables 5

    Excel and DAX: Two functional languages. 8

    Using iterators 8

    DAX requires some theory. 8

DAX for SQL developers 9

    Understanding relationship handling. 9

    DAX is a functional language. 10

    DAX as a programming and querying language 11

    Subqueries and conditions in DAX and SQL. 12

DAX for MDX developers. 13

    Multidimensional vs. Tabular 13

    DAX as a programming and querying language 13

    Hierarchies. 14

    Leaf-level calculations 15

Chapter 2   Introducing DAX   17

Understanding DAX calculations 17

    DAX data types. 18

    DAX operators 21

What do you think of this book? We want to hear from you!

Microsoft is interested in hearing your feedback so we can continually improve our
books and learning resources for you. To participate in a brief online survey, please visit:

microsoft.com/learning/booksurvey

Understanding calculated columns and measures...................22

    Calculated columns..22

    Measures..23

Variables..26

Handling errors in DAX expressions..............................26

    Conversion errors...26

    Arithmetical operations errors.............................27

    Intercepting errors.......................................30

Formatting DAX code..32

Common DAX functions..35

    Aggregate functions......................................35

    Logical functions...37

    Information functions......................................39

    Mathematical functions...................................39

    Trigonometric functions...................................40

    Text functions...40

    Conversion functions......................................41

    Date and time functions..................................42

    Relational functions......................................42

Chapter 3   Using basic table functions   45

Introducing table functions.....................................45

EVALUATE syntax...47

Using table expressions..50

Understanding *FILTER*...51

Understanding *ALL*, *ALLEXCEPT*, and *ALLNOBLANKROW*............54

Understanding *VALUES* and *DISTINCT*...........................58

    Using *VALUES* as a scalar value............................59

Chapter 4   Understanding evaluation contexts   61

Introduction to evaluation contexts..............................62

    Understanding the row context.............................66

Testing your evaluation context understanding 67

    Using *SUM* in a calculated column 67

    Using columns in a measure 68

Creating a row context with iterators 69

    Using the *EARLIER* function 70

Understanding *FILTER*, *ALL*, and context interactions 74

Working with many tables. 77

    Row contexts and relationships. 78

    Filter context and relationships. 80

    Introducing *VALUES*. 84

    Introducing *ISFILTERED*, *ISCROSSFILTERED* 85

Evaluation contexts recap 88

Creating a parameter table. 89

Chapter 5   **Understanding *CALCULATE* and *CALCULATETABLE***   **93**

Understanding *CALCULATE*. 93

    Understanding the filter context. 95

    Introducing *CALCULATE* 98

CALCULATE examples 101

    Filtering a single column. 101

    Filtering with complex conditions. 106

    Using *CALCULATETABLE*. 109

Understanding context transition 111

    Understanding context transition with measures 114

    How many rows are visible after context transition?. 116

    Understanding evaluation order of context transition 117

Variables and evaluation contexts 118

Understanding circular dependencies. 119

CALCULATE rules. 122

Introducing *ALLSELECTED* 123

Understanding *USERELATIONSHIP* 125

Chapter 6   DAX examples   **129**

Computing ratios and percentages................................129

Computing cumulative totals......................................132

Using ABC (Pareto) classification.................................136

Computing sales per day and working day........................143

Computing differences in working days...........................150

Computing static moving averages................................151

Chapter 7   Time intelligence calculations   **155**

Introduction to time intelligence.................................155

Building a Date table..156

     Using *CALENDAR* and *CALENDARAUTO*.....................157

Working with multiple dates......................................160

     Handling multiple relationships to the Date table.............161

     Handling multiple Date tables..............................162

Introduction to time intelligence.................................164

     Using Mark as Date Table..................................166

Aggregating and comparing over time............................168

     Year-to-date, quarter-to-date, month-to-date...............168

     Computing periods from prior periods.......................171

     Computing difference over previous periods.................174

     Computing the moving annual total.........................175

Closing balance over time..178

     Semi-additive measures....................................178

     OPENINGBALANCE and *CLOSINGBALANCE* functions.........184

Advanced time intelligence.......................................188

     Understanding periods to date.............................189

     Understanding *DATEADD*.................................191

     Understanding *FIRSTDATE* and *LASTDATE*.................196

     Understanding *FIRSTNONBLANK* and *LASTNONBLANK*.......199

     Using drillthrough with time intelligence...................200

Custom calendars 200

    Working with weeks 201

    Custom year-to-date, quarter-to-date, month-to-date 204

    Computing over noncontiguous periods. .206

    Custom comparison between periods 210

Chapter 8   Statistical functions   213

Using *RANKX*. 213

    Common pitfalls using *RANKX* 216

Using *RANK.EQ* 219

Computing average and moving average 220

Computing variance and standard deviation. .222

Computing median and percentiles 223

Computing interests. 225

    Alternative implementation of *PRODUCT* and *GEOMEAN*. 226

    Using internal rate of return (*XIRR*). 227

    Using net present value (*XNPV*) 228

Using Excel statistical functions 229

Sampling by using the *SAMPLE* function 230

Chapter 9   Advanced table functions   233

Understanding *EVALUATE*. 233

    Using *VAR* in *EVALUATE* 235

Understanding filter functions 236

    Using *CALCULATETABLE* 236

    Using *TOPN*. 239

Understanding projection functions 241

    Using *ADDCOLUMNS* 241

    Using *SELECTCOLUMNS* 244

    Using *ROW* 247

Understanding lineage and relationships. 248

Understanding grouping/joining functions 250

    Using *SUMMARIZE* 250

    Using *SUMMARIZECOLUMNS* 255

    Using *GROUPBY* 261

    Using *ADDMISSINGITEMS* 262

    Using *NATURALINNERJOIN* 265

    Using *NATURALLEFTOUTERJOIN* 266

Understanding set functions 267

    Using *CROSSJOIN* 267

    Using *UNION* 269

    Using *INTERSECT* 272

    Using *EXCEPT* 274

    Using *GENERATE, GENERATEALL* 275

Understanding utility functions 278

    Using *CONTAINS* 278

    Using *LOOKUPVALUE* 280

    Using *SUBSTITUTEWITHINDEX* 283

    Using *ISONORAFTER* 284

Chapter 10 Advanced evaluation context   **285**

Understanding *ALLSELECTED* 285

Understanding *KEEPFILTERS* 294

Understanding AutoExists 304

Understanding expanded tables 307

    Difference between table expansion and filtering 315

Redefining the filter context 316

    Understanding filter context intersection .318

    Understanding filter context overwrite 320

    Understanding arbitrarily shaped filters 321

Understanding the *ALL* function 326

Understanding lineage 329

Using advanced SetFilter 331

Learning and mastering evaluation contexts .338

Chapter 11 Handling hierarchies   **339**

    Computing percentages over hierarchies 339

    Handling parent-child hierarchies 346

    Handling unary operators.......................................358

        Implementing unary operators by using DAX 359

Chapter 12 Advanced relationships   **367**

    Using calculated physical relationships.........................367

        Computing multiple-column relationships 367

        Computing static segmentation 369

    Using virtual relationships......................................371

        Using dynamic segmentation 371

        Many-to-many relationships 373

        Using relationships with different granularities 378

        Differences between physical and virtual relationships 381

    Finding missing relationships...................................382

        Computing number of products not sold 383

        Computing new and returning customers 384

    Examples of complex relationships 386

        Performing currency conversion...........................386

        Frequent itemset search 392

Chapter 13 The VertiPaq engine   **399**

    Understanding database processing.............................400

    Introduction to columnar databases............................400

    Understanding VertiPaq compression 403

        Understanding value encoding............................404

        Understanding dictionary encoding........................405

        Understanding Run Length Encoding (RLE) 406

        Understanding re-encoding 409

        Finding the best sort order...............................409

        Understanding hierarchies and relationships 410

    Understanding segmentation and partitioning 412

Using Dynamic Management Views 413

Using DISCOVER_OBJECT_MEMORY_USAGE. 414

Using DISCOVER_STORAGE_TABLES. 414

Using DISCOVER_STORAGE_TABLE_COLUMNS 415

Using DISCOVER_STORAGE_TABLE_COLUMN_SEGMENTS 416

Understanding materialization. 417

Choosing hardware for VertiPaq 421

Can you choose hardware? 421

Set hardware priorities 421

CPU model. 422

Memory speed 423

Number of cores 423

Memory size 424

Disk I/O and paging. 424

Conclusions 424

Chapter 14 Optimizing data models   425

Gathering information about the data model. 425

Denormalization 434

Columns cardinality 442

Handling date and time 443

Calculated columns. 447

Optimizing complex filters with Boolean calculated columns 450

Choosing the right columns to store. 451

Optimizing column storage 453

Column split optimization 453

Optimizing high cardinality columns 454

Optimizing drill-through attributes 455

Chapter 15 Analyzing DAX query plans   **457**

    Introducing the DAX query engine 457

        Understanding the formula engine 458

        Understanding the storage engine (VertiPaq) 459

    Introducing DAX query plans 459

        Logical query plan 460

        Physical query plan 461

        Storage engine query 462

    Capturing profiling information 463

        Using the SQL Server Profiler 463

        Using DAX Studio 467

    Reading storage engine queries 470

        Introducing xmSQL syntax 470

        Understanding scan time 477

        Understanding *DISTINCTCOUNT* internals 479

        Understanding parallelism and datacache 480

        Understanding the VertiPaq cache 481

        Understanding *CallbackDataID* 483

    Reading query plans 488

Chapter 16 Optimizing DAX   **495**

    Defining optimization strategy 496

        Identifying a single DAX expression to optimize 496

        Creating a reproduction query 499

        Analyzing server timings and query plan information 500

        Identifying bottlenecks in the storage engine or
        formula engine 503

Optimizing bottlenecks in the storage engine 504

    Choosing *ADDCOLUMNS* vs. *SUMMARIZE* 505

    Reducing *CallbackDataID* impact 509

    Optimizing filter conditions 512

    Optimizing *IF* conditions. 513

    Optimizing cardinality. 515

    Optimizing nested iterators 517

Optimizing bottlenecks in the formula engine 522

    Creating repro in MDX 527

    Reducing materialization 528

Optimizing complex bottlenecks 532

Index   *537*

Foreword

Maybe you don't know our names. We spend our days writing the code for the software you use in your daily job: We are part of the development team of Power BI, SQL Server Analysis Services, and . . . yes, we are among the authors of the DAX language and the VertiPaq engine.

The language you are going to learn using this book is our creature. We spent years working on this language, optimizing the engine, finding ways to improve the optimizer, and trying to build DAX into a simple, clean, and sound language to make your life as a data analyst easier and more productive.

But hey, this is intended to be the foreword of a book, no more words about us! Why are we writing a foreword for a book published by Marco and Alberto, the SQLBI guys? Well, because when you start learning DAX, it is a matter of a few clicks and searches on the web before you find articles written by them. You start reading their papers, learning the language, and hopefully appreciate our hard work. Having met them many years ago, we have great admiration for their deep knowledge of SQL Server Analysis Services. When the DAX adventure started, they were among the first to learn and adopt this new engine and language.

The articles, papers, and blog posts they publish and share on the web became the source of learning for thousands of people. We write the code, but we do not spend much time teaching how to use it; they are the ones who spread knowledge about DAX.

Alberto and Marco's books are among the best sellers on this topic and now, with this new guide to DAX, they truly created a milestone publication about the language we author and love. We write the code, they write the books, and you learn DAX, providing unprecedented analytical power to your business. This is what we love: working all together as a team—we, they, and you—to get better insights from data.

Marius Dumitru, Architect, Power BI CTO's Office

Cristian Petculescu, Chief Architect of Power BI

Jeffrey Wang, Principal Software Engineer Manager

Introduction

We previously wrote about DAX many times: in books about Power Pivot and SSAS Tabular, in blog posts, articles, white papers, and finally in a book dedicated to DAX patterns. So why should we write (and, hopefully, you read) yet another book about DAX? Is there really so much to learn about this language? Of course, we think the answer is definitely yes.

When you write a book, the first thing that the editor wants to know is the number of pages. There are very good reasons why this is important: price, management, allocation of resources, and so on. At the end, nearly everything in a book goes back to the number of pages. As authors, this is somewhat frustrating. In fact, whenever we wrote a book, we had to carefully allocate space to the description of the product (either Power Pivot for Microsoft Excel or SSAS Tabular) and to the DAX language. This always left us with the bitter taste of not having enough pages to describe all we wanted to teach about DAX. After all, you cannot write 1,000 pages about Power Pivot; a book of such a size would be intimidating for anybody.

Thus, for some years we wrote about SSAS Tabular and Power Pivot, and we kept the project of a book completely dedicated to DAX in a drawer. Then we opened the drawer and decided to avoid choosing what to include in the next book: We wanted to explain everything about DAX, with no compromises. The result of that decision is this book.

Here you will not find a description of how to create a calculated column, or which dialog box to use to set some property. This is not a step-by-step book that teaches you how to use Microsoft Visual Studio, Power BI, or Power Pivot for Excel. Instead, this is a deep dive into the DAX language, starting from the beginning and then reaching very technical details about how to optimize your code and model.

We loved each page of this book while we were writing it. We reviewed the content so many times that we had it memorized. We continued adding content whenever we thought there was something important to include, thus increasing the page count and never cutting something because there were no pages left. Doing that, we learned more about DAX and we enjoyed every moment spent doing it.

But there is one more thing. Why should you read a book about DAX?

Come on, you thought this after the first demo of Power Pivot or Power BI. You are not alone, we thought the same the first time we tried it. DAX is so easy! It looks so similar to Excel! Moreover, if you already learned other programming and/or query languages, you are probably used to learning a new language by looking at some examples of the syntax, matching patterns you find to those you already know. We made this mistake, and we would like you to avoid doing the same.

DAX is a strong language, used in a growing number of analytical tools. It is very powerful, but it has a few concepts that are hard to understand by inductive reasoning. The evaluation context, for instance, is a topic that requires a deductive approach: You start with a theory, and then you see a few examples that demonstrate how the theory works. Deductive reasoning is the approach of this book. We know that a number of people do not like learning in this way, because they prefer a more practical approach, learning how to solve specific problems, and then with experience and practice, they understand the underlying theory with an inductive reasoning. If you are looking for that approach, this book is not for you. We wrote a book about DAX patterns, full of examples and without any explanation of why a formula works, or why a certain way of coding is better. That book is a good source for copying and pasting DAX formulas. This book has a different goal: to enable you to really master DAX. All the examples demonstrate a DAX behavior; they do not solve a specific problem. If you find formulas that you can reuse in your models, this is good for you. However, always remember that this is just a side effect, not the goal of the example. Finally, always read any note to make sure there are no possible pitfalls in the code used in examples. For educational purposes we often used code that is not the best practice.

We really hope you will enjoy spending time with us in this beautiful trip to learn DAX, at least in the same way as we enjoyed writing it.

Who this book is for

If you are a casual user of DAX, then this book is probably not the best choice for you. Many books provide a simple introduction to the tools that implement DAX and to the DAX language itself, starting from the ground and reaching a basic level of DAX programming. We know this very well, because we wrote some of those books, too!

If, on the other hand, you are serious about DAX and you really want to understand every detail of this beautiful language, then this is your book. This might be your first book about DAX; in that case you should not expect to benefit from the most advanced topics too early. We suggest you read the book from cover to cover and then read again the most complex parts once you gained some experience; it is very likely that some concepts will become clearer at that point.

DAX is useful to different people, for different purposes: Excel users can leverage DAX to author Power Pivot data models, business intelligence (BI) professionals might need to implement DAX code in BI solutions of any size, casual Power BI users might need to author some DAX formulas in their self-service BI models. In this book, we tried to provide information to all of these different kinds of people. Some of the content (specifically the optimization part) is probably more targeted to BI professionals, because the knowledge needed to optimize a DAX measure is very technical; but we believe that Excel users should understand the different performance of DAX expressions to achieve the best results for their models, too.

Finally, we wanted to write a book to study, not only a book to read. At the beginning, we try to keep it easy and follow a logical path from zero to DAX. However, when the concepts to learn start to become more complex, we stop trying to be simple, and we are realistic. DAX is not a simple language. It took years for us to master it and to understand every detail of the engine. Do not expect to be able to learn all of this content in a few days, by reading casually. This book requires your attention at a very high level. In exchange for that, of course, we offer an unprecedented depth of coverage of all aspects of DAX, giving you the option to become a real DAX expert.

Assumptions about you

We expect our reader to have a basic knowledge of Excel Pivot Tables and some experience in analysis of numbers. If you already have some exposure to the DAX language, then this is good for you, since you will read the first part faster, but knowing DAX is not necessary, of course.

There are some references in the book to MDX and SQL code, but you do not really need to know these languages, because they are just parallels between different ways of writing expressions. If you do not understand those lines of code, it is just fine, it means that that specific topic is not for you.

In the most advanced parts of the book, we discuss parallelism, memory access, CPU usage, and other exquisitely geeky topics that might not be familiar to everybody. Any developer will feel at home there, whereas Excel power users might be a bit intimidated. Nevertheless, when speaking about optimization that information is required. Thus, the most advanced part of the book is aimed more toward BI developers than to Excel users. However, we think that everybody will benefit from reading it.

Organization of this book

The book is designed to flow from introductory chapters to complex ones, in a logical way. Each chapter is written with the assumption that the previous content is fully understood; there is nearly no repetition of concepts explained earlier. For this reason, we strongly suggest that you read it from cover to cover and avoid jumping to more advanced chapters too early.

Once you have read it for the first time, it becomes useful as a reference: If, for example, you are in doubt about the behavior of *ALLSELECTED*, then you can jump straight on to that section and clarify your mind on that. Nevertheless, reading that section without having digested the previous content might result in some frustration or, worse, in an incomplete understanding of the concepts.

With that said, here is the content at a glance:

- Chapter 1 is a brief introduction to DAX, with a few sections dedicated to users who already have some knowledge of other languages, namely SQL, Excel, or MDX. We do not introduce any new concept here, we just give several hints about the difference between DAX and other languages that might be known to the reader.

- Chapter 2 introduces the DAX language itself. We cover basic concepts such as calculated columns, measures, error-handling functions, and we list most of the basic functions of the language.

- Chapter 3 is dedicated to basic table functions. Many functions in DAX work on tables and return tables as a result. In this chapter we cover the most basic functions, whereas we cover advanced ones in Chapter 9.

- Chapter 4 is dedicated to the description of evaluation contexts. Evaluation contexts are the foundation of the DAX language and this chapter, along with the next one, is probably the most important of the entire book.

- Chapter 5 covers only two functions: *CALCULATE* and *CALCULATETABLE*. These are the most important functions in DAX and they strongly rely on a good understanding of evaluation contexts.

- Chapter 6 contains some examples of DAX code. However, you should not consider it as a set of patterns to reuse. Instead, we show how to solve some common scenarios with the basic concepts learned so far.

- Chapter 7 covers time intelligence calculations at a very in-depth level. Year-to-date, month-to-date, values of the previous year, week-based periods, and custom calendars are some of the calculations covered in this chapter.

- Chapter 8 is dedicated to statistical functions such as ranking, financial calculations, and percentiles.

- Chapter 9 is the continuation of Chapter 3, where we introduce the basic table functions. In this chapter, we go forward explaining in great detail the full set of DAX functions that manipulate tables, most of which are very useful in writing DAX queries.

- Chapter 10 brings your knowledge of evaluation context one step further and discusses complex functions such as *ALLSELECTED* and *KEEPFILTERS*, with the aid of the theory of expanded tables. It is a hard chapter, which uncovers most of the secrets of complex DAX expressions.

- Chapter 11 shows you how to perform calculations over hierarchies and how to handle parent/child structures using DAX.

- Chapter 12 is about solving uncommon relationships in DAX. In fact, with the aid of DAX a data model might express any kind of relationship. In this chapter, we show many types of relationships. It is the last chapter about the DAX language; the remaining part of the book covers optimization techniques.

- Chapter 13 shows a detailed description of the VertiPaq engine; it is the most common database engine on top of which DAX runs. Understanding it is essential to learn how to get the best performance in DAX.

- Chapter 14 uses the knowledge of Chapter 13 to show possible optimizations that you can apply at the data model level. When to normalize, how to reduce cardinality of columns, what kind of relationships to set to achieve top performance and low memory usage in DAX.

- Chapter 15 teaches how to read a query plan and how to measure the performance of a DAX query with the aid of tools such as SQL Server Profiler and DAX Studio.

- Chapter 16 shows several optimization techniques, based on the content of the previous chapters about optimization. We show many DAX expressions, measure their performance, and then show and explain optimized formulas.

Conventions

The following conventions are used in this book:

- **Boldface** type is used to indicate text that you type.

- *Italic* type is used to indicate new terms, measures, calculated columns, and database names.

- The first letters of the names of dialog boxes, dialog box elements, and commands are capitalized. For example, the Save As dialog box.

- The names of ribbon tabs are given in ALL CAPS.

- Keyboard shortcuts are indicated by a plus sign (+) separating the key names. For example, Ctrl+Alt+Delete means that you press Ctrl, Alt, and Delete keys at the same time.

About the companion content

We have included companion content to enrich your learning experience. The companion content for this book can be downloaded from the following page:

http://aka.ms/GuidetoDAX/files

The companion content includes the following:

- A SQL Server backup of the Contoso Retail DW database that you can use to build the examples yourself. This is a standard demo database provided by Microsoft, which we enriched with some views, to make it easier to create a data model on top of it.

- A Power BI Desktop model that we used to generate all of the figures in the book. The database is always the same, and then for each chapter there is a document showing the steps required to reproduce the same example we used in the book. You can use this information in case you want to replicate on your system the same scenario we describe in our examples.

Acknowledgments

We have so many people to thank for this book that we know it is impossible to write a complete list. So thanks so much to all of you who contributed to this book—even if you had no idea that you were doing it. Blog comments, forum posts, email discussions, chats with attendees and speakers at technical conferences, analyzing customer scenarios and so much more have been useful to us, and many people have contributed significant ideas to this book.

That said, there are people we have to mention personally, because of their particular contributions.

We want to start with Edward Melomed: He inspired us, and we probably would not have started our journey with the DAX language without a passionate discussion that we had with him several years ago and that ended with the table of contents of our first book about Power Pivot written on a napkin.

We want to thank Microsoft Press and the people who contributed to the project: Carol Dillingham has been a great editor and greatly helped us along the process of book writing. Many others behind the scenes helped us with the complexity of authoring a book: thanks to you all.

The only job longer than writing a book is the studying you must do in preparation for writing it. A group of people that we (in all friendliness) call "ssas-insiders" helped us get ready to write this book. A few people from Microsoft deserve a special mention as well, because they spent precious time teaching us important concepts about Power Pivot and DAX: They are Marius Dumitru, Jeffrey Wang, Akshai Mirchandani, and Cristian Petculescu. Your help has been priceless, guys!

We also want to thank Amir Netz, Ashvini Sharma, Kasper De Jonge, and T. K. Anand for their contributions to the many discussions we had about the product. We feel they helped us in some strategic choices we made in this book and in our career.

Finally, a special mention goes to our technical reviewers: Gerhard Brückl and Andrea Benedetti. They double-checked all the content of our original text, searching for errors and sentences that were not clear; giving us invaluable suggestions on how to improve the book. Without their meticulous work, the book would have been much harder to read! If the book contains fewer errors than our original manuscript, it is only because of them. If it still contains errors, it is our fault, of course.

Thank you so much, folks!

Errata, updates, and book support

We've made every effort to ensure the accuracy of this book and its companion content. If you discover an error, please submit it to us at:

http://aka.ms/GuidetoDAX/errata

If you need to contact the Microsoft Press Support team, please send an email message to *mspinput@microsoft.com*.

Please note that product support for Microsoft software and hardware is not offered through the previous addresses. For help with Microsoft software or hardware, go to *http://support.microsoft.com*.

Free ebooks from Microsoft Press

From technical overviews to in-depth information on special topics, the free ebooks from Microsoft Press cover a wide range of topics. These ebooks are available in PDF, EPUB, and Mobi for Kindle formats, ready for you to download at:

http://aka.ms/mspressfree

Check back often to see what is new!

We want to hear from you

At Microsoft Press, your satisfaction is our top priority, and your feedback our most valuable asset. Please tell us what you think of this book at:

http://aka.ms/tellpress

We know you are busy, so we have kept it short with just a few questions. Your answers go directly to the editors at Microsoft Press. (No personal information will be requested.) Thanks in advance for your input!

Stay in touch

Let's keep the conversation going! We are on Twitter: *http://twitter.com/MicrosoftPress*.

CHAPTER 1

What is DAX?

D AX is the programming language of Microsoft SQL Server Analysis Services (SSAS) and Microsoft Power Pivot for Excel. It was created in 2010, with the first release of PowerPivot for Excel 2010 (yes, in 2010 PowerPivot was spelled without the space; the space was introduced in the Power Pivot name in 2013). Over time, DAX gained popularity in the Excel community, which uses DAX to create Power Pivot data models in Excel, and in the Business Intelligence (BI) community, which uses DAX to build models with SSAS.

DAX is a simple language. That said, DAX is different from most programming languages and it might take some time to become acquainted with it. In our experience, having taught DAX to thousands of people, learning the basics of DAX is straightforward: You will be able to start using it in a matter of hours. But when it comes to understanding advanced concepts like evaluation contexts, iterations, and context transition, everything will seem complex. Do not give up! Be patient. Once your brain starts to digest these concepts, you will discover that DAX is, indeed, an easy language. It just takes time to get used to.

This first chapter begins with a small recap of what a data model is, in terms of tables and relationships. We recommend readers of all experience levels read this section in order to gain familiarity with the terms we use throughout the book when referring to tables, models, and different kinds of relationships.

In the next sections, we offer advice to readers who have some experience with other programming languages—namely Excel, SQL, and MDX. Each section is for readers who already know that language and might find it useful to read a very quick introduction to DAX in which we compare it to those various languages. If you are an Excel user and find the MDX part nearly impossible to understand, that is totally expected. Just skip that part, since it contains information that is essentially meaningless to you, and move to the next chapter, where our journey into the DAX language really begins.

Understanding the data model

DAX is a language specifically designed to compute business formulas over a data model. You might already know what a data model is, but if you are not familiar with it, it is worth dedicating some pages to a description of data models and relationships, so as to create a foundation on which you will build your DAX knowledge.

A data model is a set of tables, linked by relationships.

We all know what a table is: a set of rows containing data, with each row divided into columns. Each column has a data type and contains a single piece of information. We usually refer to a row in a table as a record. Tables are a convenient way to organize your data. By itself, a table is already a data model, although in its simplest form. Thus, when you write names and numbers in an Excel workbook, you are creating a data model.

If your data model contains many tables, it is very likely that they are linked through relationships. A relationship holds between two tables. When two tables are tied with a relationship, we say that they are related. Graphically, a relationship is represented by a line connecting the two tables. Figure 1-1 shows an example of a data model.

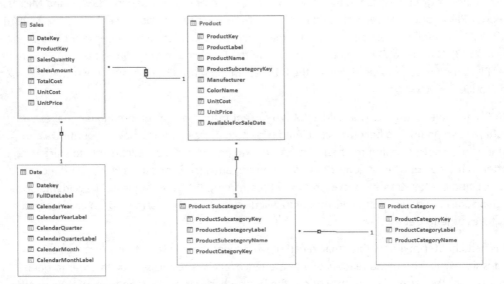

FIGURE 1-1 This is a simple example of a data model made of five tables.

Some important aspects of relationships to learn well:

- Two tables in a relationship do not have the same role. They are referred to as the one-side and many-side of the relationship. In Figure 1-1 focus on the relationship between Product and Product Subcategory. A single subcategory contains many products, while a single product has only one subcategory. Therefore, Product Subcategory is the one-side of the relationship (having one subcategory) while Product is the many-side (having many products).

- The columns used to create the relationship (which usually have the same name in both tables) are called the keys of the relationship. On the one-side of the relationship, the column needs to have a unique value for each row. On the many-side the same value can be (and often is) repeated in many different rows. When a column has a unique value for each row, it is called a key for the table. Usually, tables have a column that is the key.

- Relationships can form a chain. Each product has a subcategory and each subcategory has a category. Thus, each product has a category. In order to retrieve the category of a product, you will need to traverse a chain of two relationships. Figure 1-1 includes an example of a chain made up of three relationships, starting with Sales and continuing on to Product Category.

- In each relationship, there can be one or two small arrows. In Figure 1-1 you can see two arrows in the relationship between Sales and Product, whereas all other relationships have a single arrow. The arrow indicates the direction of the automatic filtering of the relationship. We will discuss this in much more detail in later chapters, because determining the correct direction of filters is one of the most important skills to learn.

- In the tabular data model, relationships can be created on single columns only. Multiple column relationships are not supported by the engine.

Understanding the direction of a relationship

As we said in the previous section, each relationship can have one or two directions of filtering. Filtering always happens from the one-side of the relationship to the many-side. If the relationship is bidirectional (that is, it has two arrows on it), then the filtering happens also from the many-side to the one-side.

An example might help you understand this behavior better. If you create a pivot table based on the data model previously shown in Figure 1-1, with the years on the rows and *Sum of SalesAmount* and *Count of ProductName* in the values area, you will see the result shown in Figure 1-2.

Row Labels	Sum of SalesAmount	Count of ProductName
2007	$1,010,803,395.04	1,828
2008	$849,671,203.42	2,244
2009	$857,728,031.35	2,504
Grand Total	**$2,718,202,629.81**	**2,517**

FIGURE 1-2 This pivot table shows the effect of filtering across multiple tables in action.

The Row Labels contain the years—that is, a column from the Date table. Date is on the one-side of the relationship with the Sales table. So when you put the *Sum of SalesAmount* in the pivot table, the engine filters Sales based on the year. The relationship between the Sales and Product tables is bidirectional; when you put the count of product names in the pivot table, you get, as the result, the number of products sold in each year. Said differently, the filter on the year propagates to the Product table using a chain of relationships.

If you now modify the pivot table by putting the Color on the rows and adding the *Count of FullDateLabel* in the values area, the result is somewhat harder to understand, as you can see in Figure 1-3.

Row Labels	Sum of SalesAmount	Count of ProductName	Count of FullDateLabel
Azure	$9,432,951.01	14	2556
Black	$544,932,784.76	602	2556
Blue	$221,983,165.79	200	2556
Brown	$112,311,885.56	77	2556
Gold	$39,836,201.72	50	2556
Green	$122,192,345.24	74	2556
Grey	$298,320,774.10	283	2556
Orange	$70,323,434.77	55	2556
Pink	$58,419,345.34	84	2556
Purple	$912,486.31	6	2556
Red	$94,063,709.25	99	2556
Silver	$609,853,067.20	417	2556
Silver Grey	$21,382,969.28	14	2556
Transparent	$241,181.14	1	2556
White	$505,832,783.51	505	2556
Yellow	$8,163,544.83	36	2556
Grand Total	**$2,718,202,629.81**	**2,517**	**2556**

FIGURE 1-3 This pivot table shows that if bidirectional filtering is not active, tables are not filtered.

The filter on the rows is the *Color* column in the Product table. Because Product is on the one-side of the relationship with Sales, the *Sum of SalesAmount* is correctly filtered. The *Count of ProductNames* is obviously filtered, because it is computing values from the same table that is on the rows (Product). The wrong number is the *Count of FullDateLabel*. In fact, it always shows the same value for all the rows—and by the way, this number is the total number of rows in the Date table.

The reason why the filter coming from the *Color* column does not propagate to Date is that the relationship between Date and Sales has a single arrow, pointing from Date to Sales. Thus, even if Sales has an active filter on it, the filter cannot propagate to Date, because the type of relationship prevents it.

If you change the relationship between Date and Sales to enable bidirectional filtering, then the result will be the one shown in Figure 1-4.

As you can see, the numbers are now different, reflecting the number of days on which at least one product of the particular color was sold. At first sight, it might look as if all the relationships should be defined as bidirectional, so as to let the filter propagate in any direction and always return meaningful results. As you will learn in this book, this is not always the correct way of designing a data model. In fact, depending on the scenario you are working with, you will choose the correct propagation of relationships.

Row Labels	Sum of SalesAmount	Count of ProductName	Count of FullDateLabel
Azure	$9,432,951.01	14	1033
Black	$544,932,784.76	602	1096
Blue	$221,983,165.79	200	1096
Brown	$112,311,885.56	77	1096
Gold	$39,836,201.72	50	1096
Green	$122,192,345.24	74	1096
Grey	$298,320,774.10	283	1096
Orange	$70,323,434.77	55	1096
Pink	$58,419,345.34	84	1096
Purple	$912,486.31	6	600
Red	$94,063,709.25	99	1096
Silver	$609,853,067.20	417	1096
Silver Grey	$21,382,969.28	14	1051
Transparent	$241,181.14	1	221
White	$505,832,783.51	505	1096
Yellow	$8,163,544.83	36	1095
Grand Total	**$2,718,202,629.81**	**2,517**	**2556**

FIGURE 1-4 If you enable bidirectional filtering, then the Date table is filtered using the Color column.

DAX for Excel users

Chances are you already know the Excel formula language, which DAX somewhat resembles. After all, the roots of DAX are in Power Pivot for Excel, and the development team tried to keep the two languages similar. This makes the transition to this new language easier. However, there are some very important differences.

Cells versus tables

In Excel, you perform calculations over cells. A cell is referenced using its coordinates. Thus, you write formulas as follows:

```
= (A1 * 1.25) - B2
```

DAX is different. In DAX, the concept of a cell and its coordinates does not exist. DAX works on tables and columns, not cells. So whenever you write DAX expressions, they will only refer to tables and columns. The concepts of tables and columns are not new in Excel. In fact, if you define an Excel range as a table (by using the *Format as a Table* function), you can write expressions in Excel that reference tables and columns. If you look at Figure 1-5, you see the column *SalesAmount* evaluates an expression that references columns in the same table, instead of cells in the workbook.

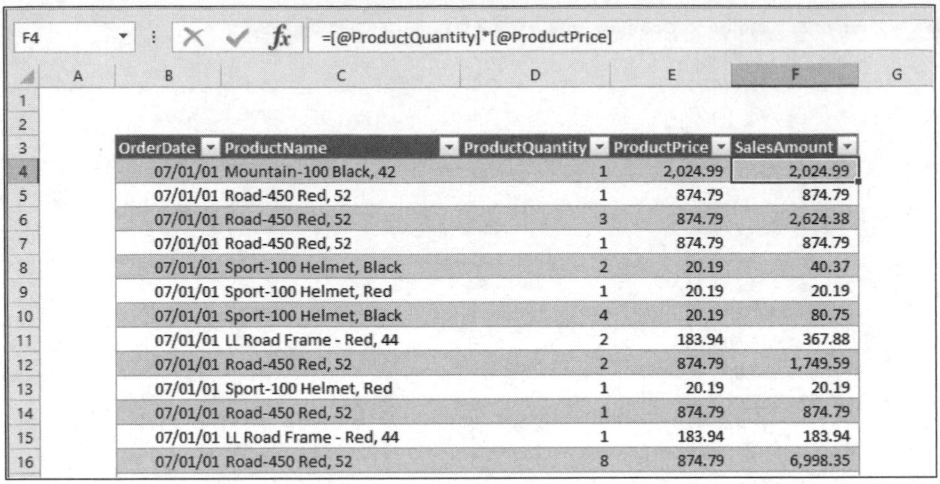

FIGURE 1-5 You can use column names in Excel tables, too.

Using Excel, you refer to columns in a table using the [@ColumnName] format, where Column-Name is the name of the column you want to use, and the @ symbol means "take the value for the current row." Although the syntax is not very intuitive, normally you do not write these expressions. They appear by simply clicking a cell and Excel takes care of inserting the right code for you.

You might think of Excel as having two different ways of performing calculations: You can use standard cell references (in which case, the formula for the cell F4 would have been E4*D4), or you can use column references, if you are working inside a table. Using column references has the advantage that you can use the same expression in all of the cells of a column and Excel computes the formula with a different value for each row.

DAX works on tables, so all of the formulas need to reference columns. For example, in DAX you write the previous multiplication in this way:

```
Sales[SalesAmount] = Sales[ProductPrice] * Sales[ProductQuantity]
```

As you can see, each column is prefixed with the name of its table. In Excel you do not provide the table name, because Excel formulas work inside a single table. In DAX, on the other hand, references need to specify the table name because DAX works on a data model containing many tables and columns in different tables, which might have the same name.

Many functions in DAX work the same as the equivalent Excel function. The *IF* function, for example, reads in the same way in DAX and in Excel:

```
Excel   IF ( [@SalesAmount] > 10, 1, 0)
DAX     IF ( Sales[SalesAmount] > 10, 1, 0)
```

One important aspect where the syntax of Excel and DAX is different is in the way you reference the entire column. You might have noticed that when writing [@ProductQuantity] the @ means "the value in the current row." When using DAX, you do not need to specify this. The default behavior of the language is to get the value of the current row. If, in Excel, you want to reference the entire column (that is, all the rows in that column), you do that by removing the @ symbol, as you can see in Figure 1-6.

G4	:	× ✓ fx	=SUM([SalesAmount])				

▲	A	B	C	D	E	F	G
1							
2							
3		OrderDate ▼	ProductName ▼	ProductQuantity ▼	ProductPrice ▼	SalesAmount ▼	AllSales ▼
4		07/01/01	Mountain-100 Black, 42	1	2,024.99	2,024.99	47,993.66
5		07/01/01	Road-450 Red, 52	1	874.79	874.79	47,993.66
6		07/01/01	Road-450 Red, 52	3	874.79	2,624.38	47,993.66
7		07/01/01	Road-450 Red, 52	1	874.79	874.79	47,993.66
8		07/01/01	Sport-100 Helmet, Black	2	20.19	40.37	47,993.66
9		07/01/01	Sport-100 Helmet, Red	1	20.19	20.19	47,993.66
10		07/01/01	Sport 100 Helmet, Black	4	20.19	80.75	47,993.66
11		07/01/01	LL Road Frame - Red, 44	2	183.94	367.88	47,993.66
12		07/01/01	Road-450 Red, 52	2	874.79	1,749.59	47,993.66
13		07/01/01	Sport-100 Helmet, Red	1	20.19	20.19	47,993.66
14		07/01/01	Road-450 Red, 52	1	874.79	874.79	47,993.66
15		07/01/01	LL Road Frame - Red, 44	1	183.94	183.94	47,993.66
16		07/01/01	Road-450 Red, 52	8	874.79	6,998.35	47,993.66
17		07/01/01	Sport-100 Helmet, Black	3	20.19	60.56	47,993.66
18		07/01/01	Sport-100 Helmet, Red	4	20.19	80.75	47,993.66
19		07/01/01	LL Road Frame - Red, 48	2	183.94	367.88	47,993.66

FIGURE 1-6 In Excel you can refer to a whole column by omitting the @ symbol before the column name.

The value of the *AllSales* column is the same in all the rows, because it is the grand total of the *SalesAmount* column. In other words, there is a syntactical difference between the value of a column in the current row and the value of the column as a whole.

DAX is different. In DAX, you write the *AllSales* expression of Figure 1-6 in this way:

```
[AllSales] := SUM ( Sales[SalesAmount] )
```

There is no syntactical difference between using a column to grab its value for a specific row and using the column as a whole. DAX understands that you want to sum all the values of the column because you used the column name inside an aggregator (in this case the *SUM* function), which requires a column name to be passed as a parameter. Thus, while Excel requires an explicit syntax to differentiate between the two types of data to retrieve, DAX does the disambiguation in an automatic way. At least at the beginning, this might be confusing.

Excel and DAX: Two functional languages

One aspect where the two languages are very similar is in the fact that both Excel and DAX are functional languages. A functional language is made of expressions that are—basically—function calls. Neither in Excel nor in DAX is there the concept of statements, loops, and jumps, which are common to many programming languages. In DAX, everything is an expression. This aspect of the language is often a challenge for programmers coming from different languages, but it should be no surprise at all for Excel users.

Using iterators

One concept that might be new to you is that of iterators. When working in Excel, you are used to performing calculations one step at a time. In the previous example, you have seen that, in order to compute the total of sales, you have created one column containing the price multiplied by the quantity and then, as a second step, you summed it to compute the total sales. This number will then be useful, for example, as a denominator to compute the percentage of sales of each product.

Using DAX, you can perform the same operation in a single step, by using iterators. An iterator does exactly what it name suggests: it iterates over a table and performs a calculation on each row of the table, aggregating the result to produce the single value you needed.

In the previous example, you can compute the sum of all sales using the *SUMX* iterator:

```
[AllSales] :=
SUMX (
    Sales,
    Sales[ProductQuantity] * Sales[ProductPrice]
)
```

Both advantages and disadvantages occur in this approach. The advantage is that you can perform many complex calculations as a single step without having to worry about adding many columns, which end up being useful only for some specific formulas. The disadvantage, on the other hand, is that programming with DAX is less visual than it is in Excel. In fact, you do not see the column computing the price multiplied by the quantity; it exists only for the lifetime of the calculation.

To tell the truth, you still have the option of creating a calculated column that computes the multiplication of price and quantity. Nevertheless, as you will learn later, this is seldom a good practice, because it uses precious memory and might slow down the calculations.

DAX requires some theory

Let's be clear: This is not a difference between programming languages; this is a difference between mindsets. Like any human on this planet, you are probably used to searching on the web for complex formulas and solution patterns for the scenarios you are trying to solve. When using Excel, chances are good that you will find a formula that does nearly what you need. You can copy the formula, customize it to fit your needs, and then use it, without having to worry too much about how it works.

For example, in one of the worksheets that I use daily, I have this formula:

```
{=SUM(IF(('Transactions'!$B$5:$B$991>=M30)*('Transactions'!$B$5:$B$991<=N30),1,0))}
```

I do not really understand exactly how the formulas in curly brackets work and how that *IF* statement is evaluated. To be honest, I only remember that I need to confirm them with a strange keyboard combination. That said, it works, it always worked and the number that it computes is of interest rather than how it internally computes the value. Thus, as an author of books and a DAX expert, I fall in this category of users, too.

This approach, which works in Excel, does not work with DAX. You will need to study some theory and understand thoroughly how evaluation contexts work before you will be able to write good DAX code. Without the proper theoretical foundation, DAX will either compute values like magic or it will compute strange numbers which make no sense. The problem is not DAX, but the fact that you have not yet understood exactly how it works.

Luckily, the theory of DAX is limited to a couple of important concepts, which are explained in Chapter 4, "Understanding evaluation contexts." When you reach that chapter, roll up your sleeves and be prepared to go back to school for some time. Once you have mastered its content, DAX will have no secrets for you, and learning it will be mainly a matter of gaining experience. However, please do not try to go further unless that piece of theory is well established. Remember: knowing is half the battle.

DAX for SQL developers

If you are used to the SQL language, then you have already worked with many tables and created joins between columns in order to set relationships. From this point of view, you will feel at home in the DAX world, because computing in DAX is a matter of querying a set of tables joined by relationships and aggregating values.

Understanding relationship handling

The first difference between SQL and DAX is in the way relationships work in the model. In SQL, you can set foreign keys between tables to declare relationships, but the engine never uses these foreign keys in queries, unless you are explicit about them. If, for example, you have a Customer table and a Sales table, where CustomerKey is a primary key in Customer and a foreign key in Sales, you can write a query such as the following:

```
SELECT
    Customers.CustomerName,
    SUM ( Sales.SalesAmount ) AS SumOfSales
FROM
    Sales
    INNER JOIN Customers
        ON Sales.CustomerKey = Customers.CustomerKey
GROUP BY
    Customers.CustomerName
```

Even if you declared the relationship in the model using foreign keys, you still need to be explicit and state the join condition in the query. Although it makes queries a little more verbose, this is useful because it lets you use different join conditions in different queries, giving you a lot of freedom in the expressivity of the queries.

In DAX, relationships are part of the model and they are all *LEFT OUTER JOINS*. Once defined in the model, you no longer need to specify the join type in the query: DAX uses an automatic *LEFT OUTER JOIN* in the query whenever you use columns related to the primary table. Thus, you would write the previous SQL query in DAX as:

```
EVALUATE
SUMMARIZE (
    Sales,
    Customers[CustomerName],
    "SumOfSales", SUM ( Sales[SalesAmount] )
)
```

Because DAX knows the existing relationship between Sales and Customers, it does the join automatically following the model. Finally, the *SUMMARIZE* function needs to perform a group by *Customers[CustomerName]*, but you do not have any keyword for that: *SUMMARIZE* automatically groups data by columns selected.

DAX is a functional language

SQL is a declarative language. You define what you need by declaring the set of data you want to retrieve using *SELECT* statements, without worrying about how the engine will actually retrieve the information. DAX, on the other hand, is a functional language.

In DAX, every expression is a function call and function parameters can be, in turn, other function calls. The evaluation of parameters might lead to very complex query plans that DAX executes in order to compute the result.

For example, if you want to retrieve only customers who live in Europe, you can write this in SQL:

```
SELECT
    Customers.CustomerName,
    SUM ( Sales.SalesAmount ) AS SumOfSales
FROM
    Sales
    INNER JOIN Customers
        ON Sales.CustomerKey = Customers.CustomerKey
WHERE
    Customers.Continent = 'Europe'
GROUP BY
    Customers.CustomerName
```

Using DAX, you do not declare the *WHERE* condition in the query. Instead, you use a specific function (*FILTER*) to filter the result:

```
EVALUATE
SUMMARIZE (
    FILTER (
        Customers,
        Customers[Continent] = "Europe"
    ),
    Customers[CustomerName],
    "SumOfSales", SUM ( Sales[SalesAmount] )
)
```

You can see that *FILTER* is a function: It will return only the customers living in Europe, producing the expected result. The order in which you nest the function and the kind of functions you use have a strong impact on the final result and also the performance of the engine. This happens in SQL, too, even if, in SQL, you trust the query optimizer to find the optimal query plan. In DAX, although the query optimizer does a great job, the programmer has more responsibility in writing good code.

DAX as a programming and querying language

In SQL, there is a clear distinction between the query language and the programming language; that is, the set of instructions used to create stored procedures, views, and other pieces of code in the database. Each SQL dialect has its own statements to let programmers enrich the data model with code. DAX, on the other hand, makes virtually no distinction between querying and programming. A rich set of functions manipulate tables and can, in turn, return tables. The *FILTER* function you have just seen in the previous query is a good example of this.

Thus, in respect to this, DAX is simpler than SQL. Once you learn it as a programming language (it is, normally, its first usage), you will know everything needed to also use it as a query language.

Subqueries and conditions in DAX and SQL

One of the most powerful features of SQL as a query language is the option of using subqueries. DAX has some similar concepts even if, in the case of DAX subqueries, they naturally arise from the functional nature of the language.

For example, in SQL, to retrieve customers and total sales for only the customers who bought more than US$100, you can write this query as follows:

```
SELECT
    CustomerName,
    SumOfSales
FROM (
    SELECT
        Customers.CustomerName,
        SUM ( Sales.SalesAmount ) AS SumOfSales
    FROM
        Sales
        INNER JOIN Customers
            ON Sales.CustomerKey = Customers.CustomerKey
    GROUP BY
        Customers.CustomerName
    ) AS SubQuery
WHERE
    SubQuery.SumOfSales > 100
```

You can obtain the same result in DAX by simply nesting function calls:

```
EVALUATE
FILTER (
    SUMMARIZE (
        Customers,
        Customers[CustomerName],
        "SumOfSales", SUM ( Sales[SalesAmount] )
    ),
    [SumOfSales] > 100
)
```

In this code, the subquery that retrieves *CustomerName* and *SumOfSales* is later fed into a *FILTER* function that retains only the rows where SumOfSales is greater than 100. Right now, this code might seem unreadable to you but, as soon as you start learning DAX, you will discover that the usage of subqueries is much easier than in SQL and it flows naturally because DAX is a functional language.

DAX for MDX developers

Many BI professionals start to learn DAX because it is the new language of SSAS Tabular and, in the past, they have used the MDX language to build and query SSAS Multidimensional models. If you are among them, be prepared to learn a completely new language: DAX and MDX do not share much. Worse, some concepts in DAX will remind you of similar existing concepts in MDX, even if they are very different.

In fact, in our experience, learning DAX after MDX is the most challenging option. In order to learn DAX you will need to free your mind from MDX; try to forget everything you know about multidimensional spaces and be prepared to learn this new language with a clear mind.

Multidimensional vs. Tabular

MDX works in the multidimensional space defined by your model. The shape of the multidimensional space is based on the architecture of dimensions and hierarchies that you define in the model and that in turn defines the set of coordinates of the multidimensional space. Intersections of sets of members in different dimensions define points in the multidimensional space. We guess it took some time for you to understand that the *[All]* member of any attribute hierarchy is indeed a point in the multidimensional space.

DAX works in a much simpler way. There are no dimensions, no members, and no points in the multidimensional space. In other words, there is no multidimensional space at all. There are hierarchies, which you can define in the model, but they are very different from hierarchies in MDX. The DAX space is built on top of tables, columns, and relationships. Each table in a tabular model is neither a measure group nor a dimension: It is just a table and to compute values you have to scan it, filter it, or sum values inside it. Everything is based on the two simple concepts of tables and relationships.

You will soon discover that, from the modeling point of view, Tabular offers fewer options than Multidimensional does. Having fewer options, in this case, does not mean being less powerful, because you have a programming language (that is, DAX) which lets you enrich the model. The real modeling power of Tabular is the tremendous speed of DAX. In fact, you are probably used to avoid using too much MDX in your model, because optimizing MDX speed is often a challenge. DAX, on the other hand, is amazingly fast. Thus, most of the complexity of the calculations will not be in the model, but in the DAX formulas instead.

DAX as a programming and querying language

DAX and MDX are both programming languages and query languages. In MDX, the difference is made clear by the presence of the MDX script. You use MDX in the MDX script, along with several special statements that can be used in the script only (for example, *SCOPE* statements) and you use MDX in queries when you write *SELECT* statements that retrieve data. In DAX, this is somewhat different. You will use DAX as a programming language to define calculated columns (a concept new to DAX, which does not exist in MDX) and measures (similar to calculated members in MDX).

You can also use DAX as a query language, for example, to retrieve data from a tabular model using Reporting Services. Nevertheless, there are no special functions in DAX that are useful only for one of these two uses of the language. Moreover, you can query a tabular model using MDX, too. Thus, the querying part of MDX works with tabular models, whereas DAX is your only option when it comes to programming a tabular model.

Hierarchies

Using MDX, you rely on hierarchies to perform most of the calculations. If, for instance, you wanted to compute the sales in the previous year, you had to retrieve the *PrevMember* of the *CurrentMember* on the Year hierarchy and use it to rewrite the MDX filter. For example, you write the formula this way to define a previous year calculation in MDX:

```
CREATE MEMBER CURRENTCUBE.[Measures].[SamePeriodPreviousYearSales] AS
    (
        [Measures].[Sales Amount],
        ParallelPeriod (
            [Date].[Calendar].[Calendar Year],
            1,
            [Date].[Calendar].CurrentMember
        )
    );
```

The measure uses the *ParallelPeriod* function, which returns the cousin of the *CurrentMember* on the Calendar hierarchy. Thus, it is based on the hierarchies defined in the model. You write the same calculation in DAX using filter contexts and standard time intelligence functions:

```
[SamePeriodPreviousYearSales] :=

CALCULATE (
    SUM ( Sales[Sales Amount] ),
    SAMEPERIODLASTYEAR ( 'Date'[Date] )
)
```

You can write the same calculation in many other ways, using *FILTER* and other DAX functions, but the idea remains the same: instead of using hierarchies, you filter tables. This difference is huge, and you will probably miss hierarchy calculations until you get used to DAX.

Another important difference is that in MDX you refer to [*Measures*].[*Sales Amount*] and the aggregation function that needs to be used is already defined in the model. In DAX, there is no predefined aggregation. In fact, as you might have noticed, the expression to compute is *SUM(Sales[Sales Amount])*. The predefined aggregation is no longer in the model; you need to define it whenever you want to use it (you can always create a measure that holds the sum of sales, but we do not want to be too wordy here).

Another important difference between DAX and MDX is that the latter makes heavy use of the *SCOPE* statement to implement business logic (again, using hierarchies), whereas the former needs a completely different approach, because hierarchy handling is missing in the language altogether.

For example, if you want to clear a measure at the Year level, in MDX you would write this statement:

```
SCOPE ( [Measures].[SamePeriodPreviousYearSales], [Date].[Month].[All] )
    THIS = NULL;
END SCOPE;
```

In DAX, there is no *SCOPE* statement. To obtain the same result, you need to check the presence of filters in the filter context and the scenario is much more complex:

```
[SamePeriodPreviousYearSales] :=
IF (
    ISFILTERED ( 'Date'[Month] ),
    CALCULATE (
        SUM ( Sales[Sales Amount] ),
        SAMEPERIODLASTYEAR ( 'Date'[Date] )
    ),
    BLANK()
)
```

You will learn later what this formula computes in detail but, intuitively, it returns a value only if the user is browsing the calendar hierarchy at the month level or below, returning a BLANK otherwise. This formula is much more error-prone than the equivalent MDX code. To be honest, hierarchy handling is one of the features that is really missing in DAX.

Leaf-level calculations

Finally, when using MDX you probably got used to avoiding leaf-level calculations. Performing leaf-level computation in MDX turns out to be so slow that you always prefer to pre-compute values and leverage aggregations to return results. In DAX, leaf-level calculations work incredibly fast and aggregations do not exist at all. This will require a shift in your mind when it will be time to build the data models. In most cases, a data model that fits perfectly in SSAS Multidimensional is not the right one for Tabular, and vice-versa.

CHAPTER 2

Introducing DAX

After the quick introduction of the previous chapter, it is now time to start talking about the DAX language. In this chapter, you learn the syntax of the language, the difference between a calculated column and a measure (also called Calculated Field, in Excel terminology), and the most commonly used functions in DAX.

As this is an introductory chapter, many functions are not covered in depth. In later sections of the book we go deeper and explain them in more detail. For now, it is enough to introduce the functions and start looking at the DAX language in general.

Understanding DAX calculations

To express complex formulas, you need to learn the basics of DAX, which includes the syntax, the different data types that DAX can handle, the basic operators, and how to refer to columns and tables. These concepts are discussed in the next few sections.

You use DAX to compute values over columns in tables. You can aggregate, calculate, and search for numbers but, at the end, all of the calculations involve tables and columns. Thus, the first syntax to learn is how to reference a column in a table.

The general format is to write the table name, enclosed in single quotes, followed by the column name, enclosed in square brackets, as in:

```
'Sales'[Quantity]
```

You can omit the single quotes if the table name does not start with a number, it does not contain spaces, and it is not a reserved word (like Date or Sum).

Note It is good practice not to use spaces in table names. This way, you avoid the quotes in formulas, which tend to make the code harder to read. Keep in mind, however, that the name of the table is the same name that you will see when browsing the model with pivot tables or any other client tool such as Power View. Thus, if you like to have spaces in the table names in your report, you need to use single quotes in your code.

You can also avoid writing the table name at all, in case you are referencing a column or a measure in the same table where you are defining the formula. Thus, *[Quantity]* is a valid column reference, if written in a calculated column or in a measure in the Sales table. Even if this technique is syntactically correct, and the user interface might suggest its use when you select a column instead of writing it, we strongly discourage you from using that. Such a syntax makes the code rather difficult to read, so it's better to always use the table name when you reference a column in a DAX expression.

DAX data types

DAX can perform computations with different numeric types, of which there are seven. In the list that follows, we show both the DAX name and the more usual name of the same data type. Boolean values, for example, are called *TRUE/FALSE* in DAX terminology. We prefer to adhere to the de-facto naming standard and we refer to them as Boolean values.

- Whole Number (*Integer*)

- Decimal Number (*Float*)

- Currency (*Currency*), a fixed decimal number internally stored as an integer

- Date (*DateTime*)

- Boolean (*TRUE/FALSE*)

- Text (*String*)

- Binary large object (*BLOB*)

DAX has a powerful type-handling system so that you do not have to worry about data types: When you write a DAX expression, the resulting type is based on the type of terms used in the expression. You need to be aware of this in case the type returned from a DAX expression is not the expected one: then you must investigate the data type of the terms used in the expression itself.

For example, if one of the terms of a sum is a date, the result is a date, too; whereas, if the same operator is used with integers, the result is an integer. This is known as *operator overloading* and you can see an example of its behavior in Figure 2-1, where the *OrderDatePlusOneWeek* column is calculated by adding 7 to the value of the *Order Date* column. The result is, as we said, a date.

Order Date	OrderDatePlusOneWeek	Quantity
5/2/2007	5/9/2007	1
5/2/2007	5/9/2007	1
5/2/2007	5/9/2007	1
5/2/2007	5/9/2007	1
7/1/2007	7/8/2007	1
7/1/2007	7/8/2007	1
7/1/2007	7/8/2007	1
7/1/2007	7/8/2007	1

f× =Sales[Order Date] + 7

FIGURE 2-1 Adding an integer to a date results in a date increased by the corresponding number of days.

In addition to operator overloading, DAX automatically converts strings into numbers and numbers into strings whenever required by the operator. For example, if you use the & operator, which concatenates strings, DAX converts its arguments into strings. If you look at the formula:

```
= 5 & 4
```

it returns "54" as a string. On the other hand, the formula:

```
= "5" + "4"
```

returns an integer result with the value of 9.

The resulting value depends on the operator and not on the source columns, which are converted following the requirements of the operator. Even if this behavior looks convenient, later in this chapter you will see what kinds of errors might happen during these automatic conversions. We suggest avoiding automatic conversions. If some kind of conversion needs to happen, then it is much better if you take control over it and make the conversion explicit. In order to be more explicit, the previous example should be:

```
= VALUE ( "5" ) + VALUE ( "4" )
```

DAX data types might be familiar to people used to working with Excel or other languages. You can find specifications of DAX data types at http://msdn.microsoft.com/en-us/library/gg492146.aspx. However, it is useful to share a few considerations about each of these data types.

Whole number (*Integer*)

DAX has only one *Integer* data type that can store a 64-bit value. All the internal calculations between integer values in DAX also use a 64-bit value.

Decimal number (*Float*)

A decimal number is always stored as a double-precision floating point value. Do not confuse this DAX data type with the *decimal* and *numeric* data type of *Transact-SQL*: The corresponding data type of a DAX decimal number in SQL is *Float*.

Currency (*Currency*)

The *Currency* data type stores a fixed decimal number. It can represent four decimal points and it is internally stored as a 64-bit integer value divided by 10,000. All calculations performed between *Currency* data types always ignore decimals beyond the fourth decimal point. If you need more accuracy, you have to do a conversion to *Decimal* data type.

The default format of the *Currency* data type includes the currency symbol. You can also apply the currency formatting to whole and decimal numbers, and you can use a format without the currency symbol for a *Currency* data type.

Date (*DateTime*)

DAX stores dates in a *DateTime* data type. This format uses a floating point number internally, wherein the integer corresponds to the number of days since December 30, 1899, and the decimal part identifies the fraction of the day. Hours, minutes, and seconds are converted to decimal fractions of a day. Thus, the following expression returns the current date plus one day (exactly 24 hours):

```
= NOW () + 1
```

Its result is the date of tomorrow at the same time of the evaluation. If you need to take only the date part of a *DateTime*, always remember to use *TRUNC* to get rid of the decimal part.

The leap year bug

Lotus 1-2-3, a popular spreadsheet released in 1983, had a bug in the handling of the *DateTime* data type. It considered 1900 a leap year, even though it is not (the final year in a century is a leap year only if the first two digits can be divided by 4 without a remainder). At that time, the development team of the first version of Excel deliberately replicated the bug, to maintain compatibility with Lotus 1-2-3. Since then, each new version of Excel maintained the bug as a feature, because of compatibility.

Now, in 2015, the bug is still in DAX, introduced for backward compatibility with Excel. The presence of the bug (should we call it a feature?) might lead to errors on periods before March 1, 1900. Thus, by design, the first officially supported date by DAX is March 1, 1900. Date calculations executed on periods before that date might lead to errors and should be considered as inaccurate.

If you need to perform calculations before 1900, you should use math to move the dates after 1900, perform your calculations, and then move the dates back in time.

Boolean (*TRUE/FALSE*)

The *Boolean* data type is used to express logical conditions. For example, a calculated column defined by the following expression is of type *Boolean*:

```
= Sales[Unit Price] > Sales[Unit Cost]
```

You can see *Boolean* data types also as numbers where *TRUE* equals 1 and *FALSE* equals 0. This might be useful sometime for sorting purposes because *TRUE > FALSE*.

Text (*String*)

Every string in DAX is stored as a *Unicode* string, where each character is stored in 16 bits. By default, the comparison between strings is case-insensitive, so the two strings "Power Pivot" and "POWER PIVOT" are considered equal.

Binary large object (*BLOB*)

The *BLOB* data type is used in the data model to store images and it is not accessible in DAX. It is mainly used by Power View or by other client tools to show pictures stored directly in the data model.

DAX operators

Having seen the importance of operators in determining the type of an expression, you can now see a list of the operators available in DAX in Table 2-1.

TABLE 2-1 Operators.

Operator Type	Symbol	Use	Example
Parenthesis	( )	Precedence order and grouping of arguments	(5 + 2) * 3
Arithmetic	+ - * /	Addition Subtraction/negation Multiplication Division	4 + 2 5 – 3 4 * 2 4 / 2
Comparison	= <> > >= < <=	Equal to Not equal to Greater than Greater than or equal to Less than Less than or equal to	[CountryRegion] = "USA" [CountryRegion] <> "USA" [Quantity] > 0 [Quantity] >= 100 [Quantity] < 0 [Quantity] <= 100
Text concatenation	&	Concatenation of strings	"Value is " & [Amount]
Logical	&& ||	AND condition between two Boolean expressions OR condition between two Boolean expressions	[CountryRegion] = "USA" && [Quantity]>0 [CountryRegion] = "USA" || [Quantity] > 0

Moreover, the logical operators are available also as DAX functions, with syntax very similar to Excel. For example, you can write:

```
AND ( [CountryRegion] = "USA", [Quantity] > 0 )
OR ( [CountryRegion] = "USA", [Quantity] > 0 )
```

that are equivalent, respectively, to:

```
[CountryRegion] = "USA" && [Quantity] > 0
[CountryRegion] = "USA" || [Quantity] > 0
```

The use of functions instead of operators for Boolean logic becomes very useful when you have to write complex conditions. In fact, when it comes to formatting large sections of code, functions are much easier to format and read than operators. However, a major drawback of functions is that you can only pass in two parameters at a time. This requires you to nest functions if you have more than two conditions to evaluate.

Understanding calculated columns and measures

Now that you know the basics of DAX syntax, you need to learn one of the most important concepts in DAX: the difference between calculated columns and measures. Even though they might appear similar at first sight because you can make some calculations both ways, they are in reality very different and understanding the difference is a key to unlock the true power of DAX.

Calculated columns

If you want to create a calculated column in Excel, for example, you can simply move to the last column of the table, which is named *Add Column*, and start writing the formula. Other tools implementing DAX might have a different user interface, of course. You create the DAX expression into the formula bar, and IntelliSense helps you during the writing of the expression.

A calculated column is just like any other column in a table and you can use it in rows, columns, filters, or values of a pivot table or any other report. You can also use a calculated column to define a relationship, if needed. The DAX expression defined for a calculated column operates in the context of the current row of the table to which it belongs. Any reference to a column returns the value of that column for the current row. You cannot directly access the values of other rows.

> **Note** As you will see later, there are DAX functions that aggregate the value of a column for the whole table. The only way to get the value of a subset of rows is to use DAX functions that return a table and then operate on it. In this way, you aggregate column values for a range of rows and possibly operating on a different row by filtering a table made of only one row. You will learn more on this topic in Chapter 4, "Understanding evaluation contexts."

One important concept that you need to remember about calculated columns is that they are computed during the database processing and then stored in the model. This might seem strange if you are accustomed to SQL-computed columns (not persisted), which are computed at query time and do not use memory. In Tabular, however, all calculated columns occupy space in memory and are computed during table processing.

This behavior is helpful whenever you create very complex calculated columns. The time required to compute them is always process time and not query time, resulting in a better user experience. Nevertheless, you always must remember that a calculated column uses precious RAM. If, for example, you have a complex formula for a calculated column, you might be tempted to separate the steps of computation in different intermediate columns. Although this technique is useful during project development, it is a bad habit in production because each intermediate calculation is stored in RAM and wastes precious space.

Measures

There is another way of defining calculations in a DAX model, useful whenever you do not want to compute values for each row but, rather, you want to aggregate values from many rows in a table. We call these calculations *measures*.

For example: You can define the *GrossMargin* column in the Sales table to compute the amount of the gross margin:

```
Sales[GrossMargin] = Sales[SalesAmount] - Sales[TotalProductCost]
```

But what happens if you want to show the gross margin as a percentage of the sales amount? You could create a calculated column with the following formula:

```
Sales[GrossMarginPct] = Sales[GrossMargin] / Sales[SalesAmount]
```

This formula computes the right value at the row level, as you can see in Figure 2-2.

Unit Discount	Unit Cost	Net Price	Quantity	GrossMargin	GrossMarginPct
€ 60.00	€ 152.94	€ 239.99	2	294.1	49.02 %
€ 39.38	€ 90.55	€ 157.52	4	425.4	54.01 %
€ 119.80	€ 275.46	€ 479.20	2	647.08	54.01 %
€ 133.19	€ 220.64	€ 532.75	2	890.6	66.87 %
€ 24.20	€ 55.64	€ 96.80	3	196.08	54.02 %
€ 65.80	€ 167.73	€ 263.20	4	645.08	49.02 %
€ 4.00	€ 10.19	€ 15.99	4	39.2	49.02 %
€ 20.00	€ 50.98	€ 79.99	4	196.04	49.01 %
€ 25.98	€ 66.23	€ 103.92	4	254.68	49.01 %

FIGURE 2-2 The *GrossMarginPct* column shows the *GrossMargin* as a percentage, calculated row by row.

Nevertheless, when you compute the aggregate value of a percentage, you cannot rely on calculated columns. In fact, you need to compute the aggregate value as the sum of gross margin divided by the sum of sales amount. Therefore, in this case, you need to compute the ratio on the aggregates; you cannot use an aggregation of calculated columns. In other words, you compute the ratio of the sum, not the sum of the ratio.

The correct implementation for the *GrossMarginPct* would be as a measure:

```
Sales[GrossMarginPct] := SUM ( Sales[GrossMargin] ) / SUM (Sales[SalesAmount] )
```

However, as we have already said, you cannot enter it into a calculated column. If you need to operate on aggregate values instead of on a row-by-row basis, you must create measures. You might have noticed that we used := to define a measure, instead of the equal sign (=). This is a standard we use throughout the book, to make it easier to differentiate between measures and columns in code.

Measures and calculated columns both use DAX expressions; the difference is the context of evaluation. A measure is evaluated in the context of the cell of the pivot table or DAX query, whereas a calculated column is computed at the row level of the table to which it belongs. The context of the cell (later in the book, you learn that this is a filter context) depends on the user selections in the pivot table or on the shape of the DAX query. So when you use *SUM(Sales[SalesAmount])* in a measure, you mean the sum of all the cells that are aggregated under this cell, whereas when you use *Sales[SalesAmount]* in a calculated column, you mean the value of the *SalesAmount* column in the current row.

A measure needs to be defined in a table. This is one of the requirements of the DAX language. However, the measure does not really belong to the table. In fact, you can move a measure from one table to another one without losing its functionality.

Differences between calculated columns and measures

Even if they look similar, there is a big difference between calculated columns and measures. The value of a calculated column is computed during data refresh and uses the current row as a context; it does not depend on user activity on the pivot table. A measure operates on aggregations of data defined by the current context. In a pivot table, for example, source tables are filtered according to the coordinates of cells, and data is aggregated and calculated using these filters. In other words, a measure always operates on aggregations of data under the evaluation context and for this reason the default execution mode does not reference any single row. The evaluation context is explained further in Chapter 4.

Choosing between calculated columns and measures

Now that you have seen the difference between calculated columns and measures, you might be wondering when to use one over the other. Sometimes either is an option, but in most situations, your computation needs determine your choice.

You have to define a calculated column whenever you want to do the following:

- Place the calculated results in an Excel Slicer, or see results in Rows or Columns in a pivot table (as opposed to the Values area), or use the result as a filter condition in a DAX query.

- Define an expression that is strictly bound to the current row. (For example, *Price * Quantity* cannot work on an average or on a sum of the two columns.)

- Categorize text or numbers. (For example, a range of values for a measure, a range of ages of customers, such as 0–18, 18–25, and so on.)

However, you must define a measure whenever you want to display resulting calculation values that reflect user selections and see them in the Values area of pivot tables, for example:

- When you calculate profit percentage of a pivot table selection.

- When you calculate ratios of a product compared to all products but keeping the filter both by year and region.

You can express some calculations both with calculated columns and with measures, even if you need to use different DAX expressions in these cases. For example, you can define the *GrossMargin* as a calculated column:

```
Sales[GrossMargin] = Sales[SalesAmount] - Sales[TotalProductCost]
```

but it can be defined as a measure, too:

```
[GrossMargin] := SUM ( Sales[SalesAmount] ) - SUM ( Sales[TotalProductCost] )
```

We suggest you use measure in this case because being evaluated at query time it does not consume memory and disk space, but this is really important only in large datasets. When the size of the model is not an issue, you can use the method you are more comfortable with.

Cross references

It is obvious that a measure can refer to one or more calculated columns. It might be less intuitive that the opposite is also true. A calculated column can refer to a measure: In this way, it forces the calculation of a measure for the context defined by the current row. This operation transforms and consolidates the result of a measure into a column, which will not be influenced by user actions. Obviously, only certain operations can produce meaningful results because usually a measure makes computations that strongly depend on the selection made by the user in the pivot table.

Variables

When writing a DAX expression, you can avoid repeating the same expression by using variables. For example, look at the following expression:

```
VAR
    TotalSales = SUM ( Sales[SalesAmount] )
RETURN
    ( TotalSales - SUM ( Sales[TotalProductCost] ) ) / TotalSales
```

You can define many variables and they are local to the expression in which you define them. Variables are very useful both to simplify the code, and because you can avoid repeating the same subexpression. Variables are computed using lazy evaluation. This means that if you define a variable that, for any reason, is not used in your code, then the variable will never be evaluated. If it needs to be computed, then this happens only once: Later usages of the variable will read the previously computed value. Thus, they are useful also as an optimization technique when you use multiple times a complex expression.

Moreover, as you will learn in Chapter 4, variables are extremely useful because they use the definition evaluation context instead of the one where the variable is used.

Handling errors in DAX expressions

Now that you have seen some of the basics of the syntax, you will learn how to handle invalid calculations gracefully. A DAX expression might contain invalid calculations because the data it references is not valid for the formula. For example, you might have a division by zero or a column value that is not a number and is used in an arithmetic operation, such as multiplication. You must learn how these errors are handled by default and how to intercept these conditions if you want some special handling.

Before you learn how to handle errors, it is worth spending a few words on describing the different kinds of errors that might appear during a DAX formula evaluation. They are:

- Conversion Errors

- Arithmetical Operations Errors

- Empty or Missing Values

Conversion errors

The first kind of error is the conversion error. As you have seen before in this chapter, DAX automatically converts values between strings and numbers whenever the operator requires it. To review the concept with examples, all of these are valid DAX expressions:

```
"10" + 32 = 42
"10" & 32 = "1032"
10 & 32 = "1032"
DATE (2010,3,25) = 3/25/2010
DATE (2010,3,25) + 14 = 4/8/2010
DATE (2010,3,25) & 14 = "3/25/201014"
```

These formulas are always correct because they operate with constant values. However, what about the following, if *VatCode* is a string?

```
SalesOrders[VatCode] + 100
```

Because the first operand of this sum is a column that, in this case, is of *Text* data type, you must be sure that DAX can convert all the values in that column to numbers. If DAX fails in converting some of the content to suit the operator needs, you will incur a conversion error. Here are typical situations:

```
"1 + 1" + 0            = Cannot convert value '1+1' of type string to a number
DATEVALUE ("25/14/2010") = Type mismatch
```

To avoid these errors, you need to add error detection logic in your DAX expressions to intercept error conditions and always return a meaningful result.

Arithmetical operations errors

The second category of errors is that of arithmetical operations, such as the division by zero or the square root of a negative number. These are not conversion-related errors: DAX raises them whenever you try to call a function or use an operator with invalid values.

The division by zero requires special handling because it behaves in such a way that is not very intuitive (except, maybe, for mathematicians). When you divide a number by zero, DAX usually returns the special value *Infinity*. Moreover, in the very special cases of 0 divided by 0 or *Infinity* divided by *Infinity*, DAX returns the special *NaN* (not a number) value.

Because this is a strange behavior, it is worth summarizing in Table 2-2.

TABLE 2-2 Special result values for division by zero.

Expression	Result
10 / 0	Infinity
7 / 0	Infinity
0 / 0	NaN
(10 / 0) / (7 / 0)	NaN

It is important to note that *Infinity* and *NaN* are not errors but special values in DAX. In fact, if you divide a number by *Infinity* the expression does not generate an error but returns 0:

```
9954 / ( 7 / 0 )    = 0
```

Apart from this special situation, DAX can return arithmetical errors when calling a function with a wrong parameter, such as the square root of a negative number:

```
SQRT ( -1 )     = An argument of function 'SQRT' has the wrong data type
                  or the result is too large or too small
```

If DAX detects errors like this, it blocks any further computation of the expression and raises an error. You can use the *ISERROR* function to check if an expression leads to an error, something that you use later in this chapter.

Finally, keep in mind that special values like *NaN* are displayed in such a way in the Power Pivot or in the Visual Studio window, but they can be displayed as errors when shown by some client tools, such as an Excel pivot table. Moreover, these special values will be detected as errors by the error detection functions.

Empty or missing values

The third category that we examine is not a specific error condition, but the presence of empty values, which might result in unexpected returns or calculation errors when combining those empty values with other elements in a calculation. You need to understand how DAX treats these special values.

DAX handles missing values, blank values, or empty cells in the same way, using the value *BLANK*. *BLANK* is not a real value but a special way to identify these conditions. You can obtain the value *BLANK* in a DAX expression by calling the *BLANK* function, which is different from an empty string. For example, the following expression always returns a blank value, which will be displayed as an empty cell in a pivot table:

```
= BLANK ()
```

On its own, this expression is useless, but the *BLANK* function itself becomes useful every time you want to return an empty value. For example, you might want to display an empty cell instead of 0, as in the following expression that calculates the total discount for a sale transaction, leaving the cell blank if the discount is 0:

```
= IF ( Sales[DiscountPerc] = 0, BLANK (), Sales[DiscountPerc] * Sales[Amount] )
```

BLANK, by itself, is not an error but an empty value. Therefore, an expression containing a *BLANK* might return a value or a blank, depending on the calculation required. For example, the following expression returns *BLANK* whenever *Sales[Amount]* is *BLANK*:

```
= 10 * Sales[Amount]
```

In other words, the result of an arithmetic product is *BLANK* whenever one or both terms are *BLANK*. This propagation of *BLANK* in a DAX expression happens in several other arithmetical and logical operations, as you can see in the following examples:

```
BLANK () + BLANK ()    = BLANK ()
10 * BLANK ()          = BLANK ()
BLANK () / 3           = BLANK ()
BLANK () / BLANK ()    = BLANK ()
BLANK () || BLANK ()   = FALSE
BLANK () && BLANK ()   = FALSE
BLANK () = BLANK ()    = TRUE
```

However, the propagation of *BLANK* in the result of an expression does not happen for all formulas. Some calculations do not propagate *BLANK* but return a value depending on the other terms of the formula. Examples of these are addition, subtraction, division by *BLANK*, and a logical operation between a *BLANK* and a valid value. In the following expressions, you can see some examples of these conditions, along with their results:

```
BLANK () - 10          = -10
18 + BLANK ()          = 18
4 / BLANK ()           = Infinity
0 / BLANK ()           = NaN
FALSE || BLANK ()      = FALSE
FALSE && BLANK ()      = FALSE
TRUE || BLANK ()       = TRUE
TRUE && BLANK ()       = FALSE
```

Empty values in Excel and SQL

Excel has a different way of handling empty values. In Excel, all empty values are considered 0 whenever they are used in a sum or in multiplication, but they return an error if they are part of division or of a logical expression.

In SQL the null values are propagated in an expression in a different way than what happens with *BLANK* in DAX. As you see in the previous examples, the presence of a *BLANK* in a DAX expression does not always result in a *BLANK* result, whereas the presence of *NULL* in SQL often evaluates to *NULL* for the entire expression.

Understanding the behavior of empty or missing values in a DAX expression and using *BLANK* to return an empty cell in a calculation are also important skills to control the results of a DAX expression. You can often use *BLANK* as a result when you detect wrong values or other errors, as you are going to learn in the next section.

Intercepting errors

Now that you have seen the various kinds of errors that can occur, you will learn the techniques to intercept errors and correct them or, at least, show an error message with some meaningful information. The presence of errors in a DAX expression frequently depends on the value contained in tables and columns referenced in the expression itself. Therefore, you might want to control the presence of these error conditions and return an error message. The standard technique is to check whether an expression returns an error and, if so, replace the error with a message or a default value. There are a few DAX functions for this.

The first of them is the *IFERROR* function, which is very similar to the *IF* function, but instead of evaluating a Boolean condition, it checks whether an expression returns an error. You can see two typical uses of the *IFERROR* function here:

```
= IFERROR ( Sales[Quantity] * Sales[Price], BLANK () )
= IFERROR ( SQRT ( Test[Omega] ), BLANK () )
```

In the first expression, if either Sales[Quantity] or Sales[Price] are strings that cannot be converted into a number, the returned expression is an empty value; otherwise the product of Quantity and Price is returned.

In the second expression, the result is an empty cell every time the *Test[Omega]* column contains a negative number.

When you use *IFERROR* this way, you follow a more general pattern that requires the use of *ISERROR* and *IF*:

```
= IF (
    ISERROR ( Sales[Quantity] * Sales[Price] ),
    BLANK (),
    Sales[Quantity] * Sales[Price]
  )

= IF (
    ISERROR ( SQRT ( Test[Omega] ) ),
    BLANK (),
    SQRT ( Test[Omega] )
  )
```

You should use *IFERROR* whenever the expression that has to be returned is the same tested for an error; you do not have to duplicate the expression in two places, and the resulting formula is more readable and safer in case of future changes. You should use *IF*, however, when you want to return the result of a different expression. For example, you can detect whether the argument for *SQRT* is a valid one, calculating the square root only for positive numbers and returning *BLANK* for negative ones:

```
= IF ( Test[Omega] >= 0, SQRT ( Test[Omega] ), BLANK () )
```

Considering that the third argument of an *IF* statement has a default value *BLANK*, you can also write the same expression as:

```
= IF ( Test[Omega] >= 0, SQRT ( Test[Omega] ) )
```

A particular case is the test against the empty value. The *ISBLANK* function detects an empty value condition, returning *TRUE* if the argument is *BLANK*. This is important especially when a missing value has a meaning different from a value set to 0. In the following example, we calculate the cost of shipping for a sales transaction, using a default shipping cost for the product if the transaction itself does not specify a weight:

```
– IF (
    ISBLANK ( Sales[Weight] ),
    Sales[DefaultShippingCost],
    Sales[Weight] * Sales[ShippingPrice]
)
```

If we had just multiplied product weight and shipping price, we would have an empty cost for all the sales transactions with missing weight data.

Try to avoid the usage of error-handling functions

Even if it is not yet time to speak about DAX code optimization, you need to be aware that error-handling functions might create severe performance issues in your code. It is not that they are slow by themselves. The problem is that the DAX engine cannot use optimized paths in its code when errors happen. In most cases, it is more efficient to check operands for possible errors instead of using the error-handling engine. For example, instead of writing this:

```
= IFERROR (
    SQRT ( Test[Omega] ),
    BLANK ()
)
```

It is much better to write this:

```
= IF (
    Test[Omega] >= 0,
    SQRT ( Test[Omega] ),
    BLANK ()
  )
```

This second expression does not need to detect the error and it is faster than the previous one. This, of course, is a general rule. For a detailed explanation, see Chapter 16, "Optimizing DAX."

Formatting DAX code

Before continuing with the explanation of the DAX language, it is useful to cover a very important aspect of DAX, that is, formatting the code. DAX is a functional language, meaning that—no matter how complex it is—a DAX expression is always a single function call with some parameters. The complexity of the code translates in the complexity of the expressions that you use as parameters to the outermost function.

For this reason, it is normal to see expressions that span over 10 lines or more. Seeing a 20-line DAX expression is not something strange and you will become acquainted with it. Nevertheless, as formulas start to grow in length and complexity, it is extremely important that you learn how to format them, so that they are human-readable.

There is no "official" standard to format DAX code, yet we believe it is important to describe the standard that we use on our code. It is probably not perfect and you might prefer something different, and we have no problem with that. The only thing you need to remember is: "format your code, never write everything on a single line, or you will be in trouble sooner than you expect."

In order to understand why formatting is very important, we show a formula that computes some time intelligence. It is a somewhat complex formula, but definitely not the most complex one you will author. Here is how the expression looks if you do not format it in some way:

```
IF (COUNTX (BalanceDate, CALCULATE (COUNT( Balances[Balance] )), ALLEXCEPT ( Balances,
BalanceDate[Date] ))) > 0, SUMX (ALL ( Balances[Account] ), CALCULATE (SUM(
Balances[Balance] ), LASTNONBLANK (DATESBETWEEN (BalanceDate[Date], BLANK(),LASTDATE(
BalanceDate[Date] )), CALCULATE ( COUNT( Balances[Balance] ))))), BLANK ())
```

Trying to understand what this formula computes is nearly impossible, because you have no clue of which is the outermost function and how DAX evaluates the different parameters to create the complete flow of execution. We have seen too many examples of formulas written in this way by customers who, at some point, ask for help in understanding why the formula returns incorrect results. Guess what? The first thing we do is format the expression; only later do we start working on it.

The same expression, properly formatted, looks like this:

```
=IF (
    COUNTX (
        BalanceDate,
        CALCULATE (
            COUNT ( Balances[Balance] ),
            ALLEXCEPT ( Balances, BalanceDate[Date] )
        )
    ) > 0,
    SUMX (
        ALL ( Balances[Account] ),
        CALCULATE (
            SUM ( Balances[Balance] ),
            LASTNONBLANK (
                DATESBETWEEN (
                    BalanceDate[Date],
                    BLANK (),
                    LASTDATE ( BalanceDate[Date] )
                ),
                CALCULATE ( COUNT ( Balances[Balance] ) )
            )
        )
    ),
    BLANK ()
)
```

The code is the same, but this time it is much easier to look at the three parameters of *IF* and, most important, following the blocks that arise naturally from indenting lines, and how they compose the complete flow of execution. Yes, the code is still hard to read, but now the problem is DAX, not the formatting.

DAXFormatter.com

We created a website that is dedicated to formatting DAX code. We did it for ourselves, because formatting the code is a time-consuming operation and we did not want to spend our time doing it for every formula we write. Once the tool was working, we decided to donate it to the public domain, so that users can format their own DAX code (by the way, we have been able to promote our formatting rules in this way).

You can find it on www.daxformatter.com. The user interface is simple: just copy your DAX code, click FORMAT, and the page refreshes showing a nicely formatted version of your code, which you can then copy and paste in the original window.

This is the set of rules that we use to format DAX:

- Keywords like *IF*, *COUNTX*, *CALCULATE* are always separated by any other term using a space and they are always written in uppercase.

- All column references are written in the form TableName[ColumnName], with no space between the table name and the opening square bracket. The table name is always included.

- All measure references are written in the form [MeasureName], without any table name.

- Commas are always followed by a space and never preceded by a space.

- If the formula fits one single line, then no other rule need be applied.

- If the formula does not fit a single line, then:

  - The function name stands on a line by itself, with the opening parenthesis.

  - All the parameters are in separate lines, indented with four spaces and with the comma at the end of the expression.

  - The closing parenthesis is aligned with the function call and stands in a line by itself.

These are the basic rules we use. A more detailed list of these rules is available at http://sql.bi/daxrules.

If you find a way to express formulas that best fits your reading method, then use it. The goal of formatting is to make the formula easier to read, so use the technique that works better for you. The most important thing to remember when defining your personal set of formatting rules is that you always need to see errors as soon as possible. If, in the unformatted code shown before, DAX complains about a missing closing parenthesis, it will be very hard to spot the place where the error is. On the formatted formula, it is much easier to see how a closing parenthesis matches the opening function calls.

Help on formatting DAX

Formatting DAX is not an easy task because you need to write it using a small font in a text box. Unfortunately, at the time of this writing, neither Excel nor Visual Studio provides a good text editor for DAX. Nevertheless, a few hints might help in writing your DAX code:

- If you want to increase the font size, you can hold down Ctrl while rotating the wheel button on the mouse, making it easier to look at the code.

- If you want to add a new line to the formula, you can press Shift+Enter.

- If editing in the text box is really a pain, you can always copy the code in another editor, like Notepad, and then paste the formula again in the text box.

Finally, whenever you look at a DAX expression, it is hard to understand, at first glance, whether it is a calculated column or a measure. Thus, we use an equal sign (=) whenever we define a calculated column and the assignment operator (:=) to define measures:

```
CalcCol  = SUM (Sales[SalesAmount])      is a calculated column
CalcFld := SUM (Sales[SalesAmount])      is a measure
```

Common DAX functions

Now that you have seen the fundamentals of DAX and how to handle error conditions, what follows is a brief tour through the most commonly used functions and expressions of DAX. In the remaining part of this chapter, you will see some of the most frequently used DAX functions, which you are likely to use in your own data models.

Aggregate functions

Almost every data model needs to operate on aggregated data. DAX offers a set of functions that aggregate the values of a column in a table and return a single value. We call this group of functions *aggregate functions*. For example, the following measure calculates the sum of all the numbers in the *SalesAmount* column of the Sales table:

```
Sales := SUM ( Sales[SalesAmount] )
```

This expression (*SUM*) aggregates all the rows of the table if it is used in a calculated column, but it considers only the rows that are filtered by slicers, row, columns, and filter conditions in a pivot table whenever it is used in a measure.

The aggregation functions (*SUM, AVERAGE, MIN, MAX, STDEV,* and *VAR*) operate only on numeric values or on dates.

Note *MIN* and *MAX* have another function: if used with two parameters, they will return the minimum or maximum of the two parameters. Thus, *MIN* (1, 2) will return 1 and *MAX* (1, 2) returns 2. This functionality, introduced in 2015, is very useful when you need to compute the minimum or maximum of complex expressions, because it avoids writing the same expression many times in *IF* statements.

Similarly to Excel, DAX offers an alternative syntax to these functions to make the calculation on columns that can contain both numeric and non-numeric values, such as a text column. That syntax simply adds the suffix A to the name of the function, just to get the same name and behavior as Excel. However, these functions are useful only for columns containing *TRUE/FALSE* values because *TRUE* is evaluated as 1 and *FALSE* as 0. Text columns are always considered 0. Therefore, no matter what is in the content of a column, if you use, for example, *MAXA* on a text column, you will always get 0 as the result. Moreover, DAX never considers empty cells when it performs the aggregation.

Even if these functions can be used on non-numeric columns without returning an error, their results are not useful because there is no automatic conversion to numbers for text columns. These functions are named *AVERAGEA*, *COUNTA*, *MINA*, and *MAXA*.

> **Note** Despite the same name of statistical functions, the difference in the way they are used in DAX and Excel exists because in DAX a column has a type, and its type determines the behavior of aggregation functions. Excel handles a different data type for each cell, whereas DAX handles a single data type for each column. DAX deals with data in tabular form with well-defined types for each column, whereas Excel formulas work on heterogeneous cell values, without well-defined types. If a column in Power Pivot has a *Numeric* data type, all the values can be only numbers or empty cells. If a column is of a text type, it is always 0 for these functions (except for *COUNTA*), even if the text can be converted to a number, whereas in Excel the value is considered a number on a cell-by-cell basis. For these reasons, these DAX functions are not very useful for Text columns.

The functions you learned before are useful to perform aggregation of values. Sometimes, you are not interested in aggregating values but only in counting them. Thus, DAX offers a set of functions that are useful to count rows or values:

- *COUNT* operates only on numeric columns
- *COUNTA* operates on any type of columns
- *COUNTBLANK* returns the number of empty cells in a column
- *COUNTROWS* returns the number of rows in a table
- *DISTINCTCOUNT* returns the number of distinct values of a column

COUNTA is the only interesting function in the group of A-suffixed functions, because it returns the number of values of the column that are not empty and works on any type of column. If you want to count all the values in a column that contain an empty value, you can use the *COUNTBLANK* function. Finally, if you want to count the number of rows of a table, you can use the *COUNTROWS* function. Beware that *COUNTROWS* requires a table as a parameter, not a column.

> **Note** For any column in any table, the result of *COUNTA(table[column])* + *COUNTBLANK(table[column])* will be always the same as *COUNTROWS (table)*.

The last function, *DISTINCTCOUNT*, is very useful because it does exactly what its name suggests: counts the distinct values of a column, which it takes as its only parameter. *DISTINCTCOUNT* counts the *BLANK* value as one of the possible values.

> **Note** *DISTINCTCOUNT* is a function introduced in the 2012 version of DAX. The earlier version of DAX did not include *DISTINCTCOUNT* and, to compute the number of distinct values of a column, you had to use *COUNTROWS(DISTINCT(table[column]))*. The two patterns return the very same result although *DISTINCTCOUNT* is easier to read, requiring only a single function call.

All the aggregation functions you learned so far work on columns (except for *COUNTROWS*, which works on tables). Therefore, they can aggregate values coming from a single column only. There are aggregation functions that can aggregate an expression, instead of a single column. This set of functions is very useful, especially when you want to make calculations using columns of different related tables. For example, if a Sales table contains all the sales transactions and a related Product table contains all the information about a product, including its cost, you might calculate the total internal cost of a sales transaction by defining a measure with this expression:

```
Cost := SUMX ( Sales, Sales[Quantity] * RELATED ( Product[StandardCost] ) )
```

This measure calculates the product of Quantity (from Sales table) and StandardCost of the sold product (from the related Product table) for each row in the Sales table. Finally, it returns the sum of all these calculated values.

All the aggregation functions ending with an X suffix behave this way: they compute an expression (the second parameter) for each of the rows of a table (the first parameter) and return a result obtained by the corresponding aggregation function (*SUM, MIN, MAX* or *COUNT*) applied to the result of those calculations.

You will learn more about this behavior further in Chapter 4 because, to understand their behavior correctly, we will need to introduce the concept of evaluation contexts. The X-suffixed functions available are *SUMX, AVERAGEX, PRODUCTX, COUNTX, COUNTAX, CONCATENATEX, MINX,* and *MAXX*. There are also iterators that do not have the X suffix, like *FILTER* and *ADDCOLUMNS*. All of them will be explained in great detail later.

Logical functions

Sometimes you want to build a logical condition in an expression—for example, to implement different calculations depending on the value of a column or to intercept an error condition. In these cases, you can use one of the logical functions in DAX. You have already learned in the previous section, "Handling errors in DAX expressions," the two most important functions of this group, which are *IF* and *IFERROR*.

Logical functions are very simple and do what their names suggest, they are *AND, FALSE, IF, IFERROR, NOT, TRUE,* and *OR*. If, for example, you want to compute the amount as quantity multiplied by price only when the *Price* column contains a correct numeric value, you can use the following pattern:

```
Amount = IFERROR ( Sales[Quantity] * Sales[Price], BLANK ( ) )
```

If you did not use the *IFERROR* and the *Price* column contains an invalid number, the result for the calculated column would be an error because if a single row generates a calculation error, the error propagates to the whole column. The usage of *IFERROR*, however, intercepts the error and replaces it with a blank value.

Another interesting function inside this category is *SWITCH*, which is useful when you have a column containing a low number of distinct values, and you want to get different behaviors, depending on its value. For example, the column *Size* in the Product table contains L, M, S, XL, and you might want to decode this value in a more meaningful column. You can obtain the result by using nested *IF* calls:

```
SizeDesc =
IF ( Product[Size] = "S", "Small",
    IF ( Product[Size] = "M", "Medium",
        IF ( Product[Size] = "L", "Large",
            IF ( Product[Size] = "XL", "Extra Large", "Other" ) ) ) )
```

A more convenient way to express the same formula, using *SWITCH*, is:

```
SizeDesc =
    SWITCH ( Product[Size],
      "S", "Small",
      "M", "Medium",
      "L", "Large",
      "XL", "Extra Large",
      "Other"
    )
```

The code in this latter expression is more readable, even if not faster, because, internally, DAX translates *SWITCH* statements into a set of nested *IF* functions.

Tip Here is an interesting way to use the *SWITCH* function to check for multiple conditions in the same expression. Because *SWITCH* is converted into a set of nested *IF*, where the first one that matches wins, you can test multiple conditions using this pattern:

```
SWITCH (
    TRUE (),
    Product[Size] = "XL" && Product[Color] = "Red", "Red and XL",
    Product[Size] = "XL" && Product[Color] = "Blue", "Blue and XL",
    Product[Size] = "L" && Product[Color] = "Green", "Green and L"
)
```

Using *TRUE* as the first parameter, in reality, says: "Return the first result where the condition evaluates to *TRUE*."

Information functions

Whenever you need to analyze the type of an expression, you can use one of the information functions. All of these functions return a *TRUE/FALSE* value and can be used in any logical expression. They are: *ISBLANK, ISERROR, ISLOGICAL, ISNONTEXT, ISNUMBER,* and *ISTEXT.*

It is important to note that when a column (instead of an expression) is passed as a parameter, the functions *ISNUMBER, ISTEXT,* and *ISNONTEXT* always return *TRUE* or *FALSE,* depending on the data type of the column and on the empty condition of each cell.

You might be wondering whether you can use *ISNUMBER* with a text column just to check whether a conversion to a number is possible. Unfortunately, you cannot use this approach; if you want to test whether a text value is convertible to a number, you must try the conversion and handle the error if it fails. For example, to test whether the column *Price* (which is of type text) contains a valid number, you must write:

```
IsPriceCorrect = NOT ( ISERROR ( Sales[Price] + 0 ) )
```

DAX tries to add a zero to the Price to force the conversion from a Text value to a number; if it succeeds, then it will return *TRUE* (because *ISERROR* will return *FALSE*), otherwise it will return *FALSE* (because *ISERROR* returns *TRUE*). The conversion will fail, for example, if for some rows the price has an "N/A" string value.

If, however, you try to use *ISNUMBER,* as in the following expression, you will always receive *FALSE* as a result:

```
IsPriceCorrect = ISNUMBER ( Sales[Price] )
```

In this case, *ISNUMBER* always returns *FALSE* because, based on metadata, the *Price* column is not a number but a string, regardless of the content of each row.

Mathematical functions

The set of mathematical functions available in DAX is very similar to the same set in Excel, with the same syntax and behavior. The mathematical functions of common use are *ABS, EXP, FACT, LN, LOG, LOG10, MOD, PI, POWER, QUOTIENT, SIGN,* and *SQRT.* Random functions are *RAND* and *RANDBETWEEN. EVEN* and *ODD* let you test numbers. *GCD* and *LCM* are useful to compute the greatest common denominator and least common multiple of two numbers. *QUOTIENT* returns you the integer division of two numbers.

Finally, there are several rounding functions that deserve an example; in fact, you might use several approaches to get the same result. Consider these calculated columns, along with their results in Figure 2-3:

```
FLOOR         = FLOOR ( Tests[Value], 0.01 )
TRUNC         = TRUNC ( Tests[Value], 2 )
ROUNDDOWN     = ROUNDDOWN ( Tests[Value], 2 )
MROUND        = MROUND ( Tests[Value], 0.01 )
ROUND         = ROUND ( Tests[Value], 2 )
CEILING       = CEILING ( Tests[Value], 0.01 )
ISO.CEILING   = ISO.CEILING ( Tests[Value], 0.01 )
ROUNDUP       = ROUNDUP ( Tests[Value], 2 )
INT           = INT ( Tests[Value] )
FIXED         = FIXED ( Tests[Value], 2, TRUE )
```

Test	Value	FLOOR	TRUNC	ROUNDDOWN	MROUND	ROUND	CEILING	ISO.CEILING	ROUNDUP	INT	FIXED
A	1.12345	1.12	1.12	1.12	1.12	1.12	1.13	1.13	1.13	1	1.12
B	1.265	1.26	1.26	1.26	1.26	1.27	1.27	1.27	1.27	1	1.27
C	1.265001	1.26	1.26	1.26	1.27	1.27	1.27	1.27	1.27	1	1.27
D	1.499999	1.49	1.49	1.49	1.5	1.5	1.5	1.5	1.5	1	1.50
E	1.51111	1.51	1.51	1.51	1.51	1.51	1.52	1.52	1.52	1	1.51
F	1.000001	1	1	1	1	1	1.01	1.01	1.01	1	1.00
G	1.999999	1.99	1.99	1.99	2	2	2	2	2	1	2.00

FIGURE 2-3 Summary of different rounding functions.

As you can see, *FLOOR*, *TRUNC*, and *ROUNDDOWN* are very similar, except in the way you can specify the number of digits to round on. In the opposite direction, *CEILING* and *ROUNDUP* are very similar in their results. You can see a few differences in the way the rounding is done between *MROUND* and *ROUND* function.

Trigonometric functions

DAX offers a rich set of trigonometric functions that are useful for some calculation. We do not go into details of these functions, since their usage, if needed, is simple. They are *COS, COSH, COT, COTH, SIN, SINH, TAN,* and *TANH*. Prefixing them with A computes the arc version (arcsine, arccosine, and so on).

DEGREES and *RADIANS* perform conversion to degrees and radians, respectively, and SQRTPI computes the square root of its parameter after multiplying for Pi.

Text functions

Almost all of the text functions available in DAX are similar to those available in Excel, with only a few exceptions: they are *CONCATENATE, EXACT, FIND, FIXED, FORMAT, LEFT, LEN, LOWER, MID, REPLACE, REPT, RIGHT, SEARCH, SUBSTITUTE, TRIM, UPPER,* and *VALUE*. These functions are useful for manipulating text and extracting data from strings that contain multiple values. For example, in Figure 2-4, you can see an example of the extraction of first and last name from a string containing these values separated by commas, with the title in the middle, which we want to remove.

Name	Comma1	Comma2	SimpleConversion	FirstLastName
Russo, Mr., Marco	6	11	Marco Russo	Marco Russo
Ferrari, Mr., Alberto	8	13	Alberto Ferrari	Alberto Ferrari
Ferrari, Alberto	8		Ferrari, Alberto Ferrari	Alberto Ferrari

FIGURE 2-4 Here you can see an example of extracting first and last names using text functions.

We start calculating the position of the two commas and then we use these numbers to extract the right part of the text. The *SimpleConversion* column implements a formula that might return wrong values if there are fewer than two commas in the string (and it raises an error if there are no commas at all), whereas the *FirstLastName* column implements a more complex expression that does not fail in case of missing commas:

```
Comma1 = IFERROR ( FIND ( ",", People[Name] ), BLANK ( ) )
Comma2 = IFERROR ( FIND ( ",", People[Name], People[Comma1] + 1 ), BLANK ( ) )
SimpleConversion = MID ( People[Name], People[Comma2] + 1, LEN ( People[Name] ) )
                 & " " & LEFT ( People[Name], People[Comma1] - 1 )
FirstLastName = TRIM (
              MID (
                  People[Name],
                  IF (
                      ISNUMBER ( People[Comma2] ),
                      People[Comma2],
                      People[Comma1]
                  ) + 1,
                  LEN ( People[Name] )
              )
          )
          & IF (
            ISNUMBER ( People[Comma1] ),
            " " & LEFT ( People[Name], People[Comma1] - 1 ),
            ""
          )
      )
```

As you can see, the *FirstLastName* column is defined by a long DAX expression, but you must use it to avoid possible errors that would propagate to the whole column if even a single value generates an error.

Conversion functions

You learned before that DAX performs automatic conversion of data types to adjust them to the need of the operators. Even if it happens automatically, a set of functions still can perform explicit conversion of types.

CURRENCY can transform an expression in a currency type, whereas *INT* transforms an expression into an integer. *DATE* and *TIME* take the date and time parts as parameters and return a correct *DATETIME*. *VALUE* transforms a string into a numeric format, whereas *FORMAT* gets a numeric value as the first parameter and a string format as its second one and can transform numeric values into strings. *FORMAT* is very commonly used with *DateTime*. For example, the following expression returns "2015 Jan 12."

```
= FORMAT ( DATE ( 2015, 01, 12 ), "yyyy mmm dd" )
```

The opposite operation, that is converting strings into *DateTime* values, is performed through the usage of the *DATEVALUE* function.

Date and time functions

Almost in every type of data analysis, handling time and date is an important part of the job. DAX has a large number of functions that operate on date and time. Some of them correspond to similar functions in Excel and make simple transformations to and from a *DateTime* data type. The date and time functions are *DATE, DATEVALUE, DAY, EDATE, EOMONTH, HOUR, MINUTE, MONTH, NOW, SECOND, TIME, TIMEVALUE, TODAY, WEEKDAY, WEEKNUM, YEAR*, and *YEARFRAC*.

To make a more complex operation on dates, such as comparing aggregated values year over year or calculating the year-to-date value of a measure, there is another set of functions called Time Intelligence Functions that will be described in Chapter 7, "Time intelligence calculations."

As mentioned before in this chapter, a *DateTime* data type internally uses a floating point number wherein the integer part corresponds to the number of days after December 30, 1899, and the decimal part indicates the fraction of the day in time. Hours, minutes, and seconds are converted into decimal fractions of the day. Thus, adding an integer number to a *DateTime* value increments the value by a corresponding amount of days. However, you will probably find it more convenient to use the conversion functions to extract day, month, and year from a date. In Figure 2-5, you can see how to extract this information from a table containing a list of dates:

```
Day    = DAY ( Calendar[Date] )
Month  = FORMAT ( Calendar[Date], "mmmm" )
Year   = YEAR ( Calendar[Date] )
```

Date	Day	Month	Year
1/1/2010	1	January	2010
1/2/2010	2	January	2010
1/3/2010	3	January	2010
1/4/2010	4	January	2010
1/5/2010	5	January	2010
1/6/2010	6	January	2010
1/7/2010	7	January	2010
1/8/2010	8	January	2010

FIGURE 2-5 Here you can see an example of extracting date information using date and time functions.

Relational functions

Two useful functions that enable you to navigate through relationships inside a DAX formula are *RELATED* and *RELATEDTABLE*.

You already know that a calculated column can reference column values of the table in which it is defined. Thus, a calculated column defined in Sales can reference any column of the same table. However, what can you do if you must refer to a column in another table? In general, you cannot use columns in other tables unless a relationship is defined in the model between the two tables. If the two tables share a relationship, then the *RELATED* function enables you to access columns in the related table.

For example, you might want to compute a calculated column in the Sales table that checks whether the product that has been sold is in the "Cell phones" category and, in that case, apply a reduction factor to the standard cost. To compute such a column, you must use a condition that checks the value of the product category, which is not in the Sales table. Nevertheless, a chain of relationships starts from Sales, reaching Product Category through Product and Product Subcategory, as you can see in Figure 2-6.

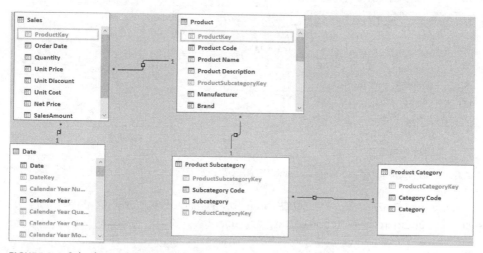

FIGURE 2-6 Sales has a chained relationship with Product Category.

It does not matter how many steps are necessary to travel from the original table to the related one, DAX will follow the complete chain of relationship and return the related column value. Thus, the formula for the AdjustedCost column can be:

```
Sales[AdjustedCost] =
IF (
    RELATED ( 'Product Category'[Category] ) = "Cell Phone",
    Sales[UnitCost] * 0.95,
    Sales[UnitCost]
)
```

In a one-to-many relationship, *RELATED* can access the one-side from the many-side because, in that case, only one row in the related table exists, if any. If no such row exists, *RELATED* simply returns *BLANK*.

If you are on the one-side of the relationship and you want to access the many-side, then *RELATED* is not helpful because many rows from the other side might be available for a single row. In that case, you can use *RELATEDTABLE*. *RELATEDTABLE* returns a table containing all the rows related to the current one. For example, if you want to know how many products are in each category, you can create a column in Product Category with this formula:

```
= COUNTROWS ( RELATEDTABLE ( Product ) )
```

This calculated column will show, for each product category, the number of products related, as you can see in Figure 2-7.

Category ...	Category	NumOfProducts
01	Audio	115
02	TV and Video	222
03	Computers	606
04	Cameras and camcorders	372
05	Cell phones	285
06	Music, Movies and Audio Books	90
07	Games and Toys	166
08	Home Appliances	661

fx =COUNTROWS (RELATEDTABLE(Product))

FIGURE 2-7 Count the number of products by using *RELATEDTABLE*.

As is the case for *RELATED*, *RELATEDTABLE* can follow a chain of relationships always starting from the one-side and going in the direction of the many-side.

CHAPTER 3

Using basic table functions

In this chapter, you will learn the difference between scalar functions and table functions in DAX. Table functions are very important for internal computations in DAX, and are useful when you write a DAX query instead of a DAX expression for a measure or a calculated column.

The goal here is to introduce the notion of table functions, but not to provide a detailed explanation of all the functions that you will see here for the first time. A deeper analysis of table functions is included in Chapter 9, "Advanced table functions." Here, we will explain the role of table functions in DAX, and how to use them in common scenarios, including in scalar DAX expressions.

Introducing table functions

DAX is a functional language, where you write expressions that produce a result after their evaluation. Until now, you have seen that a DAX expression usually returns a single value, such as a string or a number. We call such expressions *scalar expressions*. When you define a measure or a calculated column, you always write a scalar expression, as in the following examples:

```
= 4 + 3
= "DAX is a beautiful language"
= SUM ( Sales[Quantity] )
```

However, you can write a DAX expression that produces a table as a result. You cannot assign a table expression directly to a measure or to a calculated column, but table expressions are an important part of DAX. For example, there are DAX functions that receive a table expression as an argument, and a table expression is required to write a DAX query.

The simplest example of a table expression is referencing the table name in a DAX expression, such as the following expression returning the entire content (all the columns and all the rows) of the Sales table:

```
= Sales
```

However, if you try to assign the previous expression to a measure or to a calculated column, you get an error, because a measure needs a scalar value as a result. You need to manipulate the table expression in order to obtain a scalar value. This is possible by using functions that accept a table expression as an argument. For example, you count how many rows are included in a table by using *COUNTROWS*:

```
= COUNTROWS ( Sales )
```

The *COUNTROWS* function has the following definition:

```
COUNTROWS ( <table> )
```

Every time you have a DAX function that accepts a table expression as an argument, you can write the name of a table in that parameter, or you can write a function that returns a table.

We categorize DAX functions depending on their return type. We call "scalar functions" those that return a scalar value and "table functions" those that return a table. For example, *COUNTROWS* is a scalar function, because it returns a number, and accepts a table as an argument.

Many table functions usually manipulate a table, changing the rows and/or the columns of the original table. For example, you can count the number of rows in the Sales table with a unit price greater than 100 by using the following expression:

```
= COUNTROWS (
    FILTER (
        Sales,
        Sales[Unit Price] > 100
    )
)
```

In the previous expression, *FILTER* returns a table containing only the rows of Sales having a unit price greater than 100. You will learn more about the *FILTER* function later in this chapter.

Typically, you use table expressions in your code to iterate over a table's rows and aggregate some values, to return a scalar value as the result. You cannot assign a table expression directly to a measure or to a calculated column. However, you can use a table expression in a calculated table (if this feature will be available in the future) or in a DAX query, materializing the content of the table expression.

For example, you can obtain a table containing all the sales with a unit price greater than 100 by executing a table expression such as the following, which results in the content you see in Figure 3-1.

```
= FILTER (
    Sales,
    Sales[Unit Price] > 100
)
```

Order_Date	Due_Date	Delivery_Date	Quantity	Unit_Price	Unit_Discount	Unit_Cost	Net_Price
6/3/2007	6/14/2007	6/9/2007	1	229	0	116.75	229
12/17/2008	12/26/2008	12/28/2008	1	399	79.8	203.42	319.2
3/26/2009	4/1/2009	4/4/2009	1	269.9	18.893	137.6	251.007
6/11/2008	6/21/2008	6/18/2008	1	268.5	26.85	123.47	241.65
10/23/2007	11/5/2007	11/1/2007	1	791	0	363.75	791
10/24/2009	10/31/2009	10/30/2009	1	279.99	0	142.75	279.99
5/22/2007	5/30/2007	5/29/2007	1	469.97	0	216.12	469.97
2/27/2007	3/8/2007	3/7/2007	1	469.97	23.4985	216.12	446.4715

FIGURE 3-1 Content of Sales table filtered by *Unit_Price* greater than 100.

DAX also offers you the *EVALUATE* statement, which you can use to evaluate table expressions:

```
EVALUATE
FILTER (
    Sales,
    Sales[Unit Price] > 100
)
```

You can execute the DAX query above in any client tool that executes DAX queries (Microsoft Excel, DAX Studio, SQL Server Management Studio, Reporting Services, and so on). In the following section, you will see a more detailed explanation of the *EVALUATE* syntax.

EVALUATE syntax

You can use DAX both as a programming language and as a query language.

A DAX query is a DAX expression that returns a table, used with the *EVALUATE* statement. The complete DAX query syntax is as follows:

```
[DEFINE { MEASURE <tableName>[<name>] = <expression> }]
EVALUATE <table>
[ORDER BY {<expression> [{ASC | DESC}]} [, …]
    [START AT {<value>|<parameter>} [, …]] ]
```

The initial *DEFINE MEASURE* part can be useful to define measures that are local to the query (that is, they exist for the lifetime of the query). It becomes very useful when you are debugging formulas, because you can define a local measure, test it, and then put it in the model once it behaves as expected. You will see more examples of this syntax in Chapter 9.

Most of the syntax is made of optional arguments. The simplest possible query retrieves all the columns and rows from an existing table:

```
EVALUATE Product
```

You can see the result in Figure 3-2.

ProductKey	Product_Code	Product_Name	Manufacturer	Brand	Class	Style	Color
1337	501022	Contoso Expandable1-Har	Contoso, Ltd	Contoso	Regular	Product0501022	Black
1834	801008	Litware Washer & Dryer 2	Litware, Inc.	Litware	Regular	Product0801008	Silver
1308	406062	Contoso Digital Camera/C	Contoso, Ltd	Contoso	Economy	Product0406062	Purple
299	205008	SV Car Video AM/FM E100	Southridge Video	Southridge Video	Economy	Product0205008	Black
1727	702021	MGS Rise of Nations: Gold	Tailspin Toys	Tailspin Toys	Economy	Product0702021	Pink

FIGURE 3-2 Result of a query over Product table.

To control the sort order, you can use the *ORDER BY* clause:

```
EVALUATE Product
ORDER BY
    Product[Color],
    Product[Brand] ASC,
    Product[Class] DESC
```

Note Please note that the Sort By Column property defined in a model does not have an effect in a DAX query. Even if you might see sorted data by querying a single column according to the Sort By Column property, you do not have to rely on this behavior, just as you cannot rely on a clustered index in an SQL query. A client that generates a dynamic DAX query should read the Sort By Column property in a model's metadata and then generate a corresponding *ORDER BY* condition. In both DAX and SQL, you must always use an explicit *ORDER BY* condition to get sorted data as a result.

The *ASC* and *DESC* keywords are optional; if they are not present, *ASC* is used by default. You can see in Figure 3-3 the result of the previous query, where data is sorted by *Color*, *Brand*, and *Class*.

ProductKey	Product_Code	Product_Name	Manufacturer	Brand	Class	Style	Color
2422	808013	Litware 20" Box Fan E401 Ye	Litware, Inc.	Litware	Economy	Product0808013	Yellow
2481	808072	Litware 18" Oscillating Pede	Litware, Inc.	Litware	Deluxe	Product0808072	Yellow
2485	808076	Litware 18" Oscillating Pede	Litware, Inc.	Litware	Deluxe	Product0808076	Yellow
68	106003	NT Bluetooth Stereo Headp	Northwind Traders	Northwind Traders	Economy	Product0106003	Yellow
80	106015	NT Wireless Bluetooth Ster	Northwind Traders	Northwind Traders	Economy	Product0106015	Yellow
1688	701028	SV Hand Games women M4	Southridge Video	Southridge Video	Regular	Product0701028	Yellow

FIGURE 3-3 Result of a query over Product table sorted by *Color*, *Brand*, and *Class* in descending order.

The *START AT* condition is also optional and can be used only in conjunction with an *ORDER BY* clause. You can specify the starting value for each column in the *ORDER BY* statement. The *START AT* condition is useful for pagination in stateless applications that fetch only a limited number of rows from a query and then send another query when the user asks for the next page of data. For example, look at the following query:

```
EVALUATE Product
ORDER BY
    Product[Color],
    Product[Brand] ASC,
    Product[Class] DESC
START AT
    "Yellow", "Tailspin Toys"
```

The query returns the table shown in Figure 3-4 which contains only the rows starting from Yellow, Tailspin Toys.

ProductKey	Product_Code	Product_Name	Manufactu	Brand	Class	Style	Color
1664	701004	MGS Hand Games women M400	Tailspin Toys	Tailspin Toys	Regular	Product0701004	Yellow
1663	701003	MGS Hand Games men M300 Yel	Tailspin Toys	Tailspin Toys	Regular	Product0701003	Yellow
1789	702083	MGS Rise of Nations: Thrones ar	Tailspin Toys	Tailspin Toys	Economy	Product0702083	Yellow
1665	701005	MGS Hand Games for 12-16 boys	Tailspin Toys	Tailspin Toys	Economy	Product0701005	Yellow
1662	701002	MGS Hand Games for students E	Tailspin Toys	Tailspin Toys	Economy	Product0701002	Yellow
1661	701001	MGS Hand Games for kids E300 Y	Tailspin Toys	Tailspin Toys	Economy	Product0701001	Yellow
1666	701006	MGS Hand Games for Office wor	Tailspin Toys	Tailspin Toys	Deluxe	Product0701006	Yellow
108	106043	WWI Stereo Bluetooth Headpho	Wide World I	Wide World Importers	Regular	Product0106043	Yellow
56	104011	WWI 4GB Video Recording Pen >	Wide World I	Wide World Importers	Deluxe	Product0104011	Yellow

FIGURE 3-4 Result of a query over a sorted Product table skipping values until Yellow color and Tailspin Toys brand.

Please note that the notion of "starting from" depends from the order direction specified in the *ORDER BY* clause. If you specify *DESC* for *Product[Brand]* as in the following example, Wide World Importers is not included in the result, and other brands, such as Southridge Video and Northwind Traders, follow Tailspin Toys. You can see the result of the following query in Figure 3-5.

```
EVALUATE Product
ORDER BY
    Product[Color],
    Product[Brand] DESC,
    Product[Class] DESC
START AT
    "Yellow", "Tailspin Toys"
```

ProductKey	Product_Code	Product_Name	Manufacture	Brand	Class	Style	Color
1664	701004	MGS Hand Games women M400 Yel	Tailspin Toys	Tailspin Toys	Regular	Product0701004	Yellow
1663	701003	MGS Hand Games men M300 Yellow	Tailspin Toys	Tailspin Toys	Regular	Product0701003	Yellow
1665	701005	MGS Hand Games for 12-16 boys E6	Tailspin Toys	Tailspin Toys	Economy	Product0701005	Yellow
1789	702083	MGS Rise of Nations: Thrones and F	Tailspin Toys	Tailspin Toys	Economy	Product0702083	Yellow
1662	701002	MGS Hand Games for students E400	Tailspin Toys	Tailspin Toys	Economy	Product0701002	Yellow
1661	701001	MGS Hand Games for kids E300 Yell	Tailspin Toys	Tailspin Toys	Economy	Product0701001	Yellow
1666	701006	MGS Hand Games for Office worker	Tailspin Toys	Tailspin Toys	Deluxe	Product0701006	Yellow
935	308193	SV 4GB Laptop Memory M65 Yellow	Southridge Vid	Southridge Video	Regular	Product0308193	Yellow
1687	701027	SV Hand Games men M30 Yellow	Southridge Vid	Southridge Video	Regular	Product0701027	Yellow
1688	701028	SV Hand Games women M40 Yellow	Southridge Vid	Southridge Video	Regular	Product0701028	Yellow
930	308188	SV 512MB Laptop memory E800 Yell	Southridge Vid	Southridge Video	Economy	Product0308188	Yellow

FIGURE 3-5 Result of a query over a sorted Product table skipping values until Yellow color and Tailspin Toys brand, considering descending order for *Brand*.

To filter rows and change the columns returned by a DAX query, you must manipulate the table expression after the *EVALUATE* keyword by using specific table functions. This chapter introduces some of the table expressions, whereas Chapter 9 describes additional ones.

Using table expressions

As you have seen at the beginning of this chapter, you often use table expressions as arguments of other DAX functions. A typical use is in functions that iterate a table, computing a DAX expression for each row. For example, this is the case of all the aggregation functions ending with an "X", such as *SUMX*:

```
[Sales Amount] :=
SUMX (
    Sales,
    Sales[Quantity] * Sales[Unit Price]
)
```

You can replace the simple Sales table reference with a table function. For example, you can consider only sales with a quantity greater than one by using the *FILTER* function:

```
[Sales Amount Multiple Items] :=
SUMX (
    FILTER (
        Sales,
        Sales[Quantity] > 1
    ),
    Sales[Quantity] * Sales[Unit Price]
)
```

In a calculated column, you can also use the *RELATEDTABLE* function to retrieve all the rows of a table that is on the many-side of a one-to-many relationship. For example, the following calculated column in the Product table computes the sales amount of the corresponding product:

```
Product[Product Sales Amount] =
SUMX (
    RELATEDTABLE ( Sales ),
    Sales[Quantity] * Sales[Unit Price]
)
```

You can find a detailed explanation of the *RELATEDTABLE* table function in Chapter 4, "Understanding evaluation contexts," within the section "Row context and relationships."

You can nest table function calls within the same DAX expression, because any table expression can be a call to a table function. For example, the following calculated column in the Product table computes the product sales amount considering only sales with a quantity greater than one.

```
Product[Product Sales Amount Multiple Items] =
SUMX (
    FILTER (
        RELATEDTABLE ( Sales ),
        Sales[Quantity] > 1
    ),
    Sales[Quantity] * Sales[Unit Price]
)
```

When you have nested calls of table functions, DAX evaluates the innermost function first, and then evaluates the others up to the outermost one. Do not confuse this rule with the order of the evaluation of arguments of a function call.

Note As you will see later, the execution order of nested calls can be a source of confusion because *CALCULATETABLE* has a different order of evaluation than *FILTER*. In the next section, you learn the *FILTER* behavior, and you will find the *CALCULATETABLE* description in Chapter 5, "Understanding *CALCULATE* and *CALCULATETABLE*."

Understanding *FILTER*

The *FILTER* function has a simple role: It gets a table and returns a table that has the same columns as in the original table, but contains only the rows that satisfy a filter condition applied row by row.

The syntax of *FILTER* is the following:

```
FILTER ( <table>, <condition> )
```

FILTER iterates the <table> and, for each row, evaluates the <condition>, which is a Boolean expression. When the <condition> evaluates to *TRUE*, *FILTER* returns the row; otherwise, it skips it.

Note From a logical point of view, *FILTER* executes the <condition> for each of the rows in <table>. However, internal optimizations in DAX might reduce the number of these evaluations up to the number of unique values of column references included in the <condition> expression. The actual number of evaluations of the <condition> corresponds to the "granularity" of the *FILTER* operation. Such a granularity determines *FILTER* performance, and it is an important element of DAX optimizations.

For example, the following query filters products of Fabrikam brand, as you see in the result shown in Figure 3-6.

```
EVALUATE
FILTER (
    Product,
    Product[Brand] = "Fabrikam"
)
```

ProductKey	Product_Name	Brand	Class	Color	Unit_Cost	Unit_Price
1218	Fabrikam Home and Vacation Moviemake	Fabrikam	Regular	Black	293.39	638
1217	Fabrikam Home and Vacation Moviemake	Fabrikam	Regular	Black	255.68	556
1145	Fabrikam Home and Vacation Moviemake	Fabrikam	Regular	Orange	260.28	566
1239	Fabrikam Social Videographer 2/3" 17mm	Fabrikam	Economy	Blue	80.55	158
1191	Fabrikam Social Videographer 2/3" 17mm	Fabrikam	Economy	Orange	81.57	160
356	Fabrikam Laptop14.1W M4180 Red	Fabrikam	Regular	Red	210.11	456.9
2018	Fabrikam Microwave 0.8CuFt E0800 Blue	Fabrikam	Economy	Blue	48.43	94.99
1127	Fabrikam SLR Camera 35" M358 Gold	Fabrikam	Economy	Gold	150.84	328
1927	Fabrikam Refrigerator 24.7CuFt X9800 Gre	Fabrikam	Deluxe	Grey	1060.22	3199.99

FIGURE 3-6 The query filters only products of Fabrikam brand.

You can nest *FILTER* calls in another *FILTER* function, because you can use any table expression as a filter argument. The first *FILTER* executed is the innermost one. In general, nesting two filters produces the same result rather than a combination of logical conditions included in an *AND* function in the predicate. In other words, the following queries produce the same result:

```
FILTER ( <table>, AND ( <condition1>, < condition2> ) )
FILTER ( FILTER ( <table>, < condition1> ), < condition2> ) )
```

However, you might observe a different performance if the <table> has many rows and the two predicates have different complexities. For example, consider the following query, which returns Fabrikam products that have a *Unit Price* that is more than three times the *Unit Cost*, as shown in Figure 3-7.

```
EVALUATE
FILTER (
    Product,
    AND (
        Product[Brand] = "Fabrikam",
        Product[Unit Price] > Product[Unit Cost] * 3
    )
)
```

ProductKey	Product_Name	Brand	Class	Color	Unit_Cost	Unit_Price
1927	Fabrikam Refrigerator 24.7CuFt X9800 Grey	Fabrikam	Deluxe	Grey	1060.22	3199.99
1117	Fabrikam SLR Camera 35" X358 Grey	Fabrikam	Regular	Grey	144.52	436.2
1158	Fabrikam Independent Filmmaker 1/3" 8.5m	Fabrikam	Deluxe	Black	516.86	1560
1129	Fabrikam SLR Camera 35" X358 Pink	Fabrikam	Regular	Pink	144.52	436.2
1227	Fabrikam Trendsetter 2/3" 17mm X100 Oran	Fabrikam	Regular	Orange	327.34	988
1154	Fabrikam Trendsetter 1/3" 8.5mm X200 Blue	Fabrikam	Regular	Blue	330.66	998
1915	Fabrikam Refrigerator 24.7CuFt X9800 Greer	Fabrikam	Deluxe	Green	1060.22	3199.99
1207	Fabrikam Independent Filmmaker 2/3" 17m	Fabrikam	Deluxe	Grey	503.61	1520
1230	Fabrikam Independent Filmmaker 1/3" 8.5m	Fabrikam	Deluxe	Blue	506.92	1530
1109	Fabrikam SLR Camera 35" X358 Black	Fabrikam	Regular	Black	144.52	436.2

FIGURE 3-7 The query filters only products of Fabrikam brand having a Unit Price more than three times than that of Unit Cost.

Such a query might apply both conditions to all the rows of the Product table. If you have one of the two conditions that is faster and more selective, you can apply it first by using a nested *FILTER* function. For example, the following query applies the filter over *Unit Price* and *Unit Cost* in the inner-most *FILTER* function, and then filters by *Brand* only those products that satisfy the price condition.

```
EVALUATE
FILTER (
    FILTER (
        Product,
        Product[Unit Price] > Product[Unit Cost] * 3
    ),
    Product[Brand] = "Fabrikam"
)
```

If you invert the conditions, you invert also their execution order. The following query applies the price condition only to products of Fabrikam brand:

```
EVALUATE
FILTER (
    FILTER (
        Product,
        Product[Brand] = "Fabrikam"
    ),
    Product[Unit Price] > Product[Unit Cost] * 3
)
```

This knowledge will be useful when you optimize DAX expressions. You might choose the execution order to apply the most selective filter first. However, do not start optimizing DAX without a clear understanding of evaluation contexts. You will find a more complete discussion about query optimizations in Chapter 16, "Optimizing DAX." The goal of these examples was to make you aware of the order of execution of nested calls of table functions.

> **Note** Usually, the execution order of nested call functions is from the innermost to the outermost function. You will see that *CALCULATE* and *CALCULATETABLE* might be an exception to this behavior, because of the particular order used to evaluate their arguments. Because you might use *FILTER* and *CALCULATETABLE* in similar situations, be aware of this difference in case of nested calls.

Understanding *ALL*, *ALLEXCEPT*, and *ALLNOBLANKROW*

ALL is a useful function that returns all the rows of a table or all the values of a column, depending on the parameter you use. For example, the following DAX query returns all the rows in the Product table:

```
EVALUATE
ALL ( Product )
```

You cannot specify a table expression in an *ALL* argument. You have to specify either a table name or a list of column names. If you use a single column, the result is a table that has only one column containing the list of its unique values, as you can see in Figure 3-8.

```
EVALUATE
ALL ( Product[Class] )
```

FIGURE 3-8 The query over all values of a column returns a list of all unique values.

You can specify more columns from the same table in arguments of the *ALL* function. If you use many columns, the result will be a table with an equivalent number of columns, containing the list of the existing combination of values in those columns. For example, the following expression produces the result shown in Figure 3-9.

```
EVALUATE
ALL ( Product[Class], Product[Color] )
ORDER BY Product[Color]
```

Class	Color
Economy	Silver
Economy	Silver Grey
Regular	Silver Grey
Deluxe	Silver Grey
Economy	Transparent
Economy	White
Deluxe	White
Regular	White

FIGURE 3-9 The query over all values of more columns returns a list of only existing combinations of values.

In all of its variations, *ALL* ignores any existing filter to produce its result. You can use *ALL* as an argument of an iteration function, such as *SUMX* and *FILTER*, or as a filter argument in a *CALCULATE* function (which you will see later).

If you want to include most of the columns of a table in an *ALL* function call, you can use *ALLEXCEPT* instead. The syntax of *ALLEXCEPT* requires a table followed by the columns you want to exclude from the result. As a result, *ALLEXCEPT* returns a table with a unique list of existing combination of values in the other columns of the table.

In reality, *ALLEXCEPT* is a way to write a DAX expression that will automatically include in the *ALL* result any additional columns that could appear in the table in future versions. For example, if you have a Product table with five columns (*ProductKey, Product Name, Brand, Class, Color*), the following syntaxes produce the same result:

```
ALL ( Product[Product Name], Product[Brand], Product[Class] )
ALLEXCEPT ( Product, Product[ProductKey], Product[Color] )
```

However, if you later add two columns *Product[Unit Cost]* and *Product[Unit Price]*, then the result of *ALL* will ignore them, whereas the previous *ALLEXCEPT* will return the equivalent of:

```
ALL (
    Product[Product Name],
    Product[Brand],
    Product[Class],
    Product[Unit Cost],
    Product[Unit Price]
)
```

The following query returns a table that has all the columns other than *ProductKey* and *Color* from the Product table. The result in Figure 3-10 has the same number of rows of the original table, because the result includes the *Product_Name* column, which has a unique value per row. Other combinations of columns in the result might return a lower number of rows, because *ALLEXCEPT* removes duplicate combinations of values in the returned columns.

```
EVALUATE ALLEXCEPT ( Product, Product[ProductKey], Product[Color] )
```

Product_Name	Brand	Class	Unit_Cost	Unit_Price
SV Car Video LCD7 M7002 Silver	Southridge Video	Regular	169.69	369
Proseware Laser Jet Color Printer X300 Grey	Proseware	Regular	69.25	209
Contoso behind Centrex X15 Grey	Contoso	Deluxe	16.56	49.99
Contoso 2-Line Speakerphone M109 White	Contoso	Regular	16.55	35.99
Litware Home Theater System 5.1 Channel M514 Black	Litware	Regular	275.46	599
Adventure Works Desk Lamp E1200 Blue	Adventure Works	Economy	15.29	29.99
Proseware Desk Jet All-in-One Printer, Scanner, Copier M	Proseware	Regular	72.66	158
The Phone Company Microsoft Windows Mobile M200 Bl	The Phone Company	Regular	105.31	229
Fabrikam Refrigerator 9.7CuFt M5600 Blue	Fabrikam	Regular	226.71	493

FIGURE 3-10 *ALLEXCEPT* returns existing combinations of values from all the columns not specified in the arguments.

In a previous example, you have seen *ALL* in an *EVALUATE* statement, which executes the DAX expression without any existing filter. For this reason, it is better to see an example using measures that count the rows returned by *ALL* in a pivot table, where each cell evaluates the measure using a different filter. Consider the following measures:

```
[Products] := COUNTROWS ( Product )
[All Products] := COUNTROWS ( ALL ( Product ) )
[All Brands] := COUNTROWS ( ALL ( Product[Brand] ) )
```

You can see in Figure 3-11 an example of the different results for each measure.

Row Labels	Products	All Products	All Brands
Deluxe	360	2,517	12
Economy	881	2,517	12
Regular	1,275	2,517	12
(blank)		2,517	12
Grand Total	**2,516**	**2,517**	**12**

FIGURE 3-11 *All Products* and *All Brands* measures ignore the class on rows and always show the same number.

For each product class, you always have the same number in *All Products* and *All Brands* columns. The evaluation of the *ALL* statement ignores the filter defined by each cell of the pivot table.

When you call *ALL* on a parent table of a relationship, you retrieve an additional blank row if the child table contains one or more rows that do not match any values in the parent table. You can omit this special row from the result by using *ALLNOBLANKROW* instead of *ALL*.

Consider the following measures:

```
[All Products] := COUNTROWS ( ALL ( Product ) )
[All NoBlank Products] := COUNTROWS ( ALLNOBLANKROW ( Product ) )
[All Brands] := COUNTROWS ( ALL ( Product[Brand] ) )
[All NoBlank Brands] := COUNTROWS ( ALLNOBLANKROW ( Product[Brand] ) )
[All Sizes] := COUNTROWS ( ALL ( Product[Size] ) )
[All NoBlank Sizes] := COUNTROWS ( ALLNOBLANKROW ( Product[Size] ) )
```

In Figure 3-12 you can see the difference between *ALL* and *ALLNOBLANKROW* measures. The *ALL* versions of the measures return one more than the *ALLNOBLANKROW* version for the Product table and the *Products[Brand]* column. The reason is that there are rows in the Sales table that have no matching rows in the Product table, so an additional row is virtually added to the Product table and you can see the result of that in the (blank) row in Figure 3-12.

Row Labels	Products	All Products	All NoBlank Products	All Brands	All NoBlank Brands	All Sizes	All NoBlank Sizes
Deluxe	360	2,517	2,516	12	11	622	622
Economy	881	2,517	2,516	12	11	622	622
Regular	1,275	2,517	2,516	12	11	622	622
(blank)		2,517	2,516	12	11	622	622
Grand Total	2,516	2,517	2,516	12	11	622	622

FIGURE 3-12 The *All* and *All NoBlank* measures differ if the target table contains an additional blank row for unmatched values.

You should note that the *All Sizes* and *All NoBlank Sizes* measures always return the same value. Such measures query the number of values in the *Products[Size]* column. In this case *ALL* and *ALLNO-BLANKROW* functions return the same value because the *Products[Size]* column already contains a blank value for a product. In the example in Figure 3-13, there are 569 products with a blank Size, plus an additional blank product that includes references to unmatched products in the Sales table, for a total of 570. All these rows are grouped within the same (blank) value for *Products[Size]*.

Row Labels	Sales Amount	Products
⊞ (blank)	$7,772,128.09	570
⊟ 0.7 x 0.7 x 5.3	$2,200.00	1
Contoso USB Cable M250 Black	$2,200.00	1
⊟ 11 x 16 x 2	$6,728.80	2
Contoso Leather Case - case for digital photo camera X20 White	$1,276.80	1
Proseware Wireless Photo All-in-One Printer M390 Grey	$5,452.00	1
⊟ 17 x 11 x 6.1	$526.70	2
Contoso ADSL Modem Splitter/Filter X 2 E200 Black	$526.70	1
Proseware Photo smart All-in-One Printer M380 Black		1

FIGURE 3-13 The pivot table rows have Product Name values for each Size. The first (blank) value for Size includes both products with a blank size and the additional blank product for unmatched products in the Sales table.

You should use *ALLNOBLANKROW* only when you write a DAX formula that iterates values ignoring unmatched values in relationships. However, the use of *ALL* is common, whereas *ALLNOBLANKROW* is seldom used.

Understanding *VALUES* and *DISTINCT*

In the previous section, you have seen that *ALL* used with one column returns a table with all its unique values. DAX provides two other similar functions that return a list of unique values for a column: *VALUES* and *DISTINCT*.

VALUES and *DISTINCT* seem identical to *ALL* if used in an *EVALUATE* statement without any other filter operation. However, when you put these functions in a DAX measure, you can observe a different behavior because the evaluation happens in a different context for every cell of a pivot table. Consider the following measures that count the number of unique values in columns *Brand* and *Size* of the Product table.

```
[Products] := COUNTROWS ( Product )
[Values Brands] := COUNTROWS ( VALUES ( Product[Brand] ) )
[Distinct Brands] := COUNTROWS ( DISTINCT ( Product[Brand] ) )
[Values Sizes] := COUNTROWS ( VALUES ( Product[Size] ) )
[Distinct Sizes] := COUNTROWS ( DISTINCT ( Product[Size] ) )
```

VALUES returns the list of unique values that are visible in the current cell, including the optional blank row for unmatched values. *DISTINCT* does the same, without returning the blank row for unmatched values. However, both functions will include a blank row if a blank value appears as a valid value for the column. The only difference is that the blank row is added to handle missing values in a relationship.

An example might help in clarifying this difference. As you see in Figure 3-14, every product class filters a different number of products. For example, there are 360 products in Deluxe class, which has 11 unique brands and 204 unique sizes. *VALUES* and *DISTINCT* return the same number with one exception: the (blank) product class on pivot table rows. The result includes this virtually added row in order to show the value of Sales Amount for unmatched products.

Row Labels ▾	Products	Values Brands	Distinct Brands	Values Sizes	Distinct Sizes	Sales Amount
Deluxe	360	11	11	204	204	$8,584,795.18
Economy	881	11	11	377	377	$5,003,153.32
Regular	1,275	11	11	454	454	$20,102,183.11
(blank)		1		1		$16.90
Grand Total	2,516	12	11	622	622	$33,690,148.51

FIGURE 3-14 *VALUES* and *DISTINCT* differ only when a blank product is added to the model to include unmatched rows, which is visible in the (blank) row of the report.

Another difference is visible in the Grand Total of Figure 3-14. *VALUES* applied to *Product[Brand]* returns one more value than *DISTINCT* applied to the same column. However, this does not happen to *VALUES* applied to *Products[Size]*, which returns the same value as *DISTINCT* on the corresponding column. The reason is that the *Distinct Sizes* column includes a blank value for at least one product, so the added blank product does not add a new unique value to the *Distinct Sizes* column.

When there are no filters, the behavior of *DISTINCT* corresponds to *ALLNOBLANKROW*, whereas the behavior of *VALUES* corresponds to *ALL*.

VALUES also accepts a table as an argument. In that case, it returns the whole table that is visible in the current cell, optionally including the blank row for unmatched relationships. For example, consider the following measure in a data model where the Sales table has a relationship with Product and contains transactions with a product key that do not match any existing product.

```
[Products] := COUNTROWS ( Product )
[Values Products] := COUNTROWS ( VALUES ( Product ) )
[All NoBlank Products] := COUNTROWS ( ALLNOBLANKROW ( Product ) )
[All Products] := COUNTROWS ( ALL ( Product ) )
```

You can see in Figure 3-15 that also in this case the result of *VALUES* when there are no filters corresponds to the behavior of *ALL*, including the blank row added to show Sales Amount for unmatched products. In this case, you cannot use *DISTINCT* over a table; in case there are duplicated rows, you do not have a single DAX function to remove duplicated rows (you have to use *SUMMARIZE* instead, which you will see later in Chapter 9). However, the *[Products]* measure counts the number of rows in a table, ignoring a possible blank row, with a behavior corresponding to *ALLNOBLANKROW* when there are no filters.

Row Labels ▾	Products	Values Products	All NoBlank Products	All Products	Sales Amount
Deluxe	360	360	2,516	2,517	$8,584,795.18
Economy	881	881	2,516	2,517	$5,003,153.32
Regular	1,275	1,275	2,516	2,517	$20,102,183.11
(blank)		1	2,516	2,517	$16.90
Grand Total	2,516	2,517	2,516	2,517	$33,690,148.51

FIGURE 3-15 *VALUES* and *ALL* consider that added blank row in Product table for unmatched values in Sales.

Using *VALUES* as a scalar value

Even if *VALUES* is a table function, you will often use it to compute scalar values, because of a special feature in DAX you will learn in this section. For example, you can find *VALUES* in expressions such as the following one, which displays the color name in case all the products of a certain selection have the same color:

```
[Color Name] :=
IF (
    COUNTROWS ( VALUES ( Product[Color] ) ) = 1,
    VALUES ( Product[Color] )
)
```

You can see the result in Figure 3-16. When the *Color Name* column contains blank, it means that there are two or more different colors.

Row Labels	▼	Products	Sales Amount	Color Name
⊟ **A. Datum**		132	$2,293,775.20	
15 x 15.7 x 8.7		1	$3,000.00	Black
18.5 x 4.5 x 16.3		1		Black
2.6 x 5.4 x 2.8		1		Gold
3 x 5 x 2.9		1	$27,636.00	Gold
3.4 x 0.9 x 2.2		3	$25,063.00	
3.4 x 1.1 x 2.2		3	$46,811.50	
3.4 x 4.6 x 3.3		2	$59,630.00	

FIGURE 3-16 When *VALUES* returns a single row, you can use it as a scalar value, such as in *Color Name* measure.

The interesting point here is that we are using the result of *VALUES* as a scalar value, even if it returns a table. This is not a special behavior of *VALUES*, but it is a more general behavior of the DAX language:

If a table expression returns a table with one row and one column, a conversion to a scalar value is possible and done automatically if required.

In practice, you might use any table expression as a scalar value, if the result has exactly one row and one column. When the table returns more rows, you get this error at execution time: "A table of multiple values was supplied where a single value was expected." For this reason, you should always protect the conversion to a scalar value with a condition that returns a different result in case the table expression returns more rows (you should already know whether a table expression returns only one row when you write the DAX expression).

The *Color Name* measure of the previous example used *COUNTROWS* to check whether the *Color* column of the Products table has only one value selected. A simpler way to do exactly the same control is using *HASONEVALUE*, which performs the same check, returning *TRUE* if the column has only one value returned by *VALUES*, and *FALSE* otherwise. The following two syntaxes are equivalent:

```
COUNTROWS ( VALUES ( <column> ) ) = 1
HASONEVALUE ( <column> )
```

You should use *HASONEVALUE* instead of *COUNTROWS* for two reasons: It is more readable, and it could be slightly faster. The following is a better implementation of the *Color Name* measure, based on *HASONEVALUE*:

```
[Color Name] :=
IF (
    HASONEVALUE ( Product[Color] ),
    VALUES ( Product[Color] )
)
```

The reason why you will often use *VALUES* as a scalar expression is that it returns a single column, and might return a single row, depending on the execution context. The use of *VALUES* as a scalar expression is common in many DAX patterns, and it appears repeatedly in this book.

Understanding evaluation contexts

At this point in the book, you have learned the basics of the DAX language. You know how to create calculated columns and measures, and you have a good understanding of common functions used in DAX. This is the chapter where you move to the next level in this language: After learning a solid theoretical background of the DAX language, you will be able to become a real DAX champion.

With the knowledge you have gained so far, you can already create many interesting reports, but you will need to learn evaluation contexts in order to create reports that are more complex. Evaluation contexts are the basis of all of the advanced features of DAX.

We want to give a few words of warning to our readers: The concept of evaluation context is an easy one, and you will learn and understand it soon. Nevertheless, you need to thoroughly understand several subtle considerations and details. Otherwise, you will feel lost at a certain point during your DAX learning path. We teach DAX to many users in public and private classes. We know that this is absolutely normal. At a certain point—you have the feeling that formulas work like magic, because they work, but you do not understand why. Do not worry: you will be in good company. Most DAX students reach that point and many others will reach it in the future. It simply means that evaluation contexts are not clear enough to them. The solution, at that point, is an easy one: Come back to this chapter, read it again, and you will probably find something new, which you missed during your first read.

Moreover, evaluation contexts play an important role with the usage of the function *CALCULATE*, which is probably the most powerful and hard-to-learn function in DAX. We will introduce *CALCULATE* in Chapter 5, "Understanding *CALCULATE* and *CALCULATETABLE*," and then use it through the rest of the book. Understanding *CALCULATE* without having a solid background on evaluation context is problematic. On the other hand, understanding the importance of evaluation contexts without having ever tried to use *CALCULATE* is nearly impossible. Thus, this chapter and the subsequent one are the two that, in our experience with the previous books we have written, are always marked up and have the corners of pages folded over.

Introduction to evaluation contexts

Let's begin by understanding what an evaluation context is. Any DAX expression is evaluated inside a context. The context is the "environment" under which the formula is evaluated. For example, consider a very simple formula for a measure such as:

```
[Sales Amount] := SUMX ( Sales, Sales[Quantity] * Sales[UnitPrice] )
```

You already know what this formula computes: the sum of all the values of quantity multiplied by price in the Sales table. You can put this measure in a pivot table and look at the results, as you can see in Figure 4-1.

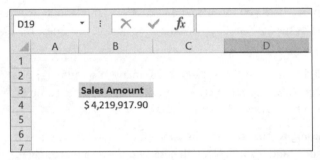

FIGURE 4-1 The measure *Sales Amount*, without a context, shows the grand total of sales.

Well, this number alone does not look interesting at all, does it? But, if you think carefully, the formula computes exactly what it is supposed to compute: the sum of all sales amount, which is a big number with no interesting meaning. This pivot table becomes more interesting as soon as we use some columns to slice the grand total and start investigating it. For example, you can take the product color, put it on the rows, and the pivot table suddenly reveals some interesting business insights, as you can see in Figure 4-2.

The grand total is still there, but now it is the sum of smaller values and each value, together with all the others, has a meaning. However, if you think carefully again, you should note that something weird is happening here: the formula is not computing what we asked.

We supposed that the formula meant "the sum of all sales amount." but inside each cell of the pivot table, the formula is not computing the sum of all sales, it is only computing the sum of sales of products with a specific color. Yet, we never specified that the computation had to work on a subset of the data model. In other words, the formula does not specify that it can work on subsets of data.

Why is the formula computing different values in different cells? The answer is very easy, indeed: because of the evaluation context under which DAX computes the formula. You can think of the evaluation context of a formula as the surrounding area of the cell where DAX evaluates the formula.

Row Labels	Sales Amount
Azure	$12,071.90
Black	$791,735.81
Blue	$294,838.55
Brown	$225,705.83
Gold	$43,292.49
Green	$202,219.08
Grey	$509,990.58
Orange	$55,324.68
Pink	$130,243.02
Purple	$286.00
Red	$126,762.21
Silver	$918,587.35
Silver Grey	$60,366.60
Transparent	$414.54
White	$841,262.48
Yellow	$6,816.78
Grand Total	**$4,219,917.90**

FIGURE 4-2 Sum of *Sales Amount*, sliced by color, looks much more interesting.

Because the product color is on the rows, each row in the pivot table can see, out of the whole database, only the subset of products of that specific color. This is the surrounding area of the formula, that is, a set of filters applied to the database prior to the formula evaluation. When the formula computes the sum of all sales amount, it does not compute it over the entire database, because it does not have the option to look at all the rows. When DAX computes the formula in the row with the value White, only white products are visible and, because of that, it only considers sales pertinent to white products. So the sum of all sales amount, when computed for a row in the pivot table that shows only white products, becomes the sum of all sales amount of white products.

Any DAX formula specifies a calculation, but DAX evaluates this calculation in a context, which defines the final value computed. The formula is always the same, but the value is different because DAX evaluates it against different subsets of data.

The only case where the formula behaves in the way it has been defined is on the grand total. At that level, because no filtering happens, the entire database is visible.

> **Note** In these examples, we are using a pivot table for the sake of simplicity. Clearly, you can define an evaluation context with queries too, and you will learn more about it in future chapters. For now, it is better to keep it simple and think of pivot tables only, so as to have a simplified and visual understanding of the concepts.

Now let's put the year on the columns, to make the pivot table even more interesting. The report is now the one shown in Figure 4-3.

Sales Amount	Column Labels			
Row Labels	CY 2007	CY 2008	CY 2009	Grand Total
Azure	$4,863.10	$4,480.80	$2,728.00	$12,071.90
Black	$282,020.06	$245,539.76	$264,175.99	$791,735.81
Blue	$142,503.18	$76,597.95	$75,737.42	$294,838.55
Brown	$68,737.05	$56,648.58	$100,320.20	$225,705.83
Gold	$9,322.00	$17,475.00	$16,495.49	$43,292.49
Green	$85,164.89	$56,495.65	$60,558.54	$202,219.08
Grey	$200,185.94	$210,735.39	$99,069.25	$509,990.58
Orange	$14,779.34	$20,215.54	$20,329.80	$55,324.68
Pink	$77,438.69	$20,174.08	$32,630.25	$130,243.02
Purple	$224.00		$62.00	$286.00
Red	$57,453.06	$26,079.59	$43,229.56	$126,762.21
Silver	$430,786.04	$216,861.80	$270,939.51	$918,587.35
Silver Grey	$34,776.00	$12,122.60	$13,468.00	$60,366.60
Transparent	$126.42	$79.38	$208.74	$414.54
White	$207,955.56	$274,919.98	$358,386.94	$841,262.48
Yellow	$1,387.28	$4,567.24	$862.26	$6,816.78
Grand Total	$1,617,722.61	$1,242,993.34	$1,359,201.95	$4,219,917.90

FIGURE 4-3 Sum of *SalesAmount* is now sliced by color and year.

The rules of the game should be clear at this point: Each cell now has a different value even if the formula is always the same, because both row and column selections of the pivot table define the context. In fact, sales for white products in year 2008 are different from sales for white products in 2007. Moreover, because you can put more than one field in both rows and columns, it is better to say that the set of fields on the rows and the set of fields on the columns define the context. Figure 4-4 makes this more evident.

Sales Amount	Column Labels			
Row Labels	CY 2007	CY 2008	CY 2009	Grand Total
⊟ Azure	$4,863.10	$4,480.80	$2,728.00	$12,071.90
A. Datum	$4,863.10	$4,480.80	$2,728.00	$12,071.90
⊟ Black	$282,020.06	$245,539.76	$264,175.99	$791,735.81
A. Datum	$13,691.00	$681.90	$10,455.00	$24,827.90
Adventure Works	$45,584.87	$29,849.86	$29,736.17	$105,170.90
Contoso	$37,330.92	$26,921.86	$55,237.03	$119,489.81
Fabrikam	$22,642.87	$49,585.00	$44,397.04	$116,624.91
Litware	$12,742.44	$9,642.05	$25,524.23	$47,908.72
Northwind Traders			$99.99	$99.99
Proseware	$46,793.84	$22,221.50	$13,912.41	$82,927.75
Southridge Video	$64,377.31	$17,329.31	$16,475.62	$98,182.24
Tailspin Toys	$831.31	$1,752.50	$4,168.63	$6,752.44
The Phone Company	$13,050.00	$21,493.00	$21,043.00	$55,586.00
Wide World Importers	$24,975.50	$66,062.78	$43,126.87	$134,165.15

FIGURE 4-4 The context is defined by the set of fields on rows and on columns.

Each cell has a different value because there are two fields on the rows, color and brand name. The complete set of fields on rows and columns defines the context. For example, the context of the cell highlighted in Figure 4-4 corresponds to color Black, brand Contoso, and Calendar Year 2007.

> **Note** It is not important whether a field is on the rows or on the columns (or on the slicer and/or page filter, or in any other kind of filter you can create with a query). All of these filters contribute to define a single context, which DAX uses to evaluate the formula. Putting a field on rows or columns has just some aesthetic consequences, but nothing changes in the way DAX computes values.

Let's see the full picture now. In Figure 4-5, we added the product category on a slicer, and the month name on a filter, where we selected December.

Month	December

Category	Sales Amount	Column Labels			
	Row Labels	CY 2007	CY 2008	CY 2009	Grand Total
Audio	⊟ Black	$2,079.58	$4,353.40	$5,327.52	$11,760.50
Cameras and camc...	Adventure Works	$479.70	$2,953.50		$3,433.20
Cell phones	Contoso	$899.95			$899.95
Computers	Fabrikam			$5,327.52	$5,327.52
Games and Toys	Litware	$699.93	$1,399.90		$2,099.83
Home Appliances	⊟ Blue	$18,570.30	$3,198.00	$7,395.00	$29,163.30
Music, Movies and ...	Litware		$3,198.00	$7,395.00	$10,593.00
TV and Video	Northwind Traders	$18,570.30			$18,570.30
	⊟ Brown	$4,199.85		$10,788.00	$14,987.85
	Litware	$4,199.85		$10,788.00	$14,987.85
	⊟ Green			$16,370.10	$16,370.10
	Northwind Traders			$16,370.10	$16,370.10

FIGURE 4-5 In a typical report, the context is defined in many ways, including slicers and filters.

It is clear at this point that the values computed in each cell have a context defined by rows, columns, slicers, and filters. All these filters contribute in the definition of a context that DAX applies to the data model prior to the formula evaluation. Moreover, it is important to learn that not all the cells have the same set of filters, not only in terms of values, but also in terms of fields. For example, the grand total on the columns contains only the filter for category, month, color, and brand, but it does not contain the filter for year. The fields for color and brand are on the rows and they do not filter the grand total. The same applies to the subtotal by color within the pivot table: for those cells there is no filter on the manufacturer, the only valid filter coming from the rows is the color.

We call this context the *Filter Context* and, as its name suggests, it is a context that filters tables. Any formula you ever author will have a different value depending on the filter context that DAX uses to perform its evaluation. This behavior, although very intuitive, needs to be well understood.

Now that you have learned what a filter context is, you know that the following DAX expression should be read as "the sum of all sales amount visible in the current filter context":

```
[Sales Amount] := SUMX ( Sales, Sales[Quantity] * Sales[UnitPrice] )
```

You will learn later how to read, modify, and clear the filter context. As of now, it is enough having a solid understanding of the fact that the filter context is always present for any cell of the pivot table or any value in your report/query. You always need to take into account the filter context in order to understand how DAX evaluates a formula.

Understanding the row context

The filter context is one of the two contexts that exist in DAX. Its companion is the row context and, in this section, you will learn what it is and how it works.

This time, we use a different formula for our considerations:

```
Sales[GrossMargin] = Sales[SalesAmount] - Sales[TotalCost]
```

You are likely to write such an expression in a calculated column, in order to compute the gross margin. As soon as you define this formula in a calculated column, you will get the resulting table, as shown in Figure 4-6.

Unit Price	Unit Cost	SalesAmount	TotalCost	GrossMargin
$32.00	$16.31	32	16.31	15.69
$32.00	$16.31	32	16.31	15.69
$147.00	$67.60	147	67.6	79.4
$308.00	$141.64	308	141.64	166.36
$190.00	$87.37	190	87.37	102.63
$43.00	$21.92	43	21.92	21.08
$43.00	$21.92	43	21.92	21.08
$43.00	$21.92	43	21.92	21.08

FIGURE 4-6 The *GrossMargin* is computed for all the rows of the table.

DAX computed the formula for all the rows of the table and, for each row, it computed a different value, as expected. In order to understand the row context, we need to be somewhat pedantic in our reading of the formula: we asked to subtract two columns, but where did we tell DAX from which row of the table to get the values of the columns? You might say that the row to use is implicit. Because it is a calculated column, DAX computes it row by row and, for each row, it evaluates a different result. This is correct, but, from the point of view of the DAX expression, the information about which row to use is still missing.

In fact, the row used to perform a calculation is not stored inside the formula. It is defined by another kind of context: the *row context*. When you defined the calculated column, DAX started an iteration from the first row of the table; it created a row context containing that row and evaluated the expression. Then it moved on to the second row and evaluated the expression again. This happens for all the rows in the table and, if you have one million rows, you can think that DAX created one million row contexts to evaluate the formula one million times. Clearly, in order to optimize calculations, this is not exactly what happens; otherwise, DAX would be a very slow language. Anyway, from the logical point of view, this is exactly how it works.

Let us try to be more precise. A row context is a context that always contains a single row and DAX automatically defines it during the creation of calculated columns. You can create a row context using other techniques, which are discussed later in this chapter, but the easiest way to explain row context is to look at calculated columns, where the engine always creates it automatically.

There are always two contexts

So far, you have learned what the row context and the filter context are. They are the only kind of contexts in DAX. Thus, they are the only way to modify the result of a formula. Any formula will be evaluated under these two distinct contexts: the row context and the filter context.

We call both contexts "evaluation contexts," because they are contexts that change the way a formula is evaluated, providing different results for the same formula.

This is one point that is very important and very hard to focus on at the beginning: *there are always two contexts and the result of a formula depends on both*. At this point of your DAX learning path, you probably think that this is obvious and very natural. You are probably right. However, later in the book, you will find formulas that will be a challenge to understand if you do not remember about the coexistence of the two contexts, each of which can change the result of the formula.

Testing your evaluation context understanding

Before we move on with more complex discussions about evaluation contexts, we would like to test your understanding of contexts with a couple of examples. Please do not look at the explanation immediately; stop after the question and try to answer it. Then read the explanation to make sense out of it.

Using *SUM* in a calculated column

The first test is a very simple one. What is happening if you define a calculated column, in Sales, with this code?

```
Sales[SumOfSalesAmount] = SUM ( Sales[SalesAmount] )
```

Because it is a calculated column, it will be computed row by row and, for each row, you will obtain a result. What number do you expect to see? Choose one from among these options:

- The value of *SalesAmount* for that row, that is, a different value for each row.

- The total of *SalesAmount* for all the rows, that is, the same value for all the rows.

- An error; you cannot use *SUM* inside a calculated column.

Stop reading, please, while we wait for your educated guess before moving on.

Now, let's elaborate on what is happening when DAX evaluates the formula. You already learned what the formula meaning is: "the sum of all sales amount as seen in the current filter context." As this is in a calculated column, DAX evaluates the formula row by row. Thus, it creates a row context for the first row, and then invokes the formula evaluation and proceeds iterating the entire table. The formula computes the sum of all sales amount values in the current filter context, so the real question is "What is the current filter context?" Answer: It is the full database, because DAX evaluates the formula outside of any pivot table or any other kind of filtering. In fact, DAX computes it as part of the definition of a calculated column, when no filter is active.

Even if there is a row context, *SUM* ignores it. Instead, it uses the filter context and the filter context right now is the full database. Thus, the second option is correct: You will get the grand total of sales amount, the same value for all the rows of Sales, as you can see in Figure 4-7.

Quantity	Unit Price	Unit Cost	SalesAmount	SumOfSalesAmount
1	$9.99	$5.09	9.99	4,219,917.90
1	$9.99	$5.09	9.99	4,219,917.90
1	$9.99	$5.09	9.99	4,219,917.90
1	$9.99	$5.09	9.99	4,219,917.90
1	$9.99	$5.09	9.99	4,219,917.90
1	$9.99	$5.09	9.99	4,219,917.90
1	$9.99	$5.09	9.99	4,219,917.90
1	$9.99	$5.09	9.99	4,219,917.90
1	$9.99	$5.09	9.99	4,219,917.90
1	$9.99	$5.09	9.99	4,219,917.90
1	$9.99	$5.09	9.99	4,219,917.90
1	$9.99	$5.09	9.99	4,219,917.90

FIGURE 4-7 *SUM (Sales[SalesAmount])*, in a calculated column, is computed against the full database.

This example shows that the two contexts exist together. They both work on the result of a formula, but in different ways. Aggregate functions like *SUM*, *MIN*, and *MAX* used in calculated columns use the filter context only and ignore the row context, which DAX uses only to determine column values. If you have chosen the first answer, as many students typically do, it is perfectly normal. The point is that you are not yet thinking that the two contexts are working together to change the formula result in different ways. The first answer is the most common, when using intuitive logic, but it is the wrong one, and now you know why.

Using columns in a measure

The second test we want to do with you is slightly different. Imagine you want to define the formula for gross margin in a measure instead of in a calculated column. You have a column with the sales amount, another column for the product cost, and you might write the following expression:

```
[GrossMargin] := Sales[SalesAmount] - Sales[ProductCost]
```

What result should you expect if you try to author such a measure?

1. The expression works correctly, we will need to test the result in a report.

2. An error, you cannot even author this formula.

3. You can define the formula, but it will give an error when used in a pivot table or in a query.

As before, stop reading, think about the answer, and then read the following explanation.

In the formula, we used *Sales[SalesAmount]*, which is a column name, that is, the value of *SalesAmount* in the Sales table. Is this definition lacking something? You should recall, from previous arguments, that the information missing here is the row from where to get the current value of *SalesAmount*. When you write this code inside a calculated column, DAX knows the row to use when it computes the expression, thanks to the row context. However, what happens for a measure? There is no iteration, there is no current row, that is, there is no row context.

Thus, the second answer is correct. You cannot even write the formula; it is syntactically wrong and you will receive an error when you try to enter it.

Remember that a column does not have a value by itself. Instead, it has a different value for each row of a table. Thus, if you want a single value, you need to specify the row to use. The only way to specify the row to use is the row context. Because inside this measure there is no row context, the formula is incorrect and DAX will refuse it.

The correct way to specify this calculation in a measure is to use aggregate functions, as in:

```
[GrossMargin] := SUM ( Sales[SalesAmount] ) - SUM ( Sales[ProductCost] )
```

Using this formula, you are now asking for an aggregation through *SUM*. Therefore, this latter formula does not depend on a row context; it only requires a filter context and it provides the correct result.

Creating a row context with iterators

You learned that DAX automatically creates a row context when you define a calculated column. In that case, the engine evaluates the DAX expression on a row-by-row basis. Now, it is time to learn how to create a row context inside a DAX expression by using iterators.

You might recall from Chapter 2, "Introducing DAX," that all the X-ending functions are iterators, that is, they iterate over a table and evaluate an expression for each row, finally aggregating the results using different algorithms. For example, look at the following DAX expression:

```
[IncreasedSales] := SUMX ( Sales, Sales[SalesAmount] * 1.1 )
```

SUMX is an iterator, it iterates the Sales table and, for each row of the table, it evaluates the sales amount adding 10 percent to its value, finally returning the sum of all these values. In order to evaluate the expression for each row, *SUMX* creates a row context on the Sales table and uses it during the iteration. DAX evaluates the inner expression (the second parameter of *SUMX*) in a row context containing the currently iterated row.

It is important to note that different parameters of *SUMX* use different contexts during the full evaluation flow. Let's look closer at the same expression:

```
= SUMX (
    Sales,                      ← External contexts
    Sales[SalesAmount] * 1.1    ← External contexts + new Row Context
)
```

The first parameter, Sales, is evaluated using the context coming from the caller (for example, it might be a pivot table cell, another measure, or part of a query), whereas the second parameter (the expression) is evaluated using both the external context plus the newly created row context.

All iterators behave in the same way:

1. Create a new row context for each row of the table received as the first parameter.

2. Evaluate the second parameter inside the newly created row context (plus any other context which existed before the iteration started), for each row of the table.

3. Aggregate the values computed during step 2.

It is important to remember that the original contexts are still valid inside the expression: Iterators only add a new row context; they do not modify existing ones in any way. This rule is usually valid, but there is an important exception: If the previous contexts already contained a row context for the same table, then the newly created row context hides the previously existing row context. We are going to discuss this in more detail in the next section.

Using the *EARLIER* function

The scenario of having many nested row contexts on the same table might seem very rare, but, in reality, it happens quite often. Let's see the concept with an example. Imagine you want to count, for each product, the number of other products with a higher price. This will produce a sort of ranking of the product based on price.

To solve this exercise, we use the *FILTER* function, which you learned in the previous chapter. As you might recall, *FILTER* is an iterator that loops through all the rows of a table and returns a new table containing only the ones that satisfy the condition defined by the second parameter. For example, if you want to retrieve the table of products with a price higher than US$100, you can use:

```
= FILTER ( Product, Product[UnitPrice] > 100 )
```

> **Note** The careful reader will have noted that *FILTER* needs to be an iterator because the expression Product[UnitPrice]>100 can be evaluated if and only if a valid row context exists for Product; otherwise the effective value of Unit Price would be indeterminate. *FILTER* is an iterator function that creates a row context for each row of the table in the first argument, which makes it possible to evaluate the condition in the second argument.

Now, let's go back to our original example: creating a calculated column that counts the number of products that have a higher price than the current one. If you would name the price of the current product **PriceOfCurrentProduct**, then it is easy to see that this pseudo-DAX formula would do what is needed:

```
Product[UnitPriceRank] =
COUNTROWS (
    FILTER (
        Product,
        Product[UnitPrice] > PriceOfCurrentProduct
    )
)
```

FILTER returns only the products with a price higher than the current one and *COUNTROWS* counts those products. The only remaining issue is a way to express the price of the current product, replacing PriceOfCurrentProduct with a valid DAX syntax. With "current," we mean the value of the column in the current row when DAX computes the column. It is harder than you might expect.

You define this new calculated column inside the Product table. Thus, DAX evaluates the expression inside a row context. However, the expression uses a *FILTER* that creates a new row context on the same table. In fact, *Product[UnitPrice]* used in the fifth row of the previous expression is the value of the unit price for the current row iterated by *FILTER - our inner iteration*. Therefore, this new row context hides the original row context introduced by the calculated column. Do you see the issue? You want to access the current value of the unit price but not use the last introduced row context. Instead, you want to use the previous row context, that is, the one of the calculated column.

DAX provides a function that makes it possible: *EARLIER*. *EARLIER* retrieves the value of a column by using the previous row context instead of the last one. So you can express the value of **PriceOfCurrentProduct** using *EARLIER(Product[UnitPrice])*.

EARLIER is one of the strangest functions in DAX. Many users feel intimidated by *EARLIER*, because they do not think in terms of row contexts and they do not take into account the fact that you can nest row contexts by creating multiple iterations over the same table. In reality, *EARLIER* is a very simple function that will be useful many times. The following code finally solves the scenario:

```
Product[UnitPriceRank] =
COUNTROWS (
    FILTER (
        Product,
        Product[UnitPrice] > EARLIER ( Product[UnitPrice] )
    )
) + 1
```

In Figure 4-8 you can see the calculated column defined in the Product table, which has been sorted using *Unit Price* in a descending order.

Product Code	Product Name	Unit Price	UnitPriceRank
0802079	Litware Refrigerator L1200 Orange	$3,199.99	1
0802073	Litware Refrigerator 24.7CuFt X980 Grey	$3,199.99	1
0802067	Litware Refrigerator 24.7CuFt X980 Blue	$3,199.99	1
0802061	Litware Refrigerator 24.7CuFt X980 Green	$3,199.99	1
0802055	Litware Refrigerator 24.7CuFt X980 Silver	$3,199.99	1
0802049	Litware Refrigerator 24.7CuFt X980 Brown	$3,199.99	1
0802043	Litware Refrigerator 24.7CuFt X980 White	$3,199.99	1
0802037	Fabrikam Refrigerator 24.7CuFt X9800 Orange	$3,199.99	1
0802031	Fabrikam Refrigerator 24.7CuFt X9800 Grey	$3,199.99	1
0802025	Fabrikam Refrigerator 24.7CuFt X9800 Blue	$3,199.99	1
0802019	Fabrikam Refrigerator 24.7CuFt X9800 Green	$3,199.99	1
0802013	Fabrikam Refrigerator 24.7CuFt X9800 Silver	$3,199.99	1
0802007	Fabrikam Refrigerator 24.7CuFt X9800 Brown	$3,199.99	1
0802001	Fabrikam Refrigerator 24.7CuFt X9800 White	$3,199.99	1
0201033	Adventure Works 52" LCD HDTV X590 Brown	$2,899.99	15
0201032	Adventure Works 52" LCD HDTV X590 White	$2,899.99	15
0201031	Adventure Works 52" LCD HDTV X590 Black	$2,899.99	15
0201030	Adventure Works 52" LCD HDTV X590 Silver	$2,899.99	15
0801036	NT Washer & Dryer 27in L2700 Green	$2,652.90	19
0801031	NT Washer & Dryer 27in L2700 Blue	$2,652.90	19

FIGURE 4-8 *UnitPriceRank* is a useful example of how *EARLIER* is useful to navigate in nested row contexts.

Because there are fourteen products with the same unit price, their rank is always one; the fifteenth product has a rank of 15, shared with other products with the same price. We suggest you study and understand this small example closely, because it is a very good test to check your ability to use and understand row contexts, how to create them using iterators (*FILTER*, in this case), and how to access values outside of them through the usage of *EARLIER*.

Note *EARLIER* accepts a second parameter, which is the number of steps to skip, so that you can skip two or more row contexts. Moreover, there is also a function named *EARLIEST* that lets you access directly the outermost row context defined for a table. To be honest, neither the second parameter of *EARLIER* nor *EARLIEST* is used often: while having two nested row contexts is a common scenario, having three or more of them is something that happens rarely.

Before leaving this example, it is worth noting that, if you want to transform this value into a better ranking (that is, a value that starts with 1 and grows of one, creating a sequence 1, 2, 3…) then counting the prices instead of counting the products is sufficient. Here, the *VALUES* function, which you learned in the previous chapter, comes to help:

```
Product[UnitPriceRankDense] =
COUNTROWS (
    FILTER (
        VALUES ( Product[UnitPrice] ),
        Product[UnitPrice] > EARLIER ( Product[UnitPrice] )
    )
) + 1
```

In Figure 4-9 you can see the new calculated column.

Product Name	Unit Price	UnitPriceRank	UnitPriceRankDense
Litware Refrigerator 24.7CuFt X980 Grey	$3,199.99	1	1
Litware Refrigerator 24.7CuFt X980 Blue	$3,199.99	1	1
Litware Refrigerator 24.7CuFt X980 Green	$3,199.99	1	1
Litware Refrigerator 24.7CuFt X980 Silver	$3,199.99	1	1
Litware Refrigerator 24.7CuFt X980 Brown	$3,199.99	1	1
Litware Refrigerator 24.7CuFt X980 White	$3,199.99	1	1
Fabrikam Refrigerator 24.7CuFt X9800 Orange	$3,199.99	1	1
Fabrikam Refrigerator 24.7CuFt X9800 Grey	$3,199.99	1	1
Fabrikam Refrigerator 24.7CuFt X9800 Blue	$3,199.99	1	1
Fabrikam Refrigerator 24.7CuFt X9800 Green	$3,199.99	1	1
Fabrikam Refrigerator 24.7CuFt X9800 Silver	$3,199.99	1	1
Fabrikam Refrigerator 24.7CuFt X9800 Brown	$3,199.99	1	1
Fabrikam Refrigerator 24.7CuFt X9800 White	$3,199.99	1	1
Adventure Works 52" LCD HDTV X590 Brown	$2,899.99	15	2
Adventure Works 52" LCD HDTV X590 White	$2,899.99	15	2
Adventure Works 52" LCD HDTV X590 Black	$2,899.99	15	2
Adventure Works 52" LCD HDTV X590 Silver	$2,899.99	15	2
NT Washer & Dryer 27in L2700 Green	$2,652.90	19	3
NT Washer & Dryer 27in L2700 Blue	$2,652.90	19	3

FIGURE 4-9 *UnitPriceRankDense* shows a better ranking, because it counts the prices, not the products.

We strongly suggest you learn and understand *EARLIER* thoroughly, because you will use it very often. Nevertheless, it is important to note that variables can be used—in many scenarios—to avoid the use of *EARLIER*. Moreover, a careful use of variables makes the code much easier to read. For example, you can compute the previous calculated column using this expression:

```
Product[UnitPriceRankDense] =
VAR
    CurrentPrice = Product[UnitPrice]
RETURN
    COUNTROWS (
        FILTER (
            VALUES ( Product[UnitPrice] ),
            Product[UnitPrice] > CurrentPrice
        )
    ) + 1
```

In this final example, using a variable, you store the current unit price in the *CurrentPrice* variable, which you use later to perform the comparison. Giving a name to the variable, you make the code easier to read, without having to traverse the stack of row contexts every time you read the expression to make sense of the evaluation flow.

Understanding *FILTER*, *ALL*, and context interactions

In the preceding example, we have used *FILTER* as a convenient way of filtering a table. *FILTER* is a very common function to use, whenever you want to apply a filter that further restricts the existing context.

Imagine that you want to create a measure that counts the number of red products. With the knowledge you gained so far, the formula is an easy one:

```
[NumOfRedProducts] :=
COUNTROWS (
    FILTER (
        Product,
        Product[Color] = "Red"
    )
)
```

This formula works fine and you can use it inside a pivot table; for example, putting the brand on the rows to produce the report shown in Figure 4-10.

Row Labels	NumOfRedProducts
Adventure Works	6
Contoso, Ltd	36
Fabrikam, Inc.	12
Litware, Inc.	12
Northwind Traders	3
Proseware, Inc.	7
Southridge Video	13
Tailspin Toys	6
Wide World Importers	4
Grand Total	**99**

FIGURE 4-10 You can easily count the number of red products using the *FILTER* function.

Before moving on with this example, it is useful to stop for a moment and think carefully how DAX computed these values. The brand is a column of the Product table. The engine evaluates *NumOfRedProducts* inside each cell, in a context defined by the brand on the rows. Thus, each cell shows the number of red products that also have the brand indicated by the corresponding row. This happens because, when you ask to iterate over the Product table, you are really asking to iterate the Product table as it is visible in the current filter context, which contains only products with that specific brand. It might seem trivial, but it is better to remember it multiple times than take a chance of forgetting it.

This is more evident if you put a slicer on the worksheet containing the color. In Figure 4-11 we have created two identical pivot tables with the slicer on color. You can see that the left one has the color Red selected, and the numbers are the same as in Figure 4-10, whereas in the right one the pivot table is empty because the slicer has the color Green selected.

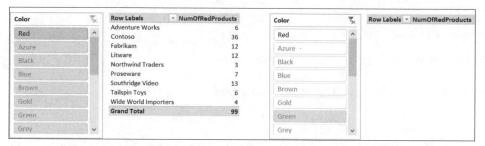

FIGURE 4-11 DAX evaluates *NumOfRedProducts* taking into account the outer context defined by the slicer.

In the right pivot table, the Product table passed into *FILTER* contains only Green products and, because there are no products that can be red and green at the same time, it always evaluates to *BLANK* (that is, *FILTER* does not return any row that *COUNTROWS* can work on).

The important part of this example is the fact that, in the same formula, there are both a filter context coming from the outside (the pivot table cell, which is affected by the slicer selection) and a row context introduced in the formula. Both contexts work at the same time and modify the formula result. DAX uses the filter context to evaluate the Product table, and the row context to filter rows during the iteration.

At this point, you might want to define another formula that returns the number of red products regardless of the selection done on the slicer. Thus, you want to ignore the selection made on the slicer and always return the number of the red products.

You can easily do this by using the *ALL* function. *ALL* returns the content of a table ignoring the filter context, that is, it always returns all the rows of a table. You can define a new measure, named *NumOfAllRedProducts*, by using this expression:

```
[NumOfAllRedProducts] :=
COUNTROWS (
    FILTER (
        ALL ( Product ),
        Product[Color] = "Red"
    )
)
```

This time, instead of referring to Product only, we use *ALL* (Product), meaning that we want to ignore the existing filter context and always iterate over all products. The result is definitely not what we would expect, as you can see in Figure 4-12.

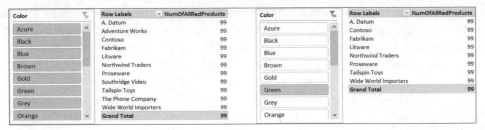

FIGURE 4-12 The *NumOfAllRedProducts* returns strange results.

There are a couple of interesting things to note in here:

- The result is always 99, regardless of the brand selected on the rows.

- The brands in the left pivot table are different from the ones in the right one.

Let us investigate both topics. First, 99 is the total number of red products in the database. Having used *ALL*, we have removed all the filters from the Product table, that is, we have removed both the filter on color and the filter on brand. This is an unwanted effect but, unfortunately, we do not have any other option with the limited knowledge we have of DAX as of now. *ALL* is very powerful, but it is an all-or-nothing function: if used, it removes all of the filters; it has no options to remove only part of them. To be more specific, we wanted to remove only the filter on color, leaving all other filters untouched. In the next chapter, you will learn how to solve this issue with the introduction of *CALCULATE*.

The second point is easier to understand: Because we have selected Green, we are seeing the manufacturers of green products, not the manufacturers of all the products. Thus, the rightmost pivot table shows green product manufacturers with the total of red products in the database. This happens because the list of manufacturers, used to populate the axis of the pivot table, is computed in the original filter context, which contains a filter on color equal to green. Once the axes have been computed, then the values are computed, always returning 99 as a result.

> **Note** This behavior of DAX is called "AutoExists logic." It looks very natural, because it hides nonexisting values, despite some internal complexity. In Chapter 10, "Advanced evaluation context," we will dedicate a section to describe the AutoExists behavior in full detail.

We do not want to solve this scenario right now. The solution will come later when you learn *CALCULATE*, which has specific features to solve scenarios like this one. As of now, we have used this example to show that you might find strange results coming from relatively simple formulas because of context interactions and the coexistence, in the same expression, of filter and row contexts.

Working with many tables

We just started learning contexts, and this led us to some interesting (and surprising) results up to now. You might have noticed that we deliberately used only one table: Product. With only one table, you need to face only interactions between row context and filter context in the same expression.

Very few data models contain just one single table. It is most likely that in your data model you will have many tables linked by relationships. Thus, an interesting question is *"How do the two contexts behave regarding relationships?"* Moreover, because relationships have a direction, we need to understand what happens on the one and on the many side of a relationship. Finally, to make things a bit harder, please recall that relationships can be unidirectional or bidirectional, depending on how you defined the cross-filter direction on relationship itself.

If you create a row context on a table on the many side of the relationship, do you expect it to let you use columns of the one side? Moreover, if you create a row context on the one side of the relationship, do you expect to be able to access columns from the table on the many side? In addition, what about the filter context? Do you expect to put a filter on the many table and see it propagated to the table on the one side? Any answer could be the correct one, but we are interested in learning how DAX behaves in these situations, that is, understand how the DAX language defines propagation of contexts through relationships. As you are going to learn, there are some subtle interactions between contexts and relationships and learning them requires some patience.

In order to examine the scenario, we use a data model containing six tables, which you can see in Figure 4-13.

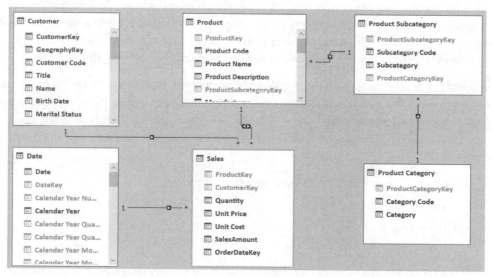

FIGURE 4-13 Here you can see the data model used to learn interaction between contexts and relationships.

There are a couple of things to note about this model:

- There is a chain of one-to-many relationships starting from *Sales* and reaching *Product Category*, through *Product* and *Product Subcategory*.

- The only bidirectional relationship is the one between *Sales* and *Product*. All remaining relationships are set to be one-way cross-filter direction.

Now that we have defined the model, let's start looking at how the contexts behave by looking at some DAX formulas.

Row contexts and relationships

The interaction of row contexts and relationships is very easy to understand, because there is nothing to understand: they do not interact in any way, at least not automatically.

Imagine you want to create a calculated column in the Sales table containing the difference between the unit price stored in the fact table and the product list price stored in the Product table. You could try this formula:

```
Sales[UnitPriceVariance] = Sales[UnitPrice] - Product[UnitPrice]
```

This expression uses two columns from two different tables and DAX evaluates it in a row context that iterates over Sales only, because you defined the calculated column within that table (Sales). Product is on the one side of a relationship with Sales (which is on the many side), so you might expect to be able to gain access to the unit price of the related row (the product sold). Unfortunately, this does not happen. The row context in Sales does not propagate automatically to Product and DAX returns an error if you try to create a calculated column by using the previous formula.

If you want to access columns on the one side of a relationship from the table on the many side of the relationship, as is the case in this example, you must use the *RELATED* function. *RELATED* accepts a column name as the parameter and retrieves the value of the column in a corresponding row that is found by following one or more relationships in the many-to-one direction, starting from the current row context.

You can correct the previous formula with the following code:

```
Sales[UnitPriceVariance] = Sales[UnitPrice] - RELATED ( Product[UnitPrice] )
```

RELATED works when you have a row context on the table on the many side of a relationship. If the row context is active on the one side of a relationship, then you cannot use it because many rows would potentially be detected by following the relationship. In this case, you need to use *RELATEDTABLE*, which is the companion of *RELATED*. You can use *RELATEDTABLE* on the one side of the relationship and it returns all the rows (of the table on the many side) that are related with the current one. For example, if you want to compute the number of sales of each product, you can use the following formula, defined as a calculated column on Product:

```
Product[NumberOfSales] = COUNTROWS ( RELATEDTABLE ( Sales ) )
```

This expression counts the number of rows in the Sales table that correspond to the current product. You can see the result in Figure 4-14.

Product Code	Product Name	NumberOfSales
0101001	Contoso 512MB MP3 Player E51 Silver	12
0101002	Contoso 512MB MP3 Player E51 Blue	9
0101003	Contoso 1G MP3 Player E100 White	4
0101004	Contoso 2G MP3 Player E200 Silver	
0101005	Contoso 2G MP3 Player E200 Red	8
0101006	Contoso 2G MP3 Player E200 Black	
0101007	Contoso 2G MP3 Player E200 Blue	10
0101008	Contoso 4G MP3 Player E400 Silver	74

FIGURE 4-14 *RELATEDTABLE* is very useful when you have a row context on the one side of the relationship.

It is worth noting that both, *RELATED* and *RELATEDTABLE,* can traverse a long chain of relationships to gather their result; they are not limited to a single hop. For example, you can create a column with the same code as before but, this time, in the Product Category table:

```
'Product Category'[NumberOfSales] = COUNTROWS ( RELATEDTABLE ( Sales ) )
```

The result is the number of sales for the category, which traverses the chain of relationships from Product Category to Product Subcategory, then to Product to finally reach the Sales table.

Note The only exception to the general rule of *RELATED* and *RELATEDTABLE* is for one-to-one relationships. If two tables share a 1:1 relationship, then you can use both *RELATED* and *RELATEDTABLE* in both tables and you will get as a result either a column value or a table with a single row, depending on the function you have used.

The only limitation—with regards to chains of relationships—is that all the relationships need to be of the same type (that is, one-to-many or many-to-one), and all of them going in the same direction. If you have two tables related through one-to-many and then many-to-one, with an intermediate bridge table in the middle, then neither *RELATED* nor *RELATEDTABLE* will work. A 1:1 relationship behaves at the same time as a one-to-many and as a many-to-one. Thus, you can have a 1:1 relationship in a chain of one-to-many without interrupting the chain.

Let's make this concept clearer with an example. You might think that Customer is related with Product because there is a one-to-many relationship between Customer and Sales, and then a many-to-one relationship between Sales and Product. Thus, a chain of relationships links the two tables. Nevertheless, the two relationships are not in the same direction.

We call this scenario a many-to-many relationship. In other words, a customer is related to many products (the ones bought) and a product is related to many customers (the ones who bought the product). You will learn the details of how to make many-to-many relationships work later; let's focus on row context, for the moment. If you try to apply *RELATEDTABLE* through a many-to-many relationship, the result could be not what you might expect. For example, consider a calculated column in Product with this formula:

```
Product[NumOfBuyingCustomers] = COUNTROWS ( RELATEDTABLE ( Customer ) )
```

You might expect to see, for each row, the number of customers who bought that product. Unexpectedly, the result will always be 18869, that is, the total number of customers in the database, as you can see in Figure 4-15.

Product Code	Product Name	NumberOfCustomers
0101001	Contoso 512MB MP3 Player E51 Silver	18869
0101002	Contoso 512MB MP3 Player E51 Blue	18869
0101003	Contoso 1G MP3 Player E100 White	18869
0101004	Contoso 2G MP3 Player E200 Silver	18869
0101005	Contoso 2G MP3 Player E200 Red	18869
0101006	Contoso 2G MP3 Player E200 Black	18869
0101007	Contoso 2G MP3 Player E200 Blue	18869
0101008	Contoso 4G MP3 Player E400 Silver	18869

FIGURE 4-15 *RELATEDTABLE* does not work if you try to traverse a many-to-many relationship.

RELATEDTABLE cannot follow the chain of relationships because they are not in the same direction: one is one-to-many, the other one is many-to-one. Thus, the filter from Product cannot reach Customers. It is worth noting that if you try the formula in the opposite direction, that is, you count, for each of the customers, the number of bought products, the result will be correct: a different number for each row representing the number of products bought by the customer. The reason for this behavior is not the propagation of a filter context but, rather, the context transition created by a hidden *CALCULATE* inside *RELATEDTABLE*. We added this final note for the sake of completeness. It is not yet time to elaborate on this: You will have a better understanding of this after reading Chapter 5, "Understanding *CALCULATE* and *CALCULATETABLE*."

Filter context and relationships

You have learned that row context does not interact with relationships and that, if you want to traverse relationships, you have two different functions to use, depending on which side of the relationship you are on while accessing the target table.

Filter contexts behave in a different way: They interact with relationships in an automatic way and they have different behaviors depending on how you set the filtering of the relationship. The general rule is that the filter context propagates through a relationship if the filtering direction set on the relationship itself makes propagation feasible.

This behavior is very easy to understand by using a simple pivot table with a few measures. In Figure 4-16 you can see a pivot table browsing the data model we have used so far, with three very simple measures defined as follows:

```
[NumOfSales]     := COUNTROWS ( Sales )
[NumOfProducts]  := COUNTROWS ( Product )
[NumOfCustomers] := COUNTROWS ( Customer )
```

Row Labels ▾	NumOfSales	NumOfProducts	NumOfCustomers
Azure	43	14	18,869
Black	3,086	602	18,869
Blue	714	200	18,869
Brown	318	77	18,869
Gold	106	50	18,869
Green	262	74	18,869
Grey	1,113	283	18,869
Orange	126	55	18,869
Pink	435	84	18,869
Purple	8	6	18,869
Red	647	99	18,869
Silver	2,595	417	18,869
Silver Grey	103	14	18,869
Transparent	100	1	18,869
White	2,679	505	18,869
Yellow	200	36	18,869
Grand Total	**12,535**	**2,517**	**18,869**

FIGURE 4-16 Here you can see the behavior of filter context and relationships.

The filter is on the product color. Product is the source of a one-to-many relationship with Sales, so the filter context propagates from Product to Sales, and you can see this because the *NumOfSales* measure counts only the sales of products with the specific color. *NumOfProducts* shows the number of products of each color, and a different value for each row (color) is what you would expect, because the filter is on the same table where we are counting.

On the other hand, *NumOfCustomers*, which counts the number of customers, always shows the same value, that is, the total number of customers. This is because the relationship between Customer and Sales, as you can see Figure 4-17, has an arrow in the direction of Sales.

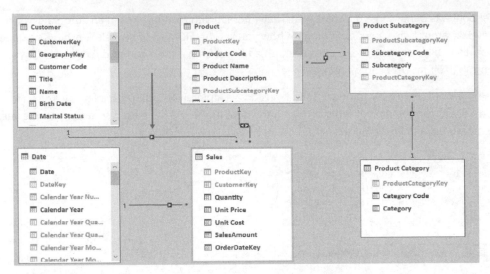

FIGURE 4-17 The relationship between *Customer* and *Sales* is a one-way relationship.

The filter started from *Product*, then propagated to *Sales* (following the arrow from *Product* to *Sales*, which is enabled) but then, when it tried to propagate to *Customer*, it did not find the arrow letting it continue. Thus, it stopped. One-way relationships permit propagation of the filter context in a single direction, not in both.

You can think that the arrows on the relationships are like semaphores. If they are enabled, then the semaphore light is green and the propagation happens. If, on the other hand, the arrow is not enabled, then the semaphore light is red and the filter cannot be propagated.

The arrow is always enabled from the one side to the many side of any relationship. You have the option of enabling it from the many side to the one side as well. If you let the arrow disable, then the propagation will not happen from the many to the one side.

You can better appreciate the behavior if you look at the pivot table shown in Figure 4-18. Instead of using the product color on the rows, this time we slice by customer education.

Row Labels	NumOfSales	NumOfProducts	NumOfCustomers
(blank)	9,826	1,039	385
Bachelors	665	119	5,356
Graduate Degree	418	72	3,189
High School	573	121	3,294
Partial College	746	121	5,064
Partial High School	307	78	1,581
Grand Total	**12,535**	**2,517**	**18,869**

FIGURE 4-18 Filtering by customer education, the Product table is filtered too.

This time the filter starts from *Customer*. It can reach the Sales table, because the arrow is enabled in the corresponding relationship. Then, from *Sales*, it can further propagate to *Product* because the relationship between *Sales* and *Product* is bidirectional.

Now you add to the model a similar measure that counts the number of subcategories, such as the following one:

```
NumOfSubcategories := COUNTROWS ( 'Product Subcategory' )
```

Adding it to the report, you will see that the number of subcategories is not filtered by the customer education, as shown in Figure 4-19.

Calendar	November 2007 🔻			
Row Labels 🔻	**NumOfSales**	**NumOfProducts**	**NumOfCustomers**	**NumOfSubcategories**
(blank)	177	33	385	44
Bachelors	30	13	5,356	44
Graduate Degree	7	5	3,189	44
High School	28	13	3,294	44
Partial College	42	14	5,064	44
Partial High School	15	7	1,581	44
Grand Total	**299**	**51**	**18,869**	**44**

FIGURE 4-19 If the relationship is unidirectional, customers cannot filter subcategories.

This is because the relationship between Product and Product Subcategory is unidirectional, that is it lets the filter propagate in a single direction. As soon as you enable the arrow starting from Product and going to Product Subcategory, you will see that the filter propagates, as you can see in Figure 4-20.

Calendar	November 2007 🔻			
Row Labels 🔻	**NumOfSales**	**NumOfProducts**	**NumOfCustomers**	**NumOfSubcategories**
(blank)	177	33	385	16
Bachelors	30	13	5,356	8
Graduate Degree	7	5	3,189	4
High School	28	13	3,294	9
Partial College	42	14	5,064	9
Partial High School	15	7	1,581	7
Grand Total	**299**	**51**	**18,869**	**21**

FIGURE 4-20 If the relationship is bidirectional, customers can filter subcategories too.

As it happened with the row context, it is not important how many steps you need to traverse to reach a table: as long as there is a chain of enabled relationships, automatic propagation happens. For example, if you put a filter on Product Category, the filter propagates to Product Subcategory, then to Product, and finally to Sales.

It is important to note that there are no functions available to access columns or values from tables following the chain of filter contexts, because propagation of the filter context in a DAX expression happens automatically, whereas propagation of row contexts does not and it is required to specify the propagation using *RELATED* and *RELATEDTABLE*.

Introducing *VALUES*

The previous example is very interesting, because it shows how to compute the number of customers who bought a product by using the direction of filtering. Nevertheless, if you are interested only in counting the number of customers, then there is an interesting alternative that we take as an opportunity to introduce as another powerful function: *VALUES*.

VALUES is a table function that returns a table of one column only, containing all the values of a column currently visible in the filter context. There are many advanced uses of *VALUES*, which we will introduce later. As of now, it is helpful to start using *VALUES* just to be acquainted with its behavior.

In the previous pivot table, you can modify the definition of *NumOfCustomers* with the following DAX expression:

```
[NumOfCustomers] := COUNTROWS ( VALUES ( Sales[CustomerKey] ) )
```

This expression does not count the number of customers in the Customer table. Instead, it counts the number of values visible in the current filter context for the *CustomerKey* column in Sales. Thus, the expression does not depend on the relationship between Sales and Customers; it uses only the Sales table.

When you put a filter on Products, it also always filters Sales, because of the propagation of the filter from Product to Sales. Therefore, not all the values of *CustomerKey* will be visible, but only the ones present in rows corresponding to sales of the filtered products.

The meaning of the expression is "count the number of customer keys for the sales related to the selected products." Because a customer key represents a customer, the expression effectively counts the number of customers who bought those products.

> **Note** You can achieve the same result using *DISTINCTCOUNT*, which counts the number of distinct values of a column. As a general rule, it is better to use *DISTINCTCOUNT* than *COUNTROWS* of *VALUES*. We used *COUNTROWS* and *VALUES*, here, for educational purposes, because *VALUES* is a useful function to learn even if its most common usages will be clear in later chapters.

Using *VALUES* instead of capitalizing on the direction of relationships comes with both advantages and disadvantages. Certainly setting the filtering in the model is much more flexible, because it uses relationships. Thus, you can count not only the customers using the *CustomerKey*, but also any other attribute of a customer (number of customer categories, for example). With that said, there might be reasons that force you to use one-way filtering or you might need to use *VALUES* for performance reasons. We will discuss these topics in much more detail in Chapter 12, "Advanced relationship handling."

Introducing *ISFILTERED, ISCROSSFILTERED*

Two functions are very useful and might help you gain a better understanding of the propagation of filter contexts. Moreover, learning them is a good way to introduce one of the most interesting concepts of pivot table computation, that is, detection of the cell for which you are computing a value from inside DAX.

These two functions aim to let you detect whether all the values of a column are visible in the current filter context or not; they are:

- *ISFILTERED*: returns *TRUE* or *FALSE*, depending on whether the column passed as an argument has a direct filter on it, that is, it has been put on rows, columns, on a slicer or filter and the filtering is happening for the current cell.

- *ISCROSSFILTERED* returns TRUE or FALSE depending on whether the column has a filter because of automatic propagation of another filter and not because of a direct filter on it.

In this section, we are interested in using the functions to understand the propagation of filter contexts. Thus, we are going to create dummy expressions, which are only useful as learning tools.

If you create a new measure with this definition:

```
[CategoryFilter] := ISFILTERED ( 'Product Category'[Category] )
```

This simple measure returns the value of the *ISFILTERED* function applied to the product category name. You can then create a second measure that makes the same test with the product color. So the code will be:

```
[ColorFilter] := ISFILTERED ( Product[Color] )
```

If you add both measures to a pivot table, placing the categories in a slicer and the colors on the rows, the result will be similar to Figure 4-21.

The interesting part is that the category is never filtered because, even if we added a slicer, we did not make a selection on it. The color, on the other hand, is always filtered on rows, because each row has a specific color, but not in the grand total, because the filter context there does not include any selection of products.

> **Note** This behavior of the grand total, that is, no filter is applied from the ones coming from rows and columns, is very useful whenever you want to modify the behavior of a formula so that, at the grand total level, it shows a different value. In fact, you will check *ISFILTERED* for an attribute present in the pivot table report in order to understand whether the cell you are evaluating is in the inner part of the pivot table or if it is at the grand total level.

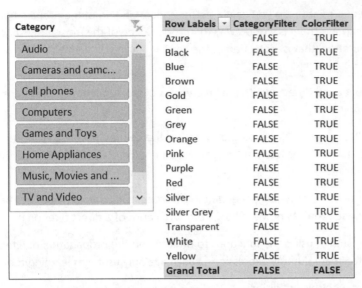

Row Labels	CategoryFilter	ColorFilter
Azure	FALSE	TRUE
Black	FALSE	TRUE
Blue	FALSE	TRUE
Brown	FALSE	TRUE
Gold	FALSE	TRUE
Green	FALSE	TRUE
Grey	FALSE	TRUE
Orange	FALSE	TRUE
Pink	FALSE	TRUE
Purple	FALSE	TRUE
Red	FALSE	TRUE
Silver	FALSE	TRUE
Silver Grey	FALSE	TRUE
Transparent	FALSE	TRUE
White	FALSE	TRUE
Yellow	FALSE	TRUE
Grand Total	**FALSE**	**FALSE**

FIGURE 4-21 You can see that Category is never filtered and Color is filtered everywhere but on the grand total.

If you now select some values from the Category slicer, the result changes. Now the category always has a filter, as you can see in Figure 4-22. In fact, the filter context introduced by the slicer is effective even at the grand total level of the pivot table.

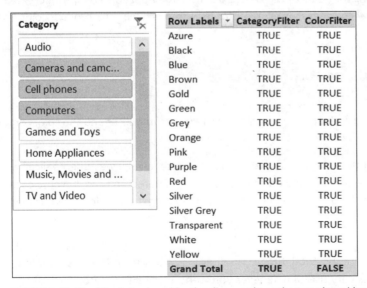

Row Labels	CategoryFilter	ColorFilter
Azure	TRUE	TRUE
Black	TRUE	TRUE
Blue	TRUE	TRUE
Brown	TRUE	TRUE
Gold	TRUE	TRUE
Green	TRUE	TRUE
Grey	TRUE	TRUE
Orange	TRUE	TRUE
Pink	TRUE	TRUE
Purple	TRUE	TRUE
Red	TRUE	TRUE
Silver	TRUE	TRUE
Silver Grey	TRUE	TRUE
Transparent	TRUE	TRUE
White	TRUE	TRUE
Yellow	TRUE	TRUE
Grand Total	**TRUE**	**FALSE**

FIGURE 4-22 The filter introduced by the slicer works at the grand total level too.

ISFILTERED is useful to detect when a direct filter is working on a column. There are situations where a column does not show all of its values, not because you are filtering the column, but because you placed a filter on another column. For example, if you filter the color and ask for the *VALUES* of the product brand, you will get as a result only the brands of products of that specific color. When a column is filtered because of a filter on another column, we say that the column is cross-filtered and the *ISCROSSFILTERED* function detects this scenario.

If you add these two new measures to the data model that check, this time, the *ISCROSSFILTERED* of color and category:

```
[CrossCategory] := ISCROSSFILTERED ( 'Product Category'[Category] )
[CrossColor] := ISCROSSFILTERED ( Product[Color] )
```

Then you will see the result shown in Figure 4-23.

Category		Row Labels	CategoryFilter	ColorFilter	CrossCategory	CrossColor
Audio	^	Azure	FALSE	TRUE	FALSE	TRUE
Cameras and camc...		Black	FALSE	TRUE	FALSE	TRUE
Cell phones		Blue	FALSE	TRUE	FALSE	TRUE
Computers		Brown	FALSE	TRUE	FALSE	TRUE
Games and Toys		Gold	FALSE	TRUE	FALSE	TRUE
Home Appliances		Green	FALSE	TRUE	FALSE	TRUE
Music, Movies and ...		Grey	FALSE	TRUE	FALSE	TRUE
TV and Video	v	Orange	FALSE	TRUE	FALSE	TRUE
		Pink	FALSE	TRUE	FALSE	TRUE
		Purple	FALSE	TRUE	FALSE	TRUE
		Red	FALSE	TRUE	FALSE	TRUE
		Silver	FALSE	TRUE	FALSE	TRUE
		Silver Grey	FALSE	TRUE	FALSE	TRUE
		Transparent	FALSE	TRUE	FALSE	TRUE
		White	FALSE	TRUE	FALSE	TRUE
		Yellow	FALSE	TRUE	FALSE	TRUE
		Grand Total	**FALSE**	**FALSE**	**FALSE**	**FALSE**

FIGURE 4-23 Cross-filtering is visible using the *ISCROSSFILTERED* function.

You can see that color is cross-filtered and category is not. An interesting question, at this point, is "Why is the category not filtered?" When you filter a color, you might expect to see only the categories of product of that specific color. To answer the question you need to remember that the category is not a column of the Product table. Instead, it is part of Product Category and the arrows on the relationship do not let the relationship propagate. If you change the data model, enabling bidirectional filtering on the full chain of relationships from Product to Product Category, then the result will be different, as is visible in Figure 4-24.

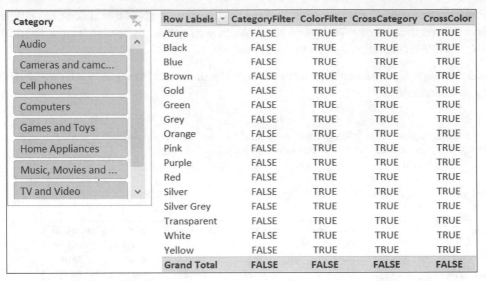

Category		Row Labels	CategoryFilter	ColorFilter	CrossCategory	CrossColor
Audio	^	Azure	FALSE	TRUE	TRUE	TRUE
Cameras and camc...		Black	FALSE	TRUE	TRUE	TRUE
Cell phones		Blue	FALSE	TRUE	TRUE	TRUE
Computers		Brown	FALSE	TRUE	TRUE	TRUE
Games and Toys		Gold	FALSE	TRUE	TRUE	TRUE
Home Appliances		Green	FALSE	TRUE	TRUE	TRUE
Music, Movies and ...		Grey	FALSE	TRUE	TRUE	TRUE
TV and Video	v	Orange	FALSE	TRUE	TRUE	TRUE
		Pink	FALSE	TRUE	TRUE	TRUE
		Purple	FALSE	TRUE	TRUE	TRUE
		Red	FALSE	TRUE	TRUE	TRUE
		Silver	FALSE	TRUE	TRUE	TRUE
		Silver Grey	FALSE	TRUE	TRUE	TRUE
		Transparent	FALSE	TRUE	TRUE	TRUE
		White	FALSE	TRUE	TRUE	TRUE
		Yellow	FALSE	TRUE	TRUE	TRUE
		Grand Total	**FALSE**	**FALSE**	**FALSE**	**FALSE**

FIGURE 4-24 Enabling two-way filtering shows that now the category is cross-filtered, even if not filtered directly.

In this section, you have seen some examples of *ISFILTERED* and *ISCROSSFILTERED*, mainly for educational purposes, because you used them only to get a better understanding of how a filter context propagates through relationships. In following chapters, by writing advanced DAX code, you will learn why these two functions are so useful.

Evaluation contexts recap

Let's recap all what we have learned about evaluation contexts.

- Evaluation context is the context that modifies the value of a DAX expression by filtering the data model and providing the concept of current row, when needed to access a column value.

- The evaluation context consists of two parts: the row context and the filter context. They co-exist and they are present for all the formulas. In order to understand a formula's behavior, you always need to take into account both contexts, because they operate at the same time.

- DAX creates a row context automatically when you define a calculated column. You can also create a row context programmatically by using iterator functions. All iterators define a row context.

- You can nest row contexts and, in such a case, the *EARLIER* function is useful to get access to the previous row context.

- DAX creates a filter context when you use a pivot table by using fields on rows, columns, slicers, and filters. There is a way to programmatically create filter contexts by using *CALCULATE*, but we still have not learned it yet. We hope that at this point you should be very curious to learn more about it!

- Row context does not propagate through relationships automatically. Propagation happens manually by using *RELATED* and *RELATEDTABLE*. You need to use these functions on the correct side of a one-to-many relationship: *RELATED* on the many side, *RELATEDTABLE* on the one side.

- Filter context automatically propagates following the filtering of the relationship. It always propagates from the one side of the relationship to the many side. In addition, you also have the option of enabling the propagation from the many side to the one side. No functions are available to force the propagation: Everything happens inside the engine in an automatic way, according to the definition of relationships in the data model.

- *VALUES* returns a table containing a one-column table with all the unique values of the column that are visible in the current filter context. You can use the resulting table as a parameter to any iterator.

At this point, you have learned the most complex conceptual topics of the DAX language. These points rule all the evaluation flows of your formulas and they are the pillars of the DAX language. Whenever you encounter an expression that does not compute what you want, there's a huge chance that was because you have not fully understood these rules.

As we said in the introduction, at a first reading all these topics look very simple. In fact, they are. What makes them complex is the fact that in a complex expression you might have several evaluation contexts active in different parts of the formula. Mastering evaluation context is a skill that you will gain with experience, and we will try to help you on this by showing many examples in the next chapters. After some DAX formulas on your own, you will intuitively know which contexts are used and which functions they require and you will finally master the DAX language.

Creating a parameter table

In this chapter, you learned many theoretical concepts about evaluation contexts. It is now time to use some of them to solve an interesting scenario and learn a very useful technique, that is, the use of parameter tables.

The idea of a parameter table is to create a table that is unrelated to the rest of the data model, but you will use it internally in DAX expressions to modify their behavior. An example might help to clarify this. Imagine you have created a report that shows the sum of sales amount and, because your company sells many goods, the numbers shown in the report are very large. Because our sample database does not suffer from this problem, instead of using the *SalesAmount* column, we have created a measure that sums the *SalesAmount* cubed, so that numbers are bigger and the described scenario is more realistic. In Figure 4-25 you can see this report.

Sales Amount	Column Labels			
Row Labels	CY 2007	CY 2008	CY 2009	Grand Total
Azure	1,960,392,451.90	705,729,904.55	316,870,144.00	2,982,992,500.45
Black	1,852,957,833,776.85	766,823,353,494.27	460,804,127,759.50	3,080,585,315,030.62
Blue	3,110,738,344,016.30	229,604,213,839.81	320,590,304,143.49	3,660,932,861,999.60
Brown	2,238,683,519,356.14	111,814,853,374.13	2,394,507,848,899.20	4,745,006,221,629.46
Gold	5,328,362,350.00	11,083,737,753.00	18,668,829,287.01	35,080,929,390.01
Green	1,384,243,448,780.78	587,763,173,943.58	527,494,290,700.17	2,499,500,913,424.52
Grey	363,642,216,140.14	1,129,486,253,197.86	121,678,591,398.79	1,614,807,060,736.79
Orange	13,053,660,871.52	9,023,532,983.06	10,442,825,120.49	32,520,018,975.07
Pink	882,892,638,974.98	24,076,918,659.84	44,266,723,593.98	951,236,281,228.80
Purple	702,464.00		61,256.00	763,720.00
Red	277,716,888,210.38	36,410,685,023.30	43,485,805,695.03	357,613,378,928.71
Silver	1,626,446,100,120.32	599,520,302,874.75	1,805,674,285,019.79	4,031,640,688,014.86
Silver Grey	62,115,060,924.00	4,721,772,262.90	13,668,050,062.00	80,504,883,248.90
Transparent	6,124.34	3,125.70	10,647.71	19,897.74
White	849,267,695,977.16	2,923,461,779,978.27	6,665,808,316,354.88	10,438,537,792,310.30
Yellow	4,851,727.20	786,150,633.51	1,631,445.55	792,633,806.26
Grand Total	12,669,051,722,266.00	6,435,282,461,048.52	12,427,408,571,527.60	31,531,742,754,842.20

FIGURE 4-25 Reading reports with big numbers is sometimes difficult.

The issue with this report is that the numbers are large and they tend to be hard to read. Are they millions, billions, trillions? Moreover, they use a lot of space in the report, without carrying much information. A common request, for this kind of report, is to show the numbers using a different scale. For example, you might want to show the values divided by a thousand or a million, so that they result in smaller numbers, still carrying the useful information.

You can easily solve this scenario by modifying the measure and dividing it by a thousand. The only problem is that, depending on the relative scale of numbers, you might want to see them as real values (if they are small enough), divided by thousands or divided by millions. Creating three measures seems cumbersome at this point and we want to find a better solution that removes the need of creating many different measures.

The idea is to let the user decide which scale to apply in the report when using a slicer. In Figure 4-26 you can see an example of the report we want to build.

ShowValueAs		ScaledSalesAmount	Column Labels			
		Row Labels	CY 2007	CY 2008	CY 2009	Grand Total
Real Value		Azure	1,960.39	705.73	316.87	2,982.99
Thousands		Black	1,852,957.83	766,823.35	460,804.13	3,080,585.32
Millions		Blue	3,110,738.34	229,604.21	320,590.30	3,660,932.86
Billions		Brown	2,238,683.52	111,814.85	2,394,507.85	4,745,006.22
		Gold	5,328.36	11,083.74	18,668.83	35,080.93
		Green	1,384,243.45	587,763.17	527,494.29	2,499,500.91
		Grey	363,642.22	1,129,486.25	121,678.59	1,614,807.06
		Orange	13,053.66	9,023.53	10,442.83	32,520.02
		Pink	882,892.64	24,076.92	44,266.72	951,236.28
		Purple	0.70		0.06	0.76
		Red	277,716.89	36,410.69	43,485.81	357,613.38
		Silver	1,626,446.10	599,520.30	1,805,674.29	4,031,640.69
		Silver Grey	62,115.06	4,721.77	13,668.05	80,504.88
		Transparent	0.01	0.00	0.01	0.02
		White	849,267.70	2,923,461.78	6,665,808.32	10,438,537.79
		Yellow	4.85	786.15	1.63	792.63
		Grand Total	12,669,051.72	6,435,282.46	12,427,408.57	31,531,742.75

FIGURE 4-26 The slicer does not filter values here. It is used to change the way numbers are shown.

The interesting idea of the report is that you do not use the *ShowValueAs* slicer to filter data. Instead, you will use it to change the scale used by the numbers. When the user selects Real Value, the actual numbers will be shown. If Thousands is selected, then the actual numbers are divided by one thousand and are shown in the same measure without having to change the layout of the pivot table. The same applies to Millions and Billions.

To create this report, the first thing that you need is a table containing the values you want to show on the slicer. In our example, made with Excel, we use an Excel table to store the scales. In a more professional solution, it would be better to store the table in an SQL database. In Figure 4-27 you can see the content of such a table.

ShowValueAs	DivideBy
Real Value	1
Thousands	1,000
Millions	1,000,000
Billions	1,000,000,000

FIGURE 4-27 This Excel table will be the source for the slicer in the report.

Obviously, you cannot create any relationship with this table, because *Sales* does not contain any column that you can use to relate to this table. Nevertheless, once the table is in the data model, you can use the *ShowValueAs* column as the source for a slicer. Yes, you end up with a slicer that does nothing, but some DAX code will perform the magic of reading user selections and further modifying the content of the report.

The DAX expression that you need to use for the measure is the following:

```
[ScaledSalesAmount] :=
IF (
    HASONEVALUE ( Scale[DivideBy] ),
    DIVIDE ( [Sales Amount], VALUES ( Scale[DivideBy] ) ),
    [Sales Amount]
)
```

There are two interesting things to note in this formula:

- The condition tested by the *IF* function is: *HASONEVALUE (Scale[ShowValueAs])*. This pattern is very common: you check whether the column of the Scale table has only one value visible. If the user did not select anything in the slicer, then all of the values of the column are visible in the current filter context; that is, *HASONEVALUE* will return *FALSE* (because the column has many different values). If, on the other hand, the user selected a single value, then only that one is visible and *HASONEVALUE* will return *TRUE*. Thus, the condition reads as: "if the user has selected a single value for *ShowValueAs* attribute."

- If a single value is selected, then you know that a single row is visible. Thus, you can compute *VALUES (Scale[DivideBy])* and you are sure that the resulting table contains only one column and one row (the one visible in the filter context). DAX will convert the one-row-one-column table returned by *VALUES* in a scalar value. If you try to use *VALUES* to read a single value when the result is a table with multiple rows, you will get an error. However, in this specific scenario, you are sure that the value returned will be only one, because of the previous condition tested by the *IF* function.

Therefore, you can read the expression as: "If the user has selected a single value in the slicer, then show the sales amount divided by the corresponding denominator, otherwise show the original sales amount." The result is a report that changes the values shown interactively, using the slicer as if it was a button. Clearly, because the report uses only standard DAX formulas, it will work when deployed to SharePoint or Power BI, too.

Parameter tables are very useful in building reports. We have shown a very simple (yet very common) example, but the only limit is your imagination. You can create parameter tables to modify the way a number is computed, to change parameters for a specific algorithm, or to perform other complex operations that change the value returned by your DAX code.

Understanding *CALCULATE* and *CALCULATETABLE*

I n this chapter we continue our journey in discovering the power of the DAX language with a detailed explanation of a single function: *CALCULATE*. In reality, the same considerations are valid also for *CALCULATETABLE*, which evaluates and returns a table instead of a scalar value. For simplicity, we will refer to *CALCULATE* in the examples, but remember that *CALCULATETABLE* has the same behavior.

It might seem strange to dedicate a full chapter to a single function, but this is essential because of its richness and side effects. *CALCULATE* is by far the most important, useful, and complex function of the DAX language. In reality, the function itself is an easy one. It only performs a few tasks, but the number of scenarios where *CALCULATE* is necessary, along with the complexity of the formulas that can be written with *CALCULATE*, make a full chapter absolutely necessary.

This, as in the previous chapter, is a tough one. We strongly suggest you read it once, get a general feeling of *CALCULATE* and then move on to the remaining part of the book. Then, as soon as you feel lost in a specific formula, come back to this chapter and read it again from the beginning. You will probably discover new information each time you read it.

Another important aspect of this chapter is that we will need to be somewhat pedantic. Thus, if at some point you find a section that looks boring and that it seems to just be stating the obvious, read it again carefully to make sure you understand it perfectly.

Understanding *CALCULATE*

You have learned in the previous chapter that there are two different contexts: row context and filter context. You have learned that you can create the row context programmatically by using iterators and you learned the *ALL* function that lets you ignore the filter context. It is important to remember that *ALL* ignores the filter context, it does not change it. Thus, in the following formula:

```
[Sales Amount Margin] :=
SUMX (
    ALL ( Sales ),
    Sales[SalesAmount] * AVERAGE ( Sales[MarginPct] )
)
```

ALL ignores the existing filter context and always returns the entire table, but it does not change in any way the evaluation of other parts of the formula. In fact, in the innermost expression, *AVERAGE* will compute the average of the *MarginPct* column in the filter context under which DAX evaluates the entire expression. There is a single function in DAX that has the ability to change a filter context, and it is *CALCULATE*.

Let's start introducing *CALCULATE* by looking at a scenario where you will find it useful. Imagine you want to build the report shown in Figure 5-1, which contains categories, subcategories, and the sum of sales amount.

Color		Row Labels	Sales Amount	SalesPct
Azure		⊞ Audio	$47,116.66	1.12 %
Black		⊟ Cameras and camcorders	$861,595.54	20.42 %
Blue		Camcorders	$327,587.00	7.76 %
Brown		Cameras & Camcorders Accessories	$108,154.54	2.56 %
Gold		Digital Cameras	$110,212.80	2.61 %
Green		Digital SLR Cameras	$315,641.20	7.48 %
Grey		⊟ Cell phones	$240,738.09	5.70 %
Orange		Cell phones Accessories	$37,487.13	0.89 %
		Home & Office Phones	$14,263.96	0.34 %
		Smart phones & PDAs	$99,069.00	2.35 %
		Touch Screen Phones	$89,918.00	2.13 %
		⊞ Computers	$903,856.11	21.42 %
		⊞ Games and Toys	$42,832.57	1.02 %
		⊞ Home Appliances	$1,426,288.26	33.80 %
		⊞ Music, Movies and Audio Books	$47,088.48	1.12 %
		⊞ TV and Video	$650,402.19	15.41 %
		Grand Total	$4,219,917.90	100.00 %

FIGURE 5-1 Here you can see a simple report showing sales divided by category and subcategory. The *SalesPct* column shows the percentage to total of the row.

The report shows the percentage of each row to the grand total. You can easily produce such a report using Microsoft Excel PivotTable features, but we are interested in computing the percentage as a measure, so that users have it available whenever they want to add it to a pivot table.

The following is a naïve solution:

```
SalesPct :=
DIVIDE (
    SUM ( Sales[SalesAmount] ),
    SUMX ( ALL ( Sales ), Sales[SalesAmount] )
)
```

The numerator is *SUM* of *SalesAmount*. The denominator ignores the filter context and always returns the grand total of *SalesAmount*, regardless of any filter. This formula works as long as you do not select anything from the slicer. For example, if you select the color Black in the slicer then the values are wrong; the percentage of the grand total is 18.76 percent instead of 100 percent since the denominator used for the percentage calculation is a higher number, as you can see in Figure 5-2.

Color		Row Labels	Sales Amount	SalesPct
Azure		⊞ Audio	$7,549.99	0.18 %
Black		⊟ Cameras and camcorders	$110,215.98	2.61 %
Blue		Camcorders	$71,794.00	1.70 %
Brown		Cameras & Camcorders Accessories	$3,568.48	0.08 %
Gold		Digital Cameras	$9,779.90	0.23 %
Green		Digital SLR Cameras	$25,073.60	0.59 %
Grey		⊟ Cell phones	$79,575.84	1.89 %
Orange		Cell phones Accessories	$8,578.93	0.20 %
		Home & Office Phones	$4,251.91	0.10 %
		Smart phones & PDAs	$36,909.00	0.87 %
		Touch Screen Phones	$29,836.00	0.71 %
		⊞ Computers	$296,695.34	7.03 %
		⊞ Games and Toys	$8,826.58	0.21 %
		⊞ Home Appliances	$110,512.81	2.62 %
		⊞ Music, Movies and Audio Books	$19,004.88	0.45 %
		⊞ TV and Video	$159,354.39	3.78 %
		Grand Total	$791,735.81	18.76 %

FIGURE 5-2 Selecting a color from the slicer shows wrong percentage results.

The problem here is easy to understand. By using *ALL*, we are ignoring the filter context. Thus, the denominator is always the grand total of all sales, whereas if you select a color, you want to keep the filter on color, clearing only the filters on category and subcategory. *ALL* and iterators are not the right choice here; you need something more powerful. In other words, you need *CALCULATE*.

Understanding the filter context

Before continuing with the description of *CALCULATE*, it is important to start a small digression to refine your understanding of a filter context. The filter context is a complex concept and you will have a final understanding of how it works only by the end of Chapter 10, "Advanced evaluation context." Before then, we give different descriptions of the filter context, in order of complexity, in order to reach the final explanation one step at a time.

In the previous chapter we gave a first definition of the filter context: "a set of filters applied to the model, which changes the rows that are visible in the entire database." Even if it is a correct definition, it is still very naïve. In order to move to the next level, you need to remember that VertiPaq (the database on which DAX works) is a columnar database. You should stop thinking about tables and think in terms of columns instead.

As an example, you can think of Product as a regular table, as in Figure 5-3.

Product

ID	Name	Color	UnitPrice
1	Camcorder	Red	112.25
2	Camera	Red	97.50
3	Smartphone	White	100.00
4	Console	Black	120.25
5	TV	Blue	1,240.85
6	CD	Red	39.99
7	Touch screen	Blue	45.12
8	PDA	Black	120.25
9	Keyboard	Black	120.50

FIGURE 5-3 You can look at the Product table as a standard table, made of rows, each divided into columns.

However, because VertiPaq is a columnar database, the correct representation of the table would be as a set of columns, not a single entity. Thus, a better visualization of the same table would be the one shown in Figure 5-4.

Product Columns

ID	Name	Color	UnitPrice
1	Camcorder	Red	112.25
2	Camera	Red	97.50
3	Smartphone	White	100.00
4	Console	Black	120.25
5	TV	Blue	1,240.85
6	CD	Red	39.99
7	Touch screen	Blue	45.12
8	PDA	Black	120.25
9	Keyboard	Black	120.50

FIGURE 5-4 The correct visualization of Product is as a set of columns, each divided into rows.

The content is the same, of course, but now it is easier to see the different columns as different items stored in memory. Obviously, the same representation works for any table in the data model. Thus, you should mentally divide each table in the model into separate columns, and you will end up with a set of columns, logically divided into tables, but each column separated from the other ones.

When you put Color in a slicer, DAX applies a filter to that column. Read this carefully, please: It does not apply a filter to the table containing the column. It applies the filter to the column only. Then, because the column is part of a table, as a result the table will have a filter, too. Nevertheless, the filter works on a single column at a time (we are describing an approximation of what really happens; we will reach the final understanding of the filter context later in the book).

When you do a selection in the slicer filtering only, say, red products, the model will have this filter as shown in Figure 5-5.

Product[Color] = "Red"

ID	Name	Color	UnitPrice
1	Camcorder	Red	112.25
2	Camera	Red	97.50
3	Smartphone	White	100.00
4	Console	Black	120.25
5	TV	Blue	1,240.85
6	CD	Red	39.99
7	Touch screen	Blue	45.12
8	PDA	Black	120.25
9	Keyboard	Black	120.50

FIGURE 5-5 Filtering the red products results in a filter applied to the *Color* column only.

You can imagine representing the filter on a single column as a bitmap over the values of the column or, in a more human-readable way, as the list of active values for the column.

We can finally state a better definition of the filter context: A filter context is a set of tables. Each table contains a single column and lists all the values for that column, which the engine considers visible in the current context. All of these filters, when put in a logical *AND*, form the filter context.

In a single cell of a pivot table, you have filters coming from slicers and filters; from the rows and from the columns. Each of these filters operate on sets of table columns. Thus, in our previous example, the filter context contains three separate filters: one for the category, one for the subcategory (both are on the rows in the pivot table), and one for the color (coming from the slicer).

All this digression leads us to a better understanding of what it means to update a filter context. If you want to update a filter context, you need to provide a new list of values for some or all of the filtered columns in the model. DAX will replace the filter on that column (and that column only) with the new list of values and, in this way, it generates a new filter context.

The two important aspects to remember are:

- A filter is a set of active values for one column.

- A filter always applies to a single column only.

Remember that this is not the correct definition of a filter context yet. You have to learn many other aspects before becoming a real master of DAX. Nevertheless, this definition will already be very useful to start working with the filter context.

Having finished the digression, you now have a better understanding of what a filter context is, and we can continue describing how *CALCULATE* can modify it.

Introducing *CALCULATE*

CALCULATE (with its companion, *CALCULATETABLE*, which you will learn later) is the only function that can modify the filter context. In reality, *CALCULATE* creates a new filter context and then evaluates an expression in that new context. Because the starting point of the new context is the existing one, we can say that it modifies the evaluation context.

Let's start examining the syntax of *CALCULATE*:

```
[Measure] := CALCULATE ( Expression, Condition1, … ConditionN )
```

CALCULATE accepts any number of parameters and the only mandatory one is the first, that is, the expression to evaluate. We call the conditions following the first parameter *filter arguments*. *CALCULATE* does the following:

- It takes the current filter context and makes a copy of it into a new filter context.

- It evaluates each filter argument and produces, for each condition, the list of valid values for that specific column.

- If two or more filter arguments affect the same column, they are merged together using an *AND* operator (or, in mathematical terms, using the set intersection).

- It uses the new condition to replace existing filters on the columns in the model. If a column already has a filter, then the new filter replaces the existing one. If, on the other hand, the column does not have a filter, then DAX simply applies the new filter to the column.

- Once the new filter context is evaluated, *CALCULATE* computes the first argument (the expression) in the new filter context. At the end, it will restore the original filter context, returning the computed result.

Note *CALCULATE* does another very important task: it transforms any existing row context into an equivalent filter context. Later in this chapter there is a more detailed discussion of this topic. The reason we mention it here is that it is better to remember this very important fact, in case you make a second reading of this section: *CALCULATE* creates a filter context out of existing row contexts.

The filters accepted by *CALCULATE* can be of two types:

- **List of values**, in the form of a table expression. In that case, you provide the exact list of values you want to see in the new filter context. The filter can be a table with a single column or with many columns, as is the case of a filter on a whole table.

- **Boolean conditions**, such as Product[Color] = "White". These filters need to work on a single column because the result has to be a list of values of a single column.

If you use the syntax with a Boolean condition, DAX will transform it into a list of values. So whenever you write:

```
[Sales Amount Red Products] :=
CALCULATE (
    SUM ( Sales[SalesAmount] ),
    Product[Color] = "Red"
)
```

DAX transforms the expression into the following one:

```
[Sales Amount Red Products] :=
CALCULATE (
    SUM ( Sales[SalesAmount] ),
    FILTER (
        ALL ( Product[Color] ),
        Product[Color] = "Red"
    )
)
```

For this reason, you can reference only one column in a filter argument with a Boolean condition. DAX has to detect the column to iterate in the *FILTER* expression, which are generated in the background automatically. If the Boolean expression references more columns, then you have to write the *FILTER* iteration in an explicit way, as you will see later.

At this point, we can go back to the example of computing the percentage of sales against the total for all the categories and subcategories, still taking into account the filter on color. You can write that measure using *CALCULATE*:

```
[SalesPctWithCalculate] :=
DIVIDE (
    SUM ( Sales[SalesAmount] ),
    CALCULATE (
        SUM ( Sales[SalesAmount] ),
        ALL ( 'Product Category' ),
        ALL ( 'Product Subcategory' )
    )
)
```

Let's focus on the use of *CALCULATE* in the denominator of this formula. The expression to compute is always the same: the sum of sales amount. However, we already know that a formula by itself can have many different values, depending on the context under which DAX evaluates it. Because the expression is inside *CALCULATE*, the context of the expression is not the original one. We only need to understand how the context is going to be and this information comes from the additional parameters of *CALCULATE*.

The first filter parameter is *ALL ('Product Category')*. *ALL* returns all the rows in a table, in this case all the categories. DAX retrieves the Product Category table and uses its values as the new filter, replacing any previously existing filter on any column of Product Category which in this example comes from the pivot table row.

The same happens, obviously, with its second filter parameter: *ALL ('Product Subcategory')* removes any filter from any column of Product Subcategory.

The important part to note is that *CALCULATE* does not replace the filter coming from the slicer, that is, the filter on Color. It only removes filters from columns of the Product Category and Product Subcategory table. Thus, the final filter context contains all the categories and subcategories, but only the selected color.

Using this new formula inside the pivot table shows correct values, as you can see in Figure 5-6.

Color		Row Labels	Sales Amount	SalesPct	SalesPctWithCalculate
Azure		⊞ Audio	$7,549.99	0.18 %	0.95 %
Black		⊟ Cameras and camcorders	$110,215.98	2.61 %	13.92 %
Blue		Camcorders	$71,794.00	1.70 %	9.07 %
Brown		Cameras & Camcorders Accessories	$3,568.48	0.08 %	0.45 %
Gold		Digital Cameras	$9,779.90	0.23 %	1.24 %
Green		Digital SLR Cameras	$25,073.60	0.59 %	3.17 %
Grey		⊟ Cell phones	$79,575.84	1.89 %	10.05 %
Orange		Cell phones Accessories	$8,578.93	0.20 %	1.08 %
		Home & Office Phones	$4,251.91	0.10 %	0.54 %
		Smart phones & PDAs	$36,909.00	0.87 %	4.66 %
		Touch Screen Phones	$29,836.00	0.71 %	3.77 %
		⊞ Computers	$296,695.34	7.03 %	37.47 %
		⊞ Games and Toys	$8,826.58	0.21 %	1.11 %
		⊞ Home Appliances	$110,512.81	2.62 %	13.96 %
		⊞ Music, Movies and Audio Books	$19,004.88	0.45 %	2.40 %
		⊞ TV and Video	$159,354.39	3.78 %	20.13 %
		Grand Total	$791,735.81	18.76 %	100.00 %

FIGURE 5-6 Percentage computed with *CALCULATE* shows correct values.

At this point, the very careful reader might stop and ask: "Well, this does not make sense. You have removed the filter from Product Category and Product Subcategory, but you are summing values from Sales. Who removed the filter from that table?" A very good question, indeed. In fact, our description is missing something very important: Once *CALCULATE* computed the new filter context, it applied it to the data model prior to evaluate the expression.

When DAX applies a filter context to a table, we already know from the previous chapter that the filter propagates through relationships following their definitions (unidirectional or bidirectional filtering). It turns out that we removed the filter from both Product Category and Product Subcategory and, when DAX applies the new filter context, it propagates it to the fact table, which is on the many-side of the chain of relationships starting from Product Category and ending at Sales.

By removing the filters from Product Category and Product Subcategory, we also removed their corresponding propagated filters on Sales.

CALCULATE examples

Now that you have seen the basics of *CALCULATE*, or at least you learned why it is so useful, the following part of the chapter is dedicated to various examples of its usage. They are important to study and understand thoroughly. In fact, *CALCULATE* by itself is a very simple function. The complexity (hence the importance we give to it) comes from the fact that, using *CALCULATE*, you are forced to think in terms of filter contexts and you might end up with several contexts in a single formula, which makes the flow of the code hard to follow. According to our experience (as trainers), learning by example is the best way to understand *CALCULATE* and filter contexts.

Filtering a single column

The simplest way to use *CALCULATE* is to filter a single column. As an example, assume you want to create a measure that always returns the sales amount of black products, regardless of the selection made on the color. The formula is very easy to author:

```
[SalesAmountBlack] :=
CALCULATE (
    SUM ( Sales[SalesAmount] ),
    Product[Color] = "Black"
)
```

If you use the previous formula in a pivot table, you will get the result shown in Figure 5-7.

Row Labels	Sales Amount	SalesAmountBlack
Azure	$12,071.90	$791,735.81
Black	$791,735.81	$791,735.81
Blue	$294,838.55	$791,735.81
Brown	$225,705.83	$791,735.81
Gold	$43,292.49	$791,735.81
Green	$202,219.08	$791,735.81
Grey	$509,990.58	$791,735.81
Orange	$55,324.68	$791,735.81
Pink	$130,243.02	$791,735.81
Purple	$286.00	$791,735.81
Red	$126,762.21	$791,735.81
Silver	$918,587.35	$791,735.81
Silver Grey	$60,366.60	$791,735.81
Transparent	$414.54	$791,735.81
White	$841,262.48	$791,735.81
Yellow	$6,816.78	$791,735.81
Grand Total	$4,219,917.90	$791,735.81

FIGURE 5-7 *SalesAmountBlack* always shows the sales of black products, regardless of the current filter context.

You can see that *SalesAmountBlack* always shows the sales for black products, even if on the rows the filter context selects different colors.

If you focus on the third row (Blue), this is what happened: The formula started the evaluation in a filter context where the only value for the color was Blue. Then, *CALCULATE* evaluated a new condition (Color = Black) and, when it had to apply it to the new filter context, it replaced the existing condition, removing the filter on Blue and replacing it with the filter on Black. This happened for all of the rows (that is, all colors) and this is the reason why you see the same number for all the rows.

Clearly, because the only column for which *CALCULATE* overrides the selection is the color, other columns maintain their filters. For example, if you put the calendar year on the columns, you see that the result is always the same for all the colors but it changes for different years, as shown in Figure 5-8.

Filtering a single column is straightforward. A less evident fact is that you can only filter one column at a time if you use conditions as filters for *CALCULATE*. For example, you might want to create a measure that computes the sales amount for only the products where the unit price is at least twice the unit cost. You can try this formula:

```
[HighProfitabilitySales] :=
CALCULATE (
    SUM ( Sales[SalesAmount] ),
    Product[Unit Price] >= Product[Unit Cost] * 2
)
```

SalesAmountBlack	Column Labels			
Row Labels	CY 2007	CY 2008	CY 2009	Grand Total
Azure	$282,020.06	$245,539.76	$264,175.99	$791,735.81
Black	$282,020.06	$245,539.76	$264,175.99	$791,735.81
Blue	$282,020.06	$245,539.76	$264,175.99	$791,735.81
Brown	$282,020.06	$245,539.76	$264,175.99	$791,735.81
Gold	$282,020.06	$245,539.76	$264,175.99	$791,735.81
Green	$282,020.06	$245,539.76	$264,175.99	$791,735.81
Grey	$282,020.06	$245,539.76	$264,175.99	$791,735.81
Orange	$282,020.06	$245,539.76	$264,175.99	$791,735.81
Pink	$282,020.06	$245,539.76	$264,175.99	$791,735.81
Purple	$282,020.06	$245,539.76	$264,175.99	$791,735.81
Red	$282,020.06	$245,539.76	$264,175.99	$791,735.81
Silver	$282,020.06	$245,539.76	$264,175.99	$791,735.81
Silver Grey	$282,020.06	$245,539.76	$264,175.99	$791,735.81
Transparent	$282,020.06	$245,539.76	$264,175.99	$791,735.81
White	$282,020.06	$245,539.76	$264,175.99	$791,735.81
Yellow	$282,020.06	$245,539.76	$264,175.99	$791,735.81
Grand Total	$282,020.06	$245,539.76	$264,175.99	$791,735.81

FIGURE 5-8 *SalesAmountBlack* overrides only the color; it still obeys the filtering on other columns (year).

You can see that, this time, the condition involves two columns: *Unit Cost* and *Unit Price*. Even if DAX can easily evaluate the condition for each product, it does not allow this syntax. The reason is that, during its evaluation algorithm, *CALCULATE* cannot determine whether the condition should replace any existing filter on *Unit Price*, on *Unit Cost*, or on none of them. In fact, if you try to write the formula above, you will get an error as a result:

```
Calculation error in measure 'Sales'[HighProfitabilitySales]: The expression contains
multiple columns, but only a single column can be used in a True/False expression that is
used as a table filter expression.
```

There is no way to author such a formula using the Boolean syntax. If you need to invoke *CALCULATE* using more than one column in the condition, you need to use a different syntax, which provides a list of values instead of a condition.

The correct way to author the previous expression is to use this syntax:

```
[HighProfitabilitySales] :=
CALCULATE (
    SUM ( Sales[SalesAmount] ),
    FILTER ( Product, Product[Unit Price] >= Product[Unit Cost] * 2 )
)
```

Instead of using a Boolean expression, this time we used the Table syntax for the filter argument of *CALCULATE*. Moreover, we did not filter only one column; we filtered the entire Product table. In Figure 5-9 you can see the *HighProfitabilitySales* measure in action.

Row Labels	Sales Amount	HighProfitabilitySales
Azure	$12,071.90	$8,980.90
Black	$791,735.81	$608,937.60
Blue	$294,838.55	$257,842.67
Brown	$225,705.83	$147,458.64
Gold	$43,292.49	$43,059.99
Green	$202,219.08	$129,221.69
Grey	$509,990.58	$466,888.26
Orange	$55,324.68	$39,400.20
Pink	$130,243.02	$66,314.37
Purple	$286.00	$34.00
Red	$126,762.21	$74,423.56
Silver	$918,587.35	$710,915.05
Silver Grey	$60,366.60	$60,366.60
Transparent	$414.54	
White	$841,262.48	$607,849.13
Yellow	$6,816.78	$5,192.16
Grand Total	**$4,219,917.90**	**$3,226,884.82**

FIGURE 5-9 *HighProfitabilitySales* shows the sales of products with a high price compared to their cost.

In this case, *CALCULATE* evaluates the condition: The result of *FILTER* is a table containing multiple columns (it contains all of the columns of Product). When the new condition is inserted into the filter context, in reality all the existing conditions on Product are replaced with this new filter. In other words, using the actual table as the first parameter of the *FILTER* function, we effectively replace all conditions on all of the columns of that table.

Having read the previous explanations, you should observe that something is not completely clear here. We said that the *FILTER* expression in *CALCULATE* replaces all of the previously existing filters on the Product table, because the table returned by *FILTER* contains all of the columns of Product. Nevertheless, the value returned by our formula is different for each row.

On the Blue row, for example, *HighProfitabilitySales* returns the sales of blue products with high profitability even if, for what we learned until now, it should return the sales of all the high profitable products, regardless of the color. Either DAX did not replace the filter on color, or something more complex is happening. Because we already know that DAX replaced the filter on color, we need to investigate more to understand the exact flow of evaluation. The following code is the formula for our measure: We numbered the lines to make it easier to reference the various parts of the formula.

```
1.   CALCULATE (
2.       SUM ( Sales[SalesAmount] ),
3.       FILTER (
4.           Product,
5.           Product[Unit Price] >= Product[Unit Cost] * 2
6.       )
7.   )
```

The first function is *CALCULATE*. We know that *CALCULATE*, as its first step, evaluates the filter arguments. Before doing anything else, *CALCULATE* evaluates the *FILTER* expression starting at line 3.

FILTER is an iterator and it iterates over the Product table (see line 4). *FILTER* will not see all the products; it will be able to see only the rows that are visible under the current filter context. Now, the question is "under which filter context does DAX evaluate Product at line 4?" Remember that *CALCULATE* still did not create its new evaluation context. It will do this later, after the evaluation of the filters. You can deduce that the filters of *CALCULATE* are evaluated under the original filter context, not under the filter context created by *CALCULATE*. While it might seem obvious, this simple consideration is one of the main sources of errors in many DAX formulas.

Product, at line 4, refers to the products that are visible under the original filter context. For the Blue row in Figure 5-9, that context shows only the blue products. Thus, *FILTER* will iterate over blue products and it will return only blue products with high profitability. Then *CALCULATE* will remove the existing filter for the color, but such a filter is now already incorporated in the result of *FILTER*, leading to the behavior you are observing. It is important to understand correctly the flow of filters and that the filter on color is replaced inside the expression evaluated by *CALCULATE* but not inside the filters of *CALCULATE*. In other words, the filter parameters of *CALCULATE* are evaluated under the previous filter context. Only later *CALCULATE* creates its new filter context, under which it computes its expression parameter.

To have a complete picture, you can check the following formula:

```
[HighProfitabilityALLSales] :=
CALCULATE (
    SUM ( Sales[SalesAmount] ),
    FILTER (
        ALL ( Product ),
        Product[Unit Price] >= Product[Unit Cost] * 2
    )
)
```

This time, instead of using *FILTER (Product)* we used *FILTER (ALL (Product))*. *FILTER* will not iterate only the blue products; it will always iterate all of the products and, because *CALCULATE* replaces the filter on color, the behavior is the one shown in Figure 5-10.

Row Labels	Sales Amount	HighProfitabilitySales	HighProfitabilityALLSales
Azure	$12,071.90	$8,980.90	$3,226,884.82
Black	$791,735.81	$608,937.60	$3,226,884.82
Blue	$294,838.55	$257,842.67	$3,226,884.82
Brown	$225,705.83	$147,458.64	$3,226,884.82
Gold	$43,292.49	$43,059.99	$3,226,884.82
Green	$202,219.08	$129,221.69	$3,226,884.82
Grey	$509,990.58	$466,888.26	$3,226,884.82
Orange	$55,324.68	$39,400.20	$3,226,884.82
Pink	$130,243.02	$66,314.37	$3,226,884.82
Purple	$286.00	$34.00	$3,226,884.82
Red	$126,762.21	$74,423.56	$3,226,884.82
Silver	$918,587.35	$710,915.05	$3,226,884.82
Silver Grey	$60,366.60	$60,366.60	$3,226,884.82
Transparent	$414.54		$3,226,884.82
White	$841,262.48	$607,849.13	$3,226,884.82
Yellow	$6,816.78	$5,192.16	$3,226,884.82
Grand Total	$4,219,917.90	$3,226,884.82	$3,226,884.82

FIGURE 5-10 *HighProfitabilityALLSales* shows that the filter on color is effectively replaced inside *CALCULATE*.

HighProfitabilityALLSales always shows the sales of all high profitability products, effectively ignoring the pre-existing filter on color.

Let's start drawing some conclusions from this first example.

- You can use Boolean conditions inside *CALCULATE*, but in order to use them, you need to reference only one column in the expression, otherwise you will get a syntax error as a result.

- You can use *FILTER* or any other table function as a filter parameter in *CALCULATE* and, in this case, all the columns in the table are part of the new filter context. This means that *CALCULATE* will replace any existing filter on those columns.

- If you use *FILTER*, then *CALCULATE* evaluates *FILTER* in the original filter context. If, on the other hand, you use a Boolean condition, then *CALCULATE* replaces the existing filter context, but only for the affected column.

Filtering with complex conditions

When you use multiple filters, *CALCULATE* performs a logical *AND* of all its filter conditions when it creates the new filter context. So if you want to filter all of the black products manufactured by Tailspin Toys, you can use an expression like this:

```
[Calculate Version] :=
CALCULATE (
    SUM ( Sales[SalesAmount] ),
    Product[Brand] = "Tailspin Toys",
    Product[Color] = "Black"
)
```

Because *CALCULATE* puts the two conditions in *AND*, you might think that this formulation of the expression is equivalent:

```
[FILTER Version] :=
CALCULATE (
    SUM ( Sales[SalesAmount]),
    FILTER (
        Product,
        AND (
            Product[Brand] = "Tailspin Toys",
            Product[Color] = "Black"
        )
    )
)
```

In reality, the two expressions are different and this section explains the reason. You have already learned this, but it is worth repeating because of the complexity of the topic and importance of the concepts that are discussed later in this section. In the formula with Boolean expressions, the existing filter context is ignored for both the brand and the color; whereas in the formula with *FILTER*, the pre-existing filter context (prior to the formula being applied) is considered for both columns.

Thus, *Calculate Version* always returns the sales amount for black Tailspin Toys, whereas *FILTER Version* returns the sales only when they are already present in the pre-existing filter context; otherwise it returns an empty value. You can observe this behavior in Figure 5-11.

Brand		Row Labels	Sales Amount	CalculateVersion	FILTER Version
Litware		⊟ Proseware	$92,264.81	$6,752.44	
Northwind Traders		Black	$82,927.75	$6,752.44	
Proseware		Blue	$9,337.06	$6,752.44	
Southridge Video		⊟ Southridge Video	$134,677.23	$6,752.44	
Tailspin Toys		Black	$98,182.24	$6,752.44	
The Phone Company		Blue	$1,481.00	$6,752.44	
Wide World Import...		Brown	$34,515.00	$6,752.44	
		Gold	$498.99	$6,752.44	
		⊟ Tailspin Toys	$17,652.88	$6,752.44	$6,752.44
		Black	$6,752.44	$6,752.44	$6,752.44
		Blue	$10,900.44	$6,752.44	
		Gold		$6,752.44	
		Grand Total	$244,594.92	$6,752.44	$6,752.44

FIGURE 5-11 The two formulas result in different computations, even if they look very similar.

The difference is because *FILTER* iterates a table filtered by the external filter context. Remember that the following formula:

```
[Sales of Tailspin Toys] :=
CALCULATE (
    SUM ( Sales[SalesAmount] ),
    Product[Brand] = "Tailspin Toys",
)
```

is equivalent to the next one:

```
[Sales of Tailspin Toys] :=
CALCULATE (
    SUM ( Sales[SalesAmount] ),
    FILTER (
        ALL ( Product[Brand] ),
        Product[Brand] = "Tailspin Toys",
    )
)
```

In the second formula, by means of using *ALL (Product[Brand])*, we explicitly ask to ignore the current filter context just for the manufacturer column. We cannot stress enough the importance of understanding the behavior of these formulas. Even if the expressions used here are for educational purposes, you will encounter similar scenarios when authoring your own expressions and be sure that, eventually, you will see strange results. In order to understand how the formula behaves, you have to understand the context behavior.

Working on a single column, the equivalence stated above works fine. In our example, we have two columns and you might be tempted to extend the equivalence to a multicolumn scenario by trying the following formula:

```
FilterAll Version :=
CALCULATE (
    SUM ( Sales[SalesAmount] ),
    FILTER (
        ALL ( Product ),
        AND (
            Product[Brand] = "Tailspin Toys",
            Product[Color] = "Black"
        )
    )
)
```

This formula does not satisfy the requirements solved by the first formula you have seen in this section. If you use *ALL (Product)*, you ignore the filter context on both columns by means of ignoring the filter context on the entire table. However, by ignoring the filter context on the entire table, you still get a different behavior. To see the effect, we need to make the pivot table more complex. In Figure 5-12 we added the category name on the rows.

Brand		Row Labels	Sales Amount	CalculateVersion	FILTER Version	FilterAllVersion
Litware	^	⊟ Computers	$80,514.44			$6,752.44
Northwind Traders		⊟ Proseware	$72,956.00			$6,752.44
Proseware		Black	$72,956.00			$6,752.44
Southridge Video		Blue				$6,752.44
Tailspin Toys		⊞ Southridge Video	$7,558.44			$6,752.44
The Phone Company		⊟ Tailspin Toys				$6,752.44
Wide World Import...		Black				$6,752.44
		Blue				$6,752.44
		Gold				$6,752.44
	v	⊟ Games and Toys	$19,727.02	$6,752.44	$6,752.44	$6,752.44
		⊟ Proseware		$6,752.44		$6,752.44
		Black		$6,752.44		$6,752.44
		Blue		$6,752.44		$6,752.44
		⊞ Southridge Video	$2,074.14	$6,752.44		$6,752.44
		⊟ Tailspin Toys	$17,652.88	$6,752.44	$6,752.44	$6,752.44
		Black	$6,752.44	$6,752.44	$6,752.44	$6,752.44
		Blue	$10,900.44	$6,752.44		$6,752.44
		Gold		$6,752.44		$6,752.44
		Grand Total	$100,241.46	$6,752.44	$6,752.44	$6,752.44

FIGURE 5-12 Using *FILTER* and *ALL* on the Product table still does not solve the scenario.

As you can see, *FilterAll Version* ignores the filter context on the entire Product table, showing the value even for the Computers category, for which *Calculate Version* shows a blank value. The reason is that the *Calculate Version* ignores the filter context for the color and model name only, whereas *FilterAll Version* ignores the filter context on the entire table, thereby ignoring the category.

In order to find the correct formula, you have to think in terms of columns instead of tables. We can neither provide the Product table to *FILTER* (because it contains the full original filter context) nor *ALL (Product)* (because it ignores all of the filters). Instead we need to compute a Product table in which we removed the filters on brand, but where any other existing filter is still active. We already know of a function that lets us work on the filter context in this very granular way: it is *CALCULATE*. The only problem is that *CALCULATE* requires an expression returning a single value and, this time, we want to return a whole table, because we need it as a parameter of the *FILTER* function. Luckily, there is a companion to *CALCULATE* that, instead of returning a single value, returns a table. It is *CALCULATETABLE*, which is introduced in the next section.

Using *CALCULATETABLE*

CALCULATETABLE works the same way as *CALCULATE*. The only difference is in the type of the result: *CALCULATE* computes a scalar value, whereas *CALCULATETABLE* evaluates a table expression and returns a table. The next formula performs exactly what we need: It removes the filter context from both, Brand and Color, but lets other filters flow inside the *FILTER* function.

```
[CalcTable Version] :=
CALCULATE (
    SUM ( Sales[SalesAmount] ),
    FILTER (
        CALCULATETABLE (
            Product,
            ALL ( Product[Brand] ),
            ALL ( Product[Color]  )
        ),
        AND (
            Product[Brand] = "Tailspin Toys",
            Product[Color] = "Black"
        )
    )
)
```

As you can see in Figure 5-13, this last formula in *CalcTable Version* computes the correct value, which is the same returned by *Calculate Version*.

Brand		Row Labels	Sales Amount	CalculateVersion	FILTER Version	FilterAllVersion	CalcTableVersion
Litware		⊟ Computers	$80,514.44			$6,752.44	
Northwind Traders		⊟ Proseware	$72,956.00			$6,752.44	
Proseware		Black	$72,956.00			$6,752.44	
Southridge Video		Blue				$6,752.44	
Tailspin Toys		⊞ Southridge Video	$7,558.44			$6,752.44	
The Phone Company		⊟ Tailspin Toys				$6,752.44	
Wide World Import...		Black				$6,752.44	
		Blue				$6,752.44	
		Gold				$6,752.44	
		⊟ Games and Toys	$19,727.02	$6,752.44	$6,752.44	$6,752.44	$6,752.44
		⊟ Proseware		$6,752.44		$6,752.44	$6,752.44
		Black		$6,752.44		$6,752.44	$6,752.44
		Blue		$6,752.44		$6,752.44	$6,752.44
		⊞ Southridge Video	$2,074.14	$6,752.44		$6,752.44	$6,752.44
		⊟ Tailspin Toys	$17,652.88	$6,752.44	$6,752.44	$6,752.44	$6,752.44
		Black	$6,752.44	$6,752.44	$6,752.44	$6,752.44	$6,752.44
		Blue	$10,900.44	$6,752.44		$6,752.44	$6,752.44
		Gold		$6,752.44		$6,752.44	$6,752.44
		Grand Total	$100,241.46	$6,752.44	$6,752.44	$6,752.44	$6,752.44

FIGURE 5-13 The use of *CALCULATETABLE* results in correct values being computed.

This digression about equivalent results is important because knowing the correct technique to transform a Boolean filter into a *FILTER* equivalent will greatly help you for conditions that are more complex. For example, if you wanted to express an *OR* condition, instead of an *AND* one, you would need to use this technique.

For example, if you want to compute the sum of all brands and colors where the condition is that the brand can be Tailspin Toys or the color is Black (*OR* condition), then you need to define it using *CALCULATETABLE*, as in the following code:

```
[CalcTable Version OR] :=
CALCULATE (
    SUM ( Sales[SalesAmount] ),
    FILTER (
        CALCULATETABLE (
            Product,
            ALL ( Product[Brand] ),
            ALL ( Product[Color]  )
        ),
        OR (
            Product[Brand] = "Tailspin Toys",
            Product[Color] = "Black"
        )
    )
)
```

In fact, using *CALCULATETABLE* is a convenient way to remove the filter from Brand and Color, keeping all other filters untouched. Thus, *AND* conditions with many columns can be easily solved with a simple *CALCULATE*, because *CALCULATE* automatically puts all its filter parameters in *AND*. On the other hand, *OR* conditions between different columns are much more complex, because you cannot rely on the automatic *AND* of *CALCULATE* and you need to manually write complex DAX code.

It is worth noting that, as an alternative formula, you can also use the following code, which uses the *ALL* function with two columns:

```
[ALL Version OR] :=
CALCULATE (
    SUM ( Sales[SalesAmount] ),
    FILTER (
        ALL ( Product[Brand], Product[Color]  ),
        OR (
            Product[Brand] = "Tailspin Toys",
            Product[Color] = "Black"
        )
    )
)
```

This latter formulation is much more elegant even if, at the beginning, it is not very intuitive.

In this section, you have seen that as soon as you use more than one column or in general make more complex conditions, the results become hard to understand. Even seasoned DAX programmers often find it hard to follow the evaluation path. Therefore, don't be scared by the complexity of this section; only experience will lead you to a natural path where you will learn how to read formulas at first glance.

Understanding context transition

We have previously anticipated that *CALCULATE* does another very important task: It transforms any existing row context into an equivalent filter context.

In order to illustrate the behavior, you create a calculated column containing a *CALCULATE* expression. The calculated column always has a row context, so this will trigger a context transition. For example, you define a calculated column in Product containing the following DAX expression:

```
Product[SumOfUnitPrice] = SUM ( Product[Unit Price] )
```

This formula sums all the list prices of all the products. The expression is evaluated within a row context and without a filter context, so it returns the grand total of unit price for all the products in the table, and not the list price of the product on which it is evaluated. You can see the behavior in Figure 5-14.

Produc...	Product Name	Unit Price	SumOfUnitPrice
1722	MGS Zoo Tycoon 2: End range Species Expansion Pack E105	$56.00	$898,141.44
1723	MGS Age of Empires III: The Asian Dynasties E106	$56.00	$898,141.44
1724	MGS Fable: The Lost Chapters E107	$56.00	$898,141.44
1725	MGS Dungeon Siege II E105	$56.00	$898,141.44
1726	MGS Zoo Tycoon 2 E108	$56.00	$898,141.44
1727	MGS Rise of Nations: Gold Edition M300	$56.00	$898,141.44
1733	MGS Halo: Combat Evolved E109	$22.79	$898,141.44
1734	MGS Zoo Tycoon Complete Collection E110	$28.00	$898,141.44
1735	MGS Flight Simulator 2004: A Century of Flight E111	$28.00	$898,141.44
1736	MGS Rise of Nations E112	$28.00	$898,141.44
1737	MGS Freelancer E113	$28.00	$898,141.44
1738	MGS Impossible Creatures E114	$28.00	$898,141.44
1739	MGS RalliSport Challenge E115	$28.00	$898,141.44
1740	MGS MechCollection E116	$28.00	$898,141.44

FIGURE 5-14 *SumOfUnitPrice*, computed inside a calculated column, returns the grand total of unit prices.

Now you can create a new calculated column with a slightly modified version of the expression, this time involving *CALCULATE*:

```
Product[SumOfUnitPriceCalc] = CALCULATE ( SUM ( Product[Unit Price] ) )
```

What? *CALCULATE* with a single expression parameter? Where have the filters gone? Nowhere. In fact, we are using *CALCULATE* in its simplest form. We said earlier that the only mandatory argument of *CALCULATE* is the first one, so it is perfectly legal to invoke *CALCULATE* without any filters. In such a case, *CALCULATE* does not change the existing filter context with other conditions, but it still performs the behavior you are learning now: It takes the existing row contexts (if any) and transforms them into an equivalent filter context. Be aware that all the existing row contexts are merged into the new filter context, as we will see in more detail later.

In the example, *CALCULATE* searches for existing row contexts and it finds that there is one on Product, because *CALCULATE* runs inside a calculated column definition. *CALCULATE* takes this row context and replaces it with a filter context that contains only the row currently iterated by the row context. We refer to this behavior as a context transition. Generally speaking, we say that *CALCULATE* performs a context transition, merging all the row contexts into a new—equivalent—filter context.

Inside *CALCULATE*, the expression *SUM (Product[Unit Price])* computes its value under a filter context that contains only the current row of Product, because of the context transition performed by *CALCULATE*. It turns out that this time the result is the same unit price of the product, as you can see in Figure 5-15.

ProductKey	Product Name	Unit Price	SumOfUnitPrice	SumOfUnitPriceCalc
1722	MGS Zoo Tycoon 2: End range Species Expansion Pack E105	$56.00	$898,141.44	$56.00
1723	MGS Age of Empires III: The Asian Dynasties E106	$56.00	$898,141.44	$56.00
1724	MGS Fable: The Lost Chapters E107	$56.00	$898,141.44	$56.00
1725	MGS Dungeon Siege II E105	$56.00	$898,141.44	$56.00
1726	MGS Zoo Tycoon 2 E108	$56.00	$898,141.44	$56.00
1727	MGS Rise of Nations: Gold Edition M300	$56.00	$898,141.44	$56.00
1733	MGS Halo: Combat Evolved E109	$22.79	$898,141.44	$22.79
1734	MGS Zoo Tycoon Complete Collection E110	$28.00	$898,141.44	$28.00
1735	MGS Flight Simulator 2004: A Century of Flight E111	$28.00	$898,141.44	$28.00
1736	MGS Rise of Nations E112	$28.00	$898,141.44	$28.00
1737	MGS Freelancer E113	$28.00	$898,141.44	$28.00
1738	MGS Impossible Creatures E114	$28.00	$898,141.44	$28.00
1739	MGS RalliSport Challenge E115	$28.00	$898,141.44	$28.00
1740	MGS MechCollection E116	$28.00	$898,141.44	$28.00

FIGURE 5-15 Using *CALCULATE*, the row context has been transformed into a filter context, changing the result.

The first time you observe this behavior, it is hard to understand why *CALCULATE* performs context transition. After you start using this feature, it is something you will love, because of the powerful formulas you will be able to author.

Moreover, there is another very important side effect of context transition. You might remember that filter context and row context behave in different ways regarding relationships: The row context does not automatically propagate through relationships, whereas the filter context propagates following the relationships. Thus, when context transition happens, the filter context automatically propagates to related tables.

You can observe this behavior if, instead of summing the list price, you create two new calculated columns, still in Product, using the following definitions:

```
Product[SalesAmount] = SUM ( Sales[SalesAmount] )

Product[SalesAmountCalc] = CALCULATE ( SUM ( Sales[SalesAmount] ) )
```

In Figure 5-16 you can see the result, which is obviously different.

ProductKey	Product Name	SalesAmount	SalesAmountCalc
1722	MGS Zoo Tycoon 2: End range Species Expansion Pack E105	$4,219,917.90	$56.00
1723	MGS Age of Empires III: The Asian Dynasties E106	$4,219,917.90	$1,008.00
1724	MGS Fable: The Lost Chapters E107	$4,219,917.90	
1725	MGS Dungeon Siege II E105	$4,219,917.90	
1726	MGS Zoo Tycoon 2 E108	$4,219,917.90	$392.00
1727	MGS Rise of Nations: Gold Edition M300	$4,219,917.90	
1733	MGS Halo: Combat Evolved E109	$4,219,917.90	
1734	MGS Zoo Tycoon Complete Collection E110	$4,219,917.90	
1735	MGS Flight Simulator 2004: A Century of Flight E111	$4,219,917.90	
1736	MGS Rise of Nations E112	$4,219,917.90	$532.00
1737	MGS Freelancer E113	$4,219,917.90	$420.00
1738	MGS Impossible Creatures E114	$4,219,917.90	

FIGURE 5-16 Context transition induced by *CALCULATE* affects filtering of related tables.

As you can see, the *SalesAmount* column contains the grand total of all sales, and *SalesAmountCalc* contains the sales of the current product. The presence of *CALCULATE* and the related context transition of the row context on Product propagates the filter to Sales, showing only the sales of one product.

Please note that context transition happens for all the row contexts that are active when *CALCULATE* is executed. In fact, you might have more than one row context on different tables. For example, if you iterate the customers using *AVERAGEX* in a calculated column created in Product, then context transition will happen for both row contexts (Product and Customer), and the Sales table will receive both filters. Consider the following expression:

```
Product[SalesWithSUMX] =
AVERAGEX (
    Customer,
    CALCULATE ( SUM ( Sales[SalesAmount] ) )
)
```

The formula computes the average amount that customers spent to buy this product (not the average price, but the average of total amount spent). *SUM* inside *CALCULATE* is executed in a filter context that shows only the sales of the current customer (iterated by *AVERAGEX*) and of the current product (iterated by calculated column evaluation). Here is an easy way to remember this rule: Inside *CALCULATE* there are no row contexts; only a filter context is present.

Understanding context transition with measures

Understanding context transition is very important because of another hidden aspect of DAX. Up to now, we have always written the expression inside *CALCULATE* using functions and columns. However, you can also write an expression that contains a measure invocation. What happens if you invoke a measure from inside a calculated column? More generally, what happens if you call a measure from inside a row context?

As an example, you can define a measure *SumOfSalesAmount* in this way:

```
[SumOfSalesAmount] := SUM ( Sales[SalesAmount] )
```

Then, you can define the *SalesWithSUMX* calculated column using this simpler code:

```
Product[SalesWithSUMX] =
SUMX (
    Customer,
    CALCULATE ( [SumOfSalesAmount] )
)
```

The presence of *CALCULATE* suggests that context transition happens. The issue is that, whenever you invoke a measure from inside another expression, DAX automatically encapsulates the measure inside *CALCULATE*. Thus, the previous expression has a behavior that is identical to the following one:

```
Product[SalesWithSUMX] =
SUMX (
    Customer,
    [SumOfSalesAmount]
)
```

This time, no *CALCULATE* is visible in the formula, yet context transition happens, because of the automatic *CALCULATE* added by DAX.

This is the reason for which it is very important that you always write your code differentiating between columns and measures. The de-facto standard used by DAX authors is to avoid putting the table name in front of measures and always prefix columns with the table name. In fact, in the previous formula, the absence of the table name before *SumOfSalesAmount* suggests that *SumOfSalesAmount* is a measure and, because of that, you know that context transition happens.

Automatic context transition makes it very easy to author formulas that perform complex calculations with iterations. With that said, it takes some time before you get acquainted to read and to use it. For example, if you want to compute the sum of sales only for the customers who bought more than the overall average, you can write a measure as in the following:

```
[SalesMoreThanAverage] :=
VAR
    AverageSales = AVERAGEX ( Customer, [SumOfSalesAmount] )
RETURN
    SUMX (
        Customer,
        IF (
            [SumOfSalesAmount] > AverageSales,
            [SumOfSalesAmount]
        )
    )
```

In the preceding code, we use *SumOfSalesAmount* as a measure inside a different row context. In the variable definition, we use it to compute the average of customer sales, whereas in the iteration with *SUMX*, we use it to check the sales of the current customer against the average, previously stored in the variable.

> **Warning** The syntax based on *VAR* is simpler to read and maintain (it could also be faster). However, it is important to understand the different behavior using different syntaxes, also without *VAR*, regardless of the version of DAX you are using. If you don't understand and master automatic context transition, you will probably end up spending a lot of frustrating time looking at a formula, without fully understanding what value is being computed.

Context transition happens automatically when calling a measure and there is no way to avoid it. This means that the only way to avoid context transition when calling a measure is to expand its code. As an example, imagine that you wrote the previous code in a different way. Instead of using a variable, you define a measure called *AverageSales* that represents the average sales of customers, as in the following code:

```
[AverageSales] := AVERAGEX ( Customer, [SumOfSalesAmount] )

[SalesMoreThanAverage] :=
SUMX (
    Customer,
    IF (
        [SumOfSalesAmount] > [AverageSales],
        [SumOfSalesAmount]
    )
)
```

In the highlighted row, you use [AverageSales] to compute the average sales of customers. The problem is that—this time—you are calling a measure inside an iteration (*SUMX*) and this makes context transition happen. Thus, the result of [AverageSales] will not be the average sales over all customers, but only over the customer you are iterating. As a result, the test will always fail and the measure returns a *BLANK*, because the true branch of *IF* is never executed. If you want to avoid context transition, you need to expand the code of the measure, as in the following example:

```
[SalesMoreThanAverage] :=
SUMX (
    Customer,
    IF (
        [SumOfSalesAmount] > AVERAGEX ( Customer, [SumOfSalesAmount] ),
        [SumOfSalesAmount]
    )
)
```

Having replaced the measure invocation with the expanded code, now *SalesMoreThanAverage* returns correct results. Moreover, it is worth it to note that—in this case—there are two nested row contexts over Customer and three measure invocations. Two of them compute the sales of the currently iterated customer by *SUMX*, the other one (inside *AVERAGEX*) computes the sales of the currently iterated customer by *AVERAGEX*.

We will use these features extensively in the next chapters, when we will start to write complex DAX code to solve specific scenarios.

How many rows are visible after context transition?

Context transition transforms a row context into an equivalent filter context. This statement requires some clarification. The row context always contains a single row, whereas the filter context that *CALCULATE* creates after context transition might contain multiple rows, and the filter created by *CALCULATE* might affect one or more columns, depending on the table structure.

If the table has a primary key, defined in the model, then *CALCULATE* creates a filter context that filters only the primary key. In fact, such a filter context contains a single row, uniquely identified by the primary key. It is worth remembering that a primary key can be defined either by using the metadata of the table or by creating a relationship that has the table as a target. In both scenarios, context transition will filter a single column and, because the column is an identity for the table, a single row.

If the table does not have a primary key, then context transition creates a filter on all of the columns of the table. This might result in a filter that contains one or many rows, depending on the table content. In fact, if all the rows are different, then the filter context uniquely identifies a row. However, if there are identical rows in the table, then all of them will be included in the filter context.

In the following example, *Wrong Sales* and *Correct Sales* result in different values returned:

```
[Sales Amount] := SUMX ( Sales, Sales[Quantity] * Sales[Unit Price] )

[Wrong Sales] := SUMX ( Sales, [Sales Amount] )

[Correct Sales] := SUMX ( Sales, Sales[Quantity] * Sales[Unit Price] )
```

In fact, *Wrong Sales* iterates over Sales and, for each row, it computes *[Sales Amount]* for all the identical rows, while *Correct Sales* computes the amount for each individual row. As a result, if there are multiple identical rows in Sales, *Wrong Sales* results in a higher value.

When working with dimension tables, this is not normally an issue, because dimensions always have a primary key. In this case, the only row that is identical to the current one is the row itself. On fact tables or—in general—on tables that do not have a primary key, you need to consider that you might have duplicated rows; otherwise you might end up with unexpected results.

Understanding evaluation order of context transition

At this point of your learning experience, you know the difference between these two calculated columns, created in the Product table:

```
Product[SumOfUnitPrice] = CALCULATE ( SUM ( Product[Unit Price] ) )

Product[SumOfAllUnitPrice] = CALCULATE ( SUM ( Product[Unit Price] ), ALL ( Product ) )
```

They are both calculated columns and they both use the *CALCULATE* function. Thus, context transition happens for both.

SumOfUnitPrice should contain the value of *Unit Price* for the current row only. However, what is the value of *SumOfAllUnitPrice*? Intuitively, because there is an *ALL (Product)*, you should expect the column to contain the sum of all the unit prices. This is exactly what it computes. Nevertheless, if you follow the rules we have described so far, you see that there is something wrong.

In fact, *ALL (Product)* returns the entire Product table, effectively removing any filter from the filter context. However, at the same time, context transition should filter Product and make only one row visible. If you put these two conditions in *AND*, the context transition is much more restrictive and, as a result, it should win. So, why is the result the sum of all unit prices, instead of the current unit price only?

Because there is an order of precedence between the filter context created by context transition and the filter context created by conditions in *CALCULATE*. *CALCULATE* executes context transition before, and it applies the filters later. Thus, any of the conditions of *CALCULATE* can override the filter created by the context transition.

This behavior is harder to describe than to use. In fact, the two formulas above compute exactly what—intuitively—one would expect. Nevertheless, it is important to understand why this happens and, most important, that filters in *CALCULATE* overwrite filters coming from context transition (in other words, filter arguments are applied later).

Variables and evaluation contexts

In Chapter 2, "Introducing DAX," we showed the concept of variables, created by using expressions such as the following one:

```
VAR Denominator = SUMX ( Sales, Sales[Line Amount] - Sales[Line Cost] )
VAR Numerator = SUM ( Sales[Line Amount] )
RETURN
    DIVIDE ( Numerator, Denominator )
```

Variables are convenient to make the code easier to read and to avoid duplicating the same subexpression multiple times, but they have another very important use because of the way they work with evaluation context. In fact, DAX computes variables in the evaluation context where you defined them, not in the one where you use them.

This feature becomes extremely useful for complex formulas where you want to refer to values based on a previous evaluation context. Let's see this with an example. Imagine you want to use a pivot table to show the categories and, for each category, the number of high sales products. You define a product as being a high sale if its sales are more than 10 percent of the total sales of the category. You can see the result to achieve in Figure 5-17.

Row Labels	SalesAmount	NumOfProducts	HighSalesProducts
Audio	22,390.06	45	4
Cameras and camcorders	12,796.10	20	4
Music, Movies and Audio Books	11,930.50	50	3
(blank)	4,172,801.24	2,402	
Grand Total	**4,219,917.90**	**2,517**	

FIGURE 5-17 This pivot table shows how many high sales products are present in each category.

This measure is very easy to compute using variables. Moreover, the use of variables makes it simpler to read, too, as you can see in the following code:

```
[HighSalesProducts] :=
VAR
    TenPercentOfSales = [SalesAmount] * 0.1
RETURN
    COUNTROWS (
        FILTER (
            Product,
            [SalesAmount] >= TenPercentOfSales
        )
    )
```

The interesting part of this formula is that DAX computes the variable *TenPercentOfSales* outside of the *FILTER* iteration. If the evaluation of *TenPercentOfSales* was inside the iteration, it would compute the 10 percent of sales of the currently iterated product due to context transition, making the whole measure fail in computing its value. Instead, DAX computes the value outside of the iteration and then uses it inside, making it possible to refer to the value of an expression outside of the current filter context. If you were to write the same measure without variables, you should have written an expression as in the following one:

```
[HighSalesProductsCalculate] :=
COUNTROWS (
    FILTER (
        Product,
        [SalesAmount] >= CALCULATE (
            [SalesAmount],
            ALL ( Product ),
            'Product Category'
        ) * 0.1
    )
)
```

This latter code is much harder to read because, basically, you need to rebuild the previous evaluation context inside the iteration and this is not an easy task, even for seasoned DAX programmers. In fact, you will learn the details of the previous expression only in Chapter 10, where we will uncover all the details of filter contexts.

Note If, when reading the previous example, you discovered that you can use variables to compute something such as *EARLIER* for evaluation context, then we can happily welcome you to the elite of DAX programmers who understand evaluation context really well. If not, do not worry. It never happens during the first read of the chapter. There is still a lot of content in the book dedicated to these complex topics that will help you in acquiring the skills needed to master evaluation contexts.

Understanding circular dependencies

When you design a data model, you should pay attention to a complex topic, which is that of circular dependencies in formulas. In this section, you are going to learn what circular dependencies are and how to avoid them in your model.

Before speaking about circular dependencies, it is worth discussing simple, linear dependencies. Let's look at an example with the following calculated column:

```
Product[Profit] = Product[Unit Price] - Product[Unit Cost]
```

The new calculated column depends on two columns of the same table. In such a case, we say that the column Profit depends on *Unit Price* and *Unit Cost*. You might then create a new column, like *ProfitPct* with the following formula:

```
Product[ProfitPct] = Product[Profit] / Product[Unit Price]
```

It is clear that *ProfitPct* depends on *Profit* and *Unit Price*. Thus, when DAX computes the calculated columns in the table, it knows that it will compute *ProfitPct* only after *Profit*. Otherwise, it will not be able to compute a valid value for the *ProfitPct* formula.

Linear dependency is not something you should normally worry about. Internally, DAX uses it to detect the correct order of computation of calculated columns during the data model refresh. In a normal data model with many calculated columns, the dependency of calculations turns into a complex graph that, again, the engine handles gracefully.

Circular dependency is a situation that happens when a loop appears in this graph. For example, a clear situation where circular dependency appears is if you try to modify the definition of *Profit* to this formula:

```
Product[Profit] := Product[ProfitPct] * Product[Unit Price]
```

Because *ProfitPct* depends on *Profit* and, in this new formula, *Profit* depends on *ProfitPct*, DAX refuses to modify the formula and shows the error "A circular dependency was detected."

Up to now, you have learned what circular dependencies are from the point of view of the formulas; that is, you have detected the existence of a dependency looking at the expression, without paying attention to the table content. Nevertheless, there is a more subtle and complex type of dependency that you can introduce by using *CALCULATE*. Let us show this scenario with an example, starting from a subset of columns of Product, as shown in Figure 5-18. Please note that—for this example—we loaded only the Product table, removing all other tables from the model, in order to make the scenario more evident.

ProductKey	Product Name	Unit Price	Unit Cost
1722	MGS Zoo Tycoon 2: End range Species Expansion Pack E105	$56.00	$28.55
1723	MGS Age of Empires III: The Asian Dynasties E106	$56.00	$28.55
1724	MGS Fable: The Lost Chapters E107	$56.00	$28.55
1725	MGS Dungeon Siege II E105	$56.00	$28.55
1726	MGS Zoo Tycoon 2 E108	$56.00	$28.55
1727	MGS Rise of Nations: Gold Edition M300	$56.00	$25.75
1733	MGS Halo: Combat Evolved E109	$22.79	$11.62
1734	MGS Zoo Tycoon Complete Collection E110	$28.00	$14.28
1735	MGS Flight Simulator 2004: A Century of Flight E111	$28.00	$14.28
1736	MGS Rise of Nations E112	$28.00	$14.28
1737	MGS Freelancer E113	$28.00	$14.28
1738	MGS Impossible Creatures E114	$28.00	$14.28

FIGURE 5-18 This subset of columns of Product table is useful to understand circular dependencies.

We are interested in understanding the dependency list for a new calculated column that makes use of the *CALCULATE* function, as in the following one:

```
Product[SumOfUnitPrice] = CALCULATE ( SUM ( Product[Unit Price] ) )
```

At first glance, it might seem that the column depends from *Unit Price* only, as this is the only column used in the formula. Nevertheless, we used *CALCULATE* to transform the current row context into a filter context. Because we have not defined any relationship with the table and we did not set the primary key for it, when *CALCULATE* makes the context transition, it filters all the columns of the table. If we expand the meaning of the *CALCULATE* call, the formula really says:

> Sum the value of Unit Price for all the rows in the Product table that have the same value for ProductKey, Product Name, Unit Cost, and Unit Price.

If you read the formula in this way, it is now clear that the code depends on all of the columns of Product because the newly introduced filter context will filter all the columns of the table. You can see the resulting table in Figure 5-19.

ProductKey	Product Name	Unit Price	Unit Cost	SumOfUnitPrice
1722	MGS Zoo Tycoon 2: End range Species Expansion Pack E105	$56.00	$28.55	$56.00
1723	MGS Age of Empires III: The Asian Dynasties E106	$56.00	$28.55	$56.00
1724	MGS Fable: The Lost Chapters E107	$56.00	$28.55	$56.00
1725	MGS Dungeon Siege II E105	$56.00	$28.55	$56.00
1726	MGS Zoo Tycoon 2 E108	$56.00	$28.55	$56.00
1727	MGS Rise of Nations: Gold Edition M300	$56.00	$25.75	$56.00
1733	MGS Halo: Combat Evolved E109	$22.79	$11.62	$22.79
1734	MGS Zoo Tycoon Complete Collection E110	$28.00	$14.28	$28.00
1735	MGS Flight Simulator 2004: A Century of Flight E111	$28.00	$14.28	$28.00
1736	MGS Rise of Nations E112	$28.00	$14.28	$28.00
1737	MGS Freelancer E113	$28.00	$14.28	$28.00
1738	MGS Impossible Creatures E114	$28.00	$14.28	$28.00

FIGURE 5-19 Here you can see the Product table with the *SumOfUnitPrice* calculated column.

You might try to define a new calculated column, using the very same formula, in the same table. Consider defining *NewSumOfUnitPrice* with the following formula, which is identical to the previous one.

```
Product[NewSumOfUnitPrice] = CALCULATE ( SUM ( Product[Unit Price] ) )
```

Surprisingly, at this point, DAX raises an error saying it detected a circular dependency. It is strange because it has detected a circular dependency in the formula that it has not detected before, with the very same code. Something has changed indeed, and it is the number of columns in the table. If we were able to add the *NewSumOfUnitPrice* to the table, we would reach a situation where the two formulas have these meanings:

- **SumOfUnitPrice** Sum the value of *Unit Price* for all the rows in the Product table that have the same value for *ProductKey, Product Name, Unit Cost,* and *Unit Price,* and *NewSumOfUnitPrice.*

- **NewSumOfUnitPrice** Sum the value of *Unit Price* for all the rows in the Product table that have the same value for *ProductKey*, *Product Name*, *Unit Cost*, and *Unit Price*, and *SumOfUnitPrice*.

Calculated columns, as with any other column in the table, become part of the filter context introduced by *CALCULATE* and, therefore, all of the calculated columns are part of the dependencies list. If you read the previous definitions, it is clear that there is a circular dependency between the two formulas and this is the reason why DAX refuses to allow the creation of *NewSumOfUnitPrice*.

Understanding this error is not very easy. However, finding a solution is straightforward, even if not very intuitive. The problem is that if the table does not have a primary key, then any calculated column containing *CALCULATE* (or a call to any measure, which adds an automatic *CALCULATE*) creates a dependency from all of the columns of the table—including calculated columns. The scenario would be different if the table had a row identifier (a primary key, in database terms). If the table had a column which acts as a row identifier, then all the columns containing a *CALCULATE* function would depend on just the row identifier, reducing their dependency list to a single column.

In Product, the *ProductKey* column can uniquely identify each row, because it is the primary key. In order to mark Product Key as a row identifier there are two options:

- You can create a relationship from any table into Product using *ProductKey* as the destination column. Performing this operation will ensure that *ProductKey* is a unique value for Product.

- You can manually set the property of a row identifier for *ProductKey* column using the Table Behavior properties.

Either one of these operations tells the DAX engine that the table has a row identifier. In such a scenario, you can define the *NewSumOfUnitPrice* column avoiding circular dependency because both calculated columns using *CALCULATE* will depend from the new key only.

CALCULATE rules

It is useful to recap the way *CALCULATE* works. You can use this set of rules to test your knowledge of *CALCULATE*: If you can read and understand all of them, then you are on the right track to becoming a real DAX master.

- *CALCULATE* and *CALCULATETABLE* are the only functions in DAX that directly manipulate the filter context.

- *CALCULATE* has only one required parameter, which is the expression to evaluate. Other parameters (also known as filter arguments) are filters that it will use to build the new filter context; they could be omitted in case you only want to invoke *CALCULATE* to perform context transition.

- Filter arguments in *CALCULATE* can have three shapes:

  (a) Boolean conditions such as *Product[Color]* = "White".

(b) List of values for one column, in the form of a one-column table, as in *ALL (Product[Color])* or with more complex *FILTER* expressions like *FILTER (ALL (Product[Color], Product[Color]) = "White")*.

(c) List of rows for one table, as in *ALL (Product)* or with more complex *FILTER* conditions, like *FILTER (ALL (Product), Product[Color] = "White")*.

Conditions written using (a) or (b) can operate on a single column only. Conditions written using the (c) shape can work on any number of columns.

- All the filter arguments of *CALCULATE* are evaluated independently, then they are put in a logical *AND* together. Finally, they are used to determine the newly created filter context.

- The filter arguments of *CALCULATE* (from the second parameter onward) are evaluated in the original filter context and they can narrow, expand, or replace the scope of a calculation. For example, when using a direct Boolean expression as a parameter, *CALCULATE* replaces the original filter context, whereas when passing an expression that uses *FILTER* on a table, *CALCULATE* takes the original filter context into account. The first parameter of *CALCULATE* (the expression to evaluate) is evaluated in the newly created filter context.

- There is a precedence order between context transition and filter arguments of *CALCULATE*. *CALCULATE* applies the filters after it has performed context transition. Thus, filters can override the context created by the transition.

Introducing *ALLSELECTED*

ALLSELECTED is a very useful function whenever you want to perform computations using the page-filter or slicer selections in the pivot table as one of the parameters. Imagine, for example, that you want to build a report such as the one shown in Figure 5-20.

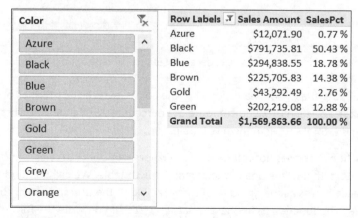

FIGURE 5-20 The percentage shown in the pivot table is computed against the total shown, not the total of all colors.

In this report, you show the percentage of the current row against the total of the column. What makes this percentage difficult to compute is the fact that the product color is used both as a slicer (in the example we removed some of the available colors) and on the rows. If you use the knowledge gained so far, you might try this formula:

```
[SalesPct] :=
DIVIDE (
    [Sales Amount],
    CALCULATE (
        [Sales Amount],
        ALL ( Product[Color] )
    )
)
```

Using *ALL (Product[Color])* you remove constraints from Color and you try to compute the total at the column level. Unfortunately, *ALL* removes all of the constraints, both the one coming from the row and the ones coming from the slicer, resulting in a wrong percentage. In Figure 5-21 you can see the result of the formula in a pivot table, where the grand total does not show 100 percent, but a smaller value.

Color		Row Labels	Sales Amount	SalesPct
		Azure	$12,071.90	0.29 %
Azure		Black	$791,735.81	18.76 %
Black		Blue	$294,838.55	6.99 %
Blue		Brown	$225,705.83	5.35 %
Brown		Gold	$43,292.49	1.03 %
Gold		Green	$202,219.08	4.79 %
Green		**Grand Total**	**$1,569,863.66**	**37.20 %**
Grey				
Orange				

FIGURE 5-21 The percentage computed using *ALL* is not correct, because it is a percentage against *ALL* colors.

The issue here is that you compute the denominator for all of the colors, even if the user has only selected some of them in the slicer. For each row, you compute the percentage of that line against a denominator that is bigger than the total shown in the pivot table.

What you need here is a function that does not return all of the colors, but only the ones selected in the original filter context, that is, the one of the complete pivot table. We call this kind of computation Visual Totals, because it uses as the grand total that is visible to the user instead of the total of the complete data model. The function to use here is *ALLSELECTED*. If you write the formula in this way:

```
[SalesPct] :=
DIVIDE (
    [Sales],
    CALCULATE (
        [Sales],
        ALLSELECTED ( Product[Color] )
    )
)
```

The result will be the correct one shown at the beginning of this section.

ALLSELECTED returns only the values that are visible in the original filter context, that is, the one of the pivot table. In other words, *ALLSELECTED* ignores filters on the rows and columns of the pivot table and considers the ones used to compute the grand total.

You can invoke *ALLSELECTED* with three different types of parameters:

- **Single column** As in *ALLSELECTED (Product[Color])*, which returns the originally selected colors.

- **Full table** As in *ALLSELECTED (Product)*, that will perform an *ALLSELECTED* operation on all the columns of the table, returning all the rows originally selected.

- **No parameters** You can also use *ALLSELECTED ()* with no parameters and it will perform *ALLSELECTED* on all of the tables in the data model, making it possible to compute the grand total of a pivot table, with no filters on rows and columns.

You will mainly use *ALLSELECTED* to compute percentages and ratios in a very dynamic way. In Chapter 10 we will go much deeper in the description of *ALLSELECTED*, which hides some complexities that we will cover later, when speaking about advanced evaluation contexts.

Understanding *USERELATIONSHIP*

Another functionality that is available with *CALCULATE* is that of activating a relationship during the evaluation of an expression. In fact, as you already know, a data model might contain both active and inactive relationships. You might have inactive relationships in the model because, for example, you have many relationships between two tables and you can keep only one active.

As an example, you might have order date and delivery date stored in your Sales table for each order. Typically, you want to perform analysis of sales based on the order date but, for some specific measures, you want to consider the delivery date. In such a case, you create two relationships between Sales and Date: one based on *OrderDateKey* and another one based on *DeliveryDateKey*. Only one of them can be active at a time and, because you typically analyze sales by their order date, you keep the relationship with *OrderDateKey* active, leaving the other one inactive. Then, you want to author a measure that shows the delivered value on a given date, in order to compare it with the ordered value. This new measure (*Delivered Amount*) should compute the sales amount using the inactive relationship, deactivating—at the same time—the relationship with the order date.

In this scenario, you can use *CALCULATE* with the *USERELATIONSHIP* keyword, as in the following code:

```
[Delivered Amount] :=
CALCULATE (
    [Sales Amount],
    USERELATIONSHIP ( Sales[DeliveryDateKey], Date[DateKey] )
)
```

The relationship between *DeliveryDateKey* and *DateKey* will be activated during the evaluation of *[Sales Amount]* and, in the meantime, the relationship with *OrderDateKey* will be deactivated. In Figure 5-22 you can see a pivot table showing the different values between *Sales Amount* based on the *OrderDateKey* and the new *Delivered Amount* measure.

Row Labels	Sales Amount	Delivered Amount
⊞ CY 2007	$1,617,722.61	$1,558,346.59
⊟ CY 2008	$1,242,993.34	$1,271,146.62
⊞ January 2008	$75,509.78	$122,078.36
⊞ February 2008	$68,983.60	$55,691.24
⊞ March 2008	$72,303.96	$76,708.71
⊞ April 2008	$127,865.28	$125,789.21
⊞ May 2008	$131,204.65	$108,230.19
⊞ June 2008	$97,021.46	$112,584.66
⊞ July 2008	$95,825.35	$103,397.66
⊞ August 2008	$152,927.10	$122,710.81
⊞ September 2008	$122,900.05	$155,754.79
⊞ October 2008	$61,768.48	$67,571.32
⊞ November 2008	$132,871.85	$117,856.05
⊞ December 2008	$103,811.78	$102,773.62
⊞ CY 2009	$1,359,201.95	$1,333,287.30
⊞ CY 2010		$57,137.39
Grand Total	$4,219,917.90	$4,219,917.90

FIGURE 5-22 The figure illustrates the difference between ordered and delivered sales.

When using *USERELATIONSHIP* to activate a relationship you need to be aware of a very important aspect: Relationships are defined when a table reference is invoked, not when *RELATED* or other relational functions are invoked.

For example, if you want to compute all amounts delivered in 2007, this formulation will not work:

```
[Delivered Amount in 2007] :=
CALCULATE (
    [Sales Amount],
    FILTER (
        Sales,
        CALCULATE (
            RELATED ( Date[CalendarYear] ),
            USERELATIONSHIP ( Sales[DeliveryDateKey], Date[DateKey] )
        ) = 2007
    )
)
```

The reason is that *FILTER* iterates the Sales table (invocation of the Sales table), and then, it evaluates the condition. During the evaluation of the condition it changes the active relationship, and then it invokes *RELATED*. However, the relationship between Sales and Date has been defined when Sales was invoked, not when *RELATED* is used.

If you want to perform a calculation such as the previous one, you need to rewrite the measure in the following way:

```
[Delivered Amount in 2007] :=
CALCULATE (
    [Sales Amount],
    FILTER (
        CALCULATETABLE (
            Sales,
            USERELATIONSHIP( Sales[DeliveryDateKey], Date[DateKey] )
        ),
        RELATED ( Date[Calendar Year] ) = 2007
    )
)
```

In this latter formulation, Sales is invoked after *CALCULATE* has activated the needed relationship. Therefore, the invocation of *RELATED* inside *FILTER* happens with the relationship with *Delivery-DateKey* active.

This behavior makes the use of nondefault relationships a complex operation in calculated columns expressions because there the invocation of the table is implicit in the calculated column definition and, therefore, you do not have control over it and you cannot change that behavior using *CALCULATE* and *USERELATIONSHIP*.

DAX examples

At this point of the book, you have a solid background in the DAX theory and it is time to start using DAX to solve some interesting scenarios. In this chapter we show some examples of DAX usage.

Be aware that the goal of the chapter is not that of providing ready-to-use patterns. For each scenario, we will build the formulas and describe the calculations with the intent of showing the process of solving a problem using DAX.

The goal of the chapter is to help you begin "thinking in DAX." In our experience, DAX becomes simple to use as soon as you acquire this unique skill. The way you describe an algorithm in DAX is very different from SQL, Microsoft Excel, MDX, or any other programming language. At the beginning, the feeling of students is always: "Yes, I understand the formula, but I would have never been able to write it alone." After some time, the feeling fades away and you will be able to write formulas more complex than those we show here.

Computing ratios and percentages

The first example is a very simple one, which we partially covered in the previous chapters. Computing percentages is probably one of the first kinds of calculation you will need to author, because it is a very common way of expressing trends and shares.

A percentage is always in the form of a division: the partial sum of a measure divided by the grand total of the same measure. For example, the percentage of sales against the total sales. A typical report containing percentages is the one shown in Figure 6-1.

In Figure 6-1, the percentage shown is the percentage against the grand total. In fact, the only cell where you can see 100 percent is the grand total. All remaining cells show a smaller percentage, that is, the contribution of that year and color to the grand total.

Color		Column Labels					
		CY 2007		CY 2008		Total Sales Amount	Total Sales %
		Row Labels	Sales Amount	Sales %	Sales Amount	Sales %	
Azure		Azure	$4,863.10	0.17 %	$4,480.80	0.16 %	$9,343.90	0.33 %
Black		Black	$282,020.06	9.86 %	$245,539.76	8.58 %	$527,559.82	18.44 %
Blue		Blue	$142,503.18	4.98 %	$76,597.95	2.68 %	$219,101.13	7.66 %
Brown		Brown	$68,737.05	2.40 %	$56,648.58	1.98 %	$125,385.63	4.38 %
Gold		Gold	$9,322.00	0.33 %	$17,475.00	0.61 %	$26,797.00	0.94 %
Green		Green	$85,164.89	2.98 %	$56,495.65	1.97 %	$141,660.54	4.95 %
Grey		Grey	$200,185.94	7.00 %	$210,735.39	7.37 %	$410,921.33	14.36 %
Orange		Orange	$14,779.34	0.52 %	$20,215.54	0.71 %	$34,994.88	1.22 %
		Pink	$77,438.69	2.71 %	$20,174.08	0.71 %	$97,612.77	3.41 %
		Purple	$224.00	0.01 %			$224.00	0.01 %
		Red	$57,453.06	2.01 %	$26,079.59	0.91 %	$83,532.65	2.92 %
		Silver	$430,786.04	15.06 %	$216,861.80	7.58 %	$647,647.84	22.64 %
		Silver Grey	$34,776.00	1.22 %	$12,122.60	0.42 %	$46,898.60	1.64 %
		Transparent	$126.42	0.00 %	$79.38	0.00 %	$205.80	0.01 %
		White	$207,955.56	7.27 %	$274,919.98	9.61 %	$482,875.54	16.88 %
		Yellow	$1,387.28	0.05 %	$4,567.24	0.16 %	$5,954.52	0.21 %
		Grand Total	$1,617,722.61	56.55 %	$1,242,993.34	43.45 %	$2,860,715.95	100.00 %

FIGURE 6-1 A typical report containing sales shown both in absolute value and as a percentage.

The canonical way of expressing such a measure is that of using a simple division:

```
[Sales %] :=
DIVIDE (
    [Sales Amount],
    CALCULATE ( [Sales Amount], ALLSELECTED () )
)
```

At the denominator, *CALCULATE* creates a filter context where the original context is visible, by using the *ALLSELECTED* function. You use *ALLSELECTED* in order to obey the filters that were set in the pivot table using slicers and filters.

Sometimes you do not want to compute only the percentage of sales against the grand total. For example, you might want to show, for each year, the percentage of sales of that color against the total of that year only, in order to produce a report such as the one in Figure 6-2.

In order to compute the total of the year, at the denominator, you need to restrict its filter context so that it contains the selected products and, for the year, only the currently visible ones. You can easily accomplish this by adding the *VALUES* function, which returns the values of a column as currently visible in the filter context:

```
[Yearly %] :=
DIVIDE (
    [Sales Amount],
    CALCULATE (
        [Sales Amount],
        ALLSELECTED (),
        VALUES ( Date[CalendarYear] )
    )
)
```

Row Labels	CY 2007 Sales Amount	Yearly %	CY 2008 Sales Amount	Yearly %	Total Sales Amount	Total Yearly %
Azure	$4,863.10	0.30 %	$4,480.80	0.36 %	$9,343.90	0.33 %
Black	$282,020.06	17.43 %	$245,539.76	19.75 %	$527,559.82	18.44 %
Blue	$142,503.18	8.81 %	$76,597.95	6.16 %	$219,101.13	7.66 %
Brown	$68,737.05	4.25 %	$56,648.58	4.56 %	$125,385.63	4.38 %
Gold	$9,322.00	0.58 %	$17,475.00	1.41 %	$26,797.00	0.94 %
Green	$85,164.89	5.26 %	$56,495.65	4.55 %	$141,660.54	4.95 %
Grey	$200,185.94	12.37 %	$210,735.39	16.95 %	$410,921.33	14.36 %
Orange	$14,779.34	0.91 %	$20,215.54	1.63 %	$34,994.88	1.22 %
Pink	$77,438.69	4.79 %	$20,174.08	1.62 %	$97,612.77	3.41 %
Purple	$224.00	0.01 %			$224.00	0.01 %
Red	$57,453.06	3.55 %	$26,079.59	2.10 %	$83,532.65	2.92 %
Silver	$430,786.04	26.63 %	$216,861.80	17.45 %	$647,647.84	22.64 %
Silver Grey	$34,776.00	2.15 %	$12,122.60	0.98 %	$46,898.60	1.64 %
Transparent	$126.42	0.01 %	$79.38	0.01 %	$205.80	0.01 %
White	$207,955.56	12.85 %	$274,919.98	22.12 %	$482,875.54	16.88 %
Yellow	$1,387.28	0.09 %	$4,567.24	0.37 %	$5,954.52	0.21 %
Grand Total	$1,617,722.61	100.00 %	$1,242,993.34	100.00 %	$2,860,715.95	100.00 %

FIGURE 6-2 In this report, the percentages shown are against the years' total, not the grand total.

It is worthwhile to remember that filters in *CALCULATE* are put in *AND* before they are applied to the model. Thus, the first *ALLSELECTED* will show the original filter context, while *VALUES* returns the currently visible years and, in each cell, it will contain that year only. The only exception will be at the grand total for the columns. There, inside each row, *VALUES* returns the two visible years.

As you have seen, so far we have used a pattern to compute the denominator:

1. Restore the original filter context.

2. Re-apply any filter to restrict the original context (for example, to the current year).

You can also apply the opposite pattern, with similar results, that is, instead of restoring the original filter and then re-applying filters, you can start with the current filter context removing filters from the columns you want to total. For example, to reproduce the report in Figure 6-1 you can restore the filters on Color and Calendar Year, leaving other filters untouched, as in:

```
[Yearly %] :=
DIVIDE (
    [Sales Amount],
    CALCULATE (
        [Sales Amount],
        ALLSELECTED ( Product[Color] ),
        ALLSELECTED ( Date[CalendarYear] )
    )
)
```

You can also obtain the measure of Figure 6-2 with this code, which removes the filter from the color only, keeping the filter on the year untouched:

```
[Yearly %-2] :=
DIVIDE (
    [Sales Amount],
    CALCULATE (
        [Sales Amount],
        ALLSELECTED ( Product[Color] )
    )
)
```

Although these measures look similar, meaning that in the pivot table shown as an example they return the same values, there is a big difference among them. In fact, this latter version of Yearly % restores the original filter on the color but keeps any other filter in place. If year is the only column filtered, the result is the same but, as soon as you add more filters on the calendar table, the two measures return different values, as you can see in Figure 6-3.

Color		Column Labels .T					
		CY 2007		CY 2008		Total Yearly %	Total Yearly %-2
Azure		Row Labels .T Yearly %	Yearly %-2	Yearly %	Yearly %-2		
Black		⊟January	17.05 %	100.00 %	7.59 %	100.00 %	13.21 %	100.00 %
Blue		Blue	16.56 %	97.13 %	6.62 %	87.20 %	12.53 %	94.81 %
Brown		Brown	0.49 %	2.87 %			0.29 %	2.20 %
Gold		Gold			0.97 %	12.80 %	0.39 %	2.99 %
Green		⊟February	0.29 %	100.00 %	5.79 %	100.00 %	2.52 %	100.00 %
Grey		Blue	0.08 %	28.11 %	3.10 %	53.61 %	1.31 %	51.87 %
Orange		Brown	0.21 %	71.89 %	2.69 %	46.39 %	1.21 %	48.13 %
		⊟March	2.88 %	100.00 %	1.48 %	100.00 %	2.31 %	100.00 %
		Blue	0.77 %	26.86 %	0.55 %	37.31 %	0.68 %	29.58 %
		Brown	0.85 %	29.69 %	0.93 %	62.69 %	0.88 %	38.28 %
		Gold	1.25 %	43.45 %			0.74 %	32.14 %

FIGURE 6-3 If you add more filters to the pivot table, the two measures return different values.

As you can see, *Yearly %* returns the percentage of sales against the year, whereas *Yearly %-2* returns the percentage against the month, because we added the month to the pivot table. It is not that one number is correct and the other one is wrong. As usual, it depends from what number you want to compute.

The important thing to remember here is that, whenever you are computing percentages, you need to be very clear on what the denominator needs to be and what should happen when the user adds more filters to the pivot table or the report.

Computing cumulative totals

Another pattern that you will probably find useful many times is the cumulative total pattern. We speak about cumulative total whenever you have a set of transactions and you are interested in accumulating their value over some sequence, typically the time. For example, you might want to compute the total sales of a product over all time, as an accumulating total, or the total number of distinct customers you had over time, again as an accumulating value.

Let's start by analyzing a simple pivot table that shows the number of products sold over time. You can see it in Figure 6-4.

Row Labels	NumOfProducts
⊟ CY 2007	5,491
⊞ January 2007	440
⊞ February 2007	472
⊞ March 2007	485
⊞ April 2007	511
⊞ May 2007	493
⊞ June 2007	425
⊞ July 2007	477
⊞ August 2007	444
⊞ September 2007	452
⊞ October 2007	389
⊞ November 2007	408
⊞ December 2007	495
⊞ CY 2008	5,058
⊞ CY 2009	6,949
Grand Total	17,498

FIGURE 6-4 This pivot table shows the total number of products sold in each year and month.

The measure shown is a very simple one:

```
[NumOfProducts] := SUM ( Sales[Quantity] )
```

You know that this measure sums the *Quantity* column from Sales for all the rows that are visible in the current filter context. If, for example, you take the value of May 2007, then the filter context has one filter on the year (2007), and one filter for the month (May 2007). The filter works on Date, which has a one-to-many relationship with Sales. Thus, it filters Sales, showing only the sales of May 2007.

If you want to compute an accumulating total, you have to find a new filter context that, instead of filtering only May 2007, filters all the periods that are before the end of May 2007. As simple as it is, this sentence hides a bigger complexity. In fact, what you need to do is:

1.   Determine the end of the current visible dates, shown in the example at the end of May 2007.

2.   Using that value, create a filter that shows all the dates that are before the end of May 2007.

The hidden complexity lies in the fact that the new filter context depends on the current one. Moreover, it is worth noting that the new filter context will be larger than the original one, because it will contain, for example, all the dates in 2007 and earlier. In Figure 6-5, you can see the set of dates that you need to retrieve in order to compute the cumulative number of products sold.

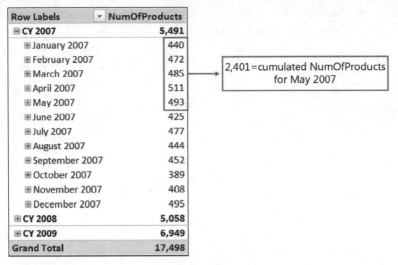

Row Labels	NumOfProducts
⊟ CY 2007	5,491
⊞ January 2007	440
⊞ February 2007	472
⊞ March 2007	485
⊞ April 2007	511
⊞ May 2007	493
⊞ June 2007	425
⊞ July 2007	477
⊞ August 2007	444
⊞ September 2007	452
⊞ October 2007	389
⊞ November 2007	408
⊞ December 2007	495
⊞ CY 2008	5,058
⊞ CY 2009	6,949
Grand Total	17,498

2,401=cumulated NumOfProducts for May 2007

FIGURE 6-5 Cumulative number of products sold needs to take into account dates before the end of the current one.

With the algorithm in mind, it is now time to look at the formula that solves the scenario:

```
[CumulativeProducts] :=
CALCULATE (
    SUM ( Sales[Quantity] ),
    FILTER (
        ALL ( 'Date' ),
        'Date'[Datekey] <= MAX ( 'Date'[Datekey] )
    )
)
```

The core of the formula is the new filter you set using *CALCULATE*, highlighted in bold. You have to focus your attention on two important points about this expression:

- The use of *ALL (Date)* in order to ignore the current context. In fact, *FILTER* iterates over the entire table, analyzing dates that are outside of the current filter context. In this way, it will return dates that are lower than or equal to the current filter (which, in our example, contains only May 2007). This also makes the calculation work with any other columns of the Date table such as *Weeks* or *Quarters*.

- The comparison of *Date[DateKey]* against *MAX (Date[DateKey])*. When you are not familiar with DAX, these expressions look strange. However, if you recall the exact meaning of *MAX*, you see that it means "the maximum value of DateKey in the current context." Because the expression is part of *CALCULATE* filters, it still works in the original filter context (that is, May 2007). Therefore, the maximum date will be the last day of May 2007. On the other hand, the expression *Date[DateKey]* is a column name, meaning "the value of DateKey in the current row context." Because the current row context is the one created by *FILTER* during its iteration, the expression reads as: "filter all the dates that are lower than or equal to the last day of May 2007."

You can see the formula in action in Figure 6-6.

Row Labels	NumOfProducts	CumulativeProducts
⊟ CY 2007	5,491	5,491
⊞ January 2007	440	440
⊞ February 2007	472	912
⊞ March 2007	485	1,397
⊞ April 2007	511	1,908
⊞ May 2007	493	2,401
⊞ June 2007	425	2,826
⊞ July 2007	477	3,303
⊞ August 2007	444	3,747
⊞ September 2007	452	4,199
⊞ October 2007	389	4,588
⊞ November 2007	408	4,996
⊞ December 2007	495	5,491
⊞ CY 2008	5,058	10,549
⊞ CY 2009	6,949	17,498
⊞ CY 2010		17,498
⊞ CY 2011		17,498
Grand Total	17,498	17,498

FIGURE 6-6 *CumulativeProducts* sums the values until the current date.

Although this formula computes correct values, accumulating products over time, it has an issue. In fact, it shows data for 2010 and later, even if there is no data in our database for 2010. In general, it will show data for future periods. Its behavior is correct because the cumulative number of products sold in the future is, with the present knowledge, the total number of sales so far. Nevertheless, you probably do not want to show these numbers.

You can remove the unwanted rows by replacing them with a blank. In fact, as you might already know, pivot tables by default hide rows where all the values are blank (same applies also to columns). To hide the rows you can simply use an *IF* function to check if there are sales in the current context, as in the following code:

```
[CumulativeProducts] :=
IF (
    COUNTROWS ( Sales ) > 0,
    CALCULATE (
        SUM ( Sales[Quantity] ),
        FILTER (
            ALL ( 'Date' ),
            'Date'[Datekey] <= MAX ( 'Date'[Datekey] )
        )
    )
)
```

In this measure, we rely on the fact that the else branch of *IF* returns a blank if it is missing. You will learn many more formulas similar to this one, in Chapter 7, "Time intelligence functions." Our goal, here, is not that of learning a pattern, but to familiarize you with the idea of computing values over different filter contexts.

Using ABC (Pareto) classification

Calculated columns are stored inside the database. This is a simple fact that you learned during the first chapters of this book, and, at this point, it should no longer surprise you. That said, this simple fact opens new ways of modeling data, and in this section you look at a scenario that you can solve very efficiently with calculated columns.

As an example of the use of calculated columns, you will learn how to solve the scenario of ABC analysis using DAX. ABC analysis is a variation of the Pareto principle, and it is also known as ABC/ Pareto Analysis. This is a very common technique to determine the core business of a company, in terms of best products or best customers. In the example, we focus on products.

The goal of ABC analysis is to assign to each product a category (A, B, or C) by which:

- Products in class A account for 70 percent of the profits.

- Products in class B account for 20 percent of the profits.

- Products in class C account for the remaining 10 percent of the profits.

The goal of ABC analysis is to identify which products have a significant impact on the overall business so that managers can focus their effort on them. You can find more information on ABC analysis at *http://en.wikipedia.org/wiki/ABC_analysis*.

The ABC class of a product needs to be stored in a physical column, because you want to use it to perform analysis on products slicing information by class. For example, in Figure 6-7 you can see a simple pivot table using ABC class on the rows.

Row Labels	NumOfProducts	Sales Amount
A	221	$2,859,704.50
B	286	$896,792.41
C	2,010	$463,420.99
Grand Total	**2,517**	**$4,219,917.90**

FIGURE 6-7 This simple pivot table shows an analysis of products and profits segmented by ABC class.

Products in class A are the core business. Products in class B are less important, but still vital for the company, whereas products in class C are good candidates for removal, because there are many of them and the profits are tiny when compared with the core products.

The definition of ABC is very simple. The implementation, on the other hand, requires some more efforts. Intuitively, you can compute the ABC class by sorting the products based on the total profit and then assign classes based on their position in the rank. The problem is that the very concept of sort order is missing in DAX. Thus, you need to find a way to determine the ranking position of a product without relying on sort. Let's follow the steps, one at a time. The first value we need is the total profit for each product. You can compute it as a calculated column in the Product table very easily:

```
Product[TotalProfit] =
CALCULATE (
    SUMX (
        Sales,
        Sales[Quantity] * ( Sales[Unit Price] - Sales[Unit Cost] )
    )
)
```

This creates a new calculated column in Product that contains the total profit for each row. As we said earlier, there is no way to physically sort the table by this column. DAX requires you to think in a slightly different way: instead of sorting, you need to think in terms of sets and filters. If a product belongs to class A, for example, it means that it contributes to the first 70 percent of the sales. The idea is to compute, for each product, the cumulative total of sales of the product and of all the products that had higher sales.

Thus, the top product's cumulative total will include only its own sales. The second top product's cumulative total will be the sum of the top product's plus its own sales. This is for all the products. Once you computed the cumulative total sales for each product, it will be easy to transform it into an ABC class. In fact, if the ratio between the cumulative sales and the total sales is less than 70 percent, then it means that the product belongs to class A. If, on the other hand, it is less than 90 percent, then it is in class B. Otherwise, if that ratio is higher than 90 percent, the product is in class C.

This part is the only complex part of ABC calculation. It is hard not because the DAX code is complex, but because it forces you to think in a different way. Let's review the code of the *IncrementalProfit* calculated column:

```
Product[IncrementalProfit] =
VAR
    CurrentProfit = Product[TotalProfit]
RETURN
    SUMX (
        FILTER (
            Product,
            Product[TotalProfit] >= CurrentProfit
        ),
        Product[TotalProfit]
    )
```

This calculated column is based on the previous one, *TotalProfit*. The inner filter retrieves the products that have a total profit higher than or equal to the current one. In other words, it retrieves the products that made more profit than the current one (including the current one). Once *FILTER* returns this list of products, the outer *SUMX* sums their total profit.

Using *EARLIER* instead of variables

You can author the previous formula without using variables, by using the *EARLIER* function, as in the following code:

```
Product[IncrementalProfit] =
SUMX (
    FILTER (
        Product,
        Product[TotalProfit] >= EARLIER (Product[TotalProfit] )
    ),
    Product[TotalProfit]
)
```

Generally, we prefer using variables whenever possible, because the code is much more readable and easy to maintain over time. However, if you use a version of DAX that does not support variables, you have to use the *EARLIER* version.

You can see the behavior of *IncrementalProfit* in Figure 6-8.

Product Name	TotalProfit	IncrementalProfit
Adventure Works 26" 720p LCD HDTV M140 Silver	$96,209.15	$96,209.15
Contoso Telephoto Conversion Lens X400 Silver	$61,270.44	$157,479.59
A. Datum SLR Camera X137 Grey	$59,534.92	$217,014.51
Fabrikam Refrigerator 24.7CuFt X9800 White	$53,494.25	$270,508.76
NT Washer & Dryer 27in L2700 Blue	$35,478.80	$305,987.56
Litware Refrigerator 24.7CuFt X980 Brown	$34,236.32	$340,223.88
NT Washer & Dryer 24in M2400 Green	$33,403.30	$373,627.18
Litware Refrigerator 24.7CuFt X980 White	$32,096.55	$405,723.73

FIGURE 6-8 *IncrementalProfit* contains the profit of all the products with a profit higher than the current one.

At this point, converting the incremental profit into the ABC class is straightforward. First, you have to transform the incremental profit into a percentage over the total profit, by making a simple division:

```
Product[IncrementalPct] =
DIVIDE (
    Product[IncrementalProfit],
    SUM ( Product[TotalProfit] )
)
```

Because *SUM* at the denominator is outside of any *CALCULATE*, such a sum is the grand total of profits, whereas the *IncrementalProfit* is the running total of the row inside which DAX evaluates the formula. The *IncrementalPct* column indicates the percentage of profits that the product produces, along with all the higher profitability products. You can see the new column in Figure 6-9.

Product Code	Product Name	TotalProfit	IncrementalProfit	IncrementalPct
0201038	Adventure Works 26" 720p LCD HDTV M140 Silver	$96,209.15	$96,209.15	3.99 %
0406047	Contoso Telephoto Conversion Lens X400 Silver	$61,270.44	$157,479.59	6.52 %
0402009	A. Datum SLR Camera X137 Grey	$59,534.92	$217,014.51	8.99 %
0802001	Fabrikam Refrigerator 24.7CuFt X9800 White	$53,494.25	$270,508.76	11.20 %
0801031	NT Washer & Dryer 27in L2700 Blue	$35,478.80	$305,987.56	12.67 %
0802049	Litware Refrigerator 24.7CuFt X980 Brown	$34,236.32	$340,223.88	14.09 %
0801038	NT Washer & Dryer 24in M2400 Green	$33,403.30	$373,627.18	15.48 %
0802043	Litware Refrigerator 24.7CuFt X980 White	$32,096.55	$405,723.73	16.81 %

FIGURE 6-9 *IncrementalPct* transforms *IncrementalProfit* in a percentage against all profits.

Reading the table, you can see that the most profitable product is responsible for 3.99 percent of total profits. The first two products, together, make 6.52 percent, and so on.

The final step is to convert this percentage in the ABC segment, which you can accomplish with a very simple *IF* statement:

```
Product[ABC Class] =
IF (
    Product[IncrementalPct] <= 0.7,
    "A",
    IF (
        Product[IncrementalPct] <= 0.9,
        "B",
        "C"
    )
)
```

Because *ABC Class* is a calculated column, it is stored inside the database, and you can use it on slicers, filters, and rows or columns to produce reports.

In case you are interested in computing the ABC class using a different measure, for example using profit of a specific year, all you need to modify is the code that computes the *TotalProfit* column, using, for example, a different filter:

```
Product[TotalProfit] =
CALCULATE (
    SUMX (
        Sales,
        Sales[Quantity] * ( Sales[Unit Price] - Sales[Unit Cost] )
    ),
    Date[Calendar Year] = "CY2008"
)
```

Other variations of ABC analysis are worth mentioning here, mostly for educational purposes. In fact, computing the ABC class for all the products is somewhat easy but simple variations typically hide much complexity.

For example, you might want to compute the ABC class for product category. The segmentation we computed so far assigns to each product the ABC class considering all the products in the classification. However, if you put a slicer for category, you will retrieve the product of that category with the global ABC class. Computing the class by category means assigning to each product its class, computing the values for that category only.

Thus, you will have ABC class for cellular phones, ABC class for TV sets, and so on. This kind of analysis lets you focus on the most important products for a specific category. We will see two variations of this analysis. The first one, which is simpler, uses a denormalized column in the Product table Category, which you can define with the following code:

```
Product[Category] =
    RELATED ( 'ProductCategory'[Category] )
```

The *TotalProfit* column definition is the same as before, because it computes the sales for a specific product. The difference starts with the calculation of *IncrementalProfit*. In fact, to compute the *IncrementalProfit* column, you take into account only products with the same category of the current one. Moreover, instead of using *SUMX* and *FILTER*, as we did in the previous example, we can now dare to write some more elegant DAX:

```
Product[IncrementalProfit] =
CALCULATE (
    SUM ( Product[TotalProfit] ),
    ALLEXCEPT ( Product, 'Product'[Category] ),
    Product[TotalProfit] >= EARLIER ( Product[TotalProfit] )
)
```

Despite being a short expression, this formula hides a lot of complexity and it is worth some words of explanation.

- The outer *CALCULATE* will perform a context transition. Its internal expression (sum of total profit) should compute the value of total profit for the current line only. However, context transition does not have precedence over the additional filters of *CALCULATE*. Thus, the goal of the additional filter will be that of creating a filter context such that the inner *SUM* will compute the incremental profit within the current category only.

- *ALLEXCEPT* removes all the filters from the table, except for the columns specified in its arguments. Because we use *ALLEXCEPT* on Product, apart from the product category, this means that all the filters coming from the context transition will be removed, keeping only the one on *ProductCategory*. In other words, we are asking to compute the sum of total profit for all the products with the same category as the current one.

- The second condition, which will be in *AND* with the first one, filters the products where the total profit is greater or equal than the current total profit, calculated with *EARLIER*. This looks strange because, as you might remember, *EARLIER* is useful whenever you have nested row contexts. In this formula, there seems to be no other row context, apart from the one created by the calculated column definition.

   However, you might also recall that the condition:

```
Product[TotalProfit] >= EARLIER ( Product[TotalProfit] )
```

   corresponds to this table expression:

```
FILTER (
    ALL ( Product[TotalProfit] ),
    Product[TotalProfit] >= EARLIER ( Product[TotalProfit] )
)
```

   In the expanded version, it is now evident that there are two nested row contexts on Product: one created by *FILTER* and one created by the calculated column definition, hence the need to use *EARLIER*.

This formula is probably not the first one that will come to your mind to solve the problem. We decided to use this formula because it shows some very common and elegant patterns to describe the sets of data on which you want to compute values. Once you get used to this way of expressing formulas, the *IncrementalPct* definition should look straightforward:

```
Product[IncrementalPct] =
DIVIDE (
    Product[IncrementalProfit],
    CALCULATE (
        SUM ( Product[TotalProfit] ),
        ALLEXCEPT ( Product, Product[Category] )
    )
)
```

In order to transform the incremental profit into a percentage, we again used *ALLEXCEPT* as the denominator to compute the sum of total profit only for the products of the current category. Take your time to carefully read and understand these formulas; they are useful to help your mind adapt to the way DAX code looks and works.

In Figure 6-10 you can see these calculated columns in the Product table.

Category	Product Name	TotalProfit	IncrementalProfit	IncrementalPct
TV and Video	Adventure Works 26" 720p LCD HDTV M140 Silver	$96,209.15	$96,209.15	27.26 %
Cameras and camcor...	Contoso Telephoto Conversion Lens X400 Silver	$61,270.44	$61,270.44	11.58 %
Cameras and camcor...	A. Datum SLR Camera X137 Grey	$59,534.92	$120,805.36	22.83 %
Home Appliances	Fabrikam Refrigerator 24.7CuFt X9800 White	$53,494.25	$53,494.25	6.64 %
Home Appliances	NT Washer & Dryer 27in L2700 Blue	$35,478.80	$88,973.05	11.04 %
Home Appliances	Litware Refrigerator 24.7CuFt X980 Brown	$34,236.32	$123,209.37	15.29 %
Home Appliances	NT Washer & Dryer 24in M2400 Green	$33,403.30	$156,612.67	19.44 %
Home Appliances	Litware Refrigerator 24.7CuFt X980 White	$32,096.55	$188,709.22	23.43 %

FIGURE 6-10 Values for ABC classification are computed for each category.

You can see that, now, the incremental percentage does not grow linearly as it did with the global ABC class. The first product, for example, is responsible for 27.67 percent of the margin on TV and Video, whereas the second one is responsible for 11.58 percent of the margin of Cameras and camcorders.

You can easily use this *ABC class* to show, for a specific category, the segmentation in classes and/or the specific products that belong to a class, as you can see in Figure 6-11.

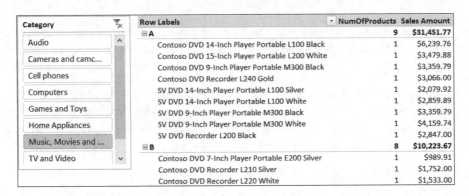

FIGURE 6-11 Using the *ABC class* for category, you can see the most important products for each category.

If your data model is more normalized, that is, you do not have columns in Product that contain the category, then the formulas tend to be a bit more complex. The reason is that you can no longer filter only Product. Instead, you will need to put (or remove) the filters on related tables. As it happened with the previous model, the only two columns requiring an adjustment are *Incremental-Profit* and *IncrementalPct*, which you can see here:

```
Product[IncrementalProfit] =
CALCULATE (
    SUM ( Product[TotalProfit] ),
    FILTER (
        Product,
        RELATED ( 'Product Category'[ProductCategoryKey] ) =
        EARLIER ( RELATED ( 'Product Category'[ProductCategoryKey] ) )
```

```
    ),
    Product[TotalProfit] >= EARLIER ( Product[TotalProfit] )
)

Product[IncrementalPct] =
DIVIDE (
    Product[IncrementalProfit],
    CALCULATE (
        SUM ( Product[TotalProfit] ),
        FILTER (
            Product,
            RELATED ( 'Product Category'[ProductCategoryKey] ) =
            EARLIER ( RELATED ( 'Product Category'[ProductCategoryKey] ) )
        )
    )
)
```

We highlighted the *FILTER* function that retrieves the product with the same category of the current one. It is worth it to note the use of *EARLIER (RELATED ( ))*, which retrieves the product category key using the relationship starting from the current row in the previous row context.

Let's briefly recap what you learned with the ABC classification example:

- The use of calculated columns as a modeling tool. In fact, you can put very complex logic in calculated columns that, being computed at process time, can execute complex calculations without affecting the speed of the model.

- Because you can neither sort data, nor retrieve values of the previous row (as you would, for example, in Excel), there is the need to define the sets on which you want to work using sets, defined with *FILTER*.

- The use of *ALLEXCEPT*, to remove all filters from a table, apart from some columns.

- *EARLIER* is very useful whenever you want to filter one table based on the current value of a column of the same table. Moreover, you can also use *EARLIER (RELATED ( ))* to grab values from related tables, using the previous row's context.

ABC is an interesting example of how to produce segmentation using calculated columns. We suggest you study this example in depth, because it contains many interesting details that will prove useful later in the book and in your everyday DAX authoring.

Computing sales per day and working day

Another interesting example of how to compute values in DAX, and that comes up frequently in the design of analytical models, is that of performing calculations over working days. In the next chapter, you will learn many details about time intelligence calculations; here we want to focus on a simpler scenario.

You want to produce a report such as the one shown in Figure 6-12.

Row Labels	Sales Amount	NumOfDays	DailySales	NumOfWorkingDays	WorkDailySales
⊟ CY 2007	$1,617,722.61	365	$4,432.12	261	$6,198.17
⊟ Q1-2007	$374,146.58	90	$4,157.18	65	$5,756.10
⊞ January 2007	$117,679.75	31	$3,796.12	23	$5,116.51
⊞ February 2007	$123,397.23	28	$4,407.04	20	$6,169.86
⊞ March 2007	$133,069.60	31	$4,292.57	22	$6,048.62
⊟ Q2-2007	$384,800.65	91	$4,228.58	65	$5,920.01
⊞ April 2007	$129,869.42	30	$4,328.98	21	$6,184.26
⊞ May 2007	$128,362.03	31	$4,140.71	23	$5,580.96
⊞ June 2007	$126,569.20	30	$4,218.97	21	$6,027.10
⊞ Q3-2007	$402,134.45	92	$4,371.03	65	$6,186.68
⊞ Q4-2007	$456,640.93	92	$4,963.49	66	$6,918.80
⊞ CY 2008	$1,242,993.34	366	$3,396.16	262	$4,744.25
Grand Total	$2,860,715.95	731	$3,913.43	523	$5,469.82

FIGURE 6-12 In this pivot table you can see sales divided by days and by working days.

The numbers shown have different meanings:

- *Sales Amount* is the total sales in the period.

- *DailySales* is the average amount sold by day.

- *WorkDailySales* is the average amount sold by working day, and it accounts for nonworking days, which are not expected to be profitable.

Following is the definition of these measures:

```
[NumOfDays] :=
COUNTROWS ( Date )

[NumOfWorkingDays] :=
CALCULATE ( [NumOfDays], Date[WorkingDay] = "WorkDay" )

[Sales Amount] :=
SUMX ( Sales, Sales[Quantity] * Sales[Unit Price] )

[DailySales] :=
DIVIDE ( [Sales Amount], [NumOfDays] )

[WorkDailySales] :=
DIVIDE ( [Sales Amount], [NumOfWorkingDays] )
```

These measures are very simple, but they hide some problems that we have to fix. In fact, in the previous picture, we filtered only two years: 2007 and 2008. The numbers made perfect sense. If we remove the filter, so as to show all the years, the problem becomes evident, as you can see in Figure 6-13.

Row Labels	Sales Amount	NumOfDays	DailySales	NumOfWorkingDays	WorkDailySales
⊞ CY 2005		365		260	
⊞ CY 2006		365		260	
⊟ CY 2007	$1,617,722.61	365	$4,432.12	261	$6,198.17
⊟ Q1-2007	$374,146.58	90	$4,157.18	65	$5,756.10
⊞ January 2007	$117,679.75	31	$3,796.12	23	$5,116.51
⊞ February 2007	$123,397.23	28	$4,407.04	20	$6,169.86
⊞ March 2007	$133,069.60	31	$4,292.57	22	$6,048.62
⊟ Q2-2007	$384,800.65	91	$4,228.58	65	$5,920.01
⊞ April 2007	$129,869.42	30	$4,328.98	21	$6,184.26
⊞ May 2007	$128,362.03	31	$4,140.71	23	$5,580.96
⊞ June 2007	$126,569.20	30	$4,218.97	21	$6,027.10
⊞ Q3-2007	$402,134.45	92	$4,371.03	65	$6,186.68
⊞ Q4-2007	$456,640.93	92	$4,963.49	66	$6,918.80
⊞ CY 2008	$1,242,993.34	366	$3,396.16	262	$4,744.25
⊟ CY 2009	$1,359,201.95	365	$3,723.84	261	$5,207.67
⊞ Q1-2009	$226,952.53	90	$2,521.69	64	$3,546.13
⊞ Q2-2009	$376,454.07	91	$4,136.86	65	$5,791.60
⊞ Q3-2009	$349,803.24	92	$3,802.21	66	$5,300.05
⊞ Q4-2009	$405,992.11	92	$4,412.96	66	$6,151.40
⊞ CY 2010		365		261	
⊞ CY 2011		365		260	
Grand Total	$4,219,917.90	2,556	$1,650.99	1,825	$2,312.28

FIGURE 6-13 The grand total of this pivot table shows wrong values.

If you look at the grand total of both *DailySales* and *WorkDailySales*, you immediately see that the numbers are wrong. In fact, they cannot be an average of the values shown in the rows. The problem should be easy to understand, because in the pivot table we are showing the number of days and the number of working days. At the grand total, we are accounting for periods in which there are no sales and, because the number of days is at the denominator, the final value is lower than expected.

Instead of showing you the correct formula immediately, in this scenario we prefer to show you several trials, in order to have the opportunity of looking at the effects of choosing the wrong solution to the problem. At the end, of course, we will provide the correct formula.

Because the two measures share the same issue, let us focus on *DailySales* and, when we have corrected this formula, we will bring the same update to *NumOfWorkingDays*.

A first trial could be clearing the number of days when there are no sales. Thus, you might try this new formula for *NumOfDays*:

```
[NumOfDays] :=
IF (
    [Sales Amount] > 0,
    COUNTROWS ( Date )
)
```

This update will make the pivot table look better, because rows with no sales will disappear from it, but it does not fix the grand total. Thus, it is not only wrong, but also misleading, because it makes the problem less evident, as you can see in Figure 6-14.

Row Labels	Sales Amount	NumOfDays	DailySales
⊟ CY 2007	$1,617,722.61	365	$4,432.12
⊞ Q1-2007	$374,146.58	90	$4,157.18
⊞ Q2-2007	$384,800.65	91	$4,228.58
⊞ Q3-2007	$402,134.45	92	$4,371.03
⊞ Q4-2007	$456,640.93	92	$4,963.49
⊞ CY 2008	$1,242,993.34	366	$3,396.16
⊟ CY 2009	$1,359,201.95	365	$3,723.84
⊞ Q1-2009	$226,952.53	90	$2,521.69
⊞ Q2-2009	$376,454.07	91	$4,136.86
⊞ Q3-2009	$349,803.24	92	$3,802.21
⊞ Q4-2009	$405,992.11	92	$4,412.96
Grand Total	$4,219,917.90	2,556	$1,650.99

FIGURE 6-14 Rows of periods without sales disappeared, but the grand total is still wrong.

As you can see, the grand total is still wrong, even if all the rows with no sales disappeared from the pivot table. They disappeared because we set *NumOfDays* to Blank, hence the pivot table hides the rows. At the grand total, on the other hand, the value of sales is greater than zero, so our formula still takes into account all of the days. The first trial is clearly going in the wrong direction.

This measure is suffering from a problem that has a clear pattern: we call it "granularity mismatch." If you look carefully at the numbers, they are correct at the month level and at the year level; they are wrong only at the grand total. The reason is that, for some years, there are no sales. We do not want to count those years. Thus, we say that at year granularity the numbers are correct, whereas at the grand total granularity the numbers are wrong. The issue, here, is that we need to compute the formula at the correct granularity, and then consolidate the results in a single value. You cannot compute this kind of measure at higher granularities.

This raises a problem: What is the correct granularity? It may be the year, the month, the day. It all depends on the business rules, and it is something you need to define in the business rules, so as to set the correct expectations. While we are looking at errors at the grand total, but we are still happy with the yearly values, we can set the granularity at the year level, using this new formula:

```
[DailySales] :=
DIVIDE (
    [Sales Amount],
    SUMX (
        VALUES ( 'Date'[Calendar Year] ),
        IF (
            [Sales Amount] > 0,
            [NumOfDays]
        )
    )
)
```

You can see that the denominator now iterates over the years and, for each year, it checks whether there are sales in that specific year. If sales are present, then the *IF* function returns the number of days; otherwise it returns a *BLANK* and does not contribute to the total number of the denominator.

> **Note** It is worthwhile to remember that the two measures *Sales Amount* and *NumOfDays* work correctly because there is a *CALCULATE* around them, automatically inserted by DAX. If that *CALCULATE* was not there, the formula would not work correctly. You can easily check it by replacing, in the previous code, *Sales Amount* and *NumOfDays* with their corresponding code in the measure definition. You will see wrong results, because a *CALCULATE* and the associated context transition will be missing.

In Figure 6-15, you can see that the result is now correct, even at the grand total.

Row Labels	Sales Amount	NumOfDays	DailySales
⊟ CY 2007	$1,617,722.61	365	$4,432.12
⊞ Q1-2007	$374,146.58	90	$4,157.18
⊞ Q2-2007	$384,800.65	91	$4,228.58
⊞ Q3-2007	$402,134.45	92	$4,371.03
⊞ Q4-2007	$456,640.93	92	$4,963.49
⊞ CY 2008	$1,242,993.34	366	$3,396.16
⊟ CY 2009	$1,359,201.95	365	$3,723.84
⊞ Q1-2009	$226,952.53	90	$2,521.69
⊞ Q2-2009	$376,454.07	91	$4,136.86
⊞ Q3-2009	$349,803.24	92	$3,802.21
⊞ Q4-2009	$405,992.11	92	$4,412.96
Grand Total	$4,219,917.90	2,556	$3,850.29

FIGURE 6-15 Adding the iteration over the years fixed the grand total.

This measure is not yet final. In fact, in the database we use for these tests, all the years are completed, meaning that there is data from January 1 up to December 31. In the real world, you are likely to produce reports for years which are not completely filled with data. For example, when you produce a report in August you have data up to August, and no information about future months.

In such a case, the measure will still report incorrect numbers. In the report in Figure 6-16 we have removed sales after August 8, 2009.

Row Labels	Sales Amount	NumOfDays	DailySales
⊞ CY 2007	$1,617,722.61	365	$4,432.12
⊞ CY 2008	$1,242,993.34	366	$3,396.16
⊟ CY 2009	$771,738.72	365	$2,114.35
⊟ Q1-2009	$226,952.53	90	$2,521.69
⊞ January 2009	$82,603.99	31	$2,664.64
⊞ February 2009	$65,389.24	28	$2,335.33
⊞ March 2009	$78,959.30	31	$2,547.07
⊟ Q2-2009	$376,454.07	91	$4,136.86
⊞ April 2009	$116,320.35	30	$3,877.35
⊞ May 2009	$163,396.26	31	$5,270.85
⊞ June 2009	$96,737.46	30	$3,224.58
⊟ Q3-2009	$168,332.12	92	$1,829.70
⊞ July 2009	$148,100.26	31	$4,777.43
⊞ August 2009	$20,231.86	31	$652.64
Grand Total	$3,632,454.67	2,556	$3,314.28

FIGURE 6-16 When a year is not complete, the measure still reports incorrect results.

You can see that August is the last month (and, by the way, it is incomplete) and all the totals above it (that is, quarter, year, and grand total) are reporting wrong numbers. The reason for this behavior is that we (intentionally) used the wrong granularity in our code. The correct granularity is not the year; it is the month. We used the year because it seemed correct at the year level but, even if we fixed the formula for the grand total, we are still experiencing the same issue at the year level, as soon as some months in the year are missing.

Thus, the correct formulation of the measure needs to account for both years and months, as in:

```
[DailySales] :=
DIVIDE (
    [Sales Amount],
    SUMX (
        VALUES ( Date[Calendar Year] ),
        SUMX (
            VALUES ( Date[Month] ),
            IF (
                [Sales Amount] > 0,
                [NumOfDays]
            )
        )
    )
)
```

Now the denominator performs two nested loops, on years and months, and checks, for each pair (year, month), if there are sales in that month of the year, correctly accumulating days for only the months where there are sales. You can see the result in Figure 6-17.

Row Labels	Sales Amount	NumOfDays	DailySales
⊞ CY 2007	$1,617,722.61	365	$4,432.12
⊞ CY 2008	$1,242,993.34	366	$3,396.16
⊟ CY 2009	$771,738.72	365	$3,175.88
⊟ Q1-2009	$226,952.53	90	$2,521.69
⊞ January 2009	$82,603.99	31	$2,664.64
⊞ February 2009	$65,389.24	28	$2,335.33
⊞ March 2009	$78,959.30	31	$2,547.07
⊟ Q2-2009	$376,454.07	91	$4,136.86
⊞ April 2009	$116,320.35	30	$3,877.35
⊞ May 2009	$163,396.26	31	$5,270.85
⊞ June 2009	$96,737.46	30	$3,224.58
⊟ Q3-2009	$168,332.12	92	$2,715.03
⊞ July 2009	$148,100.26	31	$4,777.43
⊞ August 2009	$20,231.86	31	$652.64
Grand Total	$3,632,454.67	2,556	$3,729.42

FIGURE 6-17 Once granularity is correctly set, the formula reports correct numbers.

A more elegant formulation for the same expression can be the following one, which uses *CROSSJOIN* (you will learn *CROSSJOIN* in Chapter 9, "Advanced table functions").

```
[DailySales] :=
DIVIDE (
    [Sales Amount],
    SUMX (
        CROSSJOIN (
            VALUES ( Date[Calendar Year] ),
            VALUES ( Date[Month] )
        ),
        IF (
            [Sales Amount] > 0,
            [NumOfDays]
        )
    )
)
```

The granularity mismatch issue appears often in a model design. There are measures that you can compute only at a defined granularity, and if this is the case you need to iterate over the columns that define the granularity and finally aggregate the partial results. We suggest you study this example in detail, because it will become useful in several data models.

It is worth it to note that there is still a small issue on the last month. In fact, the number of days reported by *NumOfDays* does not take into account that the month might be incomplete. In fact, if you produce a report on August 15, you should not take into account days in the future, for which sales are clearly not present. If you want to produce a correct result also in the last month, you should further restrict the Date table by removing dates which come after the last sale, as in the following example:

```
[DailySalesCorrected] :=
CALCULATE (
    DIVIDE (
        [Sales Amount],
        SUMX (
            CROSSJOIN (
                VALUES ( Date[Calendar Year] ),
                VALUES ( Date[Month] )
            ),
            IF ( [Sales Amount] > 0, [NumOfDays] )
        )
    ),
    FILTER ( 'Date', 'Date'[Date] <= MAX ( Sales[OrderDate] ) )
)
```

Computing differences in working days

The next example we want to show is a very simple one, yet it is very interesting because it shows a way to compute values, using DAX, which is not usual in other analytical engines, such as Analysis Services Multidimensional.

In the fact table, for each order, you have two dates:

- **OrderDate**   is the date at which the order was placed.

- **ShipDate**   is the date at which the order was shipped.

You might be interested in computing how many days it takes to handle an order and this is very easy to do, thanks to the way DAX stores dates. In fact, it is enough to perform a simple subtraction *ShipDate – OrderDate* to compute the number of days. With that said, a much more interesting number to compute is the number of working days between the two dates; that is, during holidays or nonworking days, when the company does not work. Thus, it is much fairer to compute the time to process an order using the working days, instead of the nonworking days.

This proves to be a bit more challenging than a simple subtraction. As in the previous example, the calendar table contains a column that indicates whether a specific day is a working day or not. You need to find a way to use that column to compute the difference between the two dates, expressed in working days.

In the data model, the Calendar table is useful to slice orders by order date, year, and so on. The relationship between the Calendar and the fact table is based on the order date. In order to solve this scenario, you need to stop thinking of the Calendar table as a dimension (something used only to filter data) and think that the Calendar table is just a table. You can use it to compute numbers in a different way other than if it was only a dimension.

For example, you can count the number of rows in the Calendar table that are between *OrderDate* and *ShipDate* and that, at the same time, are working days. If you express the algorithm in this way, it translates to DAX very quickly with a calculated column:

```
Sales[WorkinDaysHandling] =
COUNTROWS (
    FILTER (
        Date,
        AND (
            AND (
                Date[Date] >= Sales[OrderDate],
                Date[Date] <= Sales[ShipDate]
            ),
            Date[Working Day] = "WorkDay"
        )
    )
)
```

One way to express the same algorithm which is more elegant, is as follows:

```
Sales[WorkinDaysHandling] =
CALCULATE (
    COUNTROWS ( Date ),
    ALL ( Date ),
    DATESBETWEEN ( Date[Date], Sales[OrderDate], Sales[ShipDate] ),
    Date[WorkingDay] = "WorkDay"
)
```

This latter formulation makes use of the *DATESBETWEEN* function, which you will learn in the next chapter. As of now, it is enough to say that the *DATESBETWEEN* function returns a table with all the dates between the boundaries you pass as parameters. The result being a table, you can use it as a filter to *CALCULATE* to change the existing selection over time.

Computing static moving averages

Moving averages are another common pattern that you can solve in many ways using DAX. In this section, we will provide an example of how to compute moving averages in a static way. As an example, you use a stock database that contains prices for some stocks. Using this data model, you want to compute the average price of the last 50 and 200 periods. In the stock market, a common trading technique is to look at when the faster-moving average (over 50 periods) crosses the slower one (200 periods) to determine the buy and sell points.

This example has the further requirement that, because of holidays and holes in the database (as in days where the price of a stock is not determined), 50 periods do not correspond to a fixed number of days. You want to account for holes in the database and always ensure that the average covers 50 points where the stock has a defined price.

The data model to use for this example is a very simple one, containing only a Calendar table and another table holding the close price of the stock, which you can see in Figure 6-18, where there are no prices for January 6–7.

Stock	Date	Close	Volume
MICROSOFT	1/4/2001	24.2200	112,398,400
APPLE	1/4/2001	8.5300	26,407,000
MICROSOFT	1/5/2001	24.5600	93,416,400
APPLE	1/5/2001	8.1900	14,727,400
MICROSOFT	1/8/2001	24.4700	79,784,600
APPLE	1/8/2001	8.2800	13,346,800
MICROSOFT	1/9/2001	25.9100	114,965,400
APPLE	1/9/2001	8.5900	21,033,200
MICROSOFT	1/10/2001	26.4400	90,243,400
APPLE	1/10/2001	8.2800	20,742,600

FIGURE 6-18 Stock prices contain several holes, for holidays and other nonworking days.

In order to compute the averages, you can use a calculated column. The main reason is that you want to show this average on a chart and this means that DAX will need to compute hundreds of values to plot the lines. Because the average over many points might be a slow operation, you consolidate the calculation in a calculated column, in order to generate a faster chart.

You need to compute the dates to use as boundaries for the moving average, and these dates might be different from stock to stock. The first step to solve the problem is to assign to each row in the table a number that monotonically increases for each stock. Thus, you assign the number 1 to the first price of Microsoft and you do the same for Apple. The number 2 will be for the second price, and so on. The result is visible in Figure 6-19.

Stock	Date	Close	Volume	DayNumber
MICROSOFT	1/4/2001	24.22	112398400	1
APPLE	1/4/2001	8.53	26407000	1
MICROSOFT	1/5/2001	24.56	93416400	2
APPLE	1/5/2001	8.19	14727400	2
MICROSOFT	1/8/2001	24.47	79784600	3
APPLE	1/8/2001	8.28	13346800	3
MICROSOFT	1/9/2001	25.91	114965400	4
APPLE	1/9/2001	8.59	21033200	4
MICROSOFT	1/10/2001	26.44	90243400	5
APPLE	1/10/2001	8.28	20742600	5

FIGURE 6-19 The *DayNumber* column is the index of the price for the stock.

To compute this number, you simply count, for each row, the number of rows with the same stock as the current row and with an earlier date:

```
Prices[DayNumber] =
COUNTROWS (
    FILTER (
        Prices,
        AND (
            Prices[Date] <= EARLIER ( Prices[Date] ),
            Prices[Stock] = EARLIER ( Prices[Stock] )
        )
    )
)
```

The second step in solving the scenario is computing the moving average. Now that each row has an index, it is very easy to determine the boundaries of the 50 or 200 periods. In fact, it is enough to take the current *DayNumber*, subtract the number of periods you want to consider, and then take the date of the determined row.

You can use two different techniques to compute the column. The first one is easier to understand, even if the code is not optimal and less elegant than the second solution. Nevertheless, its biggest advantage is that it follows the algorithm outlined previously in a very simple way:

```
Prices[MovingAverage200] =
CALCULATE (
    AVERAGE ( Prices[Close] ),
    FILTER (
        ALL ( Prices[Date] ),
        AND (
            Prices[Date]
                >= LOOKUPVALUE (
                    Prices[Date],
                    Prices[Stock], EARLIER ( Prices[Stock] ),
                    Prices[DayNumber], EARLIER ( Prices[DayNumber] ) - 200
                ),
            Prices[Date] <= EARLIER ( Prices[Date] )
        )
    ),
    ALLEXCEPT ( Prices, Prices[Stock] )
)
```

As you can see, the core of the formula is in the innermost condition, which filters the dates between the current one and the one of *DayNumber* – 200. The outer *ALLEXCEPT* is required to restrict the calculation to only the rows of the same stock.

The second version of the formula is a better solution:

```
Prices[MovingAverage200] =
CALCULATE (
    CALCULATE (
        AVERAGE ( Prices[Close] ),
        Prices[DayNumber] > VALUES ( Prices[DayNumber] ) - 200,
        Prices[DayNumber] <= VALUES ( Prices[DayNumber] )
    ),
    ALLEXCEPT ( Prices, Prices[Stock], Prices[DayNumber] )
)
```

This version of the moving average uses two nested *CALCULATE*. The outer *CALCULATE* uses *ALLEXCEPT* to fix both the stock and the day number in the filter context. Once these two columns are set, you can safely use *VALUES* to retrieve their value, because you know that there will be a single value for both, thanks to the context transition. The inner *CALCULATE* replaces the existing filter on *DayNumber* (set by the outer *CALCULATE*) with a new filter that shows the last 200 values of *DayNumber*. Thus, the outer *CALCULATE* sets a filter on *DayNumber* that the inner *CALCULATE* immediately removes. The Stock filter, on the other hand, is set in the outer *CALCULATE* and is never removed, so that it is still effective when DAX computes the average.

Once the calculated columns for *MovingAverage200* and *MovingAverage50* are set in the model, you can easily define measures based on them:

```
[AVG 200]   := AVERAGE ( Prices[MovingAverage200] )
[AVG 50]    := AVERAGE ( Prices[MovingAverage50] )
[AVG Close] := AVERAGE ( Prices[Close] )
```

Finally you use the measures to show a chart that indicates, for each stock, the buy and sell points at the intersection of the moving averages, as you can see in Figure 6-20.

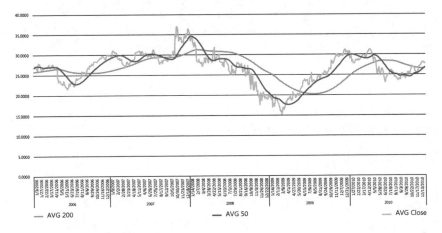

FIGURE 6-20 Moving averages are useful to show the direction of a stock over time.

Time intelligence calculations

Almost any data model includes some sort of calculation related to dates. DAX offers several functions to simplify these calculations, which work fine if the underlying data model respects some specific requirements.

In this chapter, you will learn how to implement common date-related calculations such as year-to-date, year-over-year, and comparisons over years, including nonadditive and semi-additive measures. You will learn how to compute both using specific time intelligence functions, and custom DAX code that is required for nonstandard calendars and week-based calculations.

Introduction to time intelligence

Typically, your data model will contain a calendar table. In fact, it is usually better to aggregate data by year and month using columns of a calendar table (containing one row for each day) instead of extracting the date parts from a single column of type date or datetime in calculated columns. There are a few reasons for this choice. You obtain a model wherein all date attributes are included in a separate table making it easier to browse data using a generic client, and you can use special DAX functions that perform time intelligence calculations. Moreover, most of the time intelligence functions require a separate Date table to work correctly.

Defining a separate Date table is a common practice in any star schema. You should use this technique for any model, even if you do not have a star schema as a starting point. Whenever you have a date column you want to analyze, you should create a relationship with a Date table. If you have multiple date columns in a table, you can create multiple inactive relationships to the Date table in addition to a single active one, as shown in the Sales table in Figure 7-1.

You can also choose to create a different Date table for each date column. Later in this chapter, we will discuss these two alternatives. In any case, you should always create at least one Date table in your model whenever you have one or more dates in your data.

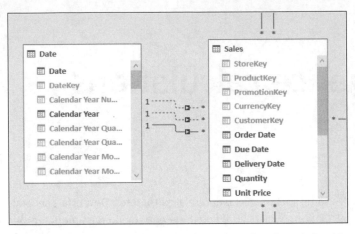

FIGURE 7-1 The Sales table has one active and two inactive relationships with the Date table.

Building a Date table

The first step for handling date calculation in a data model is to create a Date table, which simplifies any date-related calculation. Because of its importance, you should be careful when you create a Date table. In this section, you learn the best practices regarding the creation these kind of tables.

First, you need a data source that contains at least one column with all days included in the period of time you want to analyze. For example, if the minimum and maximum dates contained in sales data are July 3, 2001, and July 27, 2004, respectively, the range of dates you should consider is between January 1, 2001, and December 31, 2004. In this way, you have all the days for all the years containing sales data.

 Important Every year in a Date table must contain all the days for that year; otherwise, time intelligence functions will not work properly.

After you have a list of dates, you can choose to create other columns, such as *Day, Month,* and *Year,* and calculated columns by using DAX expressions. However, it is best to move these simple calculations in the data source reducing the use of calculated columns only when strictly needed. In this way, you obtain a better memory use for the imported columns, because imported columns result in better storage compression when compared to calculated columns.

Next, the table has to be marked as a Date table. This defines metadata used by clients and by the DAX calculation engine when it evaluates a time intelligence function. In case you have unexpected results from one of these functions, always check that the Date table has all the days for each year, and that it is marked as a Date table in the data model.

If you are building a model by using a star schema as a data source, you will probably find an existing Date table and use it (in Figure 7-2 you can see an example of the Date table used in many examples of this book). If you do not have such a table in your data source and you cannot create one there, you can generate one using the *CALENDAR* and *CALENDARAUTO* functions.

FIGURE 7-2 The Date table included in a star schema already has the columns required.

> **Note** Because the term Date is a reserved keyword in DAX (it corresponds to the function *DATE*), in previous versions of the DAX language you must embed the Date name in quotes when referring to the table name, even if there are no spaces or special characters in that name. You might prefer using Dates instead of Date as the name of the table to avoid this requirement. However, it is better to be consistent in table names, so if you use the singular form for all the other table names, it is better to keep it singular for the Date table, too.

Using *CALENDAR* and *CALENDARAUTO*

If you do not have a Date table in your data source, you can create such a table directly in the data model by adding calculated columns to a table built by using either *CALENDAR* or *CALENDARAUTO*. These functions return a table of one column of Date data type. For example, *CALENDARAUTO* automatically finds the minimum and maximum year of all the date columns included across the whole data model, and generates all the dates included between these years.

Note Not all the products supporting DAX allow you to create tables in the data model using a DAX expression. Power Pivot for Microsoft Excel does not support that in any version. Such a feature might appear in future versions of Power BI and Analysis Services Tabular.

CALENDARAUTO scans all of the date columns in your model, with the exception of calculated columns, which are not considered. For example, if you use *CALENDARAUTO* to create a Date table in a model that contains sales between 2007 and 2011 and has an *AvailableForSaleDate* column in the Product table starting in 2004, you will get all the days between January 1, 2004, and December 31, 2011. However, if the data model contains other date columns, they affect the date range considered by *CALENDARAUTO*. For example, in Figure 7-3 you can see that the range starts on January 1, 1910, because the data model includes a Customer table with a *Birth Date* column, and one customer was born in 1910.

Date
1/1/1910 12:00:00 AM
1/2/1910 12:00:00 AM
1/3/1910 12:00:00 AM
1/4/1910 12:00:00 AM
1/5/1910 12:00:00 AM
1/6/1910 12:00:00 AM
1/7/1910 12:00:00 AM
1/8/1910 12:00:00 AM
1/9/1910 12:00:00 AM
1/10/1910 12:00:00 AM
1/11/1910 12:00:00 AM
1/12/1910 12:00:00 AM
1/13/1910 12:00:00 AM
1/14/1910 12:00:00 AM
1/15/1910 12:00:00 AM
1/16/1910 12:00:00 AM
1/17/1910 12:00:00 AM
1/18/1910 12:00:00 AM
1/19/1910 12:00:00 AM

FIGURE 7-3 The Date table obtained with *CALENDARAUTO* has a *Date* column and includes all the days of the years available in date columns of tables in the data model.

You can specify a month number as an argument to *CALENDARAUTO*. If provided, it generates dates from the first day of the following months to the last day of the month indicated as an argument. This is useful when you have a fiscal year that ends in a month other than December. For example, the following expression generates a Date table for fiscal year starting on July 1 and ending on June 30, as you can see in Figure 7-4:

```
CALENDARAUTO ( 6 )
```

Date
7/1/1910 12:00:00 AM
7/2/1910 12:00:00 AM
7/3/1910 12:00:00 AM
7/4/1910 12:00:00 AM
7/5/1910 12:00:00 AM
7/6/1910 12:00:00 AM
7/7/1910 12:00:00 AM
7/8/1910 12:00:00 AM
7/9/1910 12:00:00 AM
7/10/1910 12:00:00 AM
7/11/1910 12:00:00 AM
7/12/1910 12:00:00 AM
7/13/1910 12:00:00 AM
7/14/1910 12:00:00 AM
7/15/1910 12:00:00 AM
7/16/1910 12:00:00 AM
7/17/1910 12:00:00 AM
7/18/1910 12:00:00 AM
7/19/1910 12:00:00 AM

FIGURE 7-4 The result of *CALENDARAUTO* receiving 6 as an argument starts from July 1, 1910.

As you have seen, *CALENDARAUTO* might consider date columns you want to ignore. In the previous examples, the birth date in Customer table extended the range of years even if you will never relate such a column to the Date table. In similar cases, you might want to use the *CALENDAR* function, which has two arguments: the start date and the end date. The following expression generates a date column covering all the years used in the Sales table, and its result is shown in Figure 7-5.

```
CALENDAR (
    DATE ( YEAR ( MIN ( Sales[Order Date] ) ), 1, 1 ),
    DATE ( YEAR ( MAX ( Sales[Order Date] ) ), 12, 31 )
)
```

Date
1/1/2007 12:00:00 AM
1/2/2007 12:00:00 AM
1/3/2007 12:00:00 AM
1/4/2007 12:00:00 AM
1/5/2007 12:00:00 AM
1/6/2007 12:00:00 AM
1/7/2007 12:00:00 AM
1/8/2007 12:00:00 AM
1/9/2007 12:00:00 AM
1/10/2007 12:00:00 AM
1/11/2007 12:00:00 AM
1/12/2007 12:00:00 AM
1/13/2007 12:00:00 AM
1/14/2007 12:00:00 AM
1/15/2007 12:00:00 AM
1/16/2007 12:00:00 AM
1/17/2007 12:00:00 AM
1/18/2007 12:00:00 AM
1/19/2007 12:00:00 AM

FIGURE 7-5 The result of *CALENDAR* starts from January 1, 2007, which is the year of the first date in the *Order Date* column of the Sales table.

Once you have a date column, you have to create other columns for the Date table using DAX expressions. Following is a list of commonly used expressions for this scope, with an example of their results in Figure 7-6:

```
'Date'[Year] = YEAR ( 'Date'[Date] )
'Date'[Quarter Number] = INT ( FORMAT ( [Date], "q") )
'Date'[Quarter] = "Q" & INT ( FORMAT ( [Date], "q") )
'Date'[Month Number] = MONTH ( 'Date'[Date] )
'Date'[Month] = FORMAT ( 'Date'[Date], "mmmm" )
'Date'[Week Day Number] = WEEKDAY ( 'Date'[Date] )
'Date'[Week Day] = FORMAT ( 'Date'[Date], "dddd" )
'Date'[Year Month Number] = YEAR ( 'Date'[Date] ) * 100 + MONTH ( 'Date'[Date] )
'Date'[Year Month] = FORMAT ( 'Date'[Date], "mmmm" ) & " " & YEAR ( 'Date'[Date] )
'Date'[Year Quarter Number] = YEAR ( 'Date'[Date] ) * 100 + INT ( FORMAT ( [Date], "q") )
'Date'[Year Quarter] = "Q" & FORMAT ( [Date], "q") & "-" & YEAR ( 'Date'[Date] )
```

Date	Year	Quarter Number	Quarter	Month Number	Month	Week Day Number	Week Day	Year Month Number	Year Month	Year Quarter Number	Year Quarter
1/1/2007 12:00:00 AM	2007	1	Q1	1	January	2	Monday	200701	January 2007	200701	Q1-2007
1/2/2007 12:00:00 AM	2007	1	Q1	1	January	3	Tuesday	200701	January 2007	200701	Q1-2007
1/3/2007 12:00:00 AM	2007	1	Q1	1	January	4	Wednesday	200701	January 2007	200701	Q1-2007
1/4/2007 12:00:00 AM	2007	1	Q1	1	January	5	Thursday	200701	January 2007	200701	Q1-2007
1/5/2007 12:00:00 AM	2007	1	Q1	1	January	6	Friday	200701	January 2007	200701	Q1-2007
1/6/2007 12:00:00 AM	2007	1	Q1	1	January	7	Saturday	200701	January 2007	200701	Q1-2007
1/7/2007 12:00:00 AM	2007	1	Q1	1	January	1	Sunday	200701	January 2007	200701	Q1-2007
1/8/2007 12:00:00 AM	2007	1	Q1	1	January	2	Monday	200701	January 2007	200701	Q1-2007
1/9/2007 12:00:00 AM	2007	1	Q1	1	January	3	Tuesday	200701	January 2007	200701	Q1-2007
1/10/2007 12:00:00 AM	2007	1	Q1	1	January	4	Wednesday	200701	January 2007	200701	Q1-2007
1/11/2007 12:00:00 AM	2007	1	Q1	1	January	5	Thursday	200701	January 2007	200701	Q1-2007
1/12/2007 12:00:00 AM	2007	1	Q1	1	January	6	Friday	200701	January 2007	200701	Q1-2007

FIGURE 7-6 The columns added using DAX expressions complete the Date table.

Important It is a best practice to create *natural hierarchies* for performance reasons. Hierarchies in a Date table should use columns that have unique values regardless of the parent in the hierarchy. For this reason, you should use the *Year Month* and *Year Quarter* columns as levels of hierarchies such as Year-Quarter-Month-Day. You have to sort these columns by using the *Year Month Number* and *Year Quarter Number* columns, respectively. In order to enable a pivot table with years on columns and quarters or months on rows, you can make the *Quarter* and *Month* columns visible, sorting them by using hidden columns *Quarter Number* and *Month Number*, respectively.

Working with multiple dates

You can easily relate every table that has a single date column to the Date table. However, when you have multiple date columns in the same table, you have to consider two design options: creating multiple relationships to the same Date table, or creating several Date tables, creating a relationship with a different Date table for each date column. Choosing between the two options is not simply a design decision because it also affects the DAX code you have to write in your expressions and also the kind of analysis that is possible later on.

Consider a Sales table having the following three dates for every sales transaction:

- Order Date: the date when an order has been received.

- Due Date: the date when the order was expected to be delivered.

- Delivery Date: the actual delivery date.

In the next sections, you will see how to handle these dates using the two design options and how to write the required DAX code.

Handling multiple relationships to the Date table

Even if you can create multiple relationships between two tables, only one can be active at a time. The remaining one can be used by DAX formulas calling *USERELATIONSHIP* in *CALCULATE* or *CALCULA-TETABLE*. This affects every measure that has to filter the time by using a date column other than the one used by the active relationship.

For example, consider the data model shown in Figure 7-7. There are three different relationships between Sales and Date, and only the one between *Sales[OrderDateKey]* and *Date[DateKey]* is active.

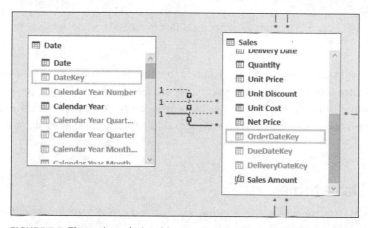

FIGURE 7-7 The active relationship connects the *OrderDateKey* column in the Sales table to the *DateKey* column in the Date table.

You can create two measures for sales amount, based on different usage of the selection on the Date table.

```
[Ordered Amount] :=
SUMX ( Sales, Sales[Unit Price] * Sales[Quantity] )

[Delivered Amount] :=
CALCULATE (
    SUMX ( Sales, Sales[Unit Price] * Sales[Quantity] ),
    USERELATIONSHIP ( Sales[DeliveryDateKey], 'Date'[DateKey] )
)
```

The first measure, *Ordered Amount*, uses the active relationship between Sales and Date, based on *Sales[OrderDateKey]*. The second measure, *Delivered Amount*, executes the same DAX expression using the relationship based on *Sales[DeliveryDateKey]*. *USERELATIONSHIP* changes the active relationship between Sales and Date in the filter context defined by *CALCULATE*. You can see in Figure 7-8 an example of a report using these measures.

Row Labels	Ordered Amount	Delivered Amount
⊟ CY 2007	**$12,457,410.85**	**$12,123,289.07**
⊞ January 2007	$912,099.00	$716,193.86
⊞ February 2007	$999,127.83	$884,789.80
⊞ March 2007	$1,073,265.17	$1,112,094.04
⊞ April 2007	$1,212,953.09	$1,249,252.19
⊞ May 2007	$964,206.51	$866,183.70
⊞ June 2007	$1,023,594.63	$1,024,670.86
⊞ July 2007	$953,675.70	$1,120,895.02
⊞ August 2007	$1,023,156.18	$830,451.90
⊞ September 2007	$1,081,595.72	$1,163,109.32
⊞ October 2007	$988,353.48	$973,715.28
⊞ November 2007	$1,009,961.54	$1,022,427.93
⊞ December 2007	$1,215,421.99	$1,159,505.16
⊞ CY 2008	**$11,031,426.30**	**$10,994,334.48**
⊞ CY 2009	**$10,201,311.36**	**$10,314,144.44**
⊞ CY 2010		**$258,380.52**
Grand Total	**$33,690,148.51**	**$33,690,148.51**

FIGURE 7-8 The *Ordered Amount* and *Delivered Amount* measures are different for each period, because the date of delivery might be in the following month.

Using multiple relationships with a single Date table increases the number of measures in the data model, but you can also define only the measures that are meaningful with certain dates. If you do not want to handle a high number of measures, or if you want to give complete freedom of using any measure with any Date, then you might consider implementing multiple Date tables, as explained in the following section.

Handling multiple Date tables

Instead of duplicating every measure, the alternative approach is that you can show the user different Date tables, one for each date you have, so that every measure aggregates data according to the date selected by the end user (or used in a query to the data model). From a maintenance point of view, this might seem a better solution because it lowers the number of measures, and it allows selecting sales that intersect two months. For example, you can easily see the total number of orders received in January and delivered in February of the same year. This approach is also known as the role-playing dimension approach. The Date table is a dimension that you duplicate once for each relationship (that is, once for each of its roles). In reality, these two options (using inactive relationships and duplicating the Date table) are complementary to each other, as you will realize after the example in Figure 7-9, which shows how to create duplicated Date tables in the model.

To create a Delivery Date table and a Due Date table, you add the same table twice in the data model. You have to rename at least the table name when doing so. You can see in Figure 7-9 the data model containing three different Date tables related to Sales.

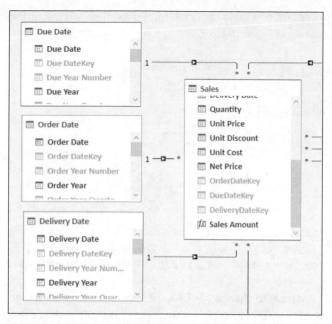

FIGURE 7-9 Each date column in Sales has a relationship with a different Date table (Due, Order, Delivery).

 Important Because you must physically duplicate the Date table, it is a best practice to create different views in the data source, one for each "role dimension," so that each Date table has different column names and different content. For example, instead of having the same column *Year* in all Date tables, it is better if you use *Order Year*, *Delivery Year*, and *Due Year*, so that it will be easier to navigate into a pivot table. This is also visible in Figure 7-9. Furthermore, it is also a good idea to change the content; for instance, by placing a prefix for the year that depends on the role of the date. As an example, you might use OY prefix for the order year and DY for the Delivery Year, so that looking at a report containing OY 2014 it is clear that it refers to order date, whereas DY 2014 refers to delivery date.

Figure 7-10 shows an example of the resulting pivot table using multiple date tables. You can see that renaming column names and content is important to produce a readable result. In order to avoid confusion between order and delivery dates, we used OY as a prefix for order years, and DY as a prefix for delivery years.

Sales Amount	Column Labels				
Row Labels	DY 2007	DY 2008	DY 2009	DY 2010	Grand Total
OY 2007	$12,123,289.07	$334,121.78			$12,457,410.85
OY 2008		$10,660,212.70	$371,213.60		$11,031,426.30
OY 2009			$9,942,930.84	$258,380.52	$10,201,311.36
Grand Total	$12,123,289.07	$10,994,334.48	$10,314,144.44	$258,380.52	$33,690,148.51

FIGURE 7-10 The different prefixes for Year help the user see which is the order year (OY) and which is the delivery year (DY).

If you do not rename columns and content of a table imported multiple times, you will obtain an almost unreadable result, as the one shown in Figure 7-11.

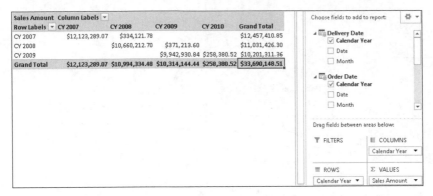

FIGURE 7-11 If you import the same table twice in the data model, the only difference is the table name. Column names (for example, Calendar Year) and their content (for example, CY 2007, CY 2008, CY 2009) are identical.

Using multiple Date tables, you do not have to change the DAX measures, so you have lower maintenance involved. However, it would be wrong to choose a single method, either duplicating tables or using multiple relationships, in handling multiple Date tables. They are both useful for different needs, and your choice should correspond to existing requirements.

Introduction to time intelligence

Having one or more Date tables in your model is an important prerequisite to perform date-based calculations such as aggregation and comparison. DAX provides a number of time intelligence functions that simplify such calculations. In reality, you can rewrite all of these special functions by using standard DAX functions such as *CALCULATE*, *CALCULATETABLE*, *FILTER*, and *VALUES*. There could be different reasons for doing so: A model using *DirectQuery* might not support the use of DAX time intelligence functions, or you might have a nonstandard calendar that existing specialized DAX functions would not handle correctly.

Before moving forward, here is a general explanation of how time intelligence functions work. Consider a simple measure: its evaluation happens in the current filter context.

```
Sales[Sales Amount] := SUMX ( Sales, Sales[Unit Price] * Sales[Quantity] )
```

The Sales table has a relationship with the Date table, so the current selection of Date determines the filter over Sales. The filter context, if propagated, uses a list of dates, which are the granularity defined by the relationship. If you want to calculate the year-to-date value, you can simply extend the selection of dates, including all the days since the beginning of the year. You can obtain this using a filter argument in a *CALCULATE* function, which returns the year-to-date up to February 2008, as you can see in Figure 7-12.

```
[Sales Amount Jan-Feb 2008] :=
CALCULATE (
    SUMX ( Sales, Sales[Unit Price] * Sales[Quantity] ),
    FILTER (
        ALL ( 'Date' ),
        AND (
            'Date'[Date] >= DATE ( 2008, 1, 1 )
            'Date'[Date] <= DATE ( 2008, 2, 29 )
        )
    )
)
```

Row Labels	Sales Amount	Sales Amount Jan-Feb 2008
⊞ CY 2007	$12,457,410.85	$1,440,010.47
⊟ CY 2008	$2,059,517.01	$1,440,010.47
⊞ January 2008	$766,917.68	$1,440,010.47
⊞ February 2008	$673,422.07	$1,440,010.47
⊞ March 2008	$619,177.26	$1,440,010.47
⊞ CY 2009	$10,201,311.36	$1,440,010.47
Grand Total	$24,718,239.22	$1,440,010.47

FIGURE 7-12 The measure *Sales Amount Jan-Feb 2008* always displays the sum of January and February of year 2008, regardless of the date range selection on rows.

The filter argument of *CALCULATE* specifies a list of days that have to be included in the filter context, replacing any existing selection of the Date table. You might rewrite the previous example by iterating in the filter only the values in the 'Date'[Date] column, instead of the entire table. In reality this does not change the cardinality of the operation (so we can expect the same performance), but it is important to understand this behavior, because it is the one used by the time intelligence functions in DAX.

Consider the following version of the previous measure. The only difference is that *FILTER* iterates the values in Date[Date], instead of iterating the entire Date table:

```
[Sales Amount Jan-Feb 2008 Single Column] :=
CALCULATE (
    SUMX ( Sales, Sales[Unit Price] * Sales[Quantity] ),
    FILTER (
        ALL ( 'Date'[Date] ),
        AND (
            'Date'[Date] >= DATE ( 2008, 1, 1 ),
            'Date'[Date] <= DATE ( 2008, 2, 29 )
        )
    )
)
```

FILTER returns a table that has only one column in this case. Thus, it replaces only that column in the filter context, keeping the other filters active. For example, if you have a selection of years and/or months in a pivot table, these filters will be still active and the resulting filter context would include them. If the relationship between Sales and Date uses a datetime data type column that you replace in the filter context, then DAX ignores all the filters in other columns of the Date table.

> **Note** Every time you apply a filter on the column that defines a one-to-many relationship with another table and such a column is of datetime data type, DAX automatically propagates the filter to the other table and overrides any other filter on other columns of the same Lookup table.

Using Mark as Date Table

Applying a filter on the date column of a calendar table works well if the date column also defines the relationship. However, you might have a relationship based on another column. Many existing Date tables could have an integer column such as the *Date[DateKey]* of our example, as you can see in Figure 7-13.

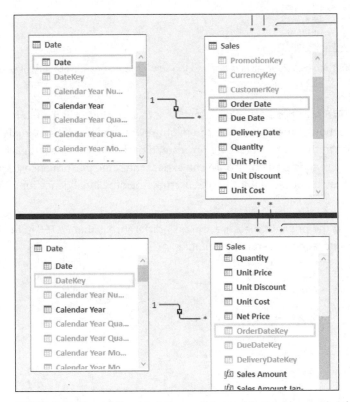

FIGURE 7-13 The relationship between Sales and Date tables previously used the *Date* column (of date data type), and now uses the *DateKey* column, which contains an integer value in the format YYYYMMDD (for example, 20080120 stands for January 20, 2008).

In this case, the Mark as Date Table feature has to be active in the Date table, otherwise the filter over the *Date[DateKey]* column does not override other existing filters active on the Date table. For example, consider the pivot table in Figure 7-14: The measure *Sales Amount Jan-Feb 2008 Single*

Column does not work, because it always returns the same value as the original *Sale Amount* measure, just filtering only data in January and February 2008 (returning blank if the selection does not include those dates).

Row Labels	Sales Amount	Sales Amount Jan-Feb 2008 Single Column
⊞ CY 2007	$12,457,410.85	
⊟ CY 2008	$2,059,517.01	$1,440,010.47
⊞ January 2008	$766,917.68	$766,917.68
⊞ February 2008	$673,422.07	$673,092.79
⊞ March 2008	$619,177.26	
⊞ CY 2009	$10,201,311.36	
Grand Total	$24,718,239.22	$1,440,010.47

FIGURE 7-14 The *Sales Amount Jan-Feb 2008 Single Column* measure does not extend the selection to days outside the row selection in the report, because it does not replace existing filters on years and months.

The reason for such behavior is that you have other filters active on the Date table, depending on the content you have on the rows of the pivot table. For example, the rows for the months January and February only show the value of each single month instead of the sum of both, whereas other months return a blank value instead of the same value duplicate in any date selection, as it was the case in Figure 7-12. If you enable the Mark as Date Table feature specifying that the date column is the *'Date'[Date]* column, then DAX automatically removes the filter from all the other columns of the Date table whenever a filter argument of a *CALCULATE* or *CALCULATETABLE* function includes a filter over that date column. (Doing that, you will obtain the same result you have seen in Figure 7-12.)

Consider the following template formula:

```
CALCULATF (
    <expr>,
    'Date'[Date] >= DATE ( 2008, 1, 1 ) && 'Date'[Date] <= DATE ( 2008, 2, 29 ),
    <filter2>,
    ...
    <filterN>
)
```

When any of the filter arguments include the date column of a table marked as a Date table, DAX removes any previous filter from that same table by using a technique corresponding to this DAX function:

```
CALCULATE (
    <expr>,
    'Date'[Date] >= DATE ( 2008, 1, 1 ) && 'Date'[Date] <= DATE ( 2008, 2, 29 ),
    <filter2>,
    ...
    <filterN>,
    ALL ( 'Date' )
)
```

The time intelligence functions work properly only if you use the Mark as Date Table feature in the correct way. If you write a time-related measure in a model that does not have the Mark as Date Table setting activated on the Date table, then you can place the *ALL ('Date')* function in the filter arguments of *CALCULATE* in order to remove the filters on other columns of the Date table that could affect the required result.

If you write a filter argument that iterates the entire Date table and not only one column, then the new filter over Date overrides any existing filter context on the Date table, and the *ALL ('Date')* function is not required. For example, you can write the previous template formula in this way, so that it will always work even if the Mark as Date Table setting is not active on the Date table:

```
CALCULATE (
    <expr>,
    FILTER (
        ALL ( 'Date' ),
        'Date'[Date] >= DATE ( 2008, 1, 1 ) && 'Date'[Date] <= DATE ( 2008, 2, 29 ),
    ),
    <filter2>,
    ...
    <filterN>
)
```

Aggregating and comparing over time

DAX provides a number of functions that simplify the aggregation and the comparison of data over time. For example, you might want to calculate the aggregated value of a measure from the beginning of the year up to the period you are selecting (also known as year-to-date aggregation). You might also want to compare the sales of this year with the sales of the previous year (also known as year-over-year). In the next sections, you see the functions available in DAX to implement measures for these and other scenarios.

 Note The time intelligence functions in DAX always apply a filter condition on the date column of a Date table. You can find some examples of how to write these calculations in DAX later in this book, and a complete list of all the time intelligence features rewritten in plain DAX at *http://www.daxpatterns.com/time-patterns/*.

Year-to-date, quarter-to-date, month-to-date

The calculations of year-to-date (YTD), quarter-to-date (QTD), and month-to-date (MTD) are all very similar. Month-to-date is meaningful only when you are looking at data at the day level, whereas you will often use year-to-date and quarter-to-date calculations to look at data at the month level.

For example, in Figure 7-15, you can see the measure *Sales Amount* aggregated by year, quarter, and month.

Row Labels	Sales Amount
⊟ CY 2007	$12,457,410.85
⊟ Q1-2007	$2,984,492.00
⊞ January 2007	$912,099.00
⊞ February 2007	$999,127.83
⊞ March 2007	$1,073,265.17
⊟ Q2-2007	$3,200,754.23
⊞ April 2007	$1,212,953.09
⊞ May 2007	$964,206.51
⊞ June 2007	$1,023,594.63
⊞ Q3-2007	$3,058,427.60
⊞ Q4-2007	$3,213,737.01
⊞ CY 2008	$11,031,426.30
⊞ CY 2009	$10,201,311.36
Grand Total	$33,690,148.51

FIGURE 7-15 The *Sales Amount* measure is aggregated by the corresponding period in each row.

You can calculate the year-to-date value of Sales for each month by modifying the filter context on dates for a range that starts on January 1 and ends on the month corresponding to the calculated cell, as in the following DAX formula:

```
[YTD Sales] := CALCULATE ( [Sales Amount], DATESYTD( 'Date'[Date] ) )
```

DATESYTD is a function that returns a list of all the dates from the beginning of the year until the last date included in the current filter context. This list is used by *CALCULATE* to set the new filter for the *Sales Amount* calculation.

> **Tip** For example, when the YTD Sales measure is evaluated for the March 2007 cell, *DATESYTD* corresponds to a filter over the date column similar to the following code.
>
> ```
> [YTD Sales] :=
> CALCULATE (
>     [Sales Amount],
>     FILTER (
>         ALL ( 'Date'[Date] ),
>         AND (
>             'Date'[Date] >= DATE ( 2007,  1,  1 ),
>             'Date'[Date] <= DATE ( 2007,  3, 31 )
>         )
>     )
> )
> ```
>
> You will find a more detailed explanation of the real underlying DAX code for the *DATESYTD* function in the section "Understanding periods to date," later in this chapter.

You can see the YTD Sales measure in action in Figure 7-16.

Row Labels	Sales Amount	YTD Sales
⊟ CY 2007	$12,457,410.85	$12,457,410.85
⊟ Q1-2007	$2,984,492.00	$2,984,492.00
⊞ January 2007	$912,099.00	$912,099.00
⊞ February 2007	$999,127.83	$1,911,226.83
⊞ March 2007	$1,073,265.17	$2,984,492.00
⊟ Q2-2007	$3,200,754.23	$6,185,246.23
⊞ April 2007	$1,212,953.09	$4,197,445.09
⊞ May 2007	$964,206.51	$5,161,651.60
⊞ June 2007	$1,023,594.63	$6,185,246.23
⊞ Q3-2007	$3,058,427.60	$9,243,673.83
⊞ Q4-2007	$3,213,737.01	$12,457,410.85
⊞ CY 2008	$11,031,426.30	$11,031,426.30
⊞ CY 2009	$10,201,311.36	$10,201,311.36
Grand Total	$33,690,148.51	

FIGURE 7-16 The *YTD Sales* measure is side by side with the regular *Sales Amount* measure.

This approach requires you to use the *CALCULATE* function, but because this pattern (using *CALCULATE* and *DATESYTD*) is very common, DAX offers a function to simplify (and make more readable) the syntax of YTD calculation: *TOTALYTD*. In the following code, you can see the same expression using *TOTALYTD*:

```
[YTD Sales] := TOTALYTD ( [Sales Amount] , 'Date'[Date] )
```

The syntax requires the expression to aggregate as the first parameter and the date column as the second parameter. The behavior is identical to the original measure, but the name *TOTALYTD* makes the behavior of the formula clearer. However, it is good to learn the behavior of the original *CALCULATE* syntax, too, because it lets you perform more advanced calculations, which you will see later in this chapter.

Similar to year-to-date, you can also define quarter-to-date and month-to-date with built-in functions, as in these measures:

```
[QTD Sales] := TOTALQTD ( [Sales Amount], 'Date'[Date] )
[QTD Sales] := CALCULATE ( [Sales Amount], DATESQTD ( 'Date'[Date] ) )

[MTD Sales] := TOTALMTD ( [Sales Amount], 'Date'[Date] )
[MTD Sales] := CALCULATE ( [Sales Amount], DATESMTD ( 'Date'[Date] ) )
```

In Figure 7-17, you can see the year-to-date and quarter-to-date measures used in a pivot table. Note that the quarter-to-date measure (*QTD Sales*) makes the year total equal to the value of *Sales Amount* of the last quarter of the year.

Row Labels	Sales Amount	YTD Sales	QTD Sales
⊟ CY 2007	$12,457,410.85	$12,457,410.85	$3,213,737.01
⊟ Q1-2007	$2,984,492.00	$2,984,492.00	$2,984,492.00
⊞ January 2007	$912,099.00	$912,099.00	$912,099.00
⊞ February 2007	$999,127.83	$1,911,226.83	$1,911,226.83
⊞ March 2007	$1,073,265.17	$2,984,492.00	$2,984,492.00
⊟ Q2-2007	$3,200,754.23	$6,185,246.23	$3,200,754.23
⊞ April 2007	$1,212,953.09	$4,197,445.09	$1,212,953.09
⊞ May 2007	$964,206.51	$5,161,651.60	$2,177,159.60
⊞ June 2007	$1,023,594.63	$6,185,246.23	$3,200,754.23
⊞ Q3-2007	$3,058,427.60	$9,243,673.83	$3,058,427.60
⊞ Q4-2007	$3,213,737.01	$12,457,410.85	$3,213,737.01
⊞ CY 2008	$11,031,426.30	$11,031,426.30	$3,303,476.73
⊞ CY 2009	$10,201,311.36	$10,201,311.36	$2,801,829.39
Grand Total	$33,690,148.51		

FIGURE 7-17 The *YTD* and *QTD Sales* measures are shown next to the regular *Sales Amount* measure.

To calculate a year-to-date measure over a fiscal year that does not end on December 31, you must use an optional third parameter that specifies the end day of the fiscal year. For example, you can calculate the fiscal year-to-date for Sales by using one of the following measures:

```
[Fiscal YTD Sales] := TOTALYTD ( [Sales Amount], 'Date'[Date], "06-30" )
[Fiscal YTD Sales] := CALCULATE ( [Sales Amount], DATESYTD ( 'Date'[Date], "06-30" ) )
```

The last parameter corresponds to June 30, that is, the end of the fiscal year. There are several time intelligence functions that have a last, optional year-end date parameter for this purpose: *STARTOFYEAR*, *ENDOFYEAR*, *PREVIOUSYEAR*, *NEXTYEAR*, *DATESYTD*, *TOTALYTD*, *OPENINGBALANCEYEAR*, and *CLOSINGBALANCEYEAR*.

> **Important** Depending on your local language settings, you might have to use the day number first:
>
> ```
> [Fiscal YTD Sales] := TOTALYTD ( [Sales Amount], 'Date'[Date], "30-06" )
> [Fiscal YTD Sales] := CALCULATE ( [Sales Amount], DATESYTD ( 'Date'[Date], "30-06" ) )
> ```

Computing periods from prior periods

Users commonly need to get a value from a period of the prior year (PY). This can be useful for making comparisons of trends during a period this year to the same period last year. You must calculate this DAX expression for that value:

```
[PY Sales] := CALCULATE ( [Sales Amount], SAMEPERIODLASTYEAR ( 'Date'[Date] ) )
```

SAMEPERIODLASTYEAR returns a set of dates shifted one year back in time. It is a specialized version of the more generic *DATEADD* function, which accepts the number and type of period to shift. The types of period supported are YEAR, QUARTER, MONTH, and DAY. For example, you can define the same *PY Sales* measure using this equivalent expression:

```
[PY Sales] := CALCULATE( [Sales Amount], DATEADD( 'Date'[Date], -1, YEAR ) )
```

In a similar way, you can compute the value from a previous quarter (PQ), month (PM), or day (PD), as you can see in the following examples:

```
[PQ Sales] := CALCULATE ( [Sales Amount], DATEADD ( 'Date'[Date], -1, QUARTER ) )

[PM Sales] := CALCULATE ( [Sales Amount], DATEADD ( 'Date'[Date], -1, MONTH ) )

[PD Sales] := CALCULATE ( [Sales Amount], DATEADD ( 'Date'[Date], -1, DAY ) )
```

Sometimes, you must look at the total amount of a measure for the previous year, usually to compare it with the year-to-date total. To do that, you can use *PARALLELPERIOD*, which is similar to *DATEADD*, but returns the full period specified in the third parameter instead of the partial period returned by *DATEADD*. You can define the *PY Sales* measure that calculates the total of sales for the previous year in this way:

```
[PY Total Sales] :=
CALCULATE ( [Sales Amount], PARALLELPERIOD ( 'Date'[Date], -1, YEAR ) )
```

In Figure 7-18, you can see the result of the *PY Sales* and *PY Total Sales* measures. The report shows the quarters' data in 2008 for the *Sales Amount* column in the respective quarters of year 2009, in the *PY Sales* column. *PY Total Sales* reports for every period the total amount of the *Sales Amount* column for the previous year.

Row Labels	Sales Amount	PY Sales	PY Total Sales	YTDOPYT Sales %	YTD Sales
⊟ CY 2008	$11,031,426.30	$12,457,410.85	$12,457,410.85	88.55 %	$11,031,426.30
⊞ Q1-2008	$2,059,517.01	$2,984,492.00	$12,457,410.85	16.53 %	$2,059,517.01
⊞ Q2-2008	$2,917,842.57	$3,200,754.23	$12,457,410.85	39.96 %	$4,977,359.58
⊞ Q3-2008	$2,750,589.99	$3,058,427.60	$12,457,410.85	62.03 %	$7,727,949.57
⊞ Q4-2008	$3,303,476.73	$3,213,737.01	$12,457,410.85	88.55 %	$11,031,426.30
⊟ CY 2009	$10,201,311.36	$11,031,426.30	$11,031,426.30	92.47 %	$10,201,311.36
⊞ Q1-2009	$1,902,822.33	$2,059,517.01	$11,031,426.30	17.25 %	$1,902,822.33
⊞ Q2-2009	$2,752,395.02	$2,917,842.57	$11,031,426.30	42.20 %	$4,655,217.35
⊞ Q3-2009	$2,744,264.62	$2,750,589.99	$11,031,426.30	67.08 %	$7,399,481.97
⊞ Q4-2009	$2,801,829.39	$3,303,476.73	$11,031,426.30	92.47 %	$10,201,311.36
Grand Total	$21,232,737.66	$23,488,837.15	$23,488,837.15	43.43 %	$10,201,311.36

FIGURE 7-18 The prior year calculations show the data shifted by one year.

The *PY Total Sales* measure can be useful to calculate the ratio between current year-to-date and total of previous year, providing a simple Key Performance Indicator (KPI) to detect whether the current

YTD sales reached the total sales of the previous year. As you see in Figure 7-18, the *YTDOPYT Sales %* measure calculates the year-to-date over the previous year's total using the following formula:

```
[YTDOPYT Sales %] := DIVIDE ( [YTD Sales], [PY Total Sales] )
```

You can also compare the year-to-date with the corresponding value in the previous year. When you want to calculate the year-to-date of the prior year, you can mix the two techniques you have seen so far. Instead of passing the *Date[Date]* parameter to *SAMEPERIODLASTYEAR*, which corresponds to the list of dates that are active in the current filter context, you can use the *DATESYTD* function to make a transformation of these dates, defining the year-to-date group first. However, you can also invert the order of these calls without affecting the result. The following two definitions of *PY YTD Sales* are equivalent, even if the second one could be slightly faster (but barely measureable).

```
[PY YTD Sales] :=
CALCULATE (
    [Sales Amount],
    SAMEPERIODLASTYEAR ( DATESYTD ( 'Date'[Date] ) )
)

[PY YTD Sales] :=
CALCULATE (
    [Sales Amount],
    DATESYTD ( SAMEPERIODLASTYEAR ( 'Date'[Date] ) )
)
```

You can also use the prior year calculation over the year-to-date measure or the year-to-date technique over the prior year measure. You can write these other two definitions of *PY YTD Sales* that are equivalent to the previous two:

```
[PY YTD Sales] :=
CALCULATE (
    [YTD Sales],
    SAMEPERIODLASTYEAR ( 'Date'[Date] )
)

[PY YTD Sales] :=
CALCULATE (
    [PY Sales],
    DATESYTD ( 'Date'[Date] )
)
```

You can see the results of the *PY YTD Sales* in Figure 7-19. The values of *YTD Sales* are reported for *PY YTD Sales* shifted by one year. In the same result, you can also see the *Fiscal YTD Sales* measure that you saw at the end of the previous section. Note that the year-to-date calculation restarts at Q3 of each year.

Row Labels .T	Sales Amount	YTD Sales	PY YTD Sales	Fiscal YTD Sales
⊟ CY 2008	$11,031,426.30	$11,031,426.30	$12,457,410.85	$6,054,066.72
⊞ Q1-2008	$2,059,517.01	$2,059,517.01	$2,984,492.00	$8,331,681.63
⊞ Q2-2008	$2,917,842.57	$4,977,359.58	$6,185,246.23	$11,249,524.20
⊞ Q3-2008	$2,750,589.99	$7,727,949.57	$9,243,673.83	$2,750,589.99
⊞ Q4-2008	$3,303,476.73	$11,031,426.30	$12,457,410.85	$6,054,066.72
⊟ CY 2009	$10,201,311.36	$10,201,311.36	$11,031,426.30	$5,546,094.01
⊞ Q1-2009	$1,902,822.33	$1,902,822.33	$2,059,517.01	$7,956,889.05
⊞ Q2-2009	$2,752,395.02	$4,655,217.35	$4,977,359.58	$10,709,284.07
⊞ Q3-2009	$2,744,264.62	$7,399,481.97	$7,727,949.57	$2,744,264.62
⊞ Q4-2009	$2,801,829.39	$10,201,311.36	$11,031,426.30	$5,546,094.01
Grand Total	$21,232,737.66	$10,201,311.36	$11,031,426.30	$5,546,094.01

FIGURE 7-19 The year-to-date calculation for prior year and fiscal year can appear in the same pivot table.

All the examples you have seen in this section can operate on year, quarter, month, and day level, but not at the week level. Time intelligence functions are not available for week-based calculations, because there are too many variations of periods based on weeks. For this reason, you have to implement DAX expressions to handle week-based calculations. You can find more details and an example of this approach in the "Custom calendars" section, later in this chapter.

Computing difference over previous periods

A common operation is calculating the difference between a measure and its value in the prior year. You can express that difference as an absolute value or as a percentage. You have already seen how to obtain the value for the prior year with the *PY Sales* measure:

```
[PY Sales] := CALCULATE ( [Sales Amount], SAMEPERIODLASTYEAR ( 'Date'[Date] ) )
```

The absolute difference of *Sales Amount* over previous year (year-over-year, YOY) is a simple subtraction. You can define a *YOY Sales* measure with the following expression:

```
[YOY Sales] := [Sales Amount] - [PY Sales]
```

The analogous calculation for comparing the year-to-date measure with a corresponding value in the prior year is a simple subtraction of two measures, *YTD Sales* and *PY YTD Sales*, which you saw in the previous section; we report it here as a reminder:

```
[YTD Sales] := TOTALYTD ( [Sales Amount], 'Date'[Date] )

[PY YTD Sales] :=
CALCULATE (
    [Sales Amount],
    DATESYTD ( SAMEPERIODLASTYEAR ( 'Date'[Date] ) )
)

[YOY YTD Sales] := [YTD Sales] - [PY YTD Sales]
```

Most of the time, the year-over-year difference is better expressed as a percentage in a report. You can define this calculation by dividing YOY Sales by the PY Sales; in this way, the difference uses the prior read value as a reference for the percentage difference (100 percent corresponds to a value that is doubled in one year). In the following expressions that define the *YOY Sales%* measure, the *DIVIDE* function avoids a divide-by-zero error if there is no corresponding data in the prior year:

```
[YOY Sales%] := DIVIDE ( [YOY Sales], [PY Sales] )
```

You can create a similar calculation to display the percentage difference of a year-over-year comparison for the year-to-date aggregation. You can define *YOY YTD Sales%* by using the following formula:

```
[YOY YTD Sales%] := DIVIDE ( [YOY YTD Sales], [PY YTD Sales] )
```

In Figure 7-20, you can see the results of these measures in a pivot table.

Row Labels	Sales Amount	PY Sales	YOY Sales	YOY YTD Sales	YOY Sales%	YOY YTD Sales%	PY YTD Sales	YTD Sales
CY 2008	$11,031,426.30	$12,457,410.85	($1,425,984.55)	($1,425,984.55)	-11.45%	-11.45%	$12,457,410.85	$11,031,426.30
Q1-2008	$2,059,517.01	$2,984,492.00	($924,974.99)	($924,974.99)	-30.99%	-30.99%	$2,984,492.00	$2,059,517.01
Q2-2008	$2,917,842.57	$3,200,754.23	($282,911.66)	($1,207,886.65)	-8.84%	-19.53%	$6,185,246.23	$4,977,359.58
Q3-2008	$2,750,589.99	$3,058,427.60	($307,837.61)	($1,515,724.27)	-10.07%	-16.40%	$9,243,673.83	$7,727,949.57
Q4-2008	$3,303,476.73	$3,213,737.01	$89,739.72	($1,425,984.55)	2.79%	-11.45%	$12,457,410.85	$11,031,426.30
CY 2009	$10,201,311.36	$11,031,426.30	($830,114.94)	($830,114.94)	-7.53%	-7.53%	$11,031,426.30	$10,201,311.36
Q1-2009	$1,902,822.33	$2,059,517.01	($156,694.68)	($156,694.68)	-7.61%	-7.61%	$2,059,517.01	$1,902,822.33
Q2-2009	$2,752,395.02	$2,917,842.57	($165,447.55)	($322,142.23)	-5.67%	-6.47%	$4,977,359.58	$4,655,217.35
Q3-2009	$2,744,264.62	$2,750,589.99	($6,325.37)	($328,467.60)	-0.23%	-4.25%	$7,727,949.57	$7,399,481.97
Q4-2009	$2,801,829.39	$3,303,476.73	($501,647.34)	($830,114.94)	-15.19%	-7.53%	$11,031,426.30	$10,201,311.36
Grand Total	$21,232,737.66	$23,488,837.15	($2,256,099.49)	($830,114.94)	-9.60%	-7.53%	$11,031,426.30	$10,201,311.36

FIGURE 7-20 All the year-over-year (YOY) measures can be used in the same report.

Computing the moving annual total

Another commonly requested calculation that eliminates seasonal changes in sales is the moving annual total (MAT), which always considers the past 12 months. For example, you can calculate the value of *MAT Sales* for March 2008 by summing the range of dates from April 2007 to March 2008. The easiest way is using the *DATESINPERIOD* function, which returns all the dates included within a period (fourth argument, YEAR, QUARTER, MONTH, or DAY) applying an offset (third parameter, a negative number gets a period in the past, a positive number in the future) to a date (second argument) existing in the column specified in the first argument.

```
[MAT Sales] :=
CALCULATE (
    [Sales Amount],
    DATESINPERIOD (
        'Date'[Date],
        LASTDATE ( 'Date'[Date] ),
        -1,
        YEAR
    )
)
```

Using *DATESINPERIOD* is usually the best option for the moving annual total calculation. For didactical purposes, it is useful to see other techniques to obtain the same filter. Consider this alternative *MAT Sales* definition, which calculates the moving annual total for Sales.

```
[MAT Sales] :=
CALCULATE (
    [Sales Amount],
    DATESBETWEEN (
        'Date'[Date],
        NEXTDAY ( SAMEPERIODLASTYEAR ( LASTDATE ( 'Date'[Date] ) ) ),
        LASTDATE ( 'Date'[Date] )
    )
)
```

The implementation of this measure requires some attention. You must use the *DATESBETWEEN* function, which returns the dates from a column included between two specified dates. Because this calculation always works at the day level, even if you are querying data at the month level, you must calculate the first day and the last day of the required interval. You can obtain the last day by calling the *LASTDATE* function, which returns the last date of a given column (always considering the current filter context). Starting from this date, you can get the first day of the interval by requesting the following day (by calling *NEXTDAY*) of the corresponding last date one year before. (You can do this by using *SAMEPERIODLASTYEAR*.)

In Figure 7-21, you can see a report that includes the moving annual total calculation. For example, the Q1-2008 value of *MAT Sales* is the result obtained by summing the *Sales Amount* value of Q2-2007, Q3-2007, Q4-2007, and Q1-2008. In the middle, you see the classic year-to-date calculation, which has the same value of moving annual total only for the last period of each year (in this case, Q4).

Row Labels	Sales Amount	YTD Sales	MAT Sales
⊟ CY 2007	$12,457,410.85	$12,457,410.85	$12,457,410.85
⊞ Q1-2007	$2,984,492.00	$2,984,492.00	$2,984,492.00
⊞ Q2-2007	$3,200,754.23	$6,185,246.23	$6,185,246.23
⊞ Q3-2007	$3,058,427.60	$9,243,673.83	$9,243,673.83
⊞ Q4-2007	$3,213,737.01	$12,457,410.85	$12,457,410.85
⊟ CY 2008	$11,031,426.30	$11,031,426.30	$11,031,426.30
⊞ Q1-2008	$2,059,517.01	$2,059,517.01	$11,532,435.86
⊞ Q2-2008	$2,917,842.57	$4,977,359.58	$11,249,524.20
⊞ Q3-2008	$2,750,589.99	$7,727,949.57	$10,941,686.58
⊞ Q4-2008	$3,303,476.73	$11,031,426.30	$11,031,426.30
⊟ CY 2009	$10,201,311.36	$10,201,311.36	$10,201,311.36
⊞ Q1-2009	$1,902,822.33	$1,902,822.33	$10,874,731.62
⊞ Q2-2009	$2,752,395.02	$4,655,217.35	$10,709,284.07
⊞ Q3-2009	$2,744,264.62	$7,399,481.97	$10,702,958.70
⊞ Q4-2009	$2,801,829.39	$10,201,311.36	$10,201,311.36
Grand Total	$33,690,148.51		

FIGURE 7-21 This report is using measures that display only days for which there is balance data.

Use the right call order for nested time intelligence functions

When you create nested calls of time intelligence functions, you might wonder what the right call order is. In the previous example, we used the following DAX expression to retrieve the first day of the "moving annual total" period:

```
NEXTDAY ( SAMEPERIODLASTYEAR ( LASTDATE ( 'Date'[Date] ) ) )
```

In this case, *LASTDATE* returns the last date of Q1-2008 (March 31, 2008), *SAMEPERIODLAS-TYEAR* returns March 31, 2007, and *NEXTDAY* returns April 1, 2007. You might invert the call order between *NEXTDAY* and *SAMEPERIODLASTYEAR*:

```
SAMEPERIODLASTYEAR ( NEXTDAY ( LASTDATE ( 'Date'[Date] ) ) )
```

It returns the same result (April 1, 2007), but you have one risk. If your Date table ends on December 31, 2011, and you consider the result for Q4-2011, this is what happens: *LASTDATE* returns the last date of Q4-2011 (December 31, 2011), *NEXTDAY* should return January 1, 2012, and *SAMEPERIODLASTYEAR* should return January 1, 2011. However, all these functions can only return existing values of the *Date[Date]* column. If the Date table does not have any row for year 2012, the *NEXTDAY* call cannot return January 1, 2012, and it would return BLANK instead. For example, consider the following wrong MAT calculation:

```
MAT Sales Wrong := CALCULATE (
    [Sales Amount],
    DATESBETWEEN (
        'Date'[Date],
        SAMEPERIODLASTYEAR ( NEXTDAY ( LASTDATE( 'Date'[Date] ) ) ),
        LASTDATE ( 'Date'[Date] )
    )
)
```

As you see in Figure 7-22, this result provides a wrong value for both Q4 2011 and for CY 2011, regardless of the fact that there are no sales in both 2010 and 2011. This happens because the lower boundary of *DATESBETWEEN* is BLANK and this creates a calculation that spans the entire range of dates available.

Row Labels	Sales Amount	YTD Sales	MAT Sales	MAT Sales Wrong
⊟ CY 2007	**$12,457,410.85**	**$12,457,410.85**	**$12,457,410.85**	**$12,457,410.85**
⊞ Q1-2007	$2,984,492.00	$2,984,492.00	$2,984,492.00	$2,984,492.00
⊞ Q2-2007	$3,200,754.23	$6,185,246.23	$6,185,246.23	$6,185,246.23
⊞ Q3-2007	$3,058,427.60	$9,243,673.83	$9,243,673.83	$9,243,673.83
⊞ Q4-2007	$3,213,737.01	$12,457,410.85	$12,457,410.85	$12,457,410.85
⊟ CY 2008	**$11,031,426.30**	**$11,031,426.30**	**$11,031,426.30**	**$11,031,426.30**
⊞ Q1-2008	$2,059,517.01	$2,059,517.01	$11,532,435.86	$11,532,435.86
⊞ Q2-2008	$2,917,842.57	$4,977,359.58	$11,249,524.20	$11,249,524.20
⊞ Q3-2008	$2,750,589.99	$7,727,949.57	$10,941,686.58	$10,941,686.58
⊞ Q4-2008	$3,303,476.73	$11,031,426.30	$11,031,426.30	$11,031,426.30
⊟ CY 2009	**$10,201,311.36**	**$10,201,311.36**	**$10,201,311.36**	**$10,201,311.36**
⊞ Q1-2009	$1,902,822.33	$1,902,822.33	$10,874,731.62	$10,874,731.62
⊞ Q2-2009	$2,752,395.02	$4,655,217.35	$10,709,284.07	$10,709,284.07
⊞ Q3-2009	$2,744,264.62	$7,399,481.97	$10,702,958.70	$10,702,958.70
⊞ Q4-2009	$2,801,829.39	$10,201,311.36	$10,201,311.36	$10,201,311.36
⊟ CY 2011				**$33,690,148.51**
⊞ Q4-2011				$33,690,148.51
Grand Total	**$33,690,148.51**			**$33,690,148.51**

FIGURE 7-22 The *MAT Sales Wrong* measure shows a value for Q4 2011 and for CY 2011 that is wrong.

In general, you should always consider that time intelligence functions work with existing values in the date column only, and are not able to handle values out of that set.

Closing balance over time

In the previous section, you saw how to create time-related aggregations in DAX. However, some measures cannot aggregate data over time. For example, you can aggregate measures such as balance account and product inventory units over any attribute but time. We call these measures semi-additive, and in this section, you will see how to define them in DAX.

Semi-additive measures

Whenever you define a measure by using either *SUM, COUNT, MIN, or MAX*, the measure is a fully additive measure because DAX uniformly applies the aggregation to all dimensions.

Sometimes you need measures to behave in a different way. For example, think about the product inventory. If you consider several products, you can calculate the quantity on hand for a product category by summing the quantities of the products belonging to that category in a particular day. However, you cannot sum quantities of the same product over multiple days, because the result would no longer represent the quantity on hand.

If you consider the Quantity column in an Inventory table, the only dimension that does not use *SUM* is the Date. The term "dimension Date" includes all the attributes of a Date table related to Inventory. For the Date attributes, you must consider only the values belonging to the last date in the evaluated period. In other words, you must implement a logic that can produce the results that you see in Figure 7-23, in which the aggregate value is the same as the last period. (For example, the value for Q1-2008 is the same as March 2008, the value for Q2-2008 is the same as June 2008, and so on.)

On Hand Quantity Simple	Column Labels	
Row Labels	Contoso In-Line Coupler E180 White	Contoso Touch Stylus Pen E150 Silver
⊞ CY 2007	20	120
⊟ CY 2008	330	40
⊟ Q1-2008	111	209
⊞ January 2008	42	200
⊞ February 2008		112
⊞ March 2008	111	209
⊟ Q2-2008	130	184
⊞ April 2008	322	434
⊞ May 2008	130	248
⊞ June 2008		184
⊟ Q3-2008	262	52
⊞ July 2008	262	158
⊞ August 2008		198
⊞ September 2008		52
⊟ Q4-2008	330	40
⊞ October 2008		201
⊞ November 2008	434	294
⊞ December 2008	330	40
⊞ CY 2009	1,062	1,144
Grand Total	1,062	1,144

FIGURE 7-23 The semi-additive *On Hand Quantity* measure is not aggregated on quarter and year.

The *On Hand Quantity Simple* measure used in Figure 7-23 displays the total of a quarter showing the value corresponding to the last month in the same quarter. In case the Inventory table has data measured every day, you might use the following measure (please note that this is not the optimal solution; the best approach is later in this section).

```
[On Hand Quantity Simple] :=
CALCULATE (
    SUM ( Inventory[Quantity] ),
    LASTDATE ( Inventory[Date] )
)
```

The definition of *On Hand Quantity Simple* uses *LASTDATE* to keep only the last date that is active in the current filter context. Therefore, only the last date for which there is available data in the filter of every cell is considered in the *CALCULATE* call.

It is interesting to note that, in this case, the *Inventory[Date]* used in *LASTDATE* is a date column in the Inventory table, which is related to the Date table for navigation on other Date attributes. By using the date column in the Inventory table, only filtered rows in Inventory are considered. This can have an interesting side effect. For every cell, only the last date available for the product selected and the period selected is considered. For example, look at the result produced in Figure 7-24, where the last column shows the Grand Total of products.

On Hand Quantity Simple	Column Labels		
Row Labels	Contoso In-Line Coupler E180 White	Contoso Touch Stylus Pen E150 Silver	Grand Total
CY 2008	330	40	40
Q1-2008	111	209	209
January 2008	42	200	42
1/12/2008		200	200
1/26/2008	42		42
February 2008		112	112
March 2008	111	209	209

FIGURE 7-24 The Grand Total of *On Hand Quantity Simple* measure does not aggregate product quantities as expected.

If you consider data in January 2008, the "Contoso In-Line Coupler E180 White" product has a quantity of 42 on January 26, whereas the "Contoso Touch Stylus Pen E150 Silver" has a quantity of 200 on January 12. The Grand Total for January 2008 displays 42, but what should be the right value? It depends on the way data is measured in the Inventory table. When you have the inventory of all the products every day, then you would not see this behavior. If a date is missing for a product, then the meaning should be that such a product does not have a quantity on hand on that day. In this common scenario, the value in the Grand Total would be correct, but the value for the "Contoso Touch Stylus Pen E150 Silver" at the month level would be wrong, because it should be blank (such a product was not in stock on January 26). In order to fix this issue, it is better to use the *Date[Date]* column instead of the *Inventory[Date]* column as the parameter passed to the *LASTDATE* function.

```
[On Hand Quantity Last Date] :=
CALCULATE (
    SUM ( Inventory[Quantity] ),
    LASTDATE ( 'Date'[Date] )
)
```

In this case, the last date in a period is the last date available in the Date table (mentioned in the preceding formula) and not the last date for which there is raw data. Thus, for January, it will always be January 31, even if there are no rows in the Inventory table. However, this might have unwanted consequences. If your data does not have values for the last day of a month, and the Date table contains all the days for that month (as it should), the *On Hand Quantity Last Date* formula defined with *LASTDATE* returns no data (a BLANK value) for that month, as you can see in Figure 7-25.

On Hand Quantity Last Date	Column Labels		
Row Labels	Contoso In-Line Coupler E180 White	Contoso Touch Stylus Pen E150 Silver	Grand Total
CY 2008			
Q1-2008			
January 2008			
1/12/2008		200	200
1/26/2008	42		42

FIGURE 7-25 The *On Hand Quantity Last Date* measure is blank in January because there is no data on January 31.

If there were Inventory data measured on January 31 and the two products in Figure 7-25 did not have units on hand, the formula based on LASTDATE would be good. However, this is not the case. The Inventory data in the Contoso database has a weekly granularity. This is visible by displaying the *On Hand Quantity Last Date* measure by aggregating all the products by date, as you can see in Figure 7-26.

Row Labels	On Hand Quantity Last Date
1/5/2008	13,927
1/12/2008	13,068
1/19/2008	12,946
1/26/2008	12,899
2/2/2008	10,239
2/9/2008	10,368
2/16/2008	9,425
2/23/2008	8,959
3/1/2008	9,584
3/8/2008	10,819
3/15/2008	9,048
3/22/2008	8,517
3/29/2008	7,860
4/5/2008	11,430

FIGURE 7-26 The *On Hand Quantity Last Date* has a weekly granularity and might not include the last day of month.

If you want to see at the month level the value of the last day with at least one transaction, ignoring days that have no transactions at all, you have to use another approach. The solution is to use the *LASTNONBLANK* function, which returns the last date for which a particular expression is not blank. This is a formula for the *On Hand Quantity* measure using the *LASTNONBLANK* function:

```
[On Hand Quantity] :=
CALCULATE (
    SUM ( Inventory[Quantity] ),
    LASTNONBLANK (
        'Date'[Date],
        CALCULATE ( COUNTROWS ( Inventory ), ALL ( Product ) )
    )
)
```

By using *On Hand Quantity*, you can see that the January month value now corresponds to January 26 for both products that we considered previously, as you can see in Figure 7-27.

On Hand Quantity	Column Labels		
Row Labels	Contoso In-Line Coupler E180 White	Contoso Touch Stylus Pen E150 Silver	Grand Total
January 2008	42		42
1/12/2008		200	200
1/26/2008	42		42

FIGURE 7-27 The *On Hand Quantity* measure correctly represents the value of January 2008 for the products selected.

In Figure 7-28 you can see that, for every product category, the month value corresponds to the last day with rows in the Inventory table.

On Hand Quantity Row Labels	Column Labels Cameras and camcorders	Cell phones	Grand Total
⊞ CY 2007	2,046	2,403	4,449
⊟ CY 2008	1,631	1,877	3,508
⊟ Q1-2008	1,349	1,058	2,407
⊟ January 2008	2,450	2,405	4,855
1/5/2008	2,510	3,279	5,789
1/12/2008	2,073	2,688	4,761
1/19/2008	1,977	1,985	3,962
1/26/2008	2,450	2,405	4,855
⊞ February 2008	1,399	1,453	2,852
⊞ March 2008	1,349	1,058	2,407
⊟ Q2-2008	1,733	3,423	5,156
⊞ April 2008	1,639	2,925	4,564
⊞ May 2008	1,309	1,838	3,147
⊞ June 2008	1,733	3,423	5,156
⊟ Q3-2008	1,930	1,661	3,591
⊞ July 2008	1,650	2,592	4,242
⊞ August 2008	1,306	1,606	2,912
⊞ September 2008	1,930	1,661	3,591
⊟ Q4-2008	1,631	1,877	3,508
⊞ October 2008	1,445	1,508	2,953
⊞ November 2008	1,768	2,914	4,682
⊞ December 2008	1,631	1,877	3,508
⊞ CY 2009	921	3,909	4,830
Grand Total	921	3,909	4,830

FIGURE 7-28 The *On Hand Quantity* measure shows the value corresponding to the last day with data in the period considered.

If the Inventory data contains a row for a product only when its quantity on hand changed since previous value, then you want to obtain the result shown in Figure 7-29.

On Hand Quantity Last Date by Product Row Labels	Column Labels Contoso In-Line Coupler E180 White	Contoso Touch Stylus Pen E150 Silver	Grand Total
⊟ January 2008	42	200	242
1/5/2008	20	120	140
1/12/2008	20	200	220
1/19/2008	20	200	220
1/26/2008	42	200	242

FIGURE 7-29 The *On Hand Quantity Last Date by Product* measure returns the last quantity on hand found in the Inventory table for each product.

In this case, the data in Inventory table eliminates duplicated rows for products that have the same quantity on hand than the previous snapshot. In practice, the quantity zero requires a specific row in the Inventory table. This method of storing data is typical of those systems that create a new inventory value for each transaction, updating only those products that had some transactions, and not all the others. You can implement this calculation by using the *On Hand Quantity Last Date by Product* measure.

The basic idea is that, for each product, you must get the last nonblank date included in the selected period. The calculation for a single account can be made by using the *CALCULATE* function and by filtering data on the LASTNONBLANK date included in the period between the first date available and the last date in the period. Notice that the date range considered begins even outside the period: You might request the balance for February and there might be no rows in that month, so you must consider also previous dates for the interval. (In Figure 7-29, the value of "Contoso Touch Stylus Pen E150 Silver" is 120 on January 5, 2008, because there is a previous transaction in 2007, even if it is not included in the selection of the report.) You use a *SUMX* function to iterate all the available products. To get the calculation only for dates that have at least one transaction (for any product), you must check whether at least one row in the Inventory table exists for any product in the current selection of dates. This is the definition of such a measure.

```
[On Hand Quantity Last Date by Product] :=
IF (
    CALCULATE ( COUNTROWS ( Inventory ), ALL ( 'Product' ) ) > 0,
    SUMX (
        'Product',
        CALCULATE (
            SUM ( Inventory[Quantity] ),
            LASTNONBLANK (
                DATESBETWEEN (
                    'Date'[Date],
                    BLANK (),
                    LASTDATE ( 'Date'[Date] )
                ),
                CALCULATE ( COUNTROWS ( Inventory ) )
            )
        )
    )
)
```

In Figure 7-30 you can see that, for every product category, the values are different from what you have seen in Figure 7-28, because in every cell the measure sums the value of the last available Inventory row for each product, even if the dates are different.

Important You have to know how the data is stored in the data model in order to choose what is the right formula to use for the *On Hand Quantity* calculation.

| On Hand Quantity Last Date by Product | Column Labels | | |
Row Labels	Cameras and camcorders	Cell phones	Grand Total
⊞ CY 2007	4,910	4,761	9,671
⊟ CY 2008	6,785	9,746	16,531
⊟ Q1-2008	5,404	7,013	12,417
⊟ January 2008	5,117	5,167	10,284
1/5/2008	5,109	5,500	10,609
1/12/2008	4,933	5,151	10,084
1/19/2008	4,825	5,444	10,269
1/26/2008	5,117	5,167	10,284
⊞ February 2008	5,130	7,100	12,230
⊞ March 2008	5,404	7,013	12,417
⊟ Q2-2008	5,556	8,356	13,912
⊞ April 2008	5,607	8,391	13,998
⊞ May 2008	5,421	7,375	12,796
⊞ June 2008	5,556	8,356	13,912
⊟ Q3-2008	6,655	8,861	15,516
⊞ July 2008	6,013	8,227	14,240
⊞ August 2008	6,088	8,465	14,553
⊞ September 2008	6,655	8,861	15,516
⊟ Q4-2008	6,785	9,746	16,531
⊞ October 2008	6,405	7,187	13,592
⊞ November 2008	6,367	9,028	15,395
⊞ December 2008	6,785	9,746	16,531
⊞ CY 2009	9,140	24,673	33,813
Grand Total	9,140	24,673	33,813

FIGURE 7-30 The result produced by *On Hand Quantity Last Date by Product* sums the last value available for each product.

Up to now, you have seen two functions that might seem similar, but have a very different behavior: *LASTDATE* and *LASTNONBLANK*. There are two other corresponding functions to get the first date, instead of the last date within a period: *FIRSTDATE* and *FIRSTNONBLANK*. You will find more examples and details about all of these functions in the "Advanced time intelligence" section, later in this chapter.

OPENINGBALANCE and *CLOSINGBALANCE* functions

DAX provides several functions to get the first and last date of a period (year, quarter, or month) that are useful whenever you need to get that value of a selection that is smaller than the whole period considered. For example, looking at the month level (which may be displayed in rows), you might want to display also the value of the end of the quarter and the end of the year in the same row, as you can see in Figure 7-31.

Note Please note that raw data used in this example includes balances for dates through December 31. For this reason, the DAX function we are going to use provides complete results because the data based on the *LASTDATE* function would not work if the last day of a period (such as month, quarter, or year) were missing.

Row Labels	LastBalance	ClosingBalanceMonth	ClosingBalanceQuarter	ClosingBalanceYear
⊟ 2010	6,686.00	6,686.00	6,686.00	6,686.00
⊟ Q1	10,667.00	10,667.00	10,667.00	6,686.00
01 - January	4,657.00	4,657.00	10,667.00	6,686.00
02 - February	7,762.00	7,762.00	10,667.00	6,686.00
03 - March	10,667.00	10,667.00	10,667.00	6,686.00
⊟ Q2	7,452.00	7,452.00	7,452.00	6,686.00
04 - April	6,210.00	6,210.00	7,452.00	6,686.00
05 - May	5,589.00	5,589.00	7,452.00	6,686.00
06 - June	7,452.00	7,452.00	7,452.00	6,686.00
⊟ Q3	7,762.00	7,762.00	7,762.00	6,686.00
07 - July	9,936.00	9,936.00	7,762.00	6,686.00
08 - August	13,972.00	13,972.00	7,762.00	6,686.00
09 - September	7,762.00	7,762.00	7,762.00	6,686.00
⊟ Q4	6,686.00	6,686.00	6,686.00	6,686.00
10 - October	6,210.00	6,210.00	6,686.00	6,686.00
11 - November	5,744.00	5,744.00	6,686.00	6,686.00
12 - December	6,686.00	6,686.00	6,686.00	6,686.00
Grand Total	6,686.00	6,686.00	6,686.00	6,686.00

FIGURE 7-31 The value at end of month, quarter, and year for each month is always the corresponding closing balance.

The formulas used to calculate *ClosingBalanceMonth*, *ClosingBalanceQuarter*, and *ClosingBalanceYear* measures are the following:

```
[ClosingBalanceMonth] :=
    CLOSINGBALANCEMONTH ( SUM ( Balances[Balance] ), 'Date'[Date] )

[ClosingBalanceQuarter] :=
    CLOSINGBALANCEQUARTER ( SUM ( Balances[Balance] ), 'Date'[Date] )

[ClosingBalanceYear] :=
    CLOSINGBALANCEYEAR ( SUM ( Balances[Balance] ), 'Date'[Date] )
```

These formulas use the *LASTDATE* function internally, but they operate on a set of dates that can extend the current selection in the pivot table. For example, the *CLOSINGBALANCEYEAR* function considers the *LASTDATE* of 'Date'[Date], which is applied to the last year period of the dates included in the filter context. So for February 2010 (and for any month or quarter of 2010), this date is December 31, 2010. The *CLOSINGBALANCEYEAR* function behaves like a *CALCULATE* expression using the *ENDOFYEAR* function as a filter. As usual, the use of *CALCULATE* is more generic and flexible, but specific DAX functions like *CLOSINGBALANCEYEAR* better express the intention of the measure designer. The following are measures equivalent to the ones previously shown using *CALCU-LATE* syntax:

```
[ClosingBalanceEOM] :=
    CALCULATE ( SUM ( Balances[Balance] ), ENDOFMONTH ( 'Date'[Date] ) )

[ClosingBalanceEOQ] :=
    CALCULATE ( SUM ( Balances[Balance] ), ENDOFQUARTER ( 'Date'[Date] ) )

[ClosingBalanceEOY] :=
    CALCULATE ( SUM ( Balances[Balance] ), ENDOFYEAR ( 'Date'[Date] ) )
```

Tip The DAX functions *OPENINGBALANCEMONTH*, *OPENINGBALANCEQUARTER*, and *OPENINGBALANCEYEAR* use the *FIRSTDATE* internally instead of the *LASTDATE* of the considered period. They correspond to the *CALCULATE* formula, which uses *STARTOFMONTH*, *STARTOFQUARTER*, and *STARTOFYEAR* internally as its filter, respectively.

An important consideration has to be made about dates for which there is available data in your model. You can see this if you drill down to data at the day level in the pivot table. Before doing that, consider the raw data set we used in this example, shown in Figure 7-32.

Name	Occupation	Country/Region	Date	Balance
Katie Jordan	Farmer	USA	1/8/2010	1,540.00
Luis Bonifaz	IT Consultant	Argentina	1/8/2010	2,310.00
Maurizio Macagno	IT Consultant	Italy	1/8/2010	1,450.00
Katie Jordan	Farmer	USA	1/15/2010	1,230.00
Luis Bonifaz	IT Consultant	Argentina	1/15/2010	2,020.00
Maurizio Macagno	IT Consultant	Italy	1/15/2010	1,120.00
Katie Jordan	Farmer	USA	1/22/2010	980.00
Luis Bonifaz	IT Consultant	Argentina	1/22/2010	1,850.00
Maurizio Macagno	IT Consultant	Italy	1/22/2010	630.00
Katie Jordan	Farmer	USA	1/31/2010	1,687.00
Luis Bonifaz	IT Consultant	Argentina	1/31/2010	1,470.00
Maurizio Macagno	IT Consultant	Italy	1/31/2010	1,500.00
Katie Jordan	Farmer	USA	2/10/2010	2,150.00

FIGURE 7-32 The balances appear many times for each month, making calculation more difficult.

As you can see, there are more balances for each month. For example, in January there are balances for days 8, 15, 22, and 31.

Note In this example, we always have a balance value for each account, as if we took a snapshot on a certain date for every account available, even if it has not changed its value since the previous date. When this condition is not true, you cannot use *OPENINGBALANCE* and *CLOSINGBALANCE* functions, and you have to rely on techniques described in the previous section "Semi-additive measures."

If you browse this data at the day level in the pivot table by using the same measures as the previous example, you see the results shown in Figure 7-33.

Row Labels	LastBalance	ClosingBalanceMonth	ClosingBalanceQuarter	ClosingBalanceYear
⊟ 2010	6,686.00	6,686.00	6,686.00	6,686.00
⊟ Q1	10,667.00	10,667.00	10,667.00	6,686.00
⊟ 01 - January	4,657.00	4,657.00	10,667.00	6,686.00
1/1/2010		4,657.00	10,667.00	6,686.00
1/2/2010		4,657.00	10,667.00	6,686.00
1/3/2010		4,657.00	10,667.00	6,686.00
1/4/2010		4,657.00	10,667.00	6,686.00
1/5/2010		4,657.00	10,667.00	6,686.00
1/6/2010		4,657.00	10,667.00	6,686.00
1/7/2010		4,657.00	10,667.00	6,686.00
1/8/2010	5,300.00	4,657.00	10,667.00	6,686.00
1/9/2010		4,657.00	10,667.00	6,686.00
1/10/2010		4,657.00	10,667.00	6,686.00
1/11/2010		4,657.00	10,667.00	6,686.00
1/12/2010		4,657.00	10,667.00	6,686.00
1/13/2010		4,657.00	10,667.00	6,686.00
1/14/2010		4,657.00	10,667.00	6,686.00
1/15/2010	4,370.00	4,657.00	10,667.00	6,686.00
1/16/2010		4,657.00	10,667.00	6,686.00
1/17/2010		4,657.00	10,667.00	6,686.00
1/18/2010		4,657.00	10,667.00	6,686.00
1/19/2010		4,657.00	10,667.00	6,686.00
1/20/2010		4,657.00	10,667.00	6,686.00
1/21/2010		4,657.00	10,667.00	6,686.00
1/22/2010	3,460.00	4,657.00	10,667.00	6,686.00
1/23/2010		4,657.00	10,667.00	6,686.00
1/24/2010		4,657.00	10,667.00	6,686.00
1/25/2010		4,657.00	10,667.00	6,686.00
1/26/2010		4,657.00	10,667.00	6,686.00
1/27/2010		4,657.00	10,667.00	6,686.00
1/28/2010		4,657.00	10,667.00	6,686.00
1/29/2010		4,657.00	10,667.00	6,686.00
1/30/2010		4,657.00	10,667.00	6,686.00
1/31/2010	4,657.00	4,657.00	10,667.00	6,686.00

FIGURE 7-33 Browsing data at the day level displays rows with no balance data.

The calculated fields defined to display values at the end of the period suffer an unpleasant side effect: all the dates are visible, even those for which there is no balance data available. If you want to display just the rows corresponding to dates with balance data defined, you have to modify the measures, checking the existence of data in the Balances table, in this way:

```
[ClosingBalanceMonth2] :=
IF (
    COUNTROWS ( Balances ) > 0,
    CLOSINGBALANCEMONTH ( SUM ( Balances[Balance] ), 'Date'[Date] )
)


[ClosingBalanceQuarter2] :=
IF (
    COUNTROWS ( Balances ) > 0,
    CLOSINGBALANCEQUARTER ( SUM ( Balances[Balance] ), 'Date'[Date] )
)


[ClosingBalanceYear2] : =
IF (
    COUNTROWS ( Balances ) > 0,
    CLOSINGBALANCEYEAR ( SUM ( Balances[Balance] ), 'Date'[Date] )
)
```

Browsing data using these measures results in a report such as the one shown in Figure 7-34.

Row Labels	LastBalance	ClosingBalanceMonth2	ClosingBalanceQuarter2	ClosingBalanceYear2
⊟ 2010	6,686.00	6,686.00	6,686.00	6,686.00
⊟ Q1	10,667.00	10,667.00	10,667.00	6,686.00
⊟ 01 - January	4,657.00	4,657.00	10,667.00	6,686.00
1/8/2010	5,300.00	4,657.00	10,667.00	6,686.00
1/15/2010	4,370.00	4,657.00	10,667.00	6,686.00
1/22/2010	3,460.00	4,657.00	10,667.00	6,686.00
1/31/2010	4,657.00	4,657.00	10,667.00	6,686.00
⊟ 02 - February	7,762.00	7,762.00	10,667.00	6,686.00
2/10/2010	6,210.00	7,762.00	10,667.00	6,686.00
2/19/2010	5,190.00	7,762.00	10,667.00	6,686.00
2/28/2010	7,762.00	7,762.00	10,667.00	6,686.00

FIGURE 7-34 This report is using measures that display only days for which there is balance data.

By default, many client tools (including the Microsoft Excel pivot table used in this example) do not display empty rows and columns. For this reason, the days containing no balance date are not shown. All the measures used in Figure 7-34 return BLANK for those days, making them disappear from the report.

Advanced time intelligence

In this section, you learn how to rewrite in plain DAX code each time intelligence calculation you have seen so far by using standard DAX functions such as *FILTER*, *ALL*, *VALUES*, *MIN*, and *MAX*. We are not suggesting doing so as a rule. Knowing the exact behavior of time intelligence functions will help you understand particular side cases you might not be able to explain at first sight, and will enable you to write custom calculations whenever the available functions do not provide the exact calculation you need. You might want to rewrite a time intelligence calculation in DAX for two main reasons.

First, you might want to use *DirectQuery*, which transforms a DAX query into a SQL query sent to the original data source and does not support the DAX time intelligence functions. When you create a Microsoft Visual Studio project enabled for *DirectQuery*, any access to these functions is blocked and you see a syntax error in DAX expressions calling them. In this case, writing the filter using standard DAX functions as described later is required.

Second, you might have a nonstandard calendar, where the first day of the year is not always the same for all the years (for example, this is the case for ISO calendars based on weeks). In this case, the assumption made by the time intelligence function (year, month, and quarter can be always extracted from the date value) is no longer true. You can write a different logic by changing the DAX code in the filter conditions, or you can simply take advantage of other columns in the Date table, so you do not have a complex DAX expression to maintain. You will find more examples of this latter approach in the section "Custom calendars," later in this chapter.

Understanding periods to date

Previously, you have seen the DAX functions that calculate month-to-date, quarter-to-date, and year-to-date. If you use *TOTALYTD*, *TOTALQTD*, or *TOTALMTD* scalar functions, their implementation determines the date filters by calling *DATESYTD*, *DATESQTD*, and *DATESMTD*. Each of these filter functions is similar to the result of a *FILTER* statement that you can write in DAX.

For example, consider the following *DATESYTD* function:

```
DATESYTD ( 'Date'[Date] )
```

It corresponds to a filter over the date column using *FILTER* called by *CALCULATETABLE*, such as in the following code:

```
CALCULATETABLE (
    FILTER (
        ALL ( 'Date'[Date] ),
        AND (
            'Date'[Date] <= MAX ( 'Date'[Date] ),
            YEAR ( 'Date'[Date] ) - YEAR ( MAX ( 'Date'[Date] ) )
        )
    )
)
```

In a similar way, the following *DATESMTD* function:

```
DATESMTD ( 'Date'[Date] )
```

corresponds to the following code:

```
CALCULATETABLE (
    FILTER (
        ALL ( 'Date'[Date] ),
        AND (
            'Date'[Date] <= MAX ( 'Date'[Date] ),
            AND (
                YEAR ( 'Date'[Date] ) = YEAR ( MAX ( 'Date'[Date] ) ),
                MONTH ( 'Date'[Date] ) = MONTH ( MAX ( 'Date'[Date] ) )
            )
        )
    )
)
```

The *DATESQTD* function would be similar to *DATESMTD*, just replacing the *MONTH* function call with *QUARTER*.

All of these alternative implementations have a common characteristic: they extract the information about year, month, and quarter, from the last day available in the current selection. The reason why *CALCULATETABLE* calls *FILTER* is to transform a row context in a filter context. However, this technique could be expensive if used in a calculated column. The internal implementation of these functions is optimized and you can use two different techniques in order to achieve better performance.

If you do not have a row context, you can simply remove *CALCULATETABLE*. Usually, this is the case for a filter argument in a *CALCULATE* call, a place where *DATESYTD* is used often. So, for *DATESYTD* you can write:

```
FILTER (
    ALL ( 'Date'[Date] ),
    AND (
        'Date'[Date] <= MAX ( 'Date'[Date] ),
        YEAR ( 'Date'[Date] ) = YEAR ( MAX ( 'Date'[Date] ) )
    )
)
```

If you have a row context for the date you want to use, for example in a calculated column, then you can use *EARLIER* instead of *MAX*:

```
FILTER (
    ALL ( 'Date'[Date] ),
    AND (
        'Date'[Date] <= EARLIER ( 'Date'[Date] ),
        YEAR ( 'Date'[Date] ) = YEAR ( EARLIER ( 'Date'[Date] ) )
    )
)
```

The second argument of *DATESYTD* allows you to specify a date that defines the year-end date. For example, for a fiscal year starting on July 1, you specify June 30 in the second argument (using one of the following versions, depending on your local language settings):

```
DATESYTD ( 'Date'[Date], "06-30" )

DATESYTD ( 'Date'[Date], "30-06" )
```

Regardless of the local language settings, let us assume you specified *<day>* and *<month>*. The corresponding *FILTER* of *DATESYTD* using these placeholders is the following:

```
FILTER (
    ALL ( 'Date'[Date] ),
    AND (
        'Date'[Date] > DATE ( YEAR ( MAX ( 'Date'[Date] ) ) - 1, <month>, <day> )
        'Date'[Date] <= MAX ( 'Date'[Date] )
    )
)
```

Understanding *DATEADD*

As you have seen, *DATEADD* is a function commonly used to get a corresponding set of dates moved by a certain offset. It is important to understand that *DATEADD* is a table function that only handles existing values in the date column passed as an argument. *DATEADD* also applies a particular logic in specific conditions, especially related to the month selection, as you will see in a few examples.

DATEADD uses only the values of the date column passed as a first argument. It ignores all other columns present in the Date table, so it has to extract other information (such as year, quarter, and day) from the available date value. Consider the following formula:

```
DATEADD ( 'Date'[Date], -1, MONTH )
```

The closest (but not correct) DAX formula we can write is the following:

```
FILTER (
    ALL ( 'Date'[Date] ),
    CONTAINS (
        VALUES ( 'Date'[Date] ),
        'Date'[Date],
        DATE ( YEAR ( 'Date'[Date] ), MONTH ( 'Date'[Date] ) - 1, DAY ( 'Date'[Date] ) )
    )
)
```

 Note In the previous example and in other formulas in this chapter we use the *CONTAINS* function, which returns true if the table passed as first argument has at least one row where the value of the column specified in the second argument corresponds to the expression passed in the third argument. You can read a more complete description of this function in Chapter 9, "Advanced table functions."

The formula is not correct because it is trying to find the corresponding days in the previous month by subtracting one from the month. However, if you start from January, you should decrease the year value and put 12 in the month argument. A slightly better version is:

```
FILTER (
    ALL ( 'Date'[Date] ),
    CONTAINS (
        VALUES ( 'Date'[Date] ),
        'Date'[Date],
        DATE (
            YEAR ( 'Date'[Date] ) - IF ( MONTH ( 'Date'[Date] ) = 1 ), 1, 0 ),
            IF ( MONTH ( 'Date'[Date] ) = 1 ), 12, MONTH ( 'Date'[Date] ) - 1 ),
            DAY ( 'Date'[Date] )
        )
    )
)
```

This version works correctly between January and December, and only with negative offsets. However, we should change the DAX expression in order to handle offsets other than –1 (for example, you might use –2 to go back two months), and we do not handle properly the shift between months with a different number of days. In fact, the last implementation works well if the destination month has a smaller number of days, but if you move from February to January, you will miss two or three days, depending on the year.

At this point, the logic becomes much more complex to implement in DAX if you do not want to rely on other columns in the Date table. In the "Custom calendars" section later in this chapter, you will find a simpler and more flexible approach to implement time intelligence in DAX based on the content of the Date table. Now, let's see what the exact behavior of *DATEADD* is. In the following descriptions the term "selection" means the values of *'Date'[Date]* active in filter context.

- *DATEADD* only works with a contiguous date selection and raises an error otherwise.

- *DATEADD* only returns days existing in the date column received as first argument.

- When a corresponding day does not exist in the corresponding month after the shift operation, the result of *DATEADD* includes the last day of the corresponding month.

- When the selection includes the last day of a month, and the selection is more than one day, then the result of *DATEADD* includes all the days between the corresponding day in the shifted month and the end of the shifted month.

A few examples are helpful to understand the effects of these behaviors. Consider the following measure: *Days* counts the number of days selected, *PM Days* counts the number of days returned by *DATEADD* shifted back one month, and *PM Day* returns the day value if the result includes only one day.

```
[Days] := COUNTROWS ( 'Date' )

[PM Days] := COUNTROWS ( DATEADD ( 'Date'[Date], -1, MONTH ) )

[PM Day] :=
IF (
    HASONEVALUE ( 'Date'[Date] ),
    DATEADD ( 'Date'[Date], -1, MONTH )
)
```

- **Rule 1** Rule 1 is simple to explain. If you try to select January 2008 and March 2008 without selecting February 2008, you get the following error:

```
Function 'DATEADD' only works with contiguous date selections.
```

If you have to handle noncontiguous date selections with time intelligence calculations, you have to write custom DAX calculations, as explained later in the "Computing over noncontiguous periods" section.

- **Rule 2** Rule 2 has effects when the selection is near the boundary of the range of dates included in the Date table. For example, by selecting the first four days in January 2008, the result includes the first four days of December 2007. As you can see in Figure 7-35, in this case the result of PM Days corresponds to Days, because no special rules apply.

Row Labels	Days	PM Days	PM Day
CY 2008	4	4	
January 2008	4	4	
1/1/2008	1	1	12/1/2007
1/2/2008	1	1	12/2/2007
1/3/2008	1	1	12/3/2007
1/4/2008	1	1	12/4/2007
Grand Total	4	4	

FIGURE 7-35 The dates selected are shifted back one month.

The Date table used in the example includes all the days between 2005 and 2011. If the initial selection includes days in January 2005 then the result is blank, because there are no values in the Date table for December 2004. You see this behavior in Figure 7-36.

Row Labels	Days	PM Days	PM Day
CY 2005	5		
January 2005	5		
1/1/2005	1		
1/2/2005	1		
1/3/2005	1		
1/4/2005	1		
1/5/2005	1		
Grand Total	5		

FIGURE 7-36 The result of *DATEADD* is blank if it should return dates not existing in the Date table.

Note The main reason why the Date table should include all the days within one year is because of *DATEADD* behavior. Remember that several time intelligence functions in DAX internally use *DATEADD*, so having a complete Date table is fundamental for a correct behavior of DAX time intelligence functions.

- **Rule 3** Rule 3 is relevant when the months have a different number of days. For example, if you select July 31, 2008, the result is June 30, 2008, as you see in Figure 7-37.

Row Labels	Days	PM Days	PM Day
⊟ CY 2008	1	1	6/30/2008
⊟ July 2008	1	1	6/30/2008
7/31/2008	1	1	6/30/2008
Grand Total	**1**	**1**	**6/30/2008**

FIGURE 7-37 A date that does not exist in the destination month is replaced by the last day of the month.

The consequence of this rule is that you might obtain as a result a lower number of days than the initial selection. This is intuitive when the selection of 31 days in March should result in a corresponding selection 28 or 29 days in February (depending on the year). However, the effect of Rule 3 is that every day always has a corresponding day, so you always compare the last day of a month with the last day of the corresponding month. In Figure 7-38 you can see that every day between March 29 and March 31 always corresponds to February 29. At the month level, an initial selection of three days (see Days column) corresponds to a resulting selection of only one day (see *PM Days*), because *DATEADD* does not return duplicates.

Row Labels	Days	PM Days	PM Day
⊟ CY 2008	3	1	
⊟ March 2008	3	1	
3/29/2008	1	1	2/29/2008
3/30/2008	1	1	2/29/2008
3/31/2008	1	1	2/29/2008
Grand Total	**3**	**1**	

FIGURE 7-38 Several days in the starting selection might result in the same day in the *DATEADD* result.

- **Rule 4** Rule 4 generates a different behavior when the last day of a month is included within a range of dates. For example, consider the initial selection of two days, June 30, 2008, and July 1, 2008. What is the result you expect by shifting the dates back one month? Considering each single day, the result is the corresponding day in the previous month (May 30, 2008, and June 1, 2008, respectively). However, when you consider the entire selection of two days, then the result will also contain the dates included between the first and the last day of the selection, which in this case corresponds to May 31, 2008. You can see in Figure 7-39 that the value returned by the *PM Days* measure is three instead of two when you consider the row CY 2008.

Row Labels	Days	PM Days	PM Day
⊟ CY 2008	2	3	
⊟ June 2008	1	1	5/30/2008
6/30/2008	1	1	5/30/2008
⊟ July 2008	1	1	6/1/2008
7/1/2008	1	1	6/1/2008
Grand Total	2	3	

FIGURE 7-39 The result of *DATEADD* includes all days between the first and the last day of the selection after the shift operation.

The result at the month level is interesting: even if you selected the last day of the month (June 30, 2008), the result only has May 30, 2008. In this case, you would not compare the last day of the month with the last day of the previous month. You can see in Figure 7-40 that the values of *Days* and *PM Days* are 1 at both the day level and the month level. However, if the selection in the month includes at least two days, then the Rule 4 effect is to add also May 31, 2008, to the selection. This is visible only in the value of *PM Days*, which is 3 in the rows June 2008 and CY 2008.

Row Labels	Days	PM Days	PM Day
⊟ CY 2008	2	3	
⊟ June 2008	2	3	
6/29/2008	1	1	5/29/2008
6/30/2008	1	1	5/30/2008
Grand Total	2	3	

FIGURE 7-40 The selection of two or more days in a month, including the last day of that month, might extend the result by adding the days until the end of the month.

An extreme case of Rule 4 is the extension from two days to five days that happens when you select February 27 and February 28 in a non-leap year, as you can see in Figure 7-41.

Row Labels	Days	PM Days	PM Day
⊟ CY 2007	2	5	
⊟ February 2007	2	5	
2/27/2007	1	1	1/27/2007
2/28/2007	1	1	1/28/2007
Grand Total	2	5	

FIGURE 7-41 The measure *PM Days* shows that the selection of two days in February results in a selection of five days in January.

The result of these rules is to provide an intuitive behavior when you operate at the month level. As you can see in Figure 7-42, when you compare the selections at the month level, the result is intuitive and expected, showing the number of days of the previous month. Understanding the rules described in this section is important to handle side conditions that might happen with partial selections of days in months. We used the number of days just to make clear the behavior, but you will certainly use other measures (for example, quantity or sales amount) in order to simplify the comparison of values between two periods (in this case, the previous month).

Row Labels	Days	PM Days	PM Day
⊟CY 2007	365	365	
⊞January 2007	31	31	
⊞February 2007	28	31	
⊞March 2007	31	28	
⊞April 2007	30	31	
⊞May 2007	31	30	
⊞June 2007	30	31	
⊞July 2007	31	30	
⊞August 2007	31	31	
⊞September 2007	30	31	
⊞October 2007	31	30	
⊞November 2007	30	31	
⊞December 2007	31	30	
Grand Total	365	365	

FIGURE 7-42 The measure *PM Days* shows the number of days of the previous month.

Understanding *FIRSTDATE* and *LASTDATE*

In the "Semi-additive measures" section earlier in this chapter, you have seen two functions that might seem similar, but have a very different behavior: *LASTDATE* and *LASTNONBLANK*. Two other corresponding functions get the first date, instead of the last date within a period: *FIRSTDATE* and *FIRSTNONBLANK*. This section describes the behavior of *FIRSTDATE* and *LASTDATE*, and the next section will explain *FIRSTNONBLANK* and *LASTNONBLANK* in detail.

FIRSTDATE and *LASTDATE* operate only on a date column and they return the first and the last date in the active filter context, respectively, ignoring the data existing in other related tables:

```
FIRSTDATE ( <dates> )
LASTDATE ( <dates> )
```

The *<dates>* argument is a table containing only one column of date data type. If you write the name of a column, a *VALUES* call is implicitly made using that column. For example, these expressions:

```
FIRSTDATE ( 'Date'[Date] )

LASTDATE ( 'Date'[Date] )
```

correspond to these expressions:

```
FIRSTDATE ( VALUES ( 'Date'[Date] ) )

LASTDATE ( VALUES ( 'Date'[Date] ) )
```

FIRSTDATE returns the minimum value of the column received in the current filter context, whereas *LASTDATE* returns the maximum value (remember that a date is internally represented as a floating-point number). The semantic difference between *FIRSTDATE/LASTDATE* and *MIN/MAX* functions is that the former returns a table and performs a context transition, whereas the latter returns a scalar value without doing any context transition. The reason for that is to simplify the DAX syntax when you place these expressions in the filter argument of a *CALCULATE* function.

For example, consider the following expression:

```
CALCULATE (
    SUM ( Inventory[Quantity] ),
    LASTDATE ( 'Date'[Date] )
)
```

You can rewrite such expressions into this equivalent DAX syntax, using *MAX* instead of *LASTDATE*, but this would result in a longer code:

```
CALCULATE (
    SUM ( Inventory[Quantity] ),
    FILTER (
        ALL ( 'Date'[Date] ),
        'Date'[Date] = MAX ( 'Date'[Date] )
    )
)
```

In reality, the *LASTDATE* function also performs a context transition. The exact correspondence of *LASTDATE* in plain DAX is as follows:

```
CALCULATE (
    SUM ( Inventory[Quantity] ),
    CALCULATETABLE (
        VALUES ( 'Date'[Date] ),
        FILTER (
            ALL ( 'Date'[Date] ),
            'Date'[Date] = MAX ( 'Date'[Date] )
        )
    )
)
```

The context transition is relevant when you execute *FIRSTDATE/LASTDATE* in a row context. The best practice is using *FIRSTDATE/LASTDATE* when you write a filter expression (because a table expression is expected), whereas *MIN/MAX* functions are better when you are writing a logical expression in a row context (which usually requires a scalar value), because *LASTDATE* implies a context transition that hides the external filter context.

For example, you will favor *FIRSTDATE/LASTDATE* over *MIN/MAX* in a filter argument of *CALCULATE/CALCULATETABLE* functions, because the syntax is simpler (we have already seen several examples of this usage). However, you should use the *MIN/MAX* approach when the context transition implied by *FIRSTDATE/LASTDATE* would modify the result. This is the case of the condition in a *FILTER* function. The following expression filters the dates for computing a running total:

```
FILTER (
    ALL ( 'Date'[Date] ),
    'Date'[Date] <= MAX ( 'Date'[Date] )
)
```

Using *MAX* is the right method to use. In fact, if you write *LASTDATE* instead of *MAX*, you would not get any syntax error, but the result would always be all the dates, regardless of the current selection. Thus, the following expression is *always wrong*:

```
FILTER (
    ALL ( 'Date'[Date] ),
    'Date'[Date] <= LASTDATE ( 'Date'[Date] )
)
```

You can see the problem by just counting the number of days returned by the two versions of the running total filter using the following measures:

```
[RT Days MAX] :=
COUNTROWS (
    FILTER (
        ALL ( 'Date'[Date] ),
        'Date'[Date] <= MAX ( 'Date'[Date] )
    )
)

[RT Days LASTDATE] :=
COUNTROWS (
    FILTER (
        ALL ( 'Date'[Date] ),
        'Date'[Date] <= LASTDATE ( 'Date'[Date] )
    )
)
```

Figure 7-43 shows that the number of days filtered for the running total is correct for the *RT Days MAX* measure, but it is wrong for *RT Days LASTDATE*. The reason is that the context transition performed by *LASTDATE* for each date always returns the same value of the current *FILTER* iteration, resulting in all the dates being returned by *FILTER*.

Row Labels	Days	RT Days MAX	RT Days LASTDATE
⊞ CY 2005	365	365	2,556
⊟ CY 2006	365	730	2,556
⊞ January 2006	31	396	2,556
⊞ February 2006	28	424	2,556
⊞ March 2006	31	455	2,556
⊞ April 2006	30	485	2,556
⊞ May 2006	31	516	2,556
⊞ June 2006	30	546	2,556
⊞ July 2006	31	577	2,556
⊞ August 2006	31	608	2,556
⊞ September 2006	30	638	2,556
⊞ October 2006	31	669	2,556
⊞ November 2006	30	699	2,556
⊞ December 2006	31	730	2,556
⊞ CY 2007	365	1,095	2,556
⊞ CY 2008	366	1,461	2,556
⊞ CY 2009	365	1,826	2,556
⊞ CY 2010	365	2,191	2,556
Grand Total	2,191	2,191	2,556

FIGURE 7-43 The *RT Days LASTDATE* measure always counts all the rows in Date table.

Understanding *FIRSTNONBLANK* and *LASTNONBLANK*

The *LASTNONBLANK* function, which you have previously seen in the "Semi-additive measures" section, has a particular behavior, shared also by *FIRSTNONBLANK*. The syntax of these functions is as follows:

```
FIRSTNONBLANK ( <column>, <expression> )
LASTNONBLANK ( <column>, <expression> )
```

These functions return the first or last value in *<column>*, filtered by the current context, wherein the *<expression>* is not blank. These functions behave like *SUMX* or similar functions in this regard, because they are iterators. They set a row context for a value of <column> and then evaluate the <expression> by using that row context. If <expression> and <column> manage data of the same table, everything works fine. However, whenever <expression> uses columns of tables other than the one to which *<column>* belongs, you have to make a context transition by using *RELATEDTABLE,* *CALCULATETABLE,* or *CALCULATE*. This is the best practice for every date-related calculation and it is a very common situation every time you have a separate Date table.

To get the right value for the last nonblank date for a given measure/table, you have to use an expression like this:

```
LASTNONBLANK ( Dates[Date], CALCULATE ( COUNT ( Inventory[Quantity] ) ) )
```

It returns the last date (in the current filter context) for which there are values for the Quantity column in the Inventory table. You can also use an equivalent formula:

```
LASTNONBLANK ( Dates[Date], COUNTROWS ( RELATEDTABLE ( Inventory ) ) )
```

The last expression returns the last date (in the current filter context) for which there is a related row in the Inventory table.

> **Note** The *FIRSTNONBLANK/LASTNONBLANK* functions accept any data type as their first argument, whereas the *FIRSTDATE/LASTDATE* functions require a column of date data type. You might also use *FIRSTNONBLANK/LASTNONBLANK* instead of *FIRSTDATE/LASTDATE* when you have a date concept expressed in another data type and you want the first or last value in the filter context, passing any nonblank expression as a second argument. However, you might consider also using the *TOPN* function in such a condition.

Using drillthrough with time intelligence

A *drillthrough* operation is a request for the data source rows corresponding to the filter context used in a certain calculation. Every time you use a time intelligence function, you change the filter context on the Date table, producing a different result for a measure from the one obtained with the initial filter context. When you use a client that performs a drillthrough action over a report, such as a pivot table in Excel, you could observe a behavior that is not what you might expect. In fact, the drillthrough operation made in MDX does not consider the changes in the filter context defined by the measure itself but only the filter context defined by rows, columns, filters, and slicers of the pivot table.

For example, the drillthrough on March 2007 always returns the same rows, regardless of the time intelligence function applied in the measure. By using *TOTALYTD* you would expect all the days from January to March 2007, by using *SAMEPERIODLASTYEAR* you would expect March 2006, and by using *LASTDATE* you would expect only the rows for March 31, 2007. However, any of these filters always returns all the rows for all the days in March 2007. Unfortunately, this behavior is by design.

Custom calendars

As you have seen so far, the standard time intelligence functions in DAX only support standard Gregorian calendars based on a solar calendar divided into 12 months, each one with a different number of days. This works well when you want to analyze the data by year, quarter, month, and day. However, you might have a different definition of periods, not corresponding to months, or you might have week-based calendars, such as the ISO week date system. Whatever the reason is, you need to rewrite the time intelligence logic in DAX when you cannot use the standard time intelligence functions.

This final section shows the main techniques to implement time intelligence calculations in DAX when you cannot use standard functions. A common technique is to move part of the business logic to the Date table. The standard DAX time intelligence functions do not read any information from the Date table other than the date column. This is a design choice of DAX, because in this way the behavior of the language does not depend on defining more metadata to identify the columns to use to determine year, quarter, and month of a date (as it was in the case with MDX and Analysis Services Multidimensional). You can make more assumptions in your code, and this helps in simplifying the code to write in order to handle custom time-related calculation.

You will find more information, examples, and DAX formulas ready to use in the following articles:

- Time Patterns: *http://www.daxpatterns.com/time-patterns/*

- Week-Based Time Intelligence in DAX: *http://sql.bi/isoweeks/*

Working with weeks

DAX does not provide any time intelligence function to handle weeks. The reason is that there are many different standards and techniques to define weeks within a year, and to define the notion of calculation over weeks. Often a single week crosses the boundaries of years, quarters, and months. You have to write the code to handle your own definition of a week-based calendar. For example, in ISO a week-date system of January 1 and January 2 in 2011 belongs to week 52 of year 2010, and the first week of 2011 starts on January 3.

Even if there are different standards, you can learn a generic approach that should work in most of the cases, moving in Date table data the assignment of a week to a month/quarter/year. Changing the rules will just require changing the content of the Date table, without modifying the DAX code of the measures.

For example, you can extend a Date table to support ISO weeks by using the following calculated columns:

```
Date[Calendar Week Number] = WEEKNUM ( 'Date'[Date], 1 )

Date [ISO Week Number] = WEEKNUM ( [Date], 21 )

Date [ISO Year Number] =
IF (
    [ISO Week Number] < 5 && [Calendar Week Number] > 50,
    [Calendar Year Number] + 1,
    IF (
        [ISO Week Number] > 50 && [Calendar Week Number] < 5,
        [Calendar Year Number] - 1,
        [Calendar Year Number]
    )
)
```

```
Date [ISO Week] = "W" & [ISO Week Number] & "-" & [ISO Year Number]

Date [ISO Week Sequential] = INT ( ( 'Date'[Date] - 2 ) / 7 )

Date [ISO Year Day Number] =
COUNTROWS (
    FILTER (
        Date,
        AND (
            'Date'[ISO Year Number] = EARLIER ( 'Date'[ISO Year Number] ),
            'Date'[Date] <= EARLIER ( 'Date'[Date] )
        )
    )
)
```

You can see in Figure 7-44 the result of these columns. The *ISO Week* column will be visible to users, whereas the *ISO Week Sequential Number* will not be visible to client tools. The *ISO Year Day Number* is the number of days since the beginning of the ISO year. Such numbers will make it easy to compare different periods.

Date	ISO Week Number	Calendar Week Number	ISO Year Number	ISO Week	ISO Week Sequential	ISO Year Day Number
12/30/2010	52	53	2010	W52-2010	5791	361
12/31/2010	52	53	2010	W52-2010	5791	362
1/1/2011	52	1	2010	W52-2010	5791	363
1/2/2011	52	2	2010	W52-2010	5791	364
1/3/2011	1	2	2011	W1-2011	5792	1
1/4/2011	1	2	2011	W1-2011	5792	2
1/5/2011	1	2	2011	W1-2011	5792	3
1/6/2011	1	2	2011	W1-2011	5792	4
1/7/2011	1	2	2011	W1-2011	5792	5
1/8/2011	1	2	2011	W1-2011	5792	6
1/9/2011	1	3	2011	W1-2011	5792	7
1/10/2011	2	3	2011	W2-2011	5793	8
1/11/2011	2	3	2011	W2 2011	5793	9

FIGURE 7-44 The calculated columns extend the Date table to support ISO weeks.

Using the new columns, you can write year-to-date aggregations by using the ISO Year Number column instead of extracting the year number from the date. The technique is the same as you have seen in the "Understanding periods to date" section earlier in this chapter. We just make sure that only one ISO Year is selected in order to execute the *VALUES* function, thus avoiding any execution error.

```
[ISO YTD Sales] :=
IF (
    HASONEVALUE ( 'Date'[ISO Year Number] ),
    CALCULATE (
        [Sales Amount],
        FILTER (
            ALL ( 'Date' ),
            AND (
                'Date'[ISO Year Number] = VALUES ( 'Date'[ISO Year Number] ),
                'Date'[Date] <= MAX ( 'Date'[Date] )
            )
        )
    )
)
```

Figure 7-45 shows the result of the *ISO YTD Sales* measure for the first week of year 2008, which includes December 31, 2007.

Row Labels	Sales Amount	ISO YTD Sales
2008	**$10,811,544.55**	**$10,811,544.55**
W1-2008	**$144,286.94**	**$144,286.94**
12/31/2007	$8,564.93	$8,564.93
1/1/2008	$20,150.87	$28,715.80
1/2/2008	$17,330.75	$46,046.55
1/3/2008	$68,198.22	$114,244.77
1/4/2008		$114,244.77
1/5/2008	$21,232.91	$135,477.68
1/6/2008	$8,809.26	$144,286.94
W2-2008	**$136,294.34**	**$280,581.28**
W3-2008	**$200,832.08**	**$481,413.36**
W4-2008	**$186,285.45**	**$667,698.81**

FIGURE 7-45 The *ISO YTD Sales* correctly includes December 31, 2007, in the first week of 2008.

The comparison with the prior year should compare the relative weeks of the year with the same weeks in the previous year. Since the dates might be very different, it is simpler to use other columns in the Date table to implement the comparison logic. The distribution of weeks within each year is very regular, because each week always has seven days, whereas calendar months have different lengths and cannot benefit from the same assumption. In week-based calendars, you can simplify the calculation by looking in the "previous" year for the same "relative" days that were selected in the current filter context.

The following *ISO PY Sales* measure filters the same selection of days in the previous year. Such a technique works also when the selection includes complete weeks, because the days are selected using the *ISO Year Day Number* value, and not the effective date.

```
[ISO PY Sales] :=
IF (
    HASONEVALUE ( 'Date'[ISO Year Number] ),
    CALCULATE (
        [Sales Amount],
        FILTER (
            ALL ( 'Date' ),
            AND (
                'Date'[ISO Year Number] = VALUES ( 'Date'[ISO Year Number] ) - 1,
                CONTAINS (
                    VALUES ( 'Date'[ISO Year Day Number] ),
                    'Date'[ISO Year Day Number], 'Date'[ISO Year Day Number]
                )
            )
        )
    )
)
```

You can see in Figure 7-46 the result produced by the *ISO PY Sales* measure.

Row Labels	Sales Amount	ISO PY Sales
⊞ 2007	$12,448,845.92	
⊞ 2008	$10,811,544.55	$12,448,845.92
⊟ 2009	$10,429,758.04	$10,811,544.55
W1-2009	$334,583.73	$144,286.94
W2-2009	$122,826.05	$136,294.34
W3-2009	$136,153.55	$200,832.08
W4-2009	$206,403.02	$186,285.45
W5-2009	$93,172.50	$178,522.17
W6-2009	$159,298.22	$204,435.72
W7-2009	$143,526.01	$86,271.44

FIGURE 7-46 The *ISO PY Sales* shows the value of the same weeks one year earlier.

The week-based calendars are simple to manage because of the assumption you can make about the symmetry between days in different years. This is usually not compatible with the calendar month, so if you want to use both hierarchies (months and weeks), you have to create different time-intelligence calculations for each hierarchy.

Custom year-to-date, quarter-to-date, month-to-date

You have seen how to rewrite *DATESYTD* and similar functions in the "Understanding periods to date" section, earlier in this chapter. In this section, we will show how to replace the logic that extracts information from the date value by using other columns of the Date table.

For example, consider the following YTD Sales measure:

```
[YTD Sales] :=
CALCULATE (
    [Sales Amount],
    DATESYTD ( 'Date'[Date] )
)
```

The corresponding syntax in DAX without time intelligence is the following one:

```
[YTD Sales] :=
CALCULATE (
    [Sales Amount],
    FILTER (
        ALL ( 'Date'[Date] ),
        AND (
            'Date'[Date] <= MAX ( 'Date'[Date] ),
            YEAR ( 'Date'[Date] ) = YEAR ( MAX ( 'Date'[Date] ) )
        )
    )
)
```

If you use a custom calendar, you have to replace the *YEAR* function call with an access to the Year column, such as in the following *YTD Sales Custom* measure. In this case, the filter iterates the Date table, so the row context can access all the columns. If the selection includes more than one year, you get the last one by using *MAX*.

```
[YTD Sales Custom] :=
CALCULATE (
    [Sales Amount],
    FILTER (
        ALL ( 'Date' ),
        AND (
            'Date'[Date] <= MAX ( 'Date'[Date] ),
            'Date'[Calendar Year Number] = MAX ( 'Date'[Calendar Year Number] )
        )
    )
)
```

You use the same template to implement quarter-to-date and month-to-date calculations. The only difference is the column used instead of *Calendar Year Number*:

```
[QTD Sales Custom] :=
CALCULATE (
    [Sales Amount],
    FILTER (
        ALL ( 'Date' ),
        AND (
            'Date'[Date] <= MAX ( 'Date'[Date] ),
            'Date'[Calendar Year Quarter Number]
                = MAX ( 'Date'[Calendar Year Quarter Number] )
        )
    )
)
[MTD Sales Custom] :=
CALCULATE (
    [Sales Amount],
    FILTER (
        ALL ( 'Date' ),
        AND (
            'Date'[Date] <= MAX ( 'Date'[Date] ),
            'Date'[Calendar Year Month Number]
                = MAX ( 'Date'[Calendar Year Month Number] )
        )
    )
)
```

You can use these formulas to implement both standard calendars (in case you have to use *DirectQuery*) and custom calendars (in case the periods are not standard).

Computing over noncontiguous periods

The standard DAX time intelligence functions do not support operations over noncontiguous periods. As you have seen in the "Understanding *DATEADD*" section earlier in this chapter, the function *DATEADD* only works with contiguous date selections. By implementing a custom DAX formula, you can also support this scenario. In an earlier section, "Working with weeks," you have already seen a technique based on *CONTAINS* that looks for the same relative day number in a previous year. However, if you have a standard calendar based on months, the implementation is more complex.

We make a few initial assumptions:

- Because the calendar is month-based, we will implement a calculation that works on one month, repeating the same calculation for every month included in the selection.

- If the selection includes all the days in a month, the shifted month will include all days, too (even when their number is different, for example, moving from 30 to 31 days or vice versa).

- If the selection includes only a few days in a month, the shifted month will include only the same relative days in the month, if they exist in the shifted month.

You create a few calculated columns to simplify the calculation in the DAX measure.

```
Date[Month Sequential Number] =
'Date'[Calendar Year Number] * 12 + 'Date'[Month Number] - 1

Date[Days in Month] =
COUNTROWS (
    FILTER (
        ALL ( Date ),
        'Date'[Month Sequential Number] = EARLIER ( 'Date'[Month Sequential Number] )
    )
)

Date[Day of Month] = DAY ( 'Date'[Date] )
```

The *Month Sequential Number* is a unique value for each combination of month and year, and it increases by one every month. This also makes it easier to move from January to December of the previous year, you just look in this column for the value of January minus one. The *Days in Month* column contains the total number of days of the month (for example, January 31, February 28 or 29, and so on). The *Day of Month* column is simply the day number within the month. You can see in Figure 7-47 an example of the content of these columns.

Date	Month Sequential Number	Days in Month	Day of Month
2/26/2008	24097	29	26
2/27/2008	24097	29	27
2/28/2008	24097	29	28
2/29/2008	24097	29	29
3/1/2008	24098	31	1
3/2/2008	24098	31	2
3/3/2008	24098	31	3
3/4/2008	24098	31	4
3/5/2008	24098	31	5

FIGURE 7-47 The calculated columns extend the Date table to support custom time intelligence calculations over noncontiguous periods.

Let's see how to build step by step the complete formula to get the value of the previous month without using *DATEADD*, which would have this syntax:

```
DATEADD ( 'Date'[Date], -1, MONTH )
```

As we said in the first assumption, we will iterate the months selected, repeating the same calculation for each month selected in the filter context:

```
SUMX (
    VALUES ( 'Date'[Month Sequential Number] ),
    <calculation for the month>
)
```

The calculation for each month is different depending on whether all the days of the month are included in the selection or not. The first part of the calculation for the month performs this check, comparing the number of days selected with the number of days in the month. Remember that this step is executed within a single month, thanks to the *SUMX* iteration over *Month Sequential Number* values.

```
IF (
    CALCULATE ( COUNTROWS ( VALUES ( 'Date'[Date] ) ) )
        = CALCULATE ( VALUES ( 'Date'[Days in Month] ) ),
    <calculation for all days selected in the month>,
    <calculation for partial selection of the days in the month>
)
```

Tip Iterating over the values of a column guarantees that for each iteration, with a context transition, there is only one value selected for the column iterated. This makes it useless to add the *HASONEVALUE* test to protect the call to *VALUES*. Nevertheless, a call to *CALCULATE* or *CALCULATETABLE* is required to perform the context transition.

If the number of days selected is equal to the number of days in the month, then we need to create a filter that selects all the days in the previous month, by subtracting one from the *Month Sequential Number* column. Please note that the following code excerpt is included within a *SUMX* iteration over the *Month Sequential Number* column of the Date table, which is the row context we want to refer to, using the *EARLIER* function.

```
CALCULATE (
    [Sales Amount],
    ALL ( 'Date' ),
    FILTER (
        ALL ( 'Date'[Month Sequential Number] ),
        'Date'[Month Sequential Number]
            = EARLIER ( 'Date'[Month Sequential Number] ) - 1
    )
)
```

Otherwise, the filter also includes the days selected in the month iterated, getting the current filtered values from the *Day of Month* column; such a filter is highlighted in the following formula:

```
CALCULATE (
    [Sales Amount],
    ALL ( 'Date' ),
    CALCULATETABLE ( VALUES ( 'Date'[Day of Month] ) ),
    FILTER (
        ALL ( 'Date'[Month Sequential Number] ),
        'Date'[Month Sequential Number]
            = EARLIER ( 'Date'[Month Sequential Number] ) - 1
    )
)
```

Tip You might be surprised to see the following syntax in a filter argument:

```
CALCULATETABLE ( VALUES ( 'Date'[Day of Month] )
```

The reason is that *CALCULATETABLE* performs a context transition, transforming the current value of *Month Sequential Number* iterated by *SUMX* in a filter context. In this way, only values of *Day of Month* corresponding to active dates in the iterated month will be included in the new filter context to evaluate *Sales Amount*.

Combining all the steps, you obtain the following complete formula for the previous month sales (*PM Sales Custom*):

```
[PM Sales Custom] :=
SUMX (
    VALUES ( 'Date'[Month Sequential Number] ),
    IF (
        CALCULATE ( COUNTROWS ( VALUES ( 'Date'[Date] ) ) )
            = CALCULATE ( VALUES ( 'Date'[Days in Month] ) ),
        CALCULATE (
            [Sales],
            ALL ( 'Date' ),
            FILTER (
                ALL ( 'Date'[Month Sequential Number] ),
                'Date'[Month Sequential Number]
                    = EARLIER ( 'Date'[Month Sequential Number] ) - 1
            )
        ),
        CALCULATE (
            [Sales],
            ALL ( 'Date' ),
            CALCULATETABLE ( VALUES ( 'Date'[Day of Month] ) ),
            FILTER (
                ALL ( 'Date'[Month Sequential Number] ),
                'Date'[Month Sequential Number]
                    = EARLIER ( 'Date'[Month Sequential Number] ) - 1
            )
        )
    )
)
```

You can see in Figure 7-48 that the measure works also with a noncontiguous selection, because months between March 2008 and August 2008 are not selected on rows. However, the column *PM Sales Custom* returns the value of December 2007 corresponding to the row January 2008, and returns the value of August 2008 corresponding to the row September 2008.

Row Labels	Sales Amount	PM Sales Custom
CY 2008	$5,798,950.75	$6,006,048.03
January 2008	$766,917.68	$1,215,421.99
February 2008	$673,422.07	$766,917.68
September 2008	$1,055,134.27	$782,352.99
October 2008	$765,578.09	$1,055,134.27
November 2008	$1,420,643.01	$765,578.09
December 2008	$1,117,255.63	$1,420,643.01
Grand Total	$5,798,950.75	$6,006,048.03

FIGURE 7-48 The *PM Sales Custom* measure shows the value of the previous month.

Using the same formulas, you can implement a comparison over the previous quarter or year by simply subtracting 3 or 12 instead of 1 from the *Month Sequential Number*.

Custom comparison between periods

In the previous section, you have seen how to implement calculations for previous periods in month-based calendars. You can apply the same technique to any period that splits a year. However, a custom calendar might require applying special rules for comparison, with exceptions for particular periods of the year (for example, Thanksgiving, Black Friday, Easter, New Year, and any other world holidays that might change the calendar day every year). In this section, you learn a technique to handle these exceptions in data instead of including special conditions in the DAX expression.

The initial assumption is that it should be possible to define, for each day, what the corresponding day is in the previous year. For example, we can assume that by default it will be the same week day, by subtracting 364 days (exactly 52 weeks) from the current day number. However, exceptions such as Thanksgiving might modify these dates (for example, it was November 27 in 2008 and November 22 in 2007). Handling the calculation of the fourth Thursday in November within the time intelligence calculation would add complexity and slow down execution time. Therefore, we define a column in the Date table that we populate with the corresponding day to use in a previous year comparison, as you see in Figure 7-49.

Date	Date Previous Year
1/1/2005	1/3/2004
1/2/2005	1/4/2004
1/3/2005	1/5/2004
1/4/2005	1/6/2004
1/5/2005	1/7/2004
1/6/2005	1/8/2004
1/7/2005	1/9/2004
1/8/2005	1/10/2004
1/9/2005	1/11/2004

FIGURE 7-49 The *Date Previous Year* column defines what is the corresponding date to use in a previous year comparison.

The formula that applies the previous year calculation using the custom formula is the following:

```
[PY Sales Custom] :=
CALCULATE (
    [Sales Amount],
    FILTER (
        ALL ( 'Date' ),
        CONTAINS (
            VALUES ( 'Date'[Date Previous Year] ),
            'Date'[Date Previous Year],
            'Date'[Date]
        )
    )
)
```

The *FILTER* function returns Date rows that correspond to active dates in the *Date Previous Year* column. For example, the user selected January 8, 2005; the current filter for *Date Previous Year* column is January 10, 2004. The *FILTER* iterates all the dates and returns one row having the Date column equal to January 10, 2004. Using *CONTAINS*, any number of dates selected is processed.

The dates returned by *FILTER* must exist in the Date column of the Date table. Moreover, the result will never include duplicated dates. If in *Date Previous Year* column the same value appears in different rows, the duplicated value will be returned only once by the filter. For these reasons, the number of rows returned by the *FILTER* might be lower than the number of dates initially selected in the filter context.

In Figure 7-50 you see the result of *PY Sales Custom*. In order to understand which range of dates is considered for the previous year, the following measures have also been added:

```
[MIN Date PY] := MIN ( 'Date'[Date Previous Year] )

[MAX Date PY] := MAX ( 'Date'[Date Previous Year] )
```

Row Labels	Sales Amount	PY Sales Custom	MIN Date PY	MAX Date PY
⊞ CY 2007	$12,457,410.85		1/2/2006	1/1/2007
⊟ CY 2008	$11,031,426.30	$12,494,892.47	1/2/2007	1/2/2008
⊟ January 2008	$766,917.68	$946,082.96	1/2/2007	2/1/2007
1/1/2008	$20,150.87	$57,230.61	1/2/2007	1/2/2007
1/2/2008	$17,330.75	$107,314.45	1/3/2007	1/3/2007
1/3/2008	$68,198.22	$15,113.79	1/4/2007	1/4/2007
1/4/2008		$66,908.39	1/5/2007	1/5/2007
1/5/2008	$21,232.91		1/6/2007	1/6/2007
1/6/2008	$8,809.26	$27,418.39	1/7/2007	1/7/2007

FIGURE 7-50 The *PY Sales Custom* returns the *Sales Amount* of the dates between *MIN Date PY* and *MAX Date PY*.

With this approach, you will never change the DAX measure to calculate the value of the previous year, and you will handle exceptions only by modifying the content of the *Date Previous Year* column in the Date table.

CHAPTER 8

Statistical functions

D AX provides a number of statistical functions that simplify the code you write to perform the corresponding calculations. New DAX versions introduced a few statistical functions not present in previous versions, so you will find corresponding workarounds and patterns in case the DAX version you use does not support the function you need.

In this chapter, you will learn how to obtain the ranking value of an element, how to calculate variances, standard deviations, and percentiles. You will also learn functions for calculating interest, computing the geometric mean, and obtaining a sample from a table.

Using *RANKX*

If you want to show the ranking value of an element according to a specific sort order, you can use the *RANKX* function. Its syntax is the following:

```
RANKX( <table>, <expression> [, <value>[, <order>[, <ties>]]]
            [, <expression> [, <value>[, <order>[, <ties>]]]] … )
```

The *<value>* argument is ranked over the values returned by *<expression>* for every row of the *<table>*. If *<value>* is omitted, *<expression>* is used to compute the value for ranking in the evaluation context that calls the *RANKX* function.

 Note Both *<expression>* and *<value>* are evaluated in different contexts. The *<expression>* argument is evaluated in a row context defined for each row of *<table>*. The *<value>* argument is evaluated in the context defined by the caller of the *RANKX* function, which could have either a row context or not. In both cases, you can use *CALCULATE* to convert a row context into a filter context (but note that a row context might not exist for the third argument). Remember that a measure implicitly performs a *CALCULATE* operation.

The *<order>* parameter is 0 or False (default) to rank in descending order and 1 or True to rank in ascending order. The *<ties>* argument is a string that can be *DENSE* or *SKIP* to control the rank value after a tie. *DENSE* always returns the next rank value after a tie, whereas *SKIP* returns a value that skips as many values as tied values. For instance, if four values are tied with a rank of 5, the next value will receive a rank of 9 for *SKIP* and a rank of 6 for *DENSE*.

For example, you can define a measure that ranks product brands in this way:

```
[Rank by Brand A] :=
RANKX ( ALL ( Product[Brand] ), [Sales Amount] )
```

The result of this measure displays a number even when more brands are selected, such as in the case of the Grand Total. You can avoid that by testing whether only one brand is selected using *HASONEVALUE*. The result of the two measures is visible in Figure 8-1.

```
[Rank by Brand B] :=
IF (
    HASONEVALUE ( Product[Brand] ),
    RANKX ( ALL ( Product[Brand] ), [Sales Amount] )
)
```

Row Labels	Sales Amount	Rank by Brand A	Rank by Brand B
Contoso	$8,098,022.18	1	1
Fabrikam	$6,118,735.01	2	2
Adventure Works	$4,424,285.42	3	3
Litware	$3,566,677.72	4	4
Proseware	$2,789,360.44	5	5
A. Datum	$2,293,775.20	6	6
Wide World Importers	$2,107,653.36	7	7
Southridge Video	$1,515,549.41	8	8
The Phone Company	$1,237,236.00	9	9
Northwind Traders	$1,181,080.38	10	10
Tailspin Toys	$357,773.39	11	11
Grand Total	**$33,690,148.51**	**1**	

FIGURE 8-1 The *Rank by Brand B* hides the ranking for Grand Total row.

It is important to consider which *<table>* parameter to pass to the *RANKX* function to obtain the desired result. In the previous query, it was necessary to specify *ALL (Product[Brand])* because you want to obtain the ranking of each brand. If you put the color on the rows, and no selection of the brand, you obtain the strange result you see in Figure 8-2.

The measure *Rank by Brand A* always returns 1, because for each color there could be one or more brands, but the *Sales Amount* displayed for each row in the report corresponds to the sum of all the brands for that color. Such a value is always greater than or equal to the value of the brands that, within that color, have the higher value. In fact, the second argument of *RANKX* is *[Sales Amount]*, which is restricted by the filter context of each cell (it is worthwhile to remind you that *RANKX* computes the value of all product brands for each cell of the report). Why do you see 1 for the *Rank by Brand B* measure only in a few rows? The reason is that when a color has products belonging to only one brand (which is the case of Azure and Transparent colors), then the *HASONEVALUE* condition is satisfied, otherwise there is more than one brand for the color, and the result forced by the *IF* condition is *BLANK*.

Row Labels	Sales Amount	Rank by Brand A	Rank by Brand B
Azure	$108,373.20	1	1
Black	$6,496,656.51	1	
Blue	$2,702,678.50	1	
Brown	$1,140,963.92	1	
Gold	$397,877.62	1	
Green	$1,554,814.88	1	
Grey	$3,839,313.05	1	
Orange	$939,207.26	1	
Pink	$916,792.73	1	
Purple	$6,565.33	1	
Red	$1,206,171.27	1	
Silver	$7,502,066.65	1	
Silver Grey	$410,846.00	1	
Transparent	$3,677.94	1	1
White	$6,363,512.53	1	
Yellow	$100,631.12	1	
Grand Total	$33,690,148.51	1	

FIGURE 8-2 The measures rank *Sales Amount* by product model, but the report splits data by product color.

The ranking computed by *Rank by Brand A* measure is an absolute ranking of all the brands. If you filter only a few brands, the ranking always considers those that are not visible. For example, in Figure 8-3 you can see that if you unselect the top three brands, the first one visible is the fourth one.

Row Labels	Sales Amount	Rank by Brand B
Litware	$3,566,677.72	4
Proseware	$2,789,360.44	5
A. Datum	$2,293,775.20	6
Wide World Importers	$2,107,653.36	7
Southridge Video	$1,515,549.41	8
The Phone Company	$1,237,236.00	9
Northwind Traders	$1,181,080.38	10
Tailspin Toys	$357,773.39	11
Grand Total	$15,049,105.90	

Brand

A. Datum	Adventure Works
Contoso	Fabrikam
Litware	Northwind Traders
Proseware	Southridge Video
Tailspin Toys	The Phone Company
Wide World Importers	

FIGURE 8-3 The first brand visible has ranking number 4, because the ranking is applied to all the brands.

If you want to calculate a ranking that considers only the visible brands, you have to use *ALLSELECTED* instead of *ALL*, as you can see in the following measure that produces the result shown in Figure 8-4.

> **Note** We introduced the *ALLSELECTED* function in Chapter 5, "Understanding *CALCULATE* and *CALCULATETABLE*," and you will see a more complete explanation of it later in Chapter 10, "Advanced evaluation context." In this context, *ALLSELECTED* removes the filter context introduced by rows and columns members in the pivot table, keeping the selection defined by slicers and filters of the pivot table.

```
[Rank by Brand C] :=
IF (
    HASONEVALUE ( Product[Brand] ),
    RANKX ( ALLSELECTED ( Product[Brand] ), [Sales Amount] )
)
```

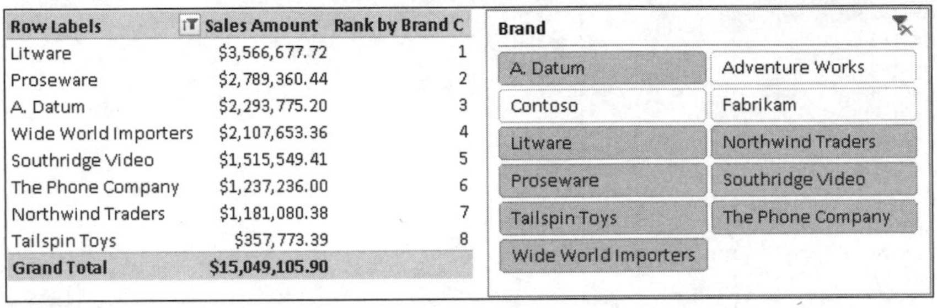

Row Labels	Sales Amount	Rank by Brand C
Litware	$3,566,677.72	1
Proseware	$2,789,360.44	2
A. Datum	$2,293,775.20	3
Wide World Importers	$2,107,653.36	4
Southridge Video	$1,515,549.41	5
The Phone Company	$1,237,236.00	6
Northwind Traders	$1,181,080.38	7
Tailspin Toys	$357,773.39	8
Grand Total	$15,049,105.90	

Brand:
A. Datum | Adventure Works
Contoso | Fabrikam
Litware | Northwind Traders
Proseware | Southridge Video
Tailspin Toys | The Phone Company
Wide World Importers

FIGURE 8-4 The first brand visible has ranking number 1, because the ranking is applied to only the visible brands.

Common pitfalls using *RANKX*

You might fall into a few common mistakes by using *RANKX* in your measures. The first pitfall is that the first argument usually contains *ALL* for a column or a table. When you use a table, you might forget to include *ALL*, something that would not happen when specifying a single column, because a table function is required and you would get an error by specifying a simple column name as the first argument.

For example, consider the following measures to compute the rank by product category. The wrong formula has Product Category table specified as a first argument of *RANKX*, whereas the correct formula uses *ALL ('Product Category')*. The results of both measures are visible in Figure 8-5.

```
[Wrong Rank by Category] :=
IF (
    HASONEVALUE ( 'Product Category' ),
    RANKX ( 'Product Category', [Sales Amount] )
)

[Rank by Category] :=
IF (
    HASONEVALUE ( 'Product Category' ),
    RANKX ( ALL ( 'Product Category' ), [Sales Amount] )
)
```

Row Labels	Sales Amount	Wrong Rank by Category	Rank by Category
Home Appliances	$10,571,029.88	1	1
Cameras and camcorders	$7,901,783.67	1	2
Computers	$7,435,548.25	1	3
TV and Video	$4,844,253.41	1	4
Cell phones	$1,771,028.66	1	5
Audio	$422,177.88	1	6
Games and Toys	$397,137.75	1	7
Music, Movies and Audio Books	$347,189.01	1	8
Grand Total	$33,690,148.51		

FIGURE 8-5 The *Wrong Rank by Category* measure always displays 1 as a result.

The other common pitfall is using a DAX formula to aggregate rows without wrapping the expression in a *CALCULATE* function. In the previous examples, we always used the measure *Sales Amount* as the expression to use in the ranking. If you use an aggregation function such as *SUMX*, you should consider that the expression is evaluated for each row of the table passed as a first argument to *RANKX*. The row context defined in this iteration is not transformed into a filter context unless a context transition is invoked by *CALCULATE*, which is an implicit operation when you evaluate a measure. Thus, for each row the filter context is always the same (that is, the existing filter in the cell where *RANKX* is evaluated), and all the items have the same rank of 1 in this way. The correct formula simply wraps the expression in a *CALCULATE* function that performs the context transition for each row of the table iterated by *RANKX*. You can see the result of the wrong and correct formulas in Figure 8-6.

```
[Wrong Rank by Quantity] :=
IF (
    HASONEVALUE ( 'Product Category' ),
    RANKX (
        ALL ( 'Product Category' ),
        SUM ( Sales[Quantity] )
    )
)

[Rank by Quantity] :=
IF (
    HASONEVALUE ( 'Product Category' ),
    RANKX (
        ALL ( 'Product Category' ),
        CALCULATE ( SUM ( Sales[Quantity] ) )
    )
)
```

Row Labels	Sum of Quantity	Wrong Rank by Quantity	Rank by Quantity
Cell phones	32,736	1	1
Home Appliances	26,348	1	2
Computers	25,722	1	3
Cameras and camcorders	18,654	1	4
Games and Toys	14,945	1	5
TV and Video	13,894	1	6
Audio	4,899	1	7
Music, Movies and Audio Books	2,982	1	8
Grand Total	140,180		

FIGURE 8-6 The *Wrong Rank by Quantity* measure always displays 1 as a result.

Using the third argument of *RANKX*

In the previous examples, you have seen *RANKX* called with only two arguments. By default, the third corresponds to the second one, and usually this is the correct choice whenever you are ranking by a DAX measure or an aggregation expression. However, if you want to perform the ranking over a table by the value of one of the columns of the table itself, then you probably need to specify a different expression in the third argument.

The second argument defines the expression to evaluate for each row of the table passed as a first argument of *RANKX*. Such an expression is always executed in a row context, so it can directly access the value of any column of the same table. However, the third argument does not have a row context if the *RANKX* is included in a measure, as in the examples you have seen so far. A row context would exist for the third argument if the *RANKX* function were part of a calculated column expression.

For example, the following measure produces a syntax error, saying that *the value for column 'Unit Price' in table 'Product' cannot be determined in the current context*:

```
[Wrong Rank by Price] :=
IF (
    HASONEVALUE ( Product ),
    RANKX (
        ALLSELECTED ( Product ),
        Product[Unit Price]
    )
)
```

The following measure is identical to the previous one, because the third argument is by default the same as the second one:

```
[Wrong Rank by Price] :=
IF (
    HASONEVALUE ( Product ),
    RANKX (
        ALLSELECTED ( Product ),
        Product[Unit Price],
        Product[Unit Price]
    )
)
```

The evaluation of the third argument requires a row context, which does not exist when the measure is evaluated in a report such as the pivot tables you have seen previously. Thus, in order to retrieve the price of the "current" product you can use *VALUES*, knowing that the *HASONEVALUE* condition does not evaluate *RANKX* in case more than one product is selected. The following measure implements such a technique, and Figure 8-7 shows the result.

```
[Rank by Price] :=
IF (
    HASONEVALUE ( Product ),
    RANKX (
        ALLSELECTED ( Product ),
        Product[Unit Price],
        VALUES ( Product[Unit Price] )
    )
)
```

Row Labels	Average Price	Rank by Price
WWI Projector 1080p DLP86 Silver	$2,499.00	1
WWI Projector 1080p DLP86 White	$2,499.00	1
WWI Projector 1080p DLP86 Black	$2,499.00	1
WWI Projector 1080p LCD86 Black	$2,295.00	4
WWI Projector 1080p LCD86 White	$2,295.00	4
WWI Projector 1080p LCD86 Silver	$2,295.00	4
WWI Laptop19W X0196 White	$1,299.00	7
WWI Laptop19W X0196 Black	$1,299.00	7
WWI Laptop19W X0196 Blue	$1,299.00	7
WWI Projector 720p DLP56 White	$999.00	10

Brand

A. Datum	Adventure Works
Contoso	Fabrikam
Litware	Northwind Traders
Proseware	Southridge Video
Tailspin Toys	The Phone Company
Wide World Importers	

FIGURE 8-7 The report shows only the product of the brand selected in the slicer. *Rank by Price* retrieves the price for the current row in the report (which has only a filter context and not a row context) using the *VALUES* function. The report contains the average price in another measure, which corresponds to the unit product of the product in each row (the measure requires the use of an aggregation function).

Using *RANK.EQ*

The *RANK.EQ* function in DAX is similar to the same function in Microsoft Excel and returns the ranking of a number in a list of numbers, offering a subset of the features available with the *RANKX* functions. You rarely use it in DAX unless you are migrating an Excel formula. It has the following syntax:

```
RANK.EQ ( <value>, <column> [, <order>] )
```

The *<value>* argument can be a DAX expression that has to be evaluated, and *<column>* is the name of an existing column against which rank will be determined. The order is optional and can be 0 for descending order and 1 for ascending order. In Excel, the same function can accept a range of cells for column argument, whereas in DAX it is often the same column used for value expression, meaning that you want to calculate the ranking of a column over itself. One scenario in which you might want to use a different column is when you have two tables, one with elements that you want to rank (for example, a specific group of products) and another with the entire set of elements to use for ranking (for example, the list of all the products). However, because of the limitations applied to the column parameter (it cannot be an expression or a column created by using *ADDCOLUMNS*, *ROW*, or *SUMMARIZE*), *RANK.EQ* is commonly used by passing the same column for value and column parameters in a calculated column expression, referring to columns of the same table as in the following example:

```
Product[Price Rank] :=
RANK.EQ ( Product[Unit Price], Product[Unit Price] )
```

If you need a more flexible or dynamic ranking, you can use *RANKX* instead of *RANK.EQ*, which is provided mainly for Excel compatibility.

Computing average and moving average

You can calculate the mean (arithmetic average) of a set of values by using one of the following DAX functions:

- **AVERAGE** returns the average of all the numbers in a numeric column.

- **AVERAGEX** calculates the average of an expression evaluated over a table.

 Note DAX provides a function called *AVERAGEA*, which returns the average of all the numbers in a text column, but you should not use it. Such a function exists in DAX for Excel compatibility only. However, when you use a text column as an argument, instead of getting an error (as it would be the case in using *AVERAGE*), you always get 0 as a result, whereas the Excel function converts each value where possible, assuming 0 for the values that are not a number.

The moving average is a calculation to analyze data points by creating a series of averages of different subsets of the full data set. You can use many DAX techniques to implement this calculation. The simplest technique is using *AVERAGEX*, iterating a table of the desired granularity and calculating for each iteration the expression that generates the single data point to use in the average.

For example, the following formulas calculate the simple average of each Sales transaction of the period selected and of the last 90 days. In the latter case, you apply the filter for the period using a *CALCULATE* function. You can see in Figure 8-8 the result of these measures:

```
[Average Sales] :=
AVERAGEX ( Sales, Sales[Quantity] * Sales[Unit Price] )

[Moving Average Sales 90 Days] :=
CALCULATE (
    AVERAGEX ( Sales, Sales[Quantity] * Sales[Unit Price] ),
    DATESINPERIOD (
        'Date'[Date],
        LASTDATE ( 'Date'[Date] ),
        -90,
        DAY
    )
)
```

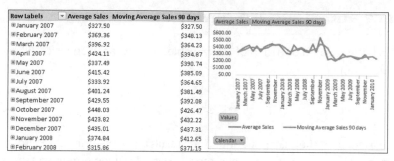

FIGURE 8-8 The line chart compares the simple average for the period selected and the moving average over 90 days.

You might want to calculate the daily average for both the period selected and the last 90 days. In this case, the *AVERAGEX* function has to iterate the days, and you can implement the filter for the moving average directly in the first argument of the *AVERAGEX* function, without relying on *CALCULATE* to do that. You can see the result of the following measures in Figure 8-9.

```
[Average Daily Sales] :=
AVERAGEX ( 'Date', [Sales Amount] )

[Moving Average Daily Sales 90 Days] :=
AVERAGEX (
    DATESINPERIOD (
        'Date'[Date],
        LASTDATE ( 'Date'[Date] ),
        -90,
        DAY
    ),
    [Sales Amount]
)
```

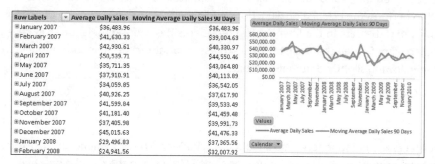

FIGURE 8-9 The line chart compares the daily average for the period selected with the daily moving average of 90 days.

Computing variance and standard deviation

The variance of a variable is the squared deviation of that variable from its mean and is calculated with the following formula:

$$\sigma^2 = \frac{1}{N}\sum_{i=1}^{N}\left(x_i - \bar{x}\right)^2$$

We indicate with $\bar{x}$ the average of the values and with Ã the resulting value of the standard deviation, which is the square root of the variance. Thus, the standard deviation is defined as follows:

$$\sigma = \sqrt{\frac{1}{N}\sum_{i=1}^{N}\left(x_i - \bar{x}\right)^2}$$

The standard deviation is expressed in the same units as the data and for this reason is simpler to use. You can read more details about its use on *http://en.wikipedia.org/wiki/Standard_deviation*.

In DAX there are several aggregation functions available to calculate variance and standard deviation of a population, beginning with *STDEV* and *VAR*, respectively. Here is the syntax of the available functions:

```
VAR.S( <column> )
VAR.P( <column> )
VARX.S( <table>, <expression> )
VARX.P( <table>, <expression> )
STDEV.S( <column> )
STDEV.P( <column> )
STDEVX.S( <table>, <expression> )
STDEVX.P( <table>, <expression> )
```

The difference between the .P and the .S suffix (which stand for Population and Sample) is in the formula used to perform the calculation. Functions ending with .P use the formulas previously described, assuming that the data in the filter context represents the entire population. You have to use functions ending with .S when the available data represents a sample of the entire population, which requires the following slightly different formula:

$$\sigma = \sqrt{\frac{1}{N-1}\sum_{i=1}^{N}\left(x_i - \bar{x}\right)^2}$$

As in the other *[Aggregate]X* functions, you should use *VARX* and *STDEVX* whenever the expression is more complex than a single column. You can use *VAR* and *STDEV* when the calculation only requires the value of one column.

For example, the following measures calculate the standard deviation of the sales quantity for each color and Figure 8-10 shows the range of values that includes 95 percent of the sales for that color.

```
[Average Qty] :=
AVERAGE ( Sales[Quantity] )

[StDev.P Qty] :=
STDEV.P ( Sales[Quantity] )

[StDev.S Qty] :=
STDEV.S ( Sales[Quantity] )

[Min Qty] :=
MIN ( Sales[Quantity] )

[Max Qty] :=
MAX ( Sales[Quantity] )

[Distribution] :=
"95% between" & ROUND ( [Average Qty] - 2 * [StDev.P Qty], 2 )
& "and" & ROUND ( [Average Qty] + 2 * [StDev.P Qty], 2 )
```

Row Labels	Average Qty	StDev.P Qty	StDev.S Qty	Min Qty	Max Qty	Distribution
Azure	1.37	0.85502	0.85610	1	4	95% between 1 and 3.08
Black	1.40	0.87538	0.87539	1	4	95% between 1 and 3.15
Blue	1.41	0.89232	0.89239	1	4	95% between 1 and 3.2
Brown	1.40	0.87426	0.87450	1	4	95% between 1 and 3.15
Gold	1.41	0.88908	0.88953	1	4	95% between 1 and 3.19
Green	1.40	0.89025	0.89045	1	4	95% between 1 and 3.19
Grey	1.40	0.87446	0.87451	1	4	95% between 1 and 3.14
Orange	1.40	0.86484	0.86511	1	4	95% between 1 and 3.13
Pink	1.40	0.87598	0.87610	1	4	95% between 1 and 3.15
Purple	1.36	0.85853	0.86431	1	4	95% between 1 and 3.08
Red	1.39	0.87098	0.87105	1	4	95% between 1 and 3.13
Silver	1.40	0.87439	0.87441	1	4	95% between 1 and 3.14
Silver Grey	1.42	0.91125	0.91193	1	4	95% between 1 and 3.24
Transparent	1.40	0.87139	0.87187	1	4	95% between 1 and 3.14
White	1.40	0.87699	0.87701	1	4	95% between 1 and 3.15
Yellow	1.42	0.90177	0.90201	1	4	95% between 1 and 3.23
Grand Total	**1.40**	**0.87720**	**0.87721**	**1**	**4**	**95% between 1 and 3.15**

FIGURE 8-10 Every color has a slightly different distribution, even when the average is identical.

As you can see, the standard deviation is calculated assuming a sample of population (*STDEV.S*) has a slightly higher value than the calculation over the entire population (*STDEV.P*). This results in extending the estimated distribution range of values obtained as a result, even if there is no apparent difference in the Distribution comment because of the rounding chosen for display.

Computing median and percentiles

Median and percentiles are two measures used in statistics. Given a population, the median is the number separating the higher half from the lower half (this is usually done using a sample of the entire population). The percentile is the value below which a corresponding percentage of values fall. For example, the twentieth percentile is the value below 20 percent of the values. The median corresponds to the fiftieth percentile.

You can calculate the median by using one of the following DAX functions, which both ignore blanks:

- **MEDIAN**   returns the median of numbers in a numeric column.

- **MEDIANX**   calculates the median number of an expression evaluated for each row in a table.

The median might be calculated as the fiftieth percentile, but it has a specific function because it can be calculated using a faster algorithm. You can calculate any percentile using one of these other DAX functions:

- **PERCENTILE.EXC**   returns the k-th percentile of values in a range, where k is in the range 0..1 exclusive.

- **PERCENTILE.INC**   returns the k-th percentile of values in a range, where k is in the range 0..1 inclusive.

- **PERCENTILEX.EXC**   returns the k-th percentile of an expression evaluated for each row in a table, where k is in the range 0..1 exclusive.

- **PERCENTILEX.INC**   returns the k-th percentile of an expression evaluated for each row in a table, where k is in the range 0..1 inclusive.

The behavior of the functions *MEDIAN*, *PERCENTILE.EXC*, and *PERCENTILE.INC* is identical to the Excel functions with the same name. For example, the following measures produce the result you can see in Figure 8-11.

```
[Median Unit Price] :=
MEDIAN ( Sales[Unit Price] )

[75 Percentile Inc] :=
PERCENTILE.INC ( Sales[Unit Price], 0.75 )

[75 Percentile Exc] :=
PERCENTILE.EXC ( Sales[Unit Price], 0.75 )
```

Row Labels	Median Unit Price	75 Percentile Inc	75 Percentile Exc
Audio	59.99	115.00	115.00
Cameras and camcorders	328.00	627.00	627.00
Cell phones	14.99	24.99	24.99
Computers	139.00	342.50	349.00
Games and Toys	16.99	43.00	43.00
Home Appliances	179.99	445.00	445.00
Music, Movies and Audio Books	109.99	219.00	219.00
TV and Video	329.00	469.97	469.97
Grand Total	109.99	299.99	299.99

FIGURE 8-11 Median and the seventy-fifth percentile calculated for each product category; the inclusive and exclusive percentiles are different only for the Computers category.

Note In case your version of DAX does not implement the functions described in this section to calculate median and percentile, you can implement the same calculation using the DAX formulas described in this article: *http://www.daxpatterns.com/statistical-patterns/*. The same article also contains the DAX measure to compute the mode, returning a result identical to the *MODE* and *MODE.SNGL* functions in Excel.

Computing interests

You can apply specific functions and formulas for interest-related calculations. For example, you can calulate compound interest and average interest rate using the following functions:

- **PRODUCT**   returns the product of numbers in a numeric column.

- **PRODUCTX**   calculates the product of an expression evaluated for each row in a table.

- **GEOMEAN**   returns the geometric mean of numbers in a numeric column.

- **GEOMEANX**   calculates the geometric mean of an expression evaluated for each row in a table.

The product of a data set $\{a_1, a_2, \dots, a_n\}$ corresponds to the products of its members:

$$p = a_1 \, a_2 \dots a_n$$

The geometric mean of the same set is given by the following equation:

$$g = \sqrt[n]{a_1 a_2 \dots a_n}$$

For example, consider the table in Figure 8-12, where each year has an interest rate.

Year	Rate
2000	8.05%
2001	6.97%
2002	6.54%
2003	5.83%
2004	5.84%
2005	5.87%
2006	6.41%
2007	6.34%
2008	6.03%
2009	5.04%
2010	4.69%
2011	4.45%
2012	3.66%
2013	3.98%
2014	4.17%

FIGURE 8-12 The table Rate contains interest rates by year.

You can use *PRODUCTX* and *GEOMEANX* to calculate the compound interest and the geometric mean. In Figure 8-13 you can see the result of these measures applied in a running total pattern, implemented using the following measures:

```
[Compound Interest] :=
PRODUCTX ( Rates, 1 + Rates[Rate] )

[Geometric Mean] :=
GEOMEAN ( Rates[Rate] )

[Running Compound Interest] :=
CALCULATE (
    [Compound Interest],
    FILTER ( ALL ( Rates ), Rates[Year] <= MAX ( Rates[Year] ) )
)

[Running Geometric Mean] :=
CALCULATE (
    [Geometric Mean],
    FILTER ( ALL ( Rates ), Rates[Year] <= MAX ( Rates[Year] ) )
)
```

Year	Rate	Values Running Compound Interest	Running Geometric Mean
2000	8.05%	8.05 %	8.05 %
2001	6.97%	15.58 %	7.49 %
2002	6.54%	23.14 %	7.16 %
2003	5.83%	30.32 %	6.80 %
2004	5.84%	37.93 %	6.60 %
2005	5.87%	46.03 %	6.47 %
2006	6.41%	55.39 %	6.46 %
2007	6.34%	65.24 %	6.45 %
2008	6.03%	75.20 %	6.40 %
2009	5.04%	84.03 %	6.25 %
2010	4.69%	92.66 %	6.09 %
2011	4.45%	101.24 %	5.93 %
2012	3.66%	108.60 %	5.71 %
2013	3.98%	116.90 %	5.57 %
2014	4.17%	125.95 %	5.46 %
Grand Total		125.95 %	5.46 %

FIGURE 8-13 The report shows the running total for compound interest and geometric mean of interest rates.

Alternative implementation of *PRODUCT* and *GEOMEAN*

If you are using a version of DAX that does not have the functions *PRODUCT* and *GEOMEAN*, you can implement them with other DAX expressions. You can implement *PRODUCTX* and *GEOMEANX* using the following measures, where *<value>* is the column containing the numbers to compute and *<table>* is the table to which the column belongs.

```
[ProductX] := POWER ( 10, SUMX ( <table>, LOG ( <value> ) ) )
[GeoMeanX] := EXP ( AVERAGEX ( <table>, LN ( <value> ) ) )
```

You have to use the *[Aggregate]X* version every time, because you have to sum the result of *LOG* or *LN* computed for each number. You can compute the measures of the previous example with the following code (which replaces the corresponding measures called by the running total in Figure 8-13):

```
[Compound Interest] :=
POWER ( 10, SUMX ( Rates, LOG ( 1 + Rates[Rate] ) ) ) - 1

[Geometric Mean] :=
EXP ( AVERAGEX ( Rates, LN ( Rates[Rate] ) ) )
```

Using internal rate of return (*XIRR*)

The internal rate of return is an indicator of profitability of investment. It is also known as effective interest rate when applied to savings and loans. In Excel, this calculation is available with the *XIRR* function. For example, a loan of 1,000 returned in a single solution paying 1,100 has an effective interest rate of 10 percent, as you can see in Figure 8-14.

Date	Amount
12/31/2014	-1,000.00
12/31/2015	1,100.00
XIRR	**10.00%**

FIGURE 8-14 An intuitive calculation of effective interest rate in Excel.

However, if the return of the same amount is in 11 monthly payments of 100, starting two months after the beginning of the loan, the resulting effective interest rate is 18.03 percent, as shown in Figure 8-15.

Date	Amount
12/31/2014	-1,000.00
2/28/2015	100.00
3/31/2015	100.00
4/30/2015	100.00
5/31/2015	100.00
6/30/2015	100.00
7/31/2015	100.00
8/31/2015	100.00
9/30/2015	100.00
10/31/2015	100.00
11/30/2015	100.00
12/31/2015	100.00
XIRR	**18.03%**

FIGURE 8-15 An example of effective interest rate for a monthly payment of a loan.

The Excel *XIRR* function has an equivalent function in recent versions of DAX, with the following syntax:

```
XIRR ( <table>, <value>, <date> [, <guess>] )
```

For each row in *<table>*, there is an evaluation of the *<value>* and *<date>* expressions, so you can use a syntax that is valid in the row context of *<table>*. The optional *<guess>* argument is a number that you guess is close to the result of *XIRR*, and if omitted it is 0.1 (10 percent) by default.

> **Tip** The guess argument might be important to improve performance of the *XIRR* function, which uses a heuristic method that attempts up to 100 tries until it finds a result that is accurate enough. Most of the time, you can omit it.

For example, if you have the data shown in Figure 8-15 in a table called LoanRates, you can obtain the effective interest rate by using the following DAX measure:

```
[Effective Interest Rate] :=
XIRR ( LoanRates, LoanRates[Amount], LoanRates[Date] )
```

Using net present value (*XNPV*)

The net present value is the sum of the present values for a schedule of cash flow, which is not necessarily periodic. In Excel, this calculation is available with the *XNPV* function (and with the *NPV* function for a periodic schedule of cash flow, but the *NPV* function is not available in DAX).

The net present value formula is useful also to evaluate the remaining balance on loan. For example, consider a loan of 1,000 at an interest rate of 10 percent. After a single payment of 1,100 one year after the loan, the net present value is zero, as you can see in Figure 8-16.

Date	Amount
12/31/2014	1,000.00
12/31/2015	-1,100.00
XNPV	0.00

FIGURE 8-16 A simple calculation of net present value in Excel.

Now consider an example similar to the one used for the internal rate of return in the previous section. You have a loan of 1,000 at an interest rate of 18.03 percent and you want to evaluate the net present value after 11 monthly payments of 100 paid regularly, starting two months after the beginning of the loan. In this case, the net present value is 84.73, which corresponds to the capital part of the loan. The last payment should be made on December 31, 2015, with a value of 100, which is exactly 84.73 (capital) plus 15.28 (interest, obtained as 18.03 percent of 84.73). You can see the calculation of net present value (*XNPV*) in Figure 8-17.

Date	Amount
12/31/2014	1,000.00
2/28/2015	-100.00
3/31/2015	-100.00
4/30/2015	-100.00
5/31/2015	-100.00
6/30/2015	-100.00
7/31/2015	-100.00
8/31/2015	-100.00
9/30/2015	-100.00
10/31/2015	-100.00
11/30/2015	-100.00
XNPV	**84.73**

FIGURE 8-17 An example of net present value for a monthly loan payment.

The Excel *XNPV* function has an equivalent function in recent versions of DAX, with the following syntax:

```
XNPV ( <table>, <value>, <date>, <rate> )
```

For each row in *<table>*, there is an evaluation of the *<value>* and *<date>* expressions, so you can use a syntax that is valid in the row context of *<table>*. The *<rate>* argument is the interest rate to apply.

For example, if you have the data shown in Figure 8-17 in a table called LoanRates, you can obtain the net present value by using the following DAX measure, where the last argument corresponds to the 18.03 percent interest rate applied to the loan:

```
[Net Present Value] :=
XNPV ( LoanRates, LoanRates[Amount], LoanRates[Date], 0.1803 )
```

Using Excel statistical functions

Recent versions of DAX include a number of statistical functions with the same behavior as their Excel counterpart. Because these functions have a specific interest only for advanced statistical calculations and they are identical to the Excel version, a complete description is out of the scope of this book and we suggest considering documentation and examples available for Excel in order to get more details about them. This is the list of these functions (which are not available in Power Pivot for Excel 2013 and in Analysis Services 2012/2014):

- **BETA.DIST**   returns the beta distribution.

- **BETA.INV** returns the inverse of the beta cumulative probability density function (BETA.DIST).

- **CHISQ.DIST** returns the chi-squared distribution.

- **CHISQ.DIST.RT** returns the right-tailed probability of the chi-squared distribution.

- **CHISQ.INV** returns the inverse of the left-tailed probability of the chi-squared distribution.

- **CHISQ.INV.RT** returns the inverse of the right-tailed probability of the chi-squared distribution.

- **COMBIN** returns the number of combinations for a given number of items.

- **COMBINA** returns the number of combinations (with repetitions) for a given number of items.

- **CONFIDENCE.NORM** returns the confidence interval for a population mean, using a normal distribution.

- **CONFIDENCE.T** returns the confidence interval for a population mean, using a Student's t distribution.

- **EXPON.DIST** returns the exponential distribution.

- **PERMUT** returns the number of permutations for a given number of objects that can be selected from number of objects.

- **POISSON.DIST** returns the Poisson distribution.

Sampling by using the *SAMPLE* function

If you need to query a sample of data from a table, you can use the *SAMPLE* function, which has the following syntax:

```
SAMPLE( <number_of_rows>, <table>,
        <columnName_0> [, <order_0>]
        [, <columnName_1> [, <order_1>]] [...] )
```

The *SAMPLE* function returns the rows defined by the *<number_of_rows>* parameter from the *<table>* specified in the second argument, which can be either a physical table or the result of a function returning a table.

The remaining arguments specify one or more columns that will be used to order data before choosing the row that will be returned as a sample. The algorithm logically sorts data according to these parameters and then divides it in *<number_of_rows>* blocks, returning one row from each block. The *<column_name>* usually corresponds to a column name, but can be any DAX expression evaluated in a row context of *<table>*. The *<order>* parameter is 0 to return data sorted by *<column>* in descendant order and 1 for ascendant order; if missing, it defaults to 0 (descendant).

For example, the following query returns just one row for every month:

```
EVALUATE SAMPLE ( 12, 'Date', 'Date'[Month] )
```

Date	DateKey	Month	Month Number	...
28/09/2009	20090928	September	9	...
21/10/2010	20101021	October	10	...
15/11/2009	20091115	November	11	...
08/05/2005	20050508	May	5	...
21/03/2005	20050321	March	3	...
15/06/2006	20060615	June	6	...
06/07/2010	20100706	July	7	...
03/01/2008	20080103	January	1	...
20/02/2011	20110220	February	2	...
20/12/2010	20101220	December	12	...
27/08/2006	20060827	August	8	...
30/04/2011	20110430	April	4	...

The *Date* column seems randomly distributed, whereas the *Month* column (other columns have been omitted for readability) is sorted in a descendant order, because by omitting the *<order>* column the default value of 0 is considered.

You can repeat *<column>* and *<order>* and you can omit *<order>* in order to specify two columns:

```
EVALUATE
SAMPLE (
    100,
    SUMMARIZE (
        'Date',
        'Date'[Date],
        'Date'[Calendar Year],
        'Date'[Month Number]
    ),
    'Date'[Month Number],
    ,
    'Date'[Calendar Year]
)
```

Date	Calendar Year	Month Number	...
25/12/2011	CY 2011	12	...
10/12/2011	CY 2011	12	...
29/12/2010	CY 2010	12	...
16/12/2009	CY 2009	12	...
05/12/2008	CY 2008	12	...
21/12/2007	CY 2007	12	...
18/12/2006	CY 2006	12	...
16/12/2006	CY 2006	12	...
02/12/2005	CY 2005	12	...
17/11/2011	CY 2011	11	...
15/11/2010	CY 2010	11	...
05/11/2009	CY 2009	11	...

If the column you specify is not regularly distributed, you should see the same distribution of data in the sample extracted. For example, consider the following query that extracts six rows from the Customer table considering the *Country/Region* for distribution.

```
EVALUATE
SAMPLE (
    6,
    SUMMARIZE (
        Customer,
        Customer[City],
        Customer[Country/Region]
    ),
    Customer[Country/Region]
)
```

City	Country/Region
Martinsville	United States
Germantown	United States
Tallahassee	United States
Warrington	United Kingdom
Boulogne-sur-Mer	France
Yerevan	Armenia

Many countries/regions are missing, whereas the United States is present several times. However, this is because there are many more cities listed for the United States and for this reason it appears more often than other countries/regions. Certain client tools use the *SAMPLE* function in order to evaluate distribution of data without having to query the whole data set and defining the axis scale accordingly.

Advanced table functions

In Chapter 3, "Using basic table functions," when you were starting to learn DAX, we introduced the notion of table functions because they are extremely important in using and understanding iterators and filters. Now that your learning experience with DAX is increasing, it is time to cover the full, extremely rich set of DAX table functions.

Because there are many table functions, we grouped them in sets, according to their scope:

- Filter functions

- Projection functions

- Grouping/Joining functions

- Set functions

- Utility functions

While learning about table functions, we want to take the opportunity to speak about an important concept: column lineage. Column lineage is important for both semantic reasons (obtaining the result you want) and performance considerations (getting faster results).

Understanding *EVALUATE*

In Chapter 3 you learned the syntax of *EVALUATE*, which is the DAX statement to evaluate and materialize a table expression. There we anticipated that the *DEFINE MEASURE* part is useful to debug a formula. We include this explanation in this chapter because usually you will use table functions as filter arguments in scalar expressions used in measures, but it is much easier to test them in environments such as SQL Server Management Studio and DAX Studio, where you have to write a query returning a table.

First, consider the syntax for *DEFINE MEASURE*:

```
[DEFINE { MEASURE <tableName>[<name>] = <expression> }]
EVALUATE <table>
```

You can define one or more measures with an *EVALUATE* statement, as in the following example:

```
DEFINE
    MEASURE Sales[Quantity] = SUM ( Sales[Quantity] )
    MEASURE Sales[Total Cost] = SUMX ( Sales, Sales[Quantity] * Sales[Unit Cost] )
EVALUATE
ADDCOLUMNS (
    VALUES ( Product[Brand] ),
    "Quantity", [Quantity],
    "Cost", [Total Cost]
)
```

You have to associate the measure to a table name, just as you define a measure within a table in the data model. If you use a name already defined in the table, you override such a name in the *EVALUATE* expression when a row context is not present. For instance, the preceding example overrides the column name *Quantity* defining a measure with the same name. The value you see in each row of the result is the sum of the *Quantity* column for all the rows aggregated for each product brand.

Brand	Quantity	Cost
Contoso	6,454,061	407,989,158.93
Wide World Importers	825,241	121,376,015.93
...	...	...

In general, it is not a good idea to override existing names in a query. Nevertheless, this is useful when you want to replace a measure defined in a data model with a temporary definition in the query, typically for debugging or optimizing reasons. For example, imagine you have a query such as the following, where the measure *Discounted Sales* is not working correctly:

```
EVALUATE
ADDCOLUMNS (
    VALUES ( Product[Brand] ),
    "Discounted Sales", [Discounted Sales]
)
```

You can create a local measure with the same name, modifying and testing it until it works, and only at that point do you copy the corrected measure in the data model:

```
DEFINE
    MEASURE Sales[Discounted Sales] =
        SUMX ( Sales, Sales[Quantity] * ( Sales[Unit Price] - Sales[Unit Discount] ) )
EVALUATE
ADDCOLUMNS (
    VALUES ( Product[Brand] ),
    "Discounted Sales", [Discounted Sales]
)
```

Overriding a measure of the data model in a query does not affect existing references to that measure in other code of the data model. For instance, consider these two measures defined in the data model:

```
[Total Sales] := SUMX ( Sales, Sales[Quantity] * Sales[Net Price] )
[Average Price] := [Total Sales] / SUM ( Sales[Quantity] )
```

If you override *Total Sales* in a query, you will not see this affecting the *Average Price* calculation, as you see in the following example:

```
DEFINE
    MEASURE Sales[Total Sales] = 0
EVALUATE
ADDCOLUMNS (
    VALUES ( Product[Brand] ),
    "Total Sales", [Total Sales],
    "Average Price", [Average Price]
)
```

Average Price returns the value computed in the data model, using the original definition of *Total Sales* instead of the one defined locally to the query.

Brand	Total Sales	Average Price
Contoso	0	135.0315
Wide World Importers	0	308.9448
...	...	...

Using *VAR* in *EVALUATE*

You can define variables in an *EVALUATE* statement with a syntax that is slightly different from the standard one used for variable definitions. Usually you define a variable using this syntax:

```
VAR
    <variableName> = <expression>
RETURN
    <expressionConsumingVariable>
```

The expression after *RETURN* can access the previously defined variable. Such a syntax can replace any scalar or table expression in DAX. However, when you write an *EVALUATE* statement, you can also define a variable in the *DEFINE* section, without having to write *RETURN* after that:

```
DEFINE
    VAR ExpensiveProducts = FILTER ( Product, Product[Unit Price] > 3000 )
EVALUATE
    CALCULATETABLE ( Product, ExpensiveProducts )
```

A more complete syntax definition for *EVALUATE* is the following:

```
[DEFINE
    [{ MEASURE <tableName>[<name>] = <expression> }]
    [{ VAR <variableName> = <expression> }]
]
EVALUATE <table>
```

In any case, the evaluation of the variable happens only if the variable is used in the table expression after *EVALUATE*, and the evaluation does not depend on filter context manipulation made after the variable definition. In other words, you might use the *VAR/RETURN* syntax as well, as in the following example:

```
EVALUATE
VAR
    ExpensiveProducts = FILTER ( Product, Product[Unit Price] > 3000 )
RETURN
    CALCULATETABLE ( Product, ExpensiveProducts )
```

Understanding filter functions

DAX has many table functions used to filter other tables. If you have an SQL background, we might say that these functions correspond to the *WHERE* condition of a *SELECT* statement in SQL, even if this is too restrictive when you consider the behavior of *CALCULATETABLE*.

Using *CALCULATETABLE*

You have seen in Chapter 5, "Understanding *CALCULATE* and *CALCULATETABLE*," a complete description of *CALCULATE* and *CALCULATETABLE*. These two functions have the same behavior. The only difference is that *CALCULATE* evaluates a scalar expression, whereas *CALCULATETABLE* evaluates a table expression.

It is useful to remember that you can combine different filter conditions in the same *CALCULATETABLE* function call, and they will be considered as in a logical *AND* condition. For example, the following query returns products of the brand Wide World Importers with a Red color:

```
EVALUATE
CALCULATETABLE (
    Product,
    Product[Brand] = "Wide World Importers",
    Product[Color] = "Red"
)
```

Particular attention goes to the evaluation order of the arguments. *CALCULATE* and *CALCULATETABLE* evaluate the first argument after all the other arguments (called filter arguments) have been evaluated. This behavior is not common in other languages and is the source of common mistakes when you have two or more *CALCULATETABLE* functions nested together. For instance, consider the following query that applies a conflicting filter over the *Color* column of the Product table:

```
EVALUATE
CALCULATETABLE (
    CALCULATETABLE (
        VALUES ( Product[Color] ),
        Product[Color] = "Blue"
    ),
    Product[Color] = "Red"
)
```

At first sight, many people new to DAX erroneously think that the result of the query is the Red color. Nevertheless, the result is Blue.

Color
Blue

The reason is that the outermost *CALCULATETABLE* expression evaluates the filter first (Color Red), then it evaluates the innermost *CALCULATETABLE*, which receives a filter (Color Red) overridden by the new filter (Color Blue). The innermost expression evaluates *VALUES* in a filter context where only the Blue color is visible. You have to get used to this way of writing and reading filter arguments of *CALCULATE* and *CALCULATETABLE* because it is the more efficient way to apply filters to table expressions.

Differences between *FILTER* and *CALCULATETABLE*

The previous example of *CALCULATETABLE* showed a way to apply filters that is not intuitive but very efficient. In fact, the evaluation of the table expression is delayed until all the filters are applied, so this guarantees a minimal cost in terms of materialization (you will read more about materialization in Chapter 13, "The VertiPaq engine"). The behavior of *FILTER* is much easier, because every call to *FILTER* returns a table that you can use in other iterators.

For instance, the following query filter returns products of the brand Wide World Importers with a Red color, just as we did with *CALCULATETABLE* at the beginning of the previous section:

```
EVALUATE
FILTER (
    Product,
    Product[Brand] = "Wide World Importers" && Product[Color] = "Red"
)
```

From a semantic point of view, you are asking to apply the filter specified in the second argument for every row of the Product table. You can use the result of a filter as an argument for another filter. Depending on the version of the DAX engine, you might see different performances, even if the result will always be the same. You will see a more complete discussion about performance in Chapter 16, "Optimizing DAX." Here you should concentrate your attention only on the different syntaxes you can use to obtain the same result.

For example, the following query filters products that sold at least 100,000 units, then filters this subset of products returning only those that are Red:

```
EVALUATE
FILTER (
    FILTER (
        Product,
        CALCULATE ( SUM ( Sales[Quantity] ) ) > 100000
    ),
    Product[Color] = "Red"
)
```

You can write the same expression inverting the filters between the two *FILTER* iterators. In this case, the filter over the Red color is the first one, and the filter over the quantity is the second one:

```
EVALUATE
FILTER (
    FILTER (
        Product,
        Product[Color] = "Red"
    ),
    CALCULATE ( SUM ( Sales[Quantity] ) ) > 100000
)
```

The result is the same for the two earlier queries, but the performance might be different. In theory, the innermost filter should apply the more restrictive filter condition, so that subsequent operations iterate a smaller number of rows. In practice, however, the DAX query engine might rearrange filters and follow a different execution pattern from the one you defined with nested iterators. Our experience is to consider different ways to obtain the same result whenever you have very complex expressions, in order to reduce the number of iterations requiring the more expensive calculations.

Using *TOPN*

The *TOPN* function filters data according to the value of one or more expressions specified in the arguments, returning only the first N elements specified in the first parameter of the function. For instance, you can filter the first product by *Weight* using the following query:

```
EVALUATE
TOPN (
    1,
    Product,
    Product[Weight]
)
```

However, this query might return more than one row, because if there are more products having the same value for *Weight*, the *TOPN* function retrieves all the rows that produce a tie.

ProductKey	Product Code	Product Name	Weight	Unit Price	...
1832	0801006	Litware Washer & Dryer 27in L420 Silver	239	2652	...
1849	0801023	NT Washer & Dryer 24in M2400 White	239	1818.9	...
1864	0801038	NT Washer & Dryer 24in M2400 Green	239	1818.9	...

You can specify the sort order using more columns, and whether the order should be descendant (default) or ascendant, as you see in the following syntax:

```
TOPN (
    <n_value>,
    <table>,
    <orderBy_expression> [, <order>
    [,<orderBy_expression> [, <order>] ]
    ...]
)
```

The <n_value> parameter specifies the number of rows that should be returned from <table> according to the sort order specified by <orderBy_expression> and <order> parameters. You can have multiple <orderBy_expression>; if multiple rows have the same value for the first <orderBy_expression>, the second one will be evaluated and so on. The <order> parameter is 0 or FALSE (default) to rank in descending order and 1 or TRUE to rank in ascending order.

You can rewrite the previous query sorting by *Weight* and *Unit Price* as follows:

```
EVALUATE
TOPN (
    1,
    Product,
    Product[Weight],
    ,
    Product[Unit Price]
)
```

In this case, the result has only one row, but you do not have a guarantee that the result is always one row; in case of ties you will have more rows.

ProductKey	Product Code	Product Name	Weight	Unit Price	...
1832	0801006	Litware Washer & Dryer 27in L420 Silver	239	2652	...

If you want an exact number of rows in the result, you have to include a unique column in the *TOPN* arguments. For example, including the *ProductKey* will retrieve the product that has the highest value for *ProductKey*, in case all the other order expressions produce a tie, as in the following query:

```
EVALUATE
TOPN (
    1,
    Product,
    Product[Weight],
    ,
    Product[Unit Price],
    ,
    Product[ProductKey]
)
```

Use of *FIRSTNONBLANK* to restrict results to a single row

In Chapter 7, "Time intelligence calculations," you have seen the use of the *FIRSTNONBLANK* function for semi-additive measures. You can also use *FIRSTNONBLANK* to retrieve a single row from a set that might contain ties, such as the result provided by *TOPN*:

```
EVALUATE
FIRSTNONBLANK ( TOPN ( 1, Product, Product[Weight] ), 0 )
```

As you see in this example, you can specify any expression in the second argument that returns a nonblank value (in this case we used the constant value 0).

Understanding projection functions

In relational algebra, a projection operation is the request of a subset of columns for an operation. DAX is not a language like SQL, designed for relational operations, but we can see many similarities in the goal of the operations you can perform with DAX table functions. In this section you will find the operations that can manipulate the columns provided by a table expression by selecting existing columns or by adding new ones to your final result.

Using *ADDCOLUMNS*

As its name implies, *ADDCOLUMNS* adds new columns to the table expression you provide as the first parameter. For each column you add, you provide a string with the column name and a scalar expression, as defined by the following syntax:

```
ADDCOLUMNS (
    <table>,
    <column_name1>, <column_expression1>
    [, <column_name2>, <column_expression2>]…
)
```

For example, you can add two columns with the number of subcategories and products for each product category by using the following syntax:

```
EVALUATE
ADDCOLUMNS (
    'Product Category',
    "Subcategories", CALCULATE ( COUNTROWS ( 'Product Subcategory' ) ),
    "Products", CALCULATE ( COUNTROWS ( Product ) )
)
```

The result includes columns from Product Category and the additional columns calculated by the *ADDCOLUMNS* iteration. You can see these new columns highlighted in italic.

ProductCategoryKey	Category Code	Category	*Subcategories*	*Products*
1	01	Audio	8	*115*
2	02	TV and Video	5	*222*
3	03	Computers	8	*2652*
…	…	…	…	…

You will see later that there is an important difference between original columns and derived columns, which we highlight in italic in this chapter. Columns highlighted in italic do not have a lineage mapping a physical column of the data model, and you cannot use them in a filter context, as we will describe in more detail in the "Understanding lineage and relationships" section, later in this chapter.

ADDCOLUMNS is an iterator that evaluates in a row context every expression specified for the added columns. In other words, *ADDCOLUMNS* provides you with the same semantics of calculated columns, but the result of the computation is local to the query and not persisted in the data model. Also for this reason, you can filter the result of *ADDCOLUMNS* accessing the new columns in other iterators (such as *FILTER* or other *ADDCOLUMNS* calls), but you cannot apply a filter argument in *CALCULATE* or *CALCULATETABLE* to such columns.

For instance, you can filter only the categories having at least 500 products using a *FILTER* that calls *ADDCOLUMNS*, as in the following example:

```
EVALUATE
FILTER (
    ADDCOLUMNS (
        'Product Category',
        "Subcategories", CALCULATE ( COUNTROWS ( 'Product Subcategory' ) ),
        "Products", CALCULATE ( COUNTROWS ( Product ) )
    ),
    [Products] > 500
)
```

The result produces a smaller number of rows.

ProductCategoryKey	Category Code	Category	Subcategories	Products
3	03	Computers	8	606
8	08	Home Appliances	8	661

In the previous example, the column *Products* had a name without a table identifier. Referencing such a name in following expressions (such as the filter condition) requires the use of the syntax we prefer to use for measure references. The column you added has the semantics of a column, but does not "belong" to a table, so it does not have a fully qualified name that includes a table name. However, you can define a column name with a fully qualified name, shown as follows:

```
EVALUATE
FILTER (
    ADDCOLUMNS (
        'Product Category',
        "Subcategories", CALCULATE ( COUNTROWS ( 'Product Subcategory' ) ),
        "'Product Category'[Products]", CALCULATE ( COUNTROWS ( Product ) )
    ),
    'Product Category'[Products] > 500
)
```

Using a fully qualified name does not add the column to the table; it simply enables the syntax to reach such a column using a fully qualified name in subsequent expressions, such as our filter. This syntax is important to enable the use of an added column by other functions, such as *SUMMARIZE* (which requires a fully qualified name for all the columns you want to group by, as you will see later in this chapter).

The name of the column needs to be unique in the result of *ADDCOLUMNS*. Thus, you can override a column name that exists in the data model if it is not part of the result, and you can output more columns with the same name but different table names. Moreover, the table name you use does not have to be a related table in the data model. Consider the table name of an added column as a placeholder. You have to use an existing table name of the data model, but we suggest you avoid inconsistent naming and avoid overriding existing names. For example, the following syntax is valid, even if it is not helpful in understanding the result (adding two columns to Product Category would be more intuitive here):

```
EVALUATE
ADDCOLUMNS (
    'Product Category',
    "'Product Subcategory'[Rows]", CALCULATE ( COUNTROWS ( 'Product Subcategory' ) ),
    "Product[Rows]", CALCULATE ( COUNTROWS ( Product ) )
)
```

The result is identical to the initial example; you just have different column names in the result.

ProductCategoryKey	Category Code	Category	'Product Subcategory'[Rows]	Product[Rows]
1	01	Audio	8	115
2	02	TV and Video	5	222
3	03	Computers	8	2652
...	...	...	...	...

Note The string you provide for a column name has to be a constant string, and you cannot use a dynamic expression for these names.

If you want to select a subset of the columns of a table, you should use *SELECTCOLUMNS*, which you will see in the next section. However, older versions of the DAX language do not have *SELECTCOLUMNS* and you can only use *ADDCOLUMNS* to manipulate the result. In this case, you should include only one or more columns that represent a unique key for a row in the table, and then add the columns you need. For example, if you want to obtain a table that has only three columns from the Product table (*ProductKey*, *Product Name*, and *Unit Price*), you can use the following query:

```
EVALUATE
ADDCOLUMNS (
    DISTINCT ( Product[ProductKey] ),
    "Product Name", CALCULATE ( VALUES ( Product[Product Name] ) ),
    "Price", CALCULATE ( VALUES ( Product[Unit Price] ) )
)
ORDER BY Product[ProductKey]
```

Please note that the result has only one column that maps to the physical table (*ProductKey*), whereas the other two are derived columns (highlighted in italic). This is important for the limitations you have in a filter context (you cannot filter derived columns through a filter context).

ProductKey	*Product Name*	*Price*
1	*Contoso 512MB MP3 Player E51 Silver*	*12.99*
2	*Contoso 512MB MP3 Player E51 Blue*	*12.99*
3	*Contoso 1G MP3 Player E100 White*	*14.52*
...	...	...

For this reason, you should use *SELECTCOLUMNS* whenever possible to select and create columns you want to project in the result.

Using *SELECTCOLUMNS*

SELECTCOLUMNS selects existing columns from and adds new columns to the ones available in a table expression. You provide a string with the column name and a scalar expression for each column you want to include in the output, as defined by the following syntax:

```
SELECTCOLUMNS (
    <table>,
    <name>, <expression>
    [, <name>, <expression>]…
)
```

 Note The *SELECTCOLUMNS* function is not available in older versions of the DAX engine.

For instance, you can rewrite the final example you have seen in *ADDCOLUMNS* using the following query:

```
EVALUATE
SELECTCOLUMNS (
    Product,
    "ProductKey", Product[ProductKey],
    "Product Name", Product[Product Name],
    "Price", Product[Unit Price]
)
ORDER BY [ProductKey]
```

The result is the same, but with an important difference: All the columns correspond to physical columns of the data model (you no longer see columns highlighted in italic). This is true for both *Product Name* and *Price* columns. The latter corresponds to *Unit Price*, even if you change the name in the output of *SELECTCOLUMNS*.

ProductKey	Product Name	Price	Category
1	Contoso 512MB MP3 Player E51 Silver	12.99	Audio
2	Contoso 512MB MP3 Player E51 Blue	12.99	Audio
3	Contoso 1G MP3 Player E100 White	14.52	Audio
...	...	...	...

SELECTCOLUMNS preserves the lineage of a column whenever possible. If you rename a column, provided that the expression simply references an existing column of the data model, the result maps that column using the same data lineage. You lose the lineage as soon as you use any expression. You will see a more detailed explanation in the section "Understanding lineage and relationships," later in this chapter.

Regardless of the lineage, any reference to columns defined by *SELECTCOLUMNS* has to use the exact name assigned to the column. Therefore, if you define columns without using fully qualified names, you have to use the syntax to access a column without the table name. For example, the following syntax is not valid:

```
EVALUATE
FILTER (
    SELECTCOLUMNS (
        Product,
        "ProductKey", Product[ProductKey],
        "Product Name", Product[Product Name],
        "Unit Price", Product[Unit Price]
    ),
    Product[Unit Price] > 10
)
ORDER BY [ProductKey]
```

The reference to *Product[Unit Price]* is not valid, because the column defined by *SELECTCOLUMNS* has *Unit Price* only as a name. It is interesting to note that *ProductKey* used in *ORDER BY* does not have this issue, because it is referenced using the column name without the table name. You can solve the problem by using the unqualified name also in the filter condition, as in the following query:

```
EVALUATE
FILTER (
    SELECTCOLUMNS (
        Product,
        "ProductKey", Product[ProductKey],
        "Product Name", Product[Product Name],
        "Unit Price", Product[Unit Price]
    ),
    [Unit Price] > 10
)
ORDER BY [ProductKey]
```

You can also use the fully qualified names in *SELECTCOLUMNS*, so that you keep the same syntax in subsequent references, as in the next example:

```
EVALUATE
FILTER (
    SELECTCOLUMNS (
        Product,
        "Product[ProductKey]", Product[ProductKey],
        "Product[Product Name]", Product[Product Name],
        "Product[Unit Price]", Product[Unit Price]
    ),
    Product[Unit Price] > 10
)
ORDER BY [ProductKey]
```

Even if you define a fully qualified name for each column, you can still reference a column using only the column name, as it is the case of *ORDER BY* referencing the *ProductKey* column. Such a syntax is valid until you do not have two columns with the same column name and different table names in the final result (you would obtain an ambiguous column reference error in that case).

You can also use *SELECTCOLUMNS* to add new columns, as you do in *ADDCOLUMNS*. The difference is that you have to reference explicitly every single column to include in the result, instead of adding new columns to the existing ones. For instance, the following query returns the number of subcategories and products for each product category, showing only the category name without other columns from the Product Category table:

```
EVALUATE
SELECTCOLUMNS (
    'Product Category',
    "Category Name", 'Product Category'[Category],
    "Subcategories", CALCULATE ( COUNTROWS ( 'Product Subcategory' ) ),
    "Products", CALCULATE ( COUNTROWS ( Product ) )
)
```

The result keeps the lineage of the *Category Name* column with the physical *Category* column in the Product Category table, adding two calculated columns highlighted in italic because they have no lineage with a physical column.

Category Name	Subcategories	Products
Audio	8	115
TV and Video	5	222
Computers	8	2652
...	...	...

Using *ROW*

The *EVALUATE* statement has to return a table. If you want to perform a computation of one or more scalar values and you do not have a corresponding table, you can use the *ROW* function, which returns a table with a single row containing the desired columns:

```
ROW (
    <column1_name>, <column1_expression>
    [,<column2_name>, <column2_expression>]…
)
```

Similar to what you do in *ADDCOLUMNS* and *SELECTCOLUMNS*, for each column you specify a name (which has to be a constant string) and the expression evaluated to provide a value for that column in the returned row. The rules for the naming convention are the same as those for the *ADDCOLUMNS* and *SELECTCOLUMNS* functions. You can add as many columns as you want.

You might consider using this function whenever you need to return more than one scalar value; instead of performing several DAX queries, you can execute just one. For example, the following query returns a row with two columns containing the quantity sold in 2008 and 2009:

```
EVALUATE
ROW (
    "Quantity 2008", CALCULATE (
        SUM ( Sales[Quantity] ),
        'Date'[Calendar Year Number] = 2008
    ),
    "Quantity 2009", CALCULATE (
        SUM ( Sales[Quantity] ),
        'Date'[Calendar Year Number] = 2009
    )
)
```

No columns included in the result have a lineage corresponding to a physical column of the data model.

Quantity 2008	Quantity 2009
5,029,924	6,956,456

You can include the *ROW* function in any DAX expression that requires a table. If available in your DAX version, you can use the *UNION* function to combine several *ROW* calls returning a table made by more rows arbitrarily defined.

Understanding lineage and relationships

Any table function returns one or more columns, each one with a particular lineage. When a column corresponds to a physical column of the data model, its lineage provides information to the engine allowing faster filter operations. The lineage does not depend on the name of the column and it is technically an internal reference that uniquely identifies the column. You cannot display the lineage of a column in DAX, but you can observe its effects.

For example, consider this initial query, which returns all the products belonging to a *Style* that sold a quantity greater than 200,000:

```
EVALUATE
CALCULATETABLE (
    Product,
    FILTER (
        VALUES ( Product[Style] ),
        CALCULATE ( SUM ( Sales[Quantity] ) ) > 200000
    )
)
```

The filter argument used in *CALCULATETABLE* is a filtered list of values for the column *Style* of the Product table. In this case, it is clear that you are applying a filter on a column of the Product table to evaluate the expression in *CALCULATETABLE*. The query above returns two rows.

ProductKey	Product Code	Product Name	Style	...
1832	0801006	Litware Washer & Dryer 27in L420 Silver	Product0202011	...
1849	0801023	NT Washer & Dryer 24in M2400 White	Product0201038	...

What happens if you apply a different filter argument using *SELECTCOLUMNS*? As we said, you will see the same result if you do not lose the lineage of the physical column. The following query applies the same filter with a different implementation. The *SELECTCOLUMNS* function generates a table with two columns (*Key* and *Sales*). The *Key* column has the same lineage of the *ProductKey* column, so it applies a filter over that column, whereas the *Sales* column does not correspond to any physical column, so it does not affect the filter context in the *CALCULATETABLE* statement:

```
EVALUATE
CALCULATETABLE (
    Product,
    FILTER (
        SELECTCOLUMNS (
            Product,
            "Key", Product[ProductKey],
            "Sales", CALCULATE ( SUM ( Sales[Quantity] ) )
        ),
        [Sales] > 200000
    )
)
```

The result is the same as for the previous query. Renaming the column does not affect the lineage.

ProductKey	Product Code	Product Name	Style	...
1832	0801006	Litware Washer & Dryer 27in L420 Silver	Product0202011	...
1849	0801023	NT Washer & Dryer 24in M2400 White	Product0201038	...

Any expression used in the column expression generates a different lineage, breaking the link to the physical column. For example, by simply adding 0 to the previous expression, you obtain a different column (regardless of the fact that we try to use the same fully qualified name):

```
EVALUATE
CALCULATETABLE (
    Product,
    FILTER (
        SELECTCOLUMNS (
            Product,
            "Product[ProductKey]", Product[ProductKey] + 0,
            "Sales", CALCULATE ( SUM ( Sales[Quantity] ) )
        ),
        [Sales] > 200000
    )
)
```

Therefore, the result of the query includes all the products, because the filter argument of *CALCULATETABLE* does not receive filters on any existing column.

ProductKey	Product Code	Product Name	Style	...
1722	0702016	MGS Zoo Tycoon 2: End range Species ...	Product0702016	...
1723	0702017	MGS Age of Empires III: The Asian ...	Product0702017	...
1724	0702018	MGS Fable: The Lost Chapters ...	Product0702018	...
...	...	...	...	...

However, the result of *RELATED* is not an expression; it is actually a keyword that enables the access to a column of the expanded table (more about this in Chapter 10, "Advanced evaluation context"). For this reason, you can create a query such as the following one, which returns the list of categories with at least one product having a Unit Price greater than 1,000:

```
EVALUATE
CALCULATETABLE (
    'Product Category',
    SELECTCOLUMNS (
        FILTER ( Product, Product[Unit Price] > 1000 ),
        "Category", RELATED ( 'Product Category'[Category] )
    )
)
```

It is interesting to note that the *SELECTCOLUMNS* function returns more than the four rows you see in the result. The table expression receives 154 rows from the *FILTER*. However, the filter argument of *CALCULATETABLE* will consider only the unique values in the *Category* column.

ProductCategoryKey	Category Code	Category
2	02	TV and Video
3	03	Computers
4	04	Cameras and camcorders
8	08	Home Appliances

Understanding grouping/joining functions

DAX has several functions that aggregate data and join tables using existing relationships in the data model. Only *SUMMARIZE* exists in all the versions of DAX, whereas other functions are present only in more recent versions of the language. Even if you will use other functions in current DAX versions, it is a good idea to familiarize yourself with *SUMMARIZE* first, also because most of the existing patterns and examples are still based on this function.

In this section, you will find functions that are similar and might be confused about their use. In general, you should heed the following best practices:

- If you write a query, such as *EVALUATE*, you should use *SUMMARIZECOLUMNS* for computing aggregates over base table columns, instead of using *SUMMARIZE* or *GROUPBY*.

- If you write a scalar expression (such as when defining a measure, or an expression used by a table expression), you should use aggregation functions from the Agg*X family, such as *SUMX* or *AVERAGEX*, instead of using *SUMMARIZE*, *GROUPBY*, and *SUMMARIZECOLUMNS*. In other words, there is no need to invoke a table-valued function to aggregate intermediate values, when an "X" scalar aggregate function can do the job instead.

- You should use *SUMMARIZECOLUMNS* instead of *SUMMARIZE* whenever possible.

- You should use *GROUPBY* only to aggregate intermediate/aggregate results returned by *SUMMARIZECOLUMNS* and *ADDCOLUMNS*, when you have to do some extra computation with measure values (created in these functions), and not over base columns.

Using *SUMMARIZE*

You can produce a summary table of data by using *SUMMARIZE*. This function groups data by one or more columns, and for each row it can add new columns that evaluate the specified expressions. The syntax is as follows:

```
SUMMARIZE (
    <table>,
    <group_by_column1>
    [,<group_by_column2>][, …]
    [,ROLLUP( <group_by_columnX> [,<group_by_columnY>] [, …] )]
    [,<column1_name>, { <column1_expression> | ISSUBTOTAL( <group_by_column> ) } ]
    [,<column2_name>, { <column2_expression> | ISSUBTOTAL( <group_by_column> ) } ][, …]
)
```

You can group the table in the first argument by using any column of any table that can be reached using a many-to-one or a one-to-one relationship. In other words, you can use any column reachable by using *RELATED*, without having to use such a function. For instance, the following query returns the quantities sold every year:

```
EVALUATE
SUMMARIZE (
    Sales,
    'Date'[Calendar Year],
    "Quantity", SUM ( Sales[Quantity] )
)
```

The result includes only values for *Calendar Year* column that have at least one corresponding row in the Sales table.

Calendar Year	Quantity
CY 2007	5,551,636
CY 2008	5,029,924
CY 2009	6,956,456

The expression you write for each column added by *SUMMARIZE* has a filter context that makes the use of *CALCULATE* unnecessary. However, *SUMMARIZE* also has a row context available that enables access to the values of the grouped columns, as you see in the following example:

```
EVALUATE
SUMMARIZE (
    Sales,
    'Date'[Calendar Year Number],
    "Short Year", 'Date'[Calendar Year Number] - 2000,
    "Quantity", SUM ( Sales[Quantity] )
)
```

You can see the result in this table.

Calendar Year Number	Short Year	Quantity
2007	7	5,551,636
2008	8	5,029,924
2009	9	6,956,456

However, for a number of reasons, mainly related to performances, it is a best practice to avoid using *SUMMARIZE* to evaluate expressions. Whenever possible, you should generate additional columns by using *ADDCOLUMNS* instead. The conversion is usually simple. You only have to add a *CALCULATE* statement for all the columns that include aggregations requiring a filter context of the rows grouped together. For instance, you can write the previous query in this more efficient way:

```
EVALUATE
ADDCOLUMNS (
    SUMMARIZE (
        Sales,
        'Date'[Calendar Year Number]
    ),
    "Short Year", 'Date'[Calendar Year Number] - 2000,
    "Quantity", CALCULATE ( SUM ( Sales[Quantity] ) )
)
```

Important You can find a longer explanation about this best practice in the following article: *http://www.sqlbi.com/articles/best-practices-using-summarize-and-addcolumns/*. However, consider using *SUMMARIZECOLUMNS* instead of *SUMMARIZE* in more recent versions of DAX when you write an *EVALUATE* statement. In general, follow the best practices described in the introduction to the grouping functions.

You can choose to include roll-up rows in the result of a *SUMMARIZE* function based on one or more of the groups you specified. In this case, you have to include a column expression within the *SUMMARIZE* syntax. The roll-up rows have a BLANK value for the column used to group results. For example, the following query adds a row with the total for all the years, identified by a BLANK value for *Calendar Year*:

```
EVALUATE
SUMMARIZE (
    Sales,
    ROLLUP ( 'Date'[Calendar Year] ),
    "Quantity", SUM ( Sales[Quantity] )
)
ORDER BY 'Date'[Calendar Year]
```

Calendar Year	Quantity
	17,538,016
CY 2007	5,551,636
CY 2008	5,029,924
CY 2009	6,956,456

Because the roll-up rows have a BLANK value for the grouping columns, if the result is sorted, you get the roll-up row before the detail rows that it represents. If you want to roll up more columns, you must specify all of them as parameters of a single *ROLLUP* call, whereas you can specify other grouping columns before or after the *ROLLUP* call. In other words, you can use only one *ROLLUP* call in a single *SUMMARIZE* statement. For example, the following query calculates rollup for *Category* and *Weight Unit Measure* of products without calculating a total for all the years. (*Calendar Year* is out of the *ROLLUP* function.)

```
EVALUATE
SUMMARIZE (
    Sales,
    'Date'[Calendar Year],
    ROLLUP ( 'Product Category'[Category], Product[Weight Unit Measure] ),
    "Quantity", SUM ( Sales[Quantity] )
)
ORDER BY
    'Date'[Calendar Year],
    'Product Category'[Category],
    Product[Weight Unit Measure]
```

Calendar Year	Category	Weight Unit Measure	Quantity
CY 2009			6,956,456
...	...	...	...
CY 2009	**Computers**		**236,026**
CY 2009	**Computers**		**1,253,907**
CY 2009	Computers	pounds	1,017,881
CY 2009	Games and Toys		487,185
CY 2009	Games and Toys		924,866
CY 2009	Games and Toys	pounds	437,681
...	...	...	...

As you can see from the previous result, just checking the BLANK value in a column is not a reliable way to identify roll-up rows. In fact, there are two rows for Computers in 2009 that have a BLANK value in the *Weight Unit Measure* column. One of these two rows corresponds to the total of Computers that does not have a Weight Unit Measure specified in the Product table, and the other row is the total of Computers in 2009 for any *Weight Unit Measure* of products. Moreover, the ordering does not guarantee the order of these two rows, and in this case the roll-up row (the one with the higher *Quantity* value) is after the row that represents only those products without a *Weight Unit Measure* specified. For these reasons, do not assume that the BLANK value in a column corresponds to a roll-up row.

> **Tip** Using a foreign key that contains only existing values in the lookup table is a best practice for a tabular model. You can apply the classic transformation used in a star schema, in which a surrogate key for "unknown" members is used in fact tables to map application keys not found in the corresponding dimension table. Relying on the built-in tabular mechanism that displays data in blank rows should be a second choice.

To understand whether a row is the roll-up result for a grouping column, you can add columns to the result by using the *ISSUBTOTAL* function, which accepts a grouping column as a parameter and returns TRUE if the row contains a subtotal value (which is the case in a roll-up row); otherwise, it returns FALSE. The following query adds two columns that identify whether the row is a roll-up row for the specified grouping column:

```
EVALUATE
SUMMARIZE (
    Sales,
    'Date'[Calendar Year],
    ROLLUP ( 'Product Category'[Category], Product[Weight Unit Measure] ),
    "Quantity", SUM ( Sales[Quantity] ),
    "Category Subtotal", ISSUBTOTAL ( 'Product Category'[Category] ),
    "W.U.M. Subtotal", ISSUBTOTAL ( Product[Weight Unit Measure] )
)
ORDER BY
    'Date'[Calendar Year],
    'Product Category'[Category],
    Product[Weight Unit Measure]
```

Calendar Year	Category	Weight Unit Measure	Quantity	Category Subtotal	W.U.M. Subtotal
CY 2009			6,956,456	True	True
...	...	...	...	...	...
CY 2009	**Computers**		**236,026**	**False**	**False**
CY 2009	**Computers**		**1,253,907**	**False**	**True**
CY 2009	Computers	pounds	1,017,881	False	False
CY 2009	Games and Toys		487,185	False	False
CY 2009	Games and Toys		924,866	False	True
CY 2009	Games and Toys	pounds	437,681	False	False
...	...	...	...	...	...

As you can see in the result, the *W.U.M. Subtotal* column contains True for the Computers in 2009 row that is a sum of all the weight unit measures of products, and contains False for the row that represents Computers in 2009 without a weight unit measure specified in the Products table. The *ISSUBTOTAL* function is useful to obtain information for conditional formatting of the result in a report.

Using *SUMMARIZECOLUMNS*

The function *SUMMARIZECOLUMNS* is a more flexible and efficient implementation of *SUMMARIZE*. It is a best practice to use *SUMMARIZECOLUMNS* instead of *SUMMARIZE*. Its syntax is as follows:

```
SUMMARIZECOLUMNS (
    <group_by_column1>
    [,<group_by_column2>][, …]
    [,<filterTable1>[,<filterTable2>] [, …]]
    [,<column1_name>, { <column1_expression> | IGNORE ( <group_by_column> ) } ]
    [,<column2_name>, { <column2_expression> | IGNORE ( <group_by_column> ) } ][, …]
)
```

For instance, you can write the first example you have seen for *SUMMARIZE* by using *SUMMARIZECOLUMNS* in this way:

```
EVALUATE
SUMMARIZECOLUMNS (
    'Date'[Calendar Year],
    "Quantity", SUM ( Sales[Quantity] )
)
```

Calendar Year	Quantity
CY 2007	5,551,636
CY 2008	5,029,924
CY 2009	6,956,456

In reality, the internal behavior is somewhat different. *SUMMARIZECOLUMNS* removes from the output all the rows that have a BLANK value for all of the supplied column expressions. For example, the previous syntax corresponds to the following:

```
EVALUATE
FILTER (
    ADDCOLUMNS (
        VALUES ( 'Date'[Calendar Year] ),
        "Quantity", CALCULATE ( SUM ( Sales[Quantity] ) )
    ),
    NOT ISBLANK ( [Quantity] )
)
```

If you do not specify any new column, the result does not filter any value present in the columns specified.

```
EVALUATE
SUMMARIZECOLUMNS (
    'Date'[Calendar Year]
)
```

Calendar Year
CY 2005
CY 2006
CY 2007
CY 2008
CY 2009
CY 2010
CY 2011

Important The following part of the *SUMMARIZECOLUMNS* explanation requires the notion of expanded tables, explained in Chapter 10. You will not use *SUMMARIZECOLUMNS* in measures, because it cannot have an outside filter context. This function is useful in DAX queries. You can continue the reading assuming that the behavior of a filter table in *SUMMARIZECOLUMNS* is similar to the table you use in *SUMMARIZE*, which can group all the columns reachable through a chain of many-to-one relationships. However, the use of filter tables in *SUMMARIZECOLUMNS* can do more, especially in data models that have relationships with bidirectional cross filters.

If you want to get only the years for which at least one row exists in a Sales table, you might want to specify such a table as a filter context. However, you cannot specify an outside filter context for *SUMMARIZECOLUMNS*, so you cannot embed it within a *CALCULATE* or *CALCULATETABLE* call. The following syntax is invalid:

```
EVALUATE
CALCULATETABLE (
    SUMMARIZECOLUMNS (
        'Date'[Calendar Year]
    ),
    Sales
)
```

Instead, you can specify one or more filter tables, which correspond to filter arguments you would specify in an external *CALCULATETABLE*:

```
EVALUATE
SUMMARIZECOLUMNS (
    'Date'[Calendar Year],
    Sales
)
```

This query returns a list of three years, which are the same filtered by the first query, where we specified an expression that was aggregating the *Quantity* column in the Sales table.

Calendar Year
CY 2007
CY 2008
CY 2009

 Important *SUMMARIZE* can have an outside filter context, whereas this is not possible for *SUMMARIZECOLUMNS*. This can be an important difference, especially if you are generating a DAX query dynamically by code. You have to implement the filter directly in the *SUMMARIZECOLUMNS* filter arguments, instead of relying on outside filter contexts defined by *CALCULATE* or *CALCULATETABLE*. However, you can filter the result of *SUMMARIZECOLUMNS* by using the *FILTER* function.

You do not have to specify a table as first argument, but you can optionally specify one or more tables after the grouping columns that become part of the filter context. You have to apply filters to evaluation here, because *SUMMARIZECOLUMNS* cannot have an outside filter context. For example, the following query returns all the combinations of calendar years and product classes available (it is a total of 21 rows):

```
EVALUATE
SUMMARIZECOLUMNS (
    'Date'[Calendar Year],
    Product[Class]
)
```

Calendar Year	Class
CY 2005	Economy
CY 2006	Economy
CY 2007	Economy
	... (total 21 rows)

> **Note** In the previous example, *SUMMARIZECOLUMNS* has the same behavior of CROSSJOIN. Usually, you will use *SUMMARIZECOLUMNS* for more complex requests, continuing to use *CROSSJOIN* for this particular case.

You can obtain only the combinations of calendar years and product classes where there is at least one corresponding row in the Sales table (the total is nine rows):

```
EVALUATE
SUMMARIZECOLUMNS (
    'Date'[Calendar Year],
    Product[Class],
    Sales
)
```

Calendar Year	Class
CY 2007	Economy
CY 2008	Economy
CY 2009	Economy
CY 2007	Regular
...	... (total 9 rows)

The following query returns the combination of calendar years and product classes for products that have a unit price greater than 3,000 (the total is seven rows):

```
EVALUATE
SUMMARIZECOLUMNS (
    'Date'[Calendar Year],
    Product[Class],
    CALCULATETABLE ( Product, Product[Unit Price] > 3000 )
)
```

Calendar Year	Class
CY 2005	Deluxe
CY 2006	Deluxe
CY 2007	Deluxe
CY 2008	Deluxe
...	... (total 7 rows)

Finally, this is the query returning the combination of calendar years and product classes for products that have a unit price greater than 3,000, considering only those combinations that have at least one corresponding row in Sales table (the total is three rows). In this case, we also add the sum of quantity in a new column:

```
EVALUATE
SUMMARIZECOLUMNS (
    'Date'[Calendar Year],
    Product[Class],
    CALCULATETABLE ( Sales, Product[Unit Price] > 3000 ),
    "Quantity", SUM ( Sales[Quantity] )
)
```

Calendar Year	Class	Quantity
CY 2007	Deluxe	5,667
CY 2008	Deluxe	10,375
CY 2009	Deluxe	14,829

If you add the column that evaluates the sum of quantity from the Sales table, you might use the previous filter that only considered the rows in Product table. In fact, *SUMMARIZECOLUMNS* removes the rows that have a BLANK result in all the column expressions you evaluate. You can keep them by using the *IGNORE* function, as you see in the following example:

```
EVALUATE
SUMMARIZECOLUMNS (
    'Date'[Calendar Year],
    Product[Class],
    CALCULATETABLE ( Product, Product[Unit Price] > 3000 ),
    "Quantity", IGNORE ( SUM ( Sales[Quantity] ) )
)
```

Calendar Year	Class	Quantity
CY 2005	Deluxe	
CY 2006	Deluxe	
CY 2007	Deluxe	5,667
CY 2008	Deluxe	10,375
CY 2009	Deluxe	14,829
CY 2010	Deluxe	
CY 2011	Deluxe	

The expression you evaluate in *SUMMARIZECOLUMNS* only has a filter context, and does not have a row context (as you have in *SUMMARIZE*). However, you can access the grouped columns by using

VALUES, which returns a table of one column and one row that is automatically converted in a scalar value, as you see in the following example.

```
EVALUATE
SUMMARIZECOLUMNS (
    'Date'[Calendar Year],
    Product[Class],
    CALCULATETABLE ( Sales, Product[Unit Price] > 3000 ),
    "Upper", UPPER ( VALUES ( Product[Class] ) ),
    "Quantity", SUM ( Sales[Quantity] )
)
```

Calendar Year	Class	Upper	Quantity
CY 2007	Deluxe	DELUXE	5,667
CY 2008	Deluxe	DELUXE	10,375
CY 2009	Deluxe	DELUXE	14,829

Using *ROLLUPADDISSUBTOTAL*, you can create subtotals adding columns with the flag that indicates whether the row is a subtotal or not for that column. This is a simplified way of combining the *ROLLUP* and *ISSUBTOTAL* functions that you have seen in the *SUMMARIZE* function. The following query adds a subtotal for the *Calendar Year* column:

```
EVALUATE
SUMMARIZECOLUMNS (
    Product[Class],
    Product[Weight Unit Measure],
    ROLLUPADDISSUBTOTAL ( 'Date'[Calendar Year], "Subtotal Year" ),
    CALCULATETABLE ( Sales, Product[Unit Price] > 3000 ),
    "Quantity", SUM ( Sales[Quantity] )
)
```

Calendar Year	Class	Weight Unit Measure	Subtotal Year	Quantity
CY 2007	Deluxe	pounds	False	5,667
CY 2008	Deluxe	pounds	False	10,375
CY 2009	Deluxe	pounds	False	14,829
	Deluxe	pounds	True	30,871

You can call *ROLLUPADDISSUBTOTAL* several times, and you can include several pairs of column references and column names in a single call to *ROLLUPADDISSUBTOTAL* (the result is identical).

If you want to create a single subtotal for two or more columns, you can use *ROLLUPGROUP*. The following query creates a single subtotal for class and weight unit measure of product, and the subtotal per year. In practice, you see the subtotal of all the products for every year, and then the total of all the years and all the products:

```
EVALUATE
SUMMARIZECOLUMNS (
    ROLLUPADDISSUBTOTAL (
        'Date'[Calendar Year], "Subtotal Year",
        ROLLUPGROUP ( Product[Class], Product[Weight Unit Measure] ), "Subtotal Product"
    ),
    CALCULATETABLE ( Sales, Product[Unit Price] > 1000 ),
    "Quantity", SUM ( Sales[Quantity] )
)
```

Calendar Year	Class	Weight Unit Measure	Subtotal Year	Subtotal Product	Quantity
CY 2007	Regular	pounds	False	False	71,763
CY 2008	Regular	pounds	False	False	83,203
CY 2009	Regular	pounds	False	False	49,332
CY 2007	Deluxe	pounds	False	False	86,883
CY 2008	Deluxe	pounds	False	False	101,219
CY 2009	Deluxe	pounds	False	False	103,386
CY 2007			False	True	158,646
CY 2008			False	True	184,422
CY 2009			False	True	152,718
			True	True	495,786

The order of arguments for *ROLLUPADDISSUBTOTAL* is important because by inverting them you would obtain the subtotal of all the years for every class and weight unit measure of product, followed by the same grand total.

Using *GROUPBY*

The *GROUPBY* function is similar to *SUMMARIZE*, but does not provide the filter context generated by *SUMMARIZE*, and does not have a row context that you can use for a context transition. Its purpose is to apply an iterator over the rows of the group thanks to the *CURRENTGROUP* function. For instance, you can write the first example of *SUMMARIZE* using *GROUPBY* in this way:

```
EVALUATE
GROUPBY (
    Sales,
    'Date'[Calendar Year Number],
    "Quantity", SUMX ( CURRENTGROUP(), Sales[Quantity] )
)
```

Calendar Year	Quantity
CY 2007	5,551,636
CY 2008	5,029,924
CY 2009	6,956,456

You must use the *CURRENTGROUP* function at the top level of table scans in the column expression, so you cannot use it in nested iterators. The *GROUPBY* function can be useful if you generate DAX queries dynamically in your code, and you want to apply a particular aggregation on the result of another table expression.

Important You should use *GROUPBY* only for post-processing small result sets obtained by other table functions, typically *SUMMARIZECOLUMNS* and *ADDCOLUMNS*. *GROUPBY* should not be used to aggregate physical tables of the data model because it does not push the computation in the storage engine (you will realize why this is important for performance in Chapter 16). Even if the name resembles the *GROUPBY* condition of SQL language, its goal is different.

Using *ADDMISSINGITEMS*

The *ADDMISSINGITEMS* function is fundamentally a tool that includes the items with no data that would be hidden in the result of *SUMMARIZECOLUMNS* because of no data in the expression for the new columns.

For example, consider the result of the following query with *SUMMARIZECOLUMNS*:

```
EVALUATE
SUMMARIZECOLUMNS (
    'Date'[Calendar Year],
    "Quantity", SUM ( Sales[Quantity] )
)
```

Calendar Year	Quantity
CY 2007	5,551,636
CY 2008	5,029,924
CY 2009	6,956,456

The Date table includes years ranging from 2005 to 2011, but *SUMMARIZECOLUMNS* only shows years that have a result in *Quantity*. You can include years without any corresponding quantity by wrapping the expression in *ADDMISSINGITEMS*, specifying the columns for which you want to include "empty" members. The next query adds the years without data to the result of *SUMMARIZE*:

```
EVALUATE
ADDMISSINGITEMS (
    'Date'[Calendar Year],
    SUMMARIZECOLUMNS (
        'Date'[Calendar Year],
        "Quantity", SUM ( Sales[Quantity] )
    ),
    'Date'[Calendar Year]
)
```

Calendar Year	Quantity
CY 2007	5,551,636
CY 2008	5,029,924
CY 2009	6,956,456
CY 2005	
CY 2006	
CY 2010	
CY 2011	

When you aggregate two or more columns, you can define individual columns for which you want to include "missing" items. For example, consider the following query that returns quantity of sales for product with a price greater than 3,000, grouped by *Stock Type* and *Gender*:

```
EVALUATE
SUMMARIZECOLUMNS (
    Product[Stock Type],
    Customer[Gender],
    CALCULATETABLE ( Sales, Product[Unit Price] > 3000 ),
    "Quantity", SUM ( Sales[Quantity] )
)
```

Stock Type	Gender	Quantity
Mid		29,106
Mid	M	926
Mid	F	839

As you see, there is only one type of stock (Mid). If you apply *ADDMISSINGITEMS* only to the *Stock Type* column, you obtain two more rows, one for each missing stock type (Low and High):

```
EVALUATE
ADDMISSINGITEMS (
    Product[Stock Type],
    SUMMARIZECOLUMNS (
        Product[Stock Type],
        Customer[Gender],
        CALCULATETABLE ( Sales, Product[Unit Price] > 3000 ),
        "Quantity", SUM ( Sales[Quantity] )
    ),
    Product[Stock Type]
)
```

Stock Type	Gender	Quantity
Mid		29,106
Mid	M	926
Mid	F	839
High		
Low		

However, you can extend the missing items also to the *Gender* column, as in the following example:

```
EVALUATE
ADDMISSINGITEMS (
    Product[Stock Type],
    Customer[Gender],
    SUMMARIZECOLUMNS (
        Product[Stock Type],
        Customer[Gender],
        CALCULATETABLE ( Sales, Product[Unit Price] > 3000 ),
        "Quantity", SUM ( Sales[Quantity] )
    ),
    Product[Stock Type],
    Customer[Gender]
)
```

Stock Type	Gender	Quantity
Mid		29,106
Mid	M	926
Mid	F	839
High		
Low		

Stock Type	Gender	Quantity
High	M	
Low	M	
High	F	
Low	F	

Using *NATURALINNERJOIN*

The *NATURALINNERJOIN* function performs an inner join between two tables. You can use tables that have no relationships because the join uses common columns between the two tables, and the data type must be identical, too. There should be at least one column with the same name and type between the two tables. The syntax is very simple; the function has two table expressions as arguments:

```
NATURALINNERJOIN ( <leftJoinTable>, <rightJoinTable> )
```

> **Important** The join condition of NATURALINNERJOIN is automatically defined by the columns having the same name and type in the two tables. You use this function when you do not have a relationship in the data model between two tables, and you can join the result of table functions, too.

In the following example, you see the join between two tables created within the query, just to demonstrate you can join any table regardless of the presence of relationships in the data model:

```
EVALUATE
VAR A =
    UNION (
        ROW ( "Name", "Audio", "Value", 1 ),
        ROW ( "Name", "Audio", "Value", 2 ),
        ROW ( "Name", "Computers", "Value", 3 ),
        ROW ( "Name", "Games", "Value", 4 ),
        ROW ( "Name", "Music", "Value", 5 )
    )
VAR B =
    UNION (
        ROW ( "Name", "Audio", "Ext", 6 ),
        ROW ( "Name", "Computers", "Ext", 7 ),
        ROW ( "Name", "Computers", "Ext", 8 ),
        ROW ( "Name", "Games", "Ext", 9 ),
        ROW ( "Name", "TV", "Ext", 10 )
    )
RETURN
    NATURALINNERJOIN ( A, B )
```

Name	Value	Ext
Audio	1	6
Audio	2	6
Computers	3	7
Computers	3	8
Games	4	9

Using *NATURALLEFTOUTERJOIN*

The *NATURALLEFTOUTERJOIN* function has a behavior similar to *NATURALINNERJOIN*, with the only difference that it executes a left outer join of the first table expression passed as argument, with the second table expression passed in the other argument. The syntax requires two table expressions as arguments, and their order is important:

```
NATURALLEFTOUTERJOIN ( <leftJoinTable>, <rightJoinTable > )
```

Important The join condition of *NATURALLEFTOUTERJOIN* is similar to *NATURALINNERJOIN*, and it is automatically defined by the columns having the same name and type in the two tables. It is common to use this function when there are no relationships in the data model between the two tables to join.

As seen here, table A is joined with B, applying a left outer join instead of an inner join:

```
EVALUATE
VAR A =
    UNION (
        ROW ( "Name", "Audio", "Value", 1 ),
        ROW ( "Name", "Audio", "Value", 2 ),
        ROW ( "Name", "Computers", "Value", 3 ),
        ROW ( "Name", "Games", "Value", 4 ),
        ROW ( "Name", "Music", "Value", 5 )
    )
VAR B =
    UNION (
        ROW ( "Name", "Audio", "Ext", 6 ),
        ROW ( "Name", "Computers", "Ext", 7 ),
        ROW ( "Name", "Computers", "Ext", 8 ),
        ROW ( "Name", "Games", "Ext", 9 ),
        ROW ( "Name", "TV", "Ext", 10 )
    )
RETURN
    NATURALLEFTOUTERJOIN ( A, B )
```

In this case the result also includes the rows in the first table (where name is equal to Music) that are not present in the second table.

Name	Value	Ext
Audio	1	6
Audio	2	6
Computers	3	7
Computers	3	8
Games	4	9
Music	5	

Understanding set functions

A number of DAX functions manipulate tables, or sets of rows. We included them in this section about sets, because you can see them as set manipulation functions (such as *UNION, INTERSECT, EXCEPT*). The expressivity of the language is higher when it provides access to all set operators (Cartesian product, union, intersection, complement).

Using *CROSSJOIN*

The *CROSSJOIN* function generates the Cartesian product between two or more tables. You can use any table expression as an argument; simply put all of them in the arguments, as in the following syntax:

```
CROSSJOIN ( <tableExpression1>, <tableExpression2> [, <tableExpressionN>] … )
```

A typical case of *CROSSJOIN* usage is combining the values of different columns, as in the following example:

```
EVALUATE
CROSSJOIN (
    VALUES ( Product[Stock Type] ),
    VALUES ( 'Product Category'[Category] )
)
```

Stock Type	Category
High	Audio
Mid	Audio
Low	Audio

Stock Type	Category
High	TV and Video
Mid	TV and Video
Low	TV and Video
...	...

The result includes all the combinations of all the rows of a table with all the rows of other tables, including all the columns of all the tables. In case there is the same column name in two or more tables used in *CROSSJOIN*, it is necessary to use the fully qualified name (including table and column name) to identify the column, as in the following example:

```
EVALUATE
CROSSJOIN ( 'Product Category', 'Product Subcategory' )
```

The column *ProductCategoryKey* is present in two columns, with two different fully qualified names.

Product Category [ProductCategoryKey]	Product Category [Category]	Product Subcategory [ProductSubcategoryKey]	Product Subcategory [ProductCategoryKey]	Product Subcategory [Subcategory]
1	Audio	1	1	MP4&MP3
2	TV and Video	1	1	MP4&MP3
3	Computers	1	1	MP4&MP3
4	Cameras and camcorders	1	1	MP4&MP3
...	...	...	...	...
1	Audio	2	1	Recorder
2	TV and Video	2	1	Recorder
3	Computers	2	1	Recorder
4	Cameras and camcorders	2	1	Recorder
...	...	...	...	...
1	Audio	9	2	Televisions
2	TV and Video	9	2	Televisions
3	Computers	9	2	Televisions
4	Cameras and camcorders	9	2	Televisions
...	...	...	...	...

If you want to duplicate a column in the result of *CROSSJOIN* without having to worry about fully qualified names, you have to rename the column in advance. For example, the following query returns all the combinations of product stock types with themselves:

```
EVALUATE
CROSSJOIN (
    VALUES ( Product[Stock Type] ),
    SELECTCOLUMNS (
        VALUES ( Product[Stock Type] ),
        "Alternate Type", Product[Stock Type]
    )
)
```

As you see in the result, it is not an issue having two columns with the same lineage in the result.

Stock Type	Alternate Type
High	High
Mid	High
Low	High
High	Mid
Mid	Mid
Low	Mid
High	Low
Mid	Low
Low	Low

Using *UNION*

UNION generates a single table using all the rows of the tables passed as arguments. The tables must have the same number of columns and the columns are combined by position in their respective tables. The first argument defines the name of the columns in the result (subsequent arguments add rows but do not affect column names):

```
UNION ( <tableExpression1>, <tableExpression2> [, <tableExpressionN>] … )
```

The result retains duplicate rows, and it preserves the lineage whenever possible. For instance, the following query keeps the lineage to the physical columns of the data model, because the two table expressions return columns from the same table and in the same position:

```
EVALUATE
UNION (
    FILTER (
        'Product Subcategory',
        'Product Subcategory'[ProductCategoryKey] = 6
    ),
    FILTER (
        'Product Subcategory',
        'Product Subcategory'[Subcategory Code] = "0602"
        || 'Product Subcategory'[Subcategory Code] = "0702"
    )
)
```

The query produces two duplicated rows, highlighted in the following result.

ProductSubcategoryKey	Subcategory Code	Subcategory	ProductCategoryKey
34	0601	Music CD	6
35	**0602**	**Movie DVD**	**6**
36	0603	Audio Books	6
35	**0602**	**Movie DVD**	**6**
39	0702	Download Games	7

The lineage is important when you use the result of *UNION* in a filter context. For example, the following query returns all the product categories having at least one of the subcategories produced by the *UNION* function, which merges two tables having different column names (*Code 1* and *Code 2*) with the same lineage:

```
EVALUATE
CALCULATETABLE (
    'Product Category',
    UNION (
        CALCULATETABLE (
            SELECTCOLUMNS (
                'Product Subcategory',
                "Code 1", 'Product Subcategory'[Subcategory Code]
            ),
            'Product Subcategory'[Subcategory Code] = "0601"
                || 'Product Subcategory'[Subcategory Code] = "0602"
        ),
        CALCULATETABLE (
            SELECTCOLUMNS (
                'Product Subcategory',
                "Code 2", 'Product Subcategory'[Subcategory Code]
            ),
            'Product Subcategory'[Subcategory Code] = "0702"
        )
    )
)
```

ProductCategoryKey	Category Code	Category
6	06	Music, Movies and Audio Books
7	07	Games and Toys

If you add a value losing the lineage, the result no longer filters the original columns. In fact, the following example has a *UNION* function that returns the same list of subcategory codes (0601, 0602, and 0702), but the use of *ROW* in the second argument of *UNION* breaks the lineage with the original column:

```
EVALUATE
CALCULATETABLE (
    'Product Category',
    UNION (
        CALCULATETABLE (
            SELECTCOLUMNS (
                'Product Subcategory',
                "Code 1", 'Product Subcategory'[Subcategory Code]
            ),
            'Product Subcategory'[ProductCategoryKey] = 6
        ),
        ROW ( "Code 2", "0702" )
    )
)
```

The result includes all of the categories, because the result of the *UNION* does not affect the filter context.

ProductCategoryKey	Category Code	Category
1	01	Audio
2	02	TV and Video
3	03	Computers
4	04	Cameras and camcorders
...	...	...

The data type of a column in the result depends on the content of all the tables merged by *UNION*, using the type that makes the implicit conversion always possible without any error. The following query merges two rows with an integer value:

```
EVALUATE
ADDCOLUMNS (
    UNION (
        ROW ( "Value", 1 ),
        ROW ( "Value", 2 )
    ),
    "IsText", ISTEXT ( [Value] ),
    "IsNumber", ISNUMBER ( [Value] )
)
```

The column *Value* in the result is a number.

Value	IsText	IsNumber
1	False	True
2	False	True

However, if one of the two rows has a string instead of a number, the result will have a string data type for the column *Value*. In the following example, the second row has a different column name:

```
EVALUATE
ADDCOLUMNS (
    UNION (
        ROW ( "Value", 1 ),
        ROW ( "AnotherName", "2" )
    ),
    "IsText", ISTEXT ( [Value] ),
    "IsNumber", ISNUMBER ( [Value] )
)
```

The column name (*Value*) depends only on the first argument of *UNION*, whereas the data type depends on the content of all the rows.

Value	IsText	IsNumber
1	True	False
2	True	False

Using *INTERSECT*

INTERSECT returns a table containing only the rows that exist in both table expressions passed as arguments. The tables must have the same number and data type of columns and the columns are combined by position in their respective tables. The first argument defines the name of the columns in the result (any ensuing arguments add rows but do not affect column names):

```
INTERSECT ( <tableExpression1>, <tableExpression2> )
```

The result keeps the lineage from the first table of the two arguments. For example, the following query keeps the lineage to the physical columns of the data model, even if the second table does not have the same lineage:

```
EVALUATE
INTERSECT (
    VALUES ( Product[Color] ),
    UNION (
        ROW ( "Color", "Red" ),
        ROW ( "Color", "Blue" )
    )
)
```

Color
Blue
Red

If you invert the two arguments, the result is the same, but you cannot use it in a filter argument because it does not have a lineage with the physical column:

```
EVALUATE
INTERSECT (
    UNION (
        ROW ( "Color", "Red" ),
        ROW ( "Color", "Blue" )
    ),
    VALUES ( Product[Color] )
)
```

Color
Blue
Red

It is important to understand how to use *INTERSECT* in a filter context, because it is one of the most frequent applications of this function. In the following example, you see how to obtain a list of customers who bought a product of the Cell phones category in both 2008 and 2009:

```
EVALUATE
CALCULATETABLE (
    VALUES ( Customer[Customer Code] ),
    INTERSECT (
        CALCULATETABLE (
            SUMMARIZE (
                Sales,
                Customer[CustomerKey],
                Product[ProductKey]
            ),
            'Date'[Calendar Year Number] = 2008,
            'Product Category'[Category] = "Cell phones"
        ),
        CALCULATETABLE (
            SUMMARIZE (
                Sales,
                Customer[CustomerKey],
                Product[ProductKey]
            ),
            'Date'[Calendar Year Number] = 2009,
            'Product Category'[Category] = "Cell phones"
        )
    )
)
```

The result has only three customers.

Customer Code
CS676
CS679
CS810

Using *EXCEPT*

The *EXCEPT* function implements the complement operators over two sets. It returns a table containing only the rows that exist in the first table expressions passed as an argument, but not in the second one. The tables must have the same number and data type of columns and the columns are combined by position in their respective tables. The first argument defines the name of the columns in the result (following arguments add rows but do not affect column names):

```
EXCEPT ( <tableExpression1>, <tableExpression2> )
```

The result keeps the lineage from the first table of the two arguments. For instance, the following query keeps the lineage to the physical columns of the data model, even if the second table does not have the same lineage:

```
EVALUATE
EXCEPT (
    VALUES ( Product[Color] ),
    UNION (
        ROW ( "Color", "Red" ),
        ROW ( "Color", "Blue" )
    )
)
```

Color
Silver
White
... (all colors but Red and Blue)

An example of *EXCEPT* usage is displaying the customer who bought a product in 2008 (code 0202011) and did not buy another product (code 0201038) in the same year.

```
EVALUATE
CALCULATETABLE (
    VALUES ( Customer[Customer Code] ),
    EXCEPT (
        CALCULATETABLE (
            SUMMARIZE (
                Sales,
                Customer[CustomerKey]
            ),
            'Date'[Calendar Year Number] = 2008,
            Product[Product Code] = "0202011"
        ),
        CALCULATETABLE (
            SUMMARIZE (
                Sales,
                Customer[CustomerKey]
            ),
            'Date'[Calendar Year Number] = 2008,
            Product[Product Code] = "0201038"
        )
    )
)
```

Customer Code
25044
25047
26676
26681

... (376 rows in total)

Using *GENERATE, GENERATEALL*

The *GENERATE* function evaluates the tableExpression2 for each row in tableExpression1, returning a Cartesian product between each row in tableExpression1 and the corresponding rows generated by tableExpression2. The syntax requires two table expressions:

```
GENERATE ( <tableExpression1>, <tableExpression2> )
```

A trivial use of *GENERATE* is the generation of a table that contains all the valid combinations of product categories and subcategories, as you can do with this query:

```
EVALUATE
GENERATE (
    'Product Category',
    RELATEDTABLE ( 'Product Subcategory' )
)
```

Category Code	Category	Subcategory Code	Subcategory	...
01	Audio	0101	MP4&MP3	...
01	Audio	0102	Recorder	...
01	Audio	0103	Radio	...
...	...	...	...	...
02	TV and Video	0201	Televisions	...
02	TV and Video	0202	VCD & DVD	...
...	...	...	...	...

The tableExpression2 in a *GENERATE* call usually contains a *RELATEDTABLE* or *CALCULATETABLE* function, in order to leverage the context transition using the row iterated in tableExpression1.

Note If you omitted the *RELATEDTABLE* function in the second parameter, you would achieve the same result you obtained by using *CROSSJOIN* instead of *GENERATE* because you would lack the transformation of a row context into a filter context provided by *RELATEDTABLE*, which is an alias for *CALCULATEDTABLE*. In fact, the following queries are equivalent:

```
EVALUATE
GENERATE( 'Product Category', 'Product Subcategory' )

EVALUATE
CROSSJOIN( 'Product Category', 'Product Subcategory' )
```

A more interesting example of *GENERATE* is how you can obtain a table that contains the top two products for each year. The following query executes the *TOPN* function for each year, calculating the ranking of products locally to each year:

```
EVALUATE
GENERATE (
    VALUES ( 'Date'[Calendar Year] ),
    TOPN (
        2,
        SUMMARIZE ( RELATEDTABLE ( Sales ), Product[Product Name] ),
        CALCULATE ( SUM ( Sales[Quantity] ) )
    )
)
```

Calendar Year	Product Name
CY 2007	SV 16xDVD M360 Black
CY 2007	Adventure Works 26" 720p LCD HDTV M140 Silver
CY 2008	Contoso Touch Stylus Pen E150 White
CY 2008	Contoso In-Line Coupler E180 Silver
CY 2009	Contoso In-Line Coupler E180 Silver
CY 2009	Headphone Adapter for Contoso Phone E130 Black

The previous query returns just those years containing at least one sale. If you want to also include years without any corresponding rows in Sales, you can use *GENERATEALL* instead of *GENERATE*, as in the following query:

```
EVALUATE
GENERATEALL (
    VALUES ( 'Date'[Calendar Year] ),
    TOPN (
        2,
        SUMMARIZE ( RELATEDTABLE ( Sales ), Product[Product Name] ),
        CALCULATE ( SUM ( Sales[Quantity] ) )
    )
)
```

Calendar Year	Product Name
CY 2005	
CY 2006	
CY 2007	SV 16xDVD M360 Black
CY 2007	Adventure Works 26" 720p LCD HDTV M140 Silver
CY 2008	Contoso Touch Stylus Pen E150 White
CY 2008	Contoso In-Line Coupler E180 Silver
CY 2009	Contoso In-Line Coupler E180 Silver
CY 2009	Headphone Adapter for Contoso Phone E130 Black
CY 2010	
CY 2011	

If you are used to SQL, you might consider the *GENERATE* function similar to the CROSS APPLY condition in SQL, whereas *GENERATEALL* is similar to OUTER APPLY in SQL.

Understanding utility functions

The DAX language includes several functions that you will use often in iterators. Two of the logical functions that you will frequently use in filter conditions are *CONTAINS* and *ISONORAFTER*. The *LOOKUPVALUE* function is very common in scenarios where you want to retrieve a value from a table when a physical relationship does not exist, but you can set a logical filter on one or more columns obtaining a single value for a column. The *SUBSTITUTEWITHINDEX* function might be useful if you generate DAX queries dynamically in your code.

Using *CONTAINS*

You can use *FILTER* and *CALCULATETABLE* functions to filter rows from a table. However, if you need to check whether at least one row exists in a table within certain conditions, you might calculate more rows than necessary by using these functions. In the table passed as first argument, the *CONTAINS* function checks the existence of at least one row that contains all the column values specified in the following parameters. This is the syntax:

```
CONTAINS (
    <table>,
    <column1_name>, <column1_expression>
    [,<column2_name>, <column2_expression>][, …]
)
```

You might also want to check whether the Sales table contains at least one sale with a unit price of 99.99. Because the result of *CONTAINS* is a scalar value, you can embed it in a *ROW* function to execute the query:

```
EVALUATE
ROW (
    "Sales Exist",
    CONTAINS (
        Sales,
        Sales[Unit Price], 99.99
    )
)
```

Sales Exists
True

The preceding query corresponds to the following:

```
EVALUATE
ROW (
    "Sales Exist",
    COUNTROWS (
        CALCULATETABLE ( Sales, Sales[Unit Price] = 99.99 )
    ) > 0
)
```

Usually *CONTAINS* provides a better performance for simple filter conditions, whereas *CALCULATETABLE* is preferable for more complex expressions. *CONTAINS* just checks for an exact match, and you must use *CALCULATETABLE*, *FILTER*, or both if you need more complex filtering conditions. However, you can combine more column conditions, and the columns can also belong to related tables. For example, the following query returns TRUE when at least one sale has been made in Australia with a unit price of 99.99:

```
EVALUATE
ROW (
    "Sales Australia",
    CONTAINS (
        Sales,
        Sales[Unit Price], 99.99,
        Customer[CountryRegion], "Australia"
    )
)
```

Sales Australia
True

In this case, the preceding query corresponds to the following:

```
EVALUATE
ROW (
    "Sales Australia",
    COUNTROWS (
        CALCULATETABLE (
            Sales,
            Sales[Unit Price] = 99.99,
            Customer[CountryRegion] = "Australia"
        )
    ) > 0
)
```

A practical use of *CONTAINS* is as a filter condition when you want to obtain a list of elements that has at least one corresponding row in another table. The following query returns the list of dates in which there has been at least one sale in the city of Columbus:

```
EVALUATE
FILTER (
    VALUES ( 'Date'[Date] ),
    CONTAINS (
        RELATEDTABLE ( Sales ),
        Customer[City], "Columbus"
    )
)
ORDER BY 'Date'[Date]
```

Date
01/22/2007
01/23/2007
01/26/2007
…

As you see, the *CONTAINS* function is executed within a different row context for each date. The row context for each date is transformed into a filter context by the *RELATEDTABLE* function, so that *CONTAINS* considers only the sales for these rows and returns TRUE when at least one row exists for the city of Columbus on that particular date.

Using *LOOKUPVALUE*

In the previous section, you saw how to check whether at least one row exists in a table. However, you will often need to decode a value in a lookup table. To do this, the *LOOKUPVALUE* function in DAX has the following syntax:

```
LOOKUPVALUE (
    <result_column_name>,
    <search_column1_name>, <search_column1_expression>
    [,<search_column2_name>, <search_column2_expression>] [, …]
)
```

The first argument is the column that contains the value to return. The other parameters are pairs of column name and value (as scalar expressions) to perform the lookup operation in the table containing the column specified in the first argument. For instance, the following query transforms the CAD currency code into the corresponding currency name:

```
EVALUATE
ROW (
    "Currency", LOOKUPVALUE (
        Currency[Currency],
        Currency[Currency Code], "CAD"
    )
)
```

Currency
Canadian Dollar

 Note The *LOOKUPVALUE* function ignores the existing filter context, performing a direct lookup in the target table. This behavior is particularly useful when you are executing an expression within a context transition during an iteration.

You can specify more columns to perform the matching operation, and you can refer to columns of related tables. The following query returns the name of the product of brand Contoso and class Deluxe that has a Silver color and belongs to the Audio category:

```
EVALUATE
ROW (
    "Product", LOOKUPVALUE (
        Product[Product Name],
        Product[Color], "Silver",
        Product[Brand], "Contoso",
        Product[Class], "Deluxe",
        'Product Category'[Category], "Audio"
    )
)
```

Product
Contoso 8GB Clock & Radio MP3 Player X850 Silver

If there are multiple rows matching the search values, the function returns an error if different values are returned in *<result_column_name>*, whereas it returns a BLANK value if there are no matching rows. However, if there is a single distinct value for *<result_column_name>*, even if multiple rows in the underlying table match the search values, the *LOOKUPVALUE* function returns only that unique value. For example, the following query returns the name of the month corresponding to the month number 3:

```
EVALUATE
ROW (
    "Month Name", LOOKUPVALUE (
        'Date'[Month],
        'Date'[Month Number], 3
    )
)
```

Month Name
March

Even if the Date table contains hundreds of rows corresponding to the month number 3 (31 days for each year in the Date table), all of them have the same value in the *Month* column (March).

> **Tip** Most of the time, a *RELATED* function performs the required lookup operation when you have a row context and you need to get the value of a column in a related table. However, if you do not have a relationship between two tables in an underlying data model, or if you have to implement a particular logic for a lookup operation, you can use *LOOKUPVALUE* instead of *RELATED*. You might also rewrite the *LOOKUPVALUE* call by using the *CALCULATE* function, even if it is not a best practice. For example, the previous query can be rewritten as follows:
>
> ```
> EVALUATE
> ROW (
>     "Month Name", CALCULATE (
>         VALUES ( 'Date'[Month] ),
>         'Date'[Month Number] = 3
>     )
> )
> ```
>
> Using *LOOKUPVALUE* instead of *CALCULATE* makes the intent more explicit. Thus, using *LOOKUPVALUE* is the preferred way to implement a lookup operation if you cannot use *RELATED*. Use *CALCULATE* only if the matching condition cannot be expressed through *LOOKUPVALUE* arguments.

Using *SUBSTITUTEWITHINDEX*

The function *SUBSTITUTEWITHINDEX* can replace those columns in a rowset corresponding to column headers of a matrix by indexes representing their positions. You might find this function useful only if you create a dynamic user interface for querying DAX. In fact, Power BI internally uses *SUBSTITUTEWITHINDEX* for matrix charts. The syntax is as follows:

```
SUBSTITUTEWITHINDEX (
    <table>,
    <columnName>,
    <indexTable>,
    <expression>
    [,<order>]
)
```

The result corresponds to the table passed as first argument, where the columns that match the ones in *<indexTable>* are replaced with a single column named according to the *<columnName>* argument. Such a column contains the index of the value in tables found in the corresponding column of *<indexTable>*. The two tables (*<table>* and *<indexTable>*) must have at least one matching column, and all the matching columns are replaced with the corresponding index. You see an example with local tables in the following query:

```
EVALUATE
SUBSTITUTEWITHINDEX (
    UNION (
        ROW ( "Name", "Marco", "Company", "Sqlbi", "User", "marcor" ),
        ROW ( "Name", "Alberto", "Company", "Sqlbi", "User", "hal" ),
        ROW ( "Name", "Bob", "Company", "Contoso", "User", "bob97" )
    ),
    "index", UNION (
        ROW ( "Company", "Sqlbi", "Name", "Alberto" ),
        ROW ( "Company", "Contoso", "Name", "Bob" ),
        ROW ( "Company", "Sqlbi", "Name", "Marco" )
    ),
    0
)
```

The result only includes the *User* column from the first table, and the *Name* and *Company* columns are replaced by the *Index* column that corresponds to the 0-based position of the values found in the *<indexTable>* argument.

User	Index
marcor	2
hal	0
bob97	1

Using *ISONORAFTER*

The *ISONORAFTER* function emulates the behavior of a *START AT* clause in *EVALUATE*, and returns TRUE when all of the values passed as argument meet the condition specified. Usually you evaluate this function in a filter condition during an iteration, applying it to the current row context:

```
ISONORAFTER (
    <scalar_expression>,
    <scalar_expression>, [sort_order]
    [,<scalar_expression>, <scalar_expression>, [sort_order]] [,…]
)
```

For example, you can filter the months greater than or equal to October 2008 by using the *ISONORAFTER* function in the filter condition of the following query:

```
EVALUATE
FILTER (
    SUMMARIZE (
        'Date',
        'Date'[Calendar Year],
        'Date'[Month],
        'Date'[Month Number]
    ),
    ISONORAFTER (
        'Date'[Calendar Year], "CY 2008", ASC,
        'Date'[Month Number], 10, ASC
    )
)
ORDER BY
    'Date'[Calendar Year],
    'Date'[Month Number]
```

The result does not have any month before October 2008. It is important to note that you can use the result of the *FILTER* in other DAX expressions, regardless of the order defined by *ORDER BY*, which is only useful to display the result in a meaningful way.

Calendar Year	Month	Month Number
CY 2008	October	10
CY 2008	November	11
CY 2008	December	12
CY 2009	January	1
CY 2009	February	2
…	…	…

Advanced evaluation context

We introduced evaluation contexts in Chapter 4, "Understanding evaluation contexts," and up to now you have learned how to use them to compute simple formulas. The definition of evaluation contexts used so far is incomplete or, rather, an approximation of what evaluation contexts really are. In order to proceed with more intricate calculations and to obtain a full understanding of how DAX evaluates expressions, you need to move to the next level and to thoroughly learn the way evaluation contexts work and how they interact.

In this chapter we are going to uncover all the complexities of evaluation contexts and show many examples of expressions that look wrong at first sight, but only because you do not have a full understanding of how they work.

This chapter is a very complex one, and chances are good that you will need to read it more than once. Nevertheless, learning these detailed topics is mandatory if you want to fully understand DAX and learn the more complicated scenarios we will present to you in later chapters. If you are curious to understand how tough it will be, you can jump to the section "Learning and mastering evaluation contexts" at the end of the chapter, and then come back here and continue reading.

Understanding *ALLSELECTED*

ALLSELECTED, which we introduced in Chapter 5, "Understanding *CALCULATE* and *CALCULATETABLE*," looks like a special function that is able to understand what the user selected in the pivot table. In fact, it lets you retrieve the original filter context under which the pivot table is running. Unfortunately, there is a big issue with this description of *ALLSELECTED*, regarding how it is possible that a DAX function knows what a user selected in a pivot table. If the source of a report is not a pivot table but a DAX query, is *ALLSELECTED* still going to work? In order to provide an answer to this (legitimate) question, we need to closely investigate the description of *ALLSELECTED* to understand exactly how it works.

Let us state this simple fact from the beginning: *ALLSELECTED* has no clue as to what the user selected in the pivot table. *ALLSELECTED* does not even know that a pivot table exists. Therefore, how does it work?

ALLSELECTED removes from the context the last filter generated from context transition.

The side effect of this operation is that—in most cases—it retrieves the original filter context. Unfortunately, this does not always happen and you might write formulas where you expect *ALLSE-LECTED* to compute a value (based on the first definition we gave for *ALLSELECTED*) and you end up with an unexpected result.

In order to fully understand the behavior of *ALLSELECTED*, we need to refine the knowledge we have about context transition a bit. In Chapter 5, you learned that context transition transforms all existing row contexts into equivalent filter contexts. Thus, you know that after context transition all row contexts are gone and they are replaced with a single filter context containing all the equivalent filters. This is not completely correct. In reality, context transition generates two new filter contexts: one containing the full iterated table and one containing the current row. Let's elaborate on this, analyzing the following simple measure:

```
AverageSales :=
AVERAGEX (
    Customer,
    CALCULATE ( SUM ( Sales[Quantity] ) )
)
```

During iteration we invoke *CALCULATE*, so context transition happens. The engine transforms the current row on Customer into two filter contexts, which are applied one after the other:

- The first one contains Customer.

- The second one contains the currently iterated row on Customer.

This behavior is transparent to your code in most cases. The reason is that the two filters are placed one after the other in the stack of filter contexts. Therefore, the last one (containing a single customer) is always more restrictive than the previous one, effectively hiding it. We refer to the first filter as the outer filter, whereas the second one is the inner filter. When *CALCULATE* ends, both filters are removed from the stack. Thus, your code typically ignores the existence of the outer filter, because it has no effect during *CALCULATE* and no effect after *CALCULATE* ends. However, as you are learning, the outer filter is extremely important to understand the behavior of *ALLSELECTED*.

Keep in mind that this behavior always happens, even if you do not notice it. Look at the following example:

```
AverageSalesInEurope :=
AVERAGEX (
    FILTER ( Customer, Customer[Contintent] = "Europe" ),
    CALCULATE ( SUM ( Sales[Quantity] ) )
)
```

In this case, iteration happens for only the customers in Europe. Thus the two filters are:

- Outer: customers in Europe.

- Inner: currently iterated customer from the ones in Europe.

Again, the currently iterated one is more restrictive than the list of all customers in Europe, so you normally ignore the existence of the outer filter. You can safely ignore it, until you start using *ALLSELECTED*. In fact, *ALLSELECTED* will remove the more restrictive filter (inner), leaving the outer one working. This behavior is somewhat complex to follow until you get used to it, so some examples might help in learning it better.

In order to understand the behavior of *ALLSELECTED*, we use a very simple data model, containing a single table (called Table) with only three rows and two columns (*Col* and *Val*), which you can see in Figure 10-1.

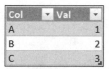

FIGURE 10-1 This is the table we will use to understand exactly how *ALLSELECTED* works.

Based on this table, you can easily create a pivot table with a slicer that selects only two rows and the *Sum of Val* in the value area, which you can see in Figure 10-2.

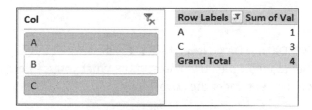

FIGURE 10-2 Here you can see a very simple pivot table based on our one table model.

There is nothing special here. We filter two values, and all the numbers are correct. Now, to introduce *ALLSELECTED*, you define a new measure, using this code:

```
[SumAllSelected] :=
CALCULATE (
    SUM ( Table[Val] ),
    ALLSELECTED ( )
)
```

Intuitively, you expect this measure to compute the value of 4 for all the rows. This is because you use *ALLSELECTED* without parameters, which means you want to retrieve the original filter context. In fact, the result is correct, as you can see in Figure 10-3.

Col
A
B
C

Row Labels	Sum of Val	SumAllSelected
A	1	4
C	3	4
Grand Total	**4**	**4**

FIGURE 10-3 Using *ALLSELECTED*, the value shown in all the rows is the grand total of our original calculation.

Even if the result is what we expected, we now know that this is not because *ALLSELECTED* retrieved the original filter context as it had no way of doing so. Let us review how the correct value came up, with the new definition of *ALLSELECTED*. Nevertheless, before moving on, we need to be a bit more accurate about how DAX computed the formula in the cells. There are two different steps in evaluating the full pivot table:

- One step computes the values for the individual rows.

- One step computes the values for the grand total.

The reason for this is that the individual rows contain a filter on Table[Col] that filters a single value (either A or C), whereas at the grand total level the filter context contains both A and C. Both steps run under a filter created by the slicer.

> **Note** In reality, the code executed is MDX, not DAX. Nevertheless, for the sake of this example, we use DAX to make it easier to follow the flow of execution. What you see here is a very good approximation of what happens under the cover.

The code for the individual rows is similar to this:

```
EVALUATE
CALCULATETABLE (
    ADDCOLUMNS (
        VALUES ( Table[Col] ),
        "Sum of Val", [Sum of Val],
        "SumAllSelected", [SumAllSelected]
    ),
    OR ( Table[Col] = "A", Table[Col] = "C" )
)
```

On the other hand, the code for the grand total looks like this:

```
EVALUATE
CALCULATETABLE (
    ROW (
        "Grand Total Sum of Val", [Sum of Val],
        "Grand Total SumAllSelected", [SumAllSelected]
    ),
    OR ( Table[Col] = "A", Table[Col] = "C" )
)
```

As you can see, even if your original code in the measures does not contain any iteration, there is a hidden iteration introduced by *ADDCOLUMNS* during the evaluation of the rows. Moreover, note that this iteration is not present during the evaluation of the grand total rows. For all practical purposes, they are two different steps of execution with different semantics.

Now let us focus on what happens during the evaluation of *SumAllSelected* for the individual rows. The outer *CALCULATETABLE* sets the original filter context to A or C. Then *ADDCOLUMNS* starts to iterate over the values of Table[Col], which contains A and C. When it is on A, it performs context transition, because it is calling a measure (*SumAllSelected*). This context transition creates two filters:

- The outer one, containing the currently iterated table: (A, C).

- The inner one, containing the currently iterated row: (A).

At this point, DAX evaluates *SumAllSelected* which again executes *CALCULATE*, this time invoking it with *ALLSELECTED*. *ALLSELECTED* removes the last filter context generated from context transition, which is the inner one, making the outer one visible. Because the outer filter context contains (A, C), it computes the sum of A and C together, generating the visual total, as expected.

At the grand total level, on the other hand, there is no filter context generated by context transition. Therefore, *ALLSELECTED* has nothing to do and it is ignored. Because the outer *CALCULATETABLE* is still in effect, the filter context still contains (A, C), generating the visual total.

You are already familiar with most of these evaluation steps. Probably the only new information you are gathering at this point is the presence of the hidden row context generated during the iteration over the fields you put on rows and columns of the pivot table. You do not really need to care about that row context in most scenarios, because the engine generates it and quickly transforms it into a filter context. Thus, from inside your code, you cannot access it. *ALLSELECTED* is the only function that interacts with it and this is the reason we are speaking in so much detail about the evaluation process of a pivot table here.

What is important to learn and to understand is that *ALLSELECTED* shows the visual totals because of the specific format of the query executed by the engine when it resolves a query coming from a pivot table. However, *ALLSELECTED* by itself has nothing to do with visual totals.

So far, it seems as if we are providing a complex explanation to a very simple behavior. To some extent this is true because you will probably use *ALLSELECTED* for a long time without ever having to recall this theory. Nevertheless, look at what happens if you write a measure that contains an iteration and another context transition, as in the following measure:

```
[SumxAllSelected] := SUMX ( Table, [SumAllSelected] )
```

It is worth remembering the code of *SumAllSelected*:

```
[SumAllSelected] :=
CALCULATE (
    SUM ( Table[Val] ),
    ALLSELECTED ( )
)
```

At this point, the scenario is much more complex. We have the hidden iteration created by the pivot table (in reality, by the MDX code generated by the pivot table), and inside it, another iteration created by *SUMX* that performs an additional context transition. The result is surprising; as you can see in Figure 10-4.

Col		Row Labels	Sum of Val	SumAllSelected	SumxAllSelected
A		A	1	4	1
B		C	3	4	3
C		**Grand Total**	**4**	**4**	**8**

FIGURE 10-4 Iterating and performing *ALLSELECTED* later produces numbers that are hard to explain.

You probably would expect *SumxAllSelected* to return 4 in each inner row of the pivot table and 8 at the grand total, because it iterates over the table (which shows one row in the inner cells and two rows at the grand total) and sums a measure of which we already know the result: It should be 4. Surprisingly, the value at the grand total makes sense, whereas the values in the inner cells seem completely wrong. Let us examine what happened by expanding the code. Since we are interested in only the last measure, *SumxAllSelected*, we are using a somewhat simplified version of the code, which ignores other measures:

```
EVALUATE
CALCULATETABLE (
    ADDCOLUMNS (
        VALUES ( Table[Col] ),
        "SumxAllSelected", [SumxAllSelected]
    ),
    OR ( Table[Col] = "A", Table[Col] = "C" )
)

EVALUATE
CALCULATETABLE (
    ROW (
        "Grand Total SumxAllSelected", [SumxAllSelected]
    ),
    OR ( Table[Col] = "A", Table[Col] = "C" )
)
```

In order to understand it even better, let us fully expand the code of *SumxAllSelected* to its definition, focusing on the portion that computes the individual rows:

```
EVALUATE
CALCULATETABLE (
    ADDCOLUMNS (
        VALUES ( Table[Col] ),
        "SumxAllSelected",
        CALCULATE (
            SUMX (
                Table,
                CALCULATE ( SUM ( Table[Val] ), ALLSELECTED () )
            )
        )
    ),
    OR ( Table[Col] = "A", Table[Col] = "C" )
)
```

With the fully expanded code, it is now more evident that the innermost *CALCULATE* is executed when there are two nested row contexts: The first one generated by the outer *ADDCOLUMNS* and the inner one generated by *SUMX*. In reality, the outer one has already been converted into a filter context by *CALCULATE* when the inner row context starts.

In Table 10.1 you can see the set of filter contexts generated by the various calls right before the innermost *CALCULATE* is executed:

TABLE 10-1 Set of filter contexts generated during the evaluation of the pivot table.

Function Call	Filter Context	Notes
CALCULATETABLE	(A, C)	
CALCULATE when iterating ADDCOLUMNS	(A, C)	Table
	(A)	Row
CALCULATE when iterating SUMX	(A)	Table
	(A)	Row

In this scenario, the innermost *CALCULATE* invokes *ALLSELECTED*, which removes the last filter context generated by context transition. As you can easily check, this time *ALLSELECTED* does not restore the original filter context. Instead, it restores a context containing only A. This is the reason why the pivot table shows the value for A or C in the value rows. Moreover, it is worth noting that the filter restored is not the original one, because the iteration started in the measure hides the row context generated by the pivot table.

At the grand total level, things are different. In fact, the fully expanded code of the grand total looks like the following:

```
EVALUATE
CALCULATETABLE (
    ROW (
        "Grand Total SumxAllSelected",
        CALCULATE (
            SUMX (
                Table,
                CALCULATE ( SUM ( Table[Val] ), ALLSELECTED () )
            )
        )
    ),
    OR ( Table[Col] = "A", Table[Col] = "C" )
)
```

In this case, the only iteration is the one introduced by *SUMX*. In Table 10-2 you can see the flow of contexts that, for the grand total, is much easier:

TABLE 10-2 Set of filter contexts generated during the evaluation of the pivot table.

Function Call	Filter Context	Notes
CALCULATETABLE	(A, C)	
CALCULATE when iterating SUMX	(A, C)	Table
	(A)	Row

The innermost *CALCULATE* performs context transition, removing the row (either A or C) and restoring the table over which *SUMX* is iterating, namely a table containing both A and C. In fact, at the grand total, you see a value of 8, which is 2 times 4.

Before leaving this topic, it is worth showing another example where a naïve interpretation of *ALLSELECTED* fails in explaining how DAX computes numbers. Look at this measure, which is basically a variation of the previous one where, instead of iterating Table, we iterate *ALL (Table)*:

```
SumxAllSelectedOnAll :=
SUMX (
    ALL ( Table ),
    CALCULATE (
        SUM ( Table[Val] ),
        ALLSELECTED ( )
    )
)
```

This time, context transition generated by *CALCULATE* will put on the filter context its two filters: the outer is *ALL (Table)* and the inner is the currently iterated row over *ALL (Table)*. What is relevant is the fact that the outer filter is now different from the original filter introduced by the slicer. Thus, *ALLSELECTED* will not restore the filter generated by the slicer. Instead, it will restore a filter containing all the rows, summing the value of all the rows, even those originally hidden by the slicer. You can see the result in Figure 10-5.

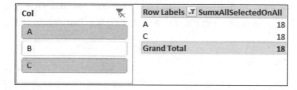

FIGURE 10-5 Iterating and performing *ALLSELECTED* later produces numbers that are difficult to explain.

Let us review this in more detail. The code for the rows of the pivot table is the following:

```
EVALUATE
CALCULATETABLE (
    ADDCOLUMNS (
        VALUES ( Table[Col] ),
        "SumxAllSelectedOnAll",
        CALCULATE (
            SUMX (
                ALL ( Table ),
                CALCULATE ( SUM ( Table[Val] ), ALLSELECTED () )
            )
        )
    ),
    OR ( Table[Col] = "A", Table[Col] = "C" )
)
```

Table 10-3 shows the set of filter contexts generated by the various calls right before the innermost *CALCULATE* is executed:

TABLE 10-3 Set of filter contexts generated during the evaluation of the pivot table.

Function Call	Filter Context	Notes
CALCULATETABLE	(A, C)	
CALCULATE when iterating ADDCOLUMNS	(A, C)	Table
	(A)	Row
CALCULATE when iterating SUMX	**ALL (Table)**	**Table**
	(A)	Row

When *ALLSELECTED* removes the last filter context containing A, it exposes the previous one, which is filtering *ALL (Table)*. Thus, the innermost *SUM* computes the sum of *Table[Val]* for all the rows, yielding a result of 6. This happens three times, because the iteration is running over *ALL (Table)* and the result is 18, which is 3 times (1+2+3).

As you see, until you understand exactly how *ALLSELECTED* works, it is nearly impossible to understand how DAX computes its values. *ALLSELECTED* works in an intuitive way only when it is used as a filter in *CALCULATE* for a measure that is used directly inside a pivot table. However, as soon as you start mixing iterations and context transitions, then deeper context transitions are generated and *ALLSELECTED* becomes very complex to follow and understand, up to a point where numbers seem to make no sense at all. *ALLSELECTED* by itself is not a complex function. What is complex is the fact that we tend to think that *ALLSELECTED* restores the original filter context of the pivot table. Once you forget about this and you think of *ALLSELECTED* as restoring the outer filter of the last context transition, numbers start to make sense again.

Understanding *KEEPFILTERS*

In the ranking of complex DAX functions, *KEEPFILTERS* has a very good position. In fact, its behavior is somewhat easy to learn and remember, but it is it is difficult to know precisely when to use it and what the result of using it will be. As it happened with *ALLSELECTED*, *KEEPFILTERS* requires you to understand exactly its semantics before you can safely use it. And, as it happened with *ALLSELECTED*, we use *KEEPFILTERS* to expose some more details about the internals of filter contexts.

The purpose of *KEEPFILTERS* is a very simple one: It combines with an *AND* the result of a new filter context with the previous one. An example helps to understand it better. In the pivot table in Figure 10-6, these are the formula definitions:

```
[Sales Amount] :=
SUMX ( Sales, Sales[Quantity] * Sales[Unit Price] )

[RedSalesCalc] :=
CALCULATE (
    [Sales Amount],
    Product[Color] = "Red"
)

[RedSalesValues] :=
CALCULATE (
    [Sales Amount],
    Product[Color] = "Red",
    VALUES ( Product[Color] )
)

[RedSalesKeepFilter] :=
CALCULATE (
    [Sales Amount],
    KEEPFILTERS ( Product[Color] = "Red" )
)
```

Row Labels	Sales Amount	RedSalesCalc	RedSalesValues	RedSalesKeepFilter
Azure	$12,071.90	$126,762.21		
Black	$791,735.81	$126,762.21		
Blue	$294,838.55	$126,762.21		
Brown	$225,705.83	$126,762.21		
Gold	$43,292.49	$126,762.21		
Green	$202,219.08	$126,762.21		
Grey	$509,990.58	$126,762.21		
Orange	$55,324.68	$126,762.21		
Pink	$130,243.02	$126,762.21		
Purple	$286.00	$126,762.21		
Red	$126,762.21	$126,762.21	$126,762.21	$126,762.21
Silver	$918,587.35	$126,762.21		
Silver Grey	$60,366.60	$126,762.21		
Transparent	$414.54	$126,762.21		
White	$841,262.48	$126,762.21		
Yellow	$6,816.78	$126,762.21		
Grand Total	$4,219,917.90	$126,762.21	$126,762.21	$126,762.21

FIGURE 10-6 In this pivot table, you can see that the last two measures compute the same value.

As you can see, *RedSalesCalc* always computes sales of red products, while *RedSalesValues* and *RedSalesKeepFilter* compute the value of red sales only when Red is already present in the filter context. However, each of them uses a different technique:

- *RedSalesValues* explicitly uses the *VALUES* function to retrieve the active colors that *CALCULATE* merges in *AND* with the condition on *Product[Color]*.

- *RedSalesKeepFilter* uses the *KEEPFILTER* function. *KEEPFILTERS* evaluates its inner condition and then puts the result in a logical *AND* with the previous filter context.

Although they look very similar and, in this example, they produce the same result, the two techniques are different:

- *KEEPFILTERS* is not a table function: Its result is not a table. In fact, you can use *KEEPFILTERS* only in *CALCULATE* or as a top-level function in iterations (a feature that we will see shortly).

- *KEEPFILTERS* puts the inner condition in *AND* with the previous filter context as a whole, whereas *VALUES* put the *AND* with a single column only. This fact is not evident in the previous example; it will become clearer with the following examples.

To appreciate the difference between using *VALUES* and using *KEEPFILTERS*, you need to mix, in the same query, context transition and complex filters. Imagine that you want to compute a measure that shows the average monthly sales. Such a measure needs to iterate over the years and months and, for each individual month, compute the total sales. You then aggregate the partial results using a standard *AVERAGEX* function, as in the following example:

```
[AvgMonthlySales] :=
AVERAGEX (
    CROSSJOIN (
        VALUES ( 'Date'[Calendar Year] ),
        VALUES ( 'Date'[Month] )
    ),
    [Sales Amount]
)
```

If you use this measure in a simple report, showing the average sales over the years, the result is correct, as you can see in Figure 10-7.

Note Please note that, for educational purposes and to make this example clearer, we modified the hierarchy Calendar on the Date table using the month name (without the year) as the second level. Technically, this modification made the hierarchy an unnatural one, resulting in a hierarchy that does not follow best practices, but we needed it to better show the effects of *KEEPFILTERS*.

AvgMonthlySales	Column Labels			
Row Labels	Blue	Green	Red	Grand Total
⊟ CY 2007	$11,875.27	$9,462.77	$4,787.76	$23,760.09
⊞ January	$36,533.96		$139.26	$36,673.22
⊞ February	$179.83	$6,587.70	$3,052.80	$9,820.33
⊞ March	$1,703.66	$7,999.50	$2,746.97	$12,450.13
⊞ April	$870.73	$3,190.00	$9,351.26	$13,411.99
⊞ May	$1,050.12	$25,598.40	$329.46	$26,977.98
⊞ June	$6,209.06	$1,822.00	$5,277.79	$13,308.85
⊞ July	$578.40	$29,497.50	$149.85	$30,225.75
⊞ August	$3,439.01	$129.99	$10,415.87	$13,984.87
⊞ September	$3,355.52		$10,392.00	$13,747.52
⊞ October	$19,908.71	$2,347.80	$2,540.00	$24,796.51
⊞ November	$38,538.74	$7,992.00	$10,908.00	$57,438.74
⊞ December	$30,135.44		$2,149.80	$32,285.24
⊟ CY 2008	$6,383.16	$7,061.96	$2,370.87	$13,264.43
⊞ January	$9,980.63	$4,264.00		$14,244.63
⊞ February	$4,679.62		$1,259.93	$5,939.55
⊞ March	$833.00	$1,493.60	$1,356.95	$3,683.55
⊞ April	$14,023.00	$26,116.30	$644.31	$40,783.61
⊞ May	$2,279.76	$1,592.00	$80.85	$3,952.61
⊞ June	$16,887.00	$224.00	$324.87	$17,435.87
⊞ July	$756.48		$7,991.94	$8,748.42
⊞ August	$11,595.86		$3,855.52	$15,451.38
⊞ September	$8,764.50	$12,236.75	$7,328.83	$28,330.08
⊞ October	$2,970.10	$1,272.00	$1,407.58	$5,649.68
⊞ November	$598.00	$9,297.00	$659.85	$10,554.85
⊞ December	$3,230.00		$1,168.96	$4,398.96
Grand Total	$9,129.21	$8,332.97	$3,631.85	$18,512.26

FIGURE 10-7 The average of monthly sales is computed correctly for the years and the grand total in this pivot table.

In order to explain why *KEEPFILTERS* is useful, you need to create a complex filter on the calendar. In doing that, you will see that the formula will stop computing the correct values. A complex filter (also known as an "arbitrarily shaped set," which we will introduce later in this chapter) is a filter containing columns that are not independently filtered.

The set visible in the report shows all the months of 2007 and 2008 and you can express it as:

```
FILTER (
    CROSSJOIN (
        VALUES ( 'Date'[Calendar Year] ),
        VALUES ( 'Date'[Month] )
    ),
    OR (
        'Date'[Calendar Year] = 2007,
        'Date'[Calendar Year] = 2008
    )
)
```

The only condition is on Calendar Year, so this is not a complex filter. You can create a complex filter by selecting the last two months of 2007 and the first two months of 2008, using, for example, the filter on the hierarchy, as you can see in Figure 10-8.

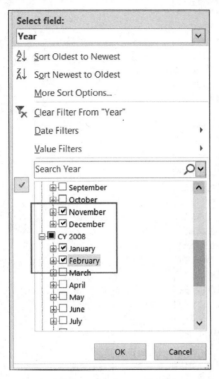

FIGURE 10-8 By selecting multiple items, you can create a complex filter.

This filter is no longer a simple one. In fact, you can write it only using a condition that includes both the year and the month in the same expression, as in:

```
FILTER (
    CROSSJOIN (
        VALUES ( 'Date'[Calendar Year] ),
        VALUES ( 'Date'[Month] )
    ),
    OR (
        OR (
            'Date'[Calendar Year] = 2007 && 'Date'[Month] = "November",
            'Date'[Calendar Year] = 2007 && 'Date'[Month] = "December"
        ),
        OR (
            'Date'[Calendar Year] = 2008 && 'Date'[Month] = "January",
            'Date'[Calendar Year] = 2008 && 'Date'[Month] = "February"
        )
    )
)
```

In other words, an arbitrarily shaped filter is a filter that expresses a relationship among the columns involved in the filter itself. These kinds of filters are not an issue by themselves; DAX can handle them smoothly. The problem arises when you combine them with other filters, as you can see in Figure 10-9, where we show the *AvgMonthlySales* projected on the filter shown in Figure 10-8.

AvgMonthlySales	Column Labels			
Row Labels	Blue	Green	Red	Grand Total
⊟ CY 2007	$34,337.09	$7,992.00	$6,528.90	$44,861.99
⊞ November	$38,538.74	$7,992.00	$10,908.00	$57,438.74
⊞ December	$30,135.44		$2,149.80	$32,285.24
⊟ CY 2008	$7,330.13	$4,264.00	$1,259.93	$10,092.09
⊞ January	$9,980.63	$4,264.00		$14,244.63
⊞ February	$4,679.62		$1,259.93	$5,939.55
Grand Total	$15,484.53	$7,035.18	$2,762.66	$21,419.44

FIGURE 10-9 The Grand Total is wrong, showing a value that is not the correct monthly average.

As you can see, the total on the column is wrong (it is worth computing the average manually because you will then see that the total shown is wrong). Before solving the issue, we need to understand better what is happening. At the column grand total, there are two years and four months visible in the filter context. Because of the relationships stated in the condition, only two months of each year are present, but if you look at the individual columns, you have the following values:

- Year: 2007, 2008

- Month: January, February, November, December

AVERAGEX iterates the *CROSSJOIN* of the two columns. Thus, *CROSSJOIN* generates eight pairs, including January and February of 2007 and November and December of 2008, which were excluded by the previous condition. Finally, context transition introduced by *CALCULATE* replaces the filter on both year and month, resulting in the evaluation of the average over the whole eight months, instead of the original four.

To put it differently, we started with a complex filter defining an implicit relationship between the columns, and because we used *CROSSJOIN* and *CALCULATE* in the measure, we ended with a simple filter that removed the relationship and restored a simple filter. Unfortunately, in doing so, we computed the wrong value. We call this scenario *complex filter reduction*. It is one of the most dangerous causes of errors in DAX code.

In such a scenario, *KEEPFILTERS* is the solution. *KEEPFILTERS* modifies the semantics of context manipulation of *CALCULATE*. The normal behavior of *CALCULATE* is to replace existing filters. *KEEP-FILTERS* instructs *CALCULATE* not to replace the filter. Instead, it will put the new filter in a logical *AND* with the previous one. Therefore, if the previous filter contained a relationship between some columns, that relationship will remain active.

In the example, if you write the *AvgMonthlySales* leveraging *KEEPFILTERS*, the result will be the correct one. So the correct formula would be this one:

```
[AvgMonthlySales] :=
AVERAGEX (
    KEEPFILTERS (
        CROSSJOIN (
            VALUES ( 'Date'[Calendar Year] ),
            VALUES ( 'Date'[Month] )
        )
    ),
    [Sales Amount]
)
```

By using this formula, the result is the expected one, as you can see in Figure 10-10.

AvgMonthlySales	Column Labels			
Row Labels	Blue	Green	Red	Grand Total
⊟ CY 2007	$34,337.09	$7,992.00	$6,528.90	$44,861.99
⊞ November	$38,538.74	$7,992.00	$10,908.00	$57,438.74
⊞ December	$30,135.44		$2,149.80	$32,285.24
⊟ CY 2008	$7,330.13	$4,264.00	$1,259.93	$10,092.09
⊞ January	$9,980.63	$4,264.00		$14,244.63
⊞ February	$4,679.62		$1,259.93	$5,939.55
Grand Total	$20,833.61	$6,128.00	$4,772.58	$27,477.04

FIGURE 10-10 Using *KEEPFILTERS*, *AVERAGEX* computes the correct result.

The presence of *KEEPFILTERS* forces the *CROSSJOIN* to put its result in *AND* with the previous filter. Thus, *CROSSJOIN* still generates eight rows, but then these rows are further filtered using the previous filter context.

At this point, you have learned the difference between *KEEPFILTERS* and *VALUES*. *VALUES*, used inside *CALCULATE* or as a parameter of a *CROSSJOIN* in a *FILTER* statement, works on a single column only. So it is not useful when the filter you want to preserve is composed of many columns with a relationship defined in an arbitrarily shaped set. *KEEPFILTERS*, on the other hand, is much more powerful.

It is not easy to decide when to use *KEEPFILTERS*. The reason is that your measure might behave in the correct way, but when used inside a complex filter, it starts to compute wrong values. Generally, you do not know in advance how your code is used in later reports, which is a major issue when authoring a formula.

When deciding whether it is worthwhile to think about adding a *KEEPFILTERS* in your code, here are two of the evidences you need to pay attention to:

- You are using iterations and leveraging context transition inside your formula.

- The user is likely to use the same columns you iterate as a complex filter.

If your formula does not include iterations, and most important, context transition at all, then *KEEPFILTERS* is not necessary. Subsequently, when having the option of using an iteration of a normal aggregator, it is always better to use the aggregator, to avoid the danger of complex filter reduction.

Beware that users might introduce complex filters in many different ways, and most of the time, they are not aware of the problem. For example, Microsoft Excel includes, among the many filtering options, a "Top 10 filter" that lets the user select the top N elements from a list of values, sorting the list with a measure.

In Figure 10-11, you can see a pivot table where the user selected the top three product names sorted by *AvgMonthlySales*.

Because the year is on the rows, the user expects to see three products each year (the top three), while the pivot table shows four products. The reason is that filter reduction changed the filter under which it computes the *AvgMonthlySales*.

In this case, the relationship stored in the condition is similar to the *TOPN* operation (the MDX function used is *TOPCOUNT*, which corresponds to the *TOPN* function in DAX). Such operation retrieves some products for each year (only the top three of that given year). It stores a relationship between years and products, and this relationship is destroyed by the filter reduction.

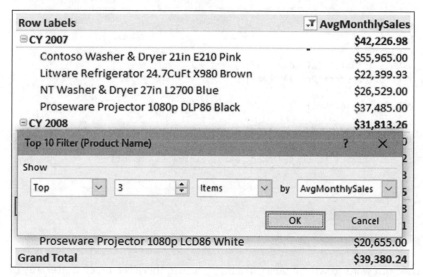

FIGURE 10-11 *TOPN* filtering frequently creates complex filters that lead to wrong results after filter reduction.

For the same pivot table, if you use the correct formula for *AvgMonthlySales* (the one using *KEEPFILTERS*), the result is the expected one, as you can see in Figure 10-12.

Row Labels	AvgMonthlySales
⊟ CY 2007	**$48,836.00**
Contoso Washer & Dryer 21in E210 Pink	$55,965.00
NT Washer & Dryer 27in L2700 Blue	$26,529.00
Proseware Projector 1080p DLP86 Black	$37,485.00
⊟ CY 2008	**$31,813.26**
Fabrikam Independent Filmmaker 1/3" 8.5mm X200 Grey	$21,840.00
Litware Refrigerator 24.7CuFt X980 Grey	$25,599.92
Litware Refrigerator 24.7CuFt X980 White	$23,999.93
⊟ CY 2009	**$43,151.55**
Fabrikam Refrigerator 24.7CuFt X9800 White	$39,999.88
Litware Refrigerator 24.7CuFt X980 Brown	$28,799.91
Proseware Projector 1080p LCD86 White	$20,655.00
Grand Total	**$41,266.94**

FIGURE 10-12 Using *KEEPFILTERS* the report shows, correctly, three products for each year.

It is finally helpful to note that *KEEPFILTERS* is useful not only in some measures, as we have demonstrated, but also in queries. As an example, look at the following query:

```
EVALUATE
FILTER (
    CALCULATETABLE (
        ADDCOLUMNS (
            CROSSJOIN (
                VALUES ( 'Date'[Calendar Year] ),
                VALUES ( Product[Product Name] )
            ),
            "Sales", [Sales Amount]
        ),
        GENERATE (
            VALUES ( 'Date'[Calendar Year] ),
            TOPN ( 3, VALUES ( Product[Product Name] ), [Sales Amount] )
        )
    ),
    NOT ( ISBLANK ( [Sales] ) )
)
ORDER BY 'Date'[Calendar Year], 'Product'[Product Name]
```

You probably would not want to write a query like this, because there is a much better way of expressing it, by making the *GENERATE* function as a parameter of *ADDCOLUMNS*, as in the following code:

```
EVALUATE
FILTER (
    CALCULATETABLE (
        ADDCOLUMNS (
            GENERATE (
                VALUES ( 'Date'[Calendar Year] ),
                TOPN ( 3, VALUES ( Product[Product Name] ), [Sales Amount] )
            ),
            "Sales", [Sales Amount]
        )
    ),
    NOT ( ISBLANK ( [Sales] ) )
)
ORDER BY 'Date'[Calendar Year], Product[Product Name]
```

Nevertheless, queries like the more complex one shown previously are very common when they are generated by code generators and other automated tools, because they clearly separate the filtering from the projection over rows and columns. In such a case, you might encounter filter reduction because the inner *ADDCOLUMNS* iterates over the same columns which are filtered by the *GENERATE* used as a parameter of *CALCULATE*. As a result, you will not retrieve the top three products of each year but, again, a larger list of products.

In such a case, the correct formulation of the query is the following:

```
EVALUATE
FILTER (
    CALCULATETABLE (
        ADDCOLUMNS (
            KEEPFILTERS (
                CROSSJOIN (
                    VALUES ( 'Date'[Calendar Year] ),
                    VALUES ( Product[Product Name] )
                )
            ),
            "Sales", [Sales Amount]
        ),
        GENERATE (
            VALUES ( 'Date'[Calendar Year] ),
            TOPN ( 3, VALUES ( Product[Product Name] ), [Sales Amount] )
        )
    ),
    NOT ( ISBLANK ( [Sales] ) )
)
ORDER BY 'Date'[Calendar Year], 'Product'[Product Name]
```

In this case, *KEEPFILTERS* has to operate on *CROSSJOIN* to retrieve, for each year, only the top three products previously selected by *GENERATE*. It is important to note that, in this specific case, iteration does not happen inside the measure but in *ADDCOLUMNS*.

Understanding AutoExists

AutoExists is a feature of the MDX language which restricts the results of a query to only existing combinations of attributes. It is a relevant topic in a book about DAX because you can use DAX to create a Tabular solution that users will query, for example, using a pivot table. Excel uses MDX to query the model. Thus, even if you authored all of your code with DAX, you still need to understand the behavior of the model when it resolves MDX queries.

In order to understand AutoExists, look at the data model in Figure 10-13.

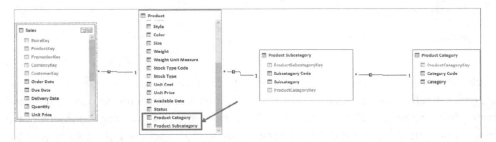

FIGURE 10-13 In this model, product category and subcategory are both normalized and denormalized.

In the model, there is the usual chain of relationships between products, subcategories, and categories. Using the *RELATED* function, we also added the denormalized category and subcategory in the Product table.

Based on this model, you can easily build two pivot tables that show sales sliced by category and subcategory. At first sight, the two results look identical, as you can see in Figure 10-14.

Normalized Model		Denormalized Model	
Row Labels	Sales Amount	Row Labels	Sales Amount
⊟ Audio	$422,177.88	⊟ Audio	$422,177.88
Bluetooth Headphones	$136,912.18	Bluetooth Headphones	$136,912.18
MP4&MP3	$185,016.40	MP4&MP3	$185,016.40
Recording Pen	$100,249.30	Recording Pen	$100,249.30
⊟ Cameras and camcorders	$7,901,783.67	⊟ Cameras and camcorders	$7,901,783.67
Camcorders	$3,491,508.00	Camcorders	$3,491,508.00
Cameras & Camcorders Accessories	$870,068.07	Cameras & Camcorders Accessories	$870,068.07
Digital Cameras	$859,119.20	Digital Cameras	$859,119.20
Digital SLR Cameras	$2,681,088.40	Digital SLR Cameras	$2,681,088.40
Grand Total	$8,323,961.55	Grand Total	$8,323,961.55

FIGURE 10-14 Browsing normalized and denormalized columns provides the same experience.

In reality, DAX computes the two pivot tables in two different ways and the identical result is the consequence of two different features that, in standard queries, provide the same result. They are *AutoExists* and *empty row removal*. AutoExists is a server feature, while empty row removal is a pivot table feature. Let us analyze them in more detail.

- AutoExists is a feature of the MDX query engine that avoids calculation over nonexisting sets. In fact, while it is meaningful to compute the amount of sales for the pair (Audio, MP4&MP3), it makes no sense to compute the same value for the pair (Audio, Camcorders), because the subcategory Camcorders does not belong to the category Audio. Thus, because there is no product that is at the same time, both Camcorders and Audio, DAX can avoid computing this value at all, reducing the overall execution time.

- Empty row removal, on the other hand, is a feature of the pivot table that automatically hides rows if all the measures are *BLANK*. For example, if there was a product that never sold a single item, then the pivot table would hide it, because that row would not contain any useful information.

It is important to highlight that AutoExists is a server feature, whereas empty row removal is a client feature of the pivot table. You can control the behavior of empty row removal by selecting the "Show items with no data on rows" check box in the pivot table options; in this way you disable blank lines removal and the two pivot tables will look very different, as you can see in Figure 10-15.

Normalized Model

Row Labels	Sales Amount
Audio	$422,177.88
Air Conditioners	
Audio Accessories	
Audio Books	
Bluetooth Headphones	$136,912.18
Boxed Games	
Camcorders	
Cameras & Camcorders Accessories	
Car Video	
Cell phones Accessories	
Coffee Machines	
Computer Setup & Service	
Computers Accessories	

Denormalized Model

Row Labels	Sales Amount
Audio	$422,177.88
Bluetooth Headphones	$136,912.18
MP4&MP3	$185,016.40
Recording Pen	$100,249.30
Cameras and camcorders	$7,901,783.67
Camcorders	$3,491,508.00
Cameras & Camcorders Accessories	$870,068.07
Digital Cameras	$859,119.20
Digital SLR Cameras	$2,681,088.40
Grand Total	$8,323,961.55

FIGURE 10-15 If you disable empty row removal, this makes the two pivot tables show different results.

If you disable empty row removal, you can see that the normalized model performs the calculation of sales even for nonexisting pairs of category and subcategory. In the denormalized model, on the other hand, calculation happens only for existing pairs. The reason why the denormalized model behaves in a different way is AutoExists. In fact, because the two columns belong to the same table, the engine performs a first step in which it determines existing combinations and only later it computes the effective values. In DAX, you would notice the same difference by using these two queries:

```
EVALUATE
ADDCOLUMNS (
    CROSSJOIN (
        VALUES ( 'Product Category'[Category] ),
        VALUES ( 'Product Subcategory'[Subcategory] )
    ),
    "Sales Amount", [Sales Amount]
)

EVALUATE
ADDCOLUMNS (
    SUMMARIZE (
        Sales,
        'Product Category'[Category],
        'Product Subcategory'[Subcategory]
    ),
    "Sales Amount", [Sales Amount]
)
```

The first one returns nonexisting pairs of category and subcategory, while the second one returns only existing combinations.

Up to this point, the difference looks subtle, but not relevant. In reality, it becomes a very important one as soon as you start to write measures that modify the filter context. Imagine, for example, that you write a measure to compute sales of the Audio category, as in:

```
[Audio Sales] :=
CALCULATE (
    [Sales Amount],
    'Product Category'[Category] = "Audio"
)
```

Clearly, the formulas will be slightly different in the two models, but the logic remains the same. Using this measure, the pivot table yields some surprising results, as you can appreciate in Figure 10-16.

Normalized Model

Row Labels	Sales Amount	Audio Sales
Audio	$422,177.88	$422,177.88
Bluetooth Headphones	$136,912.18	$136,912.18
MP4&MP3	$185,016.40	$185,016.40
Recording Pen	$100,249.30	$100,249.30
Cameras and camcorders	$7,901,783.67	$422,177.88
Bluetooth Headphones		$136,912.18
Camcorders	$3,491,508.00	
Cameras & Camcorders Accessories	$870,068.07	
Digital Cameras	$859,119.20	
Digital SLR Cameras	$2,681,088.40	
MP4&MP3		$185,016.40
Recording Pen		$100,249.30
Grand Total	$8,323,961.55	$422,177.88

Denormalized Model

Row Labels	Sales Amount	Audio Sale Denormalized
Audio	$422,177.88	$422,177.88
Bluetooth Headphones	$136,912.18	$136,912.18
MP4&MP3	$185,016.40	$185,016.40
Recording Pen	$100,249.30	$100,249.30
Cameras and camcorders	$7,901,783.67	$422,177.88
Camcorders	$3,491,508.00	
Cameras & Camcorders Accessories	$870,068.07	
Digital Cameras	$859,119.20	
Digital SLR Cameras	$2,681,088.40	
Grand Total	$8,323,961.55	$422,177.88

FIGURE 10-16 The *Audio Sales* measure shows strange results in the normalized data model.

You can see in the denormalized model that audio sales are visible only under the Audio category. On the left, in the normalized model, the pivot table shows audio sales under the Cameras and Camcorders category. This time, even with empty row removal turned on, the two results are very different.

The reason is not hard to understand. The *Audio Sales* measure replaces the filter on the category with the fixed value "Audio." In the denormalized model, this has no effect on the Cameras and Camcorders category because there, DAX computes values only for subcategories of Cameras. However, in the normalized model, DAX evaluates the measure for all the combinations of category and subcategory, regardless of their existence. When DAX computes the value for the pair (Cameras and Camcorders, Bluetooth Headphones), the measure replaces the category with Audio, resulting in (Audio, Bluetooth Headphones), which yields to a value, which is, in turn, shown in the pivot table.

AutoExists, by definition, works only with sets of columns from the same table. This is the reason why the denormalized model works as expected, while the normalized one does not.

Understanding expanded tables

As you have seen by reading all the previous sections, understanding evaluation contexts, context propagation, context transition, and filter reduction are very important skills for you to acquire in order to understand exactly how DAX evaluates expressions.

In all the previous descriptions, we gave a somewhat simplified vision of what evaluation contexts are. In fact, there was always some sort of disclaimer saying that, later in the book, you would have learned all the internals of DAX evaluation contexts. That moment has arrived: You are about to begin learning the most hidden secrets of evaluation contexts.

Before showing you the complete picture, let us recall what you have learned so far about evaluation contexts:

- There are two contexts: row context and filter context.

- Row context does not propagate through relationships.

- Row context always contains a single row and it is introduced by calculated columns or by iterations

- Filter context propagates as indicated by the relationship definition.

- Filter context can operate either on a table or on a column. If working on a column, it filters that column only. When working with a table, it filters all the columns of the table.

All the previous statements are correct, and you learned them by reading this far in the book. Nevertheless, in order to complete your evaluation context understanding, you need to understand the foundation of evaluation contexts and DAX, which is the concept of *expanded tables*.

In DAX, every table has a corresponding expanded version. The expanded version of a table contains all the columns of the original table, plus all the columns of tables that can filter the original table through many-to-one relationships.

For example, consider the model in Figure 10-17.

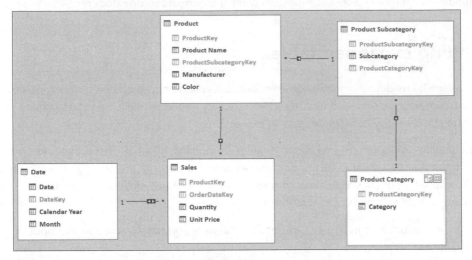

FIGURE 10-17 You use this simple model to learn the concept of expanded tables.

Sales has a many-to-one relationship with Product, so the expanded version of Sales contains all the columns of Product. Repeating the process starting from Product, you can easily see that the expanded version of Sales contains the entire data model. The expanded version of Product, on the other hand, contains all the columns of Product, Product Subcategory, and Product Category.

The Date table requires a bit more attention. In fact, it can be filtered by Sales because the relationship that links them is bidirectional. Even if the relationship is bidirectional, it is not a many-to-one: it is a one-to-many. The expanded version of Date contains only Date itself, even if Date can be filtered by Sales, Product, Product Subcategory, and Product Category. When filtering happens because a relationship is bidirectional, we do not speak about expanded columns; instead, we speak about *filtering columns*. For the sake of this description, filtering columns and expanded columns behave in the same way even if they are different. Thus, for the moment, we keep them in the same basket and only at the end of this section will we discuss in greater detail the difference between filtering columns and expanded ones.

When repeating the same exercise for the other tables in the data model, you create the expanded tables shown in Table 10-4.

TABLE 10-4 Expanded versions of the tables.

Table	Expanded Version
Date	Date. Plus the whole model as filtering columns
Sales	The whole model
Product	Product, Product Subcategory, Product Category
Product Subcategory	Product Subcategory, Product Category
Product Category	Product Category

Expanded tables are a useful concept because they show, for each table, the list of columns that propagate their filter context to the original table. If you take, for example, Product, you can easily check that if you filter any of the columns in its expanded version, then the engine will filter Product, too.

Most important, is the fact that DAX uses expanded tables to place any filter in the filter context. To understand it better, visualize the expanded tables on a chart, which you can see in Figure 10-18.

	Product Category	Product Subcategory	Product	Sales	Date
Category					
ProductCategoryKey					
ProductCategoryKey					
Subcategory					
ProductSubcategoryKey					
ProductSubcategoryKey					
Product Name					
Manufacturer					
Color					
ProductKey					
ProductKey					
Unit Price					
Quantity					
OrderDateKey					
DateKey					
Date					
Calendar Year					
Month					
Legend	Native Columns	Derived Columns	Filtering Columns		

FIGURE 10-18 Visualizing the data model on a chart makes it easier to look at expanded tables.

The chart lists all the columns in the model on the rows and each table on the columns. We colored the cells to indicate the three kinds of columns inside:

- **Native columns** are the columns that originally belong to the table.

- **Derived columns** are the columns added to the expanded table following relationships.

- **Filtering columns** are the columns that can filter the table, even if they do not belong to the expanded version of the table.

When you put a filter on a column, you can color the row containing the column, to visually indicate which tables are filtered. If you write the following:

```
[RedSales] :=
CALCULATE (
    SUM ( Sales[Quantity] ),
    Product[Color] = "Red"
)
```

Then because the filter is on the *Color* column, the corresponding chart will be the one visible in Figure 10-19.

	Product Category	Product Subcategory	Product	Sales	Date
Category					
ProductCategoryKey					
ProductCategoryKey					
Subcategory					
ProductSubcategoryKey					
ProductSubcategoryKey					
Product Name					
Manufacturer					
Color					
ProductKey					
ProductKey					
Unit Price					
Quantity					
OrderDateKey					
DateKey					
Date					
Calendar Year					
Month					

Legend	Native Columns	Derived Columns	Filtering Columns

FIGURE 10-19 Coloring the line of a column makes it evident which tables are filtered.

The filter on *Color* is a column filter, that is, a filter that operates on a single column. So we can now state the general rule for a column filter: *"A filter context placed on a column operates on all the expanded tables that contain it."* As you can see, this rule is the same as the one we stated earlier, when we were still speaking about tables and relationships. The filter context does not really "propagate" through relationships. It applies its effect to all the tables that contain the column, because it works on expanded tables.

Note Please note that the filter on *Color* propagates to Date, too, even if—technically—*Color* does not belong to the expanded version of Date. This is the effect of bidirectional filtering working. It is important to note that the filter on *Color* reaches Date through a filtering column, not through the expanded tables. Internally, DAX injects a specific filtering code to make bidirectional relationships work, whereas filtering on expanded tables happens automatically based on the way the engine works. As we said, the difference is only internal, yet it is important to point it out.

You already know that you can create both column filters, similar to the one you have seen previously, and table filters, by using the *FILTER* function passing a whole table to it. How do table filters work? They work on expanded tables, too. In fact, whenever you use a table as a filter condition in *CALCULATE*, you are—in reality—filtering the expanded table.

In order to understand it, look at these two measure definitions:

```
[NumOfCategories] :=
    COUNTROWS ( 'Product Category' )

[NumOfCategoriesFilteredByProduct] :=
    CALCULATE ( COUNTROWS ( 'Product Category' ), Product )
```

The first measure computes the number of categories. The second one computes the number of categories, but before doing so, it applies a filter context that contains the Product table (as filtered in the context, of course). The result is visible in Figure 10-20, where we used the product color on the rows.

Row Labels	NumOfCategories	NumOfCategoriesFilteredByProduct
Azure	8	1
Black	8	8
Blue	8	6
Brown	8	3
Gold	8	6
Green	8	5
Grey	8	6
Orange	8	4
Pink	8	6
Purple	8	4
Red	8	7
Silver	8	8
Silver Grey	8	1
Transparent	8	1
White	8	8
Yellow	8	6
Grand Total	8	8

FIGURE 10-20 This pivot table shows the effect of applying a table filter in *CALCULATE*.

The first column, *NumOfCategories*, always shows the same number. The reason is that we used the product color on the rows and, if you look at the expanded table diagram in Figure 10-18, the Product Category table does not contain the *Color* column. Thus, filtering the color has no effect on the number of categories visible in the filter context. However, when you put Product on the filter context, you are using the expanded version of Product. Because the expanded version of Product contains all the columns of the Product Subcategory, the number of visible categories will no longer be eight but, instead, the number of categories containing products of that specific color.

Using a table as a filter parameter in *CALCULATE* filters all the columns in the expanded version of the table. As a result, there is a big difference between the following two measures:

```
[NumOfCategoriesFilteredByColor] :=
CALCULATE (
    COUNTROWS ( 'Product Category' ),
    FILTER (
        ALL ( Product[Color] ),
        Product[Color] = "Green"
    )
)

[NumOfCategoriesFilteredByProduct] :=
CALCULATE (
    COUNTROWS ( 'Product Category' ),
    FILTER (
        ALL ( Product ),
        Product[Color] = "Green"
    )
)
```

Although the two measures look nearly identical, they are not. The first one places a filter on the *Color* column only and, because of this, its filtering effect is isolated to the expanded tables containing the *Product[Color]* column. Therefore, it has no effect on the Product Category table. The second one, however, places a filter on the entire Product expanded table. Because the expanded Product table contains the columns of *Product Category*, it turns out that the second measure computes only the number of categories containing green products, while the first one always shows the total number of categories, as you can better appreciate in Figure 10-21.

Row Labels	NumOfCategoriesFilteredByColor	NumOfCategoriesFilteredByProducct
Azure	8	5
Black	8	5
Blue	8	5
Brown	8	5
Gold	8	5
Green	8	5
Grey	8	5
Orange	8	5
Pink	8	5
Purple	8	5
Red	8	5
Silver	8	5
Silver Grey	8	5
Transparent	8	5
White	8	5
Yellow	8	5
Grand Total	**8**	**5**

FIGURE 10-21 This pivot table shows the effect of applying a table filter in *CALCULATE*.

Let us look a bit more into the difference between derived columns and filtering ones. We said earlier that the expanded version of Date, which has a bidirectional relationship with Sales, does not contain the columns of Sales. When you filter Date, you obtain a filter on Sales because the expanded version of Sales contains Date, not vice versa. This last sentence is very important, so we want to reinforce the concept by stating it again: Filtering Date filters Sales, even if the expanded version of Date does not contain Sales.

Nevertheless, because Date has a bidirectional relationship with Sales, and the expanded version of Sales contains the entire data model, we say that Date has a filtering set that represents the whole model. When you filter any column in the model, because you are filtering one of the filtering columns of Date, you are filtering Date, too. This is the reason why, if you define a simple measure such as the following:

```
[NumOfDates] := COUNTROWS ( 'Date' )
```

You can use it in a pivot table, filtering by color, and you obtain, for each color, the number of dates where that color was sold, as you can see in Figure 10-22.

Row Labels	NumOfDates
Azure	9
Black	431
Blue	130
Brown	54
Gold	22
Green	44
Grey	180
Orange	26
Pink	69
Purple	3
Red	87
Silver	372
Silver Grey	17
Transparent	10
White	367
Yellow	30
Grand Total	2556

FIGURE 10-22 The filter on color is propagated to Date because of the bidirectional relationship.

The filtering happens because the color belongs to the filtering columns of Date. Nevertheless, the expanded version of Date contains neither the *Color* column nor any other column of Product. You can verify this if you create a set of measures that count the number of products using different tables as filters:

```
[NumOfProducts] := COUNTROWS ( 'Product' )

[NumOfProductsFilteredByDate] := CALCULATE ( COUNTROWS ( 'Product' ), 'Date' )

[NumOfProductsFilteredBySales] := CALCULATE ( COUNTROWS ( 'Product' ), Sales )
```

NumOfProductsFilteredByDate uses Date as a filter argument in *CALCULATE*, which is the expanded version of Date, whereas *NumOfProductsFilteredBySales* uses the expanded version of Sales. As you can easily check in Figure 10-23, the filter reaches Products only when you use Sales in the filter. This is because the expanded version of Date does not contain columns of Product, whereas the expanded version of Sales does.

Row Labels	NumOfProducts	NumOfProductsFilteredByDate	NumOfProductsFilteredBySales
⊞ CY 2005	2,517	2,517	
⊞ CY 2006	2,517	2,517	
⊟ CY 2007	2,517	2,517	426
April	2,517	2,517	56
August	2,517	2,517	47
December	2,517	2,517	60
February	2,517	2,517	45
January	2,517	2,517	38
July	2,517	2,517	52
June	2,517	2,517	50
March	2,517	2,517	52
May	2,517	2,517	58
November	2,517	2,517	51
October	2,517	2,517	52
September	2,517	2,517	52
⊞ CY 2008	2,517	2,517	511
⊞ CY 2009	2,517	2,517	538
⊞ CY 2010	2,517	2,517	
⊞ CY 2011	2,517	2,517	
Grand Total	2,517	2,517	1,170

FIGURE 10-23 Only the last column shows the number of products sold in the period, because it uses the expanded version of Sales. The expanded version of Date does not contain any Product columns.

Expanded tables are a powerful tool to aid you in understanding the direction of filter context propagation. In fact, they are the real foundation of the theory of filter context propagation in DAX. We needed some time to introduce them, because their use is not very intuitive and we preferred to introduce other concepts before it to help you feel comfortable with the language. Once you master the use of expanded tables, you will find it very easy to understand how DAX works.

ALLEXCEPT with expanded tables

You know that *ALLEXCEPT* performs *ALL* on all the columns of a table except for the ones you pass as a parameter. What is less evident is the fact that you can use *ALLEXCEPT* with the expanded table, too. For example, the following measure works just fine:

```
[SalesOfSameColorAndCategory] :=
CALCULATETABLE (
    SUMX (
        Sales,
        Sales[Quantity] * Sales[UnitPrice]
    ),
    ALLEXCEPT ( Product, Product[Color], 'Product Category'[Category] )
)
```

In fact, the expanded version of Product contains all the columns of Product Category, too.

You can also specify one entire table instead of all the columns of a table that is part of the expanded table. For example, the following two expressions of *ALLEXCEPT* are equivalent:

```
ALLEXCEPT ( Product, 'Product Category' )
ALLEXCEPT ( Product, 'Product Category'[ProductCategoryKey], 'Product Category'[Category] )
```

The tables you specify in the second or following arguments are excluded from the *ALL* condition and have to be part of the expanded table that you specify in the first argument.

Difference between table expansion and filtering

As we said earlier, table expansion happens only from the many-side to the one-side of a relationship. Thus, even if Product had a bidirectional relationship with Product Subcategories, the expanded version of Product contains subcategories, whereas the expanded version of Product Subcategories does not contain Product.

The DAX engine injects filtering code in the expressions (as you can do using the *CROSSFILTER* function), in order to make bidirectional filtering work as if the expansion happened in both ways. Thus, in most cases, your code will work just fine as if table expansion happened in both directions. For this reason, you have seen in Figures 10-17 and 10-18 that filtering columns are different from derived columns. The filtering columns are those that apply filters, thanks to this behavior of the DAX engine, and not because of the expanded table (which they are not part of).

However, the difference becomes important with the use of *SUMMARIZE* or *RELATED*. If, for example, you use *SUMMARIZE* to perform a grouping of a table based on another one, you have to use one of the columns of the expanded version of the base table (and you cannot use filtering columns).

For instance, the following *SUMMARIZE* statement works very well:

```
EVALUATE
SUMMARIZE ( Product, 'Product Subcategory'[Subcategory] )
```

Whereas the next one, which tries to summarize subcategories based on product color, does not:

```
EVALUATE
SUMMARIZE ( 'Product Subcategory', Product[Color] )
```

The error you get as a result is "The column 'Color' specified in the '*SUMMARIZE*' function was not found in the input table," meaning that the expanded version of Product Subcategory does not contain *Product[Color]*. Similarly to *SUMMARIZE*, *RELATED* works only with columns that belong to the expanded table.

This is more evident if you try to use one of the filtering columns, which are not part of the expanded version of the table. For example, you cannot group the Date table by using columns of other tables, even if these columns are filtering columns:

```
EVALUATE
SUMMARIZE ( Date, Product[Color] )
```

There is only a special case where table expansion happens in both directions, which is a relationship defined as one to one. If a relationship is a 1:1 relationship, then both tables are expanded one into the other. This is because a one-to-one relationship makes the two tables semantically identical: Each row in one table has a direct relationship with a single row in the other table. So it is correct to think of the two tables as being a single one, split into two sets of columns.

Redefining the filter context

Now that you are confident in using expanded tables and the way they work in DAX, it is time to perform a deeper analysis of the evaluation contexts interaction and write the final definition of an evaluation context.

Let us start by defining a *tuple*. A tuple is a set of column values. For example, in the Date table, a tuple might be:

```
« Year = 2007, Month = January »
```

Columns in a tuple might belong to different tables. You can think of a tuple as being a row of a table containing columns from different tables.

A tuple defines a value for some of the columns of the model. Thus, intuitively, a tuple behaves as a filter on the data model. The tuple «2007, January», applied to a model containing sales, for example, filters the sales of January 2007.

To see an example of a tuple used as a filter, look at the following expression:

```
CALCULATE (
    ...
    FILTER (
        CROSSJOIN (
            ALL ( Date[Year] ),
            ALL ( Date[Month] )
        ),
        OR (
            AND ( Date[Year] = 2007, Date[Month] = "January" ),
            AND ( Date[Year] = 2006, Date[Month] = "December" )
        )
    )
)
```

The filter argument of *CALCULATE* is the following list of tuples:

```
« Year=2006, Month=December »
« Year=2007, Month=January »
```

A list of tuples is a filter. A filter is not yet a filter context. A filter context is, indeed, a set of filters. In fact, if you look at the following code:

```
CALCULATE (
    …
    FILTER (
        CROSSJOIN (
            ALL ( Date[Year] ),
            ALL ( Date[Month] )
        ),
        OR (
            AND ( Date[Year] = 2007, Date[Month] = "January" ),
            AND ( Date[Year] = 2006, Date[Month] = "December" )
        )
    ),
    OR ( Product[Color] = "Black", Product[Color] = "Yellow" )
)
```

The resulting filter context contains two different sets of tuples: one filtering two columns from the Date table and another one filtering the product color. Graphically, a filter is identical to a table. To make the difference between a filter and a table more evident, we use a filter icon whenever the tables in a figure represent a filter. The filter produced by the previous formula is visible in Figure 10-24.

Year	Month
2007	January
2006	December

Color
Black
Yellow

FIGURE 10-24 Filters are represented as tables, with a filter icon to highlight their role.

A set of filters, such as the one in Figure 10-24, is a filter context. A filter context is very similar to a set of tables. We say that a column is filtered by a filter context if it belongs to one of its filters. Thus, in the example the three columns, year, month, and color, belong to the filter context.

At first sight, a tuple looks like a normal row and a filter looks like a table. In reality, the two concepts are very similar but we prefer to use different names because of their use. For instance, in the previous code, the result of *FILTER* is a table. It becomes a filter context only when you use it as a filter argument for *CALCULATE*. Then DAX transforms the table into a filter context and the individual rows of the table become tuples. The difference is subtle, yet we find it useful when describing the behavior of the filter context.

For example, there is a big difference between transforming a real table or the result of a *CROSSJOIN* into a filter. When you use a *CROSSJOIN* as filter context, the filter context contains the individual columns resulting from the *CROSSJOIN*, whereas when you use a full table as a filter context, the filter context will contain all the columns of the expanded version of the original table. If you look at the following two expressions, the filter arguments used in them have different tuples as a result:

```
CALCULATE (
    SUM ( Sales[Quantity] ),
    'Product Subcategory'[Subcategory] = "Radio"
)

CALCULATE (
    SUM ( Sales[Quantity] ),
    FILTER (
        'Product Subcategory',
        'Product Subcategory'[Subcategory] = "Radio"
    )
)
```

In fact, the first filter argument generates a filter context made of tuples with a single column:

```
« Subcategory = Radio »
```

Alternately, the second expression sets the filter on the table. In this way, the resulting filter context contains tuples with all the columns of the expanded version of subcategories:

```
«
    'Product Subcategory'[Subcategory] = Radio,
    'Product Subcategory'[ProductSubcategoryKey] = 3,
    'Product Subcategory'[ProductCategoryKey] = 1,
    'Product Category'[ProductCategoryKey] = 1,
    'Product Category'[Category] = Audio
»
```

As you learn in this chapter, that difference is very important and might be the cause of misunderstandings when using tables as filters.

Now that you learned what a tuple and a filter context are, it is time to define two operators that DAX uses on filter contexts. They are *INTERSECTION* and *OVERWRITE*.

Understanding filter context intersection

Given two filter contexts, A and B, the intersection of A and B is computed by adding the filters in A to the filters in B. Intersection is used by *CALCULATE* when it needs to merge its filter arguments.

Some examples are very useful to clarify the concept. Look at the following expression:

```
CALCULATETABLE (
    …
    Date[Year] = 2008,
    OR (
        Product[Color] = "Black",
        Product[Color] = "Yellow"
    )
)
```

There are two filters, one on Year and the other one on Color. We have always said that filter arguments of *CALCULATE* are combined with *AND*, but now that we are speaking about tuples, we can be more specific and say that they are combined with intersection. In fact, the resulting filter context is visible in Figure 10-25.

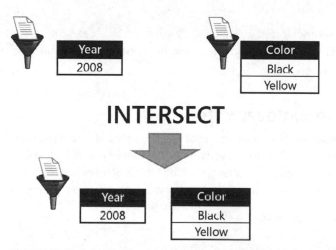

FIGURE 10-25 Intersection of two filters is the union of the filters, that is, a logical *AND* between them.

Intersection is a very simple operation and, in fact, you can think of an intersection as a simple *AND* operation between the sets defined by the filters. Moreover, an intersection has the beautiful feature that it works fine with complex filters. In fact, if you look at the following expression, you will note that the Date table is filtered by two conditions, using a completely different pattern. The first condition filters January 2007 and December 2006, and the second condition filters only dates where the quantity sold is greater than 100 (regardless of the year and month). Yet an intersection leads to a correct calculation (January 2007 and December 2006 for only the days where quantity sold is greater than the given value of 100).

```
CALCULATE (
    …
    FILTER (
        CROSSJOIN (
            ALL ( Date[Year] ),
            ALL ( Date[Month] )
        ),
        OR (
            AND ( Date[Year] = 2007, Date[Month] = "January" ),
            AND ( Date[Year] = 2006, Date[Month] = "December" )
        )
    ),
    FILTER (
        ALL ( Date[Date] ),
        CALCULATE ( SUM (Sales[Quantity] ) ) > 100)
    )
)
```

Finally, intersection is symmetric: A intersected with B leads to the same result as B intersected with A. This is expected, but as you learn in the next section, the overwrite operator is not symmetric and you will need to use it with more care.

Understanding filter context overwrite

Now that you have learned the intersection operation, it is time to introduce the second operation that DAX can perform on filter contexts: *OVERWRITE*. Overwrite is the operator used by *CALCULATE* when it merges the new filter context, computed by intersecting its filter arguments, with the previous filter context, to create the new filter context under which it computes its expression.

As an example, look at the following expression:

```
CALCULATE (
    CALCULATE (
        …,
        Product[Color] = "Yellow"
    ),
    Product[Color] = "Black"
)
```

The inner *CALCULATE* overwrites the previous filter and, in fact, DAX computes the result for the yellow color, ignoring the filter on black. This is expected but it shows that, in this case, the two filter contexts are not combined using intersection, but instead are using the overwrite operator.

Overwrite is simple in its definition but leads to very complex scenarios when used in DAX formulas whenever you have nontrivial filters. Let us start with its definition:

In computing A overwrite B, we use B for the previous filter context and A for the filter context which overwrites B. This makes it easier to read the sentence "A overwrites B" because the new filter (A) overwrites the old filter (B). In the previous example, A is yellow and B is black.

To compute A overwrite B, DAX does two operations:

1. It removes from all the filters in B the columns filtered in A, generating a new filter context that we call B-Cleaned.

2. It intersects A with B-Cleaned.

In the previous example, the B filter contained black. B-Cleaned becomes empty because DAX removes the only column present (*Color*) and finally generates the new filter context that contains only the filter on yellow. In Figure 10-26 you can see a graphical representation of the overwrite operation.

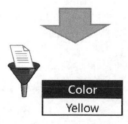

FIGURE 10-26 Overwrite semantics removes columns from B and then intersects the resulting filter with A.

Overwrite is a powerful operator, but it requires much more attention. In fact, it works in an intuitive way as long as the filters are well shaped while, for arbitrarily shaped filters, it starts to be much more complex. Before moving on with the description, it is now time to introduce arbitrarily shaped filters, because they play an important role in the explanation.

Understanding arbitrarily shaped filters

A well-shaped filter is a filter that you can express as the *CROSSJOIN* of single-column filters. An example of a well-shaped filter is as follows:

```
CALCULATETABLE (
    ...
    OR (
        Date[Year] = 2007,
        Date[Year] = 2006
    ),
    OR (
        Product[Color] = "Black",
        Product[Color] = "Yellow"
    )
)
```

In fact, the previous filter is equivalent to this one:

```
CALCULATETABLE (
    ...
    CROSSJOIN (
        FILTER (
            ALL ( Date[Year] ),
            OR (
                Date[Year] = 2007,
                Date[Year] = 2006
            )
        ),
        FILTER (
            ALL (Product[Color] ),
            OR (
                Product[Color] = "Black",
                Product[Color] = "Yellow"
            )
        )
    )
)
```

You can easily represent graphically a well-shaped filter as a set of filters on individual columns, as you can see in Figure 10-27.

Year	Color
2007	Black
2006	Yellow

FIGURE 10-27 You can represent well-shaped filters as filters on individual columns.

Well-shaped filters always lead to simple expressions and both intersection and overwrite work in an intuitive way with well-shaped filters.

An arbitrarily shaped filter, on the other hand, is a filter that is not well shaped. In other words, you cannot express arbitrarily shaped filters as the *CROSSJOIN* of filters on individual columns. We previously used (by intent) an arbitrarily shaped filter, which you can see in the following expression:

```
CALCULATE (
    ...
    FILTER (
        CROSSJOIN (
            VALUES ( Date[Year] ),
            VALUES ( Date[Month] )
        ),
        OR (
            AND ( Date[Year] = 2007, Date[Month] = "January" ),
            AND ( Date[Year] = 2006, Date[Month] = "December" )
        )
    )
)
```

The result of this filter is visible in Figure 10-28. As you can see, you cannot show the filter as two separate columns. Instead, you need to put the columns in the same table, because they have a relationship which is stored in the filter itself.

Year	Month
2007	January
2006	December

FIGURE 10-28 An arbitrarily shaped filter is not the *CROSSJOIN* of simple column filters.

You cannot express the filter containing one month in 2007 and one month in 2006 as the *CROSS-JOIN* of simpler filters. In fact, DAX can evaluate the filter only by taking into account the two columns together. That is to say, an arbitrarily shaped filter defines a relationship between its columns. In fact, we call a filter (or more generically, a table) a *relation* in academic papers. We preferred to avoid this term in the book because it conflicts with the more widely used concept of relationship between tables. Yet a table (and a filter, in this case) defines a relationship between columns.

Arbitrarily shaped filters become a problem with the overwrite semantics. In fact, while intersection works perfectly fine with arbitrarily shaped filters, overwrite leads to much more complex scenarios. As an example, let us take the previous expression and add to another condition on the year, as in:

```
CALCULATE (
    …
    FILTER (
        CROSSJOIN (
            VALUES ( Date[Year] ),
            VALUES ( Date[Month] )
        ),
        OR (
            AND ( Date[Year] = 2007, Date[Month] = "January" ),
            AND ( Date[Year] = 2006, Date[Month] = "December" )
        )
    ),
    Date[Year] = 2007
)
```

As you might expect, this expression computes the value for January 2007 because the first filter returns January 2007 and December 2006 that, intersected with the second filter, returns only January 2007. In Figure 10-29 you can see the graphical representation of intersection.

INTERSECT

FIGURE 10-29 Intersection with arbitrarily shaped filters works just fine.

Things become different if you write the same expression in this way:

```
CALCULATE (
    CALCULATE (
        …
        Date[Year] = 2007
    ),
    FILTER (
        CROSSJOIN (
            VALUES ( Date[Year] ),
            VALUES ( Date[Month] )
        ),
        OR (
            AND ( Date[Year] = 2007, Date[Month] = "January" ),
            AND ( Date[Year] = 2006, Date[Month] = "December" )
        )
    )
)
```

In this last expression, we moved the filter on the year in an inner *CALCULATE*. The difference between the previous version and this last one is that now *CALCULATE* uses overwrite to merge the two filters. Overwrite removes the calendar year from the first filter, leaving only the filter on the month label, and it then intersects this filter with the filter on the year, as you can see in Figure 10-30.

FIGURE 10-30 Applying overwrite to an arbitrarily shaped set might lead to unexpected results.

The resulting filter now contains January and December 2007, because the new filter on the *Year* removed the column *Year* from the previous filter. In doing this it destroyed the relationship stored in the filter and replaced it with a well-shaped filter, which is not what you might have expected when writing the formula.

As a rule, we can state the following: Both intersect and overwrite work in an intuitive way when used on well-shaped filters. When working with arbitrarily shaped filters, intersect preserves their shape by intersecting their results, while overwrite might disrupt the filter generating a result which lost some of the relationships stored in the original filters.

> ### More on *KEEPFILTERS*
>
> In a previous section of this chapter, you learned the behavior of *KEEPFILTERS*. We gave that description before speaking about filter contexts and operators so that we could start speaking about arbitrarily shaped filters and to avoid introducing the whole complexity of filter context before introducing *KEEPFILTERS*.
>
> Now that you have a solid understanding of filter contexts and filter context operators, you can think of *KEEPFILTERS* in a much simpler way: When you use *KEEPFILTERS* you are asking *CALCULATE* to merge the new filter context with the previous one using intersect instead of overwrite. The result is that you will keep arbitrarily shaped sets intact, because intersect preserves them, whereas overwrite potentially destroys them.

Understanding the *ALL* function

We used the *ALL* function extensively in most of the code written so far, yet there is still something to learn about it. In fact, you learned that *ALL* returns all the values of one or more columns, or of an entire table, depending on its parameter(s). While this holds true when you use *ALL* as a table function, its behavior, when used as a filter argument in *CALCULATE*, is a different one. It is so different that we think its name should have been another one, that is, *REMOVEFILTER*. Let us elaborate on this.

When you write an expression such as the following, you trust the fact that *ALL*, as a table function, returns all the values of the calendar year. This new filter replaces the previous one and produces a filter context containing all the possible values for the year:

```
CALCULATE (
    CALCULATE (
        …
        ALL ( Date[Year] )
    ),
    Date[Year] = 2007
)
```

Unfortunately, this is not the way it works. What *ALL* does, when used as a filter argument in *CALCULATE*, is not that of returning all the values of a column. Instead, it removes the column from the filter context. This is the reason why we suggested the name of *REMOVEFILTER*.

The difference is subtle but, as you learn in this section, it is an important one. If *ALL* returned all the years, you would have expected the behavior shown in Figure 10-31.

FIGURE 10-31 You might expect *ALL* to return all the values of a table, but this is not what happens.

In reality, when *ALL* is a top-level function in a filter argument of *CALCULATE*, it removes the columns on which it works from the filter context. Thus, the resulting behavior is the one shown in Figure 10-32.

FIGURE 10-32 *ALL* removes the filter from the column on which it works, resulting in an empty filter.

At first sight, it looks as if there is no difference between the two operations. In reality, the behavior is very different and to make it more evident, we need to create some complex filters. As you already learned, when a table is transformed in a filter, the filter contains the expanded version of the table. Therefore, you know that the following measure calculates the number of dates referenced in the Sales table:

```
[NumberOfSales] :=
CALCULATE (
    COUNTROWS ( 'Date' ),
    Sales
)
```

In fact, the expanded version of Sales contains all the columns of the Date table (because of the relationship). Using the whole Sales table as a filter, you effectively filter the Date table and the result (1,096) is the total number of dates in the Date table that are referenced from Sales.

What is less evident is the fact that you might expect this other formulation of the same measure to behave the same way:

```
[NumberOfSalesWithAll] :=
CALCULATE (
    COUNTROWS ( 'Date' ),
    ALL ( Sales )
)
```

The only difference is that, this time, we used *ALL* around Sales in the filter argument of *CALCULATE*. If *ALL* returned all the rows of Sales, the two measures would behave in the same way. Nevertheless, this is not what happens. You should read *ALL* as *REMOVEFILTERS*. *ALL* removes all the columns of Sales from the current filter context before evaluating *COUNTROWS*. Because the current filter context does not contain any filter, *ALL* does nothing at all, that is, it does not modify the filter context. In fact, the result of *NumberOfSalesWithAll* is not the number of referenced dates. Instead, it returns 2,556: the total number of dates in the Date table.

It is worth it to note that *ALL* behaves as *REMOVEFILTERS* only when you use it as a top-level parameter in a filter argument of *CALCULATE*. When you use it as a regular table function, it does exactly what it is supposed to do: It returns a table. Thus, if you write the measure in the following way, you will get the expected result.

```
[NumberOfSalesWithAllAndFilter] :=
CALCULATE (
    COUNTROWS ( 'Date' ),
    FILTER ( ALL ( Sales ), TRUE () )
)
```

In fact, this time you use *ALL* inside a *FILTER* operation and not as a top-level function in a filter argument. Because of this, *FILTER* iterates over the whole fact table and returns all of its rows. Then, because the full fact table is a filter argument of *CALCULATE*, it is expanded and used as a filter, in this way, reaching the Date table.

Understanding lineage

We introduced the concept of lineage in Chapter 9, "Advanced table functions." You have seen there that the result of a table function might preserve lineage or destroy it. For example, the following table preserves lineage, because it only renames a column:

```
SELECTCOLUMNS (
    Product,
    "NewNameForProductKey",
    Product[ProductKey]
)
```

If, on the other hand, you use an expression instead of a column name, then you kill the lineage of the column, meaning that the resulting table is no longer linked to the original one. For instance, the following expression is no longer a table of Product[ProductKey]. It becomes a table of values:

```
SELECTCOLUMNS (
    Product,
    "NewNameForProductKey",
    Product[ProductKey] + 0
)
```

This difference is very important when you use a table as a filter in the filter context. In fact, you can use any table as a filter in the filter context, but the columns without lineage corresponding to a physical column of the data model will be ignored.

Imagine, for example, that you write a query such as the following one:

```
EVALUATE
ROW (
    "Result", CALCULATE (
        SUM ( Sales[Quantity] ),
        UNION (
            ROW ( "Column1", "DAX" ),
            ROW ( "Column1", "IS" ),
            ROW ( "Column1", "SIMPLE" )
        )
    )
)
```

The table defined with *UNION* is just a table, so you can use it as a filter parameter in *CALCULATE*. Nevertheless, because the columns in the table have no lineage pointing to a physical column in the data model, the table has no relationships with other tables and filtering it makes no sense, because it will not affect any value in the model. Thus, when the engine analyzes the filter arguments of *CALCULATE* to create the filter context, it ignores columns with lineage not pointing to a physical column. In other words, such a filter is completely useless.

The same happens when you use a table function that makes you lose the lineage of a column. Look, for example, at the following query:

```
EVALUATE
ROW (
    "Result", CALCULATE (
        SUM ( Sales[Quantity] ),
        CALCULATETABLE (
            SELECTCOLUMNS ( Product, "MyProductBrand", Product[Brand] ),
            Product[Color] = "Red"
        )
    )
)
```

The inner *CALCULATETABLE* returns a table containing a single column, named *MyProductBrand*, which is just a renamed version of *Product[Brand]*, for only the red products. Even if the column is named *MyProductBrand*, it preserves the lineage and the engine knows that, in reality, this is a table of *Product[Brand]*. Thus, when it merges this table in the filter context, it filters Sales, returning the amount of sales for only the brands that have at least one red product.

If you change the query by replacing *Product[Brand]* with an expression, then you lose lineage and the following query returns the sales of all products, because the table resulting from *SELECTCOLUMNS* no longer has a lineage that links it to *Product[Brand]*:

```
EVALUATE
ROW (
    "Result", CALCULATE (
        SUM ( Sales[Quantity] ),
        CALCULATETABLE (
            SELECTCOLUMNS ( Product, "MyProductBrand", Product[Brand] & ""),
            Product[Color] = "Red"
        )
    )
)
```

Understanding lineage is helpful to understand why, for example, the following query returns two different values in *Inner Sales* and *Outer Sales*:

```
EVALUATE
ADDCOLUMNS (
    SELECTCOLUMNS (
        ADDCOLUMNS (
            SUMMARIZE (
                'Date',
                'Date'[Calendar Year],
                'Date'[Month]
            ),
            "YYYYMM", [Calendar Year] & " - " & [Month]
        ),
        "YYYYMM", [YYYYMM],
        "Inner Sales", CALCULATE ( SUM ( Sales[Quantity] ) )
    ),
    "Outer Sales", CALCULATE ( SUM ( Sales[Quantity] ) )
)
```

In the previous expression, *Inner Sales* runs in a filter context containing year and month, whereas *Outer Sales* has a filter context containing only the newly introduced *YYYYMM* column that, having no lineage, cannot filter Sales, as you can see in Figure 10-33.

YYYYMM	Inner Sales	Outer Sales
CY 2005 – January		17538016
CY 2006 – January		17538016
CY 2007 – January	496440	17538016
CY 2008 – January	364833	17538016
CY 2009 – January	516948	17538016
CY 2010 – January		17538016
CY 2011 – January		17538016
CY 2005 – February		17538016
CY 2006 – February		17538016
CY 2007 – February	477875	17538016
CY 2008 – February	366501	17538016
CY 2009 – February	495871	17538016

FIGURE 10-33 The result of *Inner Sales* and *Outer Sales* is different, due to different filter contexts.

Using advanced SetFilter

All the theory outlined so far becomes useful when you need to author any nontrivial formula. As an example, you are going to analyze a simple scenario, which has many complexities because of the filter context interactions.

Imagine that you receive some form of contract request (loans, for example). You receive the request, take some time to validate it and, at the end, you either approve or deny it. The data model is a very simple one, consisting of only two tables: Contracts and Date, as you can see in Figure 10-34.

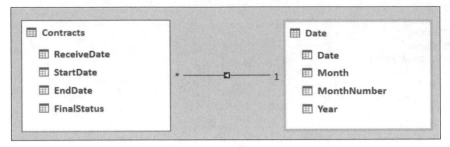

FIGURE 10-34 The example data model contains only contracts and dates.

The relationship between the two tables is based on *ReceiveDate*, to compute the number of contracts received over time. On this data model, you want to create a new measure that computes the number of pending contracts for each date. You start validating the contract at *StartDate* and the validation ends at *EndDate*. During that period, the contract is in a pending state. This number gives a rough estimate of the amount of work that the validation office has to perform. The measure should report:

■ The number of pending contracts of a date, if the date is in the pivot table.

■ The number of pending contracts as of today, on the grand total, or when the user does not select a specific date.

You start by creating two measures that compute the boundaries of the count. Using *ISFILTERED* you check if the Date table has an active filter and, based on this, you return either *TODAY* or the first or last date, with the following two measures:

```
[FirstDate] :=
IF (
    ISCROSSFILTERED ( 'Date'[Date] ),
    MIN ( 'Date'[Date] ),
    TODAY ()
)

[LastDate] :=
IF (
    ISCROSSFILTERED ( 'Date'[Date] ),
    MAX ( 'Date'[Date] ),
    TODAY ()
)
```

The next step is to count the number of contracts whose *StartDate* is earlier or equal than *FirstDate*, and *EndDate* is later or equal than *LastDate*. Instead of showing the process of writing the measure, we show first the correct result, analyzing it in detail. Then, after the correct code, we will show you several variations of the same expression, which all turn out to be wrong, due to some mistakes in the context propagation.

It would be very useful if you now take some time (10 minutes is a fair time) to think of how you would write the formula, before continuing to read.

The correct formulation of the *OpenContracts* measure is the following one:

```
1    OpenContracts :=
2    SUMX (
3        FILTER (
4            CALCULATETABLE (
5                ADDCOLUMNS (
6                    SUMMARIZE (
7                        Contracts,
8                        Contracts[StartDate],
9                        Contracts[EndDate]
10                   ),
11                   "NumOfContracts", CALCULATE ( COUNTROWS ( Contracts ) )
12               ),
13               ALL ( 'Date' )
14           ),
15           AND (
16               Contracts[StartDate] <= [FirstDate],
17               Contracts[EndDate] >= [LastDate]
18           )
19       ),
20       [NumOfContracts]
21   )
```

Let us start analyzing the code to understand how it computes the desired value.

When you analyze a DAX expression, starting from the innermost part is always a good idea. The innermost function here is *SUMMARIZE* (lines 6–10). It generates a table containing the existing combinations of *StartDate* and *EndDate* from the Contracts table. Later on, *ADDCOLUMNS* (lines 5–12) adds a column to that table with the number of contracts for each pair of dates. The result of this *ADDCOLUMNS* function call is visible in Figure 10-35.

StartDate	EndDate	NumOfContracts
1/2/2015	1/10/2015	1
1/2/2015	1/11/2015	1
1/3/2015	1/15/2015	1
1/3/2015	1/10/2015	4
1/4/2015	1/10/2015	1
1/4/2015	1/17/2015	1
1/4/2015	1/7/2015	2
1/5/2015	1/7/2015	1

FIGURE 10-35 The result of *ADDCOLUMNS* contains *StartDate*, *EndDate,* and *NumOfContracts*.

It is worth noting that *ADDCOLUMNS* is called inside a *CALCULATETABLE* that removes any filter from the date, to get rid of the filtering that might happen because the user selected a specific date or period. Thus, regardless of the outer filter on the date, this table always returns the same result.

Then *FILTER* (lines 3–19) removes from this table the rows where *StartDate* is not earlier than *FirstDate*, and *EndDate* is not later than *LastDate*, by calling the two measures defined earlier. The final step is *SUMX* (lines 2–21), which sums all the *NumOfContracts* of the remaining rows in the table, after that *FILTER* removed the unwanted ones.

The measure computes the correct values, as you can see in the report in Figure 10-36. Please note that, for the reports, we used February 17, 2015, as the date for *TODAY*.

Row Labels	OpenContracts
⊟ **February**	
2/1/2015	82
2/2/2015	77
2/3/2015	75
2/4/2015	73
2/5/2015	67
2/6/2015	63
2/7/2015	58
2/8/2015	51
2/9/2015	44
2/10/2015	38
2/11/2015	36
2/12/2015	29
2/13/2015	19
2/14/2015	16
2/15/2015	12
2/16/2015	9
2/17/2015	3
2/18/2015	2
2/19/2015	2
2/20/2015	2
2/21/2015	1
Grand Total	**3**

FIGURE 10-36 *OpenContracts* reports the number of contracts being validated in each date.

At the Grand Total, the number reported is the number of today's contracts, dates after today are a forecast. There is still a problem with February, where there is no value shown. In fact, for periods larger than one day, the number still needs a definition. Based on your specific needs, you could either use the average of the days, the value on the last day of the period, or another definition. For what concerns this exercise, we are not interested in computing values at the aggregate level (apart from the Grand Total). Rather, we want to analyze different formulations of the same measure highlighting the reasons why they will report the wrong number. Maybe the formula that you tried to write before looking at the solution falls into one of the categories we will show.

The first simple, bad formula is the following:

```
[OpenContracts] :=
COUNTROWS (
    FILTER (
        ALL ( Contracts ),
        AND (
            Contracts[StartDate] <= [FirstDate],
            Contracts[EndDate] >= [LastDate]
        )
    )
)
```

This formula always returns the same number, regardless of any selection, as you can see in the report in Figure 10-37.

OpenContracts Row Labels	Column Labels Accepted	Denied	Grand Total
⊞ January	28	28	28
⊟ February	28	28	28
2/1/2015	28	28	28
2/2/2015	28	28	28
2/3/2015	28	28	28
2/4/2015	28	28	28
2/5/2015	28	28	28
2/6/2015	28	28	28
2/7/2015	28	28	28
2/8/2015	28	28	28

FIGURE 10-37 The simplest formula of *OpenContracts* reports wrong results.

There are two different problems in this formula. First, we had to use *ALL (Contracts)* to get rid of the filter from the date (which filters the contracts based on the receive date), but this *ALL* removed the filter from the contract status, too, as you can see from the pivot table where both Accepted and Denied report the same number. You might try to solve it by replacing *ALL (Contracts)* with a more granular *CALCULATETABLE*, as in the following code:

```
OpenContracts :=
COUNTROWS (
    FILTER (
        CALCULATETABLE ( Contracts, ALL ( Date ) ),
        AND (
            Contracts[StartDate] <= [FirstDate],
            Contracts[EndDate] >= [LastDate]
        )
    )
)
```

Yet this code still does not solve the issue. In fact, context transition is happening inside the *FILTER*, so that *FirstDate* and *LastDate* show only the dates related to the current contract being filtered. In order to avoid context transition, you need to filter individual columns, not the table. This is the reason for which we used the expression:

```
SUMMARIZE (
    Contracts,
    Contracts[StartDate],
    Contracts[EndDate]
)
```

In fact, this expression contains only *StartDate* and *EndDate*. When context transition happens, it applies to the two columns only, not to the expanded table. It is worth mentioning that the expanded version of Contracts contains all the columns of Date.

Variables to avoid context transition

Using variables, you can avoid context transition by computing the value of *FirstDate* and *Last-Date* before entering the *FILTER loop*. In fact, the following code works fine (we did not show it at the beginning for educational purposes only):

```
[OpenContracts] :=
VAR First = [FirstDate]
VAR Last  = [LastDate]
RETURN
    COUNTROWS (
        FILTER (
            CALCULATETABLE ( Contracts, ALL ( Date ) ),
            AND (
                Contracts[StartDate] <= First,
                Contracts[EndDate] >= Last
            )
        )
    )
```

Using *SUMMARIZE*, you can generate a table that you can later iterate on avoiding the problem of context transition, but you still have to pay attention to some details. For example, as in the following formulation:

```
[OpenContracts] :=
SUMX (
    FILTER (
        ADDCOLUMNS (
            SUMMARIZE (
                CALCULATETABLE ( Contracts, ALL ( 'Date' ) ),
                Contracts[StartDate],
                Contracts[EndDate]
            ),
            "NumOfContracts", CALCULATE ( COUNTROWS ( Contracts ) )
        ),
        AND (
            Contracts[StartDate] <= [FirstDate],
            Contracts[EndDate] >= [LastDate]
        )
    ),
    [NumOfContracts]
)
```

This last version is very similar to the correct one. The only difference is that the *CALCULATETABLE* is put around Contracts only, as the innermost function. The problem with this formula is that the *NumOfContracts* column added by *ADDCOLUMN* is computed in a filter context that contains the current *StartDate* and *EndDate* iterated by *ADDCOLUMN* plus the original filter context of the report, which contains a single date. Thus, the resulting number of contracts will not be correct.

As you have seen with this example, DAX is particularly powerful and it can be used to compute very complex measures if you pay close attention to the details of context propagation and context transition. In fact, when authoring the code for the *OpenContracts* measure, if you slightly change the order of function calls or miss the intricacies of context transition, you are quite likely to produce a measure that does not compute a correct value.

You cannot expect, in your first try, to write a measure correctly as done in the previous example. At the beginning, you will make mistakes and might see incorrect results. With more experience, you will understand the interactions between row context, filter context, relationships, and context transition, and you will write correct formulas on your first attempt.

Learning and mastering evaluation contexts

Evaluation contexts are hard to fully understand. They not only require you to learn some new concepts, they really require you to alter what you know when writing code. This is, in our experience, the hard part of DAX: changing the way you think and start thinking in DAX.

If you found the whole chapter a tough one, and you had to read it again and again, that is very normal; you are in good company. This company includes us, the authors. We started learning DAX in 2010 and we are writing this book in 2015. Unbelievably, it took us five years to master the code of DAX and of the engine, with a lot of discussions and meetings with the development team in the meantime.

The good news is that these concepts, once fixed in your mind, are unlikely to go away and be forgotten: They will stay with you and help you come out from very complex formulas with a smile on your face—the smile of someone who knows that he or she really understands what is happening under the cover.

We did our best to explain the internals of evaluation contexts and give you a clear view of how they work, yet we know that our best is probably not enough. Our suggestion is to read this chapter multiple times, until you can read it very fast, because you totally understand it. Doing that is still hard for us, too.

Handling hierarchies

DAX does not have any built-in function that provides calculations over hierarchies between attributes and entities. However, the underlying data model can include the definition of hierarchies used by client tools to simplify the browsing experience over data. A data model supports only regular hierarchies between columns of the same table, and does not have a native support for parent-child hierarchies.

In this chapter, you will learn how to create calculations over hierarchies and how to use DAX to transform a parent-child hierarchy into a regular hierarchy managed by the data model.

Computing percentages over hierarchies

When you have a hierarchy in the data model, a common requirement is a measure that has a different behavior depending on the level of the item selected, such as a ratio to parent that displays, for each member, the percentage of that member against its parent.

For instance, consider a hierarchy made by product category, subcategory, and product name. A ratio to parent calculation shows the percentage of a category against the grand total, of a subcategory against the total of its category, and of a product against its subcategory.

You can see an example of this report in Figure 11-1.

In Microsoft Excel, you might create such a measure by using the pivot table feature Show Values As, so that the computation is performed by Excel. However, if you want to use such a calculation regardless of specific features of the client you use, you can create a new measure that performs the computation, so that the value is computed in the data model.

Row Labels	Sales Amount	PercOfParent
⊟Audio	$422,177.88	1.25%
⊞Bluetooth Headphones	$136,912.18	32.43%
⊞MP4&MP3	$185,016.40	43.82%
⊞Recording Pen	$100,249.30	23.75%
⊞Cameras and camcorders	$7,901,783.67	23.45%
⊞Cell phones	$1,771,028.66	5.26%
⊟Computers	$7,435,548.25	22.07%
⊞Computers Accessories	$373,133.70	5.02%
⊞Desktops	$1,121,379.90	15.08%
⊞Laptops	$2,119,895.65	28.51%
⊞Monitors	$655,436.00	8.81%
⊞Printers, Scanners & Fax	$556,053.00	7.48%
⊞Projectors & Screens	$2,609,650.00	35.10%
⊞Games and Toys	$397,137.75	1.18%
⊞Home Appliances	$10,571,029.88	31.38%
⊞Music, Movies and Audio Books	$347,189.01	1.03%
⊞TV and Video	$4,844,253.41	14.38%
Grand Total	$33,690,148.51	100.00%

FIGURE 11-1 The *PercOfParent* measure is useful to better understand the values in a table.

Unfortunately, performing such a calculation in DAX is not so easy. Before we start, it is worth pointing out the first big limitation that we will have in DAX: There is no way to build a generic percentage-to-parent measure that works on any arbitrary combination of columns in a report. The reason is that, inside DAX, there is no way to know how the report has been created, or how the hierarchy has been used in the client tool.

Even if you cannot write a generic formula, you can create some measures that compute the correct percentages when used in a proper way. Because the hierarchy has three levels (category, subcategory, and product), you can start with three different measures, one for each level, as in the following code:

```
[PercOfSubcategory] :=
[Sales Amount] / CALCULATE ( [Sales Amount], ALL ( Product[Product Name] ) )

[PercOfCategory] :=
[Sales Amount] / CALCULATE ( [Sales Amount], ALL ( Product[Subcategory] ) )

[PercOfTotal] :=
[Sales Amount] / CALCULATE ( [Sales Amount], ALL ( Product[Category] ) )
```

These three measures compute the needed percentages. Putting them into a pivot table leads to the result shown in Figure 11-2.

Row Labels	Sales Amount	PercOfTotal	PercOfCategory	PercOfSubcategory
⊟Audio	$422,177.88	1.25 %	100.00 %	100.00 %
⊞Bluetooth Headphones	$136,912.18	100.00 %	32.43 %	100.00 %
⊞MP4&MP3	$185,016.40	100.00 %	43.82 %	100.00 %
⊟Recording Pen	$100,249.30	100.00 %	23.75 %	100.00 %
WWI 1GB Digital Voice Recorder Pen E100 Black	$2,964.00	100.00 %	100.00 %	2.96 %
WWI 1GB Digital Voice Recorder Pen E100 Pink	$3,744.00	100.00 %	100.00 %	3.73 %
WWI 1GB Pulse Smart pen E50 Silver	$4,198.60	100.00 %	100.00 %	4.19 %
WWI 1GB Pulse Smart pen E50 White	$3,898.70	100.00 %	100.00 %	3.89 %
WWI 1GBPulse Smart pen E50 Black	$16,344.55	100.00 %	100.00 %	16.30 %
WWI 2GB Pulse Smart pen M100 Black	$5,398.65	100.00 %	100.00 %	5.39 %
WWI 2GB Pulse Smart pen M100 Blue	$5,598.60	100.00 %	100.00 %	5.58 %
WWI 2GB Pulse Smart pen M100 Silver	$20,394.90	100.00 %	100.00 %	20.34 %
WWI 2GB Pulse Smart pen M100 White	$14,796.30	100.00 %	100.00 %	14.76 %
WWI 2GB Spy Video Recorder Pen M300 Blue	$724.00	100.00 %	100.00 %	0.72 %
WWI 2GB Spy Video Recorder Pen M300 Silver	$3,258.00	100.00 %	100.00 %	3.25 %
WWI 2GB Spy Video Recorder Pen M300 White	$2,353.00	100.00 %	100.00 %	2.35 %
WWI 4GB Video Recording Pen X200 Pink	$9,176.00	100.00 %	100.00 %	9.15 %
WWI 4GB Video Recording Pen X200 Yellow	$7,400.00	100.00 %	100.00 %	7.38 %
⊞Cameras and camcorders	$7,901,783.67	23.45 %	100.00 %	100.00 %
⊞Cell phones	$1,771,028.66	5.26 %	100.00 %	100.00 %
⊟Computers	$7,435,548.25	22.07 %	100.00 %	100.00 %
⊞Computers Accessories	$373,133.70	100.00 %	5.02 %	100.00 %
⊞Desktops	$1,121,379.90	100.00 %	15.08 %	100.00 %
⊞Laptops	$2,119,895.65	100.00 %	28.51 %	100.00 %
⊞Monitors	$655,436.00	100.00 %	8.81 %	100.00 %
⊞Printers, Scanners & Fax	$556,053.00	100.00 %	7.48 %	100.00 %
⊞Projectors & Screens	$2,609,650.00	100.00 %	35.10 %	100.00 %
⊞Games and Toys	$397,137.75	1.18 %	100.00 %	100.00 %
⊞Home Appliances	$10,571,029.88	31.38 %	100.00 %	100.00 %
⊞Music, Movies and Audio Books	$347,189.01	1.03 %	100.00 %	100.00 %
⊞TV and Video	$4,844,253.41	14.38 %	100.00 %	100.00 %
Grand Total	$33,690,148.51	100.00 %	100.00 %	100.00 %

FIGURE 11-2 The three measures work fine, but only at their specific level.

You can see that the measures show correct values only where they are meaningful. Otherwise, they show a useless 100 percent. Moreover, as of now, we have three different measures, but our goal is to have only one showing different percentages at different levels.

Let's start clearing the 100 percent out of the *PercOfSubcategory* measure. What you need to do is avoid performing the calculation if the hierarchy is not showing the *Product Name* column on rows. You can test whether a column is filtered or not by using *ISFILTERED*. In fact, when the product name is on the rows, it is filtered (usually it shows only one value out of all its possible ones). Thus, you can change the formula with this new expression:

```
[PercOfSubcategory] :=
IF (
    ISFILTERED ( Product[Product Name] ),
    [Sales Amount] / CALCULATE ( [Sales Amount], ALL ( Product[Product Name] ) )
)
```

Figure 11-3 shows the pivot table using this new formula.

Row Labels	Sales Amount	PercOfTotal	PercOfCategory	PercOfSubcategory
⊟Audio	$422,177.88	1.25 %	100.00 %	
⊞Bluetooth Headphones	$136,912.18	100.00 %	32.43 %	
⊞MP4&MP3	$185,016.40	100.00 %	43.82 %	
⊟Recording Pen	$100,249.30	100.00 %	23.75 %	
WWI 1GB Digital Voice Recorder Pen E100 Black	$2,964.00	100.00 %	100.00 %	2.96 %
WWI 1GB Digital Voice Recorder Pen E100 Pink	$3,744.00	100.00 %	100.00 %	3.73 %
WWI 1GB Pulse Smart pen E50 Silver	$4,198.60	100.00 %	100.00 %	4.19 %
WWI 1GB Pulse Smart pen E50 White	$3,898.70	100.00 %	100.00 %	3.89 %
WWI 1GBPulse Smart pen E50 Black	$16,344.55	100.00 %	100.00 %	16.30 %
WWI 2GB Pulse Smart pen M100 Black	$5,398.65	100.00 %	100.00 %	5.39 %
WWI 2GB Pulse Smart pen M100 Blue	$5,598.60	100.00 %	100.00 %	5.58 %
WWI 2GB Pulse Smart pen M100 Silver	$20,394.90	100.00 %	100.00 %	20.34 %
WWI 2GB Pulse Smart pen M100 White	$14,796.30	100.00 %	100.00 %	14.76 %
WWI 2GB Spy Video Recorder Pen M300 Blue	$724.00	100.00 %	100.00 %	0.72 %
WWI 2GB Spy Video Recorder Pen M300 Silver	$3,258.00	100.00 %	100.00 %	3.25 %
WWI 2GB Spy Video Recorder Pen M300 White	$2,353.00	100.00 %	100.00 %	2.35 %
WWI 4GB Video Recording Pen X200 Pink	$9,176.00	100.00 %	100.00 %	9.15 %
WWI 4GB Video Recording Pen X200 Yellow	$7,400.00	100.00 %	100.00 %	7.38 %
⊞Cameras and camcorders	$7,901,783.67	23.45 %	100.00 %	
⊞Cell phones	$1,771,028.66	5.26 %	100.00 %	
⊟Computers	$7,435,548.25	22.07 %	100.00 %	
⊞Computers Accessories	$373,133.70	100.00 %	5.02 %	
⊞Desktops	$1,121,379.90	100.00 %	15.08 %	
⊞Laptops	$2,119,895.65	100.00 %	28.51 %	
⊞Monitors	$655,436.00	100.00 %	8.81 %	
⊞Printers, Scanners & Fax	$556,053.00	100.00 %	7.48 %	
⊞Projectors & Screens	$2,609,650.00	100.00 %	35.10 %	
⊞Games and Toys	$397,137.75	1.18 %	100.00 %	
⊞Home Appliances	$10,571,029.88	31.38 %	100.00 %	
⊞Music, Movies and Audio Books	$347,189.01	1.03 %	100.00 %	
⊞TV and Video	$4,844,253.41	14.38 %	100.00 %	
Grand Total	$33,690,148.51	100.00 %	100.00 %	

FIGURE 11-3 Using *ISFILTERED*, you remove the useless 100 percent values from the *PercOfSubcategory* column.

Using the same technique, you can remove the 100 percent from the other measures. Beware of the fact that, in *PercOfCategory*, you need to check that *Subcategory* is filtered and *Product Name* is not. This is because when you filter by *Product Name* using the hierarchy, you are also filtering a *Subcategory*, displaying a product rather than a subcategory. In order to avoid duplicated code to check these conditions, you can write a single measure that executes a different operation depending on the level of the hierarchy that is visible based on the *ISFILTERED* conditions tested from the bottom to the top of the hierarchy levels. Here is the final code for the *PercOfParent* measure:

```
PercOfParent :=
IF (
    ISFILTERED ( Product[Product Name] ),
    [Sales Amount] / CALCULATE ( [Sales Amount], ALL ( Product[Product Name] ) ),
    IF (
        ISFILTERED ( Product[Subcategory] ),
        [Sales Amount] / CALCULATE ( [Sales Amount], ALL ( Product[Subcategory] ) ),
        IF (
            ISFILTERED ( Product[Category] ),
            [Sales Amount] / CALCULATE ( [Sales Amount], ALL ( Product[Category] ) )
        )
    )
)
```

Using the *PercOfParent* measure, you obtain the desired result, which you can see in Figure 11-4.

Row Labels	Sales Amount	PercOfParent
⊟ Audio	$422,177.88	1.25 %
⊞ Bluetooth Headphones	$136,912.18	32.43 %
⊞ MP4 & MP3	$185,016.40	43.82 %
⊟ Recording Pen	$100,249.30	23.75 %
WWI 1GB Digital Voice Recorder Pen E100 Black	$2,964.00	2.96 %
WWI 1GB Digital Voice Recorder Pen E100 Pink	$3,744.00	3.73 %
WWI 1GB Pulse Smart pen E50 Silver	$4,198.60	4.19 %
WWI 1GB Pulse Smart pen E50 White	$3,898.70	3.89 %
WWI 1GB Pulse Smart pen E50 Black	$16,344.55	16.30 %
WWI 2GB Pulse Smart pen M100 Black	$5,398.65	5.39 %
WWI 2GB Pulse Smart pen M100 Blue	$5,598.60	5.58 %
WWI 2GB Pulse Smart pen M100 Silver	$20,394.90	20.34 %
WWI 2GB Pulse Smart pen M100 White	$14,796.30	14.76 %
WWI 2GB Spy Video Recorder Pen M300 Blue	$724.00	0.72 %
WWI 2GB Spy Video Recorder Pen M300 Silver	$3,258.00	3.25 %
WWI 2GB Spy Video Recorder Pen M300 White	$2,353.00	2.35 %
WWI 4GB Video Recording Pen X200 Pink	$9,176.00	9.15 %
WWI 4GB Video Recording Pen X200 Yellow	$7,400.00	7.38 %
⊞ Cameras and camcorders	$7,901,783.67	23.45 %
⊞ Cell phones	$1,771,028.66	5.26 %
⊟ Computers	$7,435,548.25	22.07 %
⊞ Computers Accessories	$373,133.70	5.02 %
⊞ Desktops	$1,121,379.90	15.08 %
⊞ Laptops	$2,119,895.65	28.51 %
⊞ Monitors	$655,436.00	8.81 %
⊞ Printers, Scanners & Fax	$556,053.00	7.48 %
⊞ Projectors & Screens	$2,609,650.00	35.10 %
⊞ Games and Toys	$397,137.75	1.18 %
⊞ Home Appliances	$10,571,029.88	31.38 %
⊞ Music, Movies and Audio Books	$347,189.01	1.03 %
⊞ TV and Video	$4,844,253.41	14.38 %
Grand Total	$33,690,148.51	

FIGURE 11-4 The *PercOfParent* measure merges the three columns computed previously into a single column.

You can delete the three measures created previously, because now you have a single measure which computes everything, putting the right value in a single column, detecting the level at which you are browsing the hierarchy by using *ISFILTERED*.

> **Note** The order of the *IF* is important. You need to start testing the innermost level of the hierarchy and then go one step at a time to outer levels. Otherwise, if you reverse the order of the conditions, you will get incorrect results. You need to remember that when the *Subcategory* is filtered through the hierarchy, the *Category* is filtered, too.

The *PercOfParent* measure written in DAX works only if you put the correct hierarchy on rows. If you replace the category hierarchy with the color, for example, you will not get the percentage ratio between selected color and all the colors. The measure you created always considers the product hierarchy, regardless of whether or not it is used in the report, resulting in a blank result when it is not used (as you see in the Grand Total row of Figure 11-4).

Moreover, because *PercOfParent* uses the *ISFILTERED* function to detect the current level of the hierarchy, it might be fooled by the presence of any additional filter (created, for example, by a slicer). This is a big issue. If, for instance, you put a slicer on *Product Name* on the report and select a few products belonging to the same subcategory, you will produce a report similar to the one shown in Figure 11-5.

FIGURE 11-5 The *PercOfParent* measure does not work if you filter the *Product Name* with a slicer.

You can easily see in Figure 11-5 that *PercOfParent* does not show correct percentages. To solve this problem, you might use a DAX trick, which is worth learning because it can prove useful in many other scenarios.

First of all, we have to investigate why the measure does not work. The percentage shown for each "1GB Pulse Smart pen" computes the percentage of sales amount for the product against all the products of the same category and, to perform this, it uses *ALL (Product[Product Name])*. By doing this it is actually removing both the filter introduced by the product on rows and the filter created by the slicer. Thus, it is removing too many filters. In fact, the sum of all percentages for products does not yield 100 percent because there are other products not shown in the report that cover the remaining percentage.

What we would like to do is to remove the filter from the *Product Name* introduced by the rows but still keep the filter introduced by the slicer. Unfortunately, because both filters operate on the same column, there is no way to differentiate between the two using the *ISFILTERED* function. In fact, *ISFILTERED* tells you whether a column is filtered, but it has no way to detect whether the filter comes from the slicer or from rows or columns.

Note The *ALLSELECTED* function is not useful here. You might try to detect if a column is filtered by counting the values of the column for the current filter and for the *ALLSELECTED* filter, mixing *COUNTROWS* and *ALLSELECTED*. However, this test would fail in the special case where a hierarchy has a level with a single value. In that case, the result will always be 1 because you are selecting, on the rows, the only visible value of the column.

The solution, which is not very intuitive, is to make the two filters operate on different columns. You create three new columns, called *H Product Name*, *H Category*, and *H Subcategory*, where the initial H stands for "Hierarchy." Then you build the hierarchy using the H columns, renaming them inside the hierarchy, and finally, you hide the H columns from client tools so that they cannot be used on slicers, rows, or columns.

In Figure 11-6, you can see the Product table with all these duplicated columns. Note that the H columns are hidden from client tools.

Product Name	Subcategory	Category	H Product Name	H Subcategory	H Category
Contoso In-Line Coupler E180 White	Cell phones Accessories	Cell phones	Contoso In-Line Coupler E180 White	Cell phones Accessories	Cell phones
Contoso In-Line Coupler E180 Black	Cell phones Accessories	Cell phones	Contoso In-Line Coupler E180 Black	Cell phones Accessories	Cell phones
Contoso In-Line Coupler E180 Silver	Cell phones Accessories	Cell phones	Contoso In-Line Coupler E180 Silver	Cell phones Accessories	Cell phones
WWI 1GB Pulse Smart pen E50 White	Recording Pen	Audio	WWI 1GB Pulse Smart pen E50 White	Recording Pen	Audio
WWI 1GBPulse Smart pen E50 Black	Recording Pen	Audio	WWI 1GBPulse Smart pen E50 Black	Recording Pen	Audio
WWI 2GB Pulse Smart pen M100 Black	Recording Pen	Audio	WWI 2GB Pulse Smart pen M100 Black	Recording Pen	Audio
WWI 2GB Pulse Smart pen M100 Blue	Recording Pen	Audio	WWI 2GB Pulse Smart pen M100 Blue	Recording Pen	Audio
WWI 2GB Pulse Smart pen M100 Silver	Recording Pen	Audio	WWI 2GB Pulse Smart pen M100 Silver	Recording Pen	Audio
WWI 4GB Video Recording Pen X200 Pink	Recording Pen	Audio	WWI 4GB Video Recording Pen X200 Pink	Recording Pen	Audio
WWI 4GB Video Recording Pen X200 Yellow	Recording Pen	Audio	WWI 4GB Video Recording Pen X200 Yellow	Recording Pen	Audio
WWI 1GB Digital Voice Recorder Pen E100 Red	Recording Pen	Audio	WWI 1GB Digital Voice Recorder Pen E100 Red	Recording Pen	Audio
WWI 1GB Digital Voice Recorder Pen E100 Pi...	Recording Pen	Audio	WWI 1GB Digital Voice Recorder Pen E100 Pink	Recording Pen	Audio

FIGURE 11-6 In order to solve the scenario, you duplicate several columns in the Product table.

In Figure 11-7, you can see the newly created hierarchy, based on the H columns.

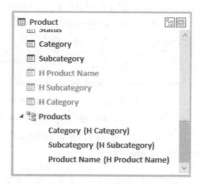

FIGURE 11-7 The Products hierarchy in the Product table is now based on the H columns.

Finally, you need to update the formula of *PercOfParent* so that it uses the H columns instead of the original ones:

```
=
IF (
    ISFILTERED ( Product[H Product Name] ),
    [Sales Amount] / CALCULATE ( [Sales Amount], ALL ( Product[H Product Name] ) ),
    IF (
        ISFILTERED ( Product[H Subcategory] ),
        [Sales Amount] / CALCULATE ( [Sales Amount], ALL ( Product[H Subcategory] ) ),
        IF (
            ISFILTERED ( Product[H Category] ),
            [Sales Amount] / CALCULATE ( [Sales Amount], ALL ( Product[H Category] ) )
        )
    )
)
```

With this new data model, the user will be able to put *Product Name* on the slicer, but this will not filter the *H Product Name* column directly. Thus, *ISFILTERED ([H Product Name])* will return *FALSE* on all the rows that do not display the product name.

In Figure 11-8, you can see both measures used in the same pivot table.

Product Name		
WWI 1GB Digital Voice Recorder Pen E100 Pink		
WWI 1GB Pulse Smart pen E50 Silver		
WWI 1GB Pulse Smart pen E50 White		
WWI 1GBPulse Smart pen E50 Black		
WWI 2GB Pulse Smart pen M100 Black		
WWI 2GB Pulse Smart pen M100 Blue		

Row Labels	Sales Amount	PercOfParent	PercOfParentCorrect
⊟Audio	$24,441.85	5.79 %	100.00 %
⊟Recording Pen	$24,441.85	24.38 %	100.00 %
WWI 1GB Pulse Smart pen E50 Silver	$4,198.60	100.00 %	17.18 %
WWI 1GB Pulse Smart pen E50 White	$3,898.70	100.00 %	15.95 %
WWI 1GBPulse Smart pen E50 Black	$16,344.55	100.00 %	66.87 %
Grand Total	$24,441.85	0.07 %	

FIGURE 11-8 *PercOfParentCorrect* now computes the correct results.

> **Note** This approach works only if the user selects regular columns for the slicer and selects the Products hierarchy on pivot table rows. If the user selects one or more levels from the hierarchy and puts them in one or more slicers, the same issue shown previously in Figure 11-5 will happen. Unfortunately, in that case, DAX does not offer you more control. You have to instruct the user to select the correct columns for the slicers.

From the point of view of the filter contexts, there is no practical difference between filtering a column from the hierarchy or from the visible ones. In fact, if the user filters a product category, only products of that category will be visible. The only notable difference is internal to DAX; that is, *ISFILTERED* will return *TRUE* only when a column of the hierarchy has been used to filter the table. Otherwise, it will return *FALSE*, even if not all the values of the column are visible.

At this point, you might think why not use the Excel built-in function "Show Values As" to obtain the same result. The reasons are that this technique defines the business logic in the data model, it does not require any user intervention to work, and it works on clients other than Excel. Moreover, the same technique of duplicating columns in hierarchies can prove useful in many different scenarios, not natively handled by Excel.

Handling parent-child hierarchies

The data model used by DAX does not support true parent/child hierarchies, as it is the case of a Multidimensional database in Analysis Services. However, there are some very useful DAX functions for flattening parent/child hierarchies into regular column-based hierarchies. This is good enough for most scenarios, although it means that you will have to make an educated guess at design time about the maximum depth of your hierarchy. In this section, you will learn how to use DAX functions and create a parent/child hierarchy, often abbreviated as P/C.

You can see an example of P/C hierarchy in Figure 11-9.

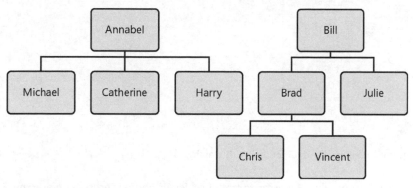

FIGURE 11-9 A graphical representation of a P/C hierarchy.

P/C hierarchies have two unique qualities:

- The number of levels in the hierarchy is not always the same. For example, the path from Annabel to Michael has a depth of two levels, whereas in the same hierarchy, the path from Bill to Chris has a depth of three levels.

- The hierarchy is normally represented in a single table, storing for each row a link to the parent.

You can see the canonical representation of P/C hierarchies in Figure 11-10.

NodeId	Node	ParentNodeId
1	Bill	
6	Annabel	
7	Catherine	6
0	Harry	6
9	Michael	6
2	Brad	1
3	Julie	1
4	Chris	2
5	Vincent	2

FIGURE 11-10 A table containing a P/C hierarchy.

It is easy to see that the *ParentNodeId* is the ID of the parent of each node. In fact, for Catherine, it stores 6, which is the ID of Annabel, her parent. The issue with this data model is that, this time, the relationship is a self-referenced one; that is, the two tables involved in the relationship are really the same table.

A data model for DAX does not support self-referencing relationships, so you have to modify the data model itself, turning the parent/child hierarchy into a regular one, based on one column for each level of the hierarchy.

Before delving into the details of how to handle the P/C hierarchies, it is worth noting one last point. Look at the table in Figure 11-11 containing the values we want to aggregate using the hierarchy.

NodeId	InvoiceId	Amount	City
2	3	200	Chicago
2	4	200	Seattle
3	5	300	Chicago
4	6	400	Seattle
5	7	500	Chicago
6	8	600	Seattle
7	9	600	Seattle
7	10	600	Chicago
8	11	400	Chicago
8	12	400	Chicago
9	13	300	Chicago
9	14	300	Seattle

FIGURE 11-11 This Sales table contains the data for the P/C hierarchy.

The rows in the Sales table contain references to both leaf-levels and nodes in the hierarchy. For example, the sixth row references NodeId 6, which is Annabel. Annabel has three children nodes, so when we look at her data, we will need to aggregate both her numbers and her children's values.

Figure 11-12 displays the result we want to achieve.

Row Labels	FinalFormula
⊟Annabel	3,200
Annabel	600
Catherine	1,200
Harry	800
Michael	600
⊟Bill	1,600
⊟Brad	1,300
Brad	400
Chris	400
Vincent	500
Julie	300
Grand Total	**4,800**

FIGURE 11-12 This report shows the result of browsing a P/C hierarchy with a pivot table.

There are many steps to cover before reaching the final goal. Once the tables have been loaded in the data model, the first step is to create a calculated column that contains, for each node, the path to reach it. In fact, because we cannot use standard relationships, we will need to use a set of special functions, available in DAX, designed for handling P/C hierarchies.

The new calculated column named *HPath* uses the *PATH* function:

```
PC[HPath] =
PATH ( PC[NodeId], PC[ParentNodeId] )
```

PATH is a function that receives two parameters. The first is the key of the table (in this case, the table name is PC), and the second is the name of the column that holds the parent node ID. The *PATH* function performs a recursive traversal of the table, and for each node it builds the path as a list of keys separated by the pipe (|) character. In Figure 11-13, you can see the PC table with the *HPath* calculated column.

NodeId			Node		ParentNodeId		HPath	
1			Bill				1	
6			Annabel				6	
7			Catherine		6		6|7	
8			Harry		6		6|8	
9			Michael		6		6|9	
2			Brad		1		1|2	
3			Julie		1		1|3	
4			Chris		2		1|2|4	
5			Vincent		2		1|2|5	

FIGURE 11-13 The *HPath* column contains, for each node, the complete path to reach it.

The *HPath* column, by itself, is not useful. It is so important because it is the basis for another set of calculated columns, which you will use to build the hierarchy. In fact, the next step is to build three calculated columns (one for each level of the hierarchy) by following this pattern:

```
PC[Level1] = LOOKUPVALUE ( PC[Node], PC[NodeId], PATHITEM ( PC[HPath], 1, INTEGER ) )
PC[Level2] = LOOKUPVALUE ( PC[Node], PC[NodeId], PATHITEM ( PC[HPath], 2, INTEGER ) )
PC[Level3] = LOOKUPVALUE ( PC[Node], PC[NodeId], PATHITEM ( PC[HPath], 3, INTEGER ) )
```

The three columns will be *Level1*, *Level2*, and *Level3*; the only change is in the second parameter to *PATHITEM*, which will be 1, 2, and 3. The calculated column uses *LOOKUPVALUE* to search a row where the NodeId equals the result of *PATHITEM* inside the PC table. *PATHITEM* returns the nth item in a column built with *PATH* (or *BLANK* if there is no such item, because you are requesting a number higher than the length of the path). The resulting table is shown in Figure 11-14.

NodeId			Node		ParentNodeId		HPath		Level1		Level2		Level3	
1			Bill				1		Bill					
6			Annabel				6		Annabel					
7			Catherine		6		6|7		Annabel		Catherine			
8			Harry		6		6|8		Annabel		Harry			
9			Michael		6		6|9		Annabel		Michael			
2			Brad		1		1|2		Bill		Brad			
3			Julie		1		1|3		Bill		Julie			
4			Chris		2		1|2|4		Bill		Brad		Chris	
5			Vincent		2		1|2|5		Bill		Brad		Vincent	

FIGURE 11-14 The *Level* columns contain the values to show in the hierarchy.

In this example, you have used three columns because the maximum depth of the hierarchy is three. In a real-world scenario, you need to count the maximum number of levels of your hierarchy and build a number of columns that is big enough to hold all the levels. Thus, you can see that even if the number of levels in a P/C hierarchy should be flexible, in order to implement them in a data model, you will need to fix it by defining its maximum number in advance. It is a good practice to add a couple more levels to create space for a future growth of the hierarchy without needing to update the data model.

Now you need to transform the set of Level columns into a hierarchy and, because none of the other columns in the PC table is useful, you should hide everything else from the client tools. Your data model will look like Figure 11-15.

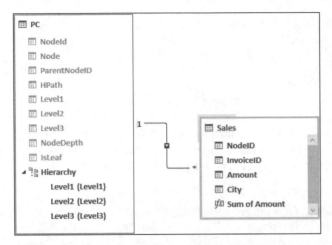

FIGURE 11-15 The data model containing the final P/C structure.

At this point, you can create a report using the hierarchy and putting the sum of amounts on the values. Figure 11-16 displays the result using a pivot table.

Row Labels	Sum of Amount
⊟Annabel	3,200
⊟(blank)	600
(blank)	600
⊟Catherine	1,200
(blank)	1,200
⊟Harry	800
(blank)	800
⊟Michael	600
(blank)	600
⊟Bill	1,600
⊟Brad	1,300
(blank)	400
Chris	400
Vincent	500
⊟Julie	300
(blank)	300
Grand Total	**4,800**

FIGURE 11-16 The P/C hierarchy is not exactly what we want because it shows too many rows.

There are several problems with this P/C hierarchy:

- Under Annabel, two blank rows contain the value of Annabel herself.

- Under Catherine, there is a blank row containing the value of Catherine herself.

The hierarchy always shows three levels, even for paths where the maximum depth should be two (such as Harry, who has no children).

Apart from these issues, which are basically visualization problems, the hierarchy computes correct values because, under the Annabel node, you can see the values of all of her children. The important aspect of this solution is that you have been able to mimic a self-referencing relationship by using the *PATH* function to create a calculated column. The remaining part is to solve the aesthetic issues, but now, at least, you are moving toward the correct solution.

The first problem to solve is the removal of all the blank values. The second row of the pivot table, for example, accounts for an amount of 600 that should be visible for Annabel, not for (blank). You can solve this by modifying the formula for the Level columns. You remove all the blanks, repeating the previous level if you reached the end of the path. Here, you can see the pattern for *Level2*:

```
PC[Level2] =
IF (
    PATHLENGTH ( PC[HPath] ) >= 2,
    LOOKUPVALUE ( PC[Node], PC[NodeId], PATHITEM ( PC[HPath], 2, INTEGER ) ),
    PC[Level1]
)
```

With this new formula, the table looks like Figure 11-17.

NodeId	Node	ParentNodeId	HPath	Level1	Level2	Level3
1	Bill		1	Bill	Bill	Bill
6	Annabel		6	Annabel	Annabel	Annabel
7	Catherine	6	6|7	Annabel	Catherine	Catherine
8	Harry	6	6|8	Annabel	Harry	Harry
9	Michael	6	6|9	Annabel	Michael	Michael
2	Brad	1	1|2	Bill	Brad	Brad
3	Julie	1	1|3	Bill	Julie	Julie
4	Chris	2	1|2|4	Bill	Brad	Chris
5	Vincent	2	1|2|5	Bill	Brad	Vincent

FIGURE 11-17 With the new formula, the Level columns never contain a blank.

If you look at this point of the pivot table, the blank rows are gone. Yet there are still too many rows. In Figure 11-18, you can see the pivot table, and, beside it, the filter context for each row.

Row Labels	Sum of Amount		Level1	Level2	Level3
⊟ Annabel	3,200		Annabel		
⊟ Annabel	600		Annabel	Annabel	
Annabel	600		Annabel	Annabel	Annabel
⊟ Catherine	1,200		Annabel	Catherine	
Catherine	1,200		Annabel	Catherine	Catherine
⊟ Harry	800		Annabel	Harry	
Harry	800		Annabel	Harry	Harry
⊟ Michael	600		Annabel	Michael	
Michael	600		Annabel	Michael	Michael
⊟ Bill	1,600		Bill		
⊟ Brad	1,300		Bill	Brad	
Brad	400		Bill	Brad	Brad
Chris	400		Bill	Brad	Chris
Vincent	500		Bill	Brad	Vincent
⊟ Julie	300		Bill	Julie	
Julie	300		Bill	Julie	Julie
Grand Total	4,800				

FIGURE 11-18 At the right of the pivot table, there is a corresponding description of the filter context for each row.

Pay attention to the second and third rows of the pivot table. In both cases, the pivot table shows a single row of the hierarchy (that is, the row of Annabel). You might want to show the second row because it contains a good value for Annabel, but you do not want to see the third row, since the hierarchy is browsing too deep and the path of Annabel is no longer valid. We need to make a more accurate search for a correct way to hide nodes.

If we assign to each row of the hierarchy the length of the path needed to reach it, it is easy to see that Annabel is a root node, which means it is a node of level 1. Catherine, on the other hand, is a node of level 2 because she is a child of Annabel. Thus, the path of Catherine is of length 2. Moreover, even if it might not be so evident, Catherine is visible at level 1 because her value is aggregated under the first node of Annabel.

At this point, we can say that each node should be visible whenever we are browsing the hierarchy up to its level. Then, when the pivot table shows a level that is too deep, we want to hide the node. In order to check this algorithm, we need two values:

- The depth of each node, which can be stored in a calculated column, because it is a fixed value for each row of the hierarchy.

- The current browsing depth of the pivot table, which is a dynamic value that depends on the current filter context, meaning that you will need a measure, because the value changes depending on the pivot table and has different values for each row. For example, Annabel is a node at level 1, but it appears in three rows, where the current depth of the pivot table has three different values.

If you could compute these two values, then the solution to the problem would be much closer. Yes, you will still need a way to hide the rows, but we can forget about this issue for now. Focus your attention on the identification of the unwanted rows.

The depth of each node is easy to compute. You can add a new calculated column to the PC table with this simple expression:

```
PC[NodeDepth] =
PATHLENGTH ( PC[HPath] )
```

PATHLENGTH returns the length of a column computed by *PATH*, and you can see that there is nothing complex here. The resulting calculated column is shown in Figure 11-19.

NodeId	Node	ParentNodeId	HPath	NodeDepth
1	Bill		1	1
6	Annabel		6	1
7	Catherine	6	6|7	2
8	Harry	6	6|8	2
9	Michael	6	6|9	2
2	Brad	1	1|2	2
3	Julie	1	1|3	2
4	Chris	2	1|2|4	3
5	Vincent	2	1|2|5	3

FIGURE 11-19 The *NodeDepth* column stores the depth of each node in a calculated column.

The *NodeDepth* column is easy to create. Computing the browsing depth is more difficult because you need to compute it in a measure. Nevertheless, the logic behind it is not very complex, and it is similar to the technique you have already learned for standard hierarchies: it uses the *ISFILTERED* function to let you discover whether a Level column is filtered or not.

The formula takes advantage of the fact that a Boolean value can be converted to a number, where *TRUE* has a value of 1 and *FALSE* has a value of 0.

```
[BrowseDepth] :=
ISFILTERED ( PC[Level1] ) +
ISFILTERED ( PC[Level2] ) +
ISFILTERED ( PC[Level3] )
```

Therefore, if only *Level1* is filtered, then the result is 1. If both *Level1* and *Level2* are filtered, but not *Level3*, then the result is 2. You can see the result for the *BrowseDepth* column in Figure 11-20.

Row Labels	Sum of Amount	BrowseDepth		Level1	Level2	Level3
Annabel	3,200	1		Annabel		
Annabel	600	2		Annabel	Annabel	
Annabel	600	3		Annabel	Annabel	Annabel
Catherine	1,200	2		Annabel	Catherine	
Catherine	1,200	3		Annabel	Catherine	Catherine
Harry	800	2		Annabel	Harry	
Harry	800	3		Annabel	Harry	Harry
Michael	600	2		Annabel	Michael	
Michael	600	3		Annabel	Michael	Michael
Bill	1,600	1		Bill		
Bill		2		Bill	Bill	
Bill		3		Bill	Bill	Bill
Brad	1,300	2		Bill	Brad	
Brad	400	3		Bill	Brad	Brad
Chris	400	3		Bill	Brad	Chris
Vincent	500	3		Bill	Brad	Vincent
Julie	300	2		Bill	Julie	
Julie	300	3		Bill	Julie	Julie
Grand Total	4,800	0				

FIGURE 11-20 The *BrowseDepth* measure computes the depth of browsing in the pivot table.

It is interesting to see that this new pivot table shows more rows than before. Now you can see that Bill has three rows, whereas in the previous reports, Bill had only one row. The reason is that in the previous report, these additional Bill rows were hidden because the value for the sum of amounts returned a BLANK value. By default, the pivot table in Excel automatically hides rows that result in a blank value for all the displayed measures. This may look like a small piece of information, but it is going to turn into a much more valuable one. In fact, it shows the path to hide a row: If the value of the measure is a BLANK, then the row will be hidden in Excel (the behavior might be different on other clients). Thus, you now have all the necessary pieces of information to complete the formula:

- The depth of each node, in the *NodeDepth* calculated column.

- The depth of the current cell in the pivot table, in the *BrowseDepth* measure.

- A way to hide unwanted columns, by means of blanking the value of the result.

It is time to merge all this information into a single measure, as follows:

```
[PC_Amount] :=
IF (
    MAX ( PC[NodeDepth] ) >= [BrowseDepth],
    SUM ( Sales[Amount] )
)
```

To understand how this measure works, look at the pivot table in Figure 11-21, where we put all the values that are useful to grab the formula behavior.

Row Labels	Sum of Amount	BrowseDepth	MaxNodeDepth	PC_Amount
Annabel	3,200	1	2	3,200
Annabel	600	2	1	
Annabel	600	3	1	
Catherine	1,200	2	2	1,200
Catherine	1,200	3	2	
Harry	800	2	2	800
Harry	800	3	2	
Michael	600	2	2	600
Michael	600	3	2	
Bill	1,600	1	3	1,600
Bill		2	1	
Bill		3	1	
Brad	1,300	2	3	1,300
Brad	400	3	2	
Chris	400	3	3	400
Vincent	500	3	3	500
Julie	300	2	2	300
Julie	300	3	2	
Grand Total	4,800	0	3	4,800

Level1	Level2	Level3
Annabel		
Annabel	Annabel	
Annabel	Annabel	Annabel
Annabel	Catherine	
Annabel	Catherine	Catherine
Annabel	Harry	
Annabel	Harry	Harry
Annabel	Michael	
Annabel	Michael	Michael
Bill		
Bill	Bill	
Bill	Bill	Bill
Bill	Brad	
Bill	Brad	Brad
Bill	Brad	Chris
Bill	Brad	Vincent
Bill	Julie	
Bill	Julie	Julie

FIGURE 11-21 This report shows the final result and all the intermediate values used by the formula.

If you look at the first row, which is Annabel, you see that *BrowseDepth* equals 1, because this is the root of the hierarchy. *MaxNodeDepth*, which is defined as *MAX (PC[NodeDepth])*, has a value of 2, meaning that the current node is showing not only data at level 1, but also data for some children that are at level 2. The current node is now showing data for some children too, and for this reason, it needs to be visible. The second line of Annabel, on the other hand, has a *BrowseDepth* of 2 and *MaxNodeDepth* of 1. The reason is that the filter context filters all the rows where *Level1* equals Annabel and *Level2* equals Annabel, and there is only one row in the hierarchy satisfying this condition, which is Annabel herself. But Annabel has a *NodeDepth* of 1 and, because the pivot table is browsing at level 2, then we need to hide the node. In fact, the *PC Amount* measure returns a BLANK.

It is useful to verify the behavior for other nodes by yourself so you can improve your understanding of how the formula is working and of its behavior. Although it is clear that you can simply return to this part of the book and copy the formula whenever you need to, understanding it is a good exercise because it forces you to think in terms of how the filter context interacts with various parts of the formula.

To reach the result, you only need to remove from the pivot table all the columns that are not needed, leaving *PC Amount* alone, and the visualization will be the desired one, as you can see in Figure 11-22.

Row Labels	PC_Amount
Annabel	3,200
Catherine	1,200
Harry	800
Michael	600
Bill	1,600
Brad	1,300
Chris	400
Vincent	500
Julie	300
Grand Total	4,800

FIGURE 11-22 Once the measure is left alone in the pivot table, all unwanted rows disappear.

CHAPTER 11 Handling hierarchies **355**

As you might imagine at this point, you will need to use the same pattern for any measure you might want to add to your pivot table when the P/C hierarchy is in place. If you put in a single measure that does not have a BLANK value for unwanted rows, then all of them will suddenly appear and disrupt the pattern.

At this point the result is already satisfactory. Yet there is still a small problem. In fact, if you look at the total of Annabel, it is 3,200. Her children, summed up, show a total of 2,600. There is a missing amount of 600, which is the value of Annabel herself. You might already be satisfied by this visualization, because the value of a node is detectable by looking at the difference between its total and the total of its children. However, if you compare this figure to the original goal (we compare them for you in Figure 11-23), you see that, there, the value of each node was clearly visible as a child of the node itself.

Row Labels	FinalFormula		Row Labels	PC_Amount
⊟Annabel	3,200		⊟Annabel	3,200
Annabel	600		Catherine	1,200
Catherine	1,200		Harry	800
Harry	800		Michael	600
Michael	600		⊟Bill	1,600
⊟Bill	1,600		⊟Brad	1,300
⊟Brad	1,300		Chris	400
Brad	400		Vincent	500
Chris	400		Julie	300
Vincent	500		**Grand Total**	**4,800**
Julie	300			
Grand Total	**4,800**			

FIGURE 11-23 The original goal represented on the left is not yet reached in the right-hand pivot table—you still need to show some rows.

At this point, the technique should be clear enough. In order to show the value for Annabel, you only need to find a suitable condition that lets you identify it as a node that should be made visible. In this case, the condition is somewhat complex. You should be aware that the nodes that must be visible can be non-leaf nodes (that is, they have some children) that have values. These nodes will be made visible for one additional level. All other nodes (that is, leaf nodes or nodes with no value associated) will follow the original rule.

First, you need to create a calculated column in the PC table that indicates whether a node is a leaf. The DAX expression is easy: leaves are nodes that are not parents of any other node. In order to check the condition, you can count the number of nodes that have the current node as the parent. If it equals zero, then you know that the current node is a leaf. The following code does this:

```
PC[IsLeaf] =
CALCULATE (
    COUNTROWS ( PC ),
    ALL ( PC ),
    PC[ParentNodeId] = EARLIER ( PC[NodeId] )
) = 0
```

In Figure 11-24, the *IsLeaf* column has been added to the data model.

NodeId	Node	ParentNodeId	HPath	IsLeaf
1	Bill		1	FALSE
6	Annabel		6	FALSE
7	Catherine	6	6|7	TRUE
8	Harry	6	6|8	TRUE
9	Michael	6	6|9	TRUE
2	Brad	1	1|2	FALSE
3	Julie	1	1|3	TRUE
4	Chris	2	1|2|4	TRUE
5	Vincent	2	1|2|5	TRUE

FIGURE 11-24 The *IsLeaf* column indicates which nodes are leaves of the hierarchy.

Now that you can identify leaves, it is time to write the final formula for handling the P/C hierarchy (you see numbers added to the lines to make them easier to identify):

```
1.   FinalFormula :=
2.      IF (
3.          [MaxNodeDepth] + 1 >= [BrowseDepth],
4.          IF (
5.              [MaxNodeDepth] + 1 = [BrowseDepth],
6.              IF (
7.                  VALUES ( PC[IsLeaf] ) = FALSE && SUM ( Sales[Amount] ) <> 0,
8.                  SUM ( Sales[Amount] )
9.              ),
10.             SUM ( Sales[Amount] )
11.         )
12.     )
```

The beginning of this formula is identical to the previous one: there is only a +1 in *[MaxNodeDepth]* at line 3 (also repeated in line 5), to take into account the next level. The reason why we add 1 to *[MaxNodeDepth]* is to allow certain nodes to show at specified browse levels; without it, the nodes that we are interested in showing will always be hidden as the *[MaxNodeDepth]* is less than their *[BrowseDepth]*. Not all the nodes should be visible at the next level—only the ones that are not leaves and have some value to show. This is the purpose of the remaining lines. On line 7, we check the special case of a node that should be made visible for one more level. If it is on that special level, then we check whether it is not a leaf (using *VALUES*, because here we are sure only a single row is visible in the P/C hierarchy) and whether there is some value to show. If this is the case, then the measure returns the sum of the amounts; otherwise, it returns BLANK, hiding the row.

It is clear that, if the data model had the ability to handle P/C hierarchies natively, then all this hard work could have been avoided. After all, this is not an easy formula to digest, because it requires a full understanding of evaluation contexts and data modeling.

Important If you create a model in Analysis Services Tabular 2012/2014, you can enable the behavior of a special property called *HideMemberIf*, which automatically hides a node under certain conditions, such as having no children. Please note that this feature is not supported by Microsoft and might change in future versions of Analysis Services. In order to turn on this setting you need the BIDS Helper Visual Studio Add-In. A complete description of how to use this property in Tabular is available at https://bidshelper.codeplex.com/wikipage?title=Tabular%20HideMemberIf.

Handling unary operators

As you have seen previously in this chapter, DAX does not have a native support of hierarchies in the underlying data model. This support exists in a Multidimensional database in Analysis Services, which also handles two other features that are not available in Tabular: unary operators and custom rollup formulas. The use of these two features is common in financial applications. Although the native data model for DAX does not include built-in support for unary operators, in this section you find out how it is possible to reproduce the functionality to a certain extent in DAX. It is not possible to re-create custom rollup formulas, unfortunately, and the only option is to write extremely long and complicated DAX expressions in measures.

Note A custom rollup formula allows you to define a different aggregation formula for each node of a hierarchy. For example, you might calculate the sum of the months for 2015 and the average of the months for 2014, and such a calculation would be applied to all of the measures. This is something that is not possible in DAX, because you cannot apply a different aggregation rule to an existing DAX expression used in a measure.

You can find in Books Online the full details about how unary operators work in the Multidimensional model: http://technet.microsoft.com/en-us/library/ms175417.aspx, but here is a quick summary. Each item in the hierarchy can be associated with an operator that controls how the total for that member aggregates up to its parent. Operators can be one of the following values:

- **+** The plus sign means the value for the current item is added to the aggregate of its siblings (that is, all the items with the same parent) that occurs before the current item on the same level of the hierarchy.

- **–** The minus sign means the value for the current item is subtracted from the value of its siblings that occurs before the current item on the same level of the hierarchy.

- ***** The asterisk means the value for the current item is multiplied by the aggregate of all the siblings that occurs before the current item on the same level of the hierarchy.

- **/** The forward slash means the value for the current item is divided by the aggregate of all the siblings that occurs before the current item on the same level of the hierarchy.

- **~** The tilde means the value for the current item is ignored when calculating the value of the parent.

- **A value between 0 and 1** This means the value of the current item is multiplied by this value when aggregation takes place, and the result is added to the aggregate of its siblings.

The DAX code for implementing unary operators gets more complex the more operators are used in a hierarchy, so for the sake of clarity and simplicity, in this section only, we use the two most common operators: the plus sign (+), and the minus sign (-). Calculations that use the forward slash and asterisk unary operators, (/) and (*), return different results, depending on the order in which they are executed, so any DAX implementation would be even more complicated. Table 11-1 shows a simple example of how these three operators behave when used in a hierarchy.

TABLE 11-1 How unary operators are calculated.

Item Name	Unary Operator	Measure Value
Profit		150
- Sales	+ (add)	100
- Other Income	+ (add)	75
- Costs	- (subtract)	25
- Headcount	~ (ignore)	493

In this example, the Sales, Other Income, Costs, and Headcount items appear as children of the Profit item in the hierarchy. The value of Profit is calculated as:

```
+ [Sales Amount] + [Other Income] - [Costs]
```

with the value of Headcount ignored, to give the total of 150.

Implementing unary operators by using DAX

The key to implementing unary operator functionality in DAX is to recalculate the value of your measure at each level of the hierarchy rather than to calculate it at a low level and aggregate it up. This means that the DAX needed can be very complicated, and it is a good idea to split the calculation into multiple steps so that you can debug it more easily.

Note The best implementation for unary operators in DAX is to avoid them, putting the sign in the table containing the values to compute instead of applying them to the members of the parent-child hierarchy table. If you cannot apply the operator to the transactions transforming data before loading the data model, you should use the technique described in this section only as a last resort.

To illustrate how to implement unary operators, you need a dimension with some unary operators on it. The table you see in Figure 11-25 defines a parent-child hierarchy of accounts in a simple profits and losses report.

AccountId	Account	ParentAccountId	UnaryOperator
1	Final Total		+
2	Revenues	1	+
3	Courses Provided	2	+
4	Instructors Cost	3	-
5	Catering	3	-
6	Attendees Revenues	3	+
7	Consultancy	2	+
8	Expenses	1	-
9	Travel	8	+
10	Travels Refund	9	-
11	Travels Paid	9	+
12	Courses Taken	8	+

FIGURE 11-25 The parent-child hierarchy has a column with a unary operator applied to each account.

Each account has a corresponding unary operator defined in the *UnaryOperator* column. For example, the account Revenues has a plus sign, whereas the account Expenses has a minus sign. Both of these accounts have the same parent, Final Total, which will return the difference between Revenues (having the plus sign) and Expenses (having the minus sign). In reality, the presence of the minus sign in the Expenses account row means that all the transactions related to the Expenses are considered with an inverted sign.

Consider how the transactions in Figure 11-26 relate to the accounts we just described.

AccountId	Description	Amount
4	Marco Russo	200
4	Alberto Ferrari	500
5	Sandwiches	300
6	Course in Seattle	800
6	Course in Boston	1200
7	Work in Microsoft	400
7	Work in Skype	500
7	Work in SQL Blog	300
10	Travel to Seattle	80
11	Travel to Boston	150
11	Travel to London	190
12	Kerberos Deep Div	1000

FIGURE 11-26 Each account has one or more transactions, always with a positive amount value.

All the transactions have a positive value, but you can see in a simple report that the resulting hierarchy has nodes reporting negative values. This is possible because the unary operator inverts the sign of a node in the hierarchy, inverting the sign of all the corresponding transactions. You can see an example of such a report in Figure 11-27.

Row Labels	AmountParentChild
⊟ Final Total	940
⊟ Expenses	-1260
Courses Taken	1000
⊟ Travel	260
Travels Paid	340
Travels Refund	-80
⊟ Revenues	2200
Consultancy	1200
⊟ Courses Provided	1000
Attendees Revenues	2000
Catering	-300
Instructors Cost	-700

FIGURE 11-27 The final report shows negative values in certain accounts because of the applied unary operators.

You create the parent-child hierarchy following the same technique described in the previous section, obtaining the calculated columns you see in Figure 11-28, which are accessible through a hierarchy in the data model built using the columns *Level1*, *Level2*, *Level3*, and *Level4*.

AccountId	Account	ParentAccountId	UnaryOperator	HierarchyPath	Level1	Level2	Level3	Level4	NodeDepth
1	Final Total		+	1	Final Total				1
2	Revenues	1	+	1|2	Final Total	Revenues			2
3	Courses Provided	2	+	1|2|3	Final Total	Revenues	Courses Provided		3
4	Instructors Cost	3	-	1|2|3|4	Final Total	Revenues	Courses Provided	Instructors Cost	4
5	Catering	3	-	1|2|3|5	Final Total	Revenues	Courses Provided	Catering	4
6	Attendees Rev...	3	+	1|2|3|6	Final Total	Revenues	Courses Provided	Attendees Re...	4
7	Consultancy	2	+	1|2|7	Final Total	Revenues	Consultancy		3
8	Expenses	1	-	1|8	Final Total	Expenses			2
9	Travel	8	+	1|8|9	Final Total	Expenses	Travel		3
10	Travels Refund	9	-	1|8|9|10	Final Total	Expenses	Travel	Travels Refund	4
11	Travels Paid	9	+	1|8|9|11	Final Total	Expenses	Travel	Travels Paid	4
12	Courses Taken	8	+	1|8|12	Final Total	Expenses	Courses Taken		3

FIGURE 11-28 The parent-child hierarchy generates a flattened hierarchy of four levels.

The DAX implementation of unary operators that you see in this section only supports plus and minus operators, which are the most common ones. In this way, you might sum or subtract every value, depending on the projection level. Because inverting a value is possible by multiplying it by -1, you will convert each operator in a corresponding multiplier, where 1 is the plus (+) operator, and -1 represents the minus (-) operator. This inversion is possible, creating the following calculation in the *Multiplier* calculated column:

```
Accounts[Multiplier] =
SWITCH (
    Accounts[UnaryOperator],
    "+", 1,
    "-", -1
)
```

Once you have the multiplier as an integer number, you can simply multiply the value of an account with its multiplier in order to apply the unary operator at the account level. Moreover, when you aggregate several accounts into a node, you can multiply each account's value for all the multipliers that you have through the hierarchy until you reach the evaluated node. For example, consider the account 10, Travels Refund. It has a minus unary operator, and its parent is the account 9, Travel, which has a plus unary operator. In this case, when grouped by the Travel node, the Travels Paid account value keeps its negative operation. In other words, you can sum the children of account Travel (Travels Refund and Travels Paid) by summing the corresponding transactions, applying the minus operator only to transactions of account Travels Refund. At this point, consider the account 8, Expenses. It groups other accounts including account 9 (Travel), and it applies the minus operator to them. Thus, the values of transactions for account Travels Refund will get two minus operators going up in the hierarchy to the Expenses level. Because applying two minus operators to a number returns the original number, we do not have to change the sign of the transactions of the Travels Refund account when we aggregate them in the Expenses account.

In order to create an efficient DAX calculation for this model, we can create a column for each level that evaluates in advance the final multiplier that you have to apply depending on the level of the hierarchy used to group transactions. In Figure 11-29 you can see that the account 10 (Travels Refund) has a multiplier −1 for its original level (*SignAtLevel4*) and for the parent level (*SignAtLevel3*, corresponding to the Travel account), whereas it has a multiplier 1 for the upper level (*SignAtLevel2*, corresponding to the Expenses account, and *SignAtLevel1*, corresponding to the Final Total account).

AccountId	Account	ParentAccountId	UnaryOperator	HierarchyPath	Multiplier	SignAtLevel1	SignAtLevel2	SignAtLevel3	SignAtLevel4
1	Final Total		+	1	1	1			
2	Revenues	1	+	1|2	1	1	1		
3	Courses Provided	2	+	1|2|3	1	1	1	1	
4	Instructors Cost	3	-	1|2|3|4	-1	-1	-1	-1	-1
5	Catering	3	-	1|2|3|5	-1	-1	-1	-1	-1
6	Attendees Rev...	3	+	1|2|3|6	1	1	1	1	1
7	Consultancy	2	+	1|2|7	1	1	1	1	
8	Expenses	1	-	1|8	-1	-1	-1		
9	Travel	8	+	1|8|9	1	-1	-1	1	
10	Travels Refund	9	-	1|8|9|10	-1	1	1	-1	-1
11	Travels Paid	9	+	1|8|9|11	1	-1	-1	1	1
12	Courses Taken	8	+	1|8|12	1	-1	-1	1	

FIGURE 11-29 Each account has a multiplier to apply when aggregating the account at that particular level.

You can create the columns *SignAtLevel<n>* as calculated columns in DAX if you cannot generate these values before importing data in the data model. When an account is displayed in its own level (the leaf-level of the hierarchy), you simply copy its multiplier; otherwise, you get the multiplier of the account in the hierarchy at the level displayed and multiply its multiplier by the multiplier you obtained for the level below. The evaluation of multipliers starts at the lowest level of the hierarchy, and then continues toward the first level. In the example in Figure 11-29, the evaluation of *SignAtLevel4* is the first one, because the *SignAtLevel3* evaluation might depend on *SignAtLevel4*.

The DAX engine automatically solves the evaluation order of calculated columns based on the DAX dependencies in formulas. Here you can see the definitions of the calculated columns for the multipliers defined for each level of the hierarchy, listed from level 1 to level 4, even if the execution order will be from level 4 to level 1 because of the dependencies between the column names highlighted in bold.

```
Accounts[SignAtLevel1] =
IF (
    Accounts[NodeDepth] = 1,
    Accounts[Multiplier],
    LOOKUPVALUE (
        Accounts[Multiplier],
        Accounts[AccountId], PATHITEM ( Accounts[HierarchyPath], 1, INTEGER )
    )
        * Accounts[SignAtLevel2]
)

Accounts[SignAtLevel2] =
IF (
    Accounts[NodeDepth] = 2,
    Accounts[Multiplier],
    LOOKUPVALUE (
        Accounts[Multiplier],
        Accounts[AccountId], PATHITEM ( Accounts[HierarchyPath], 2, INTEGER )
    )
        * [SignAtLevel3]
)

Accounts[SignAtLevel3] =
IF (
    Accounts[NodeDepth] = 3,
    Accounts[Multiplier],
    LOOKUPVALUE (
        Accounts[Multiplier],
        Accounts[AccountId], PATHITEM ( Accounts[HierarchyPath], 3, INTEGER )
    )
        * [SignAtLevel4]
)

Accounts[SignAtLevel4] =
IF ( Accounts[NodeDepth] = 4, Accounts[Multiplier] )
```

The reason why you want a multiplier defined for each level is that it simplifies the calculation of the measure that aggregates all accounts to a maximum of two groups (plus and minus) for each cell of the report. Depending on the browse depth of the report, you have to use the corresponding *SignAtLevel<n>* column to aggregate accounts based on their multipliers at that level. As you see in the following definition, the *AmountParentChild* measure performs this operation in an efficient way (the *BrowseDepth* measure applies a technique described in the previous section):

```
[BrowseDepth] :=
ISFILTERED ( Accounts[Level1] )
    + ISFILTERED ( Accounts[Level2] )
    + ISFILTERED ( Accounts[Level3] )
    + ISFILTERED ( Accounts[Level4] )

[AmountParentChild] :=
IF (
    MIN ( Accounts[NodeDepth] ) >= [BrowseDepth] && [BrowseDepth] > 0,
    ( [BrowseDepth] = 1 ) * (
        CALCULATE (
            SUM ( Transactions[Amount] ),
            Accounts[SignAtLevel1] = 1
        ) - CALCULATE (
            SUM ( Transactions[Amount] ),
            Accounts[SignAtLevel1] = -1
        )
    )
    + ( [BrowseDepth] = 2 ) * (
        CALCULATE (
            SUM ( Transactions[Amount] ),
            Accounts[SignAtLevel2] = 1
        ) - CALCULATE (
            SUM ( Transactions[Amount] ),
            Accounts[SignAtLevel2] = -1
        )
    )
    + ( [BrowseDepth] = 3 ) * (
        CALCULATE (
            SUM ( Transactions[Amount] ),
            Accounts[SignAtLevel3] = 1
        ) - CALCULATE (
            SUM ( Transactions[Amount] ),
            Accounts[SignAtLevel3] = -1
        )
    )
    + ( [BrowseDepth] = 4 ) * (
        CALCULATE (
            SUM ( Transactions[Amount] ),
            Accounts[SignAtLevel4] = 1
        ) - CALCULATE (
            SUM ( Transactions[Amount] ),
            Accounts[SignAtLevel4] = -1
        )
    )
)
```

The logic for the *AmountParentChild* calculation is as follows:

- If the item on the hierarchy is below the maximum depth that you want to display, return a BLANK value. This is the same technique described in the "Handling parent-child hierarchies" section earlier in this chapter.

- Otherwise:

- Find the sum of all leaves underneath the current item that have the multiplier 1.

- Subtract the sum of all leaves underneath the current item that have the multiplier –1.

Notice that in the code relating to the last bullet, *CALCULATE* sums all the items that have effective multipliers of 1 or –1; this is more efficient than using *SUMX()* and iterating over each individual leaf, even if that approach might be more readable.

Alternative implementations of unary operator measure

The implementation of the *AmountParentChild* measure with unary operators you have seen optimizes the performance, at the cost of a lower readability. However, newer versions of the DAX engine optimize the performance providing a way to write good performing code with a better readability. If you use Excel 2016, Power BI Designer, or Analysis Services 2016, or newer versions of these products, you might consider using one of the following alternative techniques.

For example, you can implement *AmountParentChild* by multiplying each transaction amount by the corresponding multiplier in the *SignAtLevel<n>* column of the Accounts table, as shown in the following example:

```
[AmountParentChild1] :=
IF (
    MIN ( Accounts[NodeDepth] ) >= [BrowseDepth],
    SWITCH (
        [BrowseDepth],
        1, SUMX (
            Transactions,
            Transactions[Amount] * RELATED ( Accounts[SignAtLevel1] )
        ),
        2, SUMX (
            Transactions,
            Transactions[Amount] * RELATED ( Accounts[SignAtLevel2] )
        ),
        3, SUMX (
            Transactions,
            Transactions[Amount] * RELATED ( Accounts[SignAtLevel3] )
        ),
        4, SUMX (
            Transactions,
            Transactions[Amount] * RELATED ( Accounts[SignAtLevel4] )
        )
    )
)
```

In a similar way, you can also iterate the values in the *SignAtLevel<n>* column, depending on the level displayed, and sum the corresponding transactions for that multiplier, executing only one multiplication per item displayed:

```
[AmountParentChild2] :=
IF (
    MIN ( Accounts[NodeDepth] ) >= [BrowseDepth],
    SWITCH (
        [BrowseDepth],
        1, SUMX (
            VALUES ( Accounts[SignAtLevel1] ),
            Accounts[SignAtLevel1] * CALCULATE ( SUM ( Transactions[Amount] ) )
        ),
        2, SUMX (
            VALUES ( Accounts[SignAtLevel2] ),
            Accounts[SignAtLevel2] * CALCULATE ( SUM ( Transactions[Amount] ) )
        ),
        3, SUMX (
            VALUES ( Accounts[SignAtLevel3] ),
            Accounts[SignAtLevel3] * CALCULATE ( SUM ( Transactions[Amount] ) )
        ),
        4, SUMX (
            VALUES ( Accounts[SignAtLevel4] ),
            Accounts[SignAtLevel4] * CALCULATE ( SUM ( Transactions[Amount] ) )
        )
    )
)
```

You should consider using the simplest formula that provides good performance for the version of the DAX engine you use.

Advanced relationships

This is the last chapter on DAX. The remaining part of the book covers internals of the engine and optimization techniques to make your code run faster. This means that after reading this chapter we will have shared with you all of our DAX knowledge.

In this chapter, you will learn how to handle complex relationships between tables by leveraging the DAX language. Tabular models, in fact, can handle simple or bidirectional relationships between tables and this might look somewhat limited. However, taking advantage of the DAX language, you can create very advanced models with basically any kind of relationship, including virtual ones. As usual, DAX is the key to solve complex scenarios.

We will highlight several techniques to model complex relationships. The goal of this chapter is not to give you pre-built patterns that you can use in your model. Instead, we want to show you unusual ways of using DAX to build complex models, to widen your idea of relationships, and to let you experience what you can achieve with DAX formulas.

Using calculated physical relationships

The first set of relationships you are about to learn is that of calculated physical relationships. In scenarios where the relationship cannot be set because a key is missing, or you need to compute it with complex formulas, then you can leverage calculated columns to set up the relationship. At the end, you will create a physical relationship; the only difference from a standard one is the fact that the key of the relationship is a calculated column.

Computing multiple-column relationships

The VertiPaq engine allows you to create relationships based on a single column only. It does not support relationships based on more than one column. Besides, relationships based on multiple columns are very useful and they appear in many data models. If you need to work with these kinds of models, here are two methods to do so:

- Define a calculated column containing the composition of the keys, and then use it as the new key for the relationship.

- Denormalize the columns of the target table (the "one-side" in a one-to-many relationship) using the *LOOKUPVALUE* function.

As an example, imagine that you have a special "Product of the Day" promotion. On some days, you make a special promotion for a single product with a given discount, as you can see in Figure 12-1.

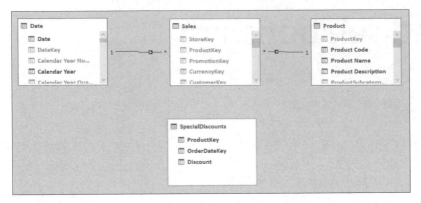

FIGURE 12-1 The SpecialDiscounts table needs a relationship based on two columns with Sales.

The table containing the promotion (SpecialDiscounts) contains three columns: *ProductKey*, *OrderDateKey*, and *Discount*. If you need to use this information to compute, for example, the amount of the discount, you face the problem that for any given sale the discount depends on *ProductKey* and *OrderDateKey*. Thus, you cannot create the relationship between Sales and SpecialDiscounts, because it would involve two columns and VertiPaq supports only single-column relationships.

You can create a new column in both the SpecialDiscount and Sales tables containing the combination of the two columns, using the following code:

```
Sales[SpecialDiscountKey] = Sales[OrderDateKey] & "-" & Sales[ProductKey]
```

You use a similar expression in SpecialDiscount, and once you defined the two columns, you can finally create the relationship between the two tables. In fact, it is always useful to remember that you can create relationships on calculated columns, too.

This solution is straightforward and works just fine. Yet there are several scenarios where this is not the best solution. It requires you to create two calculated columns (using precious RAM) that might have many different values.

Another possible solution to the same scenario is to use the *LOOKUPVALUE* function. Using *LOOKUPVALUE* you can denormalize the discount directly in the fact table, by defining a new calculated column in Sales containing:

```
Sales[SpecialDiscount] =
LOOKUPVALUE (
    SpecialDiscounts[Discount],
    SpecialDiscounts[ProductKey], Sales[ProductKey],
    SpecialDiscounts[OrderDateKey], Sales[OrderDateKey]
)
```

Following this second pattern, you do not create any relationship. Instead, you move the Discount value in the fact table performing a lookup.

Both options work fine and the choice between them depends on several factors. If *Discount* is the only column you need to use from the SpecialDiscount table, then denormalization is the best option because it reduces memory usage (you create a single calculated column, with fewer distinct values) and makes the code simple to author.

If, on the other hand, SpecialDiscounts contains many columns that you need to use in your code, then each of them would have to be denormalized in the fact table, resulting in a waste of memory and possibly in worse performance. In that case, the calculated column with the new composite key is the way to go.

This first simple example is important because it demonstrates a common and important feature of DAX: the ability to create relationships based on calculated columns. This capability shows that you can create any kind of relationship, as long as you can compute it and materialize it in a calculated column. In the next example, we show you how to create relationships based on static ranges but, by extending the concept, you can create really any kind of relationship.

Computing static segmentation

Static segmentation is a very common scenario where you have a value in a table and, rather than being interested in the analysis of the value itself (it might have hundreds or thousands of different values), you want to analyze it by splitting the value into segments. Two very common examples are the analysis of sales by customer age or by list price. Actually, it is pointless to partition sales amount by all unique values of list price, because there are too many different values in list price. However, if you group different prices in ranges, then there are very good chances that you can obtain good insights from the analysis of these groups.

In this example, you have a table containing price ranges where, for each range, you define the boundaries of the range itself, as you can see in Figure 12-2.

PriceRangeKey	PriceRange	MinPrice	MaxPrice
1	VERY LOW	0	10
2	LOW	10	30
3	MEDIUM	30	80
4	HIGH	80	150
5	VERY HIGH	150	99999

FIGURE 12-2 This is the Configuration table for the price ranges.

As it happened in the previous example, you cannot create a direct relationship between the fact table, containing sales, and this Configuration table. The reason is that the key in the Configuration table depends on a range relationship, not supported by DAX.

In this case, the solution is to denormalize the price range directly in the fact table, by using a calculated column. The pattern of the code is very similar to the previous one, the main difference being the formula:

```
Sales[PriceRange] =
CALCULATE (
    VALUES ( PriceRanges[PriceRange] ),
    FILTER (
        PriceRanges,
        AND (
            PriceRanges[MinPrice] <= Sales[Net Price],
            PriceRanges[MaxPrice] > Sales[Net Price]
        )
    )
)
```

It is interesting to note, in this code, the use of *VALUES* to retrieve a single value: *VALUES* returns a table, not a value. However, as you might recall from the DAX specifications, whenever a table contains a single row and a single column, it is automatically converted into a scalar value, if needed by the expression.

Because of the way *FILTER* computes its result, it will always return a single row from the configuration table. Thus, *VALUES* is guaranteed to always return a single row and the result of *CALCULATE* is the description of the price range containing the current net price. Obviously, this expression works fine as long as the configuration table is well designed. If, for any reason, the ranges contain holes or overlaps, then *VALUES* returns many rows and the expression might result in an error.

A better way to author the previous code is to leverage the error handling function, detect the presence of a wrong configuration, and return an appropriate message, as in the following code:

```
Sales[PriceRange] =
VAR ResultValue =
    CALCULATE (
        IFERROR (
            VALUES ( PriceRanges[PriceRange] ),
            "Overlapping Configuration"
        ),
        FILTER (
            PriceRanges,
            AND (
                PriceRanges[MinPrice] <= Sales[Net Price],
                PriceRanges[MaxPrice] > Sales[Net Price]
            )
        )
    )
RETURN
    IF (
        ISEMPTY ( ResultValue ),
        "Holes in Configuration",
        ResultValue
    )
```

The previous code detects both overlapping values (with the internal *IFERROR*) and holes in the configuration (by checking with *ISEMPTY* the result value, before returning it to the caller). Hence, it is much safer to use, because it is guaranteed to always return a good value.

Calculated physical relationships are a very powerful tool in DAX modeling, because the computation of the relationship happens during process time. Thus, they result in very good query performance, regardless of their complexity.

Using virtual relationships

There are many scenarios where you cannot set the logical relationship between tables in a static way. In these cases, you cannot use calculated static relationships. Instead, you need to define the relationship in the measure, handling the calculations in a more dynamic way. Because in this case the relationship does not belong to the model, we speak of virtual relationships, in contrast with the physical relationships you learned so far.

Using dynamic segmentation

The first example of a dynamic relationship solves a variation of the static segmentation you learned earlier in this chapter. In the static segmentation, you assigned each sale to a specific segment using a calculated column. In dynamic segmentation, the assignment happens dynamically.

Imagine that you want to cluster your customers based on the sales amount. The sales amount depends on the slicers used in the report. Therefore, the segmentation cannot be static. If, for example, you filter a single year, then a customer might belong to a specific cluster but by changing the year, the same customer will belong to a different cluster. In this scenario, you cannot rely on a physical relationship.

You start defining the Configuration table, which you can see in Figure 12-3.

SegmentCode	Segment	MinSale	MaxSale
1	Very Low	0	75
2	Low	75	100
3	Medium	100	500
4	High	500	1000
6	Very High	1000	99999999

FIGURE 12-3 Configuration table for dynamic segmentation.

The measure to compute is the number of customers belonging to a specific cluster. In other words, you want to count how many customers belong to a segment taking into account all the filters in the current filter context. The formula is a simple one:

```
CustInSegment :=
COUNTROWS (
    FILTER (
        Customer,
        AND (
            [Sales Amount] > MIN ( Segments[MinSale] ),
            [Sales Amount] <= MAX ( Segments[MaxSale] )
        )
    )
)
```

In order to understand the formula behavior, it is useful to look at a report that shows the segments on the rows, and the calendar year on columns. You can see the report in Figure 12-4.

CustInSegment Column Labels ▾				
Row Labels ▾	⊞ CY 2007	⊞ CY 2008	⊞ CY 2009	Grand Total
Very Low	351	266	255	810
Low	141	14	12	166
Medium	365	76	52	485
High	250	36	35	311
Very High	302	132	160	581
Grand Total	1409	524	514	2353

FIGURE 12-4 This pivot table shows the dynamic segmentation pattern in action.

For instance, look at the highlighted cell, which shows 76 customers belonging to the Medium cluster in 2008. The formula iterated over Customer and for each customer it checked if the value of Sales Amount for that customer falls between *MIN* of *MinSale* and *MAX* of *MaxSale*. The value of *Sales Amount* represents the sales of the individual customer, due to context transition (remember the automatic *CALCULATE* that is inserted around any measure invocation). DAX evaluates *MIN* and *MAX* in the current filter context for that specific cell, which shows only the Medium row of Segments. As a result, *MIN* is the value of *MinSale* for the Medium segment, and *MAX* is the value of *MaxSale* for the same segment. In other words, for that specific row, using *MIN*, *MAX*, or *VALUES* leads to the same result. Nevertheless, we used *MIN* and *MAX* to make the formula work at the grand total level too, where the filter context might contain multiple rows for the Segments table and *VALUES* would return an error.

The resulting measure is, as expected, additive against segments and customers and nonadditive against all other dimensions.

The formula works as long as you do not select some of the segments. If you select, for example, only Very Low and Very High (removing the three intermediate segments from the selection), then *MIN* and *MAX* will not be the correct choice, because they will enclose all the customers, resulting in wrong results in the grand total. If you want to let the user select some of the segments, then you need to write the formula in a slightly different way:

```
CustInSegmentSUMX :=
SUMX (
    Segments,
    COUNTROWS (
        FILTER (
            Customer,
            AND (
                [Sales Amount] > Segments[MinSale],
                [Sales Amount] <= Segments[MaxSale]
            )
        )
    )
)
```

This version of the formula does not suffer from the issue of partial selection of segments but it might result in worse performance, because it requires a double iteration over the tables. You can appreciate the difference between the two measures in the grand total of the report in Figure 12-5, with the two measures side by side.

Row Labels ⫟	CustInSegment	CustInSegmentSUMX
Very Low	810	810
Very High	581	581
Grand Total	2353	1391

FIGURE 12-5 At the grand total, the two measures show different values because of partial selection of segments.

Many-to-many relationships

Many-to-many relationships are a very common type of relationship that requires an additional table in the model, known as the bridge table. There are several types of many-to-many relationships. The goal of this section is to show you how to handle basic many-to-many relationships, and provide some information about more advanced ones.

As an example, we use the Promotion table in the Contoso database. Over time, Contoso makes promotions on specific products. This is a good example of a many-to-many relationship, because:

- One product can participate in many promotions over time.

- One promotion is active on many products at the same time.

The data model defines a bridge table between Product and Promotion, resulting in the diagram you can see in Figure 12-6.

You can easily handle this simple model using the bidirectional relationships of DAX. In fact, if the relationship between the bridge table and product is set bidirectional (when the model allows that), then you will be able to use Promotion to filter Products and, finally, Sales and other related tables.

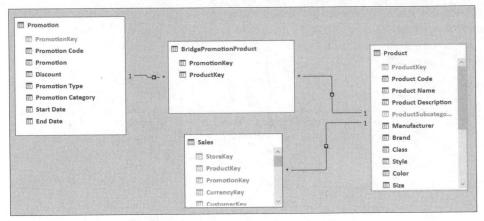

FIGURE 12-6 The diagram shows the bridge table linking Product and Promotion using a bridge table.

Note It is important to note that many-to-many relationships always lead to nonadditive measures. In fact, if you project in a report the amount sold sliced by the promotion, you will see the amount sold by all the products in promotion and, because a single product can participate in many promotions, its value will be aggregated under multiple rows. *However, in the grand total it will only be treated as a single product and so the grand total value might not be the same as the sum of all single promotions.* This is not an error. It is the normal behavior of many-to-many relationships.

As easy as this solution is, it has some drawbacks that you need to take into account when building a data model. Let's examine them in detail:

- Bidirectional relationships are not available in all versions of DAX. At the time of writing, they are supported in Power BI Desktop and in Analysis Services 2016, but not in any version of Microsoft Excel. If you do not have such a feature available, then you need to implement a different solution.

- You do not have full control over the relationship. There are models (such as the examples we provide later) where you need a finer control over the relationship, or where you want to use the relationship as a helper to compute more sophisticated expressions.

- Occasionally, in order to support a physical relationship (as in the previous example), you build a complex table preparing data before the data model (this phase is also called Extract, Transform & Load (ETL), and its implementation might correspond to an SQL query, or a Power Query transformation, or an Integration Services package). An example we will analyze later is that of temporal relationships.

In order to elaborate on the preceding topics, let's perform a deeper analysis of the data model of Figure 12-6. If you link promotions only to products, you are missing an important piece of information, that is, the period of time when the promotion was active. A more accurate data model also contains a link to the date. In fact, if you build a report based on the simple relationship outlined so far, you get a wrong result, as you can see in Figure 12-7, where it is evident that the report shows sales in years when the promotion was not active.

Sales Amount	Column Labels			
Row Labels	CY 2007	CY 2008	CY 2009	Grand Total
⊟ Asian Holiday Promotion	$885,598.85	$405,034.62	$349,782.46	$1,640,415.93
From 11/1/2007 to 1/31/2008	$764,286.28	$115,625.69	$116,964.75	$996,876.72
From 11/1/2008 to 1/31/2009	$85,229.03	$204,808.54	$132,452.14	$422,489.71
From 11/1/2009 to 1/31/2010	$69,551.84	$116,577.25	$136,650.27	$322,779.36
⊟ Asian Spring Promotion	$871,586.15	$358,683.92	$341,479.11	$1,571,749.18
From 2/1/2007 to 4/30/2007	$723,794.95	$88,835.89	$82,646.43	$895,277.27
From 2/1/2008 to 4/30/2008	$168,819.29	$193,131.73	$91,860.97	$453,811.99
From 2/1/2009 to 4/30/2009	$270,515.13	$122,312.10	$211,345.60	$604,172.83

FIGURE 12-7 If you do not take dates into account, the promotions report sales outside of their validity.

The reason is that the bridge table filters the products based on the promotion, and then the report includes all the sales of those products, even outside the promotion validity. Therefore, you need to take into account the date, too. The scenario becomes more complicated and it is worth spending some time to study it well, because it hides a lot of complexity.

A first trial might be that of expanding the bridge table by adding a date key. Clearly, you would need to create one row in the bridge table for each of the dates in the range of the promotion's validity, thus increasing the size of the bridge table. The resulting data model is the one in Figure 12-8.

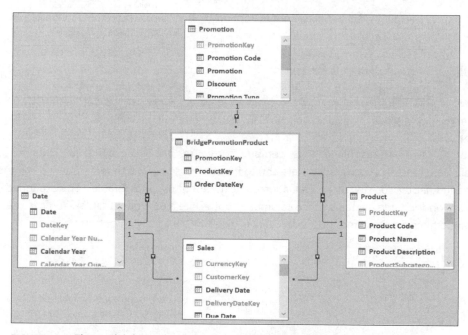

FIGURE 12-8 The model shows the expanded bridge table, with the relationship to Date.

As you can see, we have replicated the bidirectional relationship between the bridge and Product with the Date table. Unfortunately, this model cannot work because, by defining it, you create an ambiguous set of relationships, which DAX does not support. In fact, starting from Sales, you can reach the bridge table following two different paths: one from Product to BridgePromotionProduct, the other one from Date to BridgePromotionProduct. You cannot rely on the data model supporting bidirectional relationships to create this structure. It's time to get started and use DAX to compute the correct amount of sales.

First we remove the bidirectional propagation from both relationships, making all the relationships linked to the bridge table simple ones, as you can see in Figure 12-9. You can create this model with any version of DAX data models, because it does not use bidirectional relationships.

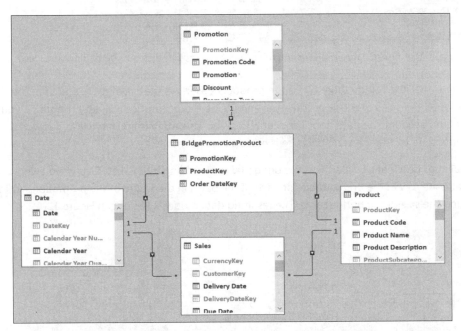

FIGURE 12-9 The model shows the expanded bridge table, with the relationship on the Date.

At this point, the measures will no longer compute correct results, because the filter from the bridge table is no longer propagated to Date and to Product. It is now worth remembering the theory you learned in Chapter 10, "Advanced evaluation context," about expanded tables. The expanded version of the bridge table contains all the columns of both Date and Product tables. You can use the bridge table to filter the Date and the Product tables by using the following pattern:

```
CALCULATE (
    …,
    CALCULATETABLE (
        Product,
        BridgePromotionProduct
    ),
    CALCULATETABLE (
        'Date',
        BridgePromotionProduct
    )
)
```

Let's briefly recall what is happening here: By using BridgePromotionProduct as a filter argument in *CALCULATE*, you are referring to the expanded bridge table. Because the expanded BridgePromotionProduct table contains the columns of Product (and Date), each *CALCULATETABLE* returns the products (or dates) referenced by the bridge table. The BridgePromotionProduct table, in turn, is already filtered in the filter context, showing only the promotions selected by the user. Thus, each *CALCULATETABLE* returns the set of products and dates of the given promotion. Once you use these two *CALCULATETABLE* to generate the filter context of the outer *CALCULATE*, they will work together as a filter on the Sales table, making it possible to aggregate sales related to the given promotion. The first version of the many-to-many formulas is the following one:

```
Sales Amount :=
CALCULATE (
    SUMX ( Sales, Sales[Quantity] * Sales[Unit Price] ),
    CALCULATETABLE ( Product, BridgePromotionProduct ),
    CALCULATETABLE ( 'Date', BridgePromotionProduct )
)
```

If you use this formula in a report and you select a single promotion, it works just fine and produces the correct result. Nevertheless, when used in a report that shows many promotions, such as the ones we have seen so far, it suffers from a major problem. The formula filters Product and Date separately, putting the filters in a logical AND on the fact table. Yet the two filters are computed separately.

Now imagine two promotions (A, B) and two products (P1, P2). P1 is in promotion A in January and February, whereas P2 is in promotion B only in February, as shown in Table 12-1.

Table 12-1 Sample set of promotions with overlapping dates.

Promotion	Product	Date
A	P1	January
A	P1	February
B	P2	February

If both promotions A and B are visible in the filter context, then the resulting filter context from the pair of *CALCULATETABLE* contains (January, February) for Date and (P1, P2) for Product. The two filters, put in *AND*, filter the entire fact table, resulting in a total amount that contains sales of all products over all periods. What you should compute, on the other hand, are the sales of January and February for P1, but only January for P2. This is because P2, in January, was not present in any promotion.

What you have to do is maintain the relationship between products and dates that is present in the bridge table, by summarizing it instead of separating it into two filters. The correct formulation for Sales Amount is the following one:

```
[Sales Amount] :=
CALCULATE (
    SUMX ( Sales, Sales[Quantity] * Sales[Unit Price] ),
    SUMMARIZE (
        BridgePromotionProduct,
        Product[ProductKey],
        'Date'[DateKey]
    )
)
```

SUMMARIZE returns the pairs of product/date that are present in the visible promotions. It will filter the fact table because the expanded version of Sales contains both product and date keys.

As you have seen, in using *SUMMARIZE* you have a finer control over how relationships are propagated. Actually, this technique gives you the option of implementing many-to-many relationships without leveraging the bidirectional propagation, which is available only in certain versions of products supporting DAX. This technique was widely used to implement many-to-many before the availability of bidirectional relationships, but you can still use it whenever you design data models with complex relationships not natively supported by the engine.

Moreover, it is worth noting that leveraging further the theory of expanded tables, you can write a more compact version of the same expression, namely:

```
[Sales Amount] :=
CALCULATE (
    SUMX ( Sales, Sales[Quantity] * Sales[Unit Price] ),
    BridgePromotionProduct
)
```

In fact, *SUMMARIZE* is not really useful there. Due to its nature, BridgePromotionProduct contains the pair of *ProductKey* and *DateKey* that filters Sales based on the selected promotions. You do not really have to use *SUMMARIZE*, because the pairs are already there, ready to be used. The expanded version of BridgePromotionProduct contains all the columns of Product and Date tables. Thus, using BridgePromotionProduct as a filter condition in *CALCULATE* provides the same result as *SUMMARIZE*.

SUMMARIZE can still be useful in case you want to further restrict the propagation of the filter from the bridge table to only a reduced number of relationships defined in the data model.

Using relationships with different granularities

Let's continue the description of dynamic relationships with a common example of relationships at different granularities. Typically, you set relationships with the primary key of the target table, but you might have to create a relationship with a different column, which is not the primary key or, to be more generic, with nonunique values. A common scenario is a data model including budgets.

For instance, suppose you have budget data at the category and month levels, instead of product and day levels that you have for sales data. In fact, you cannot easily forecast how many products you will sell of an individual product, while it makes much more sense to predict the number of products of a specific category. Moreover, it might be the case that you plan to sell new products, which are not even part of your products table, just because they do not exist yet. The same happens to the time dimension. It is nearly impossible (if not even useful) to forecast the sales on a single day, whereas it makes sense to predict sales at the month level.

As an example, look at the data model in Figure 12-10, where the Forecast table contains budget information at the category, brand, and month level.

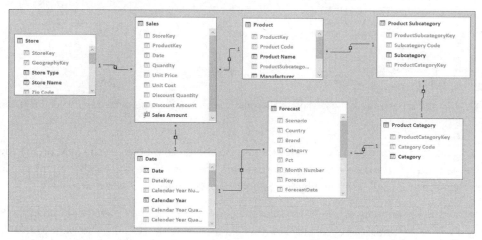

FIGURE 12-10 The model shows a typical budgeting scenario, with Forecast at a different granularity than Sales.

As you can see in the model, there are physical relationships between Forecast and both Product Category and Date. The relationship to Date is set at the first day of the month by using the *Forecast-Date* calculated column, because—originally—Forecast had only the month number. The problem is with the Brand, which is a column in Product, and Country, which is a column in Store. Both columns are not primary keys of the respective tables. Thus, you cannot create any physical relationship between these two tables.

As a result, if you build a report based on the Country, for example, you do not get meaningful results, as you can see in Figure 12-11.

Continent	Europe	

Row Labels	Sales Amount	Sum of Forecast
Denmark	$22,029,504.40	$14,415,047,217.13
France	$672,697,472.01	$14,415,047,217.13
Germany	$1,038,529,379.21	$14,415,047,217.13
Greece	$21,937,711.40	$14,415,047,217.13
Ireland	$21,956,889.02	$14,415,047,217.13
Italy	$80,379,765.46	$14,415,047,217.13
Malta	$21,746,303.76	$14,415,047,217.13
Poland	$21,932,150.75	$14,415,047,217.13
Portugal	$21,929,286.60	$14,415,047,217.13
Romania	$22,162,791.49	$14,415,047,217.13
Russia	$103,293,227.71	$14,415,047,217.13
Slovenia	$21,587,750.05	$14,415,047,217.13
Spain	$21,851,018.21	$14,415,047,217.13
Sweden	$21,494,023.28	$14,415,047,217.13
Switzerland	$21,273,245.62	$14,415,047,217.13
the Netherlands	$21,909,437.06	$14,415,047,217.13
United Kingdom	$320,947,348.44	$14,415,047,217.13
Grand Total	$2,477,657,304.47	$14,415,047,217.13

FIGURE 12-11 In this report, due to the missing relationship, the pivot table repeats the same value for all the rows.

The behavior is a very common one: Since there is no relationship between the field on the rows and the table used by *Sum of Forecast* in the values area, the pivot table repeats the same value in all the rows. Because you cannot set the physical relationship, you have to create a virtual one.

The technique to use requires you to consider the current filter on the *Country* column in the Store table and use it to generate an equivalent filter on the Forecast table. Namely, you want to take the current filter on Store and transform it into a corresponding filter on Forecast. If you modify *Sum of Forecast* using the following code, you reach this first goal:

```
[Sum of Forecast] :=
CALCULATE (
    SUM ( Forecast[Forecast] ),
    FILTER (
        VALUES ( Forecast[Country] ),
        CONTAINS (
            VALUES ( Store[Country] ),
            Store[Country],
            Forecast[Country]
        )
    )
)
```

The core of the formula is the innermost *CONTAINS*. It checks if the value of the currently iterated *Forecast[Country]* (iterated by *FILTER*) is contained in the list of visible *Store[Country]* values. As a result, it returns the forecast countries that belong to visible store countries.

> **Note** It is not yet time to speak about performance but, looking at the code, you can already make some performance considerations. *FILTER* iterates the values of *Forecast[Country]* and, for each value, it checks its presence in the values of *Store[Country]*. Thus, the complexity of this formula depends on the number of countries squared. In reality, since *CONTAINS* is faster than a full scan (you can expect logarithmic complexity on search), the complexity should be O (N * LOG (N)) where N is the number of countries. With a limited number of countries, the formula should work very fast.

This technique of using *CONTAINS* to generate a filter based on another table, is very common whenever you need to create virtual relationships moving a filter from one table to another one. The formula, by itself, does not solve the complete budgeting pattern. There are many other considerations that you should take into account to build a complete budgeting solution. Nevertheless, in this chapter we are only interested in how to manage different types of relationships. If you want to learn more about the complete budgeting solution, go to http://www.daxpatterns.com/budget-patterns/, which describes budget patterns in depth.

Before leaving the topic, it is worth looking at a version of the same formula that takes advantage of set functions and is very elegant:

```
[Sum of Forecast] :=
CALCULATE (
    SUM ( Forecast[Forecast] ),
    INTERSECT (
        VALUES ( Forecast[Country] ),
        VALUES ( Store[Country] )
    )
)
```

INTERSECT performs the set operation we need by making a set intersection. *INTERSECT* is available only in the latest versions of DAX, thus the version with *CONTAINS* might still be useful, if you need to work with an older version of DAX. It is only important to note that *ForeCast[Country]* needs to be the first column used in *INTERSECT*, because this is the column that DAX will use for lineage.

Differences between physical and virtual relationships

Virtual relationships are a powerful way to generate complex models. Working with complex scenarios, you face the choice between building a physical (maybe calculated) relationship or a virtual one.

Generally, physical relationships are a better option. There is no difference, in terms of query performance, between a standard relationship, based on a column, and a calculated one, based on a calculated column. The engine computes calculated columns at process time (when data is refreshed), so it does not really matter how complex your expression is, the relationship is a physical one and the engine can take full advantage of it.

Later in Chapter 15, "Analyzing query plans," you will learn about the Formula Engine (FE) and Storage Engine (SE), and you will learn that the Storage Engine is typically faster than the Formula Engine. Here we only anticipate that Storage Engine can use physical relationships (either calculated or not) during low-level VertiPaq queries, producing better results in terms of speed.

Virtual relationships, on the other hand, are resolved at query time. Moreover, they are not real relationships, so the engine cannot make assumptions on them and optimize the query using the notion of a relationship. Thus, whenever you have the option of doing that, prefer a physical relationship against a virtual one.

In the middle, between physical and virtual relationships, there are many-to-many relationships. You can define many-to-many relationships in the model, through bidirectional relationships (in that sense, they are physical relationships) and during calculations, leveraging table expansion. There are no differences between the two approaches. In fact, even if the relationship is marked as a bidirectional one, when the engine needs to traverse it in the opposite way, it performs the same steps that you implement using table expansion.

Therefore, regarding performance, you should choose:

1. Physical (either calculated or not) relationships to get best performance and the best use of the VertiPaq engine.

2. Bidirectional relationships or many-to-many with table expansion, as a second option. You get good performance and a good use of the engine, although not the best.

3. Virtual relationships, as the least option, because you are in danger of bad performance. Note that being in danger does not mean you will experience performance issues, but only that you need to care about different aspects of the query, which you will learn in the next chapters about optimization.

Finding missing relationships

So far, you have seen many different kinds of relationships, both physical and virtual ones. All these examples have one feature in common: You were interested in computing values when the relationship was in place. Occasionally you are interested in the opposite information, which is to compute values when the relationship does not hold.

Stated in this way, it might look surprising. In reality, missing relationships are—after all—more interesting than existing ones. Think, for example, about sales of products. If you put some products on sale, then you want to compute how many products you have sold with that special price. Nevertheless, there is another piece of information that is extremely useful: How many of those products (on sale) did not result in any sale? Because there are no sales for those products, you cannot expect to find information in the fact table about them. Yet you want to find what those products are and, maybe, evaluate the potential loss of sales.

Missing relationships is a variant that you can apply to any kind of relationship, either physical or virtual.

Computing number of products not sold

This first example where you learn about missing relationships is a somewhat simple one: finding the products not sold in a selected period. The Sales table contains information about sold products. If you want to compute the number of sold products, you can easily compute it using a measure such as the following one:

```
[NumOfProductsSold] := DISTINCTCOUNT ( Sales[ProductKey] )
```

At this point, computing the number of not sold products is as easy as subtracting, from the total number of products, the number of sold ones:

```
[NumOfProductsNotSold] := COUNTROWS ( Product ) - DISTINCTCOUNT ( Sales[ProductKey] )
```

This technique is a good choice if your goal is counting products. However, as you learn later in this section, there are many other calculations for which you do not only need to count them, but also to identify them. In *NumOfProductsNotSold*, you do not really identify the products not sold. Instead, you take advantage of the fact that you can compute the number of products not sold by a simple subtraction.

Moreover, this formula has another major drawback. If Product was a type 2 slowly changing dimension, then counting the product key in the fact table does not really produce the number of products. Instead, it computes the number of versions of products, leading to a wrong result. Instead of counting the product keys, you solve this issue by counting the number of product codes (or names), taking advantage of table expansion with *CALCULATE*. Consider the following formula:

```
[NumOfProductsSold] := CALCULATE ( DISTINCTCOUNT ( Product[Product Code] ), Sales )
```

The expansion of Sales produces a filter on Product, so that you count only the codes of products referenced by Sales. Therefore, the previous expression, although probably a bit slower than *DISTINCTCOUNT* of the product key, has two advantages:

- It counts the correct number of products, even in the case where Product is a slowly changing dimension of type 2.

- It effectively identifies the products. By leveraging table expansion, it moves the filter from Sales to Product through *CALCULATE*.

The second point is interesting because it lays out a way to compute the products not sold by performing set operations, instead of mathematical subtraction:

```
[NumOfProductsNotSold] :=
CALCULATE (
    DISTINCTCOUNT ( Product[Product Code] ),
    EXCEPT (
        VALUES ( Product[ProductKey] ),
        CALCULATETABLE (
            VALUES ( Product[ProductKey] ),
            Sales
        )
    )
)
```

This version of *NumOfProductNotSold* computes the set difference between the product keys and the set of product keys referenced by the fact table. It is worth noting that in this case, unlike in the previous example about different granularities, you are intersecting two sets built on top of the same column. Therefore, lineage is maintained and the resulting table can be used by *CALCULATE* to produce a filter context on *ProductKey*. Once the filter is in place, *DISTINCTCOUNT* computes the product codes for only the products not referenced by the fact table. In other words, with this pattern you can now navigate through a negated relationship and compute any kind of value.

Computing new and returning customers

Another example of a missing relationship is that of new and returning customers. You can use a pattern that is very similar to that of products to compute the number of customers in a period of time (that is, the distinct count of customers), the number of new customers (customers who never bought before), and returning customers (customers who bought before, and returned to buy something else).

All these calculations are very easy to author when you get used to set functions. Given a period, we use these definitions:

- **Customer** Somebody who made a purchase in the current period.

- **New customer** A customer who made a purchase in the current period and who never made purchases before the beginning of the current period.

- **Returning customer** A customer who made a purchase in the current period and already made other purchases before the beginning of the current period.

Given the previous definitions, you can define two sets:

- **Current Customers** Customers who made a purchase in the current period.

- **Previous Customers** Customers who made a purchase before the current period.

You can compute these two sets by taking advantage of table expansion:

```
VAR CurrentCustomers =
    CALCULATETABLE ( Customer, Sales )

VAR PreviousCustomers =
    CALCULATETABLE (
        Customer,
        CALCULATETABLE (
            Sales,
            FILTER (
                ALL ( 'Date' ),
                'Date'[Date] < MIN ( 'Date'[Date] )
            )
        )
    )
```

CurrentCustomer is easy to grab at first sight. *PreviousCustomers*, on the other hand, uses the same technique (table expansion) but, instead of using Sales, it takes advantage of *CALCULATETABLE* to compute Sales for periods before the beginning of the currently selected one. Note that you need to use *ALL ('Date')* to gain access to dates that are outside the current filter context.

> **Note** In this example, we are not considering selection of products. If you use these measures by filtering some products, you apply the notion of new and returning customers to the subset of considered products. In case you need another definition, you have to change the filter over products in the formulas. You can find a broader discussion of these patterns and their variations on http://www.daxpatterns.com/new-and-returning-customers/.

The two sets compute tables of Customer, so you can use set functions like *INTERSECT*, *UNION*, and *EXCEPT* to generate new filters based on them. At this point, computing the number of new customers and returning customers is a basic implementation of set logic, as you can see in the following definitions:

```
[NewCustomers] :=
CALCULATE (
    COUNTROWS ( Customer ),
    EXCEPT ( CurrentCustomers, PreviousCustomers )
)

[ReturningCustomers] :=
CALCULATE (
    COUNTROWS ( Customer ),
    INTERSECT ( CurrentCustomers, PreviousCustomers )
)
```

> **Note** Set functions have been available since the 2015 version of DAX. In previous versions, computing these values was more complex, because you had to find an optimized way of performing set logic, without leveraging the set functions. If you are interested in these calculations for previous versions of DAX, you can find them on http://www.daxpatterns.com/new-and-returning-customers/.

It is important to note that, because these set functions identify the customers, you can use the same pattern to calculate other values. For instance, if you want to compute the sales of new customers, and compare them with the sales of returning customers, you can author measures such as the following ones:

```
[SalesNewCustomers] :=
CALCULATE (
    SUM ( Sales[Amount] ),
    EXCEPT ( CurrentCustomers, PreviousCustomers )
)

[SalesOfReturningCustomers] :=
CALCULATE (
    SUM ( Sales[Amount] ),
    INTERSECT ( CurrentCustomers, PreviousCustomers )
)
```

The only difference between these two measures and the previous ones is the expression computed by *CALCULATE*. The filtering part is the same set of new or returning customers you have seen previously.

Examples of complex relationships

In this final section about the DAX language, we show you some more examples of DAX code using complex relationships and most of the functionalities you have learned so far. At the cost of repeating ourselves, please keep in mind that these are not super-optimized patterns that will solve a specific scenario. Instead, we want to show you different approaches to different scenarios, with the goal of letting you gain familiarity with DAX.

Performing currency conversion

Another example of complex relationships you are going to learn about is how to handle currency conversion in DAX. There are many techniques to implement currency conversion, and we do not pretend to explain the definitive one, because business requirements are very different when it comes to this problem. Nevertheless, because it is a good exercise, we are going to describe a solution based on the techniques you have learned so far.

There are three possible scenarios where currency conversion comes into play:

- Data collected in a single currency and you want to show, in a report, results in different currencies.

- Data collected in the original currency (that is, many of them) and you want to display results in a single one, to make comparisons.

- Data collected in the original currency (that is, many of them) and you want to display results in many currencies.

This list is just the beginning of the pain that comes when dealing with currency. Because all of the three scenarios require currency conversion, the first question is which date are you going to use to perform the conversion? Here the business rules become very complex. If the order was placed in Euros on December 1, you might be tempted to use the currency exchange rate of December 1 to perform the conversion. However, it turns out that the customer paid in Euros on December 12; money has been left in a Euro account until the end of the month and only on December 31 was it converted to USD. Which rate is the right one? December 1, 12, or 31? Only end users can advise you and decide on a business rule. Nevertheless, because we need to define a scenario and we want to use Contoso, we consider the following requirements for our example:

- Amounts stored in the fact table are always in USD. Conversion happened during the population of Sales as part of the data preparation process (ETL).

- You want to report information about sales in a user-selected currency using two different currency exchange rates:

  - At the date of the order, thus a different exchange for each order. In the demo database (Contoso), exchange rates are available at the month level. So we will use the beginning of the next month.

  - Using the last available exchange rate (which, when in production, is the current exchange rate).

As we said, this is an educational example. In the real world, business rules might be different and, in that case, you have to change the formulas and the techniques to fit your specific needs. Let's start reviewing the initial model in Figure 12-12.

There are two important points to check, regarding the data model:

- You will need two currency tables: one to select the currency of the order, which acts as a filter on the Sales table and is already visible in the diagram, and the other one to select the reporting currency. In fact, the reporting currency does not filter Sales. Instead, you use it to select the target currency for the report.

- Because currency exchange information is stored with monthly granularity, whereas orders have a daily granularity, you cannot set a relationship between Sales and ExchangeRate based on the order date.

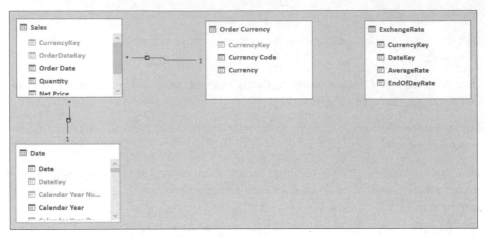

FIGURE 12-12 The starting data model for currency conversion includes Date, Sales, Order Currency, and ExchangeRate tables.

Figure 12-13 shows the data model we use for this example, where we added the Report Currency and the relationship with ExchangeRate.

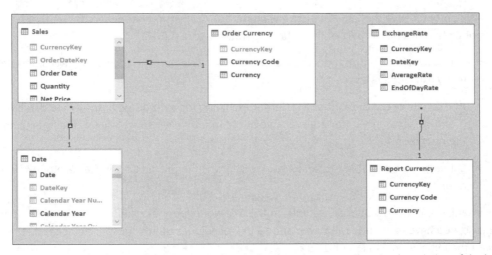

FIGURE 12-13 The data model to convert using the latest exchange rate is a simple variation of the basic one.

It is worthwhile to note that there are no relationships between Sales and ExchangeRate, because the conversion of sales from the original currency to USD already happened, and you no longer care about what was the order currency. Since you need to convert USD to a given currency, you can simply compute, for each currency, the latest exchange rate and finally multiply that number by the total sales expressed in USD.

Let's start describing the simplest kind of conversion: You have all sales in USD (already converted) and you want to report them using a different currency, applying the latest conversion rate.

The following query reports the total sales in all the different currencies:

```
DEFINE
    MEASURE Sales[SalesUSD] =
        SUMX ( Sales, Sales[Quantity] * Sales[Net Price] )
EVALUATE
ADDCOLUMNS (
    ADDCOLUMNS (
        VALUES ( 'Report Currency'[Currency] ),
        "LastAvailableExchange",
        VAR LastAvailableDate =
            CALCULATE ( MAX ( ExchangeRate[DateKey] ) )
        RETURN
            CALCULATE (
                VALUES ( ExchangeRate[EndOfDayRate] ),
                ExchangeRate[DateKey] = LastAvailableDate
            )
    ),
    "Sales in USD", [SalesUSD],
    "Currency Sales", [SalesUSD] * [LastAvailableExchange]
)
```

You can see the result of the query in Figure 12-14.

Currency	LastAvailableExchange	Sales_in_USD	Currency_Sales
US Dollar	1.00	3,805,392,024.21	3,805,392,024.21
Armenian Dram	360.10	3,805,392,024.21	1,370,321,667,919.32
Australian Dollar	1.21	3,805,392,024.21	4,602,241,114.08
Thai Baht	33.94	3,805,392,024.21	129,173,271,183.53
Canadian Dollar	1.08	3,805,392,024.21	4,100,386,013.93
Danish Krone	5.30	3,805,392,024.21	20,161,004,998.20
EURO	0.71	3,805,392,024.21	2,684,704,073.08
Hong Kong Dollar	7.75	3,805,392,024.21	29,491,940,403.34
Indian Rupee	48.21	3,805,392,024.21	183,476,595,908.26
Romanian Leu	2.98	3,805,392,024.21	11,354,528,721.85
Maltese Lira	0.29	3,805,392,024.21	1,116,502,019.90
Taiwan Dollar	32.81	3,805,392,024.21	124,864,425,794.51
Bhutan Ngultrum	48.45	3,805,392,024.21	184,377,370,254.31
Pakistan Rupee		3,805,392,024.21	
Russian Ruble	31.67	3,805,392,024.21	120,517,145,946.05
Singapore Dollar	1.44	3,805,392,024.21	5,483,950,446.09
Swedish Krona	7.31	3,805,392,024.21	27,819,889,201.82
Swiss Franc	1.08	3,805,392,024.21	4,122,723,665.11
Slovenian Tolar	161.27	3,805,392,024.21	613,695,571,744.93
British Pound	0.61	3,805,392,024.21	2,316,342,125.14
South Korean Won	1,222.74	3,805,392,024.21	4,653,005,043,686.94
Japanese Yen	95.72	3,805,392,024.21	364,255,168,871.35
Renminbi Yuan	6.83	3,805,392,024.21	25,993,453,245.88
Polish Zloty	3.00	3,805,392,024.21	11,403,618,278.96
Iranian Rial	9,917.00	3,805,392,024.21	37,738,072,704,126.30
Syrian Pound	46.04	3,805,392,024.21	175,200,248,794.79
Turkmenistan Manat		3,805,392,024.21	
Som		3,805,392,024.21	

FIGURE 12-14 The report shows total sales converted using the last available exchange rate for each currency.

It's useful to note that the query computes the last available date for each currency. Actually, for any reason, the last available date of currency conversion might be different for different currencies. Thus, you cannot rely on the maximum date in the entire table. You have to compute it inside the iteration over currencies created by *ADDCOLUMNS* over the values of *Currency*.

The scenario becomes slightly more complex if you want to report the value of sales in the original currency. In that case, you need to perform the conversion of sales with the exchange rate that was effective at the order date, because the number stored in the Sales table is the amount already converted in USD. The tricky part, here, is determining in an efficient way what the exchange rate was at the time of the order. The topic is worth elaborating a bit.

Exchange Rate contains rates at the month level, one row for each month and currency. The rate is stored on the first day of the month. So for each sale, you can use the exchange rate of the first date of the month (using the beginning of the next month would work fine, too, but you would have issues in the last month, for which there is no "next month" available). This would work well if you were sure that the exchange rate is available for each month and currency. However, if data was gathered in an imperfect way (something you should fix during ETL, if possible), then you could have some holes in the exchange rates. In that case, you can either raise an error, or use the latest exchange rate available at that date.

As you see, the calculation is not a simple one. Determining the date for each sale to use for the exchange rate is not trivial. This is a perfect scenario where calculated columns come to help. The code will be executed during the model process time, and you do not have to worry too much about performance.

You can easily compute a calculated column containing the original amount in the order currency using the following definition:

```
Sales[OriginalAmount] =
DIVIDE (
    SUMX(Sales, Sales[Quantity] * Sales[Net Price]),
    CALCULATE (
        VALUES ( ExchangeRate[EndOfDayRate] ),
        TOPN (
            1,
            CALCULATETABLE (
                VALUES ( ExchangeRate[DateKey] ),
                ExchangeRate[CurrencyKey] = EARLIER ( Sales[CurrencyKey] ),
                ExchangeRate[DateKey] <= EARLIER ( Sales[Order Date] )
            ),
            ExchangeRate[DateKey]
        ),
        ExchangeRate[CurrencyKey] = EARLIER ( Sales[CurrencyKey] )
    )
)
```

TOPN, in this case, is necessary to retrieve the latest available exchange rate at the date of the order, for the given currency. It is worth noting that *TOPN* filters only *DateKey*. This is the reason why we have to duplicate the condition on the *CurrencyKey*.

If you read the code carefully, you will recognize the calculated physical relationship pattern, where we denormalized the exchange rate to compute the original amount.

This is a suitable solution mainly because the request was to compute the value in the original currency. The scenario becomes much more complex if you need a report containing a user-defined currency, performing the conversion at the date of the order (or with the latest conversion rate at the order date). The complexity comes from the fact that, this time, you cannot rely on calculated columns, which work fine only if you need a single currency. If the report currency is selected by the user (through a slicer, or any other means), then you have to perform a similar calculation dynamically at query time.

In the following query, you can see that the execution path is a mix of the two previous scenarios:

```
DEFINE
    MEASURE Sales[SalesUSD] =
        SUMX ( Sales, Sales[Quantity] * Sales[Net Price] )
EVALUATE
ADDCOLUMNS (
    VALUES ( 'Report Currency'[Currency] ),
    "Sales in USD", [SalesUSD],
    "Currency Sales",
    SUMX (
        ADDCOLUMNS (
            SUMMARIZE (
                Sales,
                Sales[CurrencyKey],
                'Date'[Calendar Year Month Number]
            ),
            "MonthlySalesInCurrency", CALCULATE (
                VALUES ( ExchangeRate[EndOfDayRate] ),
                TOPN (
                    1,
                    CALCULATETABLE (
                        ExchangeRate,
                        FILTER (
                            VALUES ( ExchangeRate[DateKey] ),
                            ExchangeRate[DateKey] <= CALCULATE ( MAX ( 'Date'[Date] ) )
                        )
                    ),
                    ExchangeRate[DateKey]
                )
            )
            * [SalesUSD]
        ),
        [MonthlySalesInCurrency]
    )
)
```

The complexity of the query is all in the calculation of *Currency Sales*. *SUMMARIZE* group sales by currency key and month number. This table, containing currency and month, is iterated by *ADDCOLUMNS*, which computes the *MonthlySalesInCurrency* by multiplying the sales in USD by the last available exchange rate.

You might notice that, this time, when searching for the last available date, we do not filter by currency. The reason is that the full code of *MonthlySalesInCurrency* is included in *CALCULATE*, which consolidates not only the row context introduced by *ADDCOLUMNS* over the summarized fact table but, at the same time, the row context introduced by the outermost *ADDCOLUMNS*, which is iterating over the Report Currency. ExchangeRate is already filtered to show only the exchange rates of the given currency.

The result of all the monthly currency sales is aggregated by *SUMX* and transformed in a value that *ADDCOLUMNS* merges with the currency names and finally produces the result, which you can see in Figure 12-15.

Currency	Sales_in_USD	Currency_Sales
US Dollar	3,805,392,024.21	3,805,392,024.21
Armenian Dram	3,805,392,024.21	1,269,282,737,849.36
Australian Dollar	3,805,392,024.21	4,654,899,465.73
Thai Baht	3,805,392,024.21	126,320,094,175.72
Canadian Dollar	3,805,392,024.21	4,146,590,249.55
Danish Krone	3,805,392,024.21	20,229,305,593.39
EURO	3,805,392,024.21	2,709,274,745.46
Hong Kong Dollar	3,805,392,024.21	29,604,706,286.41
Indian Rupee	3,805,392,024.21	168,663,621,046.58
Romanian Leu	3,805,392,024.21	10,485,421,153.17
Maltese Lira	3,805,392,024.21	1,147,455,128.79
Taiwan Dollar	3,805,392,024.21	123,685,903,677.97
Bhutan Ngultrum	3,805,392,024.21	177,202,125,135.68
Pakistan Rupee	3,805,392,024.21	
Russian Ruble	3,805,392,024.21	104,760,299,037.85
Singapore Dollar	3,805,392,024.21	5,556,583,171.18
Swedish Krona	3,805,392,024.21	26,614,746,352.66
Swiss Franc	3,805,392,024.21	4,295,515,308.85
Slovenian Tolar	3,805,392,024.21	635,932,688,801.77
British Pound	3,805,392,024.21	2,120,316,478.09
South Korean Won	3,805,392,024.21	4,164,819,068,471.17
Japanese Yen	3,805,392,024.21	403,963,847,346.60
Renminbi Yuan	3,805,392,024.21	27,172,762,121.46
Polish Zloty	3,805,392,024.21	10,224,050,882.32
Iranian Rial	3,805,392,024.21	36,175,311,798,597.30
Syrian Pound	3,805,392,024.21	184,473,781,964.33
Turkmenistan Manat	3,805,392,024.21	
Som	3,805,392,024.21	

FIGURE 12-15 The report shows total sales converted using the exchange rate at the order date.

Frequent itemset search

Basket analysis is a very powerful analysis technique, which aims to check the correlation between sales of different products. You typically implement basket analysis using machine-learning algorithms, which are beyond the scope of this book. What we want to share here is a simplified technique of basket analysis that you can implement in DAX, creating extremely powerful data models. We call it *Frequent Itemset Search* because it searches for sets of products frequently sold together.

Imagine that you want to perform an analysis of which products frequently appear together in sales transactions made by the same customer. By "frequently," you might mean different concepts. In some businesses frequently means in the same shopping bag, while in other ones the same concept might mean in the same year. In the example we provide, we do not care about time. Thus, we search for pairs of products frequently sold together to the same customer, no matter when.

The question we want to answer is the following: Given a product A, which are the most probable products the customer is willing to buy, if he bought A? For example, we want to discover that if a customer is buying a large laptop, he might be interested in a backpack, too. Well, to be honest, we would love our algorithm to find something more useful than this, but we hope the example made the idea clear.

This time, instead of showing results in a pivot table, we want to run a query that returns, for each product in a given category, the set of the five most probable products that will be in other customer purchases.

Before writing the DAX code, let's define the variables we want to compute:

- **Support (A)** is the number of customers who bought product A.

- **Support (A and B)** is the number of customers who bought product A together with product B. Due to the nature of Contoso, we do not mind when A and B were sold. We are only interested in finding that the same customer bought both.

- **Confidence (A, B)** indicates the confidence that a customer who bought A will buy B, too. We compute it as Support (A and B) / Support (A).

The first issue in this data model is that the user selects two products (or, more generally, two categories of products). A typical question might be "show me what computer accessories (product B) are likely to be bought by a customer who is buying a laptop (product A)." In order to let the user select different products, we provide two different product tables in the data model.

 Note Multiple selection in the same product table would define an *OR* condition between different products, whereas the goal of this analysis is to define an *AND* condition between products bought by the same customer in different operations recorded in the Sales table. For this reason, two product tables are necessary.

Because both tables are related to Sales, the two relationships have to be kept inactive. Otherwise, when you select two different products in the two tables, all the rows in Sales will disappear because, obviously, no single sale can reference two different products at the same time. In Figure 12-16 you can see the data model of this example.

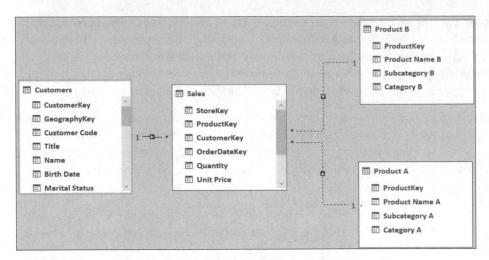

FIGURE 12-16 The relationships with the two Product tables need to be inactive.

The first measure to compute is Support (A). There are many ways to compute Support of a product. The most intuitive one is to count the values of *CustomerKey* in Sales, in a *CALCULATE* invocation that activates the correct relationship with product A, as you can see in the following code:

```
[Support A] :=
COUNTROWS (
    CALCULATETABLE (
        VALUES ( Sales[CustomerKey] ),
        USERELATIONSHIP ( Sales[ProductKey], 'Product A'[ProductKey] )
    )
)
```

This formula works well if Customer is not a slowly changing dimension, because it counts the customer keys, not the customer codes. A better approach is to use *SUMMARIZE* to retrieve the customer keys from the fact table and use them to filter Customer, as in the following code:

```
[Support A] :=
CALCULATE (
    COUNTROWS ( Customer ),
    CALCULATETABLE (
        SUMMARIZE ( Sales, Customer[CustomerKey] ),
        USERELATIONSHIP ( Sales[ProductKey], 'Product A'[ProductKey] )
    )
)
```

This latter formula has the advantage of clearly separating calculation from filtering: filter happens in *CALCULATETABLE* and computation happens in *CALCULATE*. In this instance, we use a simple *COUNTROWS* to count the customers but, in a real-world scenario, you would count the number of distinct customers using the natural key.

Computing Support (A and B) is as easy as using *INTERSECT* prior to applying the filters to the calculation, as you can see in the following code:

```
[Support A and B] :=
    CALCULATE (
        COUNTROWS ( Customer ),
        INTERSECT (
            CALCULATETABLE (
                SUMMARIZE ( Sales, Customer[CustomerKey] ),
                USERELATIONSHIP ( Sales[ProductKey], 'Product A'[ProductKey] )
            ),
            CALCULATETABLE (
                SUMMARIZE ( Sales, Customer[CustomerKey] ),
                USERELATIONSHIP ( Sales[ProductKey], 'Product B'[ProductKey] )
            )
        )
    )
```

INTERSECT works on tables containing only *Customer[CustomerKey]*. It returns a table of the customer keys who bought both products. You use the intersection result as a filter argument to *CALCULATE*.

> **Note** If you want the customers who bought product A but not B, this formula can be easily modified to return Support (A and NOT B) by using *EXCEPT* instead of *INTERSECT*. As usual, set functions in DAX provide extreme flexibility to your formulas. This is the reason why they are definitely worth learning.

At this point, you can easily define Confidence using *DIVIDE*:

```
[Confidence] := DIVIDE ( [Support A and B], [Support A] )
```

Now that we have seen the code of the measures, let's go back to our initial scenario: We want to run a query that returns, for each product of a given subcategory, the set of products of another subcategory that is more likely to be in the itemset. Here is the query:

```
CALCULATETABLE (
    GENERATE (
        ADDCOLUMNS (
            VALUES ( 'Product A'[Product Name A] ),
            "Support A", [Support A]
        ),
        TOPN (
            5,
            ADDCOLUMNS (
                VALUES ( 'Product B'[Product Name B] ),
                "Support A and B", [Support A and B],
                "Confidence", ROUND ( DIVIDE ( [Support A and B], [Support A] ) * 100, 2 )
            ),
            [Confidence]
        )
    ),
    'Product A'[Category A] = "Computers",
    'Product A'[Subcategory A] = "Laptops",
    'Product B'[Category B] = "Computers",
    'Product B'[Subcategory B] = "Computers Accessories"
)
```

These are the steps executed by this query:

1. The outermost *CALCULATETABLE* sets the filter on category and subcategory of both Product A and Product B (if customer buys a laptop, we want to see which accessories he or she is likely to buy).

2. The first *ADDCOLUMNS* generates a table with all products in the Laptop subcategory, adding a column that computes Support (A). It is useful to compute the column at this stage, because the number of rows is still small.

3. *GENERATE* iterates the list of products and, for each one, it creates a new table containing the top five products in Product B (the accessories), sorted by Confidence.

The result of this query is the list of all products in the Laptop subcategory and, for each, the five most likely itemset of two products, as you can see in Figure 12-17.

Product Name A	Support A	Product Name B	Support A and B	Confidence
Adventure Works Laptop12 M1200 Black	164	SV Keyboard E90 White	161	98,17
Adventure Works Laptop12 M1200 Black	164	Contoso Optical USB Mouse M45 White	161	98,17
Adventure Works Laptop12 M1200 Black	164	SV 40GB USB2.0 Portable Hard Disk E400 Silver	151	92,07
Adventure Works Laptop12 M1200 Black	164	Contoso Smart Battery M901 Grey	38	23,17
Adventure Works Laptop12 M1200 Black	164	Contoso Notebook Peripheral Kit M69 Grey	36	21,95
Adventure Works Laptop12 M1201 Blue	265	SV Keyboard E90 White	218	82,26
Adventure Works Laptop12 M1201 Blue	265	SV 40GB USB2.0 Portable Hard Disk E400 Silver	212	80
Adventure Works Laptop12 M1201 Blue	265	Contoso Optical USB Mouse M45 White	212	80
Adventure Works Laptop12 M1201 Blue	265	Contoso Desktop Alternative Bundle E200 Black	105	39,62
Adventure Works Laptop12 M1201 Blue	265	Contoso Notebook Peripheral Kit M69 Black	103	38,87
Adventure Works Laptop12 M1201 Red	295	SV Keyboard E90 White	257	87,12
Adventure Works Laptop12 M1201 Red	295	Contoso Optical USB Mouse M45 White	247	83,73
Adventure Works Laptop12 M1201 Red	295	SV 40GB USB2.0 Portable Hard Disk E400 Silver	224	75,93
Adventure Works Laptop12 M1201 Red	295	Contoso USB 2.0 Dock Station docking station M800 Grey	112	37,97
Adventure Works Laptop12 M1201 Red	295	Contoso Enhanced Capacity Battery M800 White	112	37,97

FIGURE 12-17 This is the result of the itemset detection on the Contoso database.

The important concepts you learned in this example are as follows:

- The use of inactive relationships if—as in this case—you need to add technical tables to the model and you then want to activate relationships on demand.

- Use of set functions to find complex conditions, such as the one we used on customers, mixing the two on-demand relationships with *INTERSECT*. In other scenarios, you can use different set functions to compute different sets.

The VertiPaq engine

At this point in the book, you have a solid understanding of the DAX language. The next step, apart from the necessary experience that you need to gain by yourself, is not only being able to write DAX, but also to write efficient DAX. Writing efficient DAX, that is, code that runs at its best possible speed, requires you to understand the internals of the engine. The next chapters aim to provide the essential knowledge to measure and improve performance of DAX code.

More specifically, this chapter is dedicated to the internal architecture of the VertiPaq engine: the in-memory columnar database that stores and hosts your model.

Before continuing with the dissertation, it is worth mentioning a quick note. The official name of the engine on top of which DAX runs is "xVelocity in-memory Analytical Engine." The name appeared later, when the engine was ready to market. During its development, it was code-named "VertiPaq." Because of the late change in the name, many white papers referred to the engine as the VertiPaq engine, and all the early adopters learned its name as VertiPaq. Moreover, internally, the engine is still known as VertiPaq (in fact, as you learn later, its query engine executes VertiPaq queries, not xVelocity queries). In order to avoid confusion in sentences such as "the xVelocity engine executes a VertiPaq query," which mixes both names in a single sentence, we decided to use VertiPaq only.

There is another important note to our readers. Starting from this chapter, we somewhat deviate from DAX and begin to discuss some low-level technical details about the implementation of DAX and the VertiPaq engine. Although this is an important topic, you need to be aware of two facts:

- Implementation details change often. We did our best to show information at a level which is not likely to change soon, carefully balancing detail level and usefulness with consistency over time. The most up-to-date information will always be available in blog posts and articles on the web.

- All the considerations about the engine and optimization techniques are useful if you rely on the VertiPaq engine. In case you are using DirectQuery, then the content of the last chapters of this book is nearly useless in your specific scenario. However, we suggest that you read and understand it anyway, because it shows many details that will help you in choosing the best engine for your analytical scenario.

Understanding database processing

DAX runs in SQL Server Analysis Services (SSAS) Tabular, Power BI service (both on server and on the local Power BI Desktop), and in the Power Pivot for Microsoft Excel add-in. Technically, Power Pivot for Excel runs a local instance of SSAS Tabular, whereas Power BI uses a separate process running a special instance of Analysis Services. Thus, speaking about different engines is somewhat artificial: Power Pivot is SSAS, even if it runs in a "hidden mode" inside Excel. In this book, we make no differences between these engines and, when we speak about SSAS, you might always mentally replace SSAS with Power Pivot or Power BI. If there are differences worth highlighting, then we will note them in the specific section.

When SSAS loads the content of a source table in memory, we say that it processes the table. This happens during the process operation of SSAS or the data refresh in Power Pivot for Excel and Power BI. During processing, the engine reads the content of your data source and transforms it in the internal VertiPaq data structure.

The steps that happen during processing are as follows:

1. Reading of the source dataset, transformation into a columnar data structure of VertiPaq, encoding and compressing each column.

2. Creation of dictionaries and indexes for each column.

3. Creation of the data structures for relationships.

4. Computation and compression of all the calculated columns.

The last two steps are not necessarily sequential. In fact, you can create a relationship based on a calculated column, or have calculated columns that depend on a relationship because they use *RELATED* or *CALCULATE*; SSAS creates a complex graph of dependencies to execute the steps in the correct order.

In the next sections, you learn many more details about these steps and the format of internal structures created by SSAS during the transformation of the data source into the VertiPaq model.

Introduction to columnar databases

VertiPaq is an in-memory columnar database. Being in-memory means that all of the data handled by a model reside in RAM, and it is an easy concept to learn. We briefly introduced the concept of a columnar database in Chapter 5, "Understanding *CALCULATE* and *CALCULATETABLE*." Now it is time to perform a deeper analysis of it.

We think of a table as a list of rows, where each row is divided into columns. Let's take, as an example, the Product table in Figure 13-1.

Product

ID	Name	Color	Unit Price
1	Camcorder	Red	112.25
2	Camera	Red	97.50
3	Smartphone	White	100.00
4	Console	Black	112.25
5	TV	Blue	1,240.85
6	CD	Red	39.99
7	Touch screen	Blue	45.12
8	PDA	Black	120.25
9	Keyboard	Black	120.50

FIGURE 13-1 The figure shows the Product table, with four columns and nine rows.

If you think of a table as a set of rows, then you are using the most natural visualization of a table structure, also known as a *row store*. In a row store, data is organized in rows and, when stored in memory, you might think that the value of the column *Name* in the first row is adjacent to the columns *ID* and *Color* in the same row. On the other hand, the column *Name* in the second row is slightly farther from *Name* in the first row because, in the middle, there are *Color, Unit Price* in the first row, and *ID* in the second row.

For example, if you need to compute the sum of *Unit Price*, you have to scan the entire table, reading many values that you are not interested in seeing. You can imagine that scanning the memory of the database sequentially: in order to read the first value of *Unit Price*, you have to read (and skip) *ID*, *Name,* and *Color* of the first row. Only then you will find an interesting value. The same process repeats for all the rows: You need to read and ignore many columns to find the interesting values to sum.

Reading and ignoring values takes time. In fact, if we asked you to compute the sum of *Unit Price*, you would not follow that algorithm. Instead, as a human being, you would probably scan the first row searching for the position of *Unit Price*, and then move your eyes vertically, reading only the values one at a time and mentally accumulating their values to produce the sum. The reason for this very natural behavior is that you save time by reading vertically instead of on a row-by-row basis.

In a columnar database, data is organized in such a way to optimize vertical scanning. To obtain this result, you need a way to make the different values of a column adjacent one to the other. In Figure 13-2 you can see the same Product table as organized by a columnar database.

Product Columns

ID	Name	Color	Unit Price
1	Camcorder	Red	112.25
2	Camera	Red	97.50
3	Smartphone	White	100.00
4	Console	Black	112.25
5	TV	Blue	1,240.85
6	CD	Red	39.99
7	Touch screen	Blue	45.12
8	PDA	Black	120.25
9	Keyboard	Black	120.50

FIGURE 13-2 The Product table organized on a column-by-column basis.

When stored in a columnar database, each column has its own data structure, and it is physically separated from the others. Thus, the different values of *Unit Price* are adjacent one to the other and distant from *Color*, *Name*, and *ID*.

On this data structure, computing the sum of *Unit Price* is much easier, because you immediately go to the column containing the *Unit Price* and then find, very near, all the values you need to perform the computation. In other words, you do not have to read and ignore other column values: In a single scan, you obtain only useful numbers and you can quickly aggregate them.

Now, imagine that, instead of asking you the sum of *Unit Price*, we asked you to compute the sum of *Unit Price* for only the Red products. Try that before you continue reading; it will help in understanding the algorithm.

This is not so easy anymore, because you cannot obtain such a number by simply scanning the *Unit Price* column. What you probably did is a scan of the *Color* column and, whenever it was Red, you grabbed the corresponding value of *Unit Price*. At the end, you summed up all the values to compute the result. This algorithm, although very natural, required you to constantly move your eyes from one column to another, possibly guiding your finger to keep the last scanned position of *Color*. It is definitely not an optimized way of computing the value! A better way, that only computers use, is to first scan the *Color* column, find the row numbers where the color is Red and then, once you know the row numbers, scan the *Unit Price* column summing only the rows you identified in the previous step.

This last algorithm is much better, because it lets you perform one scan of the first column and one scan of the second column, always accessing memory locations that are adjacent one to the other (apart from the jump between the scan of the first and second column).

For a more complex expression, such as the sum of all products that are either Blue or Black Console with a price higher than USD 50, things are even worse. This time, you have no chance of scanning the column one at a time, because the condition depends on many columns. As usual, if you try it on paper, it helps in understanding it better.

The simplest algorithm to produce such a result is to scan the table not on a column basis but, instead, on a row basis. You probably scanned the table row by row, even if the storage organization is column by column. Although it is a very simple operation when executed on paper by a human, the same operation is extremely expensive if executed by a computer in RAM, because it requires a lot of random reads of memory, leading to a worse performance than if computed doing a sequential scan.

Columnar databases provide very quick access to a single column but, as soon as you need a calculation that involves many columns, they need to spend some time—after having read the column content—to reorganize the information in such a way that the final expression can be computed. Even if this example was a very simple one, it is already very useful to highlight the most important characteristics of column stores:

- Single-column access is very fast, because it reads a single block of memory, and then it computes whatever aggregation you need on that memory block.

- If an expression uses many columns, the algorithm is more complex because it requires the engine to access different memory areas at different times, keeping track of the progress in some temporary area.

- The more columns you need to compute an expression, the harder it becomes to produce a final value, up to a point where it is easier to rebuild the row storage out of the column store to compute the expression.

Column stores aim to reduce the read time. However, they spend more CPU cycles to rearrange the data when many columns from the same table are used. Row stores, on the other hand, have a more linear algorithm to scan data, but they result in many useless reads. As a general rule, reducing reads at the cost of increasing CPU usage is a good deal, because with modern computers it is always easier (and cheaper) to increase the CPU speed versus reducing I/O (or memory access) time.

Moreover, as you learn in the next sections, columnar databases have more options to reduce the amount of time spent scanning data, that is, compression.

Understanding VertiPaq compression

In the previous section, you learned that VertiPaq stores each column in a separate data structure. This simple fact allows the engine to implement some extremely important compressions and encoding that you are about to learn in this section.

 Note Please note that the actual details of the compression algorithm of VertiPaq are proprietary and, of course, we cannot publish them in a book. Yet what we explain in this chapter is already a good approximation of what really happens in the engine and you can use it, to all effects, to understand how the VertiPaq engine stores data.

VertiPaq compression algorithms aim to reduce the memory footprint of your data model. Reducing the memory usage is a very important task for two very good reasons:

- A smaller model makes a better use of your hardware. Why spend money on 1 TB of RAM when the same model, once compressed, can be hosted in 256 GB? Saving RAM is always a good option, if feasible.

- A smaller model is faster to scan. As simple as this rule is, it is very important when speaking about performance. If a column is compressed, the engine will scan less RAM to read its content, resulting in better performance.

Understanding value encoding

Value encoding is the first kind of encoding that VertiPaq might use to reduce the memory of a column. Imagine you have a column containing the price of products, stored as integer values. The column contains many different values and, to represent all of them, you need a defined number of bits.

In the Figure 13-3 example, the maximum value of *Unit Price* is 216. Therefore, you need at least 8 bits to store each value. Nevertheless, by using a simple mathematical operation, you can reduce the storage to 5 bits.

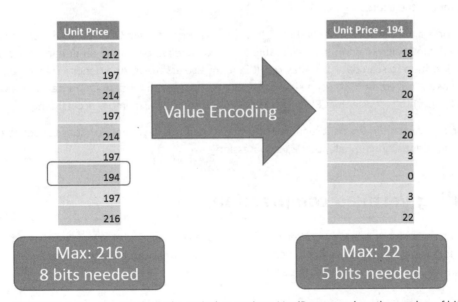

FIGURE 13-3 By using simple mathematical operations, VertiPaq can reduce the number of bits needed for a column.

In the example, VertiPaq discovered that by subtracting the minimum value (194) from all the values of the column, it could modify the range of the column, reducing it to a range from 0 to 22. Storing numbers up to 22 requires less bits than storing numbers up to 216. While 3 bits might seem a very small saving, when you multiply this for a few billion rows, it is easy to see that the difference can be an important one.

The VertiPaq engine is much more sophisticated than this. It can discover mathematical relationships between the values of a column and, when it finds them, it can use them to modify the storage, reducing its memory footprint. Obviously, when using the column, it has to re-apply the transformation in the opposite direction to again obtain the original value (depending on the transformation, this can happen before or after aggregating the values). Again, this will increase the CPU usage and reduce the amount of reads, which, as we already discussed, is a very good option.

Value encoding happens only for integer columns because, obviously, it cannot be applied on strings or floating-point values. Please consider that VertiPaq stores the currency data type of DAX in an integer value.

Understanding dictionary encoding

Dictionary encoding is another technique used by VertiPaq to reduce the number of bits required to store a column. Dictionary encoding builds a dictionary of the distinct values of a column and then it replaces the column values with indexes to the dictionary. Let's see this with an example. In Figure 13-4 you can see the *Color* column, which uses strings and, thus, cannot be value-encoded.

Replacing datatypes with dictionary and indexes

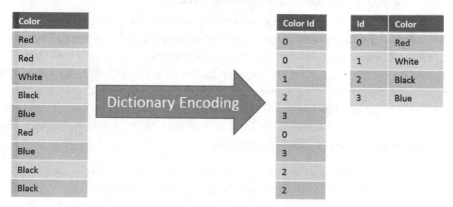

FIGURE 13-4 Dictionary encoding consists of building a dictionary and replacing values with indexes.

When VertiPaq encodes a column with dictionary encoding, it

- Builds a dictionary, containing the distinct values of the column.

- Replaces the column values with integer numbers, where each number is the dictionary index of the original value.

There are some advantages in using dictionary encoding:

- All columns contain only integer values; this makes it simpler to optimize the internal code of the engine. Moreover, it basically means that VertiPaq is datatype independent.

- The number of bits used to store a single value is the minimum number of bits necessary to store an index entry. In the example provided, having only four different values, 2 bits are sufficient.

These two aspects are of paramount importance for VertiPaq. It does not matter whether you use a string, a 64-bit integer, or a floating point to represent a value. All these datatypes will be dictionary encoded, providing the same performance, both in terms of speed of scanning and of storage space. The only difference might be in the size of the dictionary, which is typically very small when compared with the size of the column itself.

The primary factor to determine the column size is not the datatype, but it is the number of distinct values of the column. We refer to the number of distinct values of a column as its *cardinality*. Repeating a concept so important is always a good thing: Of all the various factors of an individual column, the most important one when designing a data model is its cardinality.

The lower the cardinality, the smaller the number of bits required to store a single value and, as a consequence, the smaller the memory footprint of the column. If a column is smaller, not only will it be possible to store more data in the same amount of RAM, but it will also be much faster to scan it whenever you need to aggregate its values in a DAX expression.

Understanding Run Length Encoding (RLE)

Dictionary encoding and value encoding are two very good alternative compression techniques. However, there is another complementary compression technique used by VertiPaq: Run Length Encoding (RLE). This technique aims to reduce the size of a dataset by avoiding repeated values. For example, consider a column containing the calendar quarter of a sale, stored in the Sales table. This column might have the string "Q1" repeated many times in contiguous rows, for all the sales in the same quarter. In such a case, VertiPaq avoids storing repeating values and replaces them with a slightly more complex structure that contains the value only once, with the number of contiguous rows having the same value, as you can see in Figure 13-5.

In Figure 13-5, you see *Quarter*, *Start*, and *Count*. In reality, *Start* is not required because VertiPaq can compute it by summing all the previous values of *Count*, again saving precious bytes of RAM.

RLE's efficiency strongly depends on the repetition pattern of the column. Some columns will have the same value repeated for many rows, resulting in a great compression ratio. Some others, with quickly changing values, will produce a lower compression ratio. Sorting of data is extremely important in order to improve the compression ratio of RLE, as you will see later in this chapter.

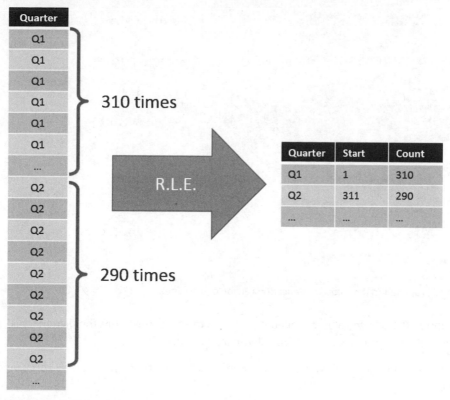

FIGURE 13-5 RLE replaces repeating values with the number of contiguous rows with the same value.

Finally, you might have a column in which content changes so often that, if you try to compress it using RLE, you end up using more space than its original one. Think, for example, of the primary key of a table. It has a different value for each row, resulting in an RLE version larger than the column itself. In such a case, VertiPaq skips the RLE compression and stores the column as it is. Thus, the VertiPaq storage of a column will never exceed the original column size. At worst, it is the same.

In the example, we have shown RLE working on the *Quarter* column containing strings. In reality, RLE processes the already dictionary-encoded version of the column. In fact, each column can have both RLE and dictionary or value encoding. Therefore, the VertiPaq storage for a column compressed with dictionary encoding consists of two distinct entities: the dictionary and the data rows. The latter is the RLE-encoded result of the dictionary-encoded version of the original column, as you can see in Figure 13-6.

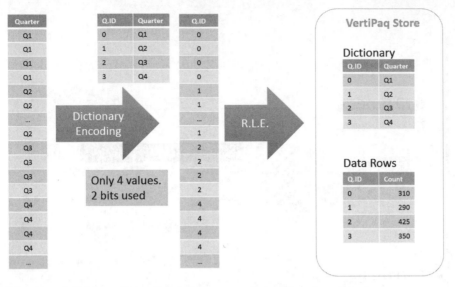

FIGURE 13-6 RLE is applied to the dictionary-encoded version of a column.

VertiPaq applies RLE also to value-encoded columns. In this case, obviously, the dictionary is missing because the column already contains value-encoded integers.

The factors to consider working with a Tabular model, regarding its compression ratio, are, in order of importance:

- The cardinality of the column, which defines the number of bits used to store a value.

- The number of repetitions, that is, the distribution of data in a column. A column with many repeated values will be compressed more than a column with very frequently changing ones.

- The number of rows in the table.

- The datatype of the column (it affects only the dictionary size).

Given all these considerations, you can see that it is nearly impossible to predict the compression ratio of a table. Moreover, while you have full control over some aspects of a table (you can limit the number of rows and change the datatypes), they are the least important ones. Yet as you will learn in the next chapter, you can work on cardinality and repetitions too, to improve the performance of a model.

Finally, it is worth noting that if you reduce the cardinality of a column, you are also increasing the chances of repetitions. For example, if you store a time column at the second granularity, then you have up to 86,400 distinct values in the column. If, on the other hand, you store the same time column at the hour granularity, then you have not only reduced the cardinality, but you have also introduced repeating values (3.600 seconds converts to the same hour), resulting in a much better compression ratio. However, changing the datatype from DateTime to Integer or also String has an irrelevant impact on the column size.

Understanding re-encoding

SSAS has to decide which algorithm to use in order to encode each column. Specifically, it needs to decide whether to use value or dictionary encoding. In reality, the patented algorithms used by SSAS are much more complex and this description is a simplification of them, yet it is enough to get a solid understanding. Anyway, how does SSAS choose the best way to compress a column? It reads a sample of rows during the first scan of the source and, depending on the values found, it chooses an algorithm.

- If the datatype of the column is not integer, then the choice is straightforward: it goes for dictionary encoding.

- For integer values, it uses some heuristics, for example:

  - If the numbers in the column increase linearly, it is probably a primary key, and value encoding is the best option.

  - If all numbers are in a defined range of values, then value encoding is the way to go.

  - If the numbers are in a very wide range of values, with values very different from another, then dictionary encoding is the best choice.

Once the decision is made, SSAS starts to compress the column using the chosen algorithm. Unfortunately, it might have made the wrong decision and discover it only very late during processing. For example, SSAS might read a few million rows where the values are in the range 100–201, so that value encoding is the best choice. After those millions of rows, suddenly an outlier appears, such as a large number like 60,000,000. Obviously, the choice was wrong because the number of bits needed to store such a large number is huge. What to do then? Instead of continuing with the wrong choice, SSAS can decide to re-encode the column. This means that the whole column is re-encoded using, in this case, dictionary encoding. This process might last for a long time, because it needs to reprocess the whole column.

For very large datasets, where processing time is important, a best practice is to provide to SSAS a good sample of data distribution in the first set of rows it reads, to reduce re-encoding to a minimum. You do so by providing a good sample in the first partition processed.

Finding the best sort order

As we already said in the previous pages, RLE's efficiency strongly depends on the sort order of the table. Obviously, all the columns in the same table are sorted in the same way because, at some point during the querying, VertiPaq might have to match different columns for the same row. So in large tables it could be important to determine the best sorting of your data to improve efficiency of RLE and reduce the memory footprint of your model.

When SSAS reads your table, it tries different sort orders to improve the compression. In a table with many columns, this is a very expensive operation. SSAS then sets an upper limit to the time it can spend finding the best sort order. The default can change with different versions of the engine, currently it is 10 seconds per million rows. You can modify its value in the *ProcessingTimeboxSecPerMRow* entry in the configuration file of the SSAS service. If using Power Pivot, you cannot change this value.

Note SSAS searches for the best sort order in data using a heuristic algorithm that certainly also considers the physical order of the rows it receives. For this reason, even if you cannot force the sort order used by VertiPaq for RLE, you can provide to the engine data sorted in an arbitrary way. The VertiPaq engine will certainly include such a sort order in the options to consider.

In order to obtain the maximum compression, you can set the value to 0, which means SSAS stops searching only when it finds the best compression factor. The benefit in terms of space usage and query speed can be very high but, at the same time, processing will take much longer.

Generally, you should try to put the least changing columns first in the sort order, because they are likely to generate many repeating values. Keep in mind, anyway, that finding the best sort order is a very complex task, and it makes sense to spend time on it only when your data model is really a large one (in the order of a few billion rows). Otherwise, the benefit you get from these extreme optimizations is limited.

Once all the columns are compressed, SSAS completes the processing by building calculated columns, hierarchies, and relationships. Hierarchies and relationships are additional data structures needed by VertiPaq to execute queries, whereas calculated columns are added to the model by using DAX expressions.

Calculated columns, like all other columns, are compressed after they are computed. Nevertheless, they are not exactly the same as standard columns. In fact, they are compressed during the final stage of processing, when all the other columns have already finished their compression. Consequently, VertiPaq does not consider them when choosing the best sort order for your table.

Imagine you create a calculated column that results in a Boolean value. Having only two values, it can be compressed very well (1 bit is enough to store a Boolean value) and it is a very good candidate to be first in the sort order list, so that the table shows first all the *TRUE* values and later only the *FALSE* ones. But, being a calculated column, the sort order is already defined and it might be the case that, with the defined sort order, the column frequently changes its value. In such a case, the column results in less-than-optimal compression.

Whenever you have the chance to compute a column in DAX or in SQL, keep in mind that computing it in SQL results in slightly better compression. Obviously, many other factors may drive you to choose DAX instead of SQL to calculate the column. For example, the engine automatically computes a calculated column in a large table depending on a column in a small table, whenever such a small table has a partial or full refresh. This happens without having to reprocess the entire large table, which would be necessary if the computation was in SQL. If you are seeking for optimal compression, this is something you have to consider.

Understanding hierarchies and relationships

As we said in the previous sections, at the end of table processing, SSAS builds two additional data structures: hierarchies and relationships.

Hierarchies are of two types: attribute hierarchies and user hierarchies. They are data structures used to improve performance of MDX queries. Because DAX does not have the concept of hierarchy in the language, hierarchies are not interesting for the topics of this book.

Relationships, on the other hand, play an important role in the VertiPaq engine and, for some extreme optimizations, it is important to understand how they work. Later in this chapter, we will cover the role of relationships in a query. Here we are only interested in defining what relationships are, in terms of VertiPaq.

A relationship is a data structure that maps IDs in one table to row numbers in another table. For example, consider the columns *ProductKey* in Sales and *ProductKey* in Products, used to build a relationship between the two tables. *Product[ProductKey]* is a primary key. You know that it used value encoding and no compression at all, because RLE could not reduce the size of a column without duplicated values. On the other end, *Sales[ProductKey]* is likely dictionary encoded and compressed, because it probably contains many repetitions. The data structures of the two columns are completely different.

Moreover, because you created the relationship, VertiPaq knows that you are likely to use it very often, placing a filter on Product and expecting to filter Sales, too. If every time it needs to move a filter from Product to Sales, VertiPaq had to retrieve values of *Product[ProductKey]*, search them in the dictionary of *Sales[ProductKey]*, and finally retrieve the IDs of *Sales[ProductKey]* to place the filter, then it would result in slow queries.

To improve query performance, VertiPaq stores relationships as pairs of IDs and row numbers. Given the ID of a *Sales[ProductKey]*, it can immediately find the corresponding rows of Product that match the relationship. Relationships are stored in memory, as any other data structure of VertiPaq. In Figure 13-7 you can see how the relationship between Sales and Product is stored.

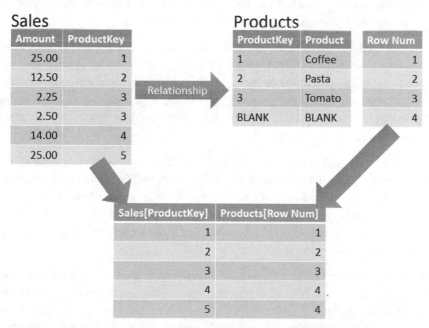

FIGURE 13-7 The figure shows the relationship between Sales and Product.

Understanding segmentation and partitioning

As you might imagine, compressing a table of several billion rows in a single step would be extremely memory-intensive and time-consuming. In fact, the table is not processed as a whole. Instead, during processing SSAS reads it into segments that, by default, contain 8 million rows each. When a segment is completely read, the engine starts to compress it while, in the meantime, it reads the next segment.

You can configure the segment size on SSAS using the *DefaultSegmentRowCount* entry in the configuration file of the service (or in the server properties in Management Studio). In Power Pivot, the segment size has a fixed value of 1 million rows. You cannot change it, because Power Pivot is optimized for smaller datasets.

Segmentation is important for several reasons:

- When querying a table, VertiPaq uses the segments as the basis for parallelism: it uses one core per segment when scanning a column. By default, SSAS always uses one single thread to scan a table with 8 million rows or less. You start observing parallelism in action only on much larger tables.

- The larger the segment, the better the compression. Having the option of analyzing more rows in a single compression step, VertiPaq can achieve better compression levels. On very large tables, it is important to test different segment sizes and measure the memory usage, so to achieve optimal compression. Keep in mind that increasing the segment size can negatively affect processing time: the larger the segment, the slower the processing.

- Although the dictionary is global to the table, bit-sizing happens at the segment level. Thus, if a column has 1,000 distinct values but, in a specific segment, only two of them are used, then that column will be compressed to a single bit for that segment.

- If segments are too small, then the parallelism at query time is increased. This is not always a good thing. In fact, while it is true that scanning the column is faster, VertiPaq needs more time at the end of the scan to aggregate partial results computed by the different threads. If a partition is too small, then the time required for managing task switching and final aggregation is more than the time needed to scan the data, with a negative impact to the overall query performance.

During processing, the first segment has a special treatment if the table has only one partition. In fact, the first segment can be larger than *DefaultSegmentRowCount*. VertiPaq reads twice the size of *DefaultSegmentRowCount* and starts to segment a table only if it contains more rows (but remember that this does not apply to a table with more than one partition). Therefore, a table with 10 million rows will be stored as a single segment, whereas a table with 20 million rows will use three segments: two containing 8 million rows, and one with only 4 million rows.

Segments cannot exceed the partition size. If you have a partitioning schema on your model that creates partitions of only 1 million rows, then all of your segments will be smaller than 1 million rows (namely, they will be same as the partition size). Over-partitioning of tables is a very common mistake of naïve VertiPaq users: remember that creating too many small partitions can only lower the performance.

Using Dynamic Management Views

SSAS lets you discover all the information about the data model using Dynamic Management Views (DMV). DMVs are extremely useful to explore how your model is compressed, the space used by different columns and tables, the number of segments in a table, or the number of bits used by columns in different segments.

You can run DMVs from inside SQL Server Management Studio or, better, using DAX Studio. Moreover, DAX Studio offers you the list of all DMV in a simpler way, without the need to remember them or to reopen this book looking for the DMV name you forgot. You can also use the free tool VertiPaq Analyzer (*http://www.sqlbi.com/tools/vertipaq-analyzer/*) to automatically retrieve data from DMVs and see them in useful reports.

Although DMVs use an SQL-like syntax, you cannot use full SQL syntax to query them, because they do not run inside SQL Server, they are a convenient way to discover the status of SSAS and to gather information about data models. Moreover, DMVs were created when SSAS supported only Multidimensional, so the information provided is not optimized for Tabular. For example, when you query the column information, you get as a result CUBE_NAME, MEASURE_GROUP_NAME, and DIMENSION_NAME, although in VertiPaq there is no concept of cube, measure group, or dimension.

There are different DMVs, divided in two main categories:

- SCHEMA views. These return information about SSAS metadata, such as database names, tables, and individual columns. They do not provide statistical information. Instead, they are used to gather information about datatypes, names, and similar data.

- DISCOVER views. They are intended to gather information about the SSAS engine and/or discover statistics information about objects in a database. For example, you can use views in the discover area to enumerate the DAX keywords, the number of connections and sessions that are currently open, or the traces running.

In this book, we do not want to describe the details of all those views, because they would be off-topic. If you need more information, you can find it in Microsoft documentation on the web. Instead, we want to give some hints and point out the most useful DMVs related to databases used by DAX, which are in the DISCOVER area.

Moreover, while many DMVs report useful information in many columns, in this book we describe the most interesting ones related to the internal structure. For example, there are DMVs to discover the datatypes of all columns, which is not interesting information from the modeling point of view (it might be useful for client tools, but it is useless for the modeler of a solution). On the other hand, knowing the number of bits used for a column in a segment is very technical and definitely useful to optimize a model, so we highlighted it.

Using DISCOVER_OBJECT_MEMORY_USAGE

The first, and probably the most useful DMV lets you discover the memory usage of all the objects in the SSAS instance. This DMV returns information about all the objects in all the databases in the SSAS instance, and it is not limited to the current database.

```
SELECT * FROM $SYSTEM.DISCOVER_OBJECT_MEMORY_USAGE
```

The output of the DMV is a table containing many rows that are very hard to read, because the structure is a parent/child hierarchy that starts with the instance name and ends with individual column information.

The most useful columns in the dataset are as follows:

- OBJECT_ID: Is the ID of the object of which it is reporting memory usage. By itself, it is not a key for the table. You need to combine it with the OBJECT_PARENT_PATH to make it a unique value working as a key.

- OBJECT_PARENT_PATH: Is the full path of the parent in the parent/child hierarchy.

- OBJECT_MEMORY_NON_SHRINKABLE: Is the amount of memory used by the object.

As we said, the raw dataset is nearly impossible to read. However, you can build a Power Pivot data model on top of this query, implementing the parent/child hierarchy structure and browse the full memory map of your instance. Kasper De Jonge published a workbook on his blog that does exactly this, and you can find it here: *http://www.powerpivotblog.nl/what-is-using-all-that-memory-on-my-analysis-server-instance/*

Using DISCOVER_STORAGE_TABLES

The DISCOVER_STORAGE_TABLES DMV is useful to quickly discover tables in a model. It returns only the tables of the current model. In reality, despite its name, it returns tables, hierarchies, and relationships, but the important information is the set of tables.

The most important columns are as follows:

- DIMENSION_NAME: Even if it is named "dimension," for Tabular models it is the table name.

- TABLE_ID: The internal ID of the table, which might be useful to create relationships, because it contains the GUID used by SSAS as a suffix on most table names. Hierarchies and relationships, reported by the same DMV, have an ID starting with H$ and R$, respectively.

- TABLE_PARTITIONS_COUNT: This represents the number of partitions of the table.

- ROWS_COUNT: It is the total number of rows of the table.

A typical usage of this DMV is to run a query similar to the following one, which returns table name and number of rows for only the tables (by checking the first characters of DIMENSION_NAME and TABLE_ID).

```
SELECT
    DIMENSION_NAME AS TABLE_NAME,
    ROWS_COUNT AS ROWS_IN_TABLE
FROM  $SYSTEM.DISCOVER_STORAGE_TABLES
WHERE DIMENSION_NAME = LEFT ( TABLE_ID, LEN ( DIMENSION_NAME ) )
ORDER BY DIMENSION_NAME
```

Note The previous query might not work on Power BI Designer and Power Pivot, because the *LEFT* and *LEN* functions could be not supported. Please consider filtering the result of the DMV in a different way in case you cannot use this technique to obtain only the rows you want.

Using DISCOVER_STORAGE_TABLE_COLUMNS

This DMV gives you detailed information about individual columns, either in tables or in relationships and hierarchies. It is useful to discover, for example, the size of the dictionary, its datatype, and the kind of encoding used for the column.

Most of the information is useful for columns, while it is of less use for hierarchies (either user or system hierarchies). Specifically, for hierarchies, the only useful information is the total size, because other attributes depend directly on the columns they use.

The most relevant columns are as follows:

- DIMENSION_NAME: Even if it is named "dimension," for Tabular models it is the table name.

- TABLE_ID: The internal ID of the table, which might be useful to create relationships, because it contains the GUID used by SSAS as a suffix on most table names. Hierarchies and relationships, reported by the same DMV, have an ID starting with H$ or R$.

- COLUMN_ID: For columns, it is the column name, while for hierarchies it indicates ID_TO_POS or POS_TO_ID, which are internal names for hierarchy structures.

- COLUMN_TYPE: Indicates the type of column. Standard columns contain BASIC_DATA, whereas hierarchies contain different internal names of no interest for this book.

- COLUMN_ENCODING: Indicates the encoding used for the column: 1 stands for hash (dictionary encoding), 2 is value encoding.

- DICTIONARY_SIZE: Is the size, in bytes, of the dictionary of the column.

For example, to retrieve table name, column name, and dictionary size of all columns in your model, you can run this query:

```
SELECT
    DIMENSION_NAME AS TABLE_NAME,
    COLUMN_ID AS COLUMN_NAME,
    DICTIONARY_SIZE AS DICTIONARY_SIZE_BYTES
FROM
    $SYSTEM.DISCOVER_STORAGE_TABLE_COLUMNS
WHERE COLUMN_TYPE = 'BASIC_DATA'
```

Using DISCOVER_STORAGE_TABLE_COLUMN_SEGMENTS

Among the various DMVs, this is the most detailed one, because it reports information about individual segments and partitions of columns. Its content is very detailed and might be overwhelming. Thus, it makes sense to use this information only when you are interested in squeezing the size of a large table, or in performing some kind of extreme optimization.

The most relevant columns are as follows:

- DIMENSION_NAME: Even if it is named "dimension," for Tabular models it is the table name.

- TABLE_ID: The internal ID of the table.

- COLUMN_ID: For columns, it is the column name, whereas for hierarchies it indicates ID_TO_POS or POS_TO_ID, which are internal names for hierarchy structures.

- SEGMENT_NUMBER: The number of the segment reported, zero-based.

- TABLE_PARTITION_NUMBER: The number of the partition to which the segment belongs.

- RECORDS_COUNT: The number of rows in the segment.

- ALLOCATED_SIZE: The size allocated for the segment.

- USED_SIZE: The size actually used for the segment.

- COMPRESSION_TYPE: Indicates the compression algorithm used for the column in the segment. Its content is private and not documented, because the algorithm is patented.

- BITS_COUNT: Number of bits used to represent the column in the segment.

- VERTIPAQ_STATE: can be SKIPPED, COMPLETED, or TIMEBOXED: And it indicates if the engine had the option to find the optimal sorting for the segment (COMPLETED), if it used the best found during the time it was allowed to use but stopped before finding the optimal one (TIMEBOXED), or if the sorting step was skipped (SKIPPED).

Understanding materialization

Now that you have a basic understanding of how VertiPaq stores data in memory, you need to learn what materialization is. Materialization is a step in query resolution that happens when using columnar databases. Understanding when and how it happens is of paramount importance.

In order to understand what materialization is, look at this simple query:

```
EVALUATE
ROW (
    "Result", COUNTROWS ( SUMMARIZE ( Sales, Sales[ProductKey] ) )
)
```

The result is the distinct count of product keys in the Sales table. Even if we have not yet covered the query engine (we will, in Chapter 15, "Analyzing DAX query plans" and Chapter 16, "Optimizing DAX"), you can already imagine how VertiPaq can execute this query. Because the only column queried is *ProductKey*, it can scan that column only, finding all the values in the compressed structure of the column. While scanning, it keeps track of values found in a bitmap index and, at the end, it only has to count the bits that are set. Thanks to parallelism at the segment level, this query can run extremely fast on very large tables and the only memory it has to allocate is the bitmap index to count the keys.

The previous query runs on the compressed version of the column. In other words, there is no need to decompress the columns and to rebuild the original table to resolve it. This optimizes the memory usage at query time and reduces the memory reads.

The same scenario happens for more complex queries, too. Look at the following one:

```
EVALUATE
ROW (
    "Result", CALCULATE (
        COUNTROWS ( Sales ),
        Product[Brand] = "Contoso"
    )
)
```

This time, we are using two different tables: Sales and Product. Solving this query requires a bit more effort. In fact, because the filter is on Product and the table to aggregate is Sales, you cannot scan a single column.

If you are not yet used to columnar databases, you probably think that, to solve the query, you have to iterate the Sales table, follow the relationship with Products, and sum 1 if the product brand is Contoso, 0 otherwise. Thus, you might think of an algorithm similar to this one:

```
EVALUATE
ROW (
    "Result", SUMX (
        Sales,
        IF ( RELATED ( Product[Brand] ) = "Contoso", 1, 0 )
    )
)
```

This is a simple algorithm, but it hides much more complexity than expected. In fact, if you carefully think of the columnar nature of VertiPaq, this query involves three different columns:

- *Product[Brand]* used to filter the Product table.

- *Product[ProductKey]* used to follow the relationship between Product and Sales.

- *Sales[ProductKey]* used on the Sales side to follow the relationship.

Iterating over *Sales[ProductKey]*, searching the row number in Products scanning *Product[ProductKey]*, and finally gathering the brand in *Product[Brand]* would be extremely expensive and require a lot of random reads to memory, negatively affecting performance. In fact, VertiPaq uses a completely different algorithm, optimized for columnar databases.

First, it scans *Product[Brand]* and retrieves the row numbers where *Product[Brand]* is Contoso. As you can see in Figure 13-8, it scans the Brand dictionary (1), retrieves the encoding of Contoso, and finally scans the segments (2) searching for the row numbers where ID equals to 0, returning the indexes to the rows found (3).

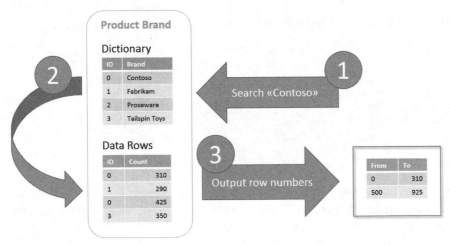

FIGURE 13-8 The output of a brand scan is the list of rows where Brand equals Contoso.

At this point, VertiPaq knows which rows in the Product table have the given brand. The relationship between Product and Sales is based on *Products[ProductKey]* and, at this point VertiPaq knows only the row numbers. Moreover, it is important to remember that the filter will be placed on Sales, not on Products. Thus, in reality, VertiPaq does not need the values of *Products[ProductKey]*, what it really needs is the set of values of *Sales[ProductKey]*, that is, the data IDs in the Sales table, not the ones in Product.

You might remember, at this point, that VertiPaq stores relationships as pairs of row numbers in Product and data IDs in *Sales[ProductKey]*. It turns out that this is the perfect data structure to move the filter from row numbers in Products to *ProductKeys* in Sales. In fact, VertiPaq performs a lookup of the selected row numbers to determine the values of *Sales[ProductKey]* valid for those rows, as you can see in Figure 13-9.

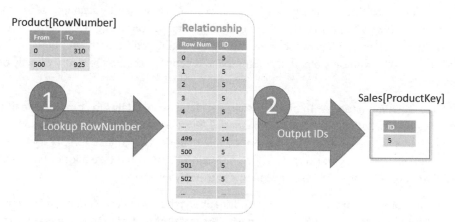

FIGURE 13-9 VertiPaq scans the product key to retrieve the IDs where brand equals Contoso.

The last step is to apply the filter on the Sales table. Since we already have the list of values of *Sales[ProductKey]*, it is enough to scan the *Sales[ProductKey]* column to transform this list of values into row numbers and finally count them. If, instead of computing a *COUNTROWS*, VertiPaq had to perform the *SUM* of a column, then it would perform another step transforming row numbers into column values to perform the last step.

As you can see, this process is made up of simple table scanning where, at each step, you access a single column. However, because data in a column is in the same memory area, VertiPaq sequentially reads blocks of memory and performs simple operations on it, producing every time as output a small data structure that is used in the following step.

The process of resolving a query in VertiPaq is very different from what common sense would suggest. At the beginning, it is very hard to think in terms of columns instead of tables. The algorithms of VertiPaq are optimized for column scanning; the concept of a table is a second-class citizen in a columnar database.

Yet there are scenarios where the engine cannot use these algorithms and reverts to table scanning. Look, for example, at the following query:

```
EVALUATE
ROW (
    "Result", COUNTROWS (
        SUMMARIZE ( Sales, Sales[ProductKey], Sales[CustomerKey] )
    )
)
```

This query looks very innocent, and in its simplicity it shows the limits of columnar databases (but also a row-oriented database faces the same challenge presented here). The query returns the count of unique pairs of product and customer. This query cannot be solved by scanning separately *ProductKey* and *CustomerKey*. The only option here is to build a table containing the unique pairs of *ProductKey* and *CustomerKey*, and finally count the rows in it. Putting it differently, this time VertiPaq has to build a table, even if with only a pair of columns, and it cannot execute the query directly on the original store.

This step, that is, building a table with partial results, which is scanned later to compute the final value, is known as *materialization*. Materialization happens for nearly every query and, by itself, it is neither good nor bad. It all depends on the size of the table materialized. In fact, temporary tables generated by materialization are not compressed (compressing them would take a lot of time, and materialization happens at query time, when latency is extremely important).

It is significant to note that materialization does not happen when you access multiple columns from a table. It all depends on what you have to do with those columns. For example, a query such as the following does not need any materialization, even if it accesses two different columns:

```
EVALUATE
ROW (
    "Result", SUMX (
        Sales, Sales[Quantity] * Sales[Net Price]
    )
)
```

VertiPaq computes the sum performing the multiplication while scanning the two columns, so there is no need to materialize a table with *Quantity* and *Net Price*. Nevertheless, if the expression becomes much more complex, or if you need the table for further processing (as it was the case in the previous example, which required a *COUNTROWS*), then materialization might be required.

In extreme scenarios, materialization might use huge amounts of RAM (sometimes more than the whole database) and generate very slow queries. When this happens, your only chance is to rewrite the calculation or modify the model in such a way that VertiPaq does not need to materialize tables to answer your queries. You will see some examples of these techniques in the following chapters of this book.

Choosing hardware for VertiPaq

Choosing the right hardware is critical for a solution based on SSAS. Spending more does not always mean having a better machine. This final section in the chapter describes how to choose the right server and, as you will see, the perfect Tabular server is not expensive.

Since the introduction of Analysis Services 2012, we helped several companies adopting the new Tabular model in their solutions. A very common issue was that, when going into production, performance was lower than expected. Worse, sometimes it was lower than in the development environments. Most of the times, the reason for that was incorrect hardware sizing, especially when the server was in a virtualized environment. As you will see, the problem is not the use of a virtual machine by itself, but the technical specs of the underlying hardware. A very complete and detailed hardware-sizing guide for Analysis Services Tabular is available in the whitepaper "Hardware Sizing a Tabular Solution (SQL Server Analysis Services)" (*http://msdn.microsoft.com/en-us/library/jj874401.aspx*). The goal of this section is to provide a shorter quick guide that will help you understand the issues affecting many data centers when they have to host a Tabular solution. If you use Power Pivot or Power BI Desktop on a personal computer, you might skip details about Non-Uniform Memory Access (NUMA) support, but all the other considerations are equally true for choosing the right hardware.

Can you choose hardware?

The first question is whether you can choose the hardware or not. The problem of using a virtual machine for a Tabular solution is that often the hardware has already been selected and installed, and you can only influence the number of cores and the amount of RAM that are assigned to your server. Unfortunately, these parameters are not so relevant for the performance. If you will have these limited choices, you should collect information about the CPU model and clock of your host server as soon as possible. If you do not have access to this information, ask a small virtual machine running on the same host server and run the Task Manager: in the Performance tab, you will see the CPU model and the clock rate. With this information, you can predict whether the performance will be worse than an average modern laptop. Unfortunately, chances are that you will be in that position, so you have to sharpen your political skills to convince the right people that running Tabular on that server is a bad idea. If you find that your host server is okay, you will only have to avoid the pitfall of running a Virtual Machine on different NUMA nodes (more on that later).

Set hardware priorities

Assuming that you can influence the hardware selection, keep in mind that you have to set priorities in this order:

1. CPU Clock and Model

2. Memory Speed

3. Number of Cores

4. Memory Size

As you see, disk I/O performance is not in the list, because it is not important at all. There is a condition (paging) where disk I/O affects performance, and we discuss it later in this section. However, you should size the RAM of the system so that you will not have paging at all. Allocate your budget on CPU and memory speed, memory size, and do not waste money on disk I/O bandwidth.

CPU model

The most important factors that affect the speed of code running in the VertiPaq are CPU clock and model. Different CPU models might have a different performance at the same clock rate, so considering the clock alone is not enough. The best practice is to run your own benchmark, measuring the different performance in queries that stress the formula engine. An example of such a query, on a model derived by Adventure Works, is the following:

```
EVALUATE
ROW (
    "Test", COUNTROWS (
        GENERATE (
            TOPN (
                8000,
                CROSSJOIN (
                    ALL ( Reseller[ResellerKey] ),
                    ALL ( Reseller[GeographyKey] )
                ),
                Reseller[ResellerKey]
            ),
            ADDCOLUMNS (
                SUMMARIZE (
                    Sales,
                    OrderDate[FullDate],
                    Products[ProductKey]
                ),
                "Sales", CALCULATE ( SUM ( Sales[SalesAmount] ) )
            )
        )
    )
)
```

You can download the sample workbook to test this query on your hardware here: *http://www.sqlbi.com/articles/choose-the-right-hardware-for-analysis-services-tabular/*. Just open the Excel workbook and run the previous query in DAX Studio, measuring the performance (more on this in Chapter 15).

You can try this query (which is intentionally slow and does not produce any meaningful result) or similar ones. Using a query of a typical workload for your data model is certainly better, because performance might vary on different hardware depending on the memory allocated to materialize intermediate results (the query in the preceding code block has a minimal use of memory).

For example, this query runs in 8.1 seconds on an Intel i7-4770K 3.5 GHz, and in 12.4 seconds on an Intel i7-2860QM 2.5 GHz. These CPUs run a desktop workstation and a notebook, respectively.

Do not presume that a server might run faster. Do your test and look at the results, because they are often surprising. If you do not have Excel on the server, you can restore the Power Pivot model on Analysis Services Tabular and run the query on SQL Server Management Studio if you do not have DAX Studio.

In general, Intel Xeon processors used on a server are E5 and E7 series, and it is very common to find clock speed around 2 GHz, even with a very high number of cores available. You should look for a clock speed of 3 GHz or more, whenever possible. Another important factor is the L2 and L3 cache size: the larger, the better. This is especially important for large tables and relationships between tables based on columns that have more than 1 million unique values.

Memory speed

The memory speed is an important factor for VertiPaq. Every operation made by the engine accesses memory at a very high speed. When the RAM bandwidth is the bottleneck, you see CPU usage instead of I/O waits. Unfortunately, we do not have a performance counter that monitors the time spent a waiting the RAM access. In Tabular, this amount of time can be relevant and it is hard to measure.

In general, you should get RAM that has at least 1,600 MHz, but if the hardware platform permits you should select faster RAM (1,833, 2,133, or 2,400 MHz). At the time of this writing (June 2015), 1,833 MHz is a fast standard on a server, whereas it is hard to find 2,133 MHz, and impossible to find 2,400 MHz unless you buy a desktop optimized to play videogames (by the way, did we mention that gaming machines are the top performers for VertiPaq?).

Number of cores

VertiPaq splits execution on multiple threads only when the table involved has multiple segments. Each segment contains 8 million rows by default (1 million on Power Pivot). If you have eight cores, you will not see all of them involved in a query unless you have at least 64 million rows.

For these reasons, scalability over multiple cores is effective only for very large tables. Raising the number of cores will improve performance for a single query only when it hits a large table (200 million of rows or more). In terms of scalability (number of concurrent users), a higher number of cores might not improve performance if users access the same tables (they would contend access to shared RAM). A better way to increase the number of concurrent users is to use more servers in a load balancing configuration.

The best practice is to get the maximum number of cores you can have on a single socket, getting the highest clock rate available. It is not good having two or more sockets on the same server. Analysis Services Tabular does not recognize the NUMA architecture, which splits memory between different sockets. NUMA requires a more expensive intersocket communication whenever a thread running on a socket accesses memory allocated by another socket—you can find more details about NUMA architecture in Hardware Sizing a Tabular Solution (SQL Server Analysis Services) at *http://msdn.microsoft.com/en-us/library/jj874401.aspx*.

Memory size

You have to store the entire database in memory. You also need RAM to execute process operations (unless you use a separate process server) and to execute queries. Usually optimized queries do not have a high request of RAM, but a single query can materialize temporary tables that could be very large (database tables have a high compression rate, whereas materialization of intermediate tables during a single query generates uncompressed data).

Having enough memory only guarantees that your queries will end returning a result, but increasing available RAM does not produce any performance improvement. Cache used by Tabular does not increase just because of more RAM available. However, a condition of low available memory might affect query performance in a negative way if the server starts paging data. You should simply have enough memory to store all the data of your database and to avoid materialization during query execution.

Disk I/O and paging

You should not allocate budget on storage I/O for Analysis Services Tabular. This is very different from Multidimensional, where random I/O operation on disk occurs very frequently, especially in certain measures. In Tabular, there are no direct storage I/O operations during a query. The only event when this might happen is when you have a low memory condition. However, it is less expensive and more effective to provide more RAM to a server than trying to improve performance by increasing storage I/O throughput when you have a systematic paging caused by low memory available.

Conclusions

You should measure performance before choosing the hardware for SSAS Tabular. It is common to observe a server running twice as slow as a development workstation, even if the server is a very new one. This is because a server designed to be scalable (especially for virtual machines) does not usually perform very well for activities made by a single thread. However, this type of workload is very common in VertiPaq. You will need time and numbers (do your benchmark) to convince your company that a "standard server" could be the weak point of the entire BI solution. Nevertheless, before convincing anybody else, keep in mind that you need to convince yourself. In this chapter, we gave you some insights about the engine. In Chapter 15, you will learn how to measure performance of queries. Take your time and do your tests. We bet they will surprise you.

Optimizing data models

I n the previous chapter, you have seen some of the internals of VertiPaq. This knowledge is useful when you design a data model and you want to optimize it for quick execution of DAX queries. While the previous chapter was more a theoretical one, in this chapter we move on to the more practical side. In fact, this chapter describes the most important guidelines for saving memory and thereby improving performance when creating data models. As you learn here, your main objective will be that of reducing the cardinality of columns in order to decrease the dictionary size, improve the compression, and speed up any iteration and filter.

The final goal of the chapter is optimizing a model. However, before going there, the first and most important skill to learn is being able to measure the pros and cons of each design choice. You do not have to follow any rules blindly without being able to evaluate their impact. For this reason, the first part of the chapter illustrates how to measure the size of each object of a model in memory, so you can evaluate the impact of each optimization, evaluating whether it was worth the effort or not.

Before moving on with the description, let us stress once more this important concept: Test all of the techniques we show on your specific data model. You already learned how data distribution is important in VertiPaq. The very same Sales table, for two different customers, may be compressed in different ways because of data distribution. Thus, any technique we show might have a different impact on different data models. Do not learn best practices. Instead, learn how to build your own best practices by learning different optimization techniques, knowing in advance that not all of them will be applicable in your specific scenario.

Gathering information about the data model

The first step for optimizing a data model is gathering information about the cost of the objects you have in the database. This section describes the tools and the techniques you have to use in order to collect all the data that will help you in prioritizing the possible optimizations of the physical structure.

You can see in Table 14-1 a list of information you should collect from each object in a database.

TABLE 14-1 Information to collect for each object in a database.

Object	Information to collect
Table	Number of rows
Column	Number of unique values Size of dictionary Size of data (total size of all segments)
Hierarchy	Size of hierarchy structure
Relationship	Size of relationship structure

In general, the size of all the objects strongly depends on the number of unique values in columns used or referenced. For this reason, the number of unique values of a column (also known as column cardinality) is the single most important information that you should gather from your database.

As you have seen in Chapter 13, "The VertiPaq engine," you can use Dynamic Management Views (DMVs) to retrieve information about the objects in the database. You can query a DMV using a SQL syntax that you can run in a connection to Analysis Services from SQL Server Management Studio or DAX Studio (which also allows you to connect to a Power Pivot model). For example, you can use this DMV query to retrieve the number of rows of each table:

```
SELECT DIMENSION_NAME, TABLE_ID, ROWS_COUNT
FROM $SYSTEM.DISCOVER_STORAGE_TABLES
```

The result of this query includes both tables and hierarchies. Every column in a table is, by default, a hierarchy that is browsable in MDX queries. In that case, the number in a *ROWS_COUNT* column minus 3 (for internal use) corresponds to the number of unique values of the column corresponding to the hierarchy. The following is an example of the result of the previous query:

DIMENSION_NAME	TABLE_ID	ROWS_COUNT
Currency	Currency_dd3bc081-2c2c-4980-a725-5c481e0f6354	105
Currency	H$Currency_dd3bc081-2c2c-4980-a725-5c481e0f6354$CurrencyKey	108
Currency	H$Currency_dd3bc081-2c2c-4980-a725-5c481e0f6354$CurrencyName	108
Currency	H$Currency_dd3bc081-2c2c-4980-a725-5c481e0f6354$CurrencyAlternateKey	108
Customer	Customer_08b41bba-8733-438e-a584-9894998b2f69	18,484
Customer	H$Customer_08b41bba-8733-438e-a584-9894998b2f69$MiddleName	46
Customer	H$Customer_08b41bba-8733-438e-a584-9894998b2f69$Gender	5

You can filter the information related to the table names by checking whether the first part of the *TABLE_ID* column corresponds to the table name. The SQL support for the DMVs is very limited and depending on the engine running DAX, certain functions might be supported or not. For example, only Analysis Services supports the following query (but neither Microsoft Excel nor Power BI Desktop support it):

```
SELECT
    DIMENSION_NAME AS TABLE_NAME,
    ROWS_COUNT AS ROWS_IN_TABLE
FROM  $SYSTEM.DISCOVER_STORAGE_TABLES
WHERE DIMENSION_NAME = LEFT ( TABLE_ID, LEN ( DIMENSION_NAME ) )
ORDER BY DIMENSION_NAME
```

Such a query produces the following result:

TABLE_NAME	ROWS_IN_TABLE
Currency	105
Customer	18,484
Date	2,191
Employee	296
Geography	655
Internet Sales	60,398

You can use another query (supported only in Analysis Services) that returns the number of unique values in each column, filtering the hierarchies based on initial name and subtracting 3 from the rows count, as in the following query:

```
-- Get number of rows for each column (remove GUID)
SELECT
    DIMENSION_NAME AS TABLE NAME,
    RIGHT ( TABLE_ID, LEN ( TABLE_ID ) - 40 - LEN ( DIMENSION_NAME ) ) AS COLUMN NAME,
    ROWS_COUNT - 3 AS COLUMN_CARDINALITY
FROM $SYSTEM.DISCOVER_STORAGE_TABLES
WHERE LEFT ( TABLE_ID, 2 ) = 'H$'
ORDER BY TABLE_ID
```

The result is the following:

TABLE_NAME	COLUMN_NAME	COLUMN_CARDINALITY
Currency	CurrencyAlternateKey	105
Currency	CurrencyKey	105
Currency	CurrencyName	105
Customer	AddressLine1	12,797
Customer	AddressLine2	166
Customer	BirthDate	8,252
Customer	LastName	375
Customer	Phone	8,890

> **Note** Analysis Services 2016 introduces the ability to disable the construction of a hierarchy on a column basis. In that case, you have to use a DAX query to retrieve the distinct count of values in a column.

You can also retrieve the size (in bytes) of the dictionary of each column by using the following query:

```
SELECT
    DIMENSION_NAME AS TABLE_NAME,
    COLUMN_ID AS COLUMN_NAME,
    DICTIONARY_SIZE AS DICTIONARY_SIZE_BYTES
FROM  $SYSTEM.DISCOVER_STORAGE_TABLE_COLUMNS
WHERE COLUMN_TYPE = 'BASIC_DATA'
```

The result is the following:

TABLE_NAME	COLUMN_NAME	DICTIONARY_SIZE_BYTES
Currency	RowNumber	88
Currency	CurrencyKey	2,796
Currency	CurrencyAlternateKey	18,616
Currency	CurrencyName	20,520
Customer	RowNumber	88
Customer	CustomerKey	598,552
Customer	GeographyKey	9,872

In case you cannot use the DMVs, you can run simple DAX queries to retrieve the number of rows in a table and the number of unique values in a column, but there is no way to create a generic DAX query that retrieves these values for all the tables and columns in a database.

For example, you can evaluate the number of rows in a table using *COUNTROWS*:

```
EVALUATE
ROW (
    "Rows in Internet Sales",
    COUNTROWS ( 'Internet Sales' )
)
```

You can get the number of unique values in a column using *DISTINCTCOUNT*:

```
EVALUATE
ROW (
    "Unique Values in Internet Sales",
    DISTINCTCOUNT ( 'Internet Sales'[Sales Order Number] )
)
```

However, a DAX query can only provide information about the cardinality of tables and columns. You need to use a DMV in order to retrieve the size of each column. The DMV used by the following query retrieves this information for all the hierarchies and relationships; the condition in the *WHERE* clause filters only the size of the data for each column, which can be split among partitions and segments:

```
SELECT
    DIMENSION_NAME AS TABLE_NAME,
    COLUMN_ID AS COLUMN_NAME,
    SEGMENT_NUMBER,
    TABLE_PARTITION_NUMBER,
    RECORDS_COUNT, USED_SIZE
FROM $SYSTEM.DISCOVER_STORAGE_TABLE_COLUMN_SEGMENTS
WHERE MEASURE_GROUP_NAME = LEFT ( TABLE_ID, LEN ( MEASURE_GROUP_NAME ) )
```

The following is an example of the result of the previous query, where the table Internet Sales has several partitions.

TABLE_NAME	COLUMN_NAME	SEGMENT_NUMBER	TABLE_PARTITION_NUMBER	RECORDS_COUNT	USED_SIZE
Internet Sales	SalesOrderNumber	0	0	1,013	1,352
Internet Sales	SalesOrderNumber	1	1	2,677	4,288
Internet Sales	SalesOrderNumber	2	2	24,443	48,888
Internet Sales	SalesOrderNumber	3	3	32,265	64,536
Internet Sales	SalesOrderNumber	4	4	0	8
Internet Sales	SalesOrderNumber	5	5	0	8
Internet Sales	SalesOrderLineNumber	0	0	1,013	8
Internet Sales	SalesOrderLineNumber	1	1	2,677	8
Internet Sales	SalesOrderLineNumber	2	2	24,443	184
Internet Sales	SalesOrderLineNumber	3	3	32,265	208

You obtain the total size used by a column by summing the *USED_SIZE* value for all the rows related to the same *COLUMN_NAME*. For example, the *SalesOrderNumber* column uses a total of 119,064 bytes, resulting from the sum of *USED_SIZE* for all the segments in all the partitions for the same *COLUMN_NAME*.

The last information related to columns is the cost of the column hierarchy. The hierarchy structures for a column in a tabular model allow the navigation in hierarchy values using MDX metadata and queries. A column with a high cardinality can have a high memory cost for these hierarchies. The following query retrieves the size of the structures used by a column hierarchy.

```
SELECT
    DIMENSION_NAME AS TABLE_NAME,
    RIGHT ( TABLE_ID, LEN ( TABLE_ID ) - LEN ( DIMENSION_NAME ) - 40 ) AS COLUMN_NAME,
    COLUMN_ID AS STRUCTURE_NAME,
    SEGMENT_NUMBER,
    TABLE_PARTITION_NUMBER,
    USED_SIZE,
    TABLE_ID AS COLUMN_HIERARCHY_ID
FROM $SYSTEM.DISCOVER_STORAGE_TABLE_COLUMN_SEGMENTS
WHERE LEFT ( TABLE_ID, 2 ) = 'H$'
```

The following table shows an example of the result of this DMV query. As you see, the size of the hierarchy is larger for columns with a higher cardinality (the *Phone* column has more unique values than the *LastName* column, and results in a larger column hierarchy, too).

TABLE_NAME	COLUMN_NAME	STRUCTURE_NAME	SEGMENT_NUMBER	TABLE_PARTITION_NUMBER	USED_SIZE	COLUMN_HIERARCHY_ID
Customer	LastName	POS_TO_ID	0	0	1,504	H$Customer_08b41bba-8733-438e-a584-9894998b2f69$LastName
Customer	LastName	POS_TO_ID	1	0	16	H$Customer_08b41bba-8733-438e-a584-9894998b2f69$LastName
Customer	LastName	ID_TO_POS	0	0	1,504	H$Customer_08b41bba-8733-438e-a584-9894998b2f69$LastName
Customer	LastName	ID_TO_POS	1	0	16	H$Customer_08b41bba-8733-438e-a584-9894998b2f69$LastName
Customer	Phone	POS_TO_ID	0	0	35,568	H$Customer_08b41bba-8733-438e-a584-9894998b2f69$Phone
Customer	Phone	POS_TO_ID	1	0	16	H$Customer_08b41bba-8733-438e-a584-9894998b2f69$Phone
Customer	Phone	ID_TO_POS	0	0	35,568	H$Customer_08b41bba-8733-438e-a584-9894998b2f69$Phone
Customer	Phone	ID_TO_POS	1	0	16	H$Customer_08b41bba-8733-438e-a584-9894998b2f69$Phone

> **Note** Analysis Services 2016 can disable the creation of a column hierarchy. If a column has a high cardinality and it is used only in measures but not as a filter condition, then disabling its column hierarchy will save the memory reported by the previous DMV query. Moreover, by disabling hierarchies for some columns, you also reduce process time, because these data structures will not be created.

Each table might have other two structures not strictly related to the columns. First, you can have user hierarchies, which usually combine two or more columns in a predefined path of navigation. Such a structure is used only by MDX queries, whereas DAX does not take advantage of it (a DAX client only uses the metadata of user hierarchies). The following query retrieves information from user hierarchies:

```
SELECT
    DIMENSION_NAME AS TABLE_NAME,
    RIGHT ( TABLE_ID, LEN ( TABLE_ID ) - LEN ( DIMENSION_NAME ) - 40 ) AS HIERARCHY_NAME,
    COLUMN_ID AS STRUCTURE_NAME,
    USED_SIZE,
    TABLE_ID AS HIERARCHY_ID
FROM $SYSTEM.DISCOVER_STORAGE_TABLE_COLUMN_SEGMENTS
WHERE LEFT ( TABLE_ID, 2 ) = 'U$'
```

You can see in the following result that each user hierarchy has four related structures, the size of which depends on the cardinality of the columns involved in the hierarchy itself.

TABLE_NAME	HIERARCHY_NAME	STRUCTURE_NAME	USED_SIZE	HIERARCHY_ID
Date	Fiscal	MULTI_LEVEL_ID	9,232	U$Date_d2c7ec3d-c72c-435d-bd43-8283714cc2dd$Fiscal
Date	Fiscal	PARENT_POS	9,232	U$Date_d2c7ec3d-c72c-435d-bd43-8283714cc2dd$Fiscal
Date	Fiscal	FIRST_CHILD_POS	9,232	U$Date_d2c7ec3d-c72c-435d-bd43-8283714cc2dd$Fiscal
Date	Fiscal	CHILD_COUNT	9,232	U$Date_d2c7ec3d-c72c-435d-bd43-8283714cc2dd$Fiscal
Date	Calendar	MULTI_LEVEL_ID	9,224	U$Date_d2c7ec3d-c72c-435d-bd43-8283714cc2dd$Calendar
Date	Calendar	PARENT_POS	9,224	U$Date_d2c7ec3d-c72c-435d-bd43-8283714cc2dd$Calendar
Date	Calendar	FIRST_CHILD_POS	9,224	U$Date_d2c7ec3d-c72c-435d-bd43-8283714cc2dd$Calendar
Date	Calendar	CHILD_COUNT	9,224	U$Date_d2c7ec3d-c72c-435d-bd43-8283714cc2dd$Calendar

The second structure not related to columns is relationships. You can retrieve their number and memory size by using the following query:

```
SELECT
    DIMENSION_NAME AS TABLE_NAME,
    USED_SIZE,
    TABLE_ID AS RELATIONSHIP_ID
FROM $SYSTEM.DISCOVER_STORAGE_TABLE_COLUMN_SEGMENTS
WHERE LEFT ( TABLE_ID, 2 ) = 'R$'
```

The information provided by this DMV does not include the columns involved in the relationship. You can see the result of the previous DMV query in the following table.

TABLE_NAME	USED_SIZE	RELATIONSHIP_ID
Product	40	R$Product_11920c93-05ae-4f1c-980e-466dfbcfca2a$9b8024a2-e51d-4a2b-9a8f-6a2199d1d2ea
Product Subcategory	8	R$Product Subcategory_ca7d6f4b-ec2c-41fa-a7e1-d771c69ec1ac$46425cb9-382b-4dfb-9b79-63bc5082c42b
Reseller	880	R$Reseller_d52b9c6f-8d2d-4e23-ae4c-2fc57c1d968a$b32d6ef8-a309-4c10-8d36-0f0e2ae84901
Internet Sales	8	R$Internet Sales_fdac9a13-4019-4773-b193-7cca3a4883eb$b3d9edf1-1e10-436b-b870-80029b0ee4f3
Internet Sales	36,976	R$Internet Sales_fdac9a13-4019-4773-b193-7cca3a4883eb$90d94b82-0243-4632-b9f7-99de63279961
Internet Sales	48,168	R$Internet Sales_fdac9a13-4019-4773-b193-7cca3a4883eb$f5617b1d-9840-4978-8860-f337cb5f852d
Internet Sales	216	R$Internet Sales_fdac9a13-4019-4773-b193-7cca3a4883eb$a5016faf-9af5-4750-92ff-505d05aefe68

In order to get the complete picture of the cost of each column in your data model, it is a good idea to collect in a single place the information from the DMVs you have seen so far. For example, we created a Power Pivot data model that connects to an Analysis Services database and executes the DMV queries presented in this chapter, organizing the result in a few Excel tables. In Figure 14-1 you can see the content of the Columns table, which provides the size used by the structures related to each column in the data model.

TABLE_NAME	COLUMN_NAME	DICTIONARY_SIZE_BYTES	GRANULARITY	SELECTIVITY	DATA_SIZE	HIERARCHY_SIZE	TOTAL_SIZE
Sales	ProductKey	75,920	2,516	0.02%	13,799,896	20,176	13,895,992
Sales	Net Price	75,812	2,469	0.02%	12,441,496	19,792	12,537,100
Sales	Due Date	46,488	1,103	0.01%	9,323,584	8,864	9,378,936
Sales	DueDateKey	21,644	1,103	0.01%	9,323,584	8,864	9,354,092
Sales	Unit Cost	10,536	480	0.00%	8,910,920	3,888	8,925,344
Sales	Unit Price	10,240	426	0.00%	8,886,792	3,456	8,900,488
Sales	Unit Discount	41,384	1,906	0.02%	8,533,808	15,296	8,590,488
Sales	CustomerKey	88	18,869	0.15%	5,937,352	75,496	6,012,936
Sales	Delivery Date	46,432	1,100	0.01%	4,970,096	8,848	5,025,376
Sales	DeliveryDateKey	21,616	1,100	0.01%	4,970,096	8,848	5,000,560
Sales	Order Date	46,368	1,096	0.01%	3,055,328	8,816	3,110,512
Sales	OrderDateKey	21,560	1,096	0.01%	3,055,328	8,816	3,085,704
Customer	Name	953,986	18,401	97.52%	36,976	147,248	1,138,210
Customer	CustomerKey	600,084	18,869	100.00%	37,744	150,992	788,820
Customer	Customer Code	457,798	18,869	100.00%	37,744	150,992	646,534

FIGURE 14-1 Each row of the Columns table shows the costs associated to each column in the data model.

If you want to see the total cost of a table, you have to sum the total size of the corresponding columns, plus the size of user hierarchies and relationships. The result is visible in Figure 14-2.

TABLE_NAME	ROWS_IN_TABLE	TABLE_SIZE	COLUMNS_SIZE	HIERARCHIES_SIZE	RELATIONSHIPS_SIZE
Sales	12,527,442	94,100,096	94,052,416		47,680
Customer	18,869	3,026,846	3,026,846		
Date	2,556	738,746	568,314	170,432	
Product	2,517	705,810	705,778		32
Store	97	191,754	191,754		
Product Subcategory	44	39,410	39,402		8
Promotion	28	72,006	72,006		
Currency	28	37,720	37,720		
Product Category	8	36,106	36,106		

FIGURE 14-2 The *TABLE_SIZE* column in the Tables table sums the cost of corresponding columns, user hierarchies, and relationships.

You can find the complete Power Pivot data model in the DMV Size Contoso Excel workbook included in the companion content. You can change the connection string pointing to a database in your Analysis Services server and refresh the tables in the data model in order to see statistics of another database. You can also download updated version of this model from *http://www.sqlbi.com/tools/vertipaq-analyzer/.*

The DMVs you have seen so far can provide more details. For example, you can see the compression type and number of bits using VertiPaq encoding for each segment and each column using the DMV named DISCOVER_STORAGE_TABLE_COLUMN_SEGMENTS. Its columns *COMPRESSION_TYPE* and *BITS_COUNT* describe the choices made by VertiPaq by compressing a column in a particular segment.

An alternative approach is using the DMV named DISCOVER_OBJECT_MEMORY_USAGE, which provides a hierarchical information about all the objects allocated in memory. Querying this DMV, you obtain a list of all the objects allocated on the server for all the databases online. Because of the hierarchical structure, its usage in a simple table is not easy. Consider the following query:

```
SELECT
    OBJECT_PARENT_PATH,
    OBJECT_ID,
    OBJECT_MEMORY_NONSHRINKABLE,
    OBJECT_MEMORY_CHILD_NONSHRINKABLE
FROM $SYSTEM.DISCOVER_OBJECT_MEMORY_USAGE
ORDER BY OBJECT_MEMORY_NONSHRINKABLE DESC
```

It returns the following result: the *OBJECT_PARENT_PATH* column contains the hierarchical position of the object, but it is not easy to navigate. You can see in the following table that the *OBJECT_MEMORY_NONSHRINKABLE* shows the amount of memory used by the specific object in the row, and *OBJECT_MEMORY_CHILD_NONSHRINKABLE* shows the memory cost summing all the child objects, at any level of the hierarchy.

OBJECT_PARENT_PATH	OBJECT_ID	OBJECT_ MEMORY_ NONSHRINKABLE	OBJECT_ MEMORY_ CHILD_ NONSHRINKABLE
HP8\TAB14.Databases.Contoso.Dimensions. Sales_001b8a59-0b80-4210-9567-facdae2142ec. In-Memory Table.Columns.OrderDateKey	Segments	3,399,392	0
HP8\TAB14.Databases.Contoso.Dimensions. Sales_001b8a59-0b80-4210-9567-facdae2142ec. In-Memory Table.Columns.Order Date	Segments	3,399,392	0
	Global	2,454,866	109,194,683
HP8\TAB14.Databases.Contoso.Dimensions. Customer_93737598-2e17-4d54-a6c1- 17f028353d90.In-Memory Table.Columns	Name	954,442	37,104
HP8\TAB14.Databases.Contoso.Cubes	Model	642,878	616,804
HP8\TAB14.Databases.Contoso.Dimensions. Customer_93737598-2e17-4d54-a6c1- 17f028353d90.In-Memory Table.Columns	CustomerKey	600,540	37,872
Global	GeneralPurpose	495,726	0

A better way to see this data is using the BISM Server Memory Report, an Excel workbook created by Kasper De Jonge that transforms the parent-child hierarchy described in the *OBJECT_PARENT_PATH* column into a regular hierarchy of a Power Pivot data model. You can download this workbook and read the entire article describing its behavior at *http://www.powerpivotblog.nl/what-is-using-all-that-memory-on-my-analysis-server-instance/*, and you can see an example of its output in Figure 14-3.

Note At the moment of writing, there is a plan for a feature in DAX Studio to retrieve size and cardinality of all the columns in a database, but it is not implemented yet. Please check whether a recent version of DAX Studio implements such a feature.

You have a number of ways to retrieve information about a data model. The most important information is always the cardinality of tables and columns, which you can retrieve with simple DAX queries. However, using DMVs can be faster and easier, providing a complete picture of all the columns and tables in a data model.

Denormalization

The first optimization you can apply to a data model is to denormalize data. Every relationship has an additional cost in terms of memory and an additional overhead when the engine transfers the filter from one table to another. We might think that an optimal model, from a pure performance point of view, would be one made of a single table. However, such an approach would be less than usable and would force having a single granularity for all of the measures. Thus, an optimal data model is the one organized as a star schema around each table defined for measures sharing the same granularity. For this reason, you should denormalize unnecessary related tables reducing the number of columns and relationships in the data model.

Row Labels	Usage MB	Pct of tota
⊟HP8\TAB14	101.94	100.0 %
⊟Databases	101.94	100.0 %
⊞(blank)	0.00	0.0 %
⊟Contoso	101.94	100.0 %
⊞(blank)	0.05	0.0 %
⊞CalculatedColumns	0.00	0.0 %
⊞Cubes	2.07	2.0 %
⊞Data Source Views	0.10	0.1 %
⊞Data Sources	0.01	0.0 %
⊟Dimensions	99.71	97.8 %
⊞(blank)	0.00	0.0 %
⊞Currency	0.09	0.1 %
⊞Customer	3.16	3.1 %
⊞Date	1.05	1.0 %
⊞Measures	0.41	0.4 %
⊞Product	0.90	0.9 %
⊞Product Category	0.09	0.1 %
⊞Product Subcategory	0.11	0.1 %
⊞Promotion	0.17	0.2 %
⊟Sales	93.33	91.6 %
⊞(blank)	0.18	0.2 %
⊟In-Memory Table	93.15	91.4 %
⊞(blank)	0.00	0.0 %
⊟Columns	92.91	91.1 %
⊞(blank)	0.00	0.0 %
⊞CurrencyKey	0.00	0.0 %
⊞CustomerKey	5.70	5.6 %
⊞Delivery Date	5.17	5.1 %
⊞DeliveryDateKey	5.14	5.0 %
⊞Due Date	9.40	9.2 %
⊞DueDateKey	9.38	9.2 %
⊞Net Price	12.14	11.9 %
⊞Order Date	3.29	3.2 %
⊞OrderDateKey	3.26	3.2 %
⊞ProductKey	13.45	13.2 %

FIGURE 14-3 BISM Server Memory Report displays the memory used by objects in a hierarchical way.

The denormalization required in a data model for DAX is usually counterintuitive for anyone with some experience in data modeling for a relational database. For instance, consider a simple data model where you have a Payment table with two columns, *Payment Code* and *Payment Description*. In a relational database, you often use a Code and Description table to avoid duplicating the description content into another table. For example, you want to avoid the duplication in a Transactions table of identical Payment Description values in different rows that have the same Payment Code value. By storing only the Payment Code, you would save space in a relational model.

Consider Table 14-2, which shows a denormalized version of the Transactions table. You can see the duplication of Credit Card and Cash strings in different rows.

TABLE 14-2 Transactions table with Payment Type denormalized in *Code* and *Description* columns.

Date	Amount	Payment Type Code	Payment Type Description
2015-06-21	100	00	Cash
2015-06-21	100	02	Credit Card
2015-06-22	200	02	Credit Card
2015-06-23	200	00	Cash
2015-06-23	100	03	Wire Transfer
2015-06-24	200	02	Credit Card
2015-06-25	100	00	Cash

If you use a separate table containing all the payment types, you can store only the Payment Type Code in the Transactions table, as you see in Table 14-3.

TABLE 14-3 Transactions table normalized, with *Payment Type Code* only.

Date	Amount	Payment Type Code
2015-06-21	100	00
2015-06-21	100	02
2015-06-22	200	02
2015-06-23	200	00
2015-06-23	100	03
2015-06-24	200	02
2015-06-25	100	00

You store the description of payment types in a separate table (see Table 14-4), which has one row for each payment type code. Such a table in a relational database reduces the total amount of space required, avoiding the duplication of a long string in the Transactions table.

TABLE 14-4 Payment Type table that normalizes *Code* and *Description*.

Payment Type Code	Payment Type Description
00	Cash
01	Debit Card
02	Credit Card
03	Wire Transfer

However, this optimization for a relational database might be a bad choice in a data model for DAX. The VertiPaq engine automatically creates a dictionary for each column, which means that the Transactions table will not pay a cost for duplicated descriptions as it happens in a relational model.

> **Note** Compression techniques based on dictionaries are available also in certain relational databases. For example, Microsoft SQL Server offers this feature in the Enterprise edition (through the clustered columnstore indexes). However, the default behavior of a relational database is to store data without compression.

In terms of space saving, you can easily compute that denormalization is always better if you denormalize a single column (please note that the denormalization of more columns might be more expensive than using a normalized model). For example, the memory cost for a normalized model is as follows:

NormalizedMemoryCost =
  ColumnCost(Transactions[Type Code]) + ColumnCost(Payments[Type Code]) +
  ColumnCost(Payments[Type Description]) + RelationshipCost(Transactions[Type Code])

The cost for the denormalized model is the following:

DenormalizedMemoryCost =
  ColumnCost(Transactions[Type Code]) + ColumnCost(Transactions[Type Description])

As you see, by denormalizing the model you remove the cost of the column *Payments[Type Code]* and the cost of the relationship on *Transactions[Type Code]*. However, you might observe that the cost of the column *Type Description* is different between Transactions and Payments tables. This is certainly true, and in a very large table, the difference might be in favor of the normalized model. However, in terms of performance, when you aggregate a column usually you see better performance with a filter applied on another column of the same table, rather than a filter on a column in another table connected through a relationship. Does this justify a complete denormalization of the data model into a single table? Absolutely not! In terms of usability, you should always consider adopting a star schema, which is a good tradeoff in terms of resource usage and performance.

In a star schema, you have a table for each entity (such as Customers and Products), and all the attributes related to an entity are completely denormalized in such tables. For example, the Products table should have attributes such as Category, Subcategory, Model, and Color. This model works well whenever the cardinality of the relationship is not too large. By large, we mean more than 1 million unique values in the entity key, but when you have more than 100,000 unique values, you already enter into a warning area in terms of performance.

In order to understand why the cardinality of a relationship is important for performance, you have to know what happens when you apply a filter on a column. Consider the schema in Figure 14-4, where you have the Sales table with relationships to the Product, Customer, and Date tables. When you query the data model filtering customers by gender, the engine transfers the filter from Customer to Sales by specifying the list of customer keys that belong to each gender type included in the query. If you have 10,000 customers, any list generated by a filter cannot be larger than this number. However, if you have 6 million customers, a filter by a single gender type might generate a list of unique keys, resulting in around 3 million unique values. A large number of keys involved in a relationship always has an impact in performance, even if in absolute terms; such impact depends also on the version of the engine and on the hardware (CPU clock, cache size, RAM speed) that you are using.

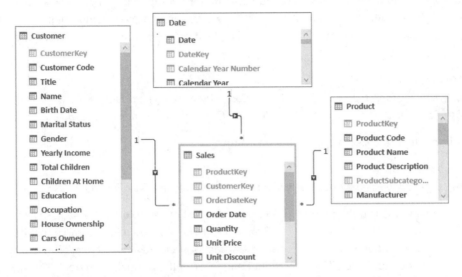

FIGURE 14-4 The Sales table has relationships with Product, Customer, and Date tables.

What can you do in order to optimize the data model when a relationship involves millions of unique values? Once you measure performance degradation not compatible with your requirements, you can consider some form of denormalization that reduces the cardinality of the relationship, or that removes the need of a relationship at all in certain queries. In the previous example, you might consider to denormalize the *Gender* column in the Sales table, in the event it is the only case where you need to optimize performance. If you have more columns to optimize, you might consider creating another table with the columns of Customer table that users query often and that have a low cardinality (and a low selectivity).

For instance, you can create a table with *Gender*, *Occupation*, and *Education*. If the cardinality of these columns is 2, 5, and 5 values, respectively, a table with all the possible combinations will have 50 rows (2 x 5 x 5). A query on any of these columns will be much faster because the filter applied to Sales will have a very short list of values. In terms of usability, the user will see two groups of attributes for the same entity, corresponding to the two tables, Customer and Customer Info. This is not an ideal situation. For this reason, you should consider this optimization only when strictly necessary. It is important that both tables have a direct relationship with the Sales table, as you can see in Figure 14-5.

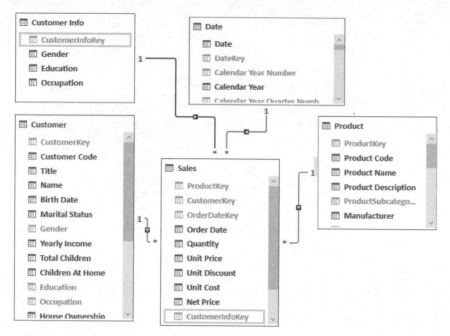

FIGURE 14-5 Both Customer and Customer Info tables have a relationship with Sales.

You should evaluate the *CustomerInfoKey* added to the Sales table before importing data in a large Sales table, so that it is a native column (as you have seen in Chapter 13, native columns are better compressed than calculated ones). However, you might obtain it in a calculated column using the following DAX expression:

```
Sales[CustomerInfoKey] =
LOOKUPVALUE (
    'Customer Info'[CustomerInfoKey],
    'Customer Info'[Gender], RELATED ( Customer[Gender] ),
    'Customer Info'[Occupation], RELATED ( Customer[Occupation] ),
    'Customer Info'[Education], RELATED ( Customer[Education] )
)
```

Talking about user experience, you should hide from the Customer table the columns denormalized in the Customer Info table. Showing the same attributes (Gender, Occupation, and Education) in two tables would generate confusion. However, if you hide these attributes from the client in the Customer table, you cannot show in a query (and especially in a pivot table) the list of Customers with a certain Occupation. If you do not want to lose this possibility, you have to complicate the model with one inactive relationship, activating it in case of need. In Figure 14-6 you can see that the Customer Info table has an active relationship with the Sales table and an inactive relationship with the Customer table.

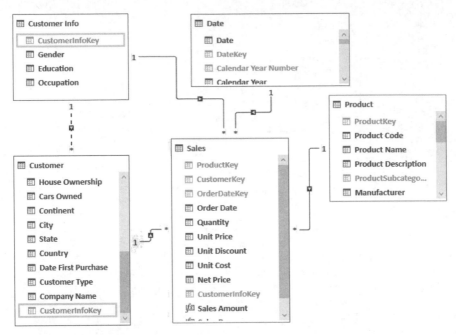

FIGURE 14-6 An inactive relationship connects Customer and Customer Info tables.

You can enable the relationship between Customer Info and Customer in case you have any other filter active in the Customer table. For example, consider the following definition of the Sales measure:

```
[Sales] :=
IF (
    ISCROSSFILTERED ( Customer[CustomerKey] ),
    CALCULATE (
        [Sales Internal],
        USERELATIONSHIP ( Customer[CustomerInfoKey], 'Customer Info'[CustomerInfoKey] )
    ),
    [Sales Internal]
)
```

The only reason why you can have an active cross filter in the Customer table (if you are not using the bidirectional filter) is when you apply a filter on any column of the Customer table. When this is true, you enable the relationship between Customer and Customer Info, automatically disabling the other relationship between Customer Info and Sales. The idea is that, since the engine has to process a list of CustomerKey values in any case, it is better to reduce such a filter by including also the attributes you moved in Customer Info. However, if you filter columns in Customer Info and not in Customer, the default active relationship uses a better relationship made with a lower number of unique values. Unfortunately, in order to optimize the usage of Customer-Sales relationship when you use both Customer Info and Customer columns in a query, you have to apply this DAX pattern to all the measures that might involve Customer Info attributes.

There is another common scenario where you have a high cardinality in a relationship and you should carefully consider some denormalization. This happens when you have a relationship between two large tables. For example, consider the data model you can see in Figure 14-7, using two tables, Sales Header and Sales Detail.

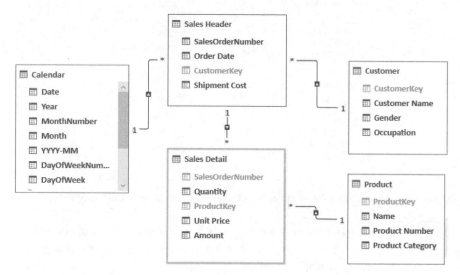

FIGURE 14-7 The Customer table filters Sales Detail transactions through relationships in Sales Header.

This situation is common because many normalized relational databases have the same design. However, the relationship between Sales Header and Sales Detail is particularly dangerous for a DAX query, because of the high number of unique values that it has. Any query grouping the *Quantity* column (from Sales Detail) by Customer Gender will transfer a filter from Sales Header to Sales Detail through the *SalesOrderNumber* column. You can obtain a better design by denormalizing in Sales Detail all the relationships you have in Sales Header. In practice, you create two star schemas sharing the same dimensions. The only purpose of the normalization is to avoid passing a filter through the relationship between Sales Header and Sales Detail, which no longer exists in the new design, as you can see in Figure 14-8.

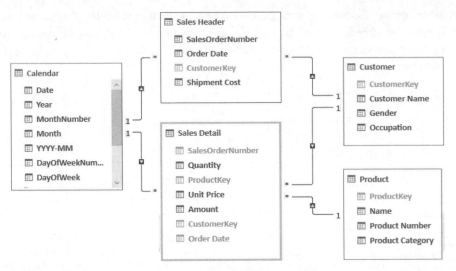

FIGURE 14-8 The Sales Header and Sales Detail tables have direct relationships with Customer and Calendar.

You have to use the right degree of denormalization in a data model for DAX, especially for performance reasons. Using the best practices described in this section, you will obtain a good balance between usability and performance.

Columns cardinality

The cardinality of a column is the number of unique values that the column contains. You have seen that this number is important to reduce the size of the column, which has a direct impact on scan performance. Another reason why you should reduce the cardinality of a column to the necessary minimum is that many DAX operations (such as iterations and filters) have an execution time that directly depends on this number. Often, cardinality of a column is more important than the number of rows of the table containing the column.

When you design a data model, you should identify the cardinality of a column and consider possible optimizations if you will use the column in relationships, filters, or calculations. There are a number of common scenarios to consider:

- **Key of a relationship**: You cannot change the cardinality of this column unless you modify the cardinality of the related table (see the "Denormalization" section in this chapter).

- **Numeric value aggregated in a measure**: You do not change the precision of a number if you have a number representing quantity or amount of a monetary transaction. However, if a number represents a measure with a floating-point value, you might consider removing the decimals that are not relevant. For example, if you are collecting temperatures, you might round the value down to the closest decimal digit (what you remove is probably lower than the precision of the measuring tool).

- **Text description**: The only impact is on dictionary size in case the column has many unique values. There are no advantages in moving the column in a separate table, because the dictionary would be the same. Keep this column if users will use it.

- **Text notes**: Potentially different for every row of the table, but it is not an issue if most of the rows have a BLANK value.

- **Pictures**: This column is required if you want to display graphics in Power View and Power BI (for example, the picture of a product). Consider a lower resolution in order to compress the space required, especially if you have many of them.

- **Transaction ID**: This column has a high cardinality in a large table. Consider removing it if it is not necessary in DAX queries. If used in drill-through operations, for example, to see the transactions that form a particular aggregation, consider splitting the number/string in two or more parts, each one with a smaller number of unique values.

- **Date and time**: Consider splitting the column in two parts (see the following section in this chapter, "Handling date and time").

- **Audit columns**: A table in a relational database often has standard columns used for auditing purposes (for instance, timestamp and user of last update). You should not import these columns in a data model, unless required for drill-through (in that case, consider splitting the timestamp following the same rules applied to date and time).

As a rule of thumb, you should consider that reducing the cardinality of a column will save memory and improve performance. Because reducing cardinality might imply losing information and/or accuracy, you have to be careful in considering the implications of these optimizations.

Handling date and time

Almost any data model has one or more date columns. Every so often, the time is also an interesting dimension of analysis. Usually these columns come from original *Datetime* columns in the data source. You should apply a number of best practices to these cases in order to optimize your data model.

First and most important, you should always split date and time in two separate columns. You do not have to use calculated columns to do this split. It should happen reading the original column in two different columns of the data model: one for the date, the other for the time. For example, if you are reading a *TransactionExecution* column from a table in SQL Server, you should use the following syntax in a T-SQL query to create two columns, *TransactionDate* and *TransactionTime*:

```
...
CAST ( TransactionExecution AS DATE ) AS TransactionDate,
CAST ( TransactionExecution AS TIME ) AS TransactionTime,
...
```

It is very important to do this split operation; otherwise you would import a column in which dictionary and cardinality would increase every day. Moreover, analyzing a timestamp in Tabular is very hard. If you have a Date table, you need an exact match with the date, and the *Datetime* column would not work correctly in a relationship with the *Date* column of a Date table.

A *Date* column usually has a good granularity: 10 years correspond to less than 3,700 unique values, and even 100 years are still in a manageable order of magnitude. Moreover, time intelligence functions require a complete calendar for each year considered, so removing days (for example, keeping only one day per month) is not an optimization to consider.

The *Time* column, on the other hand, should be subject to more considerations. When you have a *Time* column, you should consider creating a Time table, which contains one row for each point in the granularity you choose. You should also round the time to the same granularity you chose for the Time table. The Time table will make it easy to consider different periods: for example, morning and evening, or intervals of 15 minutes. Depending on the data and the analysis required, you might choose to round the data down to the closest hour or to the milliseconds (even if the latter is very unlikely). In Table 14-5 you can see the different cardinality corresponding to different precision levels.

TABLE 14-5 Cardinality corresponding to different precision levels for a *Time* column.

Precision	Cardinality
Hour	24
15 Minutes	96
5 Minutes	288
Minute	1,440
Second	86,400
Millisecond	86,400,000

It is clear that choosing the millisecond precision is usually the worst choice, and the precision down to the second has still a relative high number of unique values. Most of the time, you will choose a precision ranging between hour and minutes. At this point, you might think that the minute precision is a safe choice, because it has a relatively low cardinality. However, you have to remember that the compression of a column depends on the presence of duplicated values in contiguous rows. Thus, moving from minute to 15-minute precision can have a big impact in compression of large tables.

When you are working with time, you might choose to round to the closest second/minute, or to truncate the detail that you do not need for the analysis. The choice between these two options depends on your analytical requirements. Here is an example of the T-SQL code that truncates a time to different precision levels:

```
-- Truncate to the second
DATEADD (
    MILLISECOND,
    - DATEPART (
        MILLISECOND,
        CAST ( TransactionExecution AS TIME )
    ),
    CAST ( TransactionExecution AS TIME )
)
```

```
-- Truncate to the minute
DATEADD ( MINUTE, DATEDIFF ( MINUTE, 0, CAST ( TransactionExecution AS TIME ), 0 )

-- Truncate to 5 minute
DATEADD (
    MINUTE,
    ( DATEDIFF ( MINUTE, 0, CAST ( TransactionExecution AS TIME ) ) / 5 ) * 5,
    0
)

-- Truncate to 15 minute
DATEADD (
    MINUTE,
    ( DATEDIFF ( MINUTE, 0, CAST ( TransactionExecution AS TIME ) ) / 15 ) * 15,
    0
)

-- Truncate to hour
DATEADD ( HOUR, DATEDIFF ( HOUR, 0, CAST ( TransactionExecution AS TIME ) ), 0 )
```

If you want rounding time instead of truncating, you can use the following T-SQL code:

```
-- Round to the second
DATEADD (
    MILLISECOND,
    500 - DATEPART (
        MILLISECOND,
        CAST ( TransactionExecution AS TIME ) + '00:00:00.500'
    ),
    CAST ( TransactionExecution AS TIME )
)

-- Round to the minute
DATEADD (
    MINUTE,
    DATEDIFF (
        MINUTE,
        0,
        DATEADD (
            SECOND,
            30 - DATEPART (
                SECOND,
                TransactionExecution + '00:00:30.000'
            ),
            CAST ( TransactionExecution AS TIME )
        )
    ),
    0
)
```

```
-- Round to 5 minute
DATEADD (
    MINUTE,


    ( DATEDIFF (
        MINUTE,
        0,
        DATEADD (
            SECOND,
            150 - DATEPART (
                SECOND,
                TransactionExecution + '00:02:30.000'
            ),
            CAST ( TransactionExecution AS TIME )
        )
    ) / 5 ) * 5,
    0
)

-- Round to 15 minute
DATEADD (
    MINUTE,
    ( DATEDIFF (
        MINUTE,
        0,
        DATEADD (
            SECOND,
            150 - DATEPART (
                SECOND,
                TransactionExecution + '00:02:30.000'
            ),
            CAST ( TransactionExecution AS TIME )
        )
    ) / 15 ) * 15,
    0
)

-- Round to the hour
DATEADD (
    HOUR,
    DATEDIFF (
        HOUR,
        0,
        DATEADD (
            MINUTE,
            30 - DATEPART (
                MINUTE,
                TransactionExecution + '00:30:00.000'
            ),
            CAST ( TransactionExecution AS TIME )
        )
    ),
    0
)
```

When you store millions of new rows every day in a single table, these details can make a big difference in memory usage and performance. At the same time, do not spend too much time over optimizing a data model that does not require such a level of compression—after all, reducing the precision means removing some information that will be not available for deeper insights in case of need.

Calculated columns

A calculated column persists the result of a DAX expression evaluated row by row when you refresh a table. For this reason, you might consider it as a possible way to optimize query execution time. However, a calculated column has hidden costs and it is a good optimization technique only in specific conditions.

You should consider using a calculated column in these two situations:

- **Group or filter data**: If a calculated column returns a value used to group or filter data, you do not have any alternative other than creating the same value before importing data in the data model. For example, you might classify the price of a product in Low, Medium, and High categories, based on the product price. This value is usually a string, especially when the user displays it to make a selection.

- **Pre-calculate complex formulas**: You can store in a calculated column the result of a complex calculation that is not sensitive to filters made at query time. However, it is very hard to establish when this produces a real computational advantage, and you have to measure the presence of a real advantage at query time in order to justify its use.

You should not make the wrong assumption that any calculated column is faster than doing the same computation at query time. This is often simply a wrong statement. Other times, the advantage is barely measurable, and does not balance the cost of the calculated column. You should get a relevant performance improvement at query time in order to justify a calculated column for optimization reasons. There are also many factors to consider when you evaluate the cost/benefit ratio of a calculated column against an equivalent calculation made at run time in a measure.

A calculated column is not as optimized as a native column. It might have a lower compression rate compared to native columns of the table, because it does not take part in the heuristic that VertiPaq executes to find the optimal sort order of the data in each segment. Only a column storing a very low number of unique values might benefit from a good compression, but this is usually the result of logical conditions, and not of numeric expressions.

For example, consider the case of a simple calculated column:

```
Sales[Amount] = Sales[Quantity] * Sales[Price]
```

If you have 100 unique values in a *Quantity* column, and 1,000 unique values in a *Price* column, the resulting *Amount* column might have a cardinality included between 1 and 100,000 unique values, depending on the actual values in the columns and in their distribution across table rows. Usually, the larger the number of rows in the table, the higher is the number of unique values you will find in the *Amount* column (because of statistical distribution). With a dictionary that is one or two orders of magnitude larger than the original columns, the compression is usually worse. What about query performance? It depends, and you should measure it case by case in order to get a correct answer, considering the two possible calculations (one based on a calculated column and the other completely dynamic and based on measures).

You can sum the *Amount* calculated column in a simple measure:

```
[TotalAmountCC] := SUM ( Sales[Amount] )
```

The alternative dynamic implementation transfers the expressions of the calculated column in an iterator over the table:

```
[TotalAmountM] := SUMX ( Sales, Sales[Quantity] * Sales[Price] )
```

Is the cost of scanning the single column (*Sales[Amount]*) smaller than scanning the two original columns (*Sales[Quantity]* and *Sales[Price]*)? It is impossible to estimate this in advance, so you have to measure it. Usually the difference between these two options will be visible only in very large tables. In small tables, the performance might be very close, so the calculated column is not worth its memory footprint.

Most of the time, you can replace calculated columns (used to compute aggregated values) by using the same expressions in iterators such as *SUMX* and *AVERAGEX*. In the previous example, *TotalAmountM* is a measure that executes dynamically the same expression defined in the calculated *Amount* column, used by the simple aggregation in *TotalAmountCC*.

A different evaluation is necessary when a context transition is present in an iterator. For example, consider the following DAX measure in a model with SalesHeader and SalesDetail tables connected through a relationship:

```
[AverageOrder] :=
AVERAGEX (
    SalesHeader,
    CALCULATE (
        SUMX (
            SalesDetail,
            SalesDetail[Quantity] * SalesDetail[Unit Price]
        ),
        ALLEXCEPT ( SalesDetail, SalesHeader )
    )
)
```

In this case, the context transition within the loop can be very expensive, especially if the SalesHeader table has millions of rows or more. In this case, storing the value in a calculated column will probably save a lot of execution time.

```
SalesHeader[Amount] =
CALCULATE (
    SUMX (
        SalesDetail,
        SalesDetail[Quantity] * SalesDetail[Unit Price]
    ),
    ALLEXCEPT ( SalesDetail, SalesHeader )
)

[AverageOrder] :=
AVERAGEX (
    SalesHeader,
    SalesHeader[Amount]
)
```

We will never be tired of repeating that these examples are just indications. You should measure the performance improvements of a calculated column, and its related memory cost, in order to make a decision about using it or not.

Consider that you can avoid a calculated column if you create the same value for a native column in the data source when you populate the table (for example, using an SQL statement, or a Power Query transformation). The calculated column should leverage the VertiPaq engine, providing a faster and more flexible way to compute a column than reading the entire table again from the data source. Usually this happens when the calculated column expression aggregates rows of different tables other than the one to which it belongs.

Finally, a calculated column increases the time to refresh a data model. Even a partial refresh of a table (for example, by processing a single partition) requires recomputing all the calculated columns referencing any column of such a table. Moreover, the calculated column is computed always for the entire table, even when you refresh only one partition, and the calculated column does not depend on different data than other columns of the same row. For this reason, creating a calculated column in a large table with millions of rows is not a good idea. The process of a calculated column is a single-thread job, which iterates all the rows of the table to compute the column expression. In case there are several calculated columns, they are evaluated one at a time, making the entire operation a process bottleneck for large tables.

At this point, it should be clear that calculated columns are expensive for two reasons:

- **Memory**: The values are persisted using a nonoptimal compression.

- **Duration of Refresh**: The process of calculated columns is a sequential operation using a single thread, which results in a nonscalable operation also in large servers.

With that said, calculated columns turn useful in many scenarios. We do not want to pass on the message that calculated columns are always to be avoided. Instead, you need to be aware of their cost and make an educated decision on whether to use them or not. In the next section we describe a good example where calculated columns really shine in improving performance.

Optimizing complex filters with Boolean calculated columns

It is worth it to mention a specific case of optimization using calculated columns. You can consolidate a logical expression used to filter a high cardinality column using a calculated column that stores the result of the logical expression.

For example, consider the following measure:

```
[ExpensiveTransactions] :=
COUNTROWS (
    FILTER (
        Sales,
        RELATED ( Product[Unit Cost] ) * Sales[Quantity] > 10
    )
)
```

In case you have millions of rows in the Sales table, the filter iteration would be expensive. If the expression used in the filter does not depend on the existing filter context, as in this case, you can consolidate its result in a calculated column and apply a filter on that column in a *CALCULATE* statement instead. For example, you can rewrite the previous operation in this way:

```
Sales[CostGreaterThan10] = RELATED ( Product[Unit Cost] ) * Sales[Quantity] > 10

[ExpensiveTransactions] :=
CALCULATE (
    COUNTROWS ( Sales ),
    Sales[CostGreaterThan10] = TRUE
)
```

The calculated column containing a logical value (*TRUE* or *FALSE*) usually benefits from a good compression and has a low memory cost. It is also very effective at execution time, because it applies a direct filter to the scan of the Sales table required to count the rows. In this case, the benefit at query time is usually evident. You just have to consider if it is worth the longer processing time for the column (which you have to measure before making a final decision).

Choosing the right columns to store

In the previous section about calculated columns, you have seen that storing a column that you can compute row-by-row using other columns of the same table is not always an advantage. The same consideration is valid also for native columns of the table. When you choose the columns to store in a table, you should consider the size and the query performance. You can optimize resource allocation (and memory in particular) by doing the right evaluation in this area.

We consider the following types of columns in a table:

- **Primary or alternate keys**: The column contains a unique value for each row of the table.

- **Qualitative attributes**: The column can be text or number, used to group and/or filter rows in a table (for instance, name, color, city, country)

- **Quantitative attributes**: The number is a value used both as a filter (for example, less than a value) and as an argument in a calculation (such as price, amount, quantity).

- **Descriptive attributes**: The column contains text providing additional information about a row, but its content is never used to filter or to aggregate rows (for example, notes, comments).

- **Technical attributes**: Information recorded in the database for technical reasons, without a business value (such as username of last update, timestamp, GUID for replication).

The general principle is trying to minimize the cardinality of the columns imported in a table, not importing columns that have a high cardinality and that are not relevant for the analysis. However, every type of column deserves additional considerations.

You need the columns for **primary or alternate keys** if there are one or more one-to-many relationships with other tables. For instance, the product code and the product key columns of a table of products are certainly required columns. However, you should not include in a table a primary or alternate key column not used on the one-side of a relationship with other tables. For example, the Sales table might have a unique identifier for each row in the original table. Such a column has a cardinality that corresponds to the number of rows of the Sales table. Moreover, such a column is not necessary, because no tables target Sales for a relationship. For this reason, it is a useless column and very expensive in terms of memory and you should not import it in the data model.

You should always include in a table **qualitative attributes** that have a low cardinality, because they have a good compression and might be useful for the analysis. For example, the product category is a column that has a low cardinality, related to the Product table. In case there is a high cardinality, you should consider carefully whether to import the column or not, because its storage memory cost can be high. The high selectivity might justify the cost, but you have to check that filters in queries usually select a low number of values in that column. For instance, the production lot number might be an information included in the Sales table that you want to be able to filter at query time. Its high cost might be justified by the business need of applying this filter in certain queries.

All of the **quantitative attributes** are generally imported to guarantee any future, although you might consider skipping columns providing redundant information. Consider the columns *Quantity*, *Price*, and *Amount* of a Sales table, where the *Amount* column contains the result of the product between *Quantity* and *Price*. You probably want to create measures that aggregate each of these columns, but you will probably calculate the Price as a weighted average considering sum of amount and quantity, instead of a simple average of the Price considering each transaction at the same level. This is an example of the measure you want to define:

```
[Sum of Quantity] := SUM ( Sales[Quantity] )

[Sum of Amount] := SUM ( Sales[Amount] )

[Average Price] := DIVIDE ( [Sum of Amount], [Sum of Quantity] )
```

If you look at the measures defined, you would say that you have to import only *Quantity* and *Amount* in the data model, and you can avoid importing the *Price* column, not used by these measures. However, if you consider the cardinality of the columns, you should have some doubt. If you have 100 unique values in the *Quantity* column, and you have 10,000 unique values in the *Price* column, you might have up to 1,000,000 unique values in the *Amount* column. At this point, you might have doubts about importing only the *Quantity* and *Price* columns, using the following definition of the measures in the data model (only Sum of Amount changes, the other two measures did not change):

```
[Sum of Quantity] := SUM ( Sales[Quantity] )

[Sum of Amount] := SUMX ( Sales, Sales[Quantity] * Sales[Price] )

[Average Price] := DIVIDE ( [Sum of Amount], [Sum of Quantity] )
```

The new definition of the *Sum of Amount* measure might be slower, because it has to scan two columns instead of one. However, these columns might be smaller than the original *Amount*. Trying to predict what will be the faster option is very hard, because you should consider also the distribution of the values in the table, and not only the cardinality of the column. We suggest you measure the space used and the performance in the two cases before making a final decision. Based on our experience, removing the *Amount* column in a small data model can be more important for Power Pivot, because the memory available in computers running Excel is usually more limited and you have a faster loading time opening the file. At any rate, in a large table with billions of rows stored in an Analysis Services Tabular model, the performance penalty of the multiplication between two columns (*Quantity* and *Price*) could be larger than the increased memory scan time for the *Amount* column. In this case, the better response time for the queries justifies the higher memory cost to store the single column. Regardless, you should measure size and performance in each specific case, because the distribution of data has a key role in compression and affects any decision about this topic.

You should consider whether to import **descriptive attributes** or not. In general, they have a high storage cost for the dictionary of the column. A few examples of descriptive attributes are the Notes field in an invoice, and the *Description* column in the Product table. You use these attributes mainly to provide additional information about a specific entity. You hardly ever use this type of column to filter data. The only issue of including these columns in the data model is their memory storage cost, mainly related to the column dictionary. If the column has many blank values and a low number of rows with content in the table, then its dictionary will be small and the column cost will be more acceptable. Nevertheless, a column containing the transcription of conversations made in a call center is probably too expensive for a Service Calls table containing date, time, duration, and operator who managed the call.

A particular type of descriptive attribute is the information you want to provide as detail for transactions in a drill-through operation. For example, the invoice number or the order number of a transaction is an attribute that has a high cardinality, but that could be important for some reports. In this case, you should consider particular optimizations for drill-through attributes described in the next section.

Most of the time, there are no reasons to import columns for **technical attributes** such as timestamp, date, time, and operator of the last update. This information is mainly for auditing and forensic requirements. Unless you have a data model specifically built for auditing requirements, the need for this information is usually low in an analytical solution.

Optimizing column storage

The best optimization for a column is to remove the column from a table entirely. You have seen in the previous section when this decision makes sense, based on the type of columns of a table. Once you define the set of columns that are part of the data model, you can still use some optimization techniques in order to reduce the memory used, even if each optimization has some side effect.

Column split optimization

You can reduce the memory footprint of a column by reducing its cardinality. In certain conditions, you can achieve this result by splitting the column in two or more parts. You have to split the column before importing it into the data model. For this reason, you will see examples of the split operation in SQL, but you can use any other transformation tool (such as Power Query) to obtain the same result.

For instance, if you have a 10-character string (such as *TransactionID*), you can split the column in two parts, five characters each (as in, TransactionID_High and TransactionID_Low):

```
SELECT
    LEFT ( TransactionID, 5 ) AS TransactionID_High,
    SUBSTRING ( TransactionID, 6, LEN ( TransactionID ) - 5 ) ) AS TransactionID_Low,
    ...
```

In case of an integer value, you can use division and module for a number that creates an even distribution in the two columns. If you have an integer *TransactionID* column with numbers included between 0 and 100 million, you can divide by 10,000, as in the following example:

```
SELECT
    TransactionID / 10000 AS TransactionID_High,
    TransactionID % 10000 AS TransactionID_Low,
    ...
```

You can use a similar technique for decimal numbers. An easy split is separating integer from decimal part, even if this might not produce an even distribution. For instance, you can transform a *UnitPrice* decimal number column into *UnitPrice_Integer* and *UnitPrice_Decimal* columns:

```
SELECT
    FLOOR ( UnitPrice ) AS UnitPrice_Integer,
    UnitPrice - FLOOR ( UnitPrice ) AS UnitPrice_Decimal,
    ...
```

You can use the result of a column split as is in simple details reports, or measures that restore the original value during the calculation.

> **Important** You might use a column split to optimize numbers aggregated in measures, using the separation between integer and decimal parts as in the previous example, or use similar techniques. However, consider that the aggregation operation will have to scan more than one column, and the total time of the operation is usually larger than with a single column. If you are optimizing for performance, saving memory might be not effective in this case, unless you remove a dictionary obtaining value encoding instead of hash encoding for a currency or integer data type. Do your own measurements to validate, if such optimization works for you also from a performance point of view.

Optimizing high cardinality columns

A column with a high cardinality has a high cost because of a large dictionary, a large hierarchy structure, and a lower compression in encoding. If you have Analysis Services 2016, you can disable the construction of an attribute hierarchy for a column. Because this cost is relevant, you can reduce the memory footprint of a high cardinality column by setting the *ColumnUsage* property of the column to *DAXUsage*, which disables the creation of the hierarchy (the default is *UnrestrictedUsage*, which creates the hierarchy).

If you cannot disable the hierarchy, or if this reduction is not enough for your requirements, you can consider applying the column split optimization to a high cardinality column used in a measure. You can hide this optimization to the user by hiding the split columns and by adapting the calculation in measures. For example, if you optimized *UnitPrice* using the column split, you can create the *Sum of Amount* measure in this way:

```
Sales[Sum of Amount] :=
SUMX ( Sales, Sales[Quantity] * ( Sales[UnitPrice_Integer] + Sales[UnitPrice_Decimal] ) )
```

Remember that the calculation will be more expensive, and only an accurate measure of the performance of the two models (with and without column split optimization) can provide you with the elements to evaluate which one is better for your requirements.

Optimizing drill-through attributes

If a column contains data used only for drill-through operations, you should consider applying a column split optimization. When you do not use the column in measures, you do not have to be concerned about possible costs of the materialization of the original values. However, you cannot rebuild the original value in a DAX syntax, so you have to accept the display of the original value in two columns, or you have to implement a better visualization client-side, combining the two split values in a single one.

Analyzing DAX query plans

DAX is a functional language with a very fast execution engine. However, you can write the same calculation with different DAX expressions, possibly obtaining a different performance. In order to find a more efficient DAX expression, the first step is to identify the bottlenecks of an existing formula.

In this chapter, you will learn the architecture of the DAX query engine. You will also see how to obtain information about query plans and performance counters related to a particular DAX expression and how to read the information provided by Microsoft SQL Server Profiler and other tools. This knowledge is fundamental to optimize any DAX formula.

Introducing the DAX query engine

The DAX query engine accepts queries in both MDX and DAX, and it can work in DirectQuery or In-Memory mode. If the query is in DirectQuery mode (supported only by DAX queries, not by MDX queries), the engine converts DAX into a single SQL statement, which is then sent to the external SQL Server data source. In DirectQuery mode the query engine does not perform any computation: It returns the same results obtained by the data source. In this scenario, the optimization effort is more on the external data source than in DAX coding and, as of the time of this writing, DirectQuery can be used only when the structure of DAX queries is trivial, otherwise the SQL code is so convoluted that any optimization is nearly impossible. We do not discuss DirectQuery in this book: We focus our attention on the In-Memory mode, which is probably the most widely used.

If, on the other hand, the query targets the in-memory storage, then the query engine uses the in-memory data (the VertiPaq storage you learned about in Chapter 13, "The VertiPaq engine") to answer it. In doing so, the engine takes several steps:

1. **Build Expression Tree**. The engine transforms the query from a string to an expression tree, which is easier to manipulate for further optimizations.

2. **Build Logical Query Plan**. The engine produces a list of the logical operations required to execute the query. This tree of logical operators resembles the original DAX syntax. It is easy to find a correspondence between a DAX function and a similar operation in the logical query plan.

3. **Build Physical Query Plan**. The engine transforms the logical query plan into a set of physical operations. A physical query plan is still a tree of operators, but the resulting tree can be different from the logical query plan.

4. **Execute Physical Query Plan**. The engine finally executes the physical query plan, retrieving data from the storage engine and computing the query calculations.

Steps 1 and 4 are not of any interest, while steps 2 and 3 are very important; by reading them you will understand how the engine resolved your query. In other words, they are important to detect bottlenecks and optimization options. You will see later how to obtain and read the logical and physical query plans because, before reading them, you need to learn about the two engines that cooperate to resolve any DAX query: formula engine (FE) and storage engine (SE). The two engines have different roles and behaviors, which you will learn about in the next sections.

> **Note** Tabular does not translate MDX to DAX. MDX queries generate both a logical and a physical query plan just as DAX queries do. Keep in mind that the same query, written in DAX or in MDX, typically produces different query plans even if the result is the same. Here, we focus on the DAX language; nevertheless, you can use the information provided in this chapter to analyze how Tabular handles MDX queries as well.

Understanding the formula engine

The formula engine is the higher-level execution unit of the DAX query engine. It can handle all the operations requested by DAX functions and solve complex DAX expressions.

Each step in the physical query plan corresponds to a specific operation executed by the formula engine. Typical operators of the formula engine include joins between tables, filtering with complex conditions, aggregations, and lookups. These operators typically require data from columns of the data model. In these cases, the formula engine sends a request to the storage engine, which answers by returning a datacache. A datacache is a temporary storage area created by the storage engine and read by the formula engine. It is important to note, right from the beginning, that datacaches are not compressed (in other words, they are not VertiPaq column stores, they are plain in-memory tables).

The formula engine always works with datacaches returned by the storage engine or data structures computed by other formula engine operators. The result of a formula engine operation is not persisted in memory across different executions, even within the same session. On the other hand, datacaches are persisted and can be reused in following queries. The formula engine does not have a cache system to reuse results between different queries, and DAX relies entirely on cache features of the storage engine.

Finally, the formula engine is single threaded. This means that any operation executed in the formula engine uses only one thread and one core, no matter how many are available. The formula engine performs requests to the storage engine in a sequential way, one query at a time. A certain degree of parallelism is available only within each request to the storage engine, which has a different architecture and can take advantage of multiple cores available, as you will see in the next section.

Understanding the storage engine (VertiPaq)

The storage engine is the lower-level execution unit of the DAX query engine. Its official name is xVelocity In-Memory Analytical Engine, but it is also known as VertiPaq, which is its original code name during development.

The goal of the storage engine is to scan the VertiPaq storage and produce datacaches, which are then read by the formula engine. Every scan operation corresponds to an internal query described in a pseudo-SQL language internally called xmSQL. xmSQL is not a real query language but rather a textual representation of a storage engine query, intended to give visibility into how the formula engine is querying VertiPaq. In fact, the storage engine does not really know anything about DAX. It executes only queries allowed by its limited set of operators. In case the calculation requires a more complex evaluation within an internal scan of data, a callback to the formula engine is possible.

The storage engine is multithreaded. The operations performed by the storage engine are very efficient and can scale up on multiple cores. A single storage engine query can increase its parallelism up to one thread for each segment of a table.

The storage engine receives requests only from the formula engine, which sends them synchronously. Thus, FE waits for one SE query to be finished before sending the next one. Considering that the storage engine can use up to one thread per column segment, you can benefit from the parallelism of the storage engine only when there are many segments involved in the query. In other words, if you have eight SE queries, running on a small table (one segment), they will run sequentially one after the other, instead of all in parallel, because of the synchronous nature of communication between FE and SE.

A cache system stores the results produced by the storage engine, holding a limited number of results (typically the last 512 internal queries, but different versions of the engine might use a different number). When the storage engine receives an xmSQL query identical to one already in cache, it returns the corresponding datacache without doing any scan of data in memory. The cache is not involved in security considerations, because the row-level security system influences only the formula engine behavior, producing different xmSQL queries in case the user can see only certain rows in a table.

A scan operation made by the storage engine is usually faster than the equivalent scan performed by the formula engine, even with a single thread available. This is because the storage engine is more optimized for these operations, and because it iterates over compressed data, whereas the formula engine can only iterate datacaches, that is, uncompressed data that is usually the result of a storage engine query.

Introducing DAX query plans

Now that you are familiar with SE and FE, it is time to go back to the analysis of DAX query plans. As we said earlier, a DAX query generates both a logical and a physical query plan. These plans describe in detail the operations performed by the query engine. Unfortunately, the query plan is available only in textual representation, not graphical visualization. Because of the complexity and the length of a typical query plan, you will often use other tools and techniques to optimize a DAX expression, before starting to analyze the query plan in detail. However, it is important to understand the basics of a DAX query plan, in order to both understand the behavior of the engine and quickly spot potential bottlenecks in longer and more complex query plans.

As an example, consider this simple query:

```
EVALUATE
ROW ( "Result", SUM ( Sales[Quantity] ) )
```

The result is a table with one row and one column (*Result*), filled with the sum of the column *Quantity* for all the rows of the Sales table.

Result
17538016

In the next sections, you will see the query plans generated and executed by this DAX query. Later you will see how to obtain this information for any query. At this stage, just focus your attention on the role of the query plans, how they are structured, and the information they provide.

Logical query plan

The logical query plan is a close representation of the DAX query expression tree. This is the query plan of the previous query:

```
AddColumns: RelLogOp DependOnCols()() 0-0 RequiredCols(0)(''[Result])
        Sum_Vertipaq: ScaLogOp DependOnCols()() Integer DominantValue=BLANK
                        Table='Sales' -BlankRow Aggregations(Sum)
                Scan_Vertipaq: RelLogOp DependOnCols()() 0-127
                                RequiredCols(104)('Sales'[Quantity])
                                Table='Sales' -BlankRow
                'Sales'[Quantity]: ScaLogOp DependOnCols(104)('Sales'[Quantity])
                                Integer DominantValue=NONE
```

Each line is an operator and the following lines, indented, are the parameters of the operator. If you ignore for a moment all of the parameters for each operator, you can envision a simpler structure:

```
AddColumns:
        Sum_Vertipaq:
                Scan_Vertipaq:
                'Sales'[Quantity]:
```

The outermost operator is *AddColumns*, which creates the one-row table with the *Result* column containing the value returned by the DAX query. The *Sum_VertiPaq* operator scans the Sales table and sums the *Sales[Quantity]* column. The two operators included within *Sum_Vertipaq* are *Scan_Vertipaq* and a reference to the scanned column.

You can read this query plan, in plain English, as: "create a table with a column named *Result*, filled with the content of a *SUM* operation, performed by the storage engine by scanning the *Quantity* column in the Sales table."

The logical query plan shows what the DAX query engine plans to do in order to compute the results. Not surprisingly, it scans Sales summarizing Quantity using *SUM*. Clearly, more complex query plans will be harder to decode.

Physical query plan

The physical query plan has a similar format to the logical one: Each line is an operator and its parameters are in subsequent lines, indented with one tab. Apart from this aesthetic similarity, the two query plans use completely different operators, as you can see in the physical query plan generated by the previous DAX query:

```
AddColumns: IterPhyOp IterCols(0)(''[Result])
        SingletonTable: IterPhyOp IterCols(0)(''[Result])
        Spool: LookupPhyOp Integer #Records=1 #KeyCols=128 #ValueCols=1
                                            DominantValue=BLANK
                AggregationSpool<Cache>: SpoolPhyOp #Records=1
                        VertipaqResult: IterPhyOp #FieldCols=0 #ValueCols=1
```

Again, we can build a simplified version of the query plan, removing the parameters of each operator:

```
AddColumns:
        SingletonTable:
        Spool: LookupPhyOp
                AggregationSpool<Cache>:
                        VertipaqResult:
```

The first operator, *AddColumns*, builds the result table. Its first parameter is a *SingletonTable*, which is an operator returning a single-row table, generated by the *ROW* function. The second parameter, *Spool*, searches for a value in the datacache obtained by an xmSQL query sent to the storage engine. This is the most intricate part of DAX query plans. In fact, the physical query plan shows that it uses some data that was previously spooled by other storage engine queries, but it does not show exactly from which one. In other words, you cannot obtain the xmSQL code of a storage engine query by reading the DAX query plan. As you will see later, it is possible to retrieve the xmSQL queries sent to the storage engine, but you are able to match them with the exact point in the query plan only in simple DAX queries. In more complex (but realistic) DAX operations, this association might require longer analysis.

Before moving forward, it is important to highlight some important information included in the query plan:

```
AggregationSpool<Cache>: SpoolPhyOp #Records=1
          VertipaqResult: IterPhyOp #FieldCols=0 #ValueCols=1
```

The *VertipaqResult* operator represents an xmSQL query sent to the storage engine (you will see that in the next section). The *AggregationSpool<Cache>* operator iterates the result of the xmSQL query and you can see the total number of rows iterated (one in this case; it is reported by the #Records=1 parameter). This number is also the number of rows returned by the nested *VertipaqResult* operator.

Such a number is important for two reasons:

■ It provides you with the size (in rows) of the datacache created by VertiPaq. A large datacache consumes more memory at query time and takes more time to scan.

■ The iteration performed by *AggregationSpool<Cache>* in the formula engine runs in a single thread. When a query is slow and this number is large, it could be the indication of a bottleneck in the query execution.

Storage engine query

In the previous physical query plan, you have seen a *VertipaqResult* operator that represents an internal xmSQL query sent to the storage engine. The following is the xmSQL query generated during the execution of the example DAX query:

```
SET DC_KIND="AUTO";
SELECT
SUM([Sales_001b8a59-0b80-4210-9567-facdae2142ec].[Quantity])
FROM [Sales_001b8a59-0b80-4210-9567-facdae2142ec];
```

We can remove a few internal details that are not relevant by now. In this way, the query resembles a standard SQL syntax:

```
SELECT
SUM ( Sales[Quantity] )
FROM Sales;
```

This query aggregates all the rows of the Sales table, returning a single column with the sum of Quantity. The storage engine executes the entire aggregation operation, returning a small datacache (one row, one column) regardless of the size of the Sales table. The materialization required for this datacache is minimal. Moreover, the only data structures read by this query are those storing the

Quantity column in the Sales table. Even if the Sales table had hundreds of other columns, this would not affect the performance of this xmSQL query. The storage engine scans only columns included in the xmSQL query.

As you will see later, measuring the execution time of each xmSQL query is an important part of the optimization process. Keep in mind that performance is related to the size of the columns involved in a query, and not only on the number of rows of the table. Different columns can have different compression rates and different sizes in memory, resulting in different scan times.

Capturing profiling information

The previous section introduced you to DAX query plans. Here you learn how to capture these events and how to measure their duration, which are the first steps in DAX optimization.

The DAX engine has grown as part of Microsoft SQL Server Analysis Services. Such a service provides trace events that you can capture with the SQL Server Profiler tool. When you use DAX in other products, such as Power Pivot and Power BI, you are always using the same engine, even if you might not have the same tools available as for Analysis Services to capture trace events. For example, Power Pivot for Excel and Power BI Desktop have diagnostic options that save trace events on a file, which you can open later with the same SQL Server Profiler tool. In order to simplify the process of collecting and analyzing information using SQL Server Profiler, you can also use tracing features of DAX Studio, described later in this chapter.

Using the SQL Server Profiler

The SQL Server Profiler tool is installed as part of the SQL Server Management tools. You can connect SQL Server Profiler to an Analysis Services instance and collect all the events related to DAX query execution. You can also load a file containing a trace session produced by the same SQL Server Profiler, or by other services (such as Power Pivot for Excel and Power BI Desktop).

In order to catch DAX query plans and storage engine queries, you run a new trace session and configure it to grab the interesting events for a DAX query, as in Figure 15-1.

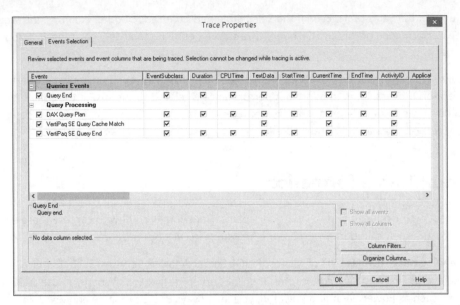

FIGURE 15-1 SQL Server Profiler settings to capture DAX query plans and storage engine queries.

You need to capture four classes of events:

- **Query End** event fired at the end of a query. You might include the *Query Begin* event too, but we suggest for you to catch only *Query End* because it contains the execution time.

- **DAX Query Plan** event fired after the query engine computed the query plan. It contains a textual representation of the query plan. This event class includes two different subclasses, *Logical Plan* and *Physical Plan*. For each query, the engine generates both classes: one logical query plan and one physical query plan.

- **VertiPaq SE Query Cache Match** event fired when a *VertiPaq* query is resolved by looking at the cache data. It is very useful in order to see how much of your query performs real computations and how much of it just does cache lookups.

- **VertiPaq SE Query End** fired when the VertiPaq engine answers a query. As with the *Query End* event, to gather timing information, we suggest you grab the end event of the queries executed by the VertiPaq Storage Engine.

Tip Once you select the events you need, it is a good idea to organize columns (pressing the Organize Columns button you see in Figure 15-1), and to save a template of the selections made. You can save a trace template by using the File / Templates / New Template menu in SQL Server Profiler.

Note In a production environment, you have to filter events of a single user session. Otherwise, you will see events of different queries executed at the same time, which makes it harder to analyze events related to a single query. If you run the Profiler in a development or test environment where you are the only active user, you will see only the events you run without any "background noise."

In order to see the sequence of events fired, we will analyze what happens when you run the following query on a very large table with more than four billion rows:

```
EVALUATE
ROW ( "Result", SUM ( Audience[Weight] ) )
```

You obtain the result shown in Figure 15-2 in the log window of the Profiler.

EventClass	EventSubclass	Duration	CPUTime
DAX Query Plan	1 - DAX VertiPaq Logical Plan		
VertiPaq SE Query End	10 - VertiPaq Scan internal	1708	13109
VertiPaq SE Query End	0 - VertiPaq Scan	1711	13109
DAX Query Plan	2 - DAX VertiPaq Physical Plan		
Query End	3 - DAXQuery	1734	31

FIGURE 15-2 Trace events captured in a SQL Server Profiler session for a simple DAX query.

Even for such a simple query, the DAX engine fires five different events:

1. A DAX *VertiPaq Logical Plan* event, which is the logical query plan.

2. An internal *VertiPaq* scan event, which corresponds to a storage engine query. You might see more than one internal event (subclass 10) for each *VertiPaq* scan event (subclass 0).

3. A *VertiPaq* scan event, which describes a single storage engine query received by the formula engine.

4. A DAX *VertiPaq Physical Plan* event, which is the physical query plan.

5. A final *Query End* event, which returns the query duration of the complete DAX query. You should ignore the CPU time reported by this event (it should be close to the time spent in the formula engine, but is not as accurate as the calculation you will see later).

All of the events show both CPU time and duration, expressed in milliseconds. CPU Time is the amount of CPU time consumed to answer the query, whereas Duration is the time the user waited for getting the result. When the Duration is lower than CPU Time, the operation has been executed in parallel on many cores. When the Duration is higher than CPU Time, the operation had to wait for other operations (usually logged in different events) to be completed.

> **Note** The accuracy of the *CPU Time* and *Duration* columns is not very reliable for values lower than 16 milliseconds, and CPU Time can be less accurate than that in conditions of high parallelism. Moreover, these timings might depend on other operations in progress on the same server. It is a common practice to be running the same test multiple times in order to create an average of execution time of single operations, especially when you need accurate numbers. However, when you only look for an order of magnitude, you might just ignore differences under 100 milliseconds.

If you consider the sequence of events, the logical query plan precedes all of the storage engine queries (VertiPaq scans), and only after their execution can you see the physical query plan. In other words, the physical query plan is an actual query plan and not an estimated one. In fact, it contains the number of rows processed by any iteration in the formula engine, even if it does not provide information about the CPU time and duration of each step in the query plan.

Logical and physical query plans do not provide any timing information, which are available only in the other events we gathered in the Profiler.

Analyzing CPU time, duration, and parallelism

Information provided in *CPU Time* and *Duration* columns is helpful to identify performance bottlenecks in a query. The first thing you want to know is whether a query spends more time in the formula engine or in the storage engine, because each engine requires different optimization techniques to improve performance.

The *Query End* event only provides you with the total elapsed time for a DAX query in the *Duration* column, summing both formula engine and storage engine duration. The *VertiPaq* scan events provide you with information about the time spent in the storage engine. You can evaluate the elapsed time in formula engine operations by subtracting the duration of all the storage engine queries from the duration of the entire DAX query (provided in the *Query End* event).

In Figure 15-2, you have seen that the *Query End* event had a Duration of 1,734 milliseconds. The time spent in the storage engine was 1,711 milliseconds. There was only one storage engine query, which lasted for 1,711 milliseconds (you only consider the VertiPaq Scan event, ignoring internal ones). The difference is 23 milliseconds, which is the amount of time spent in the formula engine. You can calculate the amount of time spent in the formula and storage engines by using the following formulas:

$$Storage\ Engine\ Duration = \sum_{k=0}^{n}(VertiPaq\ Scan\ Duration)$$

$$Formula\ Engine\ Duration = (Query\ End\ Duration) - (Storage\ Engine\ Duration)$$

Once you have measured the duration of an operation, you also have to understand the parallelism degree of a query. This information is important to understand whether you can improve the duration by increasing the parallelism (spreading the execution across more cores). If you are executing a query that already uses all the cores available, you can only optimize the performance by creating a more efficient query plan. If the query does not use all of the cores, then increasing the parallelism (if possible) might reduce the duration.

A formula engine operation always runs in a single thread, so its CPU Time corresponds to its duration (which you computed with the previous formula). You cannot increase the parallelism of a formula engine operation.

You can evaluate the parallelism of a storage engine operation by dividing the CPU Time by its Duration, assuming that the server was not executing other queries or processes (in which case, right parallelism cannot be estimated). This fraction provides you with the average number of cores used in an operation, as defined by this formula:

$$Cores\ Used\ in\ VertiPaq\ Operation = \frac{(VertiPaq\ Scan\ CPU\ Time)}{(VertiPaq\ Scan\ Duration)}$$

For example, the only VertiPaq operation you saw in Figure 15-2 has a parallelism of 7.7, obtained by dividing the CPU Time (13,109 milliseconds) by the Duration (1,711 milliseconds). When this number is close to the total number of cores in the server, you cannot improve performance by increasing the parallelism. In this example, we used a system with eight cores. Thus, the query reached the limits of the hardware. A second concurrent user would not be able to get optimal performance executing a long-running query, and would slow down other users, too.

Reading saved Profiler trace sessions

You can connect SQL Server Profiler only to Analysis Services to analyze live queries. If you want to debug events generated by the DAX engine in Power Pivot for Excel, you can save the trace session on file, reading it later with SQL Server Profiler.

In Power Pivot for Excel, you can enable the Enable Power Pivot Tracing check box for the current Excel session, which is located in the Settings dialog box. This setting generates a TRC file (TRC is the extension for trace file), which you can open in SQL Server Profiler. You cannot customize the events captured in the profiler session, so you will see more event types than those we are describing here. You can ignore them for the sake of analyzing DAX query plans.

Using DAX Studio

The community of BI developers provides a free open source tool to analyze DAX queries in a more efficient way. DAX Studio (available at *http://daxstudio.codeplex.com*) includes an editor that allows you to write and execute a query. It captures the same trace events you have seen in the SQL Server Profiler section, and displays the relevant information with a more productive user interface. DAX Studio can connect to Analysis Services Tabular, Power BI Desktop, and Power Pivot for Excel.

Before analyzing a query in DAX Studio, you have to enable the Query Plan and Server Timings options in the Traces section of the Home ribbon, as you see in Figure 15-3.

FIGURE 15-3 The Query Plan and Server Timings options enable the tracing features in DAX Studio.

Once you set these options you see a Query Plan and a Server Timings pane next to the Output and Results pane that are visible by default. DAX Studio connects to the DAX engine as if it were a profiler and it captures the same trace events described in the previous section. It automatically filters only the events related to the executed query, so you do not have to worry if there are other concurrent users active on the same server.

The Query Plan pane displays the two query plans generated by the query, as you see in Figure 15-4. You see the physical query plan in the upper half of the pane, and the logical one in the lower half. The physical query plan is usually the most important to analyze when you look for a performance bottleneck in the formula engine. For this reason, this list also provides a column that contains the number of records iterated by a spool operation (which is an iteration performed by the formula engine, usually over a datacache). In this way, you can easily recognize which operations iterate over a large number of records in a complex query plan. You will see how to use this information later in Chapter 16, "Optimizing DAX."

Line	Records	Physical Query Plan
1		AddColumns: IterPhyOp IterCols(0)("[Result])
2		SingletonTable: IterPhyOp IterCols(0)("[Result])
3	1	Spool: LookupPhyOp Integer #Records=1 #KeyCols=68 #ValueCols=1 DominantValue=BLANK
4	1	AggregationSpool<Cache>: SpoolPhyOp #Records=1
5		VertipaqResult: IterPhyOp #FieldCols=0 #ValueCols=1

Line	Logical Query Plan
1	AddColumns: RelLogOp DependOnCols()() 0-0 RequiredCols(0)("[Result])
2	Sum_Vertipaq: ScaLogOp DependOnCols()() Integer DominantValue=BLANK Table='Audience' -BlankRow Aggregations(Sum)
3	Scan_Vertipaq: RelLogOp DependOnCols()() 0-52 RequiredCols(43)('Audience'[Weight]) Table='Audience' -BlankRow
4	'Audience'[Weight]: ScaLogOp DependOnCols(43)('Audience'[Weight]) Integer DominantValue=NONE

FIGURE 15-4 The Query Plan pane displays the Physical Query Plan and the Logical Query Plan.

The Server Timings pane in Figure 15-5 shows information related to storage engine queries and how the execution time splits between the formula engine and the storage engine.

Total	SE CPU	Line	Subclass	Duration	CPU	Query		SET DC_KIND="AUTO";
1,734 ms	13,109 ms	2	Scan	1,711	13,109	SELECT SUM (Audience[Weight]) FROM Audience;		SELECT
	x7.7							SUM (Audience[Weight])
▪ FE	▪ SE							FROM Audience;
23 ms	1,711 ms							
1.3%	98.7%							
SE Queries	SE Cache							
1	0							
	0.0%							

FIGURE 15-5 The Server Timings pane displays a summary of timings information and the details of the storage engine queries.

On the left side of the Server Timings pane, you can see the following measures:

■ **Total** Elapsed time for the complete DAX query. It corresponds to the Duration of the *Query End* event.

■ **SE CPU** Sum of the CPU Time value for all the VertiPaq scan events. It also reports the degree of parallelism of VertiPaq operations (number of cores used in parallel).

■ **FE** Time elapsed in the formula engine, in milliseconds and as a percentage of the Total time.

■ **SE** Time elapsed in the storage engine, in milliseconds and as a percentage of the Total time.

■ **SE Queries** Number of queries sent to the storage engine.

■ **SE Cache** Number of storage engine queries resolved by the storage engine cache, displayed as an absolute number and as a percentage of the SE Queries value.

The list in the center shows the storage engine queries executed, and on the right side you see the complete xmSQL code of the storage engine query selected in the center list. By default, you see only one row for each query, hiding the *VertiPaq Scan Internal* events that you have seen in the SQL Server Profiler example. You can show/hide internal events by enabling the Internal button of the Server Timings section in the Home ribbon, as you see in Figure 15-6.

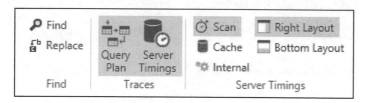

FIGURE 15-6 The Server Timings section includes options to show/hide details in the Server Timings pane.

Usually, a DAX performance analysis starts from the results displayed in the Server Timings pane. If more than 50 percent of the execution time is in FE, then you will analyze the query plans first, looking for the most expensive operations in the formula engine. Otherwise, when most of the execution time is in SE, then you will look for the most expensive storage engine queries in the center list of the Server Timings pane.

The *Duration* and *CPU* columns correspond to the *Duration* and *CPU Time* columns of the VertiPaq scan events described in the SQL Server Profiler section. You can sort the list of storage engine queries by *Duration*, so that you can easily find the most expensive one.

The xmSQL code displayed by DAX Studio is a simplified version of the original xmSQL query you can see in SQL Server Profiler. DAX Studio removes a few details, such as GUIDs included in object names, making the query easier to read.

DAX Studio makes the search of the bottlenecks in a DAX query more productive. It does not optimize DAX by itself, but it makes your job faster. In the following section of the book, we will use DAX Studio as a reference, but you should be able to find the corresponding information using SQL Server Profiler, too.

Reading storage engine queries

In this section you will learn how to read the storage engine queries and understand what happens in VertiPaq to execute an xmSQL query. You will use this information every time you have to solve a bottleneck in the storage engine. However, over time you will realize that it could be better to check the storage engine queries first, even when you have a bottleneck in the formula engine.

The storage engine task is that of scanning the VertiPaq database and generating a datacache, so that the formula engine can later use it.

Introducing xmSQL syntax

In the previous section, you have seen a simple storage engine query described in a simplified xmSQL syntax, which is the same as displayed by DAX Studio:

```
SELECT
SUM ( Sales[Quantity] )
FROM Sales;
```

This syntax would be quite similar in standard ANSI SQL:

```
SELECT
SUM ( Quantity )
FROM Sales;
```

Every xmSQL query involves a GROUP BY condition, even if this is not part of its syntax. For example, the following DAX query returns the list of unique values of the *Color* column in the Product table:

```
EVALUATE VALUES ( Product[Color] )
```

It results in this xmSQL query (note that no GROUP BY appears in the query):

```
SELECT Product[Color]
FROM Product;
```

The corresponding query in ANSI SQL would have a GROUP BY condition:

```
SELECT Color
FROM Product
GROUP BY Color
```

The reason why we compare the xmSQL to an ANSI SQL query with GROUP BY instead of DISTINCT (which would be possible for the previous example) is that most of the time xmSQL queries also include aggregated calculations. For example, consider the following DAX query:

```
EVALUATE
ADDCOLUMNS (
    VALUES ( Sales[Order Date] ),
    "Revenues", CALCULATE ( SUM ( Sales[Quantity] ) )
)
```

This is the corresponding xmSQL query sent to the storage engine:

```
SELECT Sales[Order Date], SUM ( Sales[Quantity] )
FROM Sales;
```

In ANSI SQL you would see a GROUP BY condition for the *Order Date* column:

```
SELECT [Order Date], SUM ( Quantity )
FROM Sales
GROUP BY [Order Date]
```

An xmSQL query never returns duplicated rows. When you run a DAX query over a table that does not have a unique key, the xmSQL query includes a special *RowNumber* column that keeps the rows unique. However, you cannot access the *RowNumber* column in DAX. For example, consider this DAX query:

```
EVALUATE Sales
```

It generates the following xmSQL code:

```
SELECT Sales[RowNumber], Sales[column1], Sales[column2], … ,Sales[columnN]
FROM Sales
```

Aggregation functions

xmSQL includes the following aggregation operations:

- *SUM*: sums the values of a column.

- *MIN*: returns the minimum value of a column.

- *MAX*: returns the maximum value of a column.

- *COUNT*: counts the number of rows in the current GROUP BY.

- *DCOUNT*: counts the number of distinct values of a column.

The behavior of *SUM, MIN, MAX,* and *DCOUNT* is similar. For example, the following DAX query returns the number of unique customers for each order date:

```
EVALUATE
ADDCOLUMNS (
    VALUES ( Sales[Order Date] ),
    "Customers", CALCULATE ( DISTINCTCOUNT ( Sales[CustomerKey] ) )
)
```

It generates the following xmSQL code:

```
SELECT Sales[Order Date], DCOUNT ( Sales[CustomerKey] )
FROM Sales;
```

Which corresponds to this ANSI SQL query:

```
SELECT [Order Date], COUNT ( DISTINCT CustomerKey )
FROM Sales
GROUP BY [Order Date]
```

The COUNT function does not have any argument. In fact, it computes the number of rows for the current group. For example, consider the following DAX query that counts the number of products for each color:

```
EVALUATE
ADDCOLUMNS (
    VALUES ( Product[Color] ),
    "Products", CALCULATE ( COUNTROWS ( Product ) )
)
```

This is the xmSQL code sent to the storage engine:

```
SELECT Product[Color], COUNT ( )
FROM Product;
```

A corresponding ANSI SQL query could be the following:

```
SELECT Color, COUNT ( * )
FROM Product
GROUP BY Color
```

Other aggregation functions in DAX do not have a corresponding xmSQL aggregation function. For example, consider the following DAX query using *AVERAGE*:

```
EVALUATE
ADDCOLUMNS (
    VALUES ( Product[Color] ),
    "Average Unit Price", CALCULATE ( AVERAGE ( Product[Unit Price] ) )
)
```

The corresponding xmSQL code includes two aggregations, one for the numerator and the other for the denominator of the division that will compute a simple average in the formula engine:

```
SELECT Product[Color], SUM ( Product[Unit Price] ), COUNT ( )
FROM Product;
```

Converting the xmSQL query in ANSI SQL you would obtain:

```
SELECT Color, SUM ( [Unit Price] ), COUNT ( * )
FROM Product
GROUP BY Color
```

Arithmetical operations

xmSQL includes simple arithmetical operations: +, -, *, / (sum, subtraction, multiplication, division). These operations work on single rows, whereas the formula engine usually performs arithmetical operations between the results of aggregations. It is common to see arithmetical operations in the expression used by an aggregation function. For example, the following DAX query returns the sum of the product of quantity and unit price calculated row by row for the Sales table:

```
EVALUATE
ROW (
    "Result",
    SUMX ( Sales, Sales[Quantity] * Sales[Unit Price] )
)
```

It generates the following xmSQL code:

```
SELECT
SUM ( Sales[Quantity] * Sales[Unit Price] )
FROM Sales;
```

Which corresponds to this ANSI SQL query:

```
SELECT SUM ( [Quantity] * [Unit Price] )
FROM Sales
```

xmSQL can also execute casts between data types to perform arithmetical operations. It is important to remember that these operations only happen within a row context, from the point of view of a DAX expression.

Filter operations

An xmSQL query can include filters in a WHERE condition. The performance of a filter depends on the cardinality of the conditions applied (this will be discussed in more detail later in the section, "Understanding scan time").

For example, consider the following query that returns the sum of the *Quantity* column for all the sales having a unit price equal to 10:

```
EVALUATE
CALCULATETABLE (
    ROW ( "Result", SUM ( Sales[Quantity] ) ),
    Sales[Unit Price] = 10
)
```

The resulting xmSQL query is the following:

```
SELECT SUM ( Sales[Quantity] )
FROM Sales
WHERE Sales[Unit Price] = 10;
```

The WHERE condition might include a test with more than one value. For example, consider a small variation of the previous query, where you sum the quantity or the sales having a unit price equal to 10 or 20, as in the following DAX query:

```
EVALUATE
CALCULATETABLE (
    ROW ( "Result", SUM ( Sales[Quantity] ) ),
    OR ( Sales[Unit Price] = 10, Sales[Unit Price] = 20 )
)
```

The xmSQL uses the *IN* operator to include a list of values:

```
SELECT SUM ( Sales[Quantity] )
FROM Sales
WHERE Sales[Unit Price] IN ( 10, 20 );
```

Any filter condition in xmSQL only includes existing values of the column. For example, if you apply to a DAX condition a value that does not exist in the column, the resulting xmSQL code will include a condition that will filter out all the rows. For example, if neither 10 nor 20 existed in the Sales table, the previous xmSQL query would become:

```
SELECT SUM ( Sales[Quantity] )
FROM Sales
WHERE Sales[Unit Price] IN ( );
```

The result of such an xmSQL query will be always empty.

It is important to remember that xmSQL is a textual representation of a storage engine query. The actual structure is more optimized. For example, when the list of values allowed for a column is very long, the xmSQL reports a few values, highlighting the total number of values passed internally to the query. This might happen more often than you can imagine. For example, consider the following DAX query that returns the sum of the quantity for one year of sales:

```
EVALUATE
CALCULATETABLE (
    ROW ( "Result", SUM ( Sales[Quantity] ) ),
    Sales[Order Date] >= DATE ( 2006, 1, 1 ) && Sales[Order Date] <= DATE ( 2006, 12, 31 )
)
```

Depending on the version of the DAX engine, it might generate the following xmSQL query:

```
SELECT SUM ( Sales[Quantity] )
FROM Sales
WHERE Sales[Order Date] >= 38718.000000
 VAND Sales[Order Date] <= 39082.000000
```

DAX represents date and time values as floating point numbers. For this reason, you see that the comparison of the *Order Date* column happens with two numbers corresponding to the two dates used in the filter argument of the DAX expression.

However, a different version of the DAX engine might produce the following xmSQL query instead:

```
SELECT SUM ( Sales[Quantity] )
FROM Sales
WHERE Sales[Order Date] IN ( 38732.000000, 38883.000000, 38846.000000, 38997.000000,
38809.000000, 38960.000000, 38789.000000, 38923.000000, 39074.000000, 38752.000000..[365
total values, not all displayed] ) ;
```

In this case, instead of a range condition, the xmSQL query has a bitmap index that identifies all of the values included in the filter. The WHERE / IN condition represents such a bitmap index, reporting a sample of the values followed by the total number of values in the column. In order to obtain the list of values for a range, another xmSQL query might be executed before:

```
SELECT Sales[Order Date]
FROM Sales
WHERE Sales[Order Date] >= 38718.000000
 VAND Sales[Order Date] <= 39082.000000
```

The actual xmSQL query generated in this last example might be more complex, including a callback to the formula engine in order to transform the result of the *DATE* function in the corresponding floating-point value. You will find more information about these callbacks in the section "Understanding CallbackDataID," later in this chapter.

Join operators

The xmSQL code can execute JOIN conditions when a DAX query involves multiple tables connected by relationships in the data model. For example, consider the following DAX query returning the sum of *Quantity* column in the Sales table for each Color name in the Product table:

```
EVALUATE
ADDCOLUMNS (
    VALUES ( Product [Color] ),
    "Sales", CALCULATE ( SUM ( Sales[Quantity] ) )
)
```

If you have a one-to-many relationship between the Product and Sales tables in the data model, the xmSQL code you obtain includes a LEFT OUTER JOIN between the two tables, as you see in the following storage engine query:

```
SELECT Product[Color], SUM ( Sales[Quantity] )
FROM Sales
    LEFT OUTER JOIN Product ON Sales[ProductKey] = Product[ProductKey];
```

The ON condition of the JOIN automatically includes the columns that define the relationship in the data model. You have one join for each relationship involved in the query.

Understanding scan time

Now that you have seen the syntax of xmSQL queries, it is time to consider the work performed by the storage engine to execute such statements.

VertiPaq performs a complete scan of each column involved in a storage engine query. There could be more iterations for a column, depending on the request. Because there are no indexes, the time required to complete a scan depends on the memory footprint of the column, which depends on the number of unique values in the column, their distribution across the rows and on the number of rows in the table. The importance of these factors depends on the aggregation function used in the xmSQL query. For example, consider a large table with four columns: *Date*, *Time*, *Age*, and *Score*. The table has four billion rows, so that we can observe relevant differences in execution time. We executed the following DAX queries for each column:

```
EVALUATE
ROW ( "Sum", SUM ( Example[<column name>] ) )

EVALUATE
ROW ( "Distinct Count", DISTINCTCOUNT ( Example[<column name>] ) )
```

We are not interested in the values returned by these queries, but only in the time spent in the storage engine (which, for these simple queries, is always close to the entire execution time of the DAX queries). In Table 15-1 you can see the results where we reported, for each column:

- **Memory (MB)**   the memory footprint of the column for the entire table (four billion rows).

- **Distinct Values**   the number of unique values in the column, obtained by executing the *DISTINCTCOUNT* aggregation function in DAX.

- **SUM (ms)**   the execution time of the query that applies the *SUM* aggregation to the column.

- **DISTINCTCOUNT (ms)**   the execution time of the query that applies the *DISTINCTCOUNT* aggregation to the column.

TABLE 15-1 Column size, cardinality, and execution time of aggregation functions.

Column	Memory (MB)	Distinct Values	SUM (ms)	DISTINCTCOUNT (ms)
Date	0.37	1,588	13	17
Age	203.55	96	130	103
Score	2,690.35	1,467,394	700	1,986
Time	6,192.81	1,438	1,391	844

At first sight, a few results might appear counterintuitive. Usually, the larger the number of unique values in a column, the slower the query. In this case, *Date* is faster than *Age*, which has a smaller number of unique values. Moreover, the *Time* column, which has a number of unique values similar to *Date*, has a difference in performance of at least one order of magnitude. The reasons for these differences are the different compression rates, derived by different sort orders of the columns.

The *Date* column always has the faster execution time. This is because the four billion rows have been processed as reading rows sorted by date. Even without partitioning, this created segments with one or two unique values each. Thus, all the rows in each segment had a very high compression rate, as it is clear from the memory used by the *Date* column.

The *Age* column has the second best performance for both *SUM* and *DISTINCTCOUNT*. This column has a larger memory footprint than *Date* because there are different *Age* values for each *Date*, and rows are sorted by *Date* first.

The *Score* and *Time* columns have a slower performance. Performance of *SUM* depends mainly on the memory footprint, whereas *DISTINCTCOUNT* is more sensitive to the number of distinct values in the column. The reason for that is the different calculation algorithm used for these two aggregations.

The important concept here is that you can obtain a different performance for a storage engine query depending on the memory footprint of a column. You can optimize a storage engine query by reducing the memory footprint of the columns used. You can obtain that by using columns with a smaller number of unique values, or with a different sort order of the data source, or by reducing the number of rows in the table, or by applying other techniques that you will see in the remaining part of this book.

Understanding *DISTINCTCOUNT* internals

The use of the *DISTINCTCOUNT* function in a DAX expression generates multiple *VertiPaq Scan Internal* events for a single *VertiPaq Scan* event. You can show internal events by enabling the Internal button in the Server Settings section of DAX Studio.

Consider the following DAX query:

```
EVALUATE
ROW ( "Result", DISTINCTCOUNT ( Example[Score] ) )
```

In Table 15-2 you can see the complete list of *VertiPaq Scan* events generated by the query above.

TABLE 15-2 *VertiPaq Scan* events for a DAX query with *DISTINCTCOUNT* measure.

Line	Subclass	Duration	CPU	Query
1	Internal	3,974	28,422	SELECT Example[Score] FROM Example;
2	Internal	3,974	28,422	SELECT Example[Score] FROM Example;
3	Internal	8	28,422	SELECT COUNT( ) FROM $DCOUNT_DATACACHE;
4	Scan	3,982	28,422	SELECT DCOUNT (Example[Score]) FROM Example;

The last line includes the storage engine query requested by the formula engine. In reality, internally the query is split into two subqueries. The first result is duplicated in two identical rows (see the content of *Duration* and *CPU* columns). You can see here the xmSQL code of the first internal subquery, which retrieves the list of unique values in the *Score* column of the Example table:

```
SELECT Example[Score]
FROM Example;
```

The result of this storage engine query is a list of the unique values in the *Score* column of the Example table. The next step is to count how many rows are in this list. In other words, counting the rows returned by the internal query provides the correct result to the original query. This particular xmSQL query just references a special table named *$DCOUNT_DATACACHE*, which references the previous result from a storage engine query:

```
SELECT COUNT ( )
FROM $DCOUNT_DATACACHE;
```

Table 15-2 also shows that the duration of the *Scan* event corresponds to the sum of the duration of the two internal events. As you see, the duplicated event counts only once. Regarding the CPU Time, it is always the same in all the events of the same query. The parallelism ratio (CPU Time divided by Duration) is around seven, which means that up to eight threads in parallel were executed. The next section includes a deeper discussion about the parallelism within a storage engine query.

Understanding parallelism and datacache

Every storage engine query described by an xmSQL statement returns a result called datacache, which is a single uncompressed table in memory. The result of a storage engine query can be completely materialized in memory, or its rows can be consumed during the iteration without persisting them. Usually, we refer to a datacache when this result is materialized, which is the case most of the time in complex queries.

The execution of the storage engine query can be parallelized among many cores, using different execution threads. The number of threads used depends on the hardware and on the physical structure of the columns involved in the query. The VertiPaq engine assigns one thread for each segment involved in a single scan operation (as you have seen in Chapter 13). When the operation runs on multiple threads, every thread creates a partial result. Only when all the threads complete their execution, VertiPaq will consolidate these results in a single final datacache. The formula engine will then consume the datacache in a single thread. Also for this reason, the result of a storage engine query requires such a consolidation. You can see the parallel processing and consolidation behavior described in a schema in Figure 15-7.

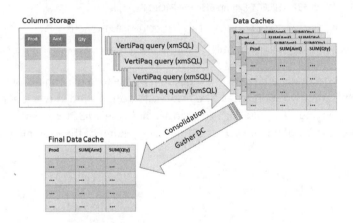

FIGURE 15-7 The final datacache is a consolidation of different datacaches created by concurrent VertiPaq queries when the engine parallelizes execution.

A segment should not be too small, because the consolidation process requires time. The efficiency of running scan operations in multiple threads should balance the overhead of the consolidation, but this is not possible if the segments are too small. As a side effect, VertiPaq operations on small tables cannot get the benefits of multiple cores: The consolidation process would be more expensive than the gain provided by parallelization of small tables.

It is useful to remember that the storage engine query only provides data to the formula engine. In a simple scenario, we have the following steps:

1. The storage engine receives an xmSQL query.

2. The storage engine executes the scan operations potentially on many threads, creating one datacache per thread.

3. The storage engine consolidates the different datacaches into a single, final datacache.

4. The formula engine consumes the datacache in a single thread.

5. The formula engine can use the same datacache in different steps of the query plan.

In the Profiler, you will always see the storage engine events before the query plan. The physical query plan always appears at the end of the events related to a query. The logical query plan can be preceded by a few storage engine queries. When this is the case, it is because the DAX engine itself sends some queries to retrieve information about size and density of columns. The DAX engine uses this information to create a better query plan. Using DAX Studio, you cannot see such a behavior, because this tool shows query plans and storage engine queries in different parts of the user interface.

Understanding the VertiPaq cache

The DAX formula engine does not have any cache, whereas the VertiPaq storage engine has one: the VertiPaq cache. Its primary goal is to improve the performance of multiple requests of the same datacache within the same query. Its secondary goal is to improve the performance of different DAX queries requesting the same datacache. It is important to understand the goals of the VertiPaq cache in order to analyze its behavior and evaluate its efficiency.

For example, consider the following DAX query:

```
EVALUATE
ADDCOLUMNS (
    VALUES ( Example[Date] ),
    "A", CALCULATE ( SUM ( Example[Score] ) ),
    "B", 2 * CALCULATE ( SUM ( Example[Score] ) )
)
```

The result of the query includes two columns, A and B, both summing the *Score* column of the Example table for each *Date*. The difference between A and B is that B multiplies this result by 2. In Table 15-3 you see a possible sequence of *Scan* events (actual events depend on the version of the DAX engine—you might observe a different execution). Within the same query, there are two VertiPaq queries that retrieve the same datacache. The second *Scan* operation (in Line 4) hits the cache, reusing (in Line 3) the previously computed datacache.

TABLE 15-3 *VertiPaq* events for a DAX query with two similar expressions.

Line	Class	Subclass	Duration	CPU	Query
1	SE Query	Internal	2,527	18,250	SELECT Example[Date], SUM (Example[Score]), COUNT ( ) FROM Example;
2	SE Query	Scan	2,528	18,250	SELECT Example[Date], SUM (Example[Score]) FROM Example;
3	SE Cache	Cache	0	0	SELECT Example[Date], SUM (Example[Score]) FROM Example;
4	SE Cache	Scan	0	0	SELECT Example[Date], SUM (Example[Score]) FROM Example;
5	SE Query	Internal	213	1,484	SELECT Example[Date], COUNT ( ) FROM Example;
6	SE Query	Scan	213	1,484	SELECT Example[Date] FROM Example;

In SQL Server Profiler, you see that a storage engine query retrieved data from the VertiPaq cache by capturing the event *VertiPaq SE Query Cache Match*. However, such an event class includes both the *Scan* and *Cache* subclasses (as you see in Lines 3 and 4 of Table 15-3). If you remove it from a profiling session, you no longer see the entire scan event if it is resolved by the VertiPaq cache.

DAX Studio always captures both subclasses of this event. You can just hide or show the *Cache* subclass event, keeping the *Scan* event visible, by enabling the Cache button of the Server Timings section in the Home ribbon. If you disable both the *Cache* and *Internal* events, DAX Studio shows three events (as shown in Table 15-4), which are the same *Scan* events you have seen in Table 15-3. DAX Studio does not completely filter out the *Scan* subclass events of the *VertiPaq SE Query Cache Match* event class. When you analyze a single query, this visualization mode is more useful than the profiler one.

TABLE 15-4 *VertiPaq Scan* events for a DAX query with two similar expressions.

Line	Class	Subclass	Duration	CPU	Query
2	SE Query	Scan	2,528	18,250	SELECT Example[Date], SUM (Example[Score]) FROM Example;
4	SE Cache	Scan	0	0	SELECT Example[Date], SUM (Example[Score]) FROM Example;
6	SE Query	Scan	213	1,484	SELECT Example[Date] FROM Example;

The VertiPaq engine reuses data in cache only when the cardinality is the same and the columns are a subset of a previous query. This algorithm is very simple because the lookup in the VertiPaq cache must not be an overhead of the memory scan operation that it is trying to avoid. For this reason, the VertiPaq cache keeps in memory only a limited number of datacaches. Therefore, there is no guarantee that a request will hit the cache, even when the query plan repeats the same storage query multiple times within the same DAX query. Nevertheless, in most conditions the VertiPaq cache satisfies most of the requests that happen in a short period, also between different DAX queries.

VertiPaq ignores row-level security settings. The DAX formula engine manages the role-based security and generates different VertiPaq storage engine queries depending on security settings and user credentials. For this reason, the VertiPaq cache is a global resource and shares the results between different users and sessions. The formula engine guarantees the correctness of the result, generating different storage engine queries depending on the requirements.

When analyzing performance, it is important to clear the cache before running a query. In order to find bottlenecks and areas of improvement for a query plan, it is better to observe the time required to complete a scan in memory, simulating the worst-case scenario (empty cache). Because of the reduced size of the VertiPaq cache, missing the cache is a frequent event on a busy server with many concurrent users running queries.

You can clear the cache in Analysis Services using the following XMLA command, which removes the cache of results related to the specified database (this example clears the cache of the Adventure Works DW database):

```
<ClearCache xmlns="http://schemas.microsoft.com/analysisservices/2003/engine">
    <Object>
        <DatabaseID>Adventure Works DW</DatabaseID>
    </Object>
</ClearCache>
```

 Note The clear cache command completely empties the VertiPaq cache of all the databases in SQL Server Analysis Services 2012 and 2014. Newer versions of Analysis Services will respect the database scope of the clear cache command.

If you are using DAX Studio, you can use the Clear Cache button in the Home ribbon to send the same command to the DAX engine.

Understanding *CallbackDataID*

The storage engine only supports a limited set of operators and functions in xmSQL. Thus, it is a formula engine task executing all the operations not directly supported by the storage engine. However, when a calculation is required within a VertiPaq iterator, the storage engine may call the formula engine using a special xmSQL function called *CallbackDataID*.

The operators supported in xmSQL include the basic mathematical operations (sum, subtraction, multiplication, and division), but do not include mathematical functions such as square root (*SQRT* in DAX), or conditional logic such as the *IF* function. If you include an expression that is not supported by xmSQL in an iterator, then the query plan generates an xmSQL syntax that contains a special function called *CallbackDataID*. During the iteration, the storage engine calls the formula engine for every row, passing the DAX expression and the values of its members as arguments.

For example, consider the sum of squares in this DAX query:

```
EVALUATE
ROW (
    "Result", SUMX ( Example, SQRT ( Example[Delta] ) )
)
```

In this case, the query plan generates the following xmSQL statement:

```
SELECT
SUM ( [ CallbackDataID ( SQRT ( Example[Delta] ) ) ] ( PFDATAID ( Example[Delta] ) ) )
FROM Example;
```

The *CallbackDataID* function contains the DAX expression that evaluates the square root of a value, which corresponds to the value of the *Delta* column in the Example table for the "current" row. (The *PFDATAID* syntax is not relevant for analyzing the logic we are describing now.) The storage engine calls the *CallbackDataID* function for each row of the Example table. The result of the xmSQL query is a datacache with only one row, corresponding to the aggregated result. Even if the formula engine is single threaded, when the storage engine calls the formula engine through *CallbackDataID*, the parallelism of the storage engine is not affected, because there could be multiple instances of the formula engine executed in parallel, one for each thread of the storage engine.

Parallelism of *CallbackDataID* and possible alternatives

In order to understand how the parallelism interacts with *CallbackDataID* and the associated cost, consider what could happen in case the *CallbackDataID* was not available. You might have a query plan requesting a datacache with the value of the *Delta* column for all the rows of the Example table, using an xmSQL query such as the following:

```
SELECT
Example[Delta], COUNT( )
FROM Example;
```

The datacache obtained by the formula engine would contain one row for each unique value of the *Delta* column, and the number of rows having such a value in the Example table. Using this information, the formula engine would apply the square root to the value of *Delta* for each row of the datacache, multiplying such a result by the number of occurrences of such a *Delta* value in the Example table. The result provided by the formula engine would be identical, but the storage engine should create a datacache much larger than the one-row datacache obtained by the xmSQL query with the *CallbackDataID* function. Remember that the storage engine often materializes the entire datacache in memory, and this would be in an uncompressed format. Then the formula engine would iterate this datacache sequentially in a single thread. This would result in poor performance.

The execution using *CallbackDataID* is less expensive in terms of memory (the datacache materialized has only one row), and is more scalable. If the *VertiPaq Scan* operation spans on multiple threads, calls made to the formula engine through *CallbackDataID* use a thread instance of the formula engine. In other words, you can imagine that every running thread (even within the same query) has its own instance of the formula engine. The only sequential operation is the consolidation made by the storage engine on the datacaches created by the running threads. However, this operation will be very fast, because it consolidates different datacaches containing only one column each.

From a performance point of view, *CallbackDataID* has three other implications:

- Expressions solved through *CallbackDataID* calls are more expensive than expressions solved by internal operators of the storage engine. There is an overhead associated with each call to *CallbackDataID*.

- In a trace session, a *VertiPaq Storage Engine* event includes the time spent in the formula engine by a *CallbackDataID* call. This is not an issue, but you have to realize that optimizing a storage engine query that has a long execution time might require you to reduce or to remove the calls to *CallbackDataID* made by xmSQL queries.

- The storage engine cache does not persist any datacache produced by an xmSQL query containing one or more *CallbackDataID* calls. Therefore, the presence of *CallbackDataID* in an xmSQL function should be carefully evaluated when the storage executes it in an iteration.

> **Important** The formula engine is single threaded, but when the storage engine calls the formula engine through *CallbackDataID*, the execution of the code in the formula engine is parallelized through the several threads created by the storage engine. The parallelism provided by this technique reduces overall Duration, but the CPU Time might increase because of the *CallbackDataID* calls overhead.

In order to understand the performance impact of *CallbackDataID*, consider the following DAX query that sums the result of a division made row by row:

```
EVALUATE
ROW (
    "Total", SUMX (
        Example,
        IF (
            Example[Denominator] <> 0,
            Example[Numerator] / Example[Denominator],
            BLANK ()
        )
    )
)
```

The *IF* function avoids a calculation error in case one row contains a zero value in the denominator column. The xmSQL query sent to the storage engine is similar to the following one:

```
SELECT
SUM ( [ CallbackDataID (
    IF (
        Example[Denominator] <> 0,
        Example[Numerator] / Example[Denominator],
        BLANK ()
    )
) ' ( PFDATAID ( Example[Numerator] ) , PFDATAID ( Example[Denominator] ) ) )
FROM Example;
```

We executed a corresponding DAX query on our Example table with four billion rows, obtaining the storage engine events that you can see in Table 15-5.

TABLE 15-5 *VertiPaq Scan* events with a *CallbackDataID* including an *IF* function in DAX.

Line	Subclass	Duration	CPU	Query
1	Internal	13,967	100,625	SELECT SUM ([CallbackDataID (IF (Example[Denominator] <> 0, ...
2	Scan	13,967	100,625	SELECT SUM ([CallbackDataID (IF (Example[Denominator] <> 0, ...

The parallelism ratio (CPU Time divided by Duration) is above seven, because we used a server with eight cores. The important point is that different threads executed parallel calls to the formula engine. In previous chapters, you have seen that in DAX the *DIVIDE* function can replace the specific *IF* condition used to check whether the denominator of a division is equal to zero. We can see what happens if we use *DIVIDE* instead of *IF* in this example. The DAX query is the following:

```
EVALUATE
ROW (
    "Total", SUMX (
        Example,
        DIVIDE ( Example[Numerator], Example[Denominator] )
    )
)
```

The *DIVIDE* function does not have a corresponding syntax in xmSQL, so also in this case we have a *CallbackDataID* in the corresponding xmSQL query sent to the storage engine:

```
SELECT
SUM ( [ CallbackDataID (
    DIVIDE ( Example[Numerator], Example[Denominator] )
) ' ( PFDATAID ( Example[Numerator] ) , PFDATAID ( Example[Denominator] ) ) )
FROM Example;
```

In Table 15-6 you can see the storage engine events obtained from running the query over the same four billion rows table used in the previous example.

TABLE 15-6 *VertiPaq Scan* events with a *CallbackDataID* including a *DIVIDE* function in DAX.

Line	Subclass	Duration	CPU	Query
1	Internal	11,662	84,203	SELECT SUM ([CallbackDataID (DIVIDE (Example[Numerator], ...
2	Scan	11,662	84,203	SELECT SUM ([CallbackDataID (DIVIDE (Example[Numerator], ...

Using *DIVIDE* instead of *IF* we obtained a 16 percent performance improvement in both Duration and CPU Time. However, despite the parallelism achieved with this technique, the overhead of *CallbackDataID* is still high, because the storage engine calls a function in the formula engine. If we remove the *CallbackDataID* completely, this overhead disappears. In this case, this is possible by simply applying a filter so that the iteration will ignore rows containing zero in the *Denominator* column. This is possible with the following DAX query:

```
EVALUATE
ROW (
    "Total", SUMX (
        FILTER ( Example, Example[Denominator] <> 0 ),
        Example[Numerator] / Example[Denominator]
    )
)
```

The entire DAX expression has a corresponding syntax in xmSQL without using *CallbackDataID*:

```
SELECT
Example[Numerator] / Example[Denominator]
FROM Example
WHERE Example[Denominator] <> 0;
```

The resulting storage engine events that you can see in Table 15-7 show an improvement close to 50 percent compared to the performance of the *DIVIDE* version.

TABLE 15-7 *VertiPaq Scan* events without *CallbackDataID* to execute a safe division in DAX.

Line	Subclass	Duration	CPU	Query
1	Internal	6,089	44,078	SELECT Example[Numerator] / Example[Denominator] ...
2	Scan	6,089	44,078	SELECT Example[Numerator] / Example[Denominator] ...

This last version also has another advantage by avoiding using *CallbackDataID*. The VertiPaq cache now keeps the datacache for future executions, which is not possible when the xmSQL query includes a *CallbackDataID* function. If you execute the last DAX query twice, the second execution produces the profiler events you can see in Table 15-8.

TABLE 15-8 *VertiPaq Scan* events without *CallbackDataID* hitting the storage engine cache.

Line	Subclass	Duration	CPU	Query
1	Cache	0	0	SELECT Example[Numerator] / Example[Denominator] ...
2	Scan	1	0	SELECT Example[Numerator] / Example[Denominator] ...

In general, you should avoid or at least reduce to a minimum the number of calls to *CallbackDataID* made by the storage engine, as you will see in Chapter 16.

Profiler limitations for *CallbackDataID* in Analysis Services 2012/2014

There are important limitations in profiler events generated by Analysis Services 2012 and 2014 when the xmSQL query includes *CallbackDataID*. The internal DAX expression passed to *CallbackDataID* might include subquery statements in DAX generating further requests to the storage engine. Unfortunately, versions of Analysis Services released before 2015 only provide information about these subqueries in the logical query plan. The physical query plan does not include the subexpression included within *CallbackDataID*. The storage engine queries executed to evaluate these subexpressions do not fire any event visible in the profiler. Analysis Services 2016, Excel 2016, and Power BI Desktop do not have this problem.

Reading query plans

At the beginning of this chapter, you have seen that there are two types of query plans in DAX: logical and physical. In reality, you will not use these query plans often, because you will focus your attention on the storage engine queries first. You can analyze performance of the storage engine queries to find issues caused by the storage engine and/or by materialization of large datacaches in memory. Storage engine queries are much easier to read than DAX query plans.

In this section, you will see some of the important behaviors to check in a query plan in order to identify performance bottlenecks. A complete and detailed coverage of all the operators used in logical and physical query plans is beyond the scope of this book. The goal here is to understand the relationships between a query plan and the storage engine queries, improving your ability to find bottlenecks, and to improve query performances.

A query plan usually generates more than one storage engine query. The formula engine combines the results of different datacaches, doing operations similar to joins between temporary tables. Consider the following DAX query that returns a table with the quantity sold for each product color:

```
EVALUATE
ADDCOLUMNS (
    ALL ( Product[Color] ),
    "Units", CALCULATE ( SUM ( Sales[Quantity] ) )
)
ORDER BY Product[Color]
```

This query returns a table with two columns similar to what you can see in Table 15-9. The point of attention is that the query includes unique values of *Color* column without any unit sold. In order to do that, the DAX engine has an approach that is different from the one you would have in plain SQL language because of the different technique used to join tables in the storage engine. We will highlight this difference later, but pay attention to the process for now.

TABLE 15-9 Number of units sold for each product color.

Color	Units
Black	9843
Blue	3970
Grey	
Multi	3926
NA	28919
Red	4949
Silver	3424
Silver/Black	
White	568
Yellow	4799

The following logical query plan includes two *Scan_Vertipaq* operations that correspond to two datacaches provided by storage engine queries:

```
Order: RelLogOp DependOnCols()() 0-1 RequiredCols(0, 1)('Product'[Color], ''[Units])
    AddColumns: RelLogOp DependOnCols()() 0-1
                RequiredCols(0, 1)('Product'[Color], ''[Units])
        Scan_Vertipaq: RelLogOp DependOnCols()() 0-0 RequiredCols(0)('Product'[Color])
        Sum_Vertipaq: ScaLogOp DependOnCols(0)('Product'[Color])
                      Integer DominantValue=BLANK
            Scan_Vertipaq: RelLogOp DependOnCols(0)('Product'[Color]) 1-37
                           RequiredCols(0, 20)('Product'[Color], 'Sales'[Quantity])
            'Sales'[Quantity]: ScaLogOp DependOnCols(20)('Sales'[Quantity])
                               Integer DominantValue=NONE
    'Product'[Color]: ScaLogOp DependOnCols(0)('Product'[Color]) String
                      DominantValue=NONE
```

The two *Scan_Vertipaq* operations require different sets of columns. The first only uses the product color, whereas the second one includes product color and sales quantity, which are two columns in two different tables. When this happens, a join between two or more tables is required.

After the logical query plan, the profiler receives the events from the storage engine. The corresponding xmSQL queries of the VertiPaq SE Query events are the following:

```
SELECT
    Product[Color],
    SUM ( Sales[Quantity] )
FROM Sales
    LEFT OUTER JOIN Product ON Sales[ProductKey]=Product[ProductKey];

SELECT
Product[Color]
FROM Product;
```

The first storage engine query retrieves a table containing one row for each color that has at least one unit sold in the Sales table. In order to do that, the query joins Sales and Product using the *ProductKey* column. The second xmSQL statement returns the list of all the product colors, independent of the Sales table. These two queries generate two different datacaches, one with two columns (product color and sum of quantity), and another one with only one column (the product color).

At this point, you might wonder why a second query is required. Why isn't the first xmSQL enough? The reason is that the *LEFT JOIN* you see in xmSQL has Sales on the left side and Product on the right side. In plain SQL code, you probably would write the following query:

```
SELECT
    Product.Color,
    SUM ( Sales.Quantity )
FROM Product
    LEFT OUTER JOIN Sales ON Sales.ProductKey = Product.ProductKey
GROUP BY Product.Color
ORDER BY Product.Color;
```

Having the Product table on the left side of a *LEFT JOIN* would produce a result that includes all of the product colors. However, the storage engine can generate queries only between tables with a relationship in the data model, and the resulting join in xmSQL always puts the table that is at the many-side of the relationship on the left side of the join condition. This guarantees that, even if there are missing product keys in the Product table, the result will include sales for those missing products, too (these sales will be included in a row with a blank value for all the product attributes, in this case the product color).

Now that you know why the DAX engine produces two storage engine queries for the simple DAX query we wrote, you can read the physical query plan, where you will find more information about the query execution:

```
PartitionIntoGroups: IterPhyOp IterCols(0, 1)('Product'[Color], ''[Units])
                  #Groups=1 #Rows=10
    AggregationSpool<Order>: SpoolPhyOp #Records=1
      AddColumns: IterPhyOp IterCols(0, 1)('Product'[Color], ''[Units])
        Spool_Iterator<Spool>: IterPhyOp IterCols(0)('Product'[Color]) #Records=10
                        #KeyCols=238 #ValueCols=0
            AggregationSpool<Cache>: SpoolPhyOp #Records=10
              VertipaqResult: IterPhyOp #FieldCols=1 #ValueCols=0
        Spool: LookupPhyOp LookupCols(0)('Product'[Color]) Integer #Records=8
              #KeyCols=238 #ValueCols=1 DominantValue=BLANK
          AggregationSpool<Cache>: SpoolPhyOp #Records=8
              VertipaqResult: IterPhyOp #FieldCols=1 #ValueCols=1
      ColPosition<'Product'[Color]>: LookupPhyOp LookupCols(0)('Product'[Color]) String
```

The physical query plan uses the *VertipaqResult* operator to indicate where it is consuming a datacache provided by the storage engine. You do not clearly see the corresponding xmSQL query for each operation. Nevertheless, at least in simple cases like the one we are considering, you can figure out this association by looking at other information. For example, one *VertipaqResult* only has one string column, whereas the other *VertipaqResult* has one string column and one integer column (the quantity). In the physical query plan, *#ValueCols* reports the number of numeric columns, whereas *#FieldCols* reports the number of other columns.

The *AggregationSpool<Cache>* operation consumes the datacaches corresponding to *VertipaqResult* nodes in the physical query plan. Here you can see important information: the number of records iterated, which corresponds to the number of rows in the datacache used. This number follows the *#Records* attribute, highlighted in the query plan. You can find the same *#Records* attribute in parent nodes of the query plan.

The physical query plan you have seen does not show in a clear way the relationships with corresponding operators in the logical query plan. This is not an issue for simple query plans, but it would be helpful information for queries that are more complex. New versions of the engine released after Analysis Services 2014 generate a richer physical query plan, such as the following one:

```
PartitionIntoGroups: IterPhyOp IterCols(0, 1)('Product'[Color], ''[Units])
                  #Groups=1 #Rows=10
    AggregationSpool<Order>: SpoolPhyOp #Records=1
      AddColumns: IterPhyOp IterCols(0, 1)('Product'[Color], ''[Units])
        Spool_Iterator<SpoolIterator>: IterPhyOp LogOp=Scan_Vertipaq
                                IterCols(0)('Products'[Color])
                                #Records=10 #KeyCols=37 #ValueCols=0
          ProjectionSpool<ProjectFusion<>>: SpoolPhyOp #Records=10
              VertipaqResult: IterPhyOp #FieldCols=1 #ValueCols=0
        SpoolLookup: LookupPhyOp LogOp=Sum_Vertipaq LookupCols(0)('Product'[Color])
              Integer #Records=8 #KeyCols=238 #ValueCols=1 DominantValue=BLANK
          ProjectionSpool<ProjectFusion<Sum>>: SpoolPhyOp #Records=8
              VertipaqResult: IterPhyOp #FieldCols=1 #ValueCols=1
      ColValue<'Product'[Color]>: LookupPhyOp LookupCols(0)('Products'[Color]) String
              LogOp=ColValue<'Products'[Color]>'Products'[Color]
```

The new version of the physical query plan uses *ProjectionSpool* operator instead of *Aggregation-Spool*, specifying the aggregation performed by the engine if there is one. In this example, the second *ProjectionSpool* operation executed a sum aggregation. The other information added to the query plan is the argument *LogOp*, which specifies for each *Spool* operation the corresponding *Vertipaq* operation in the logical query plan (you can see the highlighted *Scan_Vertipaq* and *Sum_Vertipaq* operators in the last example).

At this point, we can recap what we are reading in the query plans and the storage engine queries we have:

1.   The formula engine consumes two datacaches, corresponding to *VertipaqResult* operators in the physical query plan.

2.   The formula engine iterates over the list of product colors, which is a table containing 10 rows and one column. This is the datacache obtained by the second storage engine query. (Do not make particular assumptions about the order of the storage engine queries in the profiler.)

3.   For each row of this datacache (a product color), the formula engine executes a lookup in the other datacache containing the product colors and the quantity sold for each one.

The entire process executed by the formula engine is sequential and single threaded. The formula engine sends to the storage engine one request at a time. The storage engine might parallelize the query, but the formula engine does not send multiple requests in parallel to the storage engine.

> **Note** The formula engine and the storage engine are components subject to optimizations and improvements made in new releases. The behavior described might be different in newer versions of the DAX engine.

The formula engine can combine different results by using the lookup operation described in the previous query plan, or other set operators. In any case, the formula engine executes this operation sequentially. For this reason, you might expect longer execution times by combining large datacaches, or by performing a lookup for millions of rows in a large lookup datacache. A simple and effective way to identify these potential bottlenecks in the physical query plan is looking for the highest number of records in the operators of a logical query plan. For this reason, DAX Studio extracts such a number from the query plan, making it easier to sort query plan operators by using the number of records iterated. You can click the *Records* column shown in Figure 15-4 in order to sort the rows by this number. You will see a more detailed example of this approach in Chapter 16.

The presence of relationships in the data model is important to obtain better performance. We can examine the behavior of a join between two tables when a relationship is not available. For example, consider a query returning the same result of the previous example, but operating in a data model that does not have a relationship between Product and Sales tables. We need a DAX query such as the following one, which uses the virtual relationship pattern you have seen in Chapter 12, "Advanced relationships" in the section "Using relationships with different granularities":

```
DEFINE
    MEASURE Sales[Units] =
        CALCULATE (
            SUM ( Sales[Quantity] ),
            FILTER (
                ALL ( Sales[ProductKey] ),
                CONTAINS (
                    VALUES ( Product[ProductKey] ),
                    Product[ProductKey], 'Sales'[ProductKey]
                )
            )
        )
    )
EVALUATE
ADDCOLUMNS ( ALL ( Product[Color] ), "Units", [Units] )
ORDER BY Product[Color]
```

The function in the *Units* measure definition is equivalent to a relationship between Sales and Products. The resulting query plan is more complex than the previous one, because there are many more operations in both the logical and the physical query plan. Without doing a dump of the complete query plan, which would be too long for a book, we can summarize the behavior of the query plan in these logical steps:

1. Retrieve the list of *ProductKey* values for each product color.

2. Sum the *Quantity* value for each *ProductKey*.

3. For each color, aggregate the *Quantity* of the related *ProductKey* values.

The formula engine executes four storage engine queries, corresponding to the following xmSQL statements:

```
SELECT
Sales[ProductKey]
FROM Sales;

SELECT
Product[ProductKey], Product[Color]
FROM Product;

SELECT
Sales[ProductKey], SUM ( Sales[Quantity] )
FROM Sales
WHERE    Sales[ProductKey] IN ( 490, 479, 528, 379, 359, 332, 374, 597, 387,
                                484..[158 total values, not all displayed] );

SELECT
Product[Color]
FROM Product;
```

The WHERE condition that you see in the third storage engine queries might seem useless, because the DAX query does not apply a filter over products. However, in the real world usually you will have some other filter active on products or other tables. The query plan tries to extract only the quantities sold of products that are relevant to the query, lowering the size of the datacache returned to the formula engine. When you see a similar WHERE condition in the storage engine, the only concern is the size of the bitmap index moved back and forth between the formula engine and the storage engine.

> **Note** Different versions of the DAX engine might generate different patterns of the filters. In particular, updated versions of the engine released in products newer than Analysis Services 2014 might generate a special subclass of events in the profiler (Batch VertiPaq Scan), which defines temporary tables in the storage engine reducing the number of cases where this list of values returns to the formula engine for further processing.

Regardless of the technique used to retrieve the values from the storage engine, the formula engine has to group all the products belonging to each color. The performance of this join performed at the formula engine level depends mainly on the number of products, and secondarily on the number of colors. Once again, the size of a datacache is the first and most important element to consider when you look for a performance bottleneck in the formula engine. In this case, the optimization is using a relationship, or reducing the number of rows to consider in the join.

Analyzing complex and longer query plans would require another book, even for the length of the query plans involved. More details about the internals of the query plans are available in the white papers "Understanding DAX Query Plans" (*http://www.sqlbi.com/articles/understanding-dax-query-plans/*) and "Understanding Distinct Count in DAX Query Plans" (*http://www.sqlbi.com/articles/understanding-distinct-count-in-dax-query-plans/*).

CHAPTER 16

Optimizing DAX

This is the last chapter of the book and it is time to use all the knowledge you have gained so far to approach the most fascinating topic about DAX: optimizing formulas. You learned how the VertiPaq engine works, how to read a query plan and the internals of the formula engine and the storage engine. Now all the pieces are in place and you are ready to learn how to use that information to write fast code.

However, before approaching this chapter, there is one very important warning. Do not expect to learn best practices or a simple way to write fast code. Simply stated: there is no way in DAX to write code that is always the fastest. The speed of a DAX formula depends on many factors, the most important of which, unfortunately, is not in DAX code: It is data distribution. You already learned that VertiPaq compression strongly depends on data distribution. The size of a column (hence, the speed to scan it) depends on its cardinality: the larger, the slower. Thus, the very same formula might behave differently when executed on one column or another.

You will learn how to measure the speed of a formula and we will provide you with several examples where rewriting the expression in a different way leads to a faster execution time. Learn all these examples for what they are: examples that might help you in finding new ideas for your code. Do not take them as golden rules, because they are not.

We are not teaching you rules, we are trying to teach you how to find your own rules, in the very special scenario that is your data model. Be prepared to change them when the data model changes or when you approach a new customer. Flexibility is necessary when optimizing DAX code: flexibility, a deep technical knowledge of the engine and a good amount of madness, to be prepared to test formulas and expressions that are far from being intuitive.

Finally, all the information we provide in this book is valid at the time of printing. New versions of the engine come on the market frequently and the development team is always working on making the code better. So be prepared to measure different numbers in the version of the engine you will be running and, if this happens, be prepared to use different optimization methods. If, one day, you measure your code and reach the educated conclusion that "Marco and Alberto are wrong, this code runs much faster than their suggested one," that will be our brightest day, because we would have been able to teach you all what we know, and you are moving forward in writing better DAX code than ours.

Defining optimization strategy

The optimization process for a DAX query, expression, or measure, requires a strategy to reproduce a performance issue, identify the bottleneck, and remove it. Initially, you always observe a slowness in a complex query, but optimizing a complicated expression including several DAX measures is more involved than optimizing one measure at a time. For this reason, the approach we suggest is to isolate the slowest measure or expression first, optimizing it in a simpler query that can reproduce the issue with a shorter query plan.

This is a simple to-do list you should follow every time you want to optimize DAX:

1. Identify a single DAX expression to optimize.

2. Create a query that reproduces the issue.

3. Analyze server timings and query plan information.

4. Identify bottlenecks in the storage engine or formula engine.

5. Implement changes and rerun the test query.

You can see a more complete description of each of these steps in the following sections.

Identifying a single DAX expression to optimize

If you already know the slowest measure in your data model, you probably can skip this section and move to the following one. However, it is common to identify a performance issue initially in a report that might generate several queries, and in each of these queries, you might have several measures. The first step is to identify a single DAX expression to optimize, reducing the reproduction to a single query and possibly to a single measure exposed in the result.

A complete refresh of a report in Reporting Services, in Power View, in Power BI, or of a complete Microsoft Excel workbook, might generate more queries in either DAX or MDX (pivot tables and charts in Excel always generate the latter). When you have a complex report with many queries, you have to identify the slowest query. In general, you can optimize one query at a time, so you should reduce the optimization scope to a single query. Depending on the report source, you can measure the refresh time of each single object, or you have to collect Query End events in SQL Server Profiler and find the slowest one.

If you are using Excel, you might easily identify a single pivot table having a slow refresh time. Excel always generates MDX queries, which benefit from a formula engine cache that is not available for all the DAX expressions. This means that the simple refresh operation of a pivot table could be fast because of the MDX cache hiding an underlying performance issue in a DAX measure defined in the data model. In order to identify this, you should clear the cache before the refresh request by using the Clear Cache command in DAX Studio (which can work with Power Pivot, Power BI Desktop, and Analysis Services Tabular). If you cannot easily clear the cache, you can also try to navigate the pivot table, always choosing a different filter, and/or requesting a drill-down in a different hierarchy path. Once you identify the pivot table with low performance, you can extract the MDX query it generates by using OLAP PivotTable Extensions, a free Excel add-in available at *http://olappivottableextend. codeplex.com/*.

Once you extract the DAX or MDX query that contains the expression to optimize (which is the internal definition of a DAX measure in case you have an MDX query), you have to identify and isolate such a DAX expression, so that you will concentrate your effort on the right area. If you are using a dynamic environment (such as a pivot table in Excel, or the canvas of a Power View or Power BI report), the easiest way is to try the report with just one measure at a time, until you clearly identify the slowest one. When this is not easy or not possible, you can reduce the measures included in a query by modifying and executing it interactively in DAX Studio.

For example, consider the following DAX query generated by Power BI using a table result with four expressions (two sums and two averages) grouped by product color:

```
EVALUATE
TOPN (
    102,
    SUMMARIZECOLUMNS (
        ROLLUPADDISSUBTOTAL ( 'Product'[Color], "IsGrandTotalRowTotal" ),
        "SumQuantity", CALCULATE ( SUM ( 'Sales'[Quantity] ) ),
        "SumNet_Price", CALCULATE ( SUM ( 'Sales'[Net Price] ) ),
        "AverageUnit_Cost", CALCULATE ( AVERAGE ( 'Sales'[Unit Cost] ) ),
        "AverageUnit_Discount", CALCULATE ( AVERAGE ( 'Sales'[Unit Discount] ) )
    ),
    [IsGrandTotalRowTotal],
    0,
    'Product'[Color],
    1
)
ORDER BY
    [IsGrandTotalRowTotal] DESC, 'Product'[Color]
```

You should reduce the query by trying one calculation at a time, to locate the slower one. In this specific case, it is enough to comment or remove three of the four columns calculated in the *SUMMA-RIZECOLUMNS* function (*SumQuantity*, *SumNet_Price*, *AverageUnit_Cost*, and *AverageUnit_Discount*), finding the slowest one before proceeding. We captured this query using SQL Profiler, because we do not have a way to intercept the DAX measure generated by Power Query directly in DAX Studio.

Note You can connect SQL Profiler to Power BI Desktop and intercept all the Query End events. In order to do that, you need to know the local port used by a local instance of Analysis Services managed by Power BI Desktop. If you connect DAX Studio to Power BI Desktop, you can see such a number in the lower-right corner of the DAX Studio windows once you open the connection. The name is *localhost:<port number>*, where <port number> corresponds to an integer number that is different every time you open a new window with Power BI Desktop. When you run a trace with SQL Profiler, use this complete name (including the port number) as the server name.

Another example is the following MDX query generated by the pivot table in Excel as seen in Figure 16-1 (remember you can extract this query using the OLAP PivotTable Extension add-in):

```
SELECT
{ [Measures].[Sales Amount], [Measures].[Sales Rows] }
DIMENSION PROPERTIES PARENT_UNIQUE_NAME, MEMBER_VALUE, HIERARCHY_UNIQUE_NAME ON COLUMNS,
NON EMPTY Hierarchize ( DrilldownMember (
    { { DrilldownLevel ( { [Date].[Calendar].[All] } }, , , INCLUDE_CALC_MEMBERS ) } },
    { [Date].[Calendar].[Year].&[CY 2008] }, , , INCLUDE_CALC_MEMBERS ) )
DIMENSION PROPERTIES PARENT_UNIQUE_NAME, MEMBER_VALUE, HIERARCHY_UNIQUE_NAME ON ROWS
FROM [Model]
CELL PROPERTIES VALUE, FORMAT_STRING, LANGUAGE, BACK_COLOR, FORE_COLOR, FONT_FLAGS
```

Row Labels	Sales Amount	Sales Rows
⊞ CY 2007	$1,617,722.61	3,964
⊟ CY 2008	$1,242,993.34	3,597
⊞ January 2008	$75,509.78	257
⊞ February 2008	$68,983.60	268
⊞ March 2008	$72,303.96	259
⊞ April 2008	$127,865.28	314
⊞ May 2008	$131,204.65	317
⊞ June 2008	$97,021.46	300
⊞ July 2008	$95,825.35	337
⊞ August 2008	$152,927.10	299
⊞ September 2008	$122,900.05	296
⊞ October 2008	$61,768.48	290
⊞ November 2008	$132,871.85	324
⊞ December 2008	$103,811.78	336
⊞ CY 2009	$1,359,201.95	4,974
Grand Total	$4,219,917.90	12,535

FIGURE 16-1 Simple pivot table in Excel that generates an MDX query with two measures.

You can reduce the measures either in the pivot table or directly in the MDX code. You can manipulate the MDX code by reducing the list of measures included within braces. For example, you reduce the code to only the *Sales Amount* measure by modifying the list, as in the following initial part of the query:

```
SELECT
{ [Measures].[Sales Amount] }
DIMENSION PROPERTIES PARENT_UNIQUE_NAME, MEMBER_VALUE, HIERARCHY_UNIQUE_NAME ON COLUMNS,
...
```

Regardless of the technique you use, once you identify the DAX expression (or measure) that is responsible for a performance issue, you need a reproduction query to use in DAX Studio.

Creating a reproduction query

The optimization process requires a query that you can execute several times, possibly changing the definition of the measure in order to evaluate different performances. From this point of view, it is important to know how to define a measure that is local to the query, overriding the definition of the same measure in the data model.

If you captured a query in DAX or MDX, you already have a good starting point for the reproduction (repro) query. You should try to simplify the query as much as you can, so that it will be easier to find the bottleneck. You only have to keep a complex query structure when it is fundamental to observe the performance issue.

In simpler cases, when a measure is constantly slow, you should be able to create a repro query producing a single value as a result. Using *CALCULATE* or *CALCULATETABLE* you can apply all the filters you need. For example, you can execute the *Sales Amount* measure for April 2008 using the following code, obtaining the same result ($127,865.28) you see in Figure 16-1 for that month:

```
EVALUATE
ROW (
    "Result", CALCULATE (
        [Sales Amount],
        'Date'[Calendar Year] = "CY 2008",
        'Date'[Calendar Year Month] = "April 2008"
    )
)
```

You can also write the previous query using *CALCULATETABLE* instead of *CALCULATE*:

```
EVALUATE
CALCULATETABLE (
    ROW ( "Result", [Sales Amount] ),
    'Date'[Calendar Year] = "CY 2008",
    'Date'[Calendar Year Month] = "April 2008"
)
```

The two approaches produce the same result. You should consider *CALCULATETABLE* when the query you use to test the measure is more complex than a simple *ROW* function.

Once you have a repro for a specific measure defined in the data model, you should consider writing the DAX expression of the measure as a local one in the query, using the *MEASURE* syntax. For example, you can transform the previous repro in the following one:

```
DEFINE
    MEASURE Sales[Sales Amount] = SUMX ( Sales, Sales[Quantity] * Sales[Unit Price] )
EVALUATE
CALCULATETABLE (
    ROW ( "Result", [Sales Amount] ),
    'Date'[Calendar Year] = "CY 2008",
    'Date'[Calendar Year Month] = "April 2008"
)
```

At this point, you can apply changes to the DAX expression assigned to the measure directly into the query statement. In this way, you do not have to deploy a change to the data model before executing the query again. You can change the query, clear the cache, and run the query in DAX Studio, immediately measuring the performance results of the modified expression.

In certain conditions, you have to use an MDX query to reproduce a problem that happens only in MDX and not in DAX. The same DAX measure, executed in a DAX or in an MDX query, generates different query plans, and it might show a different behavior depending on the language of the query. However, also in this case you can define the DAX measure local to the query, so that it is more efficient to change and run again. For instance, you can define the *Sales Amount* measure local to the MDX query using the *WITH MEASURE* syntax:

```
WITH
    MEASURE Sales[Sales Amount] = SUMX ( Sales, Sales[Quantity] * Sales[Unit Price] )
SELECT
{ [Measures].[Sales Amount], [Measures].[Sales Rows] }
DIMENSION PROPERTIES PARENT_UNIQUE_NAME, MEMBER_VALUE, HIERARCHY_UNIQUE_NAME ON COLUMNS,
NON EMPTY Hierarchize ( DrilldownMember (
    { { DrilldownLevel ( { [Date].[Calendar].[All] }, , , INCLUDE_CALC_MEMBERS ) } },
    { [Date].[Calendar].[Year].&[CY 2008] }, , , INCLUDE_CALC_MEMBERS ) )
DIMENSION PROPERTIES PARENT_UNIQUE_NAME, MEMBER_VALUE, HIERARCHY_UNIQUE_NAME ON ROWS
FROM [Model]
CELL PROPERTIES VALUE, FORMAT_STRING, LANGUAGE, BACK_COLOR, FORE_COLOR, FONT_FLAGS
```

As you see, in MDX you have to use *WITH* instead of *DEFINE*; The following syntax for *MEASURE* is identical in both cases, and you will follow the same optimization process. Regardless of the repro language (either DAX or MDX), you always have a DAX expression to optimize, which you can define within a local *MEASURE* definition.

Analyzing server timings and query plan information

Once you have a repro, you have to run it and collect information about execution time and query plan. You have seen in Chapter 15, "Analyzing DAX query plans," how to read the information provided by SQL Server Profiler, and how to use DAX Studio to collect the same information in an easier way. In this section, you will see how to analyze a simple query in DAX Studio, so that you can spend more time interpreting data instead of collecting it.

For example, consider the following DAX query:

```
DEFINE
    MEASURE Sales[Sales Amount] = SUMX ( Sales, Sales[Quantity] * Sales[Unit Price] )
EVALUATE
ADDCOLUMNS (
    VALUES ( 'Date'[Calendar Year] ),
    "Result", [Sales Amount]
)
```

If you execute this query in DAX Studio after you cleared the cache and enabled Query Plan and Server Timings, you obtain a result with one row for each year in the Date table, and the total of Sales Amount for sales made in that year. The starting point for an analysis is always the Server Timings pane, which displays information about the entire query, as you can see in Figure 16-2.

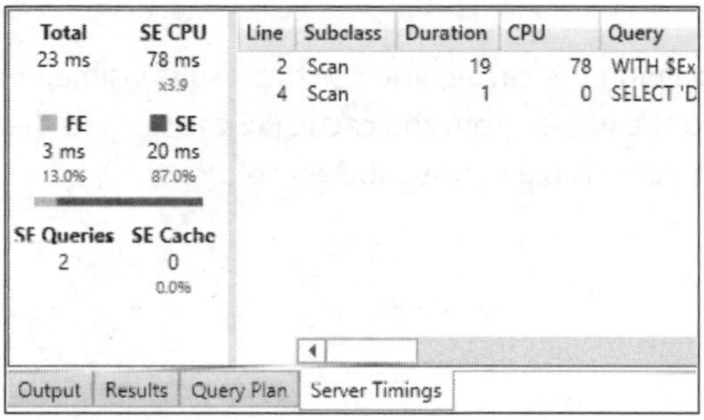

FIGURE 16-2 Server Timings pane after simple query execution.

Our query returned the result in 23 ms (Total), and it spent 87 percent of this time in the storage engine (SE), whereas the formula engine (FE) used only 3 ms of the total time. This pane does not provide much information about the formula engine internals, but it is rich in more details for storage engine activity. For example, there were two storage engine queries (SE Queries), that consumed a total of 78 ms of processing time (SE CPU). The CPU time can be larger than Duration thanks to the parallelism of the storage engine. In fact, the engine used 78 ms of cores working in parallel, so that the duration time is a fraction of that number. The hardware used in this test had 8 cores, and the parallelism degree of this query (ratio between SE CPU and SE) is 3.9. You cannot reach a parallelism higher than the number of cores you have.

In Table 16-1 you can see the way we will represent these same counters in this chapter. We will use such a compact representation to simplify comparison between different executions and to put more content in the available pages.

TABLE 16-1 Server Timings counters corresponding to data shown in Figure 16-2.

Total	FE	SE	SE CPU	SE Queries
23	3 (13%)	20 (87%)	78	2

The storage engine queries are available in the list, and you can see that a single storage engine operation (the first one) consumes the entire duration and CPU time. By enabling the display of Internal and Cache subclass events, you can see in Figure 16-3 that the two storage engine queries were actually executed by the storage engine.

Total	SE CPU	Line	Subclass	Duration	CPU	Query
23 ms	78 ms	1	Internal	19	78	WITH $Exp
	x3.9	2	Scan	19	78	WITH $Exp
▦ FE	▪ SE	3	Internal	0	0	SELECT 'D
3 ms	20 ms	4	Scan	1	0	SELECT 'D
13.0%	87.0%					
SE Queries	SE Cache					
2	0					
	0.0%					

| Output | Results | Query Plan | Server Timings |

FIGURE 16-3 Server Timings pane with internal subclass events visible.

If you execute the same query again without clearing the cache, you see the results visible in Figure 16-4. Both storage engine queries retrieved the values from the cache (SE cache), and the single storage engine queries resolved in the cache are visible in the Subclass column.

Total	SE CPU	Line	Subclass	Duration	CPU	Query
3 ms	0 ms	1	Cache	0	0	WITH $Exp
	x0.0	2	Scan	0	0	WITH $Exp
▦ FE	▪ SE	3	Cache	0	0	SELECT 'D
3 ms	0 ms	4	Scan	0	0	SELECT 'D
100.0%	0.0%					
SE Queries	SE Cache					
2	2					
	100.0%					

| Output | Results | Query Plan | Server Timings |

FIGURE 16-4 Server Timings pane with cache subclass events visible, after second execution of the same DAX query.

Usually we will use the repro with a cold cache (clearing the cache before the execution), but in some cases it is important to evaluate whether a given DAX expression can leverage the cache in a following request or not. For this reason, the Cache visualization in DAX Studio is disabled by default and you enable it on request.

At this point, you can start looking at the query plans. In Figure 16-5 you see the physical and logical query plans of the query used in the previous example.

The physical query plan is the one you will use more often. In the query of the previous example, there are two datacaches, one for each storage engine query. Every VertipaqResult row in the physical query plan consumes one of the datacaches available. However, you do not have a simple way to match the correspondence between a query plan operation and a datacache. You can infer the datacache by looking at the columns used in the operations requiring a VertipaqResult (the rows Spool_Iterator and SpoolLookup in Figure 16-5).

Line	Records	Physical Query Plan
1		AddColumns: IterPhyOp LogOp=AddColumns IterCols(0, 1)('Date'[Calendar Year], "[Result])
2	7	Spool_Iterator<SpoolIterator>: IterPhyOp LogOp=Scan_Vertipaq IterCols(0)('Date'[Calendar Year]) #Records=7 #KeyCols=143 #ValueCols=0
3	7	ProjectionSpool<ProjectFusion<>>: SpoolPhyOp #Records=7
4		VertipaqResult: IterPhyOp #FieldCols=1 #ValueCols=0
5	3	SpoolLookup: LookupPhyOp LogOp=Sum_Vertipaq LookupCols(0)('Date'[Calendar Year]) Double #Records=3 #KeyCols=143 #ValueCols=1 D(
6	3	ProjectionSpool<ProjectFusion<Sum>>: SpoolPhyOp #Records=3
7		VertipaqResult: IterPhyOp #FieldCols=1 #ValueCols=1

Line	Logical Query Plan
1	AddColumns: RelLogOp DependOnCols()() 0-1 RequiredCols(0, 1)('Date'[Calendar Year], "[Result])
2	Scan_Vertipaq: RelLogOp DependOnCols()() 0-0 RequiredCols(0)('Date'[Calendar Year])
3	Sum_Vertipaq: ScaLogOp DependOnCols(0)('Date'[Calendar Year]) Double DominantValue=BLANK
4	Scan_Vertipaq: RelLogOp DependOnCols(0)('Date'[Calendar Year]) 1-134 RequiredCols(0, 107, 108)('Date'[Calendar Year], 'Sales'[Quantity], 'Sales'[Unit Pri
5	Multiply: ScaLogOp DependOnCols(107, 108)('Sales'[Quantity], 'Sales'[Unit Price]) Double DominantValue=NONE
6	'Sales'[Quantity]: ScaLogOp DependOnCols(107)('Sales'[Quantity]) Integer DominantValue=NONE
7	'Sales'[Unit Price]: ScaLogOp DependOnCols(108)('Sales'[Unit Price]) Double DominantValue=NONE

FIGURE 16-5 Query Plan pane showing physical and logical query plan.

An important piece of information you see in the physical query plan is the column showing the number of records processed. As you will see, when optimizing bottlenecks in the formula engine it could be useful to identify the slowest operation in the formula engine by searching for the line with the largest number of records. You can sort the rows by clicking the *Records* column header, as you see in Figure 16-6. You restore the original sort order by clicking *Line* column header.

Line	Records	Physical Query Plan
2	7	Spool_Iterator<SpoolIterator>: IterPhyOp LogOp=Scan_Vertipaq IterCols(0)('Date'[Calendar Year]) #Records=7 #KeyCols=143 #ValueCols=0
3	7	ProjectionSpool<ProjectFusion<>>: SpoolPhyOp #Records=7
5	3	SpoolLookup: LookupPhyOp LogOp=Sum_Vertipaq LookupCols(0)('Date'[Calendar Year]) Double #Records=3 #KeyCols=143 #ValueCols=1 D(
6	3	ProjectionSpool<ProjectFusion<Sum>>: SpoolPhyOp #Records=3
1		AddColumns: IterPhyOp LogOp=AddColumns IterCols(0, 1)('Date'[Calendar Year], "[Result])
4		VertipaqResult: IterPhyOp #FieldCols=1 #ValueCols=0
7		VertipaqResult: IterPhyOp #FieldCols=1 #ValueCols=1

Line	Logical Query Plan
1	AddColumns: RelLogOp DependOnCols()() 0-1 RequiredCols(0, 1)('Date'[Calendar Year], "[Result])
2	Scan_Vertipaq: RelLogOp DependOnCols()() 0-0 RequiredCols(0)('Date'[Calendar Year])
3	Sum_Vertipaq: ScaLogOp DependOnCols(0)('Date'[Calendar Year]) Double DominantValue=BLANK
4	Scan_Vertipaq: RelLogOp DependOnCols(0)('Date'[Calendar Year]) 1-134 RequiredCols(0, 107, 108)('Date'[Calendar Year], 'Sales'[Quantity], 'Sales'[Unit Pri
5	Multiply: ScaLogOp DependOnCols(107, 108)('Sales'[Quantity], 'Sales'[Unit Price]) Double DominantValue=NONE
6	'Sales'[Quantity]: ScaLogOp DependOnCols(107)('Sales'[Quantity]) Integer DominantValue=NONE
7	'Sales'[Unit Price]: ScaLogOp DependOnCols(108)('Sales'[Unit Price]) Double DominantValue=NONE

FIGURE 16-6 Query Plan pane showing physical and logical query plans.

Identifying bottlenecks in the storage engine or formula engine

Usually a query has many possible optimizations. The first and most important decision is to identify whether a query spends most of the time in the formula engine or in the storage engine. You have a first indication in the percentages provided by DAX Studio for FE and SE. Usually this is a good starting point, but you also have to identify the distribution of the workload in both the formula engine and the storage engine. In complex queries, a large amount of time spent in the storage engine might correspond to a large number of small storage engine queries, or in a small number of storage engine queries that concentrate the largest amount of workload. As you will see, these differences require different approaches in optimization strategy.

When you identify the execution bottleneck of a query, you also have to prioritize the optimization areas. For example, you might have different inefficiencies in the query plan producing a large formula engine execution time. You should identify the most important one, and concentrate on that first. If you do not follow this approach, you might end up spending time optimizing an expression that affects the execution time in a marginal way only. Sometimes the more efficient optimizations are simple but hidden in unintuitive context transition or other details in DAX syntax. You should always measure execution time before and after each optimization attempt, making sure that you obtain a real advantage and are not just applying some optimization pattern you found on the web or in this book.

Finally, remember that even if you have an issue in the formula engine, you should always start your analysis by looking at the storage engine queries. They provide you with valuable information about content and size of the datacaches used by the formula engine. Reading the query plan that describes the operations made by the formula engine is a very complex process. It is easier to consider that the formula engine will use the content of datacaches and will have to do all the operations required to produce the result of a DAX query that has not been already produced by the storage engine. This approach is efficient especially for large and complex DAX queries, which might produce thousands of lines in a query plan, but a relatively small number of datacaches produced by storage engine queries.

Optimizing bottlenecks in the storage engine

A long execution time in the storage engine is usually the consequence of one or more of the following reasons (already explained in more detail in Chapter 15):

- **Long scan time**   Even for a simple aggregation, a DAX query has to scan one or more columns. The cost for this scan depends on the size of the column, which depends on the number of unique values and data distribution. Different columns in the same table can have very different execution times.

- **Large cardinality**   A large number of unique values in a column affects the *DISTINCTCOUNT* calculation and filter arguments of a *CALCULATE* statement.

- **High frequency of *CallbackDataID***   A large number of calls made by the storage engine to the formula engine can affect the overall performance of a query.

- **Large materialization**   If a storage engine query produces a large datacache, its generation requires time (allocating and writing RAM). Moreover, its consumption (made by the formula engine) is also another potential bottleneck.

In the following sections, you will see several examples of optimizations at the storage engine level. Starting with the notion you learned in previous chapters, you will see a typical problem reproduced in a simpler query and optimized.

Choosing *ADDCOLUMNS* vs. *SUMMARIZE*

A best practice writing DAX expressions is to use *SUMMARIZE* only to do joins between tables, using it as a way to obtain the result of an equivalent *SELECT DISTINCT* syntax in SQL, without using the aggregation features available in *SUMMARIZE*. In order to aggregate data, you should use *ADDCOLUMNS* and a context transition to aggregate only the desired group of rows. You can find a longer discussion at *http://www.sqlbi.com/articles/best-practices-using-summarize-and-addcolumns/.* However, it is important to understand how you can realize that the optimization is possible by analyzing the query plan and server timings information.

Consider the following DAX query:

```
DEFINE
    MEASURE Sales[Sales Amount] = SUMX ( Sales, Sales[Quantity] * Sales[Unit Price] )
EVALUATE
SUMMARIZE (
    Sales,
    'Product Category'[Category],
    "Sales", [Sales Amount]
)
```

The result is a table with one row for each product category and two columns: the *Category* of products and the *Sales Amount* for each category. The server timings pane provides the information in Table 16-2.

TABLE 16-2 Timing of a query using *SUMMARIZE* to group and aggregate data.

Query	Total	FE	SE	SE CPU	SE Queries
Summarize	63	7 (11%)	59 (89%)	297	2

The bottleneck is the storage engine (89 percent), and drilling down you see that the second storage engine query executes a request similar to the first one (see the two events in Table 16-3). The difference is that the second SE query has an higher cardinality.

TABLE 16-3 VertiPaq Scan events for query based on *SUMMARIZE* only (with simplified xmSQL code).

Line	Subclass	Duration	CPU	Query (xmSQL)
2	Scan	37	172	SELECT 'Product Category'[Category], SUM (Sales[Quantity] * Sales[Unit Price]) FROM Sales LEFT JOIN Product LEFT JOIN 'Product Subcategory' LEFT JOIN 'Product Category';
4	Scan	19	125	SELECT 'Product Category'[Category], Sales[ProductKey] FROM Sales LEFT JOIN Product LEFT JOIN 'Product Subcategory' LEFT JOIN 'Product Category';

The first datacache has one row for every product category and two columns, *Category* and *Sales*. This corresponds to the cardinality of the expected result from the DAX query. The second datacache provides a list of products used in the Sales table and two columns, *ProductKey* and *Category*. The number of rows provided by this datacache is larger: 2,516 instead of 8 in the example. You can retrieve the exact number from the physical query plan (see the following example), looking at the number of records processed by operations (ProjectionSpool) consuming results from VertipaqResult:

```
Line    Records  Physical Query Plan
1                AddColumns: IterPhyOp LogOp=AddColumns IterCols(0, 1) ...
2       8           Spool_Iterator<SpoolIterator>: IterPhyOp ...
3       8             AggregationSpool<GroupBy>: SpoolPhyOp #Records=8
4       2516            Spool_Iterator<SpoolIterator>: IterPhyOp ...
5       2516              ProjectionSpool<ProjectFusion<>>: SpoolPhyOp  ...
6                           VertipaqResult: IterPhyOp #FieldCols=2 #ValueCols=0
7       8         SpoolLookup: LookupPhyOp LogOp=Sum_Vertipaq ...
8       8           ProjectionSpool<ProjectFusion<Sum>>: SpoolPhyOp #Records=8
9                     VertipaqResult: IterPhyOp #FieldCols=1 #ValueCols=1
```

When a datacache is several orders of magnitude larger than the DAX query result, you should investigate the possible optimizations. For instance, in this case we can apply the best practice of using *ADDCOLUMNS* instead of *SUMMARIZE* to aggregate data, keeping *SUMMARIZE* to obtain the list of categories used in the Sales table.

```
DEFINE
    MEASURE Sales[Sales Amount] = SUMX ( Sales, Sales[Quantity] * Sales[Unit Price] )
EVALUATE
ADDCOLUMNS (
    SUMMARIZE ( Sales, 'Product Category'[Category] ),
    "Sales", [Sales Amount]
)
```

As you see in Table 16-4, we obtain a slightly better performance result.

TABLE 16-4 Timing of a query using *ADDCOLUMNS* and *SUMMARIZE* to group and aggregate data.

Query	Total	FE	SE	SE CPU	SE Queries
Addcolumns	54	5 (9%)	49 (92%)	266	2

You see in Table 16-5 the details of the storage engine queries.

TABLE 16-5 VertiPaq Scan events for a query based on *ADDCOLUMNS* and *SUMMARIZE*.

Line	Subclass	Duration	CPU	Query (xmSQL)
2	Scan	38	188	SELECT 'Product Category'[Category], SUM (Sales[Quantity] * Sales[Unit Price]) FROM Sales LEFT JOIN Product LEFT JOIN 'Product Subcategory' LEFT JOIN 'Product Category';
4	Scan	11	78	SELECT 'Product Category'[Category] FROM Sales LEFT JOIN Product LEFT JOIN 'Product Subcategory' LEFT JOIN 'Product Category';

As you can see in the following physical query plan, the two datacaches have the same number of rows as a result (eight records), but a different number of columns. The first datacache has two columns, (*Category* and *Sales*), whereas the second datacache has one column only (*Category*).

```
Line    Records   Physical Query Plan
1                 AddColumns: IterPhyOp LogOp=AddColumns IterCols(0, 1)
2       8             Spool_Iterator<SpoolIterator>: IterPhyOp
3       8                 ProjectionSpool<ProjectFusion<>>: SpoolPhyOp #Records=8
4                             VertipaqResult: IterPhyOp #FieldCols=1 #ValueCols=0
5       8             SpoolLookup: LookupPhyOp LogOp=Sum_Vertipaq
6       8                 ProjectionSpool<ProjectFusion<Sum>>: SpoolPhyOp #Records=8
7                             VertipaqResult: IterPhyOp #FieldCols=1 #ValueCols=1
```

The formula engine receives two datasets that have the same cardinality (eight records) as the result. However, we still have a large amount of time spent in the storage engine, and it seems useless to execute two scans of the Sales table. One possible approach is avoiding the *SUMMARIZE* operation, adding a *FILTER* that removes empty rows from the result.

```
DEFINE
    MEASURE Sales[Sales Amount] =
        SUMX ( Sales, Sales[Quantity] * Sales[Unit Price] )
EVALUATE
FILTER (
    ADDCOLUMNS (
        VALUES ( 'Product Category'[Category] ),
        "Sales", [Sales Amount]
    ),
    NOT ISBLANK ( [Sales] )
)
```

You obtain a 20 percent performance improvement, as you see in the total execution time shown in Table 16-6.

TABLE 16-6 Timing of a query using *FILTER*, *ADDCOLUMNS*, and *VALUES*.

Query	Total	FE	SE	SE CPU	SE Queries
Filter	45	5 (11%)	40 (89%)	234	2

As you see in Table 16-7, the elimination of the scan on the Sales table in the second storage engine query produced the performance improvement. This approach is efficient because the number of rows (unique values in *Category*) is relatively small. In this case, this results in a materialization of the same number of rows, but it depends on data distribution, because now you materialize all the categories, regardless of their usage in the Sales table. In a different case, with a complex Sales measure and a large number of categories, the performance result could be worse than the previous one. You always have to consider the cardinality of the operations involved and the possible occurrence of materialization.

TABLE 16-7 VertiPaq Scan events for query based on *ADDCOLUMNS* and *SUMMARIZE*.

Line	Subclass	Duration	CPU	Query (xmSQL)
2	Scan	39	234	SELECT 'Product Category'[Category], SUM (Sales[Quantity] * Sales[Unit Price]) FROM Sales LEFT JOIN Product LEFT JOIN 'Product Subcategory' LEFT JOIN 'Product Category';
4	Scan	1	0	SELECT 'Product Category'[Category] FROM 'Product Category'

If you are using a recent version of DAX, you can simplify the query by using *SUMMARIZECOLUMNS*, which removes the need of a second storage engine query. For example, consider the following DAX query:

```
DEFINE
    MEASURE Sales[Sales Amount] =
        SUMX ( Sales, Sales[Quantity] * Sales[Unit Price] )
EVALUATE
SUMMARIZECOLUMNS (
    'Product Category'[Category],
    "Sales", [Sales Amount]
)
```

It produces the server timings shown in Table 16-8.

TABLE 16-8 Timing of a query using *SUMMARIZECOLUMNS*.

Query	Total	FE	SE	SE CPU	SE Queries
SummarizeColumns	39	4 (10%)	35 (90%)	234	1

As you see also in Table 16-9, there is only one storage engine query in this case, obtaining better performance in all of the conditions.

TABLE 16-9 VertiPaq Scan events for a query based on *SUMMARIZECOLUMNS*.

Line	Subclass	Duration	CPU	Query (xmSQL)
2	Scan	35	234	SELECT 'Product Category'[Category], SUM (Sales[Quantity] * Sales[Unit Price]) FROM Sales LEFT JOIN Product LEFT JOIN 'Product Subcategory' LEFT JOIN 'Product Category';

The improvement is visible also in the query plan, which has a simple scan of the single datacache produced by the storage engine query.

```
Line    Records  Physical Query Plan
1                GroupSemijoin: IterPhyOp LogOp=GroupSemiJoin IterCols(0, 1) ...
2       8            Spool_Iterator<SpoolIterator>: IterPhyOp
3       8                ProjectionSpool<ProjectFusion<>>: SpoolPhyOp #Records=8
4                        VertipaqResult: IterPhyOp #FieldCols=1 #ValueCols=1
```

The goal of this section was to introduce you to the analysis of query plans and server timings, in order to understand the behavior of different DAX queries. You should practice this exercise with your own queries, trying to understand all the steps executed by the engine in order to produce the result. Only with this knowledge will you be able to identify the more expensive part of an expression, trying to optimize it by changing the syntax and/or the calculation logic.

Reducing *CallbackDataID* impact

You have seen in Chapter 15 that the *CallbackDataID* function in a storage engine query can have a huge performance impact, because it slows down storage engine execution, and it disables the use of the storage engine cache for the datacache produced. Identifying the *CallbackDataID* is important, because this is often the reason of a bottleneck in the storage engine, especially for models that have only a few million rows in the largest table (scan time should be typically in the order of magnitude of 10–100 milliseconds).

For example, consider the following query, where the Sales Amount computes its result rounding *Unit Price* to the nearest integer.

```
DEFINE
    MEASURE Sales[Sales Amount] =
        SUMX (
            Sales,
            Sales[Quantity] * ROUND ( Sales[Unit Price], 0 )
        )
EVALUATE
ADDCOLUMNS (
    VALUES ( Product[Color] ),
    "Sales", [Sales Amount]
)
```

You can see in Table 16-10 that the execution time of this query is slow, especially considering that the Sales table has only 12 million rows.

TABLE 16-10 Timing of a query using *ROUND*.

Query	Total	FE	SE	SE CPU	SE Queries
Simple Round	401	4 (1%)	397 (99%)	2,391	2

A single storage engine query is responsible for the slow performance.

```
SELECT 'Product[Color]',
       SUM ( Sales[Quantity] ) * [CallbackDataID ( ROUND ( Sales[Unit Price], 0 ) )] )
FROM Sales
LEFT JOIN Product ON Sales[ProductKey] = Product[ProductKey]
```

Even if the resulting datacache has only a few rows (one for each product color), the storage engine calls the formula engine more than 12 million times, one for each row in the Sales table. This happens in multiple threads, because every segment has one million rows in the example used, so the duration would be higher on a server with a lower number of cores.

You might consider creating a calculated column in the Sales table to store the result of *ROUND* function for every row. This is certainly a good approach, because it removes the need for a *CallbackDataID* call at run time. However, this comes at the cost of memory usage and it could be too high, or simply not worth the effort, especially if there are other optimizations available. Instead of completely removing the need of *CallbackDataID*, we can try to reduce the number of calls.

The Sales table has a cardinality of more than 12 million rows, but the number of unique values in the *Unit Price* column is less than 500. So why call *ROUND* more than once for each unique value in the *Unit Price* column? You reduce the execution time rewriting the code in a way that reduces the number of calls to the *ROUND* function to the minimum required.

 Note You should always use statistics of the data model during DAX optimization. A quick way to obtain these numbers for a data model is using VertiPaq Analyzer (*http://www.sqlbi.com/tools/vertipaq-analyzer/*).

At first sight, the following query looks very inefficient, because it contains two nested iterators over columns of the same table. The logic is to multiply the Unit Price by the sum of the Quantity for all the rows in Sales with the same unit price. *CALCULATE* applies a context transition that automatically filters the rows with the same unit price value.

```
DEFINE
    MEASURE Sales[Sales Amount] =
        SUMX (
            VALUES ( Sales[Unit Price] ),
            ROUND ( Sales[Unit Price], 0 )
                * CALCULATE ( SUM ( Sales[Quantity] ) )
        )
EVALUATE
ADDCOLUMNS (
    VALUES ( Product[Color] ),
    "Sales", [Sales Amount]
)
```

The initial idea is that the overhead of the double loop may be less expensive than 12 million *ROUND* invocations. As usual, you have to measure the performance in order to validate the hypothesis. The numbers in Table 16-11 show that the duration is 90 percent smaller than in the previous version.

TABLE 16-11 Timing of a query by reducing the number of *ROUND* invocations.

Query	Total	FE	SE	SE CPU	SE Queries
Optimized Round	36	7 (19%)	29 (81%)	172	2

The formula engine executes the external iterator (*SUMX*), whereas the storage engine only aggregates the quantity value for each combination of product color and unit price, as you see in the following xmSQL query. For each row of this datacache, the formula engine will call the *ROUND* function directly, passing the *Unit Price* as an argument. In this way, there will be no *CallbackDataID* required.

```
SELECT 'Product[Color]', Sales[Unit Price], SUM ( Sales[Quantity] )
FROM Sales
LEFT JOIN Product ON Sales[ProductKey] = Product[ProductKey]
```

The storage engine query has now increased the datacache, which returns 1,600 rows (one for each existing combination of color and unit price), instead of 16 rows (one for each color). You can imagine that applying this same technique to another data model might worsen the performance. For example, a materialization of millions of rows would be more expensive than an equivalent number of *CallbackDataID* invocations.

Usually two or more nested iterators do not result in a single storage engine query, requiring materialization of data produced by the innermost iterators, so that the formula engine can complete the process. However, the best choice depends on data distribution and should be measured and evaluated on a case-by-case basis.

Finally, remember that most of the scalar DAX functions that do not aggregate data require a *CallbackDataID* if executed in an iterator. For example, *DATE*, *VALUE*, most of the type conversions, *IFERROR*, *DIVIDE*, and all of the rounding, mathematical, and date/time functions are all implemented in the formula engine only. Most of the time, their presence in an iterator generates a *CallbackDataID* invocation. However, you always have to check the xmSQL query to verify whether *CallbackDataID* is present or not.

CallbackDataID with constant values

Older versions of the DAX engine might not optimize evaluation of constant values within an iterator. For example, the following DAX expression invokes a *CallbackDataID* to *ROUND* for every row of the Sales table, even if the result is always the same:

```
SUMX ( Sales, ROUND ( 1.1, 0 ) * Sales[Quantity] )
```

Recent versions of the DAX engine optimize this calculation automatically. You should always check the xmSQL code of storage engine queries to verify whether it contains an invocation to DAX functions through *CallbackDataID* in expensive loops.

Optimizing filter conditions

Applying a filter condition in an iterator or in a filter argument of a *CALCULATE/CALCULATETABLE* function might provide a different performance depending on the version of the engine. For example, consider the following implementations of a special *Sales Amount* measure, which ignores a particular customer:

```
Sales[Sales Amount Calculate] :=
CALCULATE (
    SUMX ( Sales, Sales[Quantity] * Sales[Unit Price] ),
    Customer[Customer Code] <> "11954"
)

Sales[Sales Amount Filter] :=
SUMX (
    FILTER ( Sales, RELATED ( Customer[Customer Code] ) <> "11954" ),
    Sales[Quantity] * Sales[Unit Price]
)
```

The results are identical, whereas the query plan and the related storage engine queries might be different, depending on the version of the DAX engine used. In older versions of the DAX engine, the *Sales Amount Calculate* measure produces a storage engine query that receives a filter with a list of customers (all those with a *Customer Code* other than 11954), as you can see in the following example:

```
SELECT Product[Color], SUM ( Sales[Quantity] ) * Sales[Unit Price] )
FROM Sales
    LEFT OUTER JOIN Customer ON Sales[CustomerKey] = Customer[CustomerKey]
    LEFT OUTER JOIN Product ON Sales[ProductKey] = Product[ProductKey]
WHERE
    Customer[Customer Code] IN ( '11024', '11036', '11041', '11043', '11928', '11938',
'11954'..[18868 total values, not all displayed] )
```

In this case, applying a filter condition on a column that has millions of unique values can slow down execution of storage engine queries. If you use a *FILTER* statement over Sales instead of the *CALCULATE* statement, such as in *Sales Amount Filter* measure, the query plan includes the same logical condition, and you do not have to transfer a large filter back and forth between the formula engine and the storage engine.

```
SELECT Product[Color], SUM ( Sales[Quantity] ) * Sales[Unit Price] )
FROM Sales
    LEFT OUTER JOIN Customer ON Sales[CustomerKey] = Customer[CustomerKey]
    LEFT OUTER JOIN Product ON Sales[ProductKey] = Product[ProductKey]
WHERE Customer[Customer Code] <> '11954'
```

The performance of the two statements might be different depending on the number of rows in the Sales table and on the cardinality of the *Customer Code* column in the Customer table. For example, with 2 million customers and 10 million rows in Sales, the Sales Amount Filter measure is faster. However, recent versions of the DAX engine already optimize this condition. In general, it is a good idea to test these differences in a complex expression, because a different execution strategy for the two filters might be the result of complex query plans involving other conditions.

Optimizing *IF* conditions

An *IF* function is always executed by the formula engine. When you include *IF* within an iteration, you might see a *CallbackDataID* involved in the execution. Moreover, the engine might evaluate the arguments of the *IF* regardless of the result of the condition in the first argument. Even if the result is correct, you might pay the full cost of processing all the possible solutions. As usual, you can see different behaviors depending on the version of the DAX engine you use.

For example, consider the following DAX query:

```
DEFINE
    MEASURE Sales[Sales Amount] =
        SUMX (
            Sales,
            Sales[Quantity] * Sales[Unit Price]
                * IF ( Sales[Unit Price] > 10, 0.9, 1 )
        )
EVALUATE
ADDCOLUMNS (
    VALUES ( Product[Color] ),
    "Sales", [Sales Amount]
)
```

The *IF* statement executed in the iterator produces a storage engine query with a *CallbackDataID* call, as you see in the following xmSQL code:

```
SELECT 'Product[Color]',
       SUM ( Sales[Quantity] * Sales[Unit Price]
             * [CallbackDataID ( IF ( Sales[Unit Price] > 10, 0.9, 1 ) )] )
FROM Sales
LEFT JOIN Product ON Sales[ProductKey] = Product[ProductKey]
```

The iterator calls *CallbackDataID* for each row of the Sales table, producing the execution times shown in Table 16-12.

TABLE 16-12 Timing of a query using the *IF* condition in an iterator.

Query	Total	FE	SE	SE CPU	SE Queries
IF in iterator	140	5 (4%)	135 (96%)	734	2

In a similar case, you can try to split the original iterator in two different ones, filtering each one with the conditions of the *IF* statements, as in the following example:

```
DEFINE
    MEASURE Sales[Sales Amount] =
        CALCULATE (
            SUMX ( Sales, Sales[Quantity] * Sales[Unit Price] ) * 0.9,
            Sales[Unit Price] > 10
        )
        + CALCULATE (
            SUMX ( Sales, Sales[Quantity] * Sales[Unit Price] ) * 1,
            NOT ( Sales[Unit Price] > 10 )
        )
EVALUATE
ADDCOLUMNS (
    VALUES ( Product[Color] ),
    "Sales", [Sales Amount]
)
```

In this case, the result is a marginal optimization of the execution time, as you see in Table 16-13. The results might be different depending on the data model and on the version of the DAX engine.

TABLE 16-13 Timing of a query optimizing by unfolding the *IF* condition.

Query	Total	FE	SE	SE CPU	SE Queries
Unfolded IF	104	6 (6%)	98 (94%)	672	3

This approach requires more storage engine queries, which are hopefully faster because of the lack of *CallbackDataID* calls. In fact, the following two storage engine queries replace the previous one that was using *CallbackDataID*:

```
SELECT 'Product[Color]',
       SUM ( Sales[Quantity] * Sales[Unit Price] * 0.9 )
FROM Sales
LEFT JOIN Product ON Sales[ProductKey] = Product[ProductKey]
WHERE Sales[Unit Price] > 10

SELECT 'Product[Color]',
       SUM ( Sales[Quantity] * Sales[Unit Price] * 1 )
FROM Sales
LEFT JOIN Product ON Sales[ProductKey] = Product[ProductKey]
WHERE NOT ( Sales[Unit Price] > 10 )
```

This technique is particularly useful when an expensive operation is necessary only for a small fraction of the rows involved in an aggregation. It is also worth remembering that the filter condition may affect performance depending on the cardinality of the column filtered.

Note The *SWITCH* statement in DAX is similar to a series of nested *IF* functions, and can be optimized in a similar way. You can find a longer discussion and an example of that at *http://sqlblog.com/blogs/marco_russo/archive/2014/08/18/possible-switch-optimization-in-dax-powerpivot-dax-tabular.aspx.*

Optimizing cardinality

Reducing the cardinality of any iterator in a DAX expression is always a best practice. Sometimes you can reach this goal by changing the DAX expression without changing the result. You have to think in terms of columnar storage, and always consider data distribution for a specific data model. For this reason, you will see here different techniques to write the same condition. Performance might be different depending on cardinality of columns, on distribution of values across rows, and on the version of the DAX engine used.

For example, consider the following DAX query that applies a logical *OR* condition between values of two columns. The *Sales Filtered* measure only considers rows that have a *Unit Price* greater than 10, or a *Quantity* greater or equal than 2.

```
DEFINE
    MEASURE Sales[Sales Amount] =
        SUMX ( Sales, Sales[Quantity] * Sales[Unit Price] )
    MEASURE Sales[Sales Filtered] =
        CALCULATE (
            [Sales Amount],
            FILTER (
                Sales,
                OR ( Sales[Unit Price] > 10, Sales[Quantity] >= 2 )
            )
        )
EVALUATE
ADDCOLUMNS (
    VALUES ( Product[Color] ),
    "Sales", [Sales Filtered]
)
```

You can see the server timings of this query in Table 16-14.

TABLE 16-14 Timing of a calculation using a table filter.

Query	Total	FE	SE	SE CPU	SE Queries
Table filter	239	16 (8%)	219 (92%)	1,188	3

This calculation requires three storage engine queries that you can see in Table 16-15. The first one retrieves the value of *Sales Amount* (quantity multiplied by unit price) for each combination of product, quantity, and unit price. The second one generates a similar datacache that has the list of product key, quantity, and unit price for each product color. The materialization of these two datacaches requires 9,973 rows each. The last storage engine query gets the list of product colors to display in the result.

TABLE 16-15 VertiPaq Scan events for a query based on *SUMMARIZECOLUMNS*.

Line	Subclass	Duration	CPU	Query (xmSQL)
2	Scan	116	672	SELECT Sales[ProductKey], Sales[Quantity], Sales[Unit Price], SUM (Sales[Quantity] * Sales[Unit Price]) FROM Sales WHERE Sales[Unit Price] > 10 OR Sales[Quantity] >= 2

4	Scan	103	516	SELECT Product[Color], Product[ProductKey],
				        Sales[Quantity], Sales[Unit Price]
				FROM Sales
				   LEFT JOIN Product ON Sales[ProductKey] = Product[ProductKey]
				WHERE Sales[Unit Price] > 10 AND Sales[Quantity] >= 2

6	Scan	0	0	SELECT Product[Color] FROM Product

The bottleneck in this case is in the storage engine. Even if it splits the cost among three different queries (as you see in Table 16-15), the reason is the need of materializing two datacaches with a larger cardinality than the result (9,973 rows each of the first two storage engine queries), and for each one requiring a complete scan of the Sales table (with more than 12 million rows).

Having a filter on the entire Sales table seems to be the cause of the bottleneck for this DAX query. In this case, you cannot reduce the filter to a list of single column filters, because you have to apply a filter over two columns with an *OR* condition. However, you can reduce the cardinality of the filter by creating a table with just two columns, and then using this table as a filter argument in the *CALCULATE* function. You can obtain the table with the two columns to filter by using at least three different approaches: *SUMMARIZE*, *ALL*, and *CROSSJOIN/VALUES*. The following code shows these three variations of the *Sales Filtered* measure:

```
-- Filter two columns using SUMMARIZE
   MEASURE Sales[Sales Filtered] =
      CALCULATE (
         [Sales Amount],
         FILTER (
            SUMMARIZE ( Sales, Sales[Unit Price], Sales[Quantity] ),
            OR ( Sales[Unit Price] > 10, Sales[Quantity] >= 2 )
         )
      )

-- Filter two columns using ALL
   MEASURE Sales[Sales Filtered] =
      CALCULATE (
         [Sales Amount],
```

```
        FILTER (
            ALL ( Sales[Unit Price], Sales[Quantity] ),
            OR ( Sales[Unit Price] > 10, Sales[Quantity] >= 2 )
        )
    )

-- Filter two columns using CROSSJOIN/VALUES
    MEASURE Sales[Sales Filtered] =
        CALCULATE (
            [Sales Amount],
            FILTER (
                CROSSJOIN (
                    VALUES ( Sales[Unit Price] ),
                    VALUES ( Sales[Quantity] )
                ),
                OR ( Sales[Unit Price] > 10, Sales[Quantity] >= 2 )
            )
        )
```

In Table 16-16 you can see the performance results of these three measures applied to the original query.

TABLE 16-16 Timing of a calculation using three variations of *Sales Filtered* measure.

Query	Total	FE	SE	SE CPU	SE Queries
Summarize	82	7 (8%)	75 (92%)	375	2
All	76	5 (7%)	71 (93%)	406	2
CrossJoin	143	12 (8%)	131 (92%)	625	4

It is important to remember that you do not have to consider as a best practice what is the best choice for this specific model, which is the filter based on *ALL*, even if *SUMMARIZE* in this case is very close. You might see that in other scenarios the *CROSSJOIN* option is the more efficient one, even if it is the worst in the previous example. The best choice depends on the context of the query and on data distribution of each specific model.

Optimizing nested iterators

As we have already mentioned in this chapter, nested iterators can be dangerous for performance, especially when there is a context transition between the two iterators. This condition seems simple to recognize and to avoid. In reality, it is one of the most common performance issues found in our engagements for performance optimization. The reason is that calculations split in different measures may hide this simple problem.

First, it is useful to observe the issue in a trivial case. Consider the following DAX query:

```
EVALUATE
ROW (
    "Result", SUMX (
        Product,
        CALCULATE (
            SUMX ( Sales, Sales[Quantity] * Sales[Unit Price] )
        )
    )
)
```

The result is a single value that sums all the rows of the Sales table, multiplying quantity and unit price row by row. The storage engine should resolve such a query completely, returning a datacache with just one row. However, this is not what happens. There are two storage engine queries in the server timings information, as you can see in Table 16-17.

TABLE 16-17 VertiPaq Scan events for nested iterators.

Line	Subclass	Duration	CPU	Query (xmSQL)
2	Scan	35	172	SELECT Product[ProductKey], SUM (Sales[Quantity] * Sales[Unit Price]) FROM Sales LEFT JOIN Product ON Sales[ProductKey] = Product[ProductKey]
4	Scan	2	0	SELECT SUM ([CallbackDataID (SUMX (Sales, Sales[Quantity] * Sales[Unit Price]))]) FROM Product

The external iterator is converted into a storage engine query (the one at line 4 in Table 16-17), which contains a DAX expression requiring a callback to the formula engine. The innermost *SUMX* iterator is executed as a single storage engine query for all the products (see line 2 in Table 16-17), materializing a datacache of 2,516 rows (one for every product), as you see in the following physical query plan:

```
Line    Records  Physical Query Plan
1                AddColumns: IterPhyOp LogOp=AddColumns IterCols(0)(''[Result])
2                    SingletonTable: IterPhyOp LogOp=AddColumns IterCols(0)(''[Result])
3       1            SpoolLookup: LookupPhyOp LogOp=Sum_Vertipaq Double
4       1                ProjectionSpool<ProjectFusion<Sum>>: SpoolPhyOp #Records=1
5                            VertipaqResult: IterPhyOp #FieldCols=0 #ValueCols=1
6       2516                    SpoolLookup: LookupPhyOp LogOp=Sum_Vertipaq
7       2516                        ProjectionSpool<ProjectFusion<Sum>>: SpoolPhyOp
8                                        VertipaqResult: IterPhyOp #FieldCols=1 #ValueCols=1
```

It is clear that the following DAX query would be fast without any intermediate materialization:

```
EVALUATE
ROW (
    "Result", SUMX ( Sales, Sales[Quantity] * Sales[Unit Price])
)
```

However, this is almost never a possible solution. In fact, the nested iterators with context transitions are something that most of the time happens in longer queries, where you call a measure within an iterator. For example, the following DAX query is identical to the first one presented in this section, but it uses measures instead of writing explicit calculations within the query:

```
DEFINE
    MEASURE Sales[Sales Amount] =
        SUMX ( Sales, Sales[Quantity] * Sales[Unit Price] )
    MEASURE Sales[Sales by Product] =
        SUMX ( Product, [Sales Amount] )
EVALUATE
ROW ( "Result", [Sales by Product] )
```

As you see, calling a measure within an iterator is a warning signal for performance. The engine has to materialize an intermediate result, and this might require more RAM depending on the granularity of the iterator. You can expect at least one row materialized for each row processed by the iterator, but there are conditions where this number can be higher. In general, if you cannot avoid the materialization (because it is required for a specific calculation), you should try to lower the granularity of the iterator. For instance, if we can assume that the *Sales Amount* measure can be aggregated by *Product* or by *Brand* producing the same result, we can rewrite the *Sales by Product* calculation iterating the *Brand* column:

```
DEFINE
    MEASURE Sales[Sales Amount] =
        SUMX ( Sales, Sales[Quantity] * Sales[Unit Price] )
    MEASURE Sales[Sales by Product] =
        SUMX ( VALUES ( Product[Brand] ), [Sales Amount] )
EVALUATE
ROW ( "Result", [Sales by Product] )
```

The execution requires only one storage engine query, as you see in Table 16-18.

TABLE 16-18 VertiPaq Scan events for nested iterators reducing granularity to brand instead of product.

Line	Subclass	Duration	CPU	Query (xmSQL)
2	Scan	35	188	SELECT Product[Brand], SUM (Sales[Quantity] * Sales[Unit Price]) FROM Sales LEFT JOIN Product ON Sales[ProductKey] = Product[ProductKey]

The execution time is similar, but the most important difference is that the datacache materialized has only 11 rows (one for every brand), instead of 2,516 (one for every product). When the cardinality is in the order of magnitude of millions or more, saving two orders of magnitude in materialization makes the difference.

```
Line    Records  Physical Query Plan
1                AddColumns: IterPhyOp LogOp=AddColumns IterCols(0)(''[Result])
2                  SingletonTable: IterPhyOp LogOp=AddColumns IterCols(0)(''[Result])
3       1          SpoolLookup: LookupPhyOp LogOp=SumX Double #Records=1 #KeyCols=0
4       1            AggregationSpool<Sum>: SpoolPhyOp #Records=1
5       11            Spool_Iterator<SpoolIterator>: IterPhyOp LogOp=Sum_Vertipaq
6       11              ProjectionSpool<ProjectFusion<Sum>>: SpoolPhyOp
7                        VertipaqResult: IterPhyOp #FieldCols=1 #ValueCols=1
```

The difficulty of optimizing nested iterators is identifying them when they are not so visible. For example, consider the following query that converts the amount of every transaction from USD (the currency used to store data) to EUR, applying the currency conversion rate of the beginning of the month of the order date.

```
DEFINE
    MEASURE Sales[AmountInUSD] =
        SUMX ( Sales, Sales[Quantity] * Sales[Unit Price] )
    MEASURE Sales[AmountInEUR] =
        SUMX (
            Sales,
            [AmountInUSD]
                * LOOKUPVALUE (
                    ExchangeRate[AverageRate],
                    ExchangeRate[DateKey], IF (
                        MONTH ( Sales[Order Date] ) = 12,
                        DATE ( YEAR ( Sales[Order Date] ) + 1, 1, 1 ),
                        DATE ( YEAR ( Sales[Order Date] ),
                            MONTH ( Sales[Order Date] ) + 1,
                            1 )
                    ),
                    ExchangeRate[CurrencyKey], CALCULATE (
                        VALUES ( Currency[CurrencyKey] ),
                        Currency[Currency Code] = "EUR"
                    )
                )
        )
EVALUATE
ADDCOLUMNS (
    SUMMARIZE (
        Sales,
        'Date'[Calendar Year],
        'Date'[Month Number],
        'Date'[Month]
    ),
    "Sales", [AmountInUSD],
    "Sales in EUR", [AmountInEUR]
)
ORDER BY
    'Date'[Calendar Year],
    'Date'[Month Number]
```

This query requires more than 50 seconds to complete; most of that time is spent in the storage engine, as you see in Table 16-19.

TABLE 16-19 Timing of currency conversion calculation applied to every Sales row.

Query	Total	FE	SE	SE CPU	SE Queries
Currency Start	51,486	14,102 (8%)	37,384 (92%)	90,375	8

The real problem is visible in the physical query plan, even if it has 376 rows. If you sort the rows in DAX Studio by records in a descendant order, you see that many spool operators process more than 12 million rows. Looking at the DAX query, you might imagine that the problem lies in *LOOKUPVALUE* called into an iterator. In reality, if you look at the measure *AmountInUsd*, you should realize that we have an identical situation as the one described in the previous example.

```
MEASURE Sales[AmountInUSD] =
    SUMX ( Sales, Sales[Quantity] * Sales[Unit Price] )
MEASURE Sales[AmountInEUR] =
    SUMX (
        Sales,
        [AmountInUSD]
            * LOOKUPVALUE ...
    )
```

At this point, you can apply the same optimization we have seen before. We know that the exchange rate used in this model has the same value for one day. Thus, you can iterate *Order Date* instead of Sales, obtaining the same result.

```
MEASURE Sales[AmountInUSD] =
    SUMX ( Sales, Sales[Quantity] * Sales[Unit Price] )
MEASURE Sales[AmountInEUR] =
    SUMX (
        VALUES ( Sales[Order Date] ),
        [AmountInUSD]
            * LOOKUPVALUE ...
    )
```

However, even if this optimization cuts 50 percent of execution time, it cannot avoid a materialization of the Sales table, still resulting in a long execution time, as shown in Table 16-20.

TABLE 16-20 Timing of currency conversion calculation with *Order Date* granularity.

Query	Total	FE	SE	SE CPU	SE Queries
Currency by Order Date	23,075	6,019 (26%)	17,056 (92%)	42,642	8

The reason for the complete materialization is that, even if *Order Date* is the only column of the Sales table referenced in the complete DAX query, the relationship between Sales and Date uses another column, *OrderDateKey*. This is the reason why a complete materialization of Sales was required. The datacache required the *Sales[OrderDateKey]* column, which was not an explicit part of the iterator in the *AmountInEUR* measure. Even if there is a practical one-to-one relationship between *Sales[Order Date]* and *Sales[OrderDateKey]*, the DAX engine ignores it. You can add *Sales[OrderDateKey]* in the granularity of the iterator (see the following DAX code excerpt), in order to reduce the memory footprint of the materialization required by the two nested iterators.

```
MEASURE Sales[AmountInUSD] =
    SUMX ( Sales, Sales[Quantity] * Sales[Unit Price] )
MEASURE Sales[AmountInEUR] =
    SUMX (
        SUMMARIZE ( Sales, Sales[OrderDateKey], Sales[Order Date] ),
        [AmountInUSD]
            * LOOKUPVALUE ...
    )
```

This time, the performance has a relevant improvement, reducing the execution time of two orders of magnitude, as you see in Table 16-21.

TABLE 16-21 Timing of currency conversion calculation with *Order Date* / *OrderDateKey* granularity.

Query	Total	FE	SE	SE CPU	SE Queries
Currency by OrderDateKey	210	27 (13%)	183 (87%)	907	8

You can further refine the optimization, reducing the number of *CallbackDataID* calls and trying to lower the cardinality of the intermediate result to one row per month, instead of one row per day. However, you would obtain only a marginal improvement in this specific case. Remember to give priority to optimizations that can save an order of magnitude of execution time. You should prioritize the reduction of iterations and the number of context transitions (that often generate large materialization).

Optimizing bottlenecks in the formula engine

A bottleneck in the formula engine is typically the result of long iterations resolved in the formula engine, because they consume datacaches produced by the storage engine. For this reason, it is always a good idea to start the analysis in the storage engine, then get information about the datacaches consumed by the formula engine. Once you have this knowledge, trying to read the physical query plan is more affordable.

You can practice optimization by starting with a query such as the following one, which shows the number of open orders for each date between December 20, 2009, and January 6, 2010. An open order is a row in the Sales table with an *Order Date* lower than the analyzed date, and a *Delivery Date* greater than the analyzed date:

```
EVALUATE
ADDCOLUMNS (
    DATESBETWEEN (
        'Date'[Date],
        DATE ( 2009, 12, 20 ),
        DATE ( 2010, 1, 6 )
    ),
    "Open Orders", COUNTROWS (
        FILTER (
            Sales,
            AND (
                Sales[Order Date] < 'Date'[Date],
                Sales[Delivery Date] > 'Date'[Date]
            )
        )
    )
)
```

You can see in Table 16-22 that the execution time of this query is more than 30 seconds, with 80 percent of the time spent in the formula engine.

TABLE 16-22 Timing of open orders with a simple filter.

Query	Total	FE	SE	SE CPU	SE Queries
Open Orders 1	33,723	26,943 (80%)	6,780 (20%)	13,469	2

The physical query plan shows in detail what the DAX query does: For each date returned by *DATESBETWEEN*, it iterates all the rows in the Sales table and counts how many of them satisfy the condition for an open order, analyzing *Order Date* and *Delivery Date*. This requires more than 225 million iterations, obtained by multiplying 18 days by more than 12 million rows in the Sales table.

```
Line   Records   Physical Query Plan
1                AddColumns: IterPhyOp LogOp=AddColumns IterCols(0, 1)
2                  DatesBetween: IterPhyOp LogOp=DatesBetween IterCols(0)
3                    Extend_Lookup: IterPhyOp LogOp=Constant
4                      SingletonTable: IterPhyOp LogOp=Constant
5                      Constant: LookupPhyOp LogOp=Constant DateTime 12/20/2009
6                    Constant: LookupPhyOp LogOp=Constant DateTime 1/6/2010
7      18          SpoolLookup: LookupPhyOp LogOp=CountRows LookupCols(0)
8      18            AggregationSpool<Count>: SpoolPhyOp #Records=18
9                      Filter: IterPhyOp LogOp=Filter
10                       Extend_Lookup: IterPhyOp LogOp=GreaterThan
11                         Filter: IterPhyOp LogOp=Filter
12                           Extend_Lookup: IterPhyOp LogOp=LessThan
13                             CrossApply: IterPhyOp LogOp=LessThan
14                               DatesBetween: IterPhyOp
15                                 Extend_Lookup: IterPhyOp
16                                   SingletonTable: IterPhyOp
17                                   Constant: LookupPhyOp
18                                 Constant: LookupPhyOp
```

```
19    12527442                                          Spool_Iterator<SpoolIterator>:
20    12527442                                      ProjectionSpool<ProjectFusion<>>:
21                                                     VertipaqResult: IterPhyOp
22                                        LessThan: LookupPhyOp LogOp=LessThan
23                                          ColValue<'Sales'[Order Date]>:
24                                           ColValue<'Date'[Date]>: LookupPhyOp
25                              GreaterThan: LookupPhyOp LogOp=GreaterThan
26                           ColValue<'Sales'[Delivery Date]>: LookupPhyOp
27                             ColValue<'Date'[Date]>: LookupPhyOp
```

The datacache materializes only a few columns from the Sales table: the internal row number, the *Order Date,* and the *Delivery Date* columns. Older versions of the DAX engine might also materialize other columns not used in the remaining part of the DAX query.

In order to avoid such a large materialization, the first attempt is to apply a filter over two separate columns using a *CALCULATE* function, as in the following DAX query. The *ALL* function removes a possible filter applied by the relationship between Date and Sales with the context transition generated by *CALCULATE*.

```
EVALUATE
ADDCOLUMNS (
    DATESBETWEEN (
        'Date'[Date],
        DATE ( 2009, 12, 20 ),
        DATE ( 2010, 1, 6 )
    ),
    "Open Orders", CALCULATE (
        COUNTROWS ( Sales ),
        Sales[Order Date] < EARLIER ( 'Date'[Date] ),
        Sales[Delivery Date] > EARLIER ( 'Date'[Date] ),
        ALL ( 'Date' )
    )
)
```

In Table 16-24 you see that the reduction of execution time is three orders of magnitude.

TABLE 16-24 Timing of open orders with single-column filters.

Query	Total	FE	SE	SE CPU	SE Queries
Open Orders 2	45	14 (31%)	31 (69%)	219	4

The strategy of the query plan is to get three lists of dates (*Order Date, Delivery Date,* and *Date*) and a datacache with *Order Date, Delivery Date,* and number of rows for each combination. It is the formula engine that scans this last datacache and checks whether the combination has to be considered within open orders or not. You see in Table 16-25 the four storage engine queries executed in this case.

TABLE 16-25 VertiPaq Scan events for open orders with single-column filters.

Line	Subclass	Duration	CPU	Query (xmSQL)
2	Scan	6	16	SELECT Sales[Order Date], FROM Sales
4	Scan	1	0	SELECT Date[Date] FROM Date
6	Scan	8	109	SELECT Sales[Delivery Date], FROM Sales
8	Scan	16	94	SELECT Sales[Order Date], Sales[Delivery Date], COUNT ( ) FROM Sales WHERE Sales[Order Date] IN (... 1096 total values) AND Sales[Delivery Date] IN (... 21 total values)

The last datacache only contains combinations for values in *Delivery Date* that exist in a possible range of values, thanks to a previous query made on that column only and to the condition applied in the filter context in *CALCULATE*. Please note that this level of optimization might be not available in older versions of the DAX engine, and the result might contain combinations that are certainly not valid for the filter considered.

Because the materialization is limited to one row for each combination of *Order Date* and *Delivery Date*, the storage engine execution is faster (smaller materialization) and the scan performed by the formula engine is faster, too. The query plan generated for the previous DAX query was a smart one. However, in scenarios that are more complex or in older versions of the DAX engine, it might be necessary to modify the DAX query in order to explicitly request to aggregate data at a certain level of granularity, in order to reduce materialization and speed up the execution. For example, consider the following version of the DAX query to get open orders:

```
EVALUATE
ADDCOLUMNS (
    DATESBETWEEN (
        'Date'[Date],
        DATE ( 2009, 12, 20 ),
        DATE ( 2010, 1, 6 )
    ),
    "Open Orders", SUMX (
        FILTER (
            ADDCOLUMNS (
                SUMMARIZE ( Sales, Sales[Order Date], Sales[Delivery Date] ),
                "Rows", CALCULATE (
                    COUNTROWS ( Sales ),
                    ALL ( 'Date' )
                )
            ),
            CONTAINS (
                DATESBETWEEN (
                    'Date'[Date],
                    Sales[Order Date] + 1,
                    Sales[Delivery Date] - 1
```

```
            ),
            'Date'[Date], 'Date'[Date]
        )
    ),
    [Rows]
    )
)
```

In this case, the result shown in Table 16-26 is slower than the previous version of the DAX query. However, you will see that this approach can be more convenient in different conditions.

TABLE 16-26 Timing of open orders with explicit grouping by Order Date and Delivery Date.

Query	Total	FE	SE	SE CPU	SE Queries
Open Orders 3	108	31 (29%)	77 (71%)	437	3

There are only three storage engine queries for this query plan. You can see in Table 16-27 that two of them are very similar, differing only in the third column containing the number of rows aggregated for each combination of *Order Date* and *Delivery Date*. There are no filters pushed to the storage engine, so the two datacaches with *Order Date* and *Delivery Date* have all the combinations of these two columns for the entire Sales table (6,576).

TABLE 16-27 VertiPaq Scan events for open orders with explicit grouping by Order and Delivery Date.

Line	Subclass	Duration	CPU	Query (xmSQL)
2	Scan	1	0	SELECT Date[Date] FROM Date
4	Scan	42	234	SELECT Sales[Order Date], Sales[Delivery Date], COUNT ( ) FROM Sales
6	Scan	34	203	SELECT Sales[Order Date], Sales[Delivery Date] FROM Sales

As anticipated, you should not think that the second solution is always better than the third. In fact, if you include 365 days in the result, the performance is better for the last solution, as you can see in Table 16-28. The queries are executed using a different filter for dates, as shown in the following DAX code:

```
EVALUATE
ADDCOLUMNS (
    DATESBETWEEN (
        'Date'[Date],
        DATE ( 2009, 1, 1 ),
        DATE ( 2009, 12, 31 )
    ),
    ...
```

TABLE 16-28 Timing of open orders queries for 365 days.

Query	Total	FE	SE	SE CPU	SE Queries
Open Orders 2	207	169 (82%)	38 (18%)	109	3
Open Orders 3	111	38 (34%)	73 (66%)	329	3

Creating repro in MDX

You have seen many optimizations based on DAX queries. However, if users will query a data model using MDX, you have to verify that performances of the measures are good also in that language. For instance, consider the following repro for the second and the third versions of the calculation of open orders you have seen in the previous section. The measures provide the number of open orders in the last day of the period selected (so it works also for years and months, even if in the repro only days are used):

```
-- MDX - Open Orders 2
WITH
    MEASURE Sales[Open Orders] = CALCULATE (
        COUNTROWS ( Sales ),
        FILTER ( ALL ( Sales[Order Date] ), Sales[Order Date] < MAX ( 'Date'[Date] ) ),
        FILTER ( ALL ( Sales[Delivery Date] ), Sales[Delivery Date] > MAX ( 'Date'[Date] ) ),
        ALL ( 'Date' )
    )
SELECT
    Measures.[Open Orders] ON COLUMNS,
    NON EMPTY [Date].[Date].[Date] ON ROWS
FROM [Model]
WHERE [Date].[Calendar Year].[CY 2008]


-- MDX - Open Orders 3
WITH
    MEASURE Sales[Open Orders] =
    SUMX (
        FILTER (
            ADDCOLUMNS (
                SUMMARIZE ( Sales, Sales[Order Date], Sales[Delivery Date] ),
                "Rows", CALCULATE (
                    COUNTROWS ( Sales ),
                    ALL ( 'Date' )
                )
            ),
            CONTAINS (
                DATESBETWEEN (
                    'Date'[Date],
                    Sales[Order Date] + 1,
                    Sales[Delivery Date] - 1
                ),
                'Date'[Date], MAX ( 'Date'[Date] )
            )
        ),
        [Rows]
```

```
    )
SELECT
    Measures.[Open Orders] ON COLUMNS,
    NON EMPTY [Date].[Date].[Date] ON ROWS
FROM [Model]
WHERE [Date].[Calendar Year].[CY 2008]
```

The third version performs better than the second one in MDX too, as you can see in the result in Table 16-29.

TABLE 16-29 Timing of open orders DAX measures tested in MDX queries for 365 days.

Query	Total	FE	SE	SE CPU	SE Queries
Open Orders 2	307	263 (86%)	44 (14%)	219	7
Open Orders 3	121	28 (23%)	93 (77%)	547	6

You should always create a repro in MDX when you define measures for a data model. In fact, the behavior of MDX can be very different, especially for the non-empty calculation (which is a concept that does not exist in a native DAX query). Moreover, remember that the structure of the MDX query can affect the performance, especially when you cross several dimensions in the same query.

Reducing materialization

The formula engine executes all the DAX functions that the storage engine cannot handle. Because the storage engine only supports trivial aggregations, the formula engine has to compute complex set manipulations, including internal filter and sort operations. In this case, you have to consider how to lower the cardinality and the size of the in-memory datacaches produced by the storage engine, so that the formula engine can complete its task faster.

A good example of this problem is the *TOPN* function. For instance, consider the following query that returns the top 10 customers by sum of quantity in sales:

```
EVALUATE
TOPN (
    10,
    Customer,
    CALCULATE ( SUM ( Sales[Quantity] ) )
)
```

In Table 16-30 you see the server timings result. The cost of the query is relatively small because the Customer table has less than 20,000 rows, but it is interesting to analyze the number in more detail to imagine what could happen with a larger Customer table involved in this DAX query. The storage engine cost is slightly larger than the formula engine, but when you have a 60/40 split as in this case, you should not draw any easy conclusions.

TABLE 16-30 Timing of simple *TOPN* over Customer table.

Query	Total	FE	SE	SE CPU	SE Queries
TOPN Customer	47	19 (40%)	28 (60%)	32	2

You can see the storage engine queries results in Table 16-31. In the columns *Rows* and *Size* you see the number of rows and the memory consumed by the datacache generated by each storage engine query.

TABLE 16-31 VertiPaq Scan events for *TOPN* over Customer table.

Line	Subclass	Duration	CPU	Rows	Size	Query (xmSQL)
2	Scan	19	16	18,869	301,952	SELECT Customer[CustomerKey], SUM (Sales[Quantity]) FROM Sales LEFT JOIN Customer ON Sales[CustomerKey] = Customer[CustomerKey]
4	Scan	9	16	18,869	1,962,376	SELECT $RowNumber, Customer[Key], Customer[GeographyKey], ... (all Customer columns) FROM Customer

Both storage engine queries return 18,896 rows, which correspond to the number of customers. Considering that you only have 10 rows in the result, you know that the filter operation is in charge of the formula engine. Moreover, the second query generates a datacache that materializes the entire Customer table, including all the columns. You might wonder why materializing all the values for rows that are not part of the result and are not necessary to establish who the top 10 customers are. This is exactly the problem of using *TOPN* over an entire table. You can see how the formula engine uses the two datacaches in the following physical query plan:

```
Line   Records  Physical Query Plan
1               PartitionIntoGroups: IterPhyOp LogOp=TopN
2      1           AggregationSpool<Top>: SpoolPhyOp #Records=1
3      18869          Spool_Iterator<SpoolIterator>: IterPhyOp LogOp=Scan_Vertipaq
4      18869            ProjectionSpool<ProjectFusion<>>: SpoolPhyOp
5                         VertipaqResult: IterPhyOp #FieldCols=26 #ValueCols=0
6      18869        SpoolLookup: LookupPhyOp LogOp=Sum_Vertipaq
7      18869          ProjectionSpool<ProjectFusion<Sum>>: SpoolPhyOp
8                       VertipaqResult: IterPhyOp #FieldCols=1 #ValueCols=1
9               Constant: LookupPhyOp LogOp=Constant Integer 10
```

A first optimization is trying to reduce the number of rows iterated by the pivot table. The other is trying to reduce the materialization of the columns included in the result, doing that only for the customers included in the result. You can see an example of this approach in the following DAX query, which applies the *TOPN* only to the primary key of the Customer table (*CustomerKey*), so that the materialization of the result only affects 10 rows.

```
EVALUATE
CALCULATETABLE (
    Customer,
    TOPN (
        10,
        VALUES ( Customer[CustomerKey] ),
        CALCULATE ( SUM ( Sales[Quantity] ) )
    )
)
```

You can see the server timings in Table 16-32. The execution time is lower in both the storage engine and formula engine.

TABLE 16-32 Timing of simple *TOPN* over *CustomerKey* column.

Query	Total	FE	SE	SE CPU	SE Queries
TOPN CustomerKey	35	15 (43%)	20 (57%)	94	3

The more important thing is looking at the storage engine queries executed in Table 16-33. Even if there is one more storage engine query, the overall size materialized by all the datacaches is 453,968 bytes instead of 2,264,328 bytes, saving 80 percent of memory for materialization.

TABLE 16-33 VertiPaq Scan events for *TOPN* over *CustomerKey* column.

Line	Subclass	Duration	CPU	Rows	Size	Query (xmSQL)

2	Scan	18	94	18,869	301,952	SELECT Customer[CustomerKey], SUM (Sales[Quantity])
						FROM Sales
						   LEFT JOIN Customer
						     ON Sales[CustomerKey] = Customer[CustomerKey]

4	Scan	0	0	18,869	150,976	SELECT Customer[Key] FROM Customer

6	Scan	2	0	10	1,040	SELECT $RowNumber, Customer[Key],
						     Customer[GeographyKey], ... (all Customer columns)
						FROM Customer
						WHERE Customer[CustomerKey]
						     IN (19071, 19048..[10 total values, not all displayed])

Reducing the materialization is important when you manage large tables. Consider the following DAX query that returns the top 10 transactions in the Sales table for sales amount (resulting from the product of quantity by unit price):

```
EVALUATE
TOPN (
    10,
    Sales,
    Sales[Quantity] * Sales[Unit Price]
)
```

The result is probably more than 10 rows, in case you have several transactions with the same combination of quantity and unit price. However, in a test with 12 million rows in the fact table, the result includes 1,458 rows, and it required 19 seconds to complete. You might wonder why this simple query takes so long. The server timings in Table 16-34 would suggest a bottleneck in the storage engine.

TABLE 16-34 Timing of simple *TOPN* over Sales table.

Query	Total	FE	SE	SE CPU	SE Queries
TOPN Sales	19,062	3,689 (19%)	15,373 (81%)	37,422	1

The details of the only storage engine query shown in Table 16-35 clarify that the query plan requested a materialization of the entire Sales table, requiring around 1 GB of RAM.

TABLE 16-35 VertiPaq Scan events for *TOPN* over Sales table.

Line	Subclass	Duration	CPU	Rows	Size	Query (xmSQL)
2	Scan	15,373	37,422	12,527,442	1,002,915,360	SELECT $RowNumber, Sales[OnlineSalesKey], Sales[StoreKey], ... (all Customer columns) FROM Sales

If you have a primary key column in the Sales table, such as *OnlineSalesKey* in this example, you can apply the same technique to reduce the memory footprint of the materialization, as in this DAX query:

```
EVALUATE
CALCULATETABLE (
    Sales,
    TOPN (
        10,
        VALUES ( Sales[OnlineSalesKey] ),
        CALCULATE (
            SUMX ( Sales, Sales[Quantity] * Sales[Unit Price] )
        )
    )
)
```

Apparently, based on the Server Timings result in Table 16-36, this new approach does not save execution time, and we moved more workload on the formula engine.

TABLE 16-36 Timing of simple *TOPN* over *OnlineSalesKey* column.

Query	Total	FE	SE	SE CPU	SE Queries
TOPN OnlineSalesKey	18,905	8,542 (45%)	10,363 (55%)	23,828	3

However, also in this case this approach saves 80 percent of memory for materialization, which requires around 200 MB instead of 1 GB, as you see from the storage engine queries in Table 16-37.

TABLE 16-37 VertiPaq Scan events for *TOPN* over *CustomerKey* column.

Line	Subclass	Duration	CPU	Rows	Size	Query (xmSQL)
2	Scan	5,520	12,906	12,527,442	150,329,304	SELECT Sales[OnlineSalesKey], SUM (Sales[Quantity] * Sales[Unit Price]) FROM Sales
4	Scan	4,747	10,391	18,869	50,109,768	SELECT Sales[OnlineSalesKey] FROM Sales

6	Scan	2	96	1,458	1,116,640	SELECT $RowNumber, Sales[OnlineSalesKey],
						        Sales[StoreKey], ... (all Customer columns)
						FROM Sales
						WHERE Sales[OnlineSalesKey] IN (24447319,
						        28257231,..[1458 total values, not all displayed])

Finding the right balance between materialization and formula engine is a complex decision. In this case, you always have a slow query, so probably a smaller materialization improves scalability for queries running by other users at the same time. If you do not have enough RAM on the server, reducing materialization is the only way to complete the query.

Optimizing complex bottlenecks

You can have conditions where the bottleneck is not easy to identify. Usually this happens in complex queries, but you can learn how to interpret the information available in server settings and query plans, in order to identify the possible cause that could be shared between the formula engine and storage engine. In this section, you will see an example based on *DISTINCTCOUNT*, which is a particular calculation that might hide some pitfalls.

Consider the following DAX query, which evaluates the number of unique invoices related to each product. The measure *Count of Invoices* only considers rows in the Sales table with a *Quantity* greater than zero. The presence of this filter condition is important to observe the behavior you will see shortly:

```
DEFINE
    MEASURE Sales[Count of Invoices] =
        CALCULATE (
            DISTINCTCOUNT ( Sales[Order Number] ),
            FILTER ( 'Sales', Sales[Quantity] > 0 )      -- Slow
        )
EVALUATE
CALCULATETABLE (
    ADDCOLUMNS (
        SUMMARIZE ( Sales, Product[ProductKey], Product[Product Name] ),
        "Count of Invoices", [Count of Invoices]
    ),
    Product[Color] = "Red"
)
```

The result is a table with 99 rows, one for each product of color Red. For each product, you can see the number of invoices in the last column.

ProductKey	Product Name	Count of Invoices
2505	Contoso Touch Stylus Pen E150 Red	232
1594	SV DVD 38 DVD Storage Binder E25 Red	980
1639	Contoso DVD 38 DVD Storage Binder E25 Red	948
1701	SV Hand Games for 12 16 boys E60 Red	12358
452	WWI Desktop PC1.60 E1600 Red	534
2039	Litware Microwave 1.6CuFt M125 Red	535
2359	Contoso Air conditioner 7000BTU E0260 Red	901
...	...	...

The execution of the query requires more than 4 seconds, 93 percent of it spent in the storage engine, as you see in Table 16-38.

TABLE 16-38 Timing of *Distinct Count* with filter on table.

Query	Total	FE	SE	SE CPU	SE Queries
Distinct Count with Table Filter	4,475	327 (7%)	4,148 (93%)	21,513	101

At first sight, this seems that the DAX query has a bottleneck in the storage engine. However, you can already see in Table 16-38 that there are 101 queries to the storage engine, which is a high number for a simple DAX query such as this one. If you look at the storage engine queries in Table 16-39, you see that after the first two queries there are 99 queries that differ only for the filter applied to the *ProductKey/Quantity* tuple.

TABLE 16-39 VertiPaq scan events for *Distinct Count* with filter on table.

Line	Subclass	Duration	CPU	Rows	Size	Query (xmSQL)
2	Scan	25	78	99	396	SELECT Product[ProductKey], Sales[ProductKey], Sales[Quantity] FROM Sales LEFT JOIN Product ON Sales[ProductKey] = Product[ProductKey] WHERE Product[Color] = 'Red'
4	Scan	34	234	396	1,584	SELECT Product[ProductKey], Product[ProductName] FROM Sales LEFT JOIN Product ON Sales[ProductKey] = Product[ProductKey] WHERE Product[ProductKey] IN (1889, 380, ..[99 total values, not all displayed] VAND Product[Color] = 'Red' VAND Sales[Quantity] > 0
8	Scan	39	172	1	12	SELECT DCOUNT (Sales[Order Number]) FROM Sales WHERE Product[ProductKey] IN (1889, 380, ..[99 total values, not all displayed] VAND Product[Color] = 'Red' VAND Sales[Quantity] > 0 VAND (Product[ProductKey], Sales[Quantity]) IN { (2040, 2), (2040, 3), (2040, 1), (2040, 4) }
...	...	...	...	...	...	...
400	Scan	38	250	1	12	SELECT DCOUNT (Sales[Order Number]) FROM Sales WHERE Product[ProductKey] IN (1889, 380, ..[99 total values, not all displayed] VAND Product[Color] = 'Red' VAND Sales[Quantity] > 0 VAND (Product[ProductKey], Sales[Quantity]) IN { (1700, 2), (1700, 3), (1700, 1), (1700, 4) }

In practice, there is one storage engine query for each row produced for the output of the DAX query. This is strange and certainly not efficient. The cost of every storage engine query is around 40 milliseconds, so the query execution time depends on the number of products filtered. For example, if you filter Blue products instead of the Red ones, you wait more than 10 seconds for a result of 200 rows. If you do not filter any color, returning all the products means waiting 118 seconds for 2,516 rows. Moreover, because you have 2,518 queries to the storage engine, you have no hope that a second execution of the same query will use previous datacaches from the storage engine cache. The reason is that you are exceeding the maximum number of entries available there: The storage engine keeps the last 512 queries, but this number might vary in different versions of the DAX engine.

Remember, every storage engine query originates from the query plan, so you should analyze it to understand the reason for this behavior. The following physical query plan indicates that there is one storage engine query for each row returned by the DAX query.

```
Line    Records  Physical Query Plan
1                AddColumns: IterPhyOp LogOp=AddColumns
2       99          Spool_Iterator<SpoolIterator>: IterPhyOp LogOp=GroupBy_Vertipaq
3       99            ProjectionSpool<ProjectFusion<>>: SpoolPhyOp
4                       VertipaqResult: IterPhyOp #FieldCols=2 #ValueCols=0
5       99       SpoolLookup: LookupPhyOp LogOp=Calculate
6       99          AggregationSpool<Copy>: SpoolPhyOp
7       1             Spool_Iterator<SpoolIterator>: IterPhyOp
8       1               AggregationSpool<Cache>: SpoolPhyOp #Records=1
9                         VertipaqResult: IterPhyOp #FieldCols=0 #ValueCols=1
10      1             Spool_Iterator<SpoolIterator>: IterPhyOp LogOp=DistinctCount
11      1               AggregationSpool<Cache>: SpoolPhyOp #Records=1
12                        VertipaqResult: IterPhyOp #FieldCols=0 #ValueCols=1
...     ...         ...
301     1             Spool_Iterator<SpoolIterator>: IterPhyOp LogOp=DistinctCount
302     1               AggregationSpool<Cache>: SpoolPhyOp #Records=1
303                       VertipaqResult: IterPhyOp #FieldCols=0 #ValueCols=1
```

The reason for this behavior is the filter over Sales rows, just to consider in the *DISTINCTCOUNT* operation only those sales having a quantity greater than zero (probably all the rows in Sales satisfy this condition, but the DAX engine is not able to remove such a condition from the query plan). You can obtain the same result using a column filter instead of a table filter, as in the following DAX query, which highlights the changed condition:

```
DEFINE
    MEASURE Sales[Count of Invoices] =
        CALCULATE (
            DISTINCTCOUNT ( Sales[Order Number] ),
            FILTER ( ALL ( Sales[Quantity] ), Sales[Quantity] > 0 )    -- Fast
        )
EVALUATE
CALCULATETABLE (
    ADDCOLUMNS (
        SUMMARIZE ( Sales, Product[ProductKey], Product[Product Name] ),
        "Count of Invoices", [Count of Invoices]
    ),
    Product[Color] = "Red"
)
```

Note In the previous query, the code highlighted in bold is an explicit filter over the *Quantity* column of the Sales table:

```
FILTER ( ALL ( Sales[Quantity] ), Sales[Quantity] > 0 )
```

This complete syntax is not necessary, but it was easier to compare with similar filters used in previous queries that had to be explicit. In this case, you can replace the filter with a simpler syntax:

```
Sales[Quantity] > 0
```

We used the complete syntax for educational reasons only.

This query produces a much faster execution, improving the response time of two orders of magnitude, as you see in Table 16-40.

TABLE 16-40 Timing of *Distinct Count* with filter on column.

Query	Total	FE	SE	SE CPU	SE Queries
Distinct Count with Column Filter	90	12 (13%)	78 (87%)	422	2

The storage engine is still responsible for most of the time spent by query execution, but you should focus your attention on the low number of SE queries (only two), other than the faster response. Each storage engine query does not require more than a few hundred milliseconds, as you see in Table 16-41.

TABLE 16-41 VertiPaq scan events for *Distinct Count* with filter on column.

Line	Subclass	Duration	CPU	Rows	Size	Query (xmSQL)

2	Scan	25	125	99	396	SELECT Product[ProductKey],
						Product[ProductName]
						FROM Sales
						   LEFT JOIN Product
						   ON Sales[ProductKey] = Product[ProductKey]
						WHERE Product[Color] = 'Red'

6	Scan	53	297	99	1,584	SELECT Product[ProductKey],
						     DCOUNT (Sales[Order Number])
						FROM Sales
						   LEFT JOIN Product
						   ON Sales[ProductKey] = Product[ProductKey]
						WHERE Product[ProductKey] IN (1889,
						     380, ..[99 total values, not all displayed]
						VAND Product[Color] = 'Red'
						VAND Sales[Quantity] > 0

The key difference is that with a column filter, the query plan pushed all the filters (product color and sales quantity) into the same storage engine query. The semantics of the query using a table filter creates more constraints to the query plan in order to apply such optimization.

The lesson of this example (to be honest, of the entire book) is that you have to consider all the factors that affect a query plan in order to find the real bottleneck. Looking at the percentages of FE and SE shown in server timings is a good starting point, but you should always investigate the reason why you have certain numbers. The SQL Profiler and DAX Studio tools measure the effects of a bad query plan, but these are only clues and evidences to help you find the reason behind a slow query.

Welcome to the DAX world!

Index

A

ABC (Pareto) classification, 136–143
ABS, mathematical functions, 39–40
absolute differences, 174–175
ADDCOLUMNS
    best practices, 250
    performance decisions for use, 505–509
    use of, 241–244
addition. *See also* aggregation
    DAX operators, 21–22
    xmSQL syntax for, 474
ADDMISSINGITEMS, 262–264
aggregation
    ADDCOLUMNS and SUMMARIZE, decisions about,
        505–509
    ADDMISSINGITEMS, 262–264
    aggregate functions, 35–37
    calculated columns and measures, overview, 22–25
    calculated columns and performance, 447–450
    calculated tables, use of, 50–51
    column cardinality and performance, 442
    computing differences over previous periods,
        174–175
    computing periods from prior periods, 171–174
    grouping/joining functions, 250
    MDX developers, DAX overview, 14–15
    moving annual total calculations, 175–178
    over time, 168
    semi-additive measures, 178–184
    using in calculated columns, 67–68
    xmSQL syntax for, 472–473
    year-, quarter-, and month-to-date, 168–171
AggregationSpoolCache, 462
ALL
    cardinality, optimization of, 515–517
    cumulative total calculations, 134–136
    Date table filters and, 168
    evaluation context interactions, 74–76
    filter context and, 93–95, 100–101
    RANKX and, 215–217
    understanding use of, 54–57, 326–328
ALLEXCEPT
    ABC (Pareto) classification, use of, 140–143
    expanded tables and, 314–315
    static moving averages, computing of, 153–154
    understanding use of, 54–57
ALLNOBLANKROW, 54–57
ALLOCATED SIZE, 416
ALLSELECTED
    RANKX and, 215–216
    ration and percentage calculations, 129–132
    understanding use of, 123–125, 285–294
alternate key, 451
AND
    CALCULATE, filtering with complex conditions,
        106–109
    CALCULATETABLE and, 110–111
    DAX operators, 21–22
    filter context intersections, 318–320
    KEEPFILTERS, understanding use of, 296–303
    logical functions, overview, 37–38
annual totals, calculation of, 175–178
ANSI-SQL queries
    aggregation, xmSQL syntax conversions, 472–473
    arithmetical operations, xmSQL syntax conversion,
        474
arbitrarily shaped set (filter)
    complex filter reduction, KEEPFILTERS and, 299–303
    defined, 297, 299
    understanding use of, 321–326
arithmetic operations
    DAX operators, 21–22
    error handling, overview, 26–32

arithmetic operations *continued*
  syntax overview, 39–40
  trigonometric functions, overview, 40
  xmSQL syntax, 474
arrows, data filtering, 3–4
ASC, syntax, 48
asterisk (*), use in hierarchies, 358
audit columns, performance and, 443
AutoExists, 76, 304–307
AVERAGE
  aggregate functions, overview, 35–37
  calculation of, 220–221
  static moving averages, computing of, 151–154
  xmSQL syntax, 473
AVERAGEA, 220
AVERAGEX, 37, 220–221, 250

B

BETABGBPDIST, 229
BETABGBPINV, 230
bidirectional relationships. *See also* relationships
  expanded tables, understanding use of, 307–316
  many-to-many relationships, use of, 373–378
  overview of, 3–4
  physical vs. virtual relationships, 382
BIDS Helper Visual Studio Add-In, 358
binary large object (BLOB), syntax, 18, 21
BISM Server Memory Report, 434–435
BITS COUNT, 416
BLANK
  COUNTBLANK, use of, 36–37
  error handling, overview, 28–30
  ISBLANK, use of, 31–32, 39
  relational functions, overview, 42–44
  SUMMARIZE roll-up rolls and, 252–255
  SUMMARIZECOLUMN and, 255
BLOB (binary large object), syntax, 18, 21
Boolean conditions
  CALCULATE and, 99–101, 105–106
  calculated columns and performance, 450
  DAX operators, and/or, 21–22
  syntax, overview of, 18, 20–21
  transforming a Boolean filter into FILTER, 110–111
bridge tables, many-to-many relationships, 373–378
browsing depth, filter context and, 352–358
budget patterns, 381

C

caches. *See also* formulas, optimization of
  CallbackDataID, use of, 483–488
  DAX Studio, event tracing with, 467–470
  formula engine (FE), overview, 458
  parallelism and datacache, understanding of, 480–481
  query plans, reading of, 488–494
  server timings and query plans, analysis of, 500–503
  storage engine (VertiPaq), overview, 459
  VertiPaq cache, understanding of, 481–483
  VertiPaq SE query cache match, 464
CALCULATE. *See also* evaluation contexts
  ABC (Pareto) classification, use of, 136–143
  ALL, understanding use of, 326–328
  ALLSELECTED and, 123–125
  calculated columns and performance, 447–450
  CALCULATETABLE, use of, 108–109
  circular dependencies, 119–122
  computing differences over previous periods, 174–175
  computing periods from prior periods, 171–174
  context transition
    evaluation order of, 117
    understanding of, 111–113
    visible rows, 116–117
    with measures, 114–116
  cumulative total calculations, 132–136
  filter context
    ALL and, 93–95
    filtering a single column, 101–106
    filtering with complex conditions, 106–109
    KEEPFILTERS and, 296–303
    optimization of, 512–513
    overview of, 95–98
    OVERWRITE and, 320–321
  FIRSTNOBLANK and LASTNOBLANK, 199–200
  introduction to, 98–101
  Mark as Date Table, use of, 167–168
  moving annual total calculations, 175–178
  opening and closing balances, 184–188
  periods to date, understanding, 189–191
  RANKX, common pitfalls, 217
  ratios and percentages, computing of, 129–132
  RELATEDTABLE and, 80
  reproduction query, creation of, 499–500
  rules for using, 122–123
  sales per day calculations, 143–150

time intelligence, introduction to, 164–166
USERELATIONSHIP and, 125–127, 161–162
variables and evaluation contexts, 118–119
working days, computing differences in, 150–151
year-, quarter-, and month-to-date, 168–171
CALCULATETABLE
filter conditions, optimization of, 512–513
FIRSTNOBLANK and LASTNOBLANK, 199–200
functions of, 93
introduction to, 98–101, 108–109
many-to-many relationships, filtering and, 376–378
Mark as Date Table, use of, 167–168
order of evaluation, 51
periods to date, understanding, 189–191
reproduction query, creation of, 499–500
understanding use of, 236–239
USERELATIONSHIP and, 161–162
calculations
aggregate functions, 35–37
calculated columns and measures, overview, 22–25
calculated columns and performance, 447–450
calculated physical relationships, use of, 367–371
calculated tables, use of, 50–51
conversion functions, overview, 41–42
data types, 18–21
date and time functions, overview, 42
DAX operators, 21–22
error handling, overview, 26–32
Excel users, DAX overview, 5–9
formatting DAX code, overview, 32–35
information functions, overview, 39
logical functions, overview, 37–38
mathematical functions, overview, 39–40
MDX developers, DAX overview, 14–15
relational functions, overview, 42–44
syntax, overview of, 17–22
text functions, overview, 40–41
trigonometric functions, overview, 40
variables, use of, 26
CALENDAR
Date table, building of, 156–157
use of, 157–160
Calendar table
static moving averages, computing of, 151–154
working days, computing differences, 150–151
CALENDARAUTO
Date table, building of, 156–157
use of, 157–160

calendars. *See* Date table; time intelligence
CallbackDataID
IF conditions, optimization of, 513–515
overview of, 483–488
performance optimization, reducing impact of, 509–511
Cartesian products, CROSSJOIN, 267–269
CEILING, mathematical functions, 39–40
cells. *See also* evaluation contexts
Excel users, DAX overview, 5–7
filter context, overview, 97–98
chain, relationships, 3
CHISQBGBPDIST, 230
CHISQBGBPDISTBGBPRT, 230
CHISQBGBPINV, 230
CHISQBGBPINVBGBPRT, 230
circular dependencies, 119–122
closing balance over time, 178–188
CLOSINGBALANCE, 184–188
CLOSINGBALANCEYEAR, 185–188
COLUMN ENCODING, 415
COLUMN ID, 415–416
COLUMN TYPE, 415
columnar databases, introduction to, 400–403
columns. *See also* database processing; also evaluation
contexts; also table functions
ABC (Pareto) classification, use of, 136–143
ADDCOLUMNS, 241–244
aggregate functions, 35–37
calculated columns and measures, overview, 22–25
calculated columns and performance, 447–450
column cardinality
defined, 426
finding number of unique values, 427–429
performance and, 442–447, 515–517
column storage, choosing columns for, 451–453
column storage, optimization of, 453–455
conversion functions, overview, 41–42
data models, gathering information about, 425–434
cost of a column hierarchy, 430–434
number of unique values per column, 427–429
date and time functions, overview, 42
DAX calculations, syntax overview, 17–22
derived columns, 309, 312
DISCOVER_STORAGE_TABLE_COLUMN_SEGMENTS, 416
DISCOVER_STORAGE_TABLE_COLUMNS, 415–416
dynamic segmentation, use of, 371–373

columns. *See also* database processing; also evaluation contexts; also table functions *continued*
    Excel users, DAX overview, 5–7
    expanded tables, understanding use of, 307–316
    filtering columns, 308–316
    formatting DAX code, overview, 32–35
    information functions, overview, 39
    lineage and relationships, overview of, 248–250
    logical functions, overview, 37–38
    MDX developers, DAX overview, 13–15
    multiple column relationships, computing of, 367–369
    native columns, 309
    parent-child hierarchies, handling of, 346–358
    physical vs. virtual relationships, 381–382
    relational functions, overview, 42–44
    scanning, materialization and, 417–420
    SELECTCOLUMNS, 243–246
    Sort By Column, 48
    SUMMARIZECOLUMNS, 250, 255–261, 497, 508–509
    text functions, overview, 40–41
    trigonometric functions, overview, 40
    tuples and, 316–318
    using in a measure, 68–69
    using SUM in a calculated column, 67–68
    VALUES, use of, 84
    VertiPaq, as columnar database, 95–98
COMBIN, 230
COMBINA, 230
commas, formatting DAX code, 34
commas, text functions, 40–41
comparisons
    computing differences over previous periods, 174–175
    computing periods from prior periods, 171–174
    DAX operators, 21–22
    moving annual total calculations, 175–178
    over time, 168
    year-, quarter-, and month-to-date, 168–171
complex filters. *See* arbitrarily shaped set (filter)
compound interest calculations, 225–229
compression algorithms. *See also* Dynamic Management Views (DMV)
    dictionary compression, 405–406
    re-encoding, 409
    Run Length Encoding (RLE), VertiPaq, 406–408
    segmentation and partitioning, 412
    value encoding, 404–405
    VertiPaq, overview of, 403–411
COMPRESSION TYPE, 416
CONCATENATE, text functions, 40–41
conditions
    logical functions, overview, 37–38
    SQL developers, DAX overview, 12
CONFIDENCEBGBPNORM, 230
CONFIDENCEBGBPT, 230
CONTAINS, 278–280, 380–381
context transition
    ALLSELECTED and, 286–294
    CALCULATE and, 111–113
    CALCULATE, evaluation order of, 117
    CALCULATE, visible rows, 116–117
    CALCULATE, with measures, 114–116
    KEEPFILTERS and, 299–303
    SetFilter, use of, 331–337
conversion errors, error handling overview, 26–32
conversion functions, syntax, 41–42
cores, VertiPaq hardware decisions, 423
COS, trigonometric functions, 40
COSH, trigonometric functions, 40
COT, trigonometric functions, 40
COTH, trigonometric functions, 40
COUNT, 36–37, 472–473
COUNTA, 36–37
COUNTAX, 37
COUNTBLANK, 36–37
COUNTROWS, 36–37, 46, 428
COUNTX, 37
CPU Time, for queries, 465–467, 479, 500–503
CPU, DAX Studio event tracing, 470
CPU, hardware selection, 422–423
CROSSJOIN
    KEEPFILTERS, understanding use of, 299–303
    sales per day granularity, 149–150
    use of, 267–269
    well-shaped filters and, 321–323
CROSSJOIN/VALUES, cardinality, 515–517
cross-references, calculated columns and measures, 25
cumulative totals, computing of, 132–136
Currency (Currency), syntax, 18–20
currency conversions, example of, 386–392
CURRENCY, conversion functions, 41–42
custom rollup formulas, 358
customers, new and returning, 384–386

D

data models
    calculated columns and performance, 447–450
    column cardinality and performance, 442–447
    column storage, choosing columns for, 451–453
    column storage, optimization of, 453–455
    denormalization, 434–442
    gathering information about model, 425–434
        cost of a column hierarchy, 430–434
        dictionary size for each column, 428–429
        number of rows in a table, 426–427
        number of unique values per column, 427–429
        total cost of table, 433–434
    overview of, 1–3
    relationship directions, 3–4
    VertiPaq Analyzer, performance optimization and, 510
data types
    aggregate functions, numeric and non-numeric
        values, 35–37
    DAX syntax, overview of, 18–21
    information functions, overview, 39
database processing
    columnar databases, introduction to, 400–403
    Dynamic Management Views, use of, 413–416
    materialization, 417–420
    segmentation and partitioning, 412
    VertiPaq compression, 403–411
        best sort order, finding of, 409 410
        dictionary encoding, 405–406
        hierarchies and relationships, 410–411
        re-encoding, 409
        Run Length Encoding (RLE), 406–408
        value encoding, 404–405
    VertiPaq, hardware selection, 421–424
    VertiPaq, understanding of, 400
datacaches. See also formulas, optimization of
    CallbackDataID, use of, 483–488
    DAX Studio, event tracing with, 467–470
    formula engine (FE), overview, 458
    parallelism and datacache, understanding of, 480–481
    query plans, reading of, 488–494
    server timings and query plans, analysis of, 500–503
    storage engine (VertiPaq), overview, 459
    VertiPaq cache and, 481–483
    VertiPaq SE query cache match, 464
date. See also Date table
    column cardinality and performance, 443–447

date and time functions, overview, 42
    sales per day calculations, 143–150
    time intelligence, introduction to, 155
    working days, computing differences in, 150–151
DATE
    conversion functions, overview, 41–42
    date and time functions, overview, 42
    date table names, 157
Date (DateTime), syntax, 18, 20
Date table
    aggregating and comparing over time, 168
        computing differences over previous periods,
            174–175
        computing periods from prior periods,
            171–174
        year-, quarter-, and month-to-date, 168–171
    CALENDAR and CALENDARAUTO, use of, 157–160
    closing balance over time, 178–188
    CLOSINGBALANCE, 184–188
    custom calendars, 200–201
        custom comparisons between periods,
            210–211
        noncontiguous periods, computing over,
            206–209
        weeks, working with, 201–204
        year-, quarter-, and month-to-date, 204–205
    DATEADD, use of, 191–196
    drillthrough operations, 200
    FIRSTDATE and LASTDATE, 196–199
    FIRSTNOBLANK and LASTNOBLANK, 199–200
    Mark as Date Table, use of, 166–168
    moving annual total calculations, 175–178
    multiple dates, working with, 160 164
    naming of, 157
    OPENINGBALANCE, 184–188
    periods to date, understanding, 189–191
    time intelligence, advanced functions, 188
    time intelligence, introduction to, 155, 164–166
Date, cumulative total calculations, 134–136
DATEADD
    previous year, month, quarter comparisons,
        171–174
    use of, 191–196
Date[DateKey], Mark as Date Table, 166–168
DateKey, cumulative total calculations, 134–136
DATESBETWEEN
    moving annual total calculations, 175–178
    working days, computing differences, 151

DATESMTD, 189–191

DATESQTD, 189–191

DATESYTD, 168–171, 173, 189–191

DateTime
    column cardinality and performance, 443–447
    syntax, overview of, 18, 20

DATETIME, conversion functions, 41–42

DATEVALUE, date and time functions, 42

DAX
    data models, overview of, 1–3
    data relationships, direction of, 3–4
    data types, overview, 18–21
    evaluation order and nested calls, 51
    for Excel users, overview, 5–9
    formatting DAX code, overview, 32–35
    MDX developers, overview for, 12–15
    overview of, 1
    SQL developers, overview, 9–12

DAX query engine
    formula engine (FE), overview, 458
    introduction to, 457–459
    profiling information, capture of, 463–470
    query plans, introduction to, 459–463
    query plans, reading of, 488–494
    storage engine (VertiPaq), overview, 459
        xmSQL syntax, overview of, 470–477
    storage engine queries, reading of, 470–488
        aggregation functions, 472–473
        arithmetical operations, 474
        CallbackDataID and, 483–488
        DISTINCTCOUNT internal events, 479
        filter operations, 474–476
        JOIN operators, 477
        parallelism and datacache, understanding of, 480–481
        scan time and, 477–478
        VertiPaq cache and, 481–483

DAX Studio
    event tracing, 467–470, 497
    Power BI Desktop and, 497
    server timings and query plans, analysis of, 500–503

DAXFormatter.com, 33

DAY, 42. *See also* Date table

DCOUNT, xmSQL syntax, 472–473

debugging, DEFINE MEASURE, 47. *See also* performance
    concerns

Decimal Number (Float), 18–19

DEFINE MEASURE, 47, 233–236

DEGREES, trigonometric functions, 40

DeJonge, Kasper, 434–435

denormalization of data, 434–442

DENSE rank values, 213–214

derived columns, 309, 312

DESC, syntax, 48

descriptive attributes, columns, 451, 453

dictionary
    dictionary compression, VertiPaq, 405–406
    duplicated data and, 437
    identifying size for each column, 428–429

DICTIONARY SIZE, 415

DIMENSION NAME, 414–416

DirectQuery, 188, 399, 457

DISCOVER views, 413

DISCOVER_OBJECT_MEMORY_USAGE, 414, 433

DISCOVER_STORAGE_TABLE_COLUMN_SEGMENTS, 416

DISCOVER_STORAGE_TABLE_COLUMNS, 415–416

DISCOVER_STORAGE_TABLES, 414–415

Distinct Values, 478

DISTINCT, table function overview, 58–59

DISTINCTCOUNT
    aggregate functions, overview, 36–37
    complex bottlenecks, optimization of, 532–536
    number of unique values in column, determining, 429
    queries, internal events, 479
    VALUES and, 84

DISTINCTCOUNT (ms), query execution time, 478

division
    by zero, 27–28
    DAX operators, 21–22
    error handling, overview, 26–32
    xmSQL syntax for, 474

DMV. *See* Dynamic Management Views (DMV)

drillthrough operations, 200

Duration, DAX Studio event tracing, 470

Duration, of queries, 465–467, 500–503

Dynamic Management Views (DMV), 413
    DISCOVER_OBJECT_MEMORY_USAGE, 414, 433
    DISCOVER_STORAGE_TABLE_COLUMN_SEGMENTS, 416
    DISCOVER_STORAGE_TABLE_COLUMNS, 415–416
    DISCOVER_STORAGE_TABLES, 414–415
    object information, retrieval of, 425–434

dynamic segmentation, use of, 371–373

E

EARLIER, 70–74, 138–143
EDATE, 42
effective interest rate calculations, 227–228
empty or missing values
    aggregate functions, overview, 36–37
    error handling, overview, 28–30
    information functions, overview, 39
empty row removal, 304–307
EOMONTH, date and time functions, 42
equal to, DAX operators, 21–22
error handing
    circular dependencies, 121–122
    errors in DAX expressions, overview, 26–32
    IFERROR, 30–32, 37–38, 370–371
    static segmentation, computing of, 370–371
EVALUATE
    best practices, 250
    ISONORAFTER and, 284
    ORDER BY and, 48–50
    syntax, 47–50
    understanding use of, 233–236
evaluation contexts. *See also* formulas, optimization of
    ALL, understanding use of, 74–76, 326–328
    ALLSELECTED, understanding use of, 285–294
    arbitrarily shaped filters, use of, 321–326
    AutoExists, understanding use of, 306–307
    CALCULATE, context transition and, 111–113
    CALCULATE, introduction to, 98–101
    CALCULATE, variables and evaluation context, 118–119
    columns, use in a measure, 68–69
    EARLIER function, use of, 70–74
    expanded tables, understanding use of, 307–316
    FILTER and ALL context interactions, 74–76
    filter context, 65–66
    filter context and relationship, 80–83
    filter context intersections, 318–320, 323–326
    filter contexts, tuples and, 316–318
    introduction to, 61–66
    ISFILTERED and ISCROSSFILTERED, 85–88
    KEEPFILTERS, understanding use of, 294–303
    lineage, understanding use of, 329–331
    OVERWRITE and, 320–321, 323–326
    parameter table, creation of, 89–92
    row context, 66–67, 69–70, 78–80
    SetFilter, use of, 331–337
    SUM, use in a calculated column, 67–68
    summary of, 88–89
    VALUES, use of, 84
    well-shaped filters, 321–323
    working with many tables, 77–80
evaluation order, 51
    CALCULATE context transitions, 117
    FILTER and, 52–54
EVEN, mathematical functions, 39–40
event tracing
    DAX Studio, use of, 467–470
    DISTINCTCOUNT internal events, 479
    identifying expressions to optimize, 496–498
    SQL Server Profiler, 463–467
    VertiPaq cache and, 481–483
EXACT, text functions, 40–41
Excel. *See* Microsoft Excel
EXCEPT, 274–275, 385–386
EXP, mathematical functions, 39–40
expanded tables, understanding use of, 307–316
EXPONBGBPDIST, 230
expression trees, DAX query engine, 457
Extract, Transform & Load (ETL), 374

F

FACT, mathematical functions, 39–40
FALSE, logical functions, 37–38
FE. *See* formula engine (FE)
FE Time, DAX Studio, 469
FILTER
    ABC (Pareto) classification, use of, 136–143
    CALCULATE, filtering a single column, 104–106
    calculated tables, use of, 50–51
    EARLIER function, use of, 70–74
    evaluation context interactions, 74–76
    MDX developers, DAX overview, 14–15
    overview, 46–47
    SQL developers, DAX overview, 11–12
    static segmentation, computing of, 369–371
    syntax, 51–54
    vsBGBP CALCULATETABLE, 237–239
filter contexts. *See also* data models; also evaluation contexts; also formulas, optimization of
    ADDCOLUMNS, use of, 242–244
    ALL, ALLEXCEPT, and ALLNOBLANKROW, 54–57
    ALL, understanding use of, 55, 93–95, 326–328

filter contexts. *See also* data models; also evaluation
    contexts; also formulas, optimization of
    continued
    ALLSELECTED, understanding use of, 123–125,
        285–294
    arbitrarily shaped filters, 297, 299–303, 321–326
    AutoExists, understanding use of, 75, 306–307
    browsing depth and, 352–358
    CALCULATE
        context transition evaluation order, 117
        context transitions and, 111–113
        filtering with complex conditions, 106–109
        introduction to, 98–101
        rules for using, 122–123
        single column filtering, 101–106
    calculated columns and measures, overview, 22–25
    calculated columns and performance, 447–450
    complex filter, defined, 297, 299
    computing percentages over hierarchies, 341–346
    CONTAINS, use of, 278–280
    cumulative total calculations, 132–136
    data models, overview, 3
    data relationships, direction of, 3–4
    defined, 65–66, 97–98
    drillthrough operations, 200
    dynamic segmentation, use of, 371–373
    expanded tables vs. filtering, 315–316
    expanded tables, understanding use of, 307–316
    filter conditions, optimization of, 512–513
    filter context intersections, 318–320, 323–326
    filter functions, understanding of, 236–240
    filtering columns, 308–316
    FIRSTDATE and LASTDATE, use of, 196–199
    formula engine bottlenecks, optimization of,
        522–527
    GROUPBY, 261–262
    IF conditions, optimization of, 513–515
    INTERSECT, use of, 272–274
    ISFILTERED and ISCROSSFILTERED, use of, 85–88
    ISONORAFTER, use of, 284
    KEEPFILTERS, understanding use of, 294–303
    lineage, understanding use of, 248–250, 329–331
    LOOKUPVALUE, use of, 280–282
    many-to-many relationships, use of, 376–378
    Mark as Date Table, use of, 166–168
    materialization, reducing, 528–532
    MIN/MAX, use of, 196–199
    moving annual total calculations, 175–178

    OVERWRITE and, 320–321, 323–326
    periods to date, understanding, 189–191
    RANKX, common pitfalls, 216–219
    RANKX, use of, 213–216
    ratio and percentage calculations, 129–132
    relationship and, 80–83, 248–250
    relationships with different granularities, 378–381
    SetFilter, use of, 331–337
    static moving averages, computing of, 151–154
    SUMMARIZE and, 250–255
    SUMMARIZECOLUMNS and, 255–261
    time intelligence, introduction to, 164–166
    tuples, 316–318
    understanding use of, 95–98
    UNION, use of, 269–272
    well-shaped filters, 321–323
    working days, computing differences in, 150–151
filter operations, xmSQL syntax for, 474–476
FilterAll Version, 108–109
FIND, text functions, 40–41
FIRSTDATE, 196–199
FIRSTNOBLANK, 199–200, 240
fiscal years
    Date table generation for, 158–160
    previous year comparisons, 173–174
    year-to-date measures, 171
FIXED, text functions, 40–41
Float, syntax, 18–19
FLOOR, mathematical functions, 39–40
foreign keys, SQL developers, 9–12
FORMAT
    conversion functions, overview, 41–42
    text functions, overview, 40–41
formatting DAX code, overview, 32–35. *See also* syntax;
    also specific function names
formula engine (FE)
    bottlenecks
        complex bottlenecks, optimization of, 532–536
        identification of, 503–504, 522–527
        IF conditions, optimization of, 513–515
        materialization, reducing, 528–532
        repro, creating in MDX, 527–528
    event tracing, 463–470
    iterations, AggregationSpoolCache, 462
    overview, 458
    query plans, reading of, 488–494
    server timings and query plans, analysis of,
        500–503

formulas. *See also* evaluation contexts; also formulas, optimization of
 aggregate functions, 35–37
 calculated columns and measures, overview, 22–25
 circular dependencies, 119–122
 conversion functions, overview, 41–42
 data types, 18–21
 date and time functions, overview, 42
 DAX operators, 21–22
 DAX syntax, overview of, 17–22
 DEFINE MEASURE, 47
 error handling, overview, 26–32
 Excel users, DAX overview, 5–9
 formatting DAX code, overview, 32–35
 information functions, overview, 39
 logical functions, overview, 37–38
 mathematical functions, overview, 39–40
 relational functions, overview, 42–44
 text functions, overview, 40–41
 trigonometric functions, overview, 40
 variables, use of, 26
formulas, optimization of
 complex bottlenecks, optimization of, 532–536
 formula engine bottlenecks
  identification of, 503–504, 522–527
  materialization, reducing, 528–532
  repro, creating in MDX, 527–528
 identifying expressions to optimize, 496–498
 optimization strategy, defining of, 496–504
 overview, 495
 reproduction query, creation of, 499–500
 server timings and query plans, analysis of, 500–503
 storage engine bottlenecks
  ADDCOLUMNS and SUMMARIZE, decisions about, 505–509
  CallbackDataID, reducing impact of, 509–511
  cardinality, optimization of, 515–517
  filter conditions, optimization of, 512–513
  identification of, 503–504
  IF conditions, optimization of, 513–515
  nested iterators, optimization of, 517–522
forward slash (/), use in hierarchies, 359
Frequent Itemset Search, 392–397
fully qualified names, 242–243, 246
function calls, SQL developers, 10–12
function parameters, SQL developers, 10–11
functional languages

 Excel users, DAX overview, 8
 formatting DAX code, overview, 32–35
 SQL developers, DAX overview, 10–11
functions, DAX operators and, 22

G

GCD, mathematical functions, 39–40
GENERATE, 275–277
GENERATEALL, 275–277
GEOMEAN, 225–229
GEOMEANX, 225–229
geometric mean, calculation of, 225–229
granularity
 relationships with different granularities, 378–381
 sales per day calculations, 146–150
graphics, performance and, 443
greater than, DAX operators, 21–22
grouping functions
 ADDMISSINGITEMS, 262–264
 GROUPBY, 250, 261–262
 overview of, 250
 SUMMARIZE, 250–255
 SUMMARIZECOLUMNS, 255–261

H

hardware decision, VertiPaq, 421–424
HASNOVALUE, 60, 214
HASONEVALUE, 91–92
HideMemberIf, 358
hierarchies
 column hierarchies, determining cost of, 430–434
 computing percentages over hierarchies, 339–346
 data models, gathering information about, 425–434
 Date tables and, 160
 MDX developers, DAX overview, 13–15
 parent-child hierarchies, handling of, 346–358
 unary operators
  alternative implementations, 365–366
  handling of, 358–366
  implementing using DAX, 359–365
  values and definitions list, 358–359
 VertiPaq compression and, 410–411
HOUR, date and time functions, overview, 42

I

IF
ABC (Pareto) classification, use of, 139
computing percentages over hierarchies, 343
cumulative total calculations, 135–136
Excel users, DAX overview, 6
IF conditions, optimization of, 513–515
logical functions, overview, 37–38
IFERROR
intercepting errors, 30–32
logical functions, overview, 37–38
static segmentation, computing of, 370–371
IGNORE, 259
IN, xmSQL filter operations syntax, 474–476
IncrementalPct, 141–143
IncrementalProfit, 136–143
indexes, SUBSTITUTEWITHINDEX, 283
Infinity, division by zero, 27–28
information functions, syntax overview, 39
In-Memory. *See* VertiPaq (storage engine)
INT, conversion functions, 41–42
Integer, syntax, 18–19
interest calculations, 225–229
internal rate of return, calculation of, 227–228
INTERSECT, 272–274, 381, 385–386
inventory tables
closing balance over time, 179–184
CLOSINGBALANCE, 184–188
OPENINGBALANCE, 184–188
ISBLANK, 31–32, 39
ISCROSSFILTERED, 85–88
ISEMPTY, 370–371
ISERROR, 39
ISFILTERED, 85–88, 341–346
IsLeaf, 356–357
ISLOGICAL, 39
ISNONTEXT, 39
ISNUMBER, 39
ISO weeks, custom calendars, 201–204
ISONORAFTER, 284
ISSUBTOTAL, 254–255, 260–261
ISTEXT, 39
iterations
ADDCOLUMNS, use of, 241–244
CALCULATE, context transition with measures, 114–116
calculated columns and performance, 448–450
CallbackDataID, reducing impact of, 509–511
CallbackDataID, use of, 483–488
cardinality, optimization of, 515–517
creating a row context, 69–70
EARLIER function, use of, 70–74
Excel users, DAX overview, 8
FILTER as, 104–106
formula engine bottlenecks, 462, 522–527
granularity, sales per day, 149–150
GROUPBY, use of, 261–262
IF conditions, optimization of, 513–515
KEEPFILTERS, understanding use of, 296–303
materialization and, 417–420
nested iterators, optimization of, 517–522

J

joining functions
CROSSJOIN, 267–269
JOIN, xmSQL syntax, 477
NATURALINNERJOIN, 265
NATURALLEFTOUTERJOIN, 266–267
overview of, 250
SQL developers, DAX overview, 9–12

K

KEEPFILTERS, 294–303
Key Performance Indicators (KPI), 172–173
keys of relationship
column cardinality and performance, 442, 451
column storage, choosing columns for, 451
data models, overview of, 2–3
multiple column relationships, computing of, 367–369
relationships with different granularities, 378–381
static segmentation, computing of, 369–371

L

LASTDATE
closing balance over time, 179–184
moving annual total calculations, 175–178
nested calls and time intelligence functions, 177–178

opening and closing balances, 184–188
use of, 196–199
LASTNOBLANK, 181–184, 199–200
LCM, mathematical functions, 39–40
Leaf, 356–357. *See also* parent-child (P/C) hierarchies
leaf-level-calculations, MDX developers, 15
leap year, 20
LEFT OUTER JOINS, SQL developers, 10
LEFT, text functions, 40–41
LEN, text functions, 40–41
less than, DAX operators, 21–22
lineage
    CROSSJOIN and, 269
    EXCEPT, use of, 274–275
    INTERSECT and, 272–274
    overview of, 248–250
    SELECTCOLUMNS and, 245–246
    understanding of, 329–331
    UNION use of, 269–272
linear dependencies, 119–120
list of values, CALCULATE, 99–101
LN, mathematical functions, 39–40
localhost
    port number, 497
LOG, mathematical functions, 39–40
LOG10, mathematical functions, 39–40
logical functions
    information functions, overview, 39
    logical operators, DAX, 21–22
    syntax, overview, 37–38
Logical Plan event, 464–465
logical query plan
    DAX query engine, overview of, 457
    DAX Studio, event tracing with, 467–470
    overview, 460–461
    query plans, reading of, 488–494
    server timings and query plans, analysis of, 500–503
    SQL Server Profiler, event tracing, 464
LOOKUPVALUE
    multiple column relationships, computing of, 368–369
    parent-child hierarchies and, 349
    use of, 280–282
Lotus 1-2-3, leap year bug, 20
LOWER, text functions, 40–41

M

many-side relationships
    data models, overview of, 2–3
    expanded tables, use of, 307–316
many-to-many relationships
    physical vs. virtual relationships, 382
    row contexts and, 78–80
    use of, 373–378
many-to-one relationships, 78–80
Mark as Date Table, 166–168
MAT (moving annual total) calculations, 175–178
materialization
    EVALUATE, use of, 233–236
    formula engine bottlenecks and, 522–527
    nested iterators, optimization of, 519–522
    overview, 417–420
    reducing materialization, 528–532
mathematical functions
    syntax overview, 39–40
    trigonometric functions, overview, 40
MAX
    aggregate functions, overview, 35–37
    cumulative total calculations, 134–136
    dynamic segmentation, use of, 371–373
    using in calculated columns, 68
    xmSQL syntax, 472–473
MAXX, 37
MDX developers
    AutoExists, understanding use of, 304–307
    DAX overview, 12–15
    DAX query engine, overview of, 458
    identifying expressions to optimize, 498
    repro, creation of, 527–528
    reproduction query, creation of, 500
mean, geometric, 225–229
MEASURE, 499–500
measures
    CALCULATE, context transitions and, 114–116
    calculated columns and measures, overview, 22–25
MEDIAN, 223–225
MEDIANX, 223–225
memory. *See also* DAX query engine; also performance concerns
    BISM Server Memory Report, 434–435
    calculated columns and performance, 447–450

memory. *See also* DAX query engine; also performance
    concerns *continued*
    CallbackDataID, use of, 484–488
    column storage, choosing columns for, 451–453
    column storage, optimization of, 453–455
    data models, gathering information about, 425–434
    DAX query engine, overview of, 457–459
    denormalization of data, 434–442
    hardware selection, VertiPaq, 423–424
    materialization and, 417–420
    parallelism and datacache, understanding of, 480–481
Memory (MB), query execution time, 478
Microsoft Excel
    aggregate functions, overview, 35–37
    BISM Server Memory Report, 434–435
    cells vs. tables, 5–7
    date and time functions, overview, 42
    DAX overview, 5–9
    debugging trace events in Power Pivot, 467
    empty values, handling of, 29–30
    leap year bug, 20
    mathematical functions, overview, 39–40
    median and percentile calculations, 224–225
    NPV and XNPV, use of, 228–229
    OLAP PivotTable Extension add-in, 498
    Power Pivot add-in, 400
    RANK.EQ, use of, 219–220
    Show Values As, 339–340, 346
    statistical functions available in DAX, 229–230
    text functions, overview, 40–41
    Top 10 filter, 301
    XIRR calculations, 227–228
Microsoft Excel Slicer, calculated columns and
    measures, 25
Microsoft Press resources, 5555
MID, text functions, 40–41
MIN
    aggregate functions, overview, 35–37
    dynamic segmentation, use of, 371–373
    using in calculated columns, 68
    xmSQL syntax, 472–473
MIN/MAX, FIRSTDATE and LASTDATE use, 196–199
minus sign (–), use in hierarchies, 358–365
MINUTE, date and time functions, 42
MINX, aggregate functions, 37
missing values. *See also* BLANK
    error handling, overview, 28–30
    information functions, overview, 39

MOD, mathematical functions, 39–40
MONTH, 42. *See also* Date table
MonthSequentialNumber, 206–209
month-to-date calculations (MTD), 168–171, 189–191,
    204–205
moving annual total (MAT) calculations, 175–178
moving averages
    calculation of, 220–221
    static, computing of, 151–154
MROUND, mathematical functions, 39–40
multidimensional spaces, MDX developers, 12–15
multiplication
    DAX operators, 21–22
    xmSQL syntax for, 474

N

NaN (not a number), division by zero, 27–28
native columns, 309
natural hierarchies, Date tables and, 160. *See also*
    hierarchies
NATURALINNERJOIN, 265
NATURALLEFTOUTERJOIN, 266–267
nested calls
    ALLSELECTED understanding use of, 290–294
    EARLIER function, use of, 70–74
    evaluation order, 51
    FILTER, 52–54
    nested iterators, optimization of, 517–522
    SWITCH use of, 515
    time intelligence functions and, 177–178
net present value formula, 228–229
new customers, computing, 384–386
NEXTDAY, 177–178
Nodes, 356–357. *See also* Parent-child (P/C) hierarchies
noncontiguous periods, computing over, 206–209
non-numeric values
    aggregate functions, overview, 35–37
    information functions, overview, 39
nonstandard calendars, time intelligence, 188
not equal to, DAX operators, 21–22
NOT, logical functions, 37–38
NOW, date and time functions, 42
number of products not sold, computing, 383–384
numeric values
    aggregate functions, overview, 35–37
    parameter tables, creation of, 89–92

O

objects
    data models, gathering information about, 425–434
    OBJECT MEMORY NON SHRINKABLE, 414
    OBJECT PARENT PATH, 414
    OBJECT_ID, 414
    OBJECT_MEMORY_CHILD_NONSHRINKABLE, 433
    OBJECT_MEMORY_NONSHRINKABLE, 433
    OBJECT_PARENT_PATH, 433
ODD, mathematical functions, 39–40
OLAP PivotTable Extension add-in, 498
one-side relationships. *See also* relationships
    data models, overview of, 2–3
    expanded tables, understanding use of, 307–316
one-to-many relationships, 78–80
OnHandQuantity, 179–184
OPENINGBALANCE, 184–188
operating overloading, 18
operators
    DAX syntax, overview of, 21–22
    error handling, overview, 26–32
OR
    CALCULATETABLE and, 110–111
    DAX operators, 21–22
    logical functions, overview, 37–38
ORDER BY, 48–50
order of evaluation, 51. *See also* evaluation contexts
    FILTER and, 52–54
OVERWRITE, 320–321, 323–326

P

P/C. *See* Parent-child (P/C) hierarchies
parallelism and datacache
    CallbackDataID, use of, 483–488
    parallelism degree of query, 467
    understanding of, 480–481
PARALLELPERIOD, 171–172
parameter table, creation of, 89–92
parameters, SQL developers, 10–11
parent-child (P/C) hierarchies
    handling of, 346–358
    PATH function, use of, 348–349
    unary operators, implementing in DAX, 359–365
parenthesis, DAX operators, 21–22
Pareto (ABC) classification, 136–143

partitions
    determining size of table columns, 429
    partitioning, VertiPaq and, 412
PATH, 348–349
PATHITEM, 349
percentages
    computing of, 129–132
    computing percentages over hierarchies, 339–346
    differences over previous periods, 174–175
PERCENTILEBGBPEXE, 223–225
PERCENTILEBGBPINC, 223–225
performance concerns. *See also* query engine, DAX
    calculated columns and performance, 447–450
    column cardinality and performance, 442–447
    column storage, choosing columns for, 451–453
    column storage, optimization of, 453–455
    data models, gathering information about, 425–434
        cost of a column hierarchy, 430–434
        dictionary size for each column, 428–429
        number of rows in a table, 426–427
        number of unique values per column, 427–429
        total cost of table, 433–434
    denormalization of data, 434–442
    formula engine bottlenecks
        complex bottlenecks, optimization of, 532–536
        identification of, 503–504, 522–527
        materialization, reducing, 528–532
        repro, creating in MDX, 527–528
    hardware selection, VertiPaq, 421–424
    hierarchies and relationships, VertiPaq compression and, 411
    materialization, 417–420
    optimizing formulas
        identifying expressions to optimize, 496–498
        optimization strategy, defining of, 496–504
        overview of, 495
        reproduction query, creation of, 499–500
        server timings and query plans, analysis of, 500–503
    physical vs. virtual relationships, 382
    query plans, reading of, 488–494
    segmentation and partitioning, VertiPaq, 412
    star schemas, benefits of, 437
    storage engine bottlenecks
        ADDCOLUMNS and SUMMARIZE, decisions about, 505–509
        CallbackDataID, reducing impact of, 509–511
        cardinality, optimization of, 515–517

performance concerns. *See also* query engine, DAX
    continued
      complex bottlenecks, optimization of, 532–536
      filter conditions, optimization of, 512–513
      identification of, 503–504
      IF conditions, optimization of, 513–515
      nested iterators, optimization of, 517–522
    VertiPaq Analyzer, optimization and, 510
PERMUT, 230
Physical Plan event, 464–465
physical query plan, 461–462
    DAX query engine, overview of, 458–459
    DAX Studio, event tracing with, 467–470
    formula engine (FE), overview, 458
    query plans, reading of, 488–494
    server timings and query plans, analysis of, 500–503
PI, mathematical functions, 39
Pi, trigonometric functions, 40
pictures, performance and, 443
pivot tables. *See also* evaluation contexts
    ABC (Pareto) classification, use of, 136–143
    ALL statements and filters, 56–57
    ALLSELECTED, overview, 123–125, 215
    AutoExists, understanding use of, 304–307
    browsing depth, filter context and, 352–358
    calculated columns and measures, overview, 22–25
    cumulative total calculations, 132–136
    FILTER and ALL context interactions, 74–76
    filter context and relationship, 80–83
    filter context, overview of, 94–98
    ISFILTERED and ISCROSSFILTERED, use of, 85–88
    multiple date tables, use of, 163–164
    OLAP PivotTable Extension add-in, 498
    Power Pivot, debugging trace events, 467
    ratio and percentage calculations, 132
    relationships, direction of, 3–4
    removing unwanted rows, 352–354
    sales per day calculations, 143–150
plus sign (+)
    implementing in DAX, 359–365
    use in hierarchies, 358–359
POISSONBGBPDIST, 230
Power BI
    database processing, overview, 400
    DISCOVER_STORAGE_TABLES, use of, 415
    graphics display, 443
    hardware for VertiPaq and, 421
    optimizing DAX expressions, 496–498

profiling information, capture of, 463
refresh reports, 496
SUBSTITUTEWITHINDEX, matrix charts and, 283
unary operators and, 365
Power BI Desktop, Query End event capture, 497
Power Pivot, 400
    debugging trace events, 467
POWER, mathematical functions, 39–40
precedence
    CALCULATE context transitions, 117
    DAX operators, overview of, 21–22
previous customers, computing, 384–386
previous year, month, quarter comparisons, 171–175
primary key
    CALCULATE and context transitions, 116–117
    column storage, choosing columns for, 451
prior time period comparisons (year, month), 171–174
PRODUCT, interest calculations, 225–229
products not sold, computing of, 383–384
PRODUCTX
    aggregate functions, overview, 37
    interest calculations, 225–229
profiling information, capture of, 463–470
programming languages
    MDX developers, DAX overview, 13–15
    SQL developers, DAX overview, 11
projection functions, 241–247
PY YTD, 173–174

Q

qualitative attributes, columns, 451
quantitative attributes, columns, 451–452
quarter-to-date calculations (QTD), 168–171, 189–191
    custom calendars, 204–205
queries. *See also* formulas, optimization of; also table
    functions
    AutoExists, understanding use of, 304–307
    data models, gathering information about, 425–434
    EVALUATE statements, 47–50
    evaluation order, 51–54
    KEEPFILTERS, understanding of, 302–303
    lineage, understanding use of, 329–331
    materialization, 417–420
    MDX developers, DAX overview, 13–15
    reproduction query, creation of, 499–500
    SAMPLE function, 230–232

segmentation and partitioning, performance and, 412

SQL developers, DAX overview, 9–12, 457

table expressions, overview, 45–47

Query End, 464–465, 497

query engine, DAX

formula engine (FE), overview, 458

introduction to, 457–459

profiling information, capture of, 463–470

query plans, introduction to, 459–463

query plans, reading of, 488–494

storage engine (VertiPaq), overview, 459

xmSQL syntax, overview of, 470–477

storage engine queries, reading of, 470–488

aggregation functions, 472–473

arithmetical operations, 474

CallbackDataID and, 483–488

DISTINCTCOUNT internal events, 479

filter operations, 474–476

JOIN operators, 477

parallelism and datacache, understanding of, 480–481

scan time and, 477–478

VertiPaq cache and, 481–483

Query Plan and Server Timings, DAX Studio analysis of, 500–503

Query Plan, DAX Studio, 467–470

QUOTIENT, mathematical functions, 39–40

R

RADIANS, trigonometric functions, 40

RAND, mathematical functions, 39–40

RANDBETWEEN, mathematical functions, 39–40

RANKBGBPEQ, use of, 219–220

ranking, ABC (Pareto) classification and, 136–143

RANKX

common pitfalls, 216–219

introduction to using, 213–216

ratios, computing of, 129–132

RECORDS COUNT, 416

re-encoding, VertiPaq, 409

refresh

calculated columns and performance, 449–450

identifying expressions to optimize, 496–497

RELATED, 249–250

relational functions, overview, 42–44

table expansion vs. filtering, 315–316

vsBGBP LOOKUPVALUE, 282

working with many tables, row contexts and, 78–80

RELATEDTABLE

calculated tables, use of, 50–51

FIRSTNOBLANK and LASTNOBLANK, 199–200

relational functions, overview, 42–44

working with many tables, row contexts and, 78–80

relational functions

filter context and, 80–83

syntax overview, 42–44

relationships

arbitrarily shaped filters and, 323–326

calculated physical relationships, use of, 367–371

column cardinality and performance, 442–447

column hierarchies, determining cost of, 430–434

currency conversions, 386–392

data models

direction of relationships, 3–4

gathering information about, 425–434

overview, 1–3

expanded tables, understanding use of, 307–316

finding missing relationships, 382–386

Frequent Itemset Search, 392–397

MDX developers, DAX overview, 13–15

multiple column relationships, computing of, 367–369

NATURALINNERJOIN, 265

NATURALLEFTOUTERJOIN, 266–267

overview of, 248–250

physical vs. virtual relationships, 381–382

query plans, reading of, 492–494

SQL developers, DAX overview, 9–12

static segmentation, computing of, 369–371

USERELATIONSHIP, 123–127, 161–162

VertiPaq compression and, 410–411

virtual relationships, use of, 371–382

dynamic segmentation, use of, 371–373

many-to-many relationships, 373–378

relationships with different granularities, 378–381

REMOVEFILTERS, 326–328

REPLACE, text functions, 40–41

Reporting Services, MDX developers, 13–14

repro, creating in MDX, 527–528

reproduction query, creation of, 499–500

REPT, text functions, 40–41

resources, Microsoft Press, 5555

returning customers, computing, 384–386

RIGHT, text functions, 40–41

RLE (Run Length Encoding), VertiPaq, 406–408
role-playing dimension approach, 162–164
ROLLUP, 260–261
rollup formulas, custom, 358
roll-up rows, SUMMARIZE and, 252–255
ROLLUPADDISSUBTOTAL, 260–261
ROLLUPGROUP, 260–261
ROUND
    CallbackDataID, reducing impact of, 510–511
    mathematical functions, overview, 39–40
ROUNDDOWN, mathematical functions, 39–40
ROUNDUP, mathematical functions, 39–40
row context, 66–67
    CALCULATE, context transitions and, 111–113
    creating with iterators, 69–70
    EARLIER function, use of, 70–74
    expanded tables, understanding use of, 307–316
    working with many tables, relationships and, 78–80
ROW, use of, 247
rows. *See also* database processing; also evaluation
        contexts; also table functions
    calculated columns and measures, overview, 22–25
    CONTAINS, use of, 278–280
    data models, gathering information about, 425–434
        number of rows in a table, 426–427
    SUMMARIZE and, 252–255
ROWS COUNT, 414
Run Length Encoding (RLE), VertiPaq, 406–408

S

sales per day calculations, 143–150
SAMEPERIODLASTYEAR, 171–174, 176–178
SAMPLE, 230–232
scalar expressions, defined, 45
scalar functions, defined, 46
scalar values
    parameter table, creation of, 89–92
    table expressions and, 46–47, 60
    VALUES as a scalar value, 59–60
scan time, storage engine (VertiPaq) queries and, 477–478
SCHEMA views, 413
SCOPE, MDX developers, 15
SE Cache, DAX Studio, 469
SE CPU, DAX Studio, 469. *See also* storage engine (SE)
    (VertiPaq)

SE Queries, DAX Studio, 469. *See also* storage engine
    (SE) (VertiPaq)
SE Time, DAX Studio, 469. *See also* storage engine (SE)
    (VertiPaq)
SEARCH, text functions, 40–41
SECOND, date and time functions, 42
SEGMENT NUMBER, 416
segmentations, VertiPaq and, 412
SELECT, SQL developers, 10–11
SELECTCOLUMNS, 243–246
Server Timings pane, DAX Studio, 467–470
SetFilter, use of, 331–337
SIGN, mathematical functions, 39–40
SIN, trigonometric functions, 40
SINH, trigonometric functions, 40
SKIP, rank value, 213–214
sorting
    ABC (Pareto) classification, use of, 136–143
    ORDER BY, 48–50
    RANKX, use of, 213–216
    SAMPLE function, use of, 230–232
    Sort By Column, 48
    Top 10 filter, 301
    TOPN, use of, 239–240
    VertiPaq compression, best sort order, 409–410
SQL developers
    DAX overview, 9–12
    empty values, handling of, 29–30
    GENERATE and GENERATEALL, use of, 277
    GROUPBY, use of, 262
    xmSQL, 459
SQL Server Analysis Services (SSAS)
    AutoExists, understanding use of, 304–307
    best sort order, 409–410
SQL Server Analysis Services (SSAS) Tabular
    Date table, use of, 155
    HideMemberIf, 358
    MDX developers, DAX overview, 13–15
    MDX queries, 458
    VertiPaq database processing, 400
SQL Server Profiler, 463–467
    Query End events, capture of, 497
SQRT, mathematical functions, 39–40
SQRTPI, trigonometric functions, 40
SSAS. *See* SQL Server Analysis Services (SSAS)
standard deviation calculations, 222–223

star schema
    Date table, use of, 155
    performance benefits of, 437
START AT, 48–50
    ISONORAFTER and, 284
static moving averages, computing of, 151–154
static segmentation, computing of, 369–371
statistical functions. *See also* specific function names
    average and moving average calculations, 35–37,
        151–154, 220–221, 250, 473
    Excel functions, use of, 229–230
    interest calculations, 225–229
    median and percentiles, 223–225
    RANKBGBPEQ, use of, 219–220
    RANKX, common pitfalls, 216–219
    RANKX, use of, 213–216
    SAMPLE, 230–232
    variance and standard deviation calculations,
        35–37, 222–223
STDEV
    aggregate functions, overview, 35–37
    use of, 222–223
stocks, static moving average calculations, 151–154
Storage Engine (SE), 382
storage engine (SE) (VertiPaq), 459
    best sort order, finding of, 409–410
    bottlenecks
        ADDCOLUMNS and SUMMARIZE, decisions
            about, 505–509
        CallbackDataID, reducing impact of, 509–511
        complex bottlenecks, optimization of, 532–536
        filter conditions, optimization of, 512–513
        identification of, 503–504
        IF conditions, optimization of, 513–515
        materialization, reducing, 528–532
        nested iterators, optimization of, 517–522
    columnar databases, introduction to, 400–403
    compression, understanding of, 403–411
    database processing, understanding of, 400
    DAX query engine, overview of, 457–459
    dictionary encoding, 405–406
    DirectQuery and, 399
    Dynamic Management Views (DMV), use of, 413–416
    event tracing, 463–470
    filter contexts and, 95–98
    formula engine (FE), overview, 458
    hardware selection, 421–424
    hierarchies and relationships, understanding of,
        410–411

materialization, understanding of, 417–420
physical query plan and, 382, 462–463
queries, reading of, 470–488
    aggregation functions, 472–473
    arithmetical operations, 474
    CallbackDataID and, 483–488
    DISTINCTCOUNT internal events, 479
    filter operations, 474–476
    JOIN operators, 477
    parallelism and datacache, understanding of,
        480–481
    scan time and, 477–478
    VertiPaq cache and, 481–483
    xmSQL syntax, overview of, 470–477
query cache match, 464
query end, 464
query plans, reading of, 488–494
re-encoding, 409
Run Length Encoding (RLE), 406–408
segmentation and partitioning, 412
server timings and query plans, analysis of, 500–503
use of term, 399
value encoding, 404–405
VertipaqResult, 462–463
storage tables
    DISCOVER_STORAGE_TABLE_COLUMN_SEGMENTS, 416
    DISCOVER_STORAGE_TABLE_COLUMNS, 415–416
    DISCOVER_STORAGE_TABLES, 414–415
strings
    syntax, overview of, 18–21
    text concatenation, 21–22
subqueries, SQL developers, 12
SUBSTITUTE, text functions, 40–41
SUBSTITUTEWITHINDEX, 283
subtraction
    DAX operators, 21–22
    xmSQL syntax for, 474
sum. *See also* aggregation
    DAX operators, 21–22
    xmSQL syntax for, 474
SUM (ms), query execution time, 478
SUM function
    ABC (Pareto) classification, use of, 136–143
    aggregate functions, overview, 35–37
    cumulative total calculations, 132–136
    Excel users, DAX overview, 7
    using a calculated column, 67–68
    xmSQL syntax, 472–473

SUMMARIZE
   cardinality, optimization of, 515–517
   many-to-many relationships, filtering and, 377–378
   performance decisions for use, 505–509
   SQL developers, DAX overview, 10
   syntax, 250–251
   table expansion vs. filtering, 315–316
   understanding use of, 250–255
SUMMARIZECOLUMNS, 250, 255–261, 497, 508–509
SUMX
   ABC (Pareto) classification, use of, 136–143
   aggregate functions, overview, 37
   best practices, 250
   sales per day calculations, 143–150
SWITCH, 37–38, 515
syntax. *See also* formulas, optimization of; also specific
         function names
   aggregate functions, 35–37, 472–473
   automatic context transition, 115
   binary large objects (BLOBs), 18, 21
   calculated tables, use of, 50–51
   calculations, error handling, 26–32
   calculations, overview, 17–22
   conversion functions, overview, 41–42
   data types, 18–21
   date and time functions, overview, 42
   date table names, 157
   DAX operators, 21–22
   error handling, overview, 26–32
   formatting DAX code, 32–35
   information functions, overview, 39
   logical functions, overview, 37–38
   mathematical functions, overview, 39–40
   relational functions, overview, 42–44
   text functions, overview, 40–41
   trigonometric functions, overview, 40
   variables, use of, 26
   xmSQL syntax overview, 470–477
   year-to-date (YTD) calculations, 170

T

table functions. *See also* specific function names
   ADDCOLUMNS, 241–244
   ADDMISSINGITEMS, 262–264
   ALL, ALLEXCEPT, and ALLNOBLANKROW, 54–57
   calculated tables, use of, 50–51

   CALCULATETABLE, 236–239
   CROSSJOIN, 267–269
   EVALUATE, 233–236
   EXCEPT, 274–275
   expanded tables, understanding use of, 307–316
   filter functions, 236–240
   FILTER, overview of, 51–54, 237–239
   FIRSTNOBLANK, 240
   GENERATE and GENERATEALL, 275–277
   GROUPBY, 261–262
   grouping/joining functions, 250–267
   INTERSECT, 272–274
   ISONORAFTER, 284
   lineage and relationships, overview of, 248–250
   LOOKUPVALUE, 280–282
   NATURALINNERJOIN, 265
   NATURALLEFTOUTERJOIN, 266–267
   overview of, 45–47
   projection functions, 241–247
   ROW, 247
   SELECTCOLUMNS, 243–246
   set functions, 267–277
   SUBSTITUTEWITHINDEX, 283
   SUMMARIZE, 250–255
   SUMMARIZECOLUMNS, 255–261
   table expansion vs. filtering, 315–316
   TOPN, 239–240
   UNION, 269–272
   utility functions, 278–284
   VALUES and DISTINCT, 58–59
   VALUES as a scalar value, 59–60
TABLE ID, 414–416
TABLE PARTITION COUNT, 414
TABLE PARTITION NUMBER, 416
tables. *See also* database processing; also evaluation
         contexts
   aggregate functions, 35–37
   calculated columns and measures, overview, 22–25
   calculation error handing, overview, 26–32
   conversion functions, overview, 41–42
   data models
      gathering information about, 425–434
      overview, 1–3
      total cost of table, 433–434
   data types, 18–21
   date and time functions, overview, 42
   DAX calculations, syntax overview, 17–22
   denormalization of data, 434–442

DISCOVER_STORAGE_TABLE_COLUMN_SEGMENTS, 416

DISCOVER_STORAGE_TABLE_COLUMNS, 415–416

DISCOVER_STORAGE_TABLES, 414–415

Excel users, DAX overview, 5–7

filter context, overview of, 97–98

formatting DAX code, overview, 32–35

information functions, overview, 39

logical functions, overview, 37–38

MDX developers, DAX overview, 13–15

naming of, 17–18

parameter table, creation of, 89–92

relational functions, overview, 42–44

relationships, advanced

    calculated physical relationships, use of, 367–371

    currency conversions, 386–392

    dynamic segmentation, use of, 371–373

    finding missing relationships, 382–386

    Frequent Itemset Search, 392–397

    many-to-many relationships, 373–378

    multiple column relationships, computing of, 367–369

    physical vs. virtual relationships, 381–382

    relationships with different granularities, 378–381

    static segmentation, computing of, 369–371

    virtual relationships, use of, 371–382

scanning, materialization and, 417–420

text functions, overview, 40–41

trigonometric functions, overview, 40

variables, use of, 26

VertiPaq, as columnar database, 95–98

Tabular. See SQL Server Analysis Services (SSAS) Tabular

TAN, trigonometric functions, 40

TANH, trigonometric functions, 40

technical attributes, columns, 451, 453

text

    aggregate functions, overview, 35–37

    AVERAGEA, use of, 220

    column cardinality and performance, 443

    information functions, overview, 39

    text concatenation, DAX operators, 21–22

    text functions, overview, 40–41

Text (String), syntax of, 20–21

Text, syntax of, 18

TIME

    conversion functions, overview, 41–42

    date and time functions, overview, 42

time intelligence

    advanced functions, use of, 188

    aggregating and comparing over time, 168

        computing differences over previous periods, 174–175

        computing periods from prior periods, 171–174

        moving annual total calculations, 175–178

        year-, quarter-, and month-to-date, 168–171

    CALENDAR and CALENDARAUTO, use of, 157–160

    closing balance over time, 178–188

    CLOSINGBALANCE, 184–188

    custom calendars, 200–201

        custom comparisons between periods, 210–211

        noncontiguous periods, computing over, 206–209

        weeks, working with, 201–204

        year-, quarter-, and month-to-date, 204–205

    date and time functions, overview, 42

    Date table, use of, 156–157

    Date tables, working with multiple dates, 160–164

    DATEADD, use of, 191–196

    drillthrough and, 200

    FIRSTDATE and LASTDATE, 196–199

    FIRSTNOBLANK and LASTNOBLANK, 199–200

    introduction to, 155, 164–166

    Mark as Date Table, use of, 166–168

    OPENINGBALANCE, 184–188

    periods to date, understanding, 189–191

    working days, computing differences in, 150–151

time, performance and

    column cardinality and performance, 443–447

    CPU Time and Duration, 465–467

    DAX Studio event tracing, 470

    rounding vs. truncating, 444–447

    scan time, storage engine (VertiPaq) queries, 477–478

    server timings and query plans, analysis of, 500–503

    Total Elapsed Time, DAX Studio, 469

TIMEVALUE, date and time functions, 42

TODAY, date and time functions, 42

Top 10 filter, Excel, 301

TOPCOUNT, 301

TOPN, 239–240, 301, 528–532

Total Elapsed Time, DAX Studio, 469

TotalProfit, 139–143

totals, cumulative, 132–136

trace events

    DAX Studio, use of, 467–470

    DISTINCTCOUNT internal events, 479

trace events *continued*
 identifying expressions to optimize, 496–498
 SQL Server Profiler, 463–467
 VertiPaq cache and, 481–483
transaction ID, 443
trigonometric functions, syntax overview, 40
TRIM, text functions, 40–41
TRUE, logical functions, 37–38
TRUE/FALSE
 information functions, overview, 39
 syntax, overview of, 18, 20–21
TRUNC, mathematical functions, 39–40
tuple, overview of, 316–318
Twitter, Microsoft Press, 5555

U

unary operators
 alternative implementations, 365–366
 handling of, 358–366
 implementing using DAX, 359–365
 values and definitions, list of, 358–359
Unicode, string syntax, 20–21
UNION
 new and returning customers, computing, 385–386
 use of, 269–272
UPPER, text functions, 40–41
USED_SIZE, 416, 429
USERELATIONSHIP, 125–127, 161–162

V

VALUE
 conversion functions, overview, 41–42
 text functions, overview, 40–41
value encoding, VertiPaq, 404–405
VALUES
 as a scalar value, 59–60
 evaluation context and, 84
 grouped columns and, 259–260
 KEEPFILTERS, understanding use of, 296–303
 parameter table, creation of, 92
 ratio and percentage calculations, 130–132
 static moving averages, computing of, 154
 static segmentation, computing of, 369–371
 table function overview, 58–59

values between 0 and 1, use in hierarchies, 359
VAR
 aggregate functions, overview, 35–37
 syntax for, 222, 235
 use in EVALUATE, 235–236
 use of, 222–223
variables. *See also* formulas; also formulas, optimization of
 CALCULATE, variables and evaluation context, 118–119
 context transition, avoidance of, 336–337
 EARLIER, use of, 138–143
 EVALUATE and, 235–236
variance calculations, 222–223
VertiPaq (storage engine), 459
 best sort order, finding of, 409–410
 bottlenecks
  ADDCOLUMNS and SUMMARIZE, decisions about, 505–509
  CallbackDataID, reducing impact of, 509–511
  complex bottlenecks, optimization of, 532–536
  filter conditions, optimization of, 512–513
  identification of, 503–504
  IF conditions, optimization of, 513–515
  materialization, reducing, 528–532
  nested iterators, optimization of, 517–522
 columnar databases, introduction to, 400–403
 compression, understanding of, 403–411
 database processing, understanding of, 400
 DAX query engine, overview of, 457–459
 dictionary encoding, 405–406
 DirectQuery and, 399
 Dynamic Management Views (DMV), use of, 413–416
 event tracing, 463–470
 filter contexts and, 95–98
 hardware selection, 421–424
 hierarchies and relationships, understanding of, 410–411
 materialization, understanding of, 417–420
 physical query plan and, 382, 462–463
 query cache match, 464
 query end, 464
 query plans, reading of, 488–494
 re-encoding, 409
 Run Length Encoding (RLE), 406–408
 segmentation and partitioning, 412
 server timings and query plans, analysis of, 500–503
 storage engine queries, reading of, 470–488
  aggregation functions, 472–473
  arithmetical operations, 474

CallbackDataID and, 483–488
DISTINCTCOUNT internal events, 479
filter operations, 474–476
JOIN operators, 477
parallelism and datacache, understanding of, 480–481
scan time and, 477–478
VertiPaq cache and, 481–483
xmSQL syntax, overview of, 470–477
use of term, 399
value encoding, 404–405
VertipaqResult, 462–463
VertiPaq Analyzer, 510
VertiPaq cache, 481–483
VertiPaq Logical Plan event, 464–465
VertiPaq Physical Plan event, 465
VertiPaq Scan, 479
VertiPaq scan event, 465
VertiPaq Scan Internal, 479
VERTIPAQ STATE, 416
virtual relationships, 371
dynamic segmentation, use of, 371–373
many-to-many relationships, 373–378
physical vs. virtual relationships, 381–382
relationships with different granularities, 378–381

W

WEEKDAY, date and time functions, 42
WEEKNUM, date and time functions, 42
weeks, custom calendars, 201–204

WHERE
determining size of table columns, 429
SQL developers, DAX overview, 11
xmSQL filter operations syntax, 474–476
Whole Number (Integer), syntax, 18–19
WITHMEASURE, 500
working day
computing differences in, 150–151
sales per day calculations, 143–150
static moving averages, computing of, 151–154

X

XIRR, internal rate of return calculations, 227–228
xmSQL, 459. *See also* syntax
aggregation functions, syntax for, 472–473
arithmetic operations, syntax for, 474
filter operations syntax, 474–476
JOIN operators syntax, 477
syntax, overview of, 470–477
xVelocity In-Memory Analytical Engine, 399. *See also* VertiPaq (storage engine)

Y

YEAR, 42. *See also* Date table
YEARFRAC, date and time functions, 42
year-over-year differences, calculation of, 174–175
year-to-date calculations (YTD), 168–171, 189–191
custom calendars, 204–205

About the authors

MARCO RUSSO and **ALBERTO FERRARI** are the founders of sqlbi.com, where they regularly publish articles about Microsoft Power Pivot, Power BI, DAX, and SQL Server Analysis Services. They have worked with DAX since the first beta version of Power Pivot in 2009 and, during these years, sqlbi.com became one of the major sources for DAX articles and tutorials.

Marco Russo and Alberto Ferrari

They both provide consultancy and mentoring on business intelligence (BI), with a particular specialization in the Microsoft technologies related to BI. They have written several books and papers about these topics, with a particular mention of "SQLBI methodology," which is a complete methodology for designing and implementing the back end of a BI solution. They also wrote popular white papers such as "The Many-to-Many Revolution" (about modeling patterns using many-to-many relationships) and "Using Tabular Models in a Large-scale Commercial Solution" (a case study of Analysis Services adoption published by Microsoft).

Marco and Alberto are also regular speakers at major international conferences, including Microsoft Ignite, PASS Summit, and SQLBits. Contact Marco at marco.russo@sqlbi.com and contact Alberto at alberto.ferrari@sqlbi.com.

From technical overviews to drilldowns on special topics, get *free* ebooks from Microsoft Press at:

www.microsoftvirtualacademy.com/ebooks

Download your free ebooks in PDF, EPUB, and/or Mobi for Kindle formats.

Look for other great resources at Microsoft Virtual Academy, where you can learn new skills and help advance your career with free Microsoft training delivered by experts.

Now that you've read the book...

Tell us what you think!

Was it useful?
Did it teach you what you wanted to learn?
Was there room for improvement?

Let us know at http://aka.ms/tellpress

Your feedback goes directly to the staff at Microsoft Press,
and we read every one of your responses. Thanks in advance!

 Microsoft